Remote
Beyond
Compare

Diego de Vargas, the only known portrait.
Capilla de San Isidro, Madrid. Photograph by
Estudio Portillo, Madrid, April 1985. Courtesy of J.
Manuel Espinosa and the Museum of New Mexico.

Remote Beyond Compare

Letters of don Diego de Vargas
to His Family
from New Spain and New Mexico,
1675–1706

John L. Kessell, EDITOR
The Journals of don Diego de Vargas

Rick Hendricks, ASSISTANT EDITOR
Meredith D. Dodge, RESEARCH ASSOCIATE
Larry D. Miller, RESEARCH ASSISTANT
Eleanor B. Adams, RESEARCH CONSULTANT

UNIVERSITY OF NEW MEXICO PRESS : *Albuquerque*

A volume published in conjunction with the centennial observation of the University of New Mexico.

The preparation of this volume was made possible in part by grants from the Division of Research Programs of the National Endowment for the Humanities and the National Historical Publications and Records Commission.

Library of Congress Cataloging-in-Publication Data

Vargas, Diego de, 1643–1704.
    [Correspondence. English & Spanish]
    Remote beyond compare :   letters of don Diego de Vargas to his family from New Spain and New Mexico,
1675–1706 / John L. Kessell, editor.
        p.   cm.
    English and Spanish.
    Bibliography: p.
    Includes index.
    ISBN 0-8263-1112-1
    1. Vargas, Diego de, 1643–1704—Correspondence.   2. New Mexico—Governors—Correspondence.   3. New Mexico—History—To 1848.   4. Spaniards—New Mexico—History—18th century.   I. Kessell, John L. II. Title.
F799.V28413 1989
978.9′02′0924—dc19   88-27651
                                                                       CIP

Illustrations by Maria Carmen Gambliel.
Maps on pages 14, 36, and 54 drafted by Jerry L. Livingston.

Contents

Illustrations and Maps

Preface

Born to the middle-ranking nobility of Madrid in 1643—the same year a French army at Rocroi routed the once-invincible pikemen of Spain—Diego de Vargas lived through some of his country's darkest hours. Yet always, during a long career as royal administrator in the Indies, he held firmly to the honored tradition of warrior-knight. Once at least, in the reconquest of the kingdom and provinces of New Mexico, don Diego knew glory in an inglorious age. Here he battled and conquered an apostate foe for God and king. For the most part, however, he made adjustments to survive in a new world, sought preferment commensurate with his aristocratic values, and borrowed money at interest.

Don Diego's early life, despite the surrounding landscape of crisis and despair, was not as hard as that of most Spaniards. His birthplace and his noble status favored him. "Sólo Madrid es corte." Only Madrid is the court, the saying went. Supplied with bread and bullion from the rest of Spain and the empire, providentially spared the recurrent wars, famine, and pestilence of the seventeenth century, the capital grew as the country declined. Madrid, with its royal ostentation, proliferating government bureaucracy, and easier credit, became increasingly the haven and playground of the nobility.

To the adventurous and the hopeful, however, the empire still beckoned. Don Diego's grandfather, his father, and he, each in turn, responded to the call. Each sought to further enhance the noble house of Vargas and break the family's chain of indebtedness through royal service in the Indies, where opportunities appeared more promising. The first, though, died before embarking, and the second, a widower, remarried and settled down in Guatemala. In contrast, Diego de Vargas, always the Spaniard in America, dreamed of an honorable return home. In the end, however, after thirty punishing years in New Spain, he, too, succumbed, apparently to dysentery. Death overtook him in 1704 as he campaigned against Apache Indians, half a world from the Spain he longed to see again.

––––––

Don Diego de Vargas was a habitual if not prolific writer of letters home. Corresponding with his family in Spain, he expressed concerns that were immediate and personal. A proud and often troubled paterfamilias away in the service of the crown, he sought dutifully to govern his household from afar, win promotion and get out of debt, and, ultimately, return to Madrid, in his words, "crown of all the world." He prayed that his daughter would give birth safely, promised to send money on her dowry as soon as he was able, and offered advice about the most favorable time of year to sell the produce from his Granada properties. "May God keep you," he wished his son-in-law, "many happy years in the company of my beloved daughter." Only incidentally did he comment on the ruggedness of the American terrain or the tally of Apache prisoners.

Although he was intensely and pragmatically interested in his New World surroundings, Vargas saw no reason to express that interest to his relatives in Spain. If he was curious or enthusiastic about what he was experiencing, he did not share such sentiments with them. He never became, for the benefit or entertainment of his family, a chronicler of the Spanish Indies. Another matter don Diego chose not to mention was his personal life in New Spain. Not long after he learned of the death of his wife back home, he met and began living with another woman. Over the years, he had at least three natural children with her.

What emerges from the personal correspondence of don Diego de Vargas is a picture, more detailed in some areas than in others, of a tradition-bound member of the old middle aristocracy coping with seventeenth-century conditions as a royal official in New Spain. In his letters, he reveals much about himself. He is in turn grimly resolved, tender, frustrated, indignant, anxious, and nostalgic. In the official record, don Diego casts for himself a bronze image. As he writes home, however, it falls away, and we see the recolonizer of New Mexico in a more human light.

––––––

Because the known body of Diego de Vargas's personal correspondence is small, in contrast to his public correspondence, it is published here in its entirety, in English translation and Spanish transcript. Repetitive passages and letters convey something of the weight he attached to certain topics. Of the sixty letters and four enclosures, forty-nine are by don Diego himself; the rest are addressed to him or written about him by relatives or associates. From internal references to missing letters and from the several lacunae, it is obvious that the collection is fragmentary, especially for the first sixteen years Vargas spent in New Spain. Most of what follows he wrote while his life was caught up in the governorship of New Mexico, a colony, in his words, "remote beyond compare."

From Santa Fe to Madrid and back, an exchange of correspondence might take as little time as nine months, if the reply was immediate and the letters happened to arrive at Veracruz or Cadiz just as the flota or a packet boat was sailing. More often, an answer took a year or longer. It was customary, because of the perils of the mail, to send two or three signed, original copies by different ships, while retaining a draft or personal copy. Most of don Diego's letters are originals from America kept by his family in Spain. Unfortunately, no similar collection of the correspondence he received in New Spain has come to light.

———

Our guiding principle and goal in translating these letters has been historical accuracy—spirit over the letter—refined by sensibility to mood, intention, and context, so far as we have been able to determine them. Diego de Vargas's style is a study in convolution (all the more evident when compared with the writings of his correspondents).

To aid the reader, we have supplied paragraphing, punctuation, and specific nouns where distant or unclear antecedents might confuse. We have modernized Spanish names and used *Webster's New Geographical Dictionary* as our standard for place-names. Hence, Cadiz appears without an accent. Explanations of all Spanish words and phrases retained in the English text—such as dehesa and plaza de armas—including terms for money, weights, and measures, are provided in the glossary or notes. According to *Webster's Third New International Dictionary of the English Language Unabridged*, which we have taken as our authority, certain words, accented in Spanish, are now accepted as English words of Spanish origin, without accents. Examples are alferez, cedula, and vellon. A note on the complex subject of Spanish money is included.

The names of Spanish kings and titles of Spanish nobles we have retained in Spanish, while rendering in English the names and titles of kings and nobles of other nationalities. Offices or military titles are abbreviated when they occur with the individual's full name; they are spelled out when only the surname is used. We have left saints' names in English, unless they are mentioned as part of the name of Spanish churches, organizations, or places.

For readers of the Spanish language and for linguists, who should not be satisfied with anyone's translation, we have included complete Spanish transcripts.

The biographical introduction and the notes are meant to supply a context for the letters. People or places not further identified remain, at this stage of our research, regrettably just that— names in the text.

————

The main intent of the Vargas Project at the University of New Mexico is to publish in multivolume scholarly translation *The Journals of don Diego de Vargas, 1691–1704,* accompanied by a microfiche edition of the Spanish transcripts. These journals are the principal archives of Vargas's administration as governor and recolonizer of New Mexico. The present volume of personal correspondence, although not properly part of the official journals, will serve as a biographical preface and complement. We may never learn much more about Vargas, the man, about his personality and his motivations, but here, in letters addressed to his family in Spain we come closer than we have before.

The Vargas journals, together with other documents bearing on this pivotal period, are held today by a number of repositories in the United States, Spain, and Mexico. Our task of collecting photocopies has been greatly facilitated by the ready cooperation of the staffs of the State Records Center and Archives, Santa Fe, New Mexico; The Bancroft Library, University of California, Berkeley; The Huntington Library, San Marino, California; The Newberry Library, Chicago, Illinois; Benson Latin American Collection, The University of Texas, Austin; Beinecke Rare Book and Manuscript Library, Yale University, New Haven, Connecticut; Library of Congress, Washington, D.C.; Archivo General de Indias, Seville; Archivo Histórico Nacional, Madrid; Archivo Histórico de Protocolos de Madrid; and Archivo General de la Nación and Archivo General de Notarías, both in Mexico City.

Begun as a solo endeavor in 1980 by the editor, John L. Kessell, the Vargas Project received initial funding from the John Simon Guggenheim Memorial Foundation and the National Historical Publications and Records Commission (NHPRC), the nation's chief advocate of preserving and publishing our documentary heritage. We are grateful that the NHPRC has continued its aid and counsel. The University of New Mexico also supplied research monies, and in 1983 the Translations Program of the National Endowment for the Humanities lent its support, matched in large part by The University of New Mexico Foundation. We especially appreciate the additional financial aid provided by Marco Jesús González Peán del Valle y Rivera and his family of Richmond, California.

In the realm of ideas, we are grateful to the directors of two innovative, computer-oriented projects who have generously shared their knowledge and enthusiasm. From the beginning, Charles W. Polzer, S.J., of the Documentary Relations of the Southwest at the University of Arizona, Tucson, has given sound advice and timely encouragement. John J. Nitti, who heads the Dictionary of the Old Spanish Language Project at the University of Wisconsin, Madison, turned the Vargas Project around by inspiring our assistant editor, Rick Hendricks, to become a computer professional. He also introduced us to the form of transcription we now use, which is set forth in David Mackenzie's *A Manual of Manuscript Transcription for the Dictionary of the Old Spanish Language*, 4th ed. (Madison, 1986).

Our debt to historian J. Manuel Espinosa, for his personal interest and a legacy of exacting scholarship, is exceptional. He led the way with *First Expedition of Vargas into New Mexico, 1692* and *Crusaders of the Río Grande: The Story of Don Diego de Vargas and the Reconquest and Refounding of New Mexico*.

On our own campus, where the Vargas Project is seen as a major component of the UNM Centennial (1989), Zimmerman Library and Special Collections, the Department of History, and the Computer and Information Resources and Technology Center have each contributed in a variety of ways. All the while, Anne D. McGoey, the program specialist, kept our budget balanced and the office running smoothly. Consultant Paul A. Baye raised our consciousness of computer applications. Graduate students Kevin R. Clawson and Braden K. Frieder and undergraduates Solange García Alford, Mary Jo Luján, and Stefanie Baaken, the latter a genuine volunteer, willingly helped out when needed. We would also like to extend a special thanks to Maria Carmen Gambliel for her original artwork. At the University of New Mexico Press, Elizabeth C. Hadas, the director; David V. Holtby, associate director and editor; and Emmy Ezzell, art and production manager, with skill and steady good cheer have seen this pilot volume through to book form.

When the project began, no one in New Mexico knew that any private correspondence of Diego de Vargas existed. Still, the possibility made a pilgrimage to Madrid irresistible. Late in 1982, thanks to a travel grant from the Comité Conjunto Hispano-Norteamericano para Asuntos Educativos y Culturales, the editor made the first of three research trips to don Diego's birthplace. There, an interested relative, Manuel Cabrera Kábana, and two dedicated Americanists, Atilio O. Scarpa Araujo from Uruguay and his wife, Aída Helena Macedo Miraballes, aided in the quest.

Locating the letters published in this volume was the consummation devoutly wished, and it happened only because of the extreme kindness of descendants of Diego de Vargas. Joaquín Dorado y Aguilar, XII Marqués de la Nava de Barcinas (don Diego was the first of the title), and his family, and the family of the late Spanish diplomat, Rafael Gasset Dorado, especially Ignacio Gasset Dorado, gave access to their archives and permission to microfilm. To them and to Teresa and José Pérez Balsera Caballero, her brother, great-great-great-great-great-granddaughter and -grandson of the recolonizer, this prefatory volume is gratefully dedicated.

To all above, for their assistance, we express our thanks. To ourselves, the editors, for any errors, we assign the blame.

Note on Spanish Monies

The text that follows contains frequent mention of a variety of denominations of Spanish currency and reflects an often confusing monetary system. Many coins of different and inconstant values circulated in the Spanish empire. To provide consistency in accounting, monies of account were employed.

Money of account is a denominator of value used for the keeping of financial records; there may or may not be an equivalent coin. In the case of Spain, the basic accounting denomination was the maravedi. A secondary denomination, the vellon real, equaled 34 maravedis.

The table below is based on values assigned to currency by the 1686 pragmatic and on calculations of figures contained in the documents themselves.

1 ducado = 11 silver reales
1 vellon real = 34 maravedis
1 doblon = 60 vellon reales
1 silver real = 2.5 vellon reales
1 piece of eight (silver reales) = 15 vellon reales
1 ducado = 374 maravedis
1 escudo = 340 maravedis
1 peso = 1 escudo
1 escudo = 10 silver reales

Although the American peso had a nominal—therefore accounting—value higher in maravedis than the ducado, in practice it was considered in Spain to be of roughly equal value. A similar situation existed with respect to the ducado and the escudo, so that the documents refer to all three denominations interchangeably while noting differences in nominal values as expressed in monies of account.

From the examples that have been coming to light one can deduce that letter-writing among private individuals was a well-established custom in both Spain and the Indies (as the Spaniards persisted in calling America). Correspondents acknowledge previous letters, complain of lack of mail, speak of the cheapness of paper and ink, and in other ways betray that it was customary to write letters to absent relatives and friends. . . . Stereotypes and bias are no less evident in letters like these than in official reports, and must be equally discounted, or rather taken as such. Even so, there is much immediacy, reality, sobriety and simple informativeness in them. They are very human documents, in which the Spaniard of the Indies appears in roles intuitively familiar to us, as son, brother, immigrant, tradesman, European, anything but some exotic "conquistador" "thirsty for gold."

—James Lockhart and Enrique Otte,
Letters and Peoples of the Spanish Indies

Out of such consideration, I could have done no more than to have exiled myself to this kingdom, at the ends of the earth and remote beyond compare.

—Don Diego de Vargas to his son-in-law,
El Paso del Río del Norte, 9 April 1692

Part 1

The convento of San Francisco, Madrid.
After the 1656 Texeira map. Maria Carmen Gambliel.

Introduction

The Vargases
of Madrid

"Los Vargas son gavilanes."

"The Vargases are hawks." Of obscure origin, the saying was old
and proud. Spaniards had long likened nobles of impeccable qualities to hawks. But why hawks? Writing of the ancient and acclaimed
house of Vargas in Madrid, sixteenth-century chronicler Gonzalo
Fernández de Oviedo offered an explanation, one he personally
doubted.

In winter the hawk, according to fable, keeps alive the bird captured at dusk and, without harming it, holds it all night in its talons,
drawing warmth from it. When morning comes, in return for the
favor and so as not to stain the nest with the blood of its guest, the
hawk releases the other bird, watching which way it flies, then wings
off in the opposite direction to avoid hunting the same prey. Honor,
prowess, gratitude, mercy—whatever young Diego de Vargas made
of the tale, he knew that his family, if not among the richest or most
influential of the capital in his day, was surely one of the oldest and
most illustrious. [1]

For six centuries chroniclers had lauded his ancestors: warrior-
knights, bishops, counselors of kings, and friends of the saints. In
1083, three Vargas brothers fought for King Alfonso VI to wrest Madrid
from the Moors. The blessed farmer Isidore, later honored as patron
saint of the city, devoted his life to cultivating the land of Iván de
Vargas, a witness to his miracles. In the early thirteenth century,
when Francis of Assisi passed through Madrid and chose the site for
the Franciscan friary, a Vargas gave him the land.

Striding down a crooked block and turning right at the broad Calle
de San Francisco, don Diego could reach the friars' sprawling complex in minutes. Here, in the main church, the Vargas family chapel on the gospel side had been rebuilt in 1459 by his namesake seven
generations removed. That well-known knight, don Diego de Vargas

BREVE
DESCRIPCION
GENEALOGICA
DE LA ILUSTRE,
QUANTO ANTIQUISSIMA CASA
DE LOS VARGAS
DE MADRID,
CUYO POSSEEDOR ACTUAL, O LEGITIMO TRONCO
verdadero es Don Diego Joseph Lopez de Zarate Vargas Pimentèl Zapata y Lujàn Ponze de Leon Zepeda Alvarez Contreras y Salinas , Marquès de Villanueva , y de la Nava de Varcinas , Capitan Vivo de Infanteria , agregado al Estado mayor de la Plaza de Cadiz , y Alferez en las Reales Guardias de Infanteria Española de su Magestad.

DIVIDIDA EN DOS PARTES.
EN LA PRIMERA SE JUSTIFICA LA LEGITIMIDAD del referido Marquès de Villanueva , y ser Tronco de dicha Casa de Vargas.

EN LA SEGUNDA
SE DA UNA SUCINTA RECOPILACION de varias noticias de las hazañas y empleos de diferentes Cavalleros del Apellido de Vargas.

A genealogy of the Vargas family of Madrid written by don Diego's grandson, 1740.

Real Academia de la Historia, Madrid.

Mejía, councilman of Madrid, and his wife, doña María Alfonso de Medina y Velasco, praying in stone effigy, presided over stately rows of Vargas tombs. Here, when the future recolonizer of New Mexico was only five, they buried his mother in 1649 and, later the same year, his grandfather, and here he too must have expected to lie enshrined.[2]

On the way home, he would pass the Bishop's Chapel, next to which the new church of San Andrés was under construction. His uncle six generations back, the famed Lic. Francisco de Vargas, had begun the chapel as a final resting place for the remains of holy Isidore, long considered a saint in Madrid, but not by Rome until 1622. Such a wise and trusted counselor was Francisco de Vargas to their Catholic Majesties, Fernando and Isabel, and to the Emperor Charles V that a new proverbial expression entered the language: "Averígüelo Vargas." "Get Vargas to verify it." The saying gave dramatist Tirso de Molina the title for another play. After don Francisco died in 1524, his son, don Gutierre de Vargas Carvajal, who as bishop of Plasencia would attend the Council of Trent, finished the chapel. Inside, on a sumptuous alabaster sepulcher, a statue immortalized the bishop, kneeling in prayer, attended by pages, choirboys, and weeping women.[3]

Diego de Vargas, who would inherit the principal house of Vargas in the oldest part of the city, could recite the feats of other legendary Vargases, heroes of the Catholic Reconquest of Spain from the infidel Moor. There was Diego Pérez de Vargas. That redoubtable fighter, having lost sword and lance in battle, put his shield on his back, ripped off a big olive branch, and with two-handed grip began swinging the butt end of it around and around, flattening his assailants left and right. So delighted by the sound of the blows was a fellow-knight that he cheered him on, shouting, "Así, así, Diego; machuca, machuca." "That's the way, Diego; pound, pound." From then on, his name was Vargas Machuca. During the reconquest of New Mexico, in fact, Diego de Vargas carried a military manual by Bernardo de Vargas Machuca, a descendant of Vargas the Pounder.[4]

Four generations in succession of don Diego's direct male antecedents, including his father, were knights of the prestigious Spanish military Order of Santiago. Though they were captains and minor governors, not generals and viceroys, their membership in the order served to authenticate their pure and noble ancestry. It also offered them the surest prospect of advancement to higher rank. Since the

early sixteenth century, the old crusading orders of Santiago, Calatrava, and Alcántara had been incorporated into the crown and
become sources of royal patronage. During the lifetime of don Diego's father, sale of membership reached shameful proportions, after
which reforms were instituted. Later, from the New World, don Diego would bid for knighthood in the Order of Santiago and fail.[5]

His great-great-grandfather, don Lorenzo de Vargas y Luján, still
alive in 1580, had been rewarded with the robe of Santiago in 1564
after years of campaigning in the wars of Carlos I and Felipe II. Don
Francisco de Vargas y Salinas, baptized in 1557 in the venerable
parish church of San Pedro el Real, half a block from the family
home in Madrid, served long and bravely as an infantry captain. He
married his first cousin, doña Juana de Sotomayor y Salinas. And
on 31 May 1589, in the parish church of San Andrés, their eldest
son was baptized and given the name Lorenzo. This Lorenzo would
be don Diego's grandfather, a veteran campaigner with stories to tell.

As a young officer, don Lorenzo had seen action on the Neapolitan galleys against the Ottoman Turk, Spain's traditional maritime
foe in the Mediterranean. Beginning in 1611, he served four years
under don Alvaro de Bazán, Marqués de Santa Cruz, son of the
admiral who proposed the invincible armada of 1588. Lorenzo de
Vargas was with the land-sea force in 1611 that assaulted the Kerkenna
Islands off the Tunisian coast, fighting ashore in the first wave. The
next year, the marqués chose him as one of a raiding party to burn
the Turkish ships that lay in the shadow of La Goletta, the fortress
guarding the city of Tunis. He sailed in relief of Gozo and Malta.
He knew the ports of the Levant.[6]

Citing his record, Lorenzo de Vargas petitioned the crown for
knighthood in the Order of Santiago. By royal order, dated at Madrid
on 6 December 1613, Felipe III bade the Marqués de Santa Cruz to
invest don Lorenzo in Naples. The solemn rite took place before the
main altar of the church of Santiago on 19 March 1614. Don Gonzalo
de Córdoba, brother of the Duque de Sesa and descendant of don
Gonzalo Fernández de Córdoba, the Gran Capitán, acted as don
Lorenzo's sponsor. Other knights, clad in white robes emblazoned
with the red dagger cross of their order, and many witnesses attended. At a dramatic point in the ceremony, two Neapolitan knights
stepped forward and

> put a pair of golden spurs on don Lorenzo de Vargas Zapata, and the
> lord Marqués de Santa Cruz girded him with a gilded sword. With

sword thus girded, the lord marqués drew it from the sheath and with it bare in his hand said to don Lorenzo de Vargas Zapata, "Do you wish to be a knight?" Don Lorenzo replied, "Yes, I wish it." And the lord marqués said, "May God and the Apostle James make you a good knight."

After repeating the formula three times, the marqués touched don Lorenzo's head and shoulder with the blade and returned it to the sheath. The new knight then made his confession, received communion, and was vested in the robe of Santiago.[7]

In 1620, Lorenzo de Vargas entered Naples in the entourage of the new viceroy, Cardinal Antonio Zapata de Mendoza, who entrusted to him command of a company of Spanish infantry in the tercio of Naples. Later, in the mountainous, pastoral kingdom, the cardinal and subsequent Spanish viceroys, among them the Duque de Alba and the Conde de Monterrey, named don Lorenzo to a succession of provincial governorships, "always affirming," according to a great-great-grandson, "the illustriousness of his nobility and the singleness of his esteemed valor in these and many other offices and governments he attained."[8] Repeatedly, he was given additional military commissions to combat bands of outlaws in the countryside. His success in capturing many of these highwaymen, even several of their leaders, earned Lorenzo de Vargas further commendations.[9]

While don Lorenzo served in Italy his wife was with him. As a knight, he had been required to request royal permission to wed. It had come in 1618. The bride, born in the city of La Santísima Trinidad de los Muzos while her father governed that emerald-rich district in New Granada, was doña Antonia Cepeda Ponce de León of the house of the Duque de Arcos. It was through her that properties in Granada came into possession of the Vargases of Madrid.[10]

Late in 1621, don Lorenzo assumed the governorship of the provinces of Capitanata and the Duchy of Molise. There, while he and Antonia were in the historic town and episcopal see of Lucena, set on a high plateau just in from the Achilles tendon in the boot of Italy, she gave birth to their first son, Alonso, don Diego's father. Because the boy was born while don Lorenzo served the king in a foreign country, his legal birthplace was considered to be the royal court at Madrid.[11]

Before he was twelve, the eldest son of Lorenzo de Vargas had been sent to Spain. There, in 1633, through the influence of the Marqués de Santa Cruz, who was by then serving as Felipe IV's chief

The Vargas residence and the parish church of San Pedro el Real.
After the 1656 Texeira map. Maria Carmen Gambliel.

mayordomo, the prepossessing Alonso became a menino to Queen Isabel de Borbón. Meninos and meninas waited on the queen and were companions to the children of her household.[12] On 1 April 1636, when Alonso de Vargas was about fourteen, he was granted membership in the Order of Santiago. The ritual of knighthood and the profession of his vows would come later.[13]

Earlier the same year, 1636, in the city of Salerno, Alonso's mother took to her deathbed. In her will, dated 11 January, she requested that her body be returned to Spain for burial in the Vargas family chapel, where her deceased children already reposed and where her husband and heir would one day be interred. After providing for the maintenance of her mother, doña Juana Venegas Ponce de León, and forgiving the dowry her husband still owed her, doña Antonia made an additional bequest for the education of Manuel de Vargas, a bastard son of don Lorenzo. Among the religious paintings, personal effects, and money stipulated for relatives and servants, she wished that her black, embroidered silk dress go to doña Mariana de Vera, wife of Gaspar Ibáñez, tutor of her elder son, Alonso, the queen's menino. After don Lorenzo, she listed as her heirs the four surviving, legitimate children of their marriage: Alonso, Francisco, Juana, and Antonia.[14] Evidently, doña Antonia Cepeda Ponce de León had lived such an exemplary and virtuous life that someone later wrote a biography of her.[15]

In Madrid, meanwhile, don Alonso de Vargas played his small role among the glamorous courtiers who sat for portraits by Velázquez. It was a world unto itself, presided over, ever more frenetically, by the dark, heavy-set Conde-Duque de Olivares, while the king took his pleasure with women and hunting. Outside, the Thirty Years' War ebbed and flowed. Olivares's demand that other parts of the vast Spanish empire, not just Castile, pay the mounting costs, brought resistance, then open rebellion in Catalonia and Portugal. France took full advantage of the situation, sending troops across the border to the aid of the Catalans.[16]

———

Soon after his wife died, don Lorenzo de Vargas had returned to Madrid. When French forces invaded the Basque provinces in 1638, he fought valiantly, and at his own expense. "He was one of the first officers the Admiral of Castile chose for the assault on the stronghold of Fuenterrabía. Yet he was not rewarded, even though that action was of great danger to his life and cost to his estate."[17] After that, he came home again.

The family residence, a number of contiguous buildings and apartments, mostly of two stories, fronted on the Calle del Almendro and ran on down the narrow, unnamed street to the parish church of San Pedro el Real. It enclosed a patio and fountain. Don Lorenzo's mother-in-law, doña Juana Venegas Ponce de León; his younger son, Francisco; his daughters, Juana and Antonia; a contingent of servants; and some tenants, on the lower floor, also lived in the Vargas complex. Adjoining the principal residence on the Calle del Almendro were other houses inherited from don Lorenzo's wife. They abutted those owned by don Fadrique Enríquez and formed a corner at the little street behind the papal nuncio's residence.[18]

In 1638, don Lorenzo discussed with don Alonso, his son at court and his heir, then about sixteen years old, the inheritance the young man was entitled to from his recently deceased mother. His father asked him to legally renounce his one-quarter share in favor of his sister, Juana de Vargas Ponce de León, in order that she might have a sufficient dowry to marry well. In the event of Juana's early demise, the double share would pass to their younger sister, Antonia. Alonso complied.[19]

Perhaps because of the uncertainty of the times, don Lorenzo arranged an early marriage for Alonso. The ceremony took place on 6 January 1641, the Epiphany, at the home of the bride on the Calle de Alcalá. A native of Toledo, María Margarita Contreras y Arráiz was not quite eighteen. The queen's page she was marrying may have been a year older. Her father, don Diego de Contreras Sotelo, a treasurer in the chief royal accounting office, had offered a dowry of 30,000 ducados, which her husband would try in vain until the end of his life to collect in full. Four days after the wedding, in a rite of passage that reminded don Lorenzo of his own, the same Marqués de Santa Cruz confirmed the membership of Alonso de Vargas in the Order of Santiago, girding him with the sword of knighthood.[20]

Don Alonso would join an infantry company raised by his father, part of a tercio to be provided by the nobility of the capital. The war in Catalonia had taken on dangerous proportions. During the summer of 1640, a mob had murdered the Spanish king's viceroy on the beach at Barcelona. Now, in 1642, Capt. Alonso de Vargas marched with an ill-provisioned army of uninspired, untried troops impressed in Castile and led by incompetents. Olivares was gambling the fate of his administration on this expeditionary force. Even the king took the field. Don Alonso's two royal commissions, received scarcely a month apart, were indicative of the urgency of the moment. The first named him captain of an infantry company at a salary of 40 escudos a month, and the second promoted him to captain of a company of heavy cavalry at 110 escudos a month. Near Lérida in October, the Spaniards met a French army and suffered a ghastly defeat, losing five thousand men. Fortunately, Captain Vargas survived. [21]

Even if don Alonso was never tempted to pay a mercenary to fight in his place, as many knights did, war was seasonal, and the young officer spent part of the year in Madrid with María Margarita. Their first child, born late in 1641 or in 1642, they named Lorenzo after his grandfather. Little is known of the boy. He lived only to the age of seventeen or eighteen, not long enough to inherit his father's house. Dead by 1660, he was survived by a younger brother, Diego, who would become not only master of the house of Vargas of Madrid, but also recolonizer of New Mexico and the first Marqués de la Nava de Barcinas. [22]

Don Diego de Vargas
in Spain

On 8 November 1643, a Wednesday, twenty-year-old doña María Margarita, accompanied by her parents, presented her second son, Diego José de Vargas Zapata Luján Ponce de León y Contreras, for baptism. Evidently the priest, Lic. Juan Pedro de la Carra, administered the sacrament not in the Vargas family parish of San Pedro el Real, but in the church of San Luis, which her father and mother, the child's godparents, attended. [23] Doña María Margarita may have been living with them at the time, while her husband was away on campaign. She and her two infant sons may, in fact, have stayed with her parents until 1646 or 1647, when Capt. Alonso de Vargas moved with his family into a furnished upstairs suite of three rooms in the ancestral Vargas residence on the Calle del Almendro. [24]

Although he did not die until 1649, don Lorenzo de Vargas had not been well. In 1642, he had finally arranged the division of his deceased wife's estate among the children and, in 1643, ill in bed,

Felipe IV of Spain (1621–65).
Rivera Cambas, *Los gobernantes*.

dictated his last will and testament. Valued at 20,736 ducados, less 2,000 for an endowment at the parish of San Pedro el Real and 300 for Manuel de Vargas's education, Antonia Cepeda Ponce de León's estate divided into four equal shares of 4,609. Because don Alonso had renounced his share, doña Juana received a double share, which included a perpetual loan valued at 5,000 ducados on the revenues of the city of Granada. Don Francisco got his mother's houses and store on the Plaza Mayor, and doña Antonia the houses next to the Vargas complex on the Calle del Almendro.[25]

Don Lorenzo, by his 1643 will, bequeathed household items, personal possessions, and sums of cash to members of his family, friends and associates, and servants. He provided for the payment of his various debts. Then, he named his four children— Alonso, married to María de Contreras; Francisco; Juana, recently married to don Alonso de Anaya y Toledo; and Antonia—equal heirs to the rest of his estate.

He especially enjoined don Alonso as the new paterfamilias to look after his grandmother, doña Juana Venegas Ponce de León, "who, it can be said, is the only mother he has known." He should do the same for his uncle, Father Sebastián de Vargas, and love and care for his brother and sisters. As for his bastard half-brother, don Manuel, Alonso should see that the 300 ducados were paid and favor the young man, who seemed inclined to become a religious. Finally, there was the matter of don Lorenzo's natural son, don Pedro, the product of his union with a widow, "a noblewoman and the daughter of very respected parents." She was, in fact, pregnant again. Alonso was to aid these half-siblings however he could and provide whatever assistance their mother might need to enter a convent. In the event that she chose not to do so, she was to be given 200 ducados. Regardless, she should have the trunk containing her clothes. If need be, the Jesuit, Father Andrés Manuel, could identify it.[26]

At home and abroad, the first decade of Diego de Vargas's protected life was a depressing time for Spain. A two-front war on the peninsula, wars elsewhere, rampant inflation, collapse of the transatlantic trade, overtaxation of everyone but the nobles, government bankruptcy, the loss of tens of thousands of people in the recurrent plague of 1647–52—the list went on and on. In January of 1643, the year don Diego was born, Felipe IV, compelled by defeat on the Catalan frontier in 1642 and the fading prospect of peace with France or the separatists, gave Olivares leave to resign. Late in May came jarring news from Rocroi in northeastern France: the best of the Span-

- Valladolid
- Lérida
- Barcelona
- Guadalajara
- **MADRID**
- Ocaña
- Sevilla
- Cortijo de Barcinas
- Iznalloz
- Granada
- Cortijo de la Nava
- Cadiz

0   50   100
miles

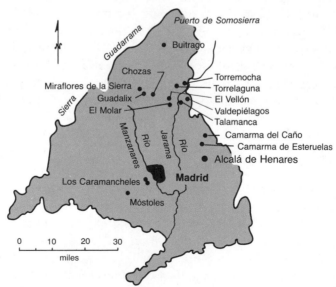

Puerto de Somosierra
Guadarrama
- Buitrago
- Chozas
- Torremocha
- Miraflores de la Sierra
- Torrelaguna
- Guadalix
- El Vellón
Sierra
- El Molar
- Valdepiélagos
- Talamanca
- Camarma del Caño
Rio Manzanares
Rio Jarama
Rio
- Camarma de Esteruelas
- Alcalá de Henares
- Los Caramancheles
Madrid
- Móstoles

0   10   20   30
miles

The Province of Madrid.

ish army cut to pieces by French artillery, six thousand veterans and their general dead. That year, too, Vargas's most famous contemporary, the French king, Louis XIV, then only five years old, began a triumphant reign that would last for more than seven decades.[27]

On 17 April 1649, when don Diego himself was five years old, his mother died, leaving him; his older brother, Lorenzo; and their baby sister, Antonia. Doña María Margarita, twenty-six years old, was buried in the Vargas chapel at the Convento de San Francisco.[28] A month later, don Lorenzo de Vargas took legal measures to prevent his widowed son's creditors from seizing the furnishings in the apartment don Alonso occupied. The West Indian, granadilla-wood bed, ebony desk, paintings, and armorial hangings were things he had brought from Naples. Because of their grandfather's stature and the resulting pomp, the children would have remembered his funeral, which took place the following November: the twelve Franciscan friars who accompanied his coffin in procession; the mass and vigil with the body present; the burial at night; the one hundred candles, organ music, sung masses; and tolling bells.[29]

The estate don Alonso de Vargas inherited from his father was fairly diversified, but not very profitable. Its entails were concentrated in and around three urban centers—Madrid, where don Lorenzo had entailed Vargas holdings; Granada, with houses, stores, and land from don Lorenzo's wife; and the villa of Torrelaguna, north of Madrid, properties in the family since the sixteenth century. There were buildings, vineyards, olive orchards, enclosed pastures, cropland, as well as revenues and privileges from religious and secular corporations. The income, together with loans on the assets, seemed to have been enough to keep the family's standard of living up to the level expected of the middle-ranking nobility in the capital. It was not, however, enough to finance higher aspirations—a title of marqués or conde, or a truly lucrative office.[30]

For don Alonso, just as for his father, the empire was the way of advancement. In 1647, two years before his death, Lorenzo de Vargas, reviewing thirty years of service, had petitioned the crown for a new appointment. He had wanted the governorship of Calabria in the kingdom of Naples, where, that same year, bread riots turned into a determined revolt against Spanish rule. Instead, he had received a royal grant appointing him corregidor of Zacatecas, New Spain's silver city. Don Lorenzo had died, however, before setting out.[31]

His father's appointment in the Indies must have set don Alonso

Capt. Alonso de Vargas Zapata.
Ballesteros Robles, *Diccionario biográfico matritense*.

thinking. He had lost his wife and his father the same year. Although it is difficult from the evidence at hand to assess his motives for seeking employment in the New World, economics, honor, and personality all seem to have played a part.

No penniless lord, don Alonso de Vargas may have heartily disliked the business of managing his estate. Besides, he had accrued considerable debts. He had been buying sheep and now owed his business agent, don Alonso de Santander y Mercado, 7,175 ducados. To pay off this large sum, he obligated to Santander six years' income from the Madrid and Granada entails "in administration." The agent, by terms of the contract, would see that he and other creditors received regular payment and that the family had an appropriate allowance. Vargas exempted the apartments where his grandmother, his sister, and his children lived.[32]

Anticipating the excitement of the Indies may have helped him deal with the death of his young wife, doña María Margarita. Still in his twenties, a captain of heavy cavalry since 1642, don Alonso de Vargas took stock of his mortgaged estate, the lawsuit to collect his deceased wife's dowry, and his chances for preferment in Spain. Morale in the military was lower than ever. There seemed to be little choice. He had no university degree. He could delegate to others authority to manage his affairs at home, and doña Juana Venegas Ponce de León, his aged grandmother, with help from the rest of the family, could care for his children. And rent from the downstairs apartments could go toward a dowry for his sister, Antonia.[33]

Captain Vargas's royal appointment as alcalde mayor of Chiapa, then in the jurisdiction of Guatemala, was issued on 13 April 1650. Two weeks later, don Alonso was in Seville. There, amid the eager bedlam of the House of Trade, he secured permission to depart for the Indies for himself and his three unmarried male servants. They sailed the same year.[34]

In the 1650s, Madrid, where don Diego grew up, was a teeming, exciting, dirty, dangerous place. It was, travelers agreed, the filthiest capital in Europe, a great urban mix, with the palaces and mansions of the wealthy interspersed in a sea of close-built tenements on "very nasty and foul" streets filled with beggars, idlers, bureaucrats, students and priests, transients and foreigners. Like a magnet, the city,

confident, easy of access, and the king's residence, drew into its puls-
ing orb of public spectacles, religious processions, markets, and alms-
houses all manner of people dispossessed by the country's ills. The
population of Madrid—approximately 125,000 in the 1650s—had
risen from 65,000 in 1600 and would reach 150,000 by 1700 (as
compared to London's 500,000 and the 400,000 of Paris). Meantime, in contrast to the villa and court, the general population of Spain
declined from around 8,000,000 in 1600 to fewer than 7,000,000
in 1700.[35]

Evidently, neither young Diego nor his older brother, Lorenzo,
possessed the natural gifts to be chosen a noble page at court, as their
father had been. By 1662, when he petitioned the crown for permission to act legally for himself, don Diego de Vargas had known three
guardians. His aged great-grandmother, doña Juana Venegas Ponce
de León, must have died, after which the responsibility of guardian-
ship had passed to one of his father's cousins, Gabriel de Barrionuevo
y Peralta. Don Gabriel died on 1 October 1659, and for a year litigation tied up Diego's allowance.

Describing himself as younger than twenty-five, the legal age where
property was concerned, but older than sixteen, don Diego had
requested in September 1660 that Lic. José de Castro Castillo, an
official of the Council of the Treasury, be named his legal guardian
and manage the 700 ducados a year provided through his father's
agent. The allowance was, in Vargas's words, "for sustenance, education, and upbringing appropriate to my station."[36] Later, when the
eighteen-year-old Vargas obtained the permission to act for himself,
Castro Castillo rendered an accounting that revealed certain mun-
dane yet interesting details of the young man's life.

The first two items covered sustenance, a servant, and two suits
each, one velvet and the other black wool, for don Diego and his
older brother, Lorenzo, described in the document as "now deceased."
Evidently the latter had died early in 1660 from a cause not mentioned. For a year and a half, the surviving brother studied Latin
with a tutor, don Sebastián de Vidaurreta y Tejada, whose fee was
120 reales a month. Food for don Diego and his manservant also
cost 120 reales a month, and the servant's monthly wage was 100
reales.

Don Diego dressed in style. A master tailor made him suits for
winter, spring, and summer. He wore fancy hats and silk stockings
and gloves. The linen merchant provided yardage for his underwear,

handkerchiefs, sheets, and pillows. Twenty-two pairs of shoes, two plain pairs for dancing lessons, and ribbons for ties, came to 286 reales. For ten months of instruction, the dancing master charged 240 reales. When young Vargas was ill in the spring of 1661, treatment had included making a small issue to drain fluids. Total costs for medication, two physicians, one surgeon, and incidentals amounted to 375 reales. Securing the permission to act on his own had cost 1,612 reales. Books for his studies at secondary school, bedding, expenses for two months, and moving his clothing totaled 235 reales. During one four-month period, don Diego spent another 322 "seeing bullfights and theatrical performances and for other trifling minor expenses."[37]

The sole surviving son of Capt. Alonso de Vargas may have aspired to office in the councils of the royal bureaucracy, a goal regularly achieved in his day after attendance at a university. Even the best of Spain's universities—Salamanca, Valladolid, and Alcalá— had by the seventeenth century evolved from centers of Renaissance learning into conservative schools for the bureaucratic elite, emphasizing the production of lawyers, "or, at the very least, of gentlemen lightly schooled in the law for reasons of practicality and prestige."[38]

Early in November 1662, just as he turned nineteen, don Diego executed a power of attorney in favor of his sixty-four-year-old great-uncle, don Sebastián de Vargas, resident at the Colegio Imperial in Madrid. In the instrument he stated that, "to continue my studies, I need to go to the University of Valladolid, for which I am about to leave."[39] Although he did not earn a degree, years later, writing to the viceroy of New Spain, he recalled having "trod the grounds of the University of Valladolid, where I studied my first years."[40] Then, it would appear, courtship and marriage intervened.

A handsome, sixteenth-century stone mansion, the Vargas country place stood in the walled medieval villa of Torrelaguna, some thirty miles north of Madrid in the open valley of the Río Jarama. It offered the family a convenient retreat from the suffocating summer heat and the turmoil of the capital, and it was the seat of their scattered holdings in the area. Almost adjoining the Vargas house on the Coso, a small plaza just inside one of the old town gates, was the Pimentel residence. Don Juan Pimentel de Prado, of the well-known family of soldiers, administrators, and diplomats, had three sons, all of them, like their father, knights of the Order of Santiago, and one daughter.[41]

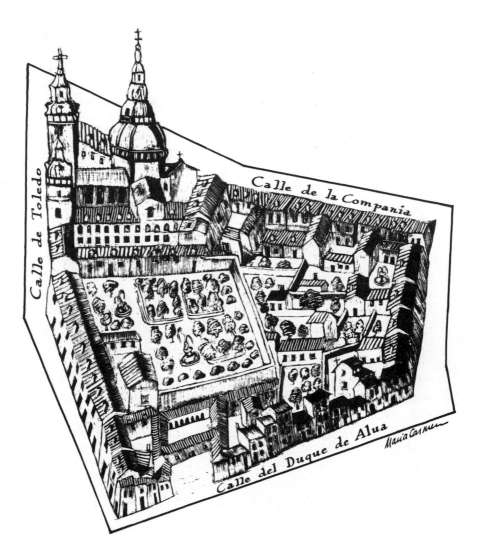

The Colegio Imperial, Madrid.
    After the 1656 Texeira map. Maria Carmen Gambliel.

On the first day of April 1664, doña Beatriz Pimentel de Prado Vélez de Olazábal, twenty-two years of age, and don Diego de Vargas, twenty, went to the notary and signed a marriage contract. As a groom's gift Diego pledged 4,000 ducados, purportedly one-tenth of his worth, the maximum set by law. The couple's banns were read on three successive days during Easter week in the towering Gothic church of Santa María Magdalena, and the wedding followed on 5 May. By permission of Dr. Antonio de León, the local pastor, don Diego's great-uncle performed the ceremony.[42]

In the Indies, meantime, don Alonso de Vargas's career had gone well enough. He had adapted himself to the verdant, largely Indian kingdom of Guatemala, serving competently on the northern periphery in remote Ciudad Real, seat of his alcaldía mayor of Chiapa. Built at the end of a poorly drained mountain valley, the community had suffered major floods in 1651 and 1652, during which don Alonso had responded heroically. Next, the Conde de Santiago de

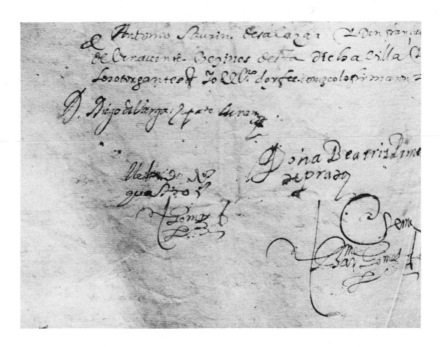

The signatures of don Diego and doña Beatriz on their marriage contract, Torrelaguna, 1 April 1664.
Archivo de Notarías, Torrelaguna.

Calimaya, president and captain general of the Audiencia of Guatemala (1654–57), had appointed him corregidor of Totonicapán, one district closer to the capital. Finally, don Martín Carlos de Mencos (1659–68), a respected president accused of illegal trade in indigo with the Dutch, brought don Alonso to Santiago de Guatemala as maestre de campo. As "the only soldier in those provinces," Vargas would understand how to deal with the robberies plaguing the capital. [43]

About 1659, don Alonso, a widower in his late thirties, remarried. The bride, doña Jerónima de Guinea y Murga, a nineteen-or twenty-year-old criolla, was the daughter of a prominent family of the capital. Her dowry of 30,000 pesos in cash, valuables, and slaves would add to the approximately 40,000 he claimed as his worth. She bore him three children: Pedro Alonso, Francisco, and Antonia. Apparently, don Alonso solved the problem of the robberies, sat as an alcalde ordinario, dealt in indigo, and settled into a happy and comfortable life with his young second wife. It lasted only six years. On 14 August 1665, the ailing Alonso de Vargas made a will. He died the next day. [44]

———

A month after don Alonso's death in the city of Santiago de Guatemala, his king, Felipe IV, died in Madrid. His desperate, incessant wars to keep together the disintegrating Habsburg empire— in the Low Countries, Italy, and the imperial corridor between; around the Mediterranean; in Catalonia and Portugal; in the New World— had been waged at the expense of the Castilian people. They had been mercilessly taxed and conscripted, and they received little in return. [45]

Despite the insecurities of his times, Diego de Vargas seemingly continued along the path to full responsibility as a landed gentleman. After he married doña Beatriz, he resided mostly in Torrelaguna, where all their children—five in six years—were born and, within a few weeks, baptized by Dr. León. Their first child made her appearance on 9 February 1665, just nine months and four days after the wedding. They named her Isabel María, adding Polonia for St. Apollonia, whose feast day it was. Don Gregorio Pimentel de Prado, Beatriz's older brother, stood as godfather, which he did for each of the subsequent children: Juana Viviana (born 2 December 1666); María Antonia (18 December 1667), who died as a baby; Francisco

Alonso (4 October 1669), also called Francisco Iván; and, last, Juan Manuel (20 December 1670).[46]

The death in 1664 of don Alonso de Santander y Mercado, his father's agent, had thrust don Diego into active management of family affairs. Named administrator that summer, Vargas took his duties seriously, despite an evident dislike for the details. These included keeping the accounts, seeing to maintenance and repair of the properties, and pursuing a variety of lawsuits, the curse on persons of property in Spain's litigious society. There was, for example, the long-standing action to recover the 18,000 ducados his maternal grandfather had failed to pay on his deceased mother's dowry. When his aunt, Antonia, through her husband, don Juan Chacón Bullón, challenged his administration of don Alonso's affairs, don Diego had to go to court to prove his right.[47]

By mid-1666, the family had word of the death of Alonso de Vargas. His will was explicit about the properties in Spain. They went to don Diego. Only in the event of the latter's demise without heirs would Pedro Alonso, the four-year-old half-brother, succeed.

One item in the debts-and-credits section of don Alonso's will stated that he had in Guatemala 10,000 pesos in cash and as much again in "wrought silver, valuables, slaves, and other items," all of which he had ordered inventoried. This, and whatever else remained, don Diego and his three criollo half-siblings were to inherit jointly, except for the standard, second-son bequest to Pedro Alonso. Meantime, Sancho de Guinea Bracamonte, a Jesuit and the brother of don Alonso's young widow, wrote to a superior in Madrid, asking that he seek out a worthy gentleman, preferably of the house of Vargas, for her to remarry. She was, he averred, a very young mother of three at twenty-five or twenty-six, with a dowry that had grown to 40,000 or 50,000 pesos.[48]

———

Later, from the Indies, don Diego would admit his distress, after the first days of managing his estate, at the number of debts, encumbrances, and repairs that demanded his attention. He traveled to Granada to inspect the houses and stores in the city and the two extensive rural properties to the north, the cortijos of Barcinas and La Nava, arranging for repairs and improvements and retaining local overseers and revenue collectors. The Madrid and Torrelaguna holdings too, particularly the main houses, were deteriorating badly as a result of neglect and the weather. From Queen Mariana, widow of Felipe IV, reigning as regent for her infirm, infant son, don Diego obtained permission in July 1667 to borrow up to 4,000 ducados against the revenues of the estate. The stated purpose was to make major repairs to the family residence on the Calle del Almendro and the mansion and a mill in Torrelaguna.[49]

Don Diego's most famous tenant in the renovated house on the Calle del Almendro was forty-eight-year-old don Francisco de Herrera the Younger, flamboyant, strikingly handsome, and tempestuous court painter. For an undisclosed reason, the artist as a favor made Vargas a loan of 137 1/2 doblones of two gold escudos each (the equivalent, says the contract, of 11,000 vellon reales, or 1,000 ducados). As security, don Diego entered into a contract with Herrera on 31 July 1670, leasing to him for four years at no cost the apartment on the patio "composed of various rooms: the three they call the mezzanine and the four above them, together with the one at the top of the stairs from these four, and also the kitchen downstairs and the little patio in it . . . with the use of the fountain, cellar, well, and a stall in the large stable of these houses."[50]

By 1670, the role of gentleman proprietor had worn thin. Yet, Vargas's career options were limited. The highest reaches of government—prestigious ambassadorships, viceroyalties, and presidencies of government councils—were monopolized by men of greater wealth and status. Without a law degree, don Diego had virtually no hope of securing a judgeship or council membership on the peninsula. What he, as a member of the middling nobility, could realistically strive for initially were lesser civil-military offices overseas. Accordingly, in 1670, he submitted a memorial to the crown, reviewing the considerable services of his father and grandfather, both knights of Santiago, and asking for a post for himself.[51]

On the eve of his departure for the Indies, Diego de Vargas said in a statement years later that he was serving as a soldier of the Regiment of His Majesty's Guard, in the company commanded by Luis Enríquez.[52] Still, without the requisite high-level influence, liquid assets, or a university degree, he had little chance of lucrative advancement. Twenty years earlier, his father had obtained an appointment in the Indies, setting the precedent. Moreover, Alonso de Vargas's death in Guatemala had given Diego de Vargas a specific reason to follow—settlement of his share of the overseas estate.

Royal Service in New Spain

It was a fairly common belief in Spain that the climate of the Indies relaxed moral fiber and dulled the intellect. Although he may have dismissed such notions when pondering his future, don Diego would later write letters from New Spain meant to convince his family that he had not succumbed.

By the summer of 1672, it was definite. He was going. The reason for his upcoming "absence" in the Indies, he reiterated in a power of attorney to Father Sebastián de Vargas, was "to settle affairs and his share of the inheritance resulting from his father's death."[53]

To prove that he was the legitimate and sole male heir of his father's first marriage, don Diego had legal proof drawn up. "I am about to leave for the city of Santiago de Guatemala," he wrote in his unstudied hand, "to collect the unrestricted estate my father left, together with the maternal legitim owed to me." He presented four witnesses who testified under oath that Diego de Vargas was indeed his father's son. Using practically the same words, each gave the required, brief physical description of him. He was a young man, they stated, of average stature, straight hair, and broad face. His most distinguishing feature was not a scar, a mole, or a limp, but an abnormality in speech. Don Diego could not pronounce certain words correctly. He lisped.[54]

As was usual for travelers about to embark on a long journey, Vargas made a will. It contained no surprises. He named doña Beatriz guardian of their four children, the eldest of whom, Isabel María, was now seven years old. The elder son, Francisco Iván, not yet three, would inherit the estate should Vargas die. Juan Manuel, not quite twenty months old, would get the usual token for a second son. In addition to Beatriz, don Diego appointed as executors his seventy-four-year-old great-uncle, Sebastián; Father Antonio Mejía, another Jesuit; his brother-in-law, don Gregorio Pimentel de Prado of Torrelaguna; and his good friend, don José de Liñán, also of Torrelaguna.[55]

Don Diego also obtained leave from the colonel of the palace guard. Last, just before bidding his family farewell, he compiled a twenty-six-page inventory of his estate. More than a simple listing, it included advice on improvements, surveys, and legal actions.[56] He entrusted this document to the godfather of his children, his brother-in-law, don Gregorio, whom, of all the relatives, he trusted most.

Parish church of Santa María Magdalena, Torrelaguna.
Maria Carmen Gambliel.

Vargas could not remember a time when he did not know Gregorio
Pimentel. Neighbors in Torrelaguna, they had grown up together.
On the feast day of St. Lawrence, 10 August 1654, when Diego was
an impressionable ten years old, Gregorio, then sixteen, had been
received into the Order of Santiago during a solemn ceremony in
the parish church. The honor devolved upon Gregorio after his older brother, Lorenzo, was killed while serving under their uncle's command in Flanders.[57] Eldest of the surviving Pimentel children, don
Gregorio became a gentleman of Torrelaguna in the fashion of his
father.

Beyond the immediate excuse of settling his father's estate, don
Diego may have had personal reasons to leave his home and family
in Torrelaguna for the uncertainties of the Indies. We know very

little about the family. Surely don Diego's own temperament influenced his decision. Later, by his actions in New Spain, he would prove that he was a man of deeds. He was proud, strong-willed, tenacious, and at times hasty in judgment. In Vargas's case, financial worries— which he expressed repeatedly—combined with a compelling sense of honor and self-worth. Wherever he found himself, don Diego sought obstinately to uphold the illustrious heritage of the house of Vargas.

By the 1660s and 1670s, Castile's twin economic woes—spiraling inflation and debased copper currency, or vellon—had driven prices, even on staples such as wheat and cheese, almost beyond the reach of most Castilians. The weather contributed. There was a severe winter in 1666–67, followed by drought in Old Castile; drought in Valencia in 1668, in Catalonia in 1670, and over most of Spain in 1671; then the floods of 1671–72; and another parched year in 1672. [58]

Not that don Diego and his family were ever hungry. Still, inflation and the weather hurt the propertied, especially those dependent on fixed incomes, as well as the poor. Although his own indebtedness might have served Vargas well, with the chance to pay back in cheaper money, it is clear that he did not understand this. His unswerving financial goal was to disencumber his estate.

———

The royal cedula recommending don Diego de Vargas to the viceroy of New Spain and the president of the Audiencia of Guatemala could only have been obtained at court by making the customary "contributions." It was signed on 12 August 1672 by or for the queen regent, Mariana. An "unstable, ignorant and obstinate woman," in the words of one historian, the queen was supposed to govern with the advice of a high-level junta provided for in Felipe IV's will. At first, she had relied more on her Jesuit confessor, Juan Everardo Nithard, making him, in effect, a kind of prime minister, until a faction of the upper nobility in 1669 forced his dismissal. By 1672, it was rumored at court that the queen had found someone new to depend on, the dashing adventurer don Fernando de Valenzuela. Not until 1675 would her son, Carlos II, reach his majority at age fourteen, after which, writes the same historian, "he was always ailing, often close to death, and increasingly neurotic in his behavior." This was the king, dubbed the Bewitched, Vargas would serve in the New World. [59]

Mariana, Queen Regent of Spain (1665–77).
Rivera Cambas, *Los gobernantes*.

To see him across the Atlantic, don Diego secured a one-time appointment as royal courier to the viceroy of New Spain. His orders were to leave immediately for the port of Cadiz to await the dispatches that would go in his care. He received payment for expenses and, after making the rounds to bid good-bye to his relatives, left Madrid in mid-August. Days later, a fire that killed thirty people and injured more than sixty swept dozens of the connecting, five-story houses on the Plaza Mayor. The one his uncle, Francisco, had bequeathed to his aunt, Juana de Vargas, and he would inherit, with its twelve and a half balconies, stood unharmed in a section the fire did not reach.[60]

In the bright, bustling city of Cadiz, Diego de Vargas waited. Months passed. He spent his expense allowance and what he had brought along for the trip. By January 1673, he was forced to petition the queen for an additional payment. "I am at present," he confessed, "in great need and with small means to prepare several things necessary for the journey." The Council of the Indies provided for 200 pesos more, and the dispatches arrived soon after.[61]

The Atlantic crossing, nearly 5,000 miles, took eight or nine weeks, more or less, depending on the weather. Don Diego did not have to wait for the annual flota to New Spain that had to sail by July to make port before hurricane season began in the Gulf of Mexico. He went earlier, probably in early March, on the packet boat that reached New Spain late in April 1673. Aboard was news of the conflagration in the Plaza Mayor of Madrid, the fierce storms of the previous September, a fire in London that destroyed great quantities of brandy, and an earthquake in Italy.[62]

For the first time, don Diego experienced a long ocean voyage, the blue Caribbean, and the harbor of dank and drab Veracruz guarded by its island fortress of San Juan de Ulúa. On the ride up from the tropical coast to the city of Mexico, he beheld natural wonders: soaring, white-capped volcanoes; lush plants with exotic fruits and flowers; and the breathtaking setting of the city built on an island in Lake Texcoco in a bowl-shaped valley ringed by majestic peaks.

His first impressions of Mexico City were likely mixed. To someone from Madrid, the streets of the viceregal capital must have seemed uncommonly straight and wide. The public buildings and the cathedral, its interior finally completed during the administration of the reigning viceroy, compared favorably. Not even the royal court could match the number or the opulence of Mexico's coaches, trimmed

The Marqués de
Mancera, Viceroy of
New Spain (1664–73).
Rivera Cambas, *Los
gobernantes*.

Sor Juana Inés de la Cruz.
Romero Flores,
Iconografía colonial.

in gold, silver, and Chinese silk. And the fetid canals, choked with canoes and flat-bottomed scows—Madrid had nothing like them. The contrast between squalid, crowded barrios and the spacious park known as the Alameda, where the aristocrats promenaded, should have been no surprise to Vargas. He may not have anticipated the racial variety in the population, however. By the 1670s there were probably twenty thousand Spaniards in the city, and perhaps six or seven times as many Indians, Blacks, and people of mixed blood.[63]

Don Diego went first to the long, fortresslike palace of the viceroy, where the incumbent, don Antonio Sebastián de Toledo Molina y Salazar, Marqués de Mancera, the twenty-fifth person to hold the office in New Spain, awaited the royal dispatches. Ruler of the vast jurisdiction since 1664—the year before Vargas's father had died in Guatemala—Mancera was about to return to Spain after nine energetic and personally profitable years in office.[64]

Although he probably did not have the pleasure of meeting them during his initial visit to the viceregal court, don Diego would later hear of two gifted residents of Mexico City. One, a lovely and witty young woman who had been the Marquesa de Mancera's favorite maid-in-waiting and the darling of the court, had since entered a

Don Carlos de Sigüenza y Góngora.
Mercurio volante.

Jeronymite convent where, as Sor Juana Inés de la Cruz, she would continue her voracious reading, study the emerging scientific disciplines, and write the sonnets and lyric poems that would make her "the supreme poet of her time in Castilian." The other, don Carlos de Sigüenza y Góngora, who as a student had been expelled from the Society of Jesus for sneaking out of his dormitory at night, had the year before, in 1672, by a brilliant display of his learning, won the chair of mathematics and astrology at the University of Mexico. Twenty years later, he would write a short book in praise of don Diego de Vargas.[65]

Evidently, Vargas petitioned the Marqués de Mancera for employment in New Spain, and the viceroy responded by appointing him justicia mayor of the mining district of Teutila. The post lay some two hundred miles southeast of the capital in the rugged, green mountains of Oaxaca, in the direction of—but not quite one-third of the way to—the city of Santiago de Guatemala. Toward the end of 1673, as Mancera began the long journey home, his wife died and was buried in the imposing Franciscan church at Tepeaca on the road to Veracruz. Although he too had been in poor health, the man who named don Diego to his first post lived on in Spain for more than forty years, to the incredible age of one hundred and six.[66]

Capt. Diego de Vargas, as he now styled himself, likely had the names of trustworthy Madrileños doing business and residing in Mexico City. On 17 July 1673, he signed a one-year promissory note, along with his bondsman, don José de Alcocer, for the 2,200 pesos he was borrowing from Juan de Esquibel Maldonado to outfit himself for his new post.[67] He was about to begin duty in the Indies, an adventure he thought would make him a richer man, and, soon enough, see him bound again for Madrid. Instead, it lasted a lifetime.

———

It was a strange and alien world, rugged beyond anything Diego de Vargas had ever experienced. Heavy rains sustained a dense forest growth and turned roads into impassable mires. The district of his alcaldía mayor, some seventeen thousand square miles, was located in the north-central part of today's Mexican state of Oaxaca. Steep, green mountains rose to more than 8,500 feet in the west. Amid their broken vastness, deep in the valley of the Río Papaloapan, lay the town of Teutila. Placer mining along the streams in the area yielded gold. To the east the mountains dropped down precipitously onto hot, lowland plains sparsely inhabited by Spaniards on sprawling cattle ranches. Throughout Vargas's jurisdiction there were scattered communities of Cuicatec, Chinantec, and Mazatec Indians, amounting to several thousand persons who owed tribute to the crown.

As early as 1520, Spaniards had penetrated the region in search of gold. By 1560, Dominican friars had erected the mission of San Pedro at Teutila, and by 1572, with the growth of the non-Indian community, a parish priest had taken over. There may have been several dozen persons who called themselves Spaniards living in and around Teutila during don Diego's tenure, as well as some Blacks and mixed-bloods, and a larger number of Indians.[68]

The title justicia mayor meant that Capt. don Diego de Vargas's initial appointment to the alcaldía mayor of Teutila was an interim one. By 1674, however, he had a regular appointment, at the modest annual salary of 250 pesos.[69] As alcalde mayor, don Diego exercised judicial and political authority over the mixed population of his district. His duties included law enforcement, supervision of tribute collection, protection of Indian communities from exploitation by Spaniards, and judgment of legal disputes.

Alcaldías mayores, particularly in the seventeenth century, were eagerly sought after because of the ready opportunities they offered for illicit, personal gain. Since these offices were almost always purchased, and the salaries were low, holders of them understandably sought to recover their investment and make a profit. Most of the 2,200 pesos Vargas had borrowed in Mexico City in July of 1673 likely went for the required contribution to the crown. The system encouraged illegal practices. Alcaldes mayores could use their posts to extract unremunerated services and demand food, to force sale of goods at inflated prices, and to collect fees for the performance of official duties. Some diverted tribute funds to their personal use. Unless such peculation reached notable proportions, it was frequently overlooked. An appropriate bribe to the official who conducted the customary judicial review of one's term could mean a favorable judgment.[70]

While Diego de Vargas administered the king's justice at Teutila, sad news reached him from home. On 10 July 1674, his wife had died, so suddenly that she did not receive the last rites. They had buried her in her family's exquisite chapel of San Gregorio in the parish church, and don Gregorio Pimentel had arranged for a thou-

Fray Payo de Rivera Enríquez, Viceroy of New Spain (1673–80).
Rivera Cambas, *Los gobernantes*.

sand masses for the repose of her soul. Doña Beatriz was thirty-two. Writing to don Gregorio from Teutila on 22 October 1675, Vargas gave instructions regarding the care of his four children. Already he seemed to be weighing the responsibility he felt for his family in Spain against the personal sacrifice he was making by serving in this isolated corner of the empire.[71]

By this time, however, the possibility of advancement in the Indies looked promising. When he underwent the initial judicial review of his tenure, don Diego was found to be, in the words of his service record, a "good, upright, and disinterested judge, deserving that his majesty and his viceroys honor and employ him in posts in the royal service."[72]

During Vargas's second term at Teutila, an act of God tested his mettle. On the night of the feast of St. Mary Magdalene, 22 July 1676, a frightening electrical storm descended on Teutila. Between eleven and twelve o'clock, lightning struck the house occupied by Lic. Jorge Méndez Pinelo, the curate, and set it afire. Everyone came running. The flames leaped to the thatched roof of the adjoining parish church. Curate Méndez Pinelo, thankful that he had escaped the fire in his house, was standing on the steps of the church, begging for God's mercy, when don Diego reached the scene.

Acting at once, Vargas ordered the priest to accompany him into the burning building. "Emboldened by the grace of God, their hopes entrusted to His mercy, together they risked their lives, entering the church." Amid the flames, they managed to rescue the carved statue of the patron, St. Peter, and others of saints "whose intercession was enough to save them, but neither church nor house, both of which were utterly destroyed." Afterward, don Diego and the priest helped Indian leaders draw up a request to the viceroy-archbishop, fray Payo de Rivera Enríquez. As a result, the natives of Teutila and the pueblos in its district were exempted from all tribute and royal service for two years. During that time, they were to rebuild their church and roof it with tile or brick to prevent a recurrence of the fire.[73]

Vargas's heroic act at Teutila in 1676 was long remembered. The incident apparently gave rise years later to the apocryphal story found inscribed on the only known portrait of him. The place was changed, to Bernalillo in New Mexico, where don Diego died of an illness in 1704, and the circumstances were embellished. He lost his life during open warfare, claimed the inscription, saving the sacred vessels.[74]

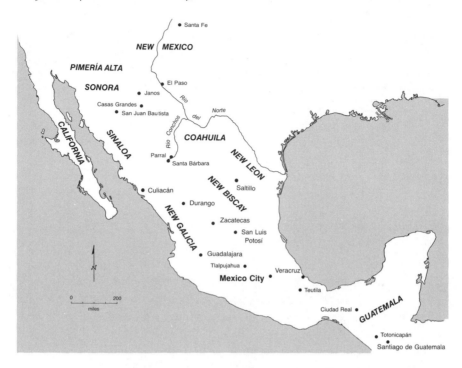

New Spain.

Although don Diego's administration of Teutila lasted five and a half years, until January 1679, it did not imply permanent residence there. He was in Mexico City on several occasions and may also have traveled south to Guatemala. Whatever the disposition of his father's estate, Diego de Vargas did not book passage home.

———

His transfer in 1679 to the alcaldía mayor of Tlalpujahua offered Vargas a challenge. This major silver- and gold-mining district spread along the north slope of high, oak- and pine-clad mountains, fewer than a hundred miles northwest of Mexico City, at an elevation of nine thousand feet. Thirty years before don Diego took over, the population numbered forty Spanish citizens and more than a thousand Indians, Blacks, and mestizos. Ore from several rich veins in the vicinity had kept six water-powered and thirteen animal-powered stamp mills operating at the end of the sixteenth century. By 1679, however, production and morale had fallen. In response to complaints by representatives and miners of Tlalpujahua, who swore that the mines were in desperate straits, the viceroy-archbishop, fray Payo de Rivera Enríquez, named Diego de Vargas justicia mayor.[75]

From Vargas's standpoint, Tlalpujahua had several advantages over Teutila. It was a more important alcaldía mayor and therefore a promotion. Its potential for profit was greater. And the proximity to Mexico City provided readier access to the viceregal court. Moreover, his personal life in the Indies, something he never mentioned in his letters to his family in Spain, now bound him to the capital.

By the late 1670s, he was maintaining a residence in Mexico City. A census of the cathedral's Sagrario parish in 1689 listed the house of Diego de Vargas on the Plazuela de las Gayas, several blocks south of the Zócalo, the city's vast and cluttered main square. The death of his wife in 1674 had made don Diego a widower at thirty. By 1679 or 1680, based on the age of the eldest natural child he recognized on his deathbed in 1704, he was living with a woman. Her name may have been Nicolasa Rincón. Vargas never married her, he explained later, because he always hoped to return to Madrid and marry someone of his own social rank.[76]

We know virtually nothing at this point about Diego de Vargas's New World companion. Whatever her circumstances, she bore him at least three children. After Juan Manuel—the same name as his second son in Spain—she gave birth to Alonso (in 1681–82) and to María Teresa (1685–86).[77]

Another family responsibility had fallen to don Diego in Mexico City. He was supporting his two criollo half-brothers, don Pedro Alonso and don Francisco, born in Guatemala to his father and doña Jerónima Guinea y Murga. Not long after don Alonso's death, doña Jerónima had remarried and gone to live with her second husband, Capt. Gabriel Ugarte y Ayala, knight of the Order of Santiago, at Guazacapán, in a rich cacao-growing region south of Santiago de Guatemala.

In 1682, Pedro Alonso, twenty years old and a law student in Mexico City, and Francisco, eighteen or nineteen, who was with don Diego in Tlalpujahua, named an attorney to act for them in a suit against their mother. They needed their inheritance promptly for two reasons. First, don Diego's wealth, distributed on account to the miners of Tlalpujahua, was by no means secure. Second, he might soon be returning to Spain.[78]

The Conde de Paredes, Viceroy of New Spain (1680–86).
Rivera Cambas, *Los gobernantes*.

Tlalpujahua.
Maria Carmen Gambliel.

Because he was often in Mexico City, and because his noble status gave him access, Diego de Vargas knew personally the first six viceroys under whom he served. Two of them, both members of the close circle of Castile's most powerful families, actively promoted his career. The first of these, don Tomás Antonio de la Cerda y Aragón, Conde de Paredes, governed for two consecutive three-year terms, from 1680 to 1686.[79]

Recognizing Vargas's excellent record at Tlalpujahua, where he had been acting in an interim capacity as justicia mayor, Paredes made him alcalde mayor. Don Diego was, in the viceroy's words, "the right person and indispensable to the development of these mines."[80] A royal cedula, dated 16 February 1683, further recommended Vargas.[81] In response to it and figures from the Treasury office in Mexico City, Paredes on 3 April 1685 addressed an especially favorable letter to the king, proposing that Diego de Vargas be considered for higher office.

The Conde de Monclova, Viceroy of New Spain (1686–88).
Rivera Cambas, *Los gobernantes*.

Under his able administration, the Tlalpujahua district had experienced a remarkable recovery. Between 1679 and 1684, the viceroy reported, Vargas had tripled crown revenue from its silver mines. Such revenue derived from two main sources. The first was a direct tax on production, levied by Treasury officials at 10 percent, with an additional 1 percent for administration. The second was the royal monopoly on mercury, an essential ingredient in the patio process of refining ore.

As alcalde mayor, Vargas was responsible for distributing the mercury to miners in his district. Before he took over, the annual amount transported to Tlalpujahua had not totaled 55 hundredweight, even in a good year. During don Diego's five years, it had averaged nearly 122 hundredweight. Furthermore, he had been prompt in paying for his consignments of mercury, valued in total at almost 85,000 pesos.[82]

Vargas also saw to matters concerning the labor force. At one point, he received a confusing order from the Tribunal of Accounts in Mexico City. The free Indians working in the mines at Tlalpujahua had long been exempt from paying tribute. The order seemed to say that they should not have been exempt. For clarification, don Diego wrote to the Conde de Paredes. His query went through the bureaucracy, causing the viceroy's advisers to cite conflicting laws. Finally, on the basis of a cedula by Felipe II, dated in Lisbon on 4 July 1582, and its reaffirmation in New Spain by a general junta of 22 November 1603, Paredes upheld the customary exemption and ordered that Vargas be so informed.[83]

Don Diego's ability to borrow large sums of money during his career in the royal service was of prime importance to him. By 1680, he had associated himself with Capt. Luis Sáenz de Tagle, a powerful member of the Consulado in Mexico City and a large-scale buyer of unminted silver from the miners he supplied with goods and credit. Through Sáenz de Tagle, who loaned him money, served as his supplier, and became his friend, Vargas gained access to a network of bankers and merchants linking Mexico City to other financial centers in Spain and the empire.[84]

Late in 1686—the year the Conde de Paredes turned over the government of New Spain to his successor, the Conde de Monclova—don Diego suffered a severe reverse. Sáenz de Tagle had sent him a large shipment of cash. Twenty-five miles short of Tlalpujahua, at a place called El Bosque, one Rafael Gómez Fajardo, or Jurado, and his gang fell upon the freighters and stole the money.

Vargas reacted swiftly. Reminding the new viceroy that he had restored Tlalpujahua and tripled royal revenue from its mines, don Diego sought extraordinary powers to deal with the thieves. The robbery, he averred, had all but ruined him. He and an armed party had failed to discover the gang's hiding place. Having determined that the criminals had not come into Mexico City, he now wanted authority not only to pursue them anywhere in the kingdom of New Spain, but also to try them on the spot and execute them without appeal. The viceroy's legal counsel, doubting neither Vargas's motives nor his conduct, pointed out the danger of error should the wrong people be executed. Accordingly, on 1 January 1687, Monclova commissioned Captain Vargas to apprehend the criminals and bring them back for trial and punishment. He was not to execute them. How the episode ended we do not know.[85]

By early 1687, don Diego was no longer serving as alcalde mayor of Tlalpujahua. Through don Juan González Calderón, a businessman registered with the Council of the Indies and his agent at court in Madrid, Vargas was seeking a higher post—the governorship of New Mexico. Earlier, he had sent González Calderón a power of attorney to press for a post in Guatemala or Peru. Now, having arranged through don Juan to submit a petition and to pay at Cadiz 2,500 pesos into the treasury of the Council of the Indies, he secured the New Mexico appointment.[86]

The Spanish crown's acceptance of cash contributions from office seekers was a polite fiction reflecting theoretical disapproval of the sale of office. Nevertheless, the government's mounting expenses and exhausted tax base encouraged the spread of the practice in the seventeenth century until escribanías of all sorts, treasury posts, some low-level audiencia positions, alcaldías mayores, certain governorships, and, in the end, even viceroyalties were for sale. Buyers might be fully qualified, or they might not, but the critical need for revenue blurred the distinction.[87]

Don Diego's royal title, dated at Madrid on 18 June 1688, ten days after payment of the 2,500 pesos, cited his commendable record at Tlalpujahua, his known nobility, and the fact that he was in Mexico City "without any post at all" but eager to continue in the royal service. His term as political and military governor of "the castle, provinces, and lands of New Mexico" was to run for five years from the day he acceded. He would receive the same annual salary as his predecessors, 2,000 pesos. The appointment was to be acted on immediately by the viceroy, even if the term of an incumbent viceregal appointee had not yet expired. In the event of don Diego's death or some other eventuality that prevented him from taking office, the 2,500 pesos were to be refunded to Luis Sáenz de Tagle in Mexico City.[88]

———

Before word of Vargas's promotion reached New Spain, another viceroy did. Don Gaspar de la Cerda Sandoval Silva y Mendoza, Conde de Galve, accompanied by the usual large and colorful entourage, made his public entry into Mexico City on 4 December 1688. Received at the cathedral by the archbishop, he proceeded to a reception in the palace of the Marqueses del Valle hosted by the former viceroy and vicereine. Related to the Conde de Paredes and sharing the surname Cerda, don Gaspar, who occupied the highest office in New Spain for seven years, was the second of the viceroys especially well disposed toward Diego de Vargas.

Although we have at present no direct evidence that Galve and Vargas knew each other in Madrid, it is likely they did, since they lived as close neighbors for some fifteen years. Galve and his mother, the Duquesa del Infantado, attended the church of San Andrés, which adjoined the Bishop's Chapel built by Vargas's ancestors. Because don Diego was ten years older than don Gaspar, they probably were not childhood friends, but certainly their families were acquainted. Moreover, the mayordomo of Galve's household, don Amadeo Isidro Zeyol, was a good friend of Diego de Vargas.[89]

Early in 1689, the Conde de Galve, still unaware of the grant bestowing the governorship of New Mexico on don Diego, reappointed him to Tlalpujahua. In the meantime, the crown had given that alcaldía mayor to someone else. When the rival, don Agustín de Hierro, appeared later in the year with a royal title containing the familiar clause permitting him to accede immediately, Vargas found himself abruptly displaced. At about the same time, however, he had good news from home. His elder daughter had married well.[90]

———

The Conde de Galve, Viceroy of New Spain (1688–96).

The wedding in Madrid, on 13 December 1688, of Isabel María de Vargas Pimentel, twenty-three years old, to don Ignacio López de Zárate y Alvarez de Medina, knight of the Order of Santiago, king's councilor, and fiscal of the Council of War, forty-one, was a gala and costly occasion. The entire court attended the ceremony, don Ignacio recalled later.

Doña Isabel María was lady of the house of Vargas, and don Ignacio the second son of the deceased don Iñigo López de Zárate y Balaguer, city councilman of Madrid and king's councilor. Both families belonged to the parish of San Pedro el Real. The López de Zárates were leaders in the Third Order of St. Francis, and don Iñigo had endowed a chapel at the Franciscan convento where the Vargases also had their chapel. By agreement, don Ignacio moved into the Vargas family home. Writing to Diego de Vargas in New Mexico years later, López de Zárate made it very clear that he had not married doña Isabel María for her money.[91]

In the absence of don Diego, his widowed aunt, doña Juana de Vargas Ponce de León, carried on the nuptial negotiations, along with doña Isabel María and her eighteen-year-old brother, don Juan Manuel. Vargas, writing from the Indies, had entrusted to doña Juana the arrangement of an appropriate marriage for Isabel María, who had been living with her great-aunt in the houses on the Plaza Mayor. He had also empowered doña Juana to offer as much as 9,000 pesos as a dowry.

Accordingly, on 15 November 1688, doña Juana, acting with Isabel María and Juan Manuel, entered into a marriage contract with don Ignacio López de Zárate. Doña Juana, in Vargas's name, offered the full 9,000 pesos and an additional 1,000 for wedding expenses, in effect, a 10,000-peso dowry. The entire amount was due within two years of the wedding date and payable in a lump sum in pesos, or, as they were known in Spain, escudos of 10 silver reales each. New World silver, as everyone knew, had greater buying power than Castile's vellon currency. Meantime, annual interest, payable every six months, would accrue at the rate of 5 percent.

Don Ignacio was also to receive 1,500 ducados from Isabel María's grandmother, doña Isabel de Olazábal Vélez de Guevara of Torrelaguna. In addition, he would collect 500 ducados annually for five years in income from the Vargas houses on the Calle del Almendro, where he and his bride were to live. During this period, Vargas was obligated to pay for all repairs, major and minor.

Doña Juana was the third person to exercise don Diego's general power of attorney since his departure for the Indies, succeeding his wife, doña Beatriz, and his brother-in-law, don Gregorio. Now, in the marriage contract, she committed as security all the revenue from the Vargas entails; her houses on the Plaza Mayor, which she had inherited from her brother, Francisco; and the 5,000-ducado censo she held on the revenues of the city of Granada. Moreover, if the dowry and interest were not paid within the stipulated two years, she agreed to substitute don Ignacio for herself in Diego de Vargas's general power of attorney. López de Zárate would then administer the Vargas entails and collect whatever income they might yield until the full dowry was paid.

For his part, don Ignacio pledged 4,000 ducados for wedding outfit and groom's gift, which he claimed was one-tenth of his worth. He also agreed to pay 300 ducados annually for Isabel María's personal household expenses. Among the witnesses to the contract was don Gregorio Pimentel de Prado, Vargas's trusted brother-in-law.[92]

Once the contract was signed, don Ignacio tried to borrow the full 10,000 pesos against it. Failing in this, and faced with the immediacy of the wedding, he turned to his influential older brother, don Juan Antonio, first Marqués de Villanueva de la Sagra. With part of the 4,000 pesos don Juan Antonio loaned him, don Ignacio covered the 1,000 he had already turned over to doña Juana for wedding expenses.[93]

———

Vargas's new son-in-law was only four years his junior. Don Ignacio had a law degree, a good position at court, and relatives in high places. A mark of don Diego's courteous respect was his imprecise use of the title doctor in the first letters he addressed to him. López de Zárate had graduated from the University of Salamanca, but he had not gone on to earn a doctorate. Along with most of his classmates, he had embarked on a career in office. He had held several positions in the Kingdom of Naples, among them governor of Capua and president of the Council of Santa Clara. Upon his return to Spain, he had been named legal adviser to the Council of War, of which his brother, don Juan Antonio, was secretary.[94] When writing to them, don Diego always used the formal mode of address.

Diego de Vargas and Ignacio López de Zárate were both members of the middle-ranking nobility, both eager for preferment, but there was a difference. Don Diego, true to his family's tradition of service in the civil-military hierarchy overseas, was proving himself in the Indies as a man of action. He probably felt superior to the bureaucrats, who held university degrees and staffed the king's councils at home as did don Ignacio. In part, at least, the old distinction between the nobility of the sword and the nobility of the robe—along with family dynamics, financial pressures, and don Diego's endless requests for favors at court— may explain the tension one senses in the correspondence between the two men.

A more specific cause of discord was the dowry. There was no way, don Diego professed in letters to don Ignacio, that he could pay promptly the 10,000 pesos his aunt had promised. He simply did not have that much cash. Although he certainly had the credit, Vargas chose not to borrow the lump sum from don Luis Sáenz de Tagle. Instead, earlier in 1690 than the marriage contract required, he turned over to López de Zárate by power of attorney the management of his properties in Spain. Although he had recently described how little these holdings had been worth to him, he may have believed that his son-in-law could restore them to profitable operation. [95]

Don Diego also asked don Ignacio to act as substitute father to the children he had not seen in sixteen years. Sometime after 1675, Francisco Iván, Vargas's elder son, had died, leaving Juan Manuel as the sole, legitimate, male heir of the house of Vargas. Don Diego was especially concerned that his son be given firm guidance. [96]

From all indications, Juan Manuel was an attractive youth. Following in the tradition of his grandfather, don Alonso de Vargas, he had been placed at court as a noble page to María Luisa de Borbón, the first queen of Carlos II. A niece of Louis XIV of France, María Luisa had formally entered Madrid as a bride in 1680. [97]

Everyone in the queen's household answered ultimately to her mayordomo. Interestingly enough, the Conde de Paredes, who as viceroy of New Spain recommended Diego de Vargas so highly, had returned to Spain in 1687 and become chief mayordomo of María Luisa. [98] Even though the queen was surrounded by her meninos and other servants, she lived a lonely existence and did not produce the desired heir to the throne. In February 1689, she suffered a short and violent illness, which she believed was the result of poison. Within days, it proved fatal.

Another royal marriage was arranged almost immediately. Mariana de Neoburgo, sister of Emperor Leopold I, wed Carlos II by

Carlos II of Spain (1677–1700).
Rivera Cambas, *Los gobernantes*.

proxy in August 1689, and then in person at Valladolid the following May.[99] Her lavish, initial entrance into Madrid, for which members of the royal household turned out in the finest attire, cost Juan
Manuel's family more than did any other event during his years as a
menino.[100]

As a noble page at court, don Juan Manuel occupied a position
superior to that of pages who served in the palaces of other great
lords. Still, the personal qualifications were similar. Late in the reign
of Carlos II, a wealthy merchant of Cadiz, believing that his youn-
gest son was well qualified, sent him to Madrid to become a page to
a powerful noble. "He had a splendid appearance for it," wrote the
merchant, "being as everybody knows very charming and having all
the right skills, such as dancing, playing a guitar with great skill,
carrying a sword well, well written, very well spoken and very courteous. In short, all my friends advised me to do it. But he did nothing more than spend money and bear himself like the son of a great
lord, whereupon I decided to bring him back."[101]

Juan Manuel, already the son and heir of a middle-ranking lord,
lived for years amid the opulence of the royal household. From the
Indies, don Diego encouraged him to continue serving at the royal
palace until he could obtain a commission as captain of cavalry, just
as his grandfather had. One thing Vargas forbade. Under no circumstances was his son to join him in New Spain.[102]

The Recolonization of New Mexico

Unexpectedly replaced as alcalde mayor of Tlalpujahua in 1689,
Diego de Vargas fumed for a year. The necessity of collecting early
payment for the five tons of mercury he was responsible for—valued
at as much as 14,000 pesos—caused him to fear that his credit would
be ruined. He was hard pressed to settle with the various miners and
their agents and, at the same time, prepare for his governorship in
New Mexico. Not until 25 September 1690 did he receive the dispatches from the Conde de Galve ordering that he accede to the
northern post. The Treasury office, on 12 October, disbursed in the
new governor's name two years' salary in advance, 4,000 pesos, and
an additional 800 pesos for travel and moving expenses.

Early in November, Vargas wrote a brief letter to Isabel María in Madrid, assuring her that he was providing for her dowry. He then took leave of his household in Mexico City and set out with his attendants for New Mexico. The long road north would have given him time to reflect on the recent history of the colony and the opportunity of his appointment. [103]

———

New Mexico had been for years a colony in exile. More than a decade had passed since that Thursday, 20 March 1681, when the Conde de Paredes and his entourage had attended the solemn memorial service in Mexico City for twenty-one Franciscan missionaries slain in an uprising of the Pueblo Indians. After more than eighty years of Spanish domination, the Indians of the kingdom and provinces of New Mexico had rebelled on the feast day of St. Lawrence, 10 August 1680, killing not only the friars, but also hundreds of colonists and their native sympathizers. The governor, don Antonio de Otermín, and the other survivors had fled. They had abandoned Santa Fe, the capital, and taken refuge in the El Paso area, more than three hundred miles to the south. Late in 1681, an attempted reconquest had failed ignominiously. [104]

Responding to the emergency, which left the northern mines more vulnerable to native and foreign incursions, Paredes had established a fifty-man presidial garrison at El Paso, seat of New Mexico's government-in-exile. He also thought of sending a colony of three hundred Spanish and mulatto families to Santa Fe, but that project was lost amid the other crises of the 1680s. [105]

In May 1683, pirates, a growing curse on both coasts of New Spain, had brutally assaulted the port of Veracruz and held it for ransom, eventually sailing away with immense quantities of booty. At this same time, the touted expedition to occupy Baja California was struggling to gain a permanent foothold in that hostile environment. Its secular leader, don Isidro de Atondo y Antillón, and his missionary counterpart, the Jesuit, Father Eusebio Francisco Kino, had done all they could, at a cost of 225,000 pesos, only to learn in 1686 that further funds had been diverted and the enterprise abandoned. Defense of the mining colony of New Biscay had taken priority. There, rebellious Upper Tarahumaras and other Indians, emboldened by the success of the Pueblos of New Mexico, had intensified their depredations.

English and French buccaneers, meanwhile, kept up their raiding.[106]

French colonists, however, not pirates, had posed the most serious threat during Paredes's tenure. Through diplomatic channels, Spanish authorities knew that a disgruntled former governor of New Mexico, don Diego de Peñalosa, had been at the court of Louis XIV urging a French invasion of New Spain from the Gulf of Mexico across the plains via New Mexico. By 1685, the viceroy had more specific reports. A French expedition under the command of René Robert Cavelier, Sieur de la Salle, had set sail for America to establish a colony on the Gulf coast. In response, Paredes ordered expeditions to counter the intruders.[107]

For the security of the entire frontier, and especially the mines, the crown had decreed as early as 1683 that New Mexico must be restored, and with as little expense to the royal treasury as possible.[108] Several enterprising subjects had responded. The most elaborate plan had come from one Capt. Toribio de la Huerta, a former resident of the colony. In 1689, he offered to restore what had been lost and, in addition, secure the fabled, mercury- and silver-rich Sierra Azul and Cerro Colorado. In return, he asked for the title marqués and what amounted to proprietary control over the colony. Although the crown had recommended Huerta to the viceroy of New Spain—by then the Conde de Galve—nothing came of his scheme. Another contender was don Domingo Jironza Petrís de Cruzate, the man Vargas would replace as governor of New Mexico. Jironza, who had served from 1684 to 1686 and again from 1689 to 1691, was seeking reappointment on the strength of an impressive victory in 1689 over the Indians at the fortified pueblo of Zia. By the time a royal decree in his favor reached Mexico City, however, don Diego had taken over at El Paso.[109]

———

The Conde de Galve had put his trust in Vargas. Restoration of New Mexico figured prominently in the viceroy's plan to turn back the French challenge in North America. Galve, in fact, sought systematically to defend New Spain from imperial rivals by fortifying ports, waging war on piracy, and countering foreign incursions with strategic military colonies. He encouraged Father Kino's explorations on the northwestern frontier. The several overland expeditions of Alonso de León and the voyages of Andrés de Pez to locate the remains

The southwest corner of the main plaza, Pecos pueblo.
  Artist's restoration by S. P. Moorehead. Kessell, *Kiva, Cross, and Crown*.

of La Salle's ill-starred colony on the Texas coast and to establish a
Spanish presence in that area were all components of the same plan.[110]

For his part, don Diego knew what the reconquest of New Mexico could mean in terms of promotion and honors. Acceding to office on 22 February 1691, he found the colony of exiles in deplorable condition, which he reported to Galve. The presidial garrison had neither protective leather jackets nor swords. In El Paso and the four settlements strung out southeastward along the valley of the Río del Norte, there were scarcely one hundred Spanish citizens, by which he must have meant heads of household or adult males capable of bearing arms. The population of Christian Indians did not total a thousand. The soldiers had only 132 horses, the rest of the populace perhaps 200 horses and mules. There were no cattle and only 600 sheep, more or less, most of them belonging to the missionaries. If don Diego did not send for flour to Parral, the mining center more than three hundred miles south, he would be reduced to eating tortillas made from the meager local supply of maize.

Vargas asked the viceroy for forty or fifty modern muskets to arm the citizens for campaigns, as well as two new chambers for the bronze mortars he had found. He would do all he could to rectify the shortages of provisions and horses. His plan was to reconnoiter the villa of Santa Fe at the earliest opportunity. He was ready, he assured Galve, to restore the Pueblo Indians to the empire and the church, without treachery, even though it might cost him his life.[111]

In 1691 the population of the Pueblo Indians upriver in the former kingdom of New Mexico may have been 25,000. First contacted by Europeans of Francisco Vázquez de Coronado's exploring expedition in 1540, they were so named because they lived in pueblos, in contrast to the semisedentary hunters and gatherers who sparsely inhabited the surrounding vastness. Characteristically close-built around one or more central plazas, these rock and earth communal dwellings rose in height to as many as five stories, each level set back, one upon the other, in truncated pyramid form. Each pueblo housed from several hundred to more than 2,000 people and, although there was much ceremonial and commercial intercourse, each acted on its own.

The territory of the Pueblo Indians, divided by the Spaniards into seven or eight provinces corresponding to the different languages they spoke, centered on the Rio Grande and its tributaries and extended from the Piro communities south of present-day Albuquerque to Tiwa-speaking Taos in the north. East of the Rio Grande lay the Salinas province and the populous pueblo of Pecos. To the west, atop a great, sheer-sided rock, stood Acoma, and beyond, the most distant provinces of the Zuñi and Hopi pueblos. During the seventeenth century, Spanish Franciscan friars had taken up residence in most of the pueblos. Until 1680, Spain had maintained New Mexico, which lacked readily exploitable wealth, primarily as a missionary colony to convert the Pueblo Indians to Christianity.[112]

Before he could return the Pueblos of New Mexico to the fold, however, Vargas had to deal with problems closer at hand. Next to food, Indian affairs were the new governor's most urgent concern. He had begun immediately to learn about the complex, shifting alliances of the native peoples in the El Paso area—the Mansos, Sumas,

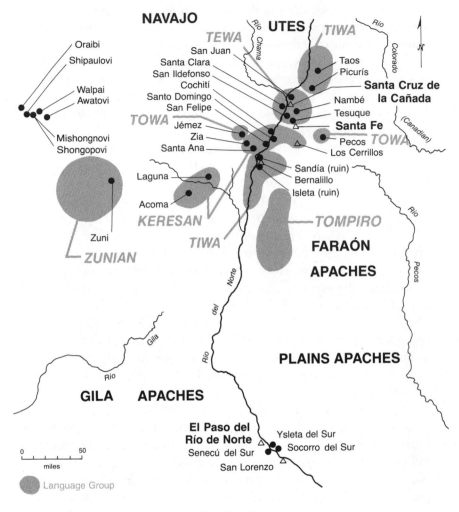

New Mexico.

and several hundred Pueblo refugees—and those in the expanse of semiarid, basin-and-range country to the west in the direction of the province of Sonora—the Janos, Jocomes, Gila Apaches, and others.[113]

In the fall of 1691, Vargas found himself drawn, against his will, into a frustrating joint campaign to the west with units from New Biscay and Sonora. He helped the Franciscans found a new mission community for the inconstant Suma Indians and, from time to time, pursued Apaches. Yet, despite the demands, details, and emergencies, don Diego kept sight of his primary goal.[114]

Corresponding with the viceroy and with Gov. Juan Isidro de Pardiñas of New Biscay, he pressed for the loan of an additional fifty presidial soldiers to reinforce his meager garrison on the reconnaissance as far as Santa Fe. He urged that former New Mexico colonists now relocated in New Biscay be forced, or given incentives, to join him in recolonizing their former homeland. On 9 April 1692, the same day he wrote to his son-in-law in Spain, he addressed another letter to Pardiñas, requesting that the latter make known the following offer. To mounted citizens who accompanied him on the reentry, don Diego was prepared to provide arms, munitions, food (including chocolate), light duty, and a share in any distribution of captives.[115]

Finally, on the feast day of St. Lawrence, 10 August 1692, the twelfth anniversary of the Pueblo Revolt, Vargas ordered the expedition proclaimed at El Paso. For don Diego, a native of Madrid, that day had broader significance. Spaniards still celebrated on 10 August their glorious victory in 1557 over French forces at Saint-Quentin. Felipe II, the king who made Madrid his court, had commemorated this day monumentally in the construction of San Lorenzo del Escorial, his massive royal monastery-mausoleum outside the capital.[116]

On 17 August 1692, the Spanish governor forded the river and rode north with the fifty presidial soldiers of El Paso and their officers, ten armed citizens, a hundred of the Pueblo Indians settled in the El Paso area, three Franciscan friars, pack animals, livestock, several wagons carrying provisions, a small cannon, and a mortar. The fifty soldiers he had requested from New Biscay had not reached El Paso in time. He left orders for them to follow.[117]

———

The column, dwarfed by the jagged ranges along its route, kept to the old road in the trough of the Río del Norte. It made good time, averaging about twelve miles a day for almost four weeks. Upriver, the expedition passed by pueblos that lay ominously deserted. In contrast, Santa Fe, set in a bowl of rolling piñon- and juniper-studded hills at the base of high mountains, teemed with a thousand or more Indian occupants. They had made over the former Spanish government buildings on the north side of the main plaza into a multistory, fortified Indian pueblo, and they awaited the outnumbered invaders defiantly.

During a day of tense negotiations, Vargas appealed to Pueblo leaders through his interpreters to submit peacefully. As they stalled, and other Pueblo Indians began arriving from the surrounding area, the Spanish governor ordered his men to cut the ditch supplying water to the stronghold. The threat of a siege brought some of the Indians out to sue for peace. Don Diego reiterated his offer of pardon and told the leaders to have their people hang small crosses around their necks and set up a large cross in the central patio. Then both sides spent a vigilant night.

The next morning, 14 September, feast of the Exaltation of the Holy Cross, don Diego de Vargas, brushing aside a warning that he should dress and arm himself as if for battle, emerged from his campaign tent in his finest court attire. Accompanied by his officers, the blue-robed friars, and the civilians, with the alferez holding aloft the royal banner, he entered through the single, narrow gate of the native stronghold. When the Indians had come down from their houses and assembled around him, the resplendent Spanish governor performed the customary ritual act of possession.[118]

> I assured them through the interpreters that they should now be more at ease, recognizing my good will, and content to find themselves pardoned and restored to our holy faith and to the king, our lord (may God keep him), of whom they were formerly vassals. I told them that I had returned in his royal name to reconfirm and reclaim the possession he held, not only of this kingdom, its provinces, and all the land, but also of them. He was their lord, their natural king, and no other, and they should consider themselves fortunate to be vassals of such a king and lord and sovereign monarch.
>
> At the same time, I ordered the alferez to raise the royal banner three times as I, the governor and captain general, proclaimed and ordered all to repeat three times, "Long live the king, our lord (may God keep him), Carlos II, king of the Spains, of all this new world, and of the kingdom and provinces of New Mexico." I affirmed three times that this kingdom of New Mexico and its provinces are his, and

these vassals, newly conquered and restored, responded three times, "Long live the king, and may he rule happily." Jubilantly, as a demonstration of joy, they tossed their hats into the air. The reverend missionary fathers fell to their knees in prayers of thanksgiving, and the entire crowd there before the Holy Cross heard the praying of the Te Deum Laudamus.[119]

The three Franciscans then absolved the Indians of their apostasy and the next day, under an arbor set up for the purpose, celebrated the first mass in Santa Fe in more than a dozen years. After a second mass two days later, they baptized 122 children born since 1680. Diego de Vargas served as godfather of the principal leader's three daughters and of most of the others.

Vargas, as much as any Spanish governor of New Mexico, and more than most, recognized the effectiveness of diplomacy and personal relations with the Pueblo Indian peoples. His willingness to deal personally with the natives of New Mexico seems to represent a gradual change of attitude on his part during long service in the Indies. Sixteen years earlier, he had written from Teutila to his son-in-law that living among Indians was "the same thing as being in a wilderness."[120]

In the next four weeks, Vargas carried his bold reconnaissance to the northern pueblos, repeating in each the same ritual acts. By 16 October he was back at Santa Fe. As a courier made ready to carry south the detailed, daily journal of the expedition thus far, don Diego summarized for the Conde de Galve his triumphs to date: 13 pueblos, including the former villa of Santa Fe, newly possessed; thousands of souls absolved; and 969 children baptized. Still, to make the reconquest permanent, he cautioned, five hundred families of colonists and a hundred presidial soldiers would be required. If fewer came, the result would be, in Vargas's words, "like casting a grain of salt into the sea." Meanwhile, he was planning to extend his victorious tour to the other pueblos, even those of the provinces of the Zuñis and Hopis far to the west. "I shall remain satisfied, even elated," he boasted, "that no one has been so daring as to undertake what, by divine will, I have achieved thus far."[121]

Vargas's insistence that he was reconquering New Mexico at his own expense has led to two assumptions long after the fact: first, that this must have been something out of the ordinary; and, second, that don Diego must have been enormously wealthy. Neither was true. The Spanish crown had long demanded that discovery and conquest be privately financed. Only by special permission were royal funds to be expended on such endeavors. Following the lead of his predecessor, Jironza, who claimed to have undertaken five relief actions and twelve campaigns at his own expense, don Diego paid to outfit and supply the 1692 reconnaissance expedition. His monotonous reiteration of the fact served to remind a continually straitened government that he had done his duty according to the royal will, without subsidy, in the great tradition of Spanish conquest. [122]

Yet even that, in a sense, was a fiction. The fifty soldiers and their officers from the El Paso presidio were salaried, as were the fifty reinforcements from New Biscay, who had eventually overtaken Vargas near Santa Fe on 22 September. Their dress, weapons, munitions, and horses would have been supplied at government expense. Frontier governors and their captains received lump sums on account from the royal treasury, paid and equipped the garrisons in their jurisdictions, and were subject to audit at the end of their terms. The three Franciscan friars received royal stipends through their order.

Most of the cost to Vargas personally, therefore, was for food and other essentials—meat, biscuit, maize, chocolate, tobacco— for the ten civilians and one hundred Indian auxiliaries, that is, the unsalaried, irregular forces, as well as for any servants, muleteers, herders, and cooks. Don Diego probably also loaned weapons, munitions, and horses to those participants who lacked them. The greatest incentive to the irregulars was, of course, the prospect of spoils: captives, livestock, weapons, food, and other possessions of the enemy.

At the rate of 1.5 reales per person per day—the allowance for colonists traveling to New Mexico in 1693 and 1694—the total for one hundred and fifty people for 128 days would have amounted to 3,600 pesos. Vargas probably did not have to spend even that much. His route was through the country of sedentary native farmers. Although he was at pains in his journal to certify that he did not take food from them, he did mention barter and gifts. His Indian auxiliaries, perhaps more used to hunting and foraging than other members of the column, may not have required much in the way of provisions. Had don Diego spent thousands of pesos on this expedition, he would surely have supplied the figure. [123]

Whatever the reconnaissance of 1692 cost Diego de Vargas, it made him a hero. Receipt in Mexico City of the news from "newly restored" Santa Fe set off a notable celebration. An occasion to rejoice in the shadow of famine and disease and the frightening food riots of the previous summer was especially welcome. The Conde de Galve ordered the pealing of the bells of the city and, on Saturday, 22 November, the illumination of the cathedral. Accompanied by members of the audiencia, Galve joined the archbishop in a grand service of thanksgiving. Two days later, the viceroy presided at a junta that praised and thanked don Diego. As evidence of their confidence in him, the ministers authorized an open draft in Vargas's name in the amount of 12,000 pesos to be used for the maintenance and defense of what he had won. Viewed from Mexico City, the reconquest of New Mexico had already been achieved and "without blood or fire."[124]

Vargas's courageous leadership and the sacrifice required of his small force were everywhere evident in the campaign journal. Responding on 24 November, the Conde de Galve and the ministers of the junta acknowledged that don Diego,

> having promised the vindication of his noble blood and most honorable qualities in the expedition to the villa of Santa Fe of the provinces of New Mexico and its restoration, embarked upon, gained, and won it by such extraordinary measures, expedients, and devices that his resounding triumph, in such circumstances, is worthy of admiration. Every step and every eventuality he accepted as providential, overcoming them discreetly in order to attain his goal, making himself thereby worthier of such felicitous success to the glory of God Our Lord and the greatest pleasure of his majesty. Many and repeated thanks are his. It is impossible to convey to him the exhilaration and joy he has caused throughout the entire kingdom. He has earned the highest appreciation and esteem of his excellency and the ministers of the junta, who bear him in mind to attend and honor him as a person who by his own deeds proclaims and repeats those of his ancestors.[125]

By mid-December 1692, don Diego and his men were back in El Paso, having extended the reconnaissance to the remaining Rio Grande pueblos, Acoma, and the Zuñi and Hopi pueblos in the west. Relying on the disunity of the native peoples and the boldness of Vargas, they had carried out in four months the symbolic reconquest of all New Mexico.

MERCURIO
VOLANTE
CON LA NOTICIA

de la recuperacion de las
PROVINCIAS DEL NVEVO MEXICO
CONSEGVIDA

Por D. DIEGO DE VARGAS, ZAPATA, Y LUXAN
PONZE DE LEON,

Governador y Capitan General de aquel Reyno.

ESCRIVIOLA

Por especial orden de el Excelentissimo Señor CONDE DE
GALVE VIRREY, GOVERNADOR, Y CAPITAN
GENERAL DE LA NUEVA-ESPAñA, &c.

DON *CARLOS DE SIGVENZA, Y*
GONGORA, *Cosmographo mayor de su Ma=*
gestad en estos Reynos, y Cathedratico Iubilado de Mathe-
maticas en la Academia Mexicana.

Con licencia en Mexico:
EN LA IMPRENTA DE ANTUERPIA
de los Herederos de la Viuda de Bernardo Calderon, año de 1693.

Mercurio volante by don Carlos de Sigüenza y Góngora, 1693.
Courtesy of The Huntington Library, San Marino, California.

When the viceroy received the second half of Vargas's journal, he commissioned don Carlos Sigüenza y Góngora, acting as court chronicler, to write a tract celebrating the feat. The resulting thirty-six-page *Mercurio Volante*, published in Mexico City in 1693, recounted the campaign in stirring detail. Vargas had, in the words of Sigüenza y Góngora, restored a whole kingdom "without wasting a single ounce of powder or unsheathing a sword and (what is most worthy of consideration and regard) without having cost the royal treasury a single maravedi."[126]

Vargas knew the difference between ritual reconquest and actual reoccupation. Nevertheless, while devoting himself vigorously to plans for the proposed colonizing expedition later in 1693, he took full advantage of his new fame. In a lengthy memorial to the king, written from Zacatecas in May during a recruiting and supply trip, he asked for a noble title of Castile, suggesting Marqués de los Caramancheles, after the two villages near Madrid from which he derived certain revenue. In addition, he wanted appointment to the governorship of Guatemala, the Philippines, Chile, or the Río de la Plata.[127]

Don Diego worked toward both ends—the recolonization of New Mexico and personal preferment—with characteristic zeal, but neither came easily.

———

The collection of Diego de Vargas's personal correspondence that follows contains no letter from the three most active years of his recolonization of New Mexico. It is not likely, even with the exigencies of duty, that he stopped writing home. For some reason, these letters are missing.[128]

On 25 February 1696, from Santa Fe, Vargas appealed to don Martín Solís y Miranda, an old acquaintance who had just been appointed to the Council of the Indies. Without dissembling, he pressed his case for advancement. The year before, Juan González Calderón, acting for Vargas at court, had presented a memorial to the king requesting reappointment, the noble title of marqués, and a 6,000-peso encomienda to be collected annually in tribute from the Pueblo Indians. Vargas's five-year term as governor of New Mexico, which began when he acceded at El Paso on 22 February 1691, had expired, although he was still in office. Through agents in Mexico City, he was seeking to block his designated successor, don Pedro

Rodríguez Cubero, who had held an appointment to the New Mexico post since 1692. Don Diego, before surrendering his governorship, wanted assurance of a new appointment or, failing that, another term in New Mexico.[129]

His case was a good one. With the full cooperation of the Conde de Galve and his junta, who allowed him carte blanche to draw on the royal treasury, Vargas had recruited soldiers and settlers, outfitted them, and led them late in 1693 to Santa Fe. When, in the biting cold and snow of December, the Pueblo Indian occupants refused to vacate the former capital, and lengthy negotiations brought only exposure, malnutrition, and death to a number of the colonists camped outside the walls, don Diego resorted to war without quarter. He knew the Pueblos were divided. Aided by a contingent of fighting men from Pecos, the Spaniards stormed and won the stronghold in a bloody, two-day battle. As a lesson to all the Indians, Vargas ordered seventy of the defenders executed and four hundred men, women, and children who surrendered distributed among the colonists for ten years of servitude.[130]

The bloodless reconquest had proved illusory. Although the natives of some of the pueblos, notably Pecos, Zia, Santa Ana, and San Felipe, sided with the Spaniards, most did not. In a series of campaigns aimed at bringing the estranged Indians down off the mesas, where they had fled after the battle of Santa Fe, and, at the same time, appropriating from their temporarily abandoned pueblos maize and other foodstuffs to keep the colonists from starving, Vargas managed to reimpose a semblance of Spanish rule. He felt confident enough, after two more decisive victories, to reinstall Franciscan missionaries in some fifteen of the Rio Grande pueblos. Two additional contingents of colonists arrived, bringing the total Hispanic population, including captive Indian servants, to perhaps seventeen hundred people. In April 1695, don Diego presided at the founding of the colony's second upriver villa, Santa Cruz de la Cañada, twenty-five miles north of Santa Fe, near present-day Española. Although the site had been occupied by Spaniards before 1680, the Indians displaced in 1695 sullenly resented the colonists' return.[131]

The winter of 1695–96 in New Mexico was one of misery and want. Near-starvation, an epidemic of "plague," and rumors of an impending Pueblo uprising oppressed the isolated colony. In December, Vargas himself fell ill, probably with typhus, and almost died.[132] A number of the colonists did die, and by late March, when he appealed to a new viceroy, the governor calculated that he had only 276 families, many fewer than the 500 he insisted were necessary for the colony's security. In addition to more colonists, he urgently requested fifteen hundred beef cattle a year, clothing for the settlers, and five hundred yoke of oxen for plowing.[133]

Vargas knew by this time that his patron, the Conde de Galve, had retired. On 28 March 1696, the same day he addressed his initial appeal to don Juan de Ortega Montañés, a rigid churchman serving ad interim as viceroy, don Diego wrote to Galve, wishing him good health and, apparently, asking that he remember him in Spain. Vargas's letter reached the failing Galve at Veracruz. Responding cordially, gentleman to gentleman, the former viceroy reassured don Diego. "You can be very certain that I shall recommend you everywhere, and especially to his majesty and to the lords of the council, so as to bring about your best advancements and reward."[134]

Vargas, meantime, fought desperately to preserve the very kingdom and reputation he had won. For six months, the missionaries had complained of insolence and plotting among their Pueblo Indian charges, and the governor, citing his meager military resources, had taken what measures he deemed expedient. Nevertheless, on 4 June 1696, most of the Pueblos rose again in a war to rid their homeland of the Spaniards, killing at the outset five Franciscans and twenty-one settlers. Only Pecos; the three Keresan-speaking pueblos of Zia, Santa Ana, and San Felipe; and Tesuque, just north of Santa Fe, chose not to join in the uprising. The beleaguered colonists, many of whom wanted to abandon New Mexico, found themselves confined in three pockets: at Santa Fe; Bernalillo, downriver forty miles; and Santa Cruz to the north, nearest the scene of the initial killings.

The war lasted from June until November. Vargas's fierce resolve and his example, combined with the bravery of some of the soldiers and settlers, the support of fighting men from the five allied pueblos, a drought, and the coming of winter, prevented the Indians from repeating their success of 1680. Again, don Diego's strategy, later approved in Mexico City and Madrid, was to appeal to the warring factions to accept pardon and turn over the instigators, or to face war without quarter, which meant battle and loss of their foodstuffs.

In a sense, the hard-won war of 1696, which saw Vargas himself in the field most of the time, assured Spain's continued presence in New Mexico. It not only convinced the viceroy to send needed aid to the struggling colony, but it also dispersed Pueblo Indian resis-

Don Juan de Ortega Montañés, Viceroy of New Spain (1696, 1701–02).
Rivera Cambas, *Los gobernantes*.

tance. Many of the unreconciled natives, after months of shifting for survival, took up residence at the western pueblos or among the Navajos and Apaches. Considerably diminished in population, the Rio Grande pueblos never again united in war against the Spaniards.[135]

By all rights, don Diego should have been rewarded by a grateful king, and, belatedly, he was. In the meantime, however, he suffered, in his words, "six lost years," three in confinement at Santa Fe and three defending himself in Mexico City. The course of events was almost inconceivable, from his vantage, considering the outstanding record he had achieved during twenty-three years in the royal service. There were several causes. The first was his own grandiose conviction that having reconquered New Mexico gave him a proprietary right to the governorship. Another was the inopportune retirement of the Conde de Galve, who, as viceroy, had put unmitigated trust in Vargas and encouraged his aspirations. Galve, moreover, died upon reaching Spain, depriving don Diego of his most effective advocate at court. In Madrid, uncertainties about who would succeed the sickly Carlos II on the Spanish throne and the resulting factionalism may have impeded the workings of an already sluggish bureaucracy. Finally, in distant New Mexico, the long-suffering colonists, who existed at the mercy of their governor, found themselves encouraged by the new executive to testify in legal proceedings against the aristocratic and unbending Diego de Vargas.

If Vargas had a character flaw, as perceived by those beneath him on the social scale, it was arrogance—or overconfidence— perhaps as much a quality of his class as of his person. Certain of the colonists must have hated him. At least twice, in their eyes, his contemptuous refusal to heed the advice of experienced observers had cost the lives of relatives. The poorly supplied expedition of 1693 should never have left El Paso so late in the year. And in 1696, don Diego should have listened to the friars; they knew that the Pueblos were about to revolt again. Moreover, in the case of Vargas, the colonists were not only subject to the virtually unassailable authority of their governor, but also dependent upon him for distribution of booty, provisions, and supplies during the recolonization. Over the years, they stored up their grievances.

If ever Vargas needed his friend Galve, it was in 1697. Don Juan de Ortega Montañés, bishop of Michoacán, who served as interim viceroy from February until December 1696, had known don Diego personally as alcalde mayor of Tlalpujahua and later celebrated his reconquest of New Mexico.[136] But the next viceroy did not know Vargas. Addressing José Sarmiento Valladares, Conde de Moctezuma y de Tula, don Diego had to introduce himself and reiterate his case. In March 1697, when Pedro Rodríguez Cubero's appointment to the governorship of New Mexico was presented to the viceroy, Vargas's attorney, Francisco Díaz de Tagle, objected. Moctezuma heard both arguments and, having no word from the crown to the contrary and no personal reason to favor don Diego, issued the requisite dispatches authorizing Rodríguez Cubero to exercise the royal appointment he had obtained in 1692.[137]

Nothing that has yet come to light suggests that the forty-year-old, long-time veteran of the royal service, Pedro Rodríguez Cubero, a native of Huéscar in Granada and previously castellan of the fortress of San Salvador de La Punta in Havana, was predisposed to mistreat Diego de Vargas.[138] That would come later. Vargas, on the other hand, convinced that the record of his deeds must have reached the king's ears and been rewarded, looked upon Rodríguez Cubero as a vile usurper. Still, he was unable legally to prevent his successor from acceding to office in Santa Fe on 2 July 1697. If don Diego resorted to intimidation, threats, and disobedience, as he was later charged, he encountered a stubborn adversary in don Pedro. During the long and vicious struggle that ensued, the truth was rarely evident in the accusations the two men and their partisans hurled at each other. That, in fact, was the eventual conclusion of the royal officials who decided the matter.[139]

Rodríguez Cubero had begun, in legal form, by proclaiming the residencia of his predecessor's administration. Anyone who had a complaint to file against the former governor was encouraged to come forward during a thirty-day period, from 12 July to 11 August 1697. Apparently this resulted in no charges of record against Vargas.[140]

Next, on 23 September, a criminal complaint was brought against don Diego by the six-member Santa Fe cabildo, which functioned not only as the municipal council but also as an advisory body to the governor. The charges against Vargas in this and subsequent proceedings ranged from misappropriation of royal funds and fomenting Indian resistance to favoritism and condoning concubinage. Whether Rodríguez Cubero coerced the colonists who served on the cabildo, as Vargas alleged, he allowed the proceedings. On 2

October, he ordered don Diego confined to quarters and his property, including his two Black slaves, mules, and clothing, confiscated
and sold at public auction to cover the costs of the trial. He also had
Juan Páez Hurtado, the former lieutenant governor, arrested.

From October 1697 until July 1700, the reconqueror of New Mexico remained under house arrest. The intrigue was intense, with the
ruling governor and his household and the former governor and his
household competing for the allegiance of several hundred colonists.
Twice at least, Rodríguez Cubero tightened Vargas's confinement.
Early in March 1700, as a result of repeated accusations that don
Diego was inciting people by telling them that the king had granted
him a title of nobility and reappointed him to the governorship,
Rodríguez Cubero decreed that Vargas was to be held incommuni-
cado except for members of his immediate household. When the
accused challenged the governor as his competent judge and refused
to listen to the reading of the decree, Rodríguez Cubero had him
put in leg irons.

Finally, after viceregal officials had considered the spate of conflicting testimony from New Mexico, they ordered Vargas released
under bond to appear in Mexico City for an investigation by the Tribunal of Accounts. The most serious charges against him were those
alleging that he had misspent royal monies meant for support of the
colonists. When the order for his release was read to him in Santa
Fe, don Diego protested. A son of the ancient and noble house of
Vargas should not be subjected to the humiliation of posting bond.
Not until 20 July 1700, after a compromise had been agreed upon,
did the former governor and his party ride south out of Santa Fe. As
some of the settlers who had testified against him feared, they had
not seen the last of Diego de Vargas. [141]

While don Diego suffered the indignity of imprisonment in Santa
Fe, his legitimate son and heir, don Juan Manuel de Vargas Pimentel,
was preparing to come to the Indies without his father's permission.
The younger Vargas, who reached the age of twenty-five on 20
December 1695, had left the queen's household late that year for
military service in the War of the League of Augsburg, a conflict
pitting most of the rest of Western Europe against the expanding
France of Louis XIV.

As his grandfather had a half-century before, Juan Manuel found himself in Catalonia fighting the French. Previously, he had volunteered to serve in the Tercio de los Colorados, an infantry unit. Then, during a call for reinforcements, he secured his commission as captain of heavy cavalry and traveled to Barcelona. He saw action with the mounted militia regiment of Rosellón, leading his company bravely, especially during the French siege of Barcelona in 1697.[142]

After the war, Captain Vargas had returned to Madrid where, as the heir of his father's house, he comported himself lavishly and, according to one observer, was not as considerate of his siblings as he might have been. He disapproved of his brother-in-law's management of the family's affairs. Yet, when don Juan Manuel decided to go to the Indies to convince his father to come home, he obligated for five years the revenue from several Vargas properties to pay for passage for himself and his servants.[143]

The appearance in Madrid in 1698 of an ambitious protégé of his father may have influenced the young Vargas. Capt. Antonio Valverde y Cosío, allegedly a merchant of Sombrerete who had joined don Diego in 1693 and risen to the rank of captain of the Santa Fe presidio, had secured permission, by pleading ill health, to leave New Mexico during the summer of 1697, before Rodríguez Cubero's arrest of Vargas. Evidently he learned of it in Mexico City and brought word to the family. He also carried, along with don Diego's latest bid for honors, a petition of his own for the captaincy of the presidio at El Paso.[144]

Actually, the process of honoring don Diego had been under way for some time. Reappointment to the governorship of New Mexico, which he sought in case he did not secure another appointment, had been granted in succession after Rodríguez Cubero, but no one had paid the required fees and picked up the official dispatch.[145]

There was more. In early January 1697, the fiscal of the Council of the Indies, considering Vargas's request for a title of nobility and a 6,000-peso encomienda, had cited an enabling law but suggested moderation. "While the services are very great, the petition seems quite excessive."[146] Next, the Cámara of the Council, a seven-member, special subcommittee, took the matter under advisement. Two of the councilors, Martín de Solís y Miranda and Pedro de Bastida, had served in New Spain and knew don Diego personally. On 25 February, the Cámara recommended to the king that he might reward Vargas with the title marqués or conde, the honorific pacificator, and a 4,000-peso encomienda. Approving the first two promptly, the king withheld the third. Still, no agent came around in Vargas's behalf to choose the title marqués or conde.[147]

Because his title of nobility was not granted with any revenue of its own, Diego de Vargas counted on the encomienda. On 28 July 1698, another petition to the king in Vargas's name came before the Council of the Indies. While gratefully accepting the honors previously bestowed, the petitioner reiterated how he had risked his life in the royal service and spent even the patrimony he had inherited from his father in the Indies. He cited his obligations for his many children and grandchildren. The Cámara, lauding don Diego once more for his restoration of New Mexico and pointing out that he lacked the means to maintain the luster of his rank and the title of Castile already granted to him, again recommended favorably. This time, the king consented, authorizing an encomienda of 4,000 pesos to be collected annually from the Indians of New Mexico reconquered by don Diego. It was to run for two generations, beginning with don Juan Manuel. If for some reason, however, the Indians of New Mexico ceased their vassalage to the Spanish crown, the grant would be null.[148]

The earliest word Diego de Vargas had of the honors bestowed upon him in Spain reached him during his captivity in Santa Fe, causing him considerable grief. A letter from his son-in-law, Ignacio López de Zárate, opened and read by Pedro Rodríguez Cubero, contained the news, but not the official dispatches. As a consequence, according to Vargas, the ruling governor used the threat of don Diego's reappointment to wring additional false testimony from the colonists in hopes of having him disqualified. When Vargas learned that Rodríguez Cubero had received a letter from his cousin, Alonso de Buendía, comptroller of the Council of the Indies, saying that no agent of don Diego had picked up the dispatches in Madrid, he began to doubt his son-in-law's good will.[149]

Aside from Vargas family dynamics, one reason don Ignacio had not presented himself to claim his father-in-law's grants was money. Not only did a claimant have to pay to have the documents issued, but there were also other royal fees, such as the media anata. Don Ignacio, who bemoaned his debts, had received nothing toward his wife's dowry or the expenses of the wedding nearly ten years before. Finally, in 1697 or 1698, sums of 4,000 and 6,000 pesos had arrived from Vargas through the good offices of Luis Sáenz de Tagle. That money, combined with Valverde's appearance in Madrid and don Juan Manuel's desire to visit his father, at last broke the stalemate.[150]

Capt. Juan Manuel de Vargas Pimentel gave as his reason for wanting to travel to the Indies "to seek don Diego de Vargas Zapata, my father, who may be in Mexico City." Along with his weapons, don Juan Manuel was taking a valet and a groom, both bachelors, Francisco García of La Corunna, described as "of medium height, round face, with curly, dark-chestnut hair," and Francisco Martel from Barcelona, also of medium height, but "hawk-faced, with short, blond hair." They were cleared on 6 July 1699 to embark on any warship of the flota scheduled to sail later that month.[151] Capt. Antonio Valverde was also returning in the same flota, having obtained royal appointment as captain of the presidio at El Paso, "safeguard of the province of New Biscay." Ironically, the order in Valverde's favor was signed by Alonso de Buendía.[152]

The passage from Cadiz to Veracruz lasted some eighty days. On 9 October 1699, word reached Mexico City that the flota was putting in at Veracruz. Juan Manuel complained about the trip up from the coast. Once in the capital, he went immediately to see Luis Sáenz de Tagle, who informed him that his father was still being held in Santa Fe. Don Luis laid the blame for the impasse squarely on Ignacio López de Zárate for having sent word of don Diego's reappointment instead of the necessary dispatches. Reporting this to López de Zárate in a letter on 2 November, Juan Manuel mentioned that he had received an interesting caller, a half-brother named Juan Manuel, as if he had not known of him before. A student, this son of his father was, according to the Castilian Juan Manuel, "as big as I am and very like me in appearance." The young man had come with a message of welcome from his mother. But the sole, surviving, legitimate son and heir of Diego de Vargas dismissed the gesture. He would not see her.[153]

He wrote to his father in Santa Fe. Don Diego, who had the letter by mid-December 1699, tried to respond. At least one copy of the reply, in which Vargas likened Pedro Rodríguez Cubero to a basilisk—the storied serpent so venomous its very eyes or breath could kill—fell into his adversary's hands during the course of their legal struggle. When finally, in late October 1700, don Diego, who had not seen his son in twenty-seven years, was reunited with don Juan Manuel on the outskirts of Mexico City, he was so overcome he could not speak. The younger man noted that his father's acquaint-

The Conde de Moctezuma
y de Tula, Viceroy of
New Spain (1696–1701).
Rivera Cambas,
Los gobernantes.

ances could not believe how well don Diego looked, considering his
long ordeal. During the nineteen months they were both in the capital, Diego de Vargas took immense pleasure and pride in his dashing son.[154]

Legal Defense in Mexico City and Reappointment to New Mexico

Don Diego said he entered Mexico City on 30 October 1700, Juan
Manuel said it was the day before, and a chronicler dated the event
5 November.[155] Whatever the precise date, the former governor of New
Mexico resided in the city for nearly three years, without royal appointment, accepting the generous financial assistance of his friends and
pursuing single-mindedly his exoneration. In Spain and the empire,
this period saw dynastic change and war, and, in Vargas's personal
sphere, one of the most tragic occurrences of his life.

Felipe V of Spain (1700–46).
Rivera Cambas, *Los gobernantes*.

The day after his arrival in the capital, don Diego strode with don Juan Manuel through the luxurious anterooms of the viceregal palace to an audience with the Conde de Moctezuma, a man he had not met before. Describing his reception for his son-in-law several months later, Vargas recalled that the ruler of New Spain had shown him every courtesy. Juan Manuel, on the contrary, thought the viceroy was typically insincere. Evidently, the younger Vargas resented the fact that Moctezuma, in more than a year, had not offered him a post. There may have been another reason. The conde, who had requested permission to retire from office, was known to favor the Habsburg party in the matter of a successor to the failing Carlos II. [156]

The last of the Spanish Habsburg kings died on 1 November 1700. In his final will, which had been the subject of intense diplomatic negotiations, he left his crown to the Bourbon pretender, Philip of Anjou, a grandson of Louis XIV of France and a great-grandson of Felipe IV of Spain. Philip acceded to the Spanish throne as Felipe V at the age of seventeen. The dynastic struggle that ensued altered traditional European alliances. During a dozen years of widespread but sporadic fighting, known collectively as the War of the Spanish Succession, Spaniards and Frenchmen, uncharacteristically, found themselves on the same side.

Not until Sunday morning, 6 March 1701, did a courier rein up before the viceregal palace with word that a dispatch boat, shrouded in black and booming a salute every half hour, had made Veracruz with news of the king's death. Juan Manuel thought the ceremony of allegiance to the new king, held on 4 April in Mexico City and featuring the release into the air of a multitude of birds, must have been more impressive than its counterpart in Madrid. Neither he nor his father was disappointed when the order arrived later in the year relieving the suspect Conde de Moctezuma and substituting as interim viceroy for the second time Juan de Ortega Montañés, already archbishop of Mexico. By 4 November 1701, when the formal transfer of office took place, don Diego had been back in Mexico City a full year. [157]

He had not been idle. With characteristic vigor, Vargas had begun to straighten out his professional and his personal affairs. He took full advantage of his new status. Socially, he had moved up from

Coat of arms of the Marqués de la Nava de Barcinas.
    Espinosa, *Crusaders of the Rio Grande.*

the untitled nobility to the titled, an elite with no more than several hundred members in all the empire. Carlos II, the late king, had nearly doubled the titled nobility, creating, by one account, 12 new vizcondes, 80 condes, and 236 marqueses—many of them for money. In contrast, Vargas had earned his title. He had cause to be proud. Within days of reestablishing residence in Mexico City, don Diego presented himself as the Marqués de la Nava de Barcinas, a name derived from two rural properties in the family's entail of Granada, the cortijos of La Nava and Barcinas. From then on, he signed everything, from legal documents to personal letters, with his title only.[158]

The honor that had escaped don Diego was the one he seemed to have taken for granted: membership in the military Order of Santiago. His father, his grandfather, his brothers-in-law, and many other kinsmen, living and dead, were knights of Santiago. Moreover, his son-in-law, Ignacio López de Zárate, also a knight of Santiago, had been a member since 1694 of the royal Council of the Orders, the body that regulated the three military orders.

Vargas particularly wanted knighthood in the Order of Santiago. During the reconquest of New Mexico, he had won two important victories on or about the feast day of St. James, 25 July. He had vowed to visit the saint's shrine at Compostela whenever he returned to Spain. As early as 1697, he had written to don Ignacio, almost matter-of-factly, requesting that his son-in-law handle the details in

Madrid and send along the necessary royal decree. Years later, as the Marqués de la Nava de Barcinas, he was still waiting.[159]

Although the criteria for admission to the Order of Santiago were applied in a somewhat arbitrary manner during the reign of Carlos II, none of the traditional reasons for disqualification— illegitimacy, Jewish or Moorish blood, defective nobility of parents or grandparents, conviction of family members or ancestors by the Inquisition, pursuit of base occupations, homicide, notorious impropriety, or disabling physical or mental impairment— should have kept Vargas out. There must have been other circumstances.[160]

Don Ignacio may never have submitted a petition in his father-in-law's behalf. The process of gathering the required information on every candidate for knighthood was costly. Furthermore, Diego de Vargas had bitter enemies in the Order of Santiago. Don Alonso de Buendía y Ortega and his brother, don Pedro, natives of Huéscar and first cousins of don Pedro Rodríguez Cubero, had been knights of Santiago since the 1680s. Their opposition alone probably explains why the recolonizer of New Mexico, despite his unquestioned service to the crown, never wore the red dagger cross of the Order of Santiago.[161]

By October 1701, the new king, Felipe V, on the advice of the Council of the Indies, had ordered the viceroy and the audiencia on at least three different occasions to render justice in the legal action against Diego de Vargas. If found innocent, he was to be allowed to exercise his reappointment to the governorship of New Mexico, but not to take the residencia of Pedro Rodríguez Cubero. The latter, the cabildo of Santa Fe, and several agents had kept up their accusations. They charged Vargas with defrauding the royal treasury of as much as 224,000 pesos and urged that he not be reappointed and allowed to take vengeance on those who had testified against him. Don Diego, meantime, presented his accounts and sought to influence the bureaucracy in his favor. Still, everything took so long and depended on so many different people.[162]

The new marqués also tried to put his house in order in Spain. First, he settled the 4,000-peso encomienda on Juan Manuel. Then, accepting at face value the distressing report his son had brought from Madrid, he relieved Ignacio López de Zárate of the management of the Vargas estate and, by general power of attorney, put Juan Manuel in charge. Not only had don Ignacio allowed the family entails to drift further into debt, according to this report, but he had also been remiss in providing for Juan Manuel. [163]

Despite his frustration over don Ignacio's seeming indifference, Vargas did not choose to dispense with the services of his influential son-in-law altogether. In fact, he became increasingly importunate. The day after he assigned management of the family's properties to Juan Manuel, don Diego executed a power of attorney naming López de Zárate to enter petitions on his behalf. He then suggested that his son-in-law seek for him the governorship of Guatemala, Santa Fe de Bogotá, Chile, Buenos Aires, the Philippines, Havana, or Tucumán. His appointment to one of these posts, he hastened to add, would be of benefit to the whole family. [164]

While Vargas expressed his dissatisfaction with don Ignacio, the favored, self-serving don Juan Manuel could do no wrong in his father's eyes. Don Diego doted on his legitimate son and overlooked his excesses. Only later did he admit that Juan Manuel, while in Mexico City, had fallen precipitously in love with a woman who bore him a child. The elder Vargas learned of the affair after she had died giving birth, when he was asked to pay for the burial and for the baby's support. [165]

Don Juan Manuel had to accept his father's adamant resolve to stay in the Indies until he had met and overcome every challenge to his honor. The court, in fact, had decreed that he not leave New Spain until his case had been heard. Whether don Diego truly wanted to return to Spain as much as he professed in his letters to the family may never be known. He seemed to consider Juan Manuel's urging an impertinence. Because he took great pride in his son's military record, however, he must have appreciated the gallant captain's impatience to get back to Madrid and put himself at the service of the new king.

But the war kept don Juan Manuel in New Spain. On orders from the king, the flota, which had not sailed for two years, was to await an escort of French warships. Finally, in early May 1702, they appeared. The Conde de Moctezuma and his family made ready to depart the capital, along with many other people whose trip to Spain had been delayed, among them Capt. Juan Manuel de Vargas Pimentel. Although Diego de Vargas worried that he could not pay for Juan Manuel's passage, when the time came, he borrowed enough to provide for him lavishly. "Not even the son of a grandee of Spain," Vargas recalled later, "could have gone with more abundance and splendor." At that, his father, knowing the younger man's nature, entrusted Juan Manuel only with drafts for certain payments in Spain, not with cash.[166]

When the flota put out to sea at last on 11 and 12 June, it passed in the channel a packet boat coming from Spain. The king and queen were well in Barcelona, and he was about to travel to Naples to take command of the Spanish armies there. The pope, meanwhile, had dispatched three cardinals to Germany to discuss peace with Emperor Leopold I. When another packet boat reached Veracruz in September, it carried news of the flota, which had made Havana on 7 July. During the three-week crossing, plague had broken out aboard the ships. Among the fatalities noted, which included a son of the Conde de Moctezuma, was Juan de Vargas. From a letter written by his sister several years later, it appeared that don Juan Manuel had succumbed to a respiratory disorder.[167]

The news from Havana that his beloved son and heir, on whom he had placed all his hopes for the house of Vargas, had died was almost too much for don Diego. In a pathetic and rambling letter to Ignacio López de Zárate, he poured out his cup of woes, bitter enough, he implied, to poison the will to go on living. After all, when he considered the path he had chosen on 11 August 1672—the day he left that "delightful villa of Madrid, crown of all the world"—the past thirty years now seemed a cruel waste. Only his Spartan concern for his honor forced him to endure, but endure he would.

Since Juan Manuel had been granted entry into one of the three military orders, Vargas wanted to know why this honor should not now devolve upon him. In addition, since preliminary judgment had been rendered in his favor and he would soon return to New Mexico, he called upon don Ignacio to press at court for a salary equal to that of the governor of New Biscay. López de Zárate should also see to the restoration of El Paso, severed from the jurisdiction of the governor of New Mexico by the grant in 1698 to Antonio Valverde. Here, amply demonstrating his concern for the future, don Diego took a position contrary to the one he had taken six years earlier. Then, he had opposed Pedro Rodríguez Cubero's 1692 appointment, arguing that it applied only to the El Paso district. Now, he argued that the El Paso district was and always had been an integral part of New Mexico.[168]

The Duque de Alburquerque, Viceroy of New Spain (1702–11).
Rivera Cambas, *Los gobernantes*.

At first, when he learned in mid-1702 that another viceroy was en route to New Spain, don Diego believed that the transition would delay and confuse the settlement of his case. The proceedings seemed to be moving haltingly toward a conclusion under the archbishop-viceroy, Juan de Ortega Montañés. With the advent of don Francisco Fernández de la Cueva Enríquez, Duque de Alburquerque, however, Vargas changed his mind. In November, he rode out with the city's dignitaries to meet and welcome the new viceroy, only to find that don Francisco knew of him and his case. Alburquerque, in fact, took a personal interest. At the hearings held on 13 February and 9 March 1703, the viceroy himself was present. The verdict could not have been more favorable.[169]

The cloud of accusations that had hung over Vargas for nearly six years lifted at last, and he found himself fully exonerated. The vicious personal charges against him had been thrown out for having come after the legal term of his residencia in unauthorized proceedings. An exhaustive investigation of his finances showed that, far from having embezzled large sums, Vargas enjoyed a credit balance in the royal treasury. Of the more than 217,000 pesos authorized between 1691 and 1697 for the reconquest and recolonization of New Mexico, just under 199,000 had actually been paid out through the Treasury offices in Mexico City, Durango, and Zacatecas. That left an adjusted balance of nearly 18,000 pesos still owed to don Diego. His accusers, moreover, were ordered to pay court costs.[170]

The decision in his favor cleared the way for Vargas to exercise his 1699 reappointment to New Mexico for five years, succeeding Pedro Rodríguez Cubero. When he went to secure the necessary dispatches and a salary advance, viceregal officials admonished don Diego to put aside any ill feelings toward the cabildo and people of the colony and govern impartially. Evidence to the contrary, he should understand, would result in his immediate removal.[171]

The vicissitudes Diego de Vargas had experienced during the fifteen years since his first appointment to the governorship of New Mexico illustrate how, to a large extent, personal relations— who an individual knew and what those in authority thought of him—could dictate a career in the royal service. Acknowledging that fact, don Diego urged his relatives in Spain to write to the Duque and Duquesa de Alburquerque and to every member of the Audiencia of Mexico, thanking them for his vindication. From Madrid, Ignacio López de

Zárate assured his father-in-law that they would comply promptly, adding to the list the archbishop of Mexico.[172]

———

In the summer of 1703, Diego de Vargas made ready to return to New Mexico. His honor demanded that he do so. Since no other assignment had reached him, he had no choice but to serve in the post to which he had been reappointed. On 1 June, a week before his departure, he had a will drawn up. In it, he named his legitimate, elder daughter, Isabel María, as heir to his title of nobility, entails, and encomienda. Her children were to follow in succession, or, in the event of their inability, the children of his younger daughter, Juana Viviana. Adding a standard clause, don Diego stipulated that if he should remarry and have more children, they would succeed before his grandchildren. As executors in Mexico City, he appointed Diego de Suazo Coscojales, archdeacon of the metropolitan cathedral, and Miguel de Ubilla, knight of the Order of Santiago, gentleman of his majesty's bedchamber, and retired comptroller of the Tribunal of Accounts.[173]

His will in order, Vargas next made the necessary financial arrangements for his governorship. From Luis Sáenz de Tagle, he borrowed 12,354 pesos, obligating himself to repay the principal and costs in eight months. As in the past, he gave his power of attorney to Francisco Díaz de Tagle to expend 40,000 pesos on supplying him and the one-hundred-man presidial garrison of Santa Fe. Exercising the power of attorney a month later, Díaz de Tagle bound Vargas to pay Sáenz de Tagle 25,552 pesos for items purchased. Don Diego could not have been dealing with a more solvent pair. When Felipe V decided to appeal personally to some of the richest men in New Spain for contributions to the war effort, the king wrote directly to Luis Sáenz de Tagle.[174]

After all he had been through, Vargas, now fifty-nine years old, cannot have relished the thousand-mile ride back to New Mexico. Nevertheless, on 8 June 1703, he and his party set out on the long journey north. This time, he was taking his two natural sons: Juan Manuel, now twenty-three or twenty-four years old and serving as his father's adjutant; and Alonso, one year younger. By mid-September, they were in desolate El Paso, where eleven years earlier he had launched the reconquest.[175]

Although he was eager to confront the colony's leading citizens in

Santa Fe, Vargas took time at El Paso to write another insistent letter to his son-in-law in Madrid, supplying duplicates of the supporting documentation he had sent previously. He enclosed two draft memorials for López de Zárate to put in final form for presentation to the king. In the first, as a reward for his services in New Mexico, don Diego sought appointment to the governorship of the Philippines, Guatemala, or Santa Fe de Bogotá. For the first time, he added to the list the governorship of New Biscay. His command of the joint campaign in 1691, he pointed out, qualified him especially for the last-mentioned post. In the second memorial, he again justified his request for a salary equal to that of the governor of New Biscay.

Vargas asked that López de Zárate secure Felipe V's confirmation of the New Mexico encomienda for the second generation, along with a royal order to expedite the collection of its revenue. He wanted to know the latest concerning the registration of his title of nobility, his son's grant of knighthood, and the three cases of chocolate he had sent to Spain in the ill-fated flota of 1702. Finally, don Diego cautioned don Ignacio to be on his guard against further perverse reports by Pedro Rodríguez Cubero.[176]

Unknown to Vargas, Ignacio López de Zárate was responding in Madrid to his father-in-law's earlier letters at about the same time don Diego was writing from El Paso. Maintaining the most rigorous courtesy, López de Zárate explained that he had not ignored any of his father-in-law's requests. Proceedings in the Council of the Indies simply took time. In response to the allegation that he had mismanaged the Vargas entails, don Ignacio was preparing a detailed financial statement of his administration. Don Diego had been misinformed by don Juan Manuel. Regardless, López de Zárate was pleased to abide by his father-in-law's powers of attorney to others. In conclusion, he reminded Vargas that he had borne for fifteen years the debts incurred for his wedding. Still, he had faith that don Diego would help extricate him financially and make life easier for the family. As for further threats from Pedro Rodríguez Cubero, which seemed unlikely, he reassured his father-in-law that he would remain vigilant.[177]

Rodríguez Cubero, Vargas's mortal enemy, had in fact left New Mexico, with the viceroy's permission, and traveled a westerly route so that he would not encounter the Marqués de la Nava de Barcinas. Although don Diego kept damning his adversary until they both died and urging that don Pedro be prosecuted and never allowed to hold office again, royal officials did not share his partisan contempt. There were two sides to the case. Vargas had been high-handed in opposing Rodríguez Cubero's appointment and wrong in whatever he did to make the ruling governor's life miserable. Instead of punishing the man who had held Vargas in confinement, the king confirmed don Pedro's earlier appointment to the governorship of Maracaibo, Mérida, and La Grita in present-day northwestern Venezuela. Death in Mexico City in 1704, however, prevented Rodríguez Cubero from serving again.[178]

According to don Diego's own account, he and his entourage entered Santa Fe to popular acclaim and rejoicing. Members of the cabildo, at least three of whom had testified against him earlier, were now at pains to honor the marqués, who acceded to the governorship for the second time on 10 November 1703. The colony, he alleged, was in shocking condition, all but defenseless, as a result of Rodríguez Cubero's neglect. The villa of Santa Fe, which Vargas had fortified and left secure with a population of more than fifteen hundred residents, now lay exposed, partially in ruins, with its garrison scattered. The villa of Santa Cruz de la Cañada and the pueblo of Galisteo had been abandoned. The Zuñi and Hopi pueblos were hostile, and the Apaches emboldened. "It was the intention of the castellan, my predecessor as governor, don Pedro Rodríguez Cubero," charged Vargas, "to destroy and erase from memory everything I had done." The cabildo, at Vargas's request, concurred dutifully, excoriating Rodríguez Cubero.[179]

As he received the congratulations of the colonists and resumed the routine business of governing, don Diego de Vargas apparently experienced a foreboding that he did not have long to live. Between 8 and 13 January 1704, he wrote a number of letters from Santa Fe to members of his family. He was clearly putting his affairs in order. More than once, he alluded to his own mortality. He summoned local officials to his quarters in the governor's palace to draw up a power of attorney in favor of José de Vargas, the husband of his second daughter, Juana Viviana, for the administration of the Torrelaguna entail. This, he told José and Juana in separate letters, was his way of providing a belated dowry. In a long letter to his other son-in-law, Ignacio López de Zárate, he did not belie his bitterness. That winter, don Diego reflected on his career in the Indies, his misfortunes of the previous six years, and the loss of his beloved son, don Juan Manuel. He thought long about the people and places back home.[180]

He was not to die in his bed in Madrid or Torrelaguna, in Mexico City, or even in Santa Fe. Death overtook sixty-year-old Diego de Vargas in the early spring of 1704 on campaign. It resulted not from an enemy arrow or musketball, as he might have preferred, but from a brief, virulent illness.

Since don Diego's return, the Apaches, particularly the Faraones who lived around the sierras known today as the Sandia and Manzano Mountains, had been raiding Spanish settlements in the nearby Rio Grande Valley. When they fell upon Bernalillo, some forty-five miles south of Santa Fe, and drove off one hundred head of cattle belonging to Fernando Durán y Chaves, Vargas proclaimed the campaign that Durán y Chaves and his neighbors had been waiting for.

On Thursday, 27 March, at about ten o'clock in the morning, the redoubtable governor led a column of fifty-odd soldiers and officers, including his natural son, Juan Manuel, as royal standard bearer, out of the capital and down along the Río Santa Fe toward the pueblo of Cochití, which they reached that afternoon. Already one soldier had been sent back to Santa Fe seriously ill. The following day, Vargas had to order his long-time secretary, Alfonso Rael de Aguilar, and another soldier, both of them ailing, to return home. As interim secretary, he named Antonio Macario Maldonado Zapata, a relative he had brought with him from Mexico City.

Proceeding to Bernalillo, the governor reviewed his expedition, swelled by 140 or 150 Pueblo Indian auxiliaries who had been ordered to rendezvous there. On Sunday, 30 March, the combined force moved south ten or twelve miles, making camp in the vicinity of present-day Alameda. During the next three days, while contingents of Pueblo Indian scouts ranged along the foothills to pick up the trails of Apaches, Vargas and his column rode on down the valley with the meandering, tree-lined river on their right and the tannish-gray mountains to their left. Wednesday night, 2 April, they camped fifteen leagues, about forty miles, south of Bernalillo en route to the abandoned, seventeenth-century hacienda of Las Barrancas. At that point, the campaign journal ceased abruptly.

A sudden illness struck Diego de Vargas the following day. He could hardly sit his saddle. Fray Juan de Garaicoechea, the Franciscan chaplain, urged him to turn back. The governor protested, but, too weak to ride, allowed himself to be carried by some of the Pueblo Indian auxiliaries north toward Bernalillo. Word of the misfortune was sent ahead by rider to Juan Páez Hurtado, Vargas's lieutenant governor and closest associate, who galloped south from Santa Fe with medication. On 5 April, don Diego was put to bed in Bernalillo, likely at don Fernando Durán y Chaves's home, the most substantial and comfortable in the settlement, where Páez Hurtado found him. The governor did not respond to the medication, but grew worse. Ministered to by Father Garaicoechea, don Diego confessed repeatedly and asked that he be received into the Third Order of St. Francis. The friar complied.[181]

On 7 April, Diego de Vargas dictated a twenty-page last will and testament.[182] He had already named his daughter, Isabel María, heir to his title, properties in Spain, and encomienda in the will he had executed in Mexico City the year before, which he left in effect. As her husband, don Ignacio López de Zárate would take possession of the Vargas estate in her name. Now, on his deathbed, don Diego provided for his own last rites.

First, he requested that a mass be celebrated with his body present in the church at Bernalillo. After that, the body should be carried to Santa Fe and placed in his draped bed, which would serve as a bier. "In the same bed, let my body be borne to the church of said villa of Santa Fe and buried in said church in the main chapel beneath the platform where the priest stands. This I ask as a favor. In a coffin lined with simple woollen cloth, let it be buried according to military honors and the privileges of a titled nobleman of Castile, leading by the bridle two horses caparisoned with the same cloth that lines the coffin."[183] In a subsequent clause, Vargas asked that the parochial fees be paid to the Franciscan in charge for nine masses with the body present. He further stipulated that for the first day there be one hundred candles for the bier and fifty for the altars and for the friars to carry. In partial payment, he offered some nine arrobas of the fine chocolate he himself drank. Don Diego ordered that, on the day of his burial, fifty fanegas of maize and twelve beefs be distributed to the poor of Santa Fe.

Next, Vargas arranged for repayment to the royal treasury of the unearned portion of his salary. Before leaving Mexico City, he had received 4,000 pesos in advance for two years. He did not want his three bondsmen to be responsible for any part of this sum. As did most people of his rank, don Diego owned domestic slaves. He now ordered that his two young Black coachmen, for whom he had paid 660 pesos, be sold, along with a light-skinned mulatta, Juana de la Cruz, twenty-two years old and married to Ignacio, one of the two coachmen.[184] In addition, he provided that his New Mexico executor,

Juan Páez Hurtado, send his personal silverware and jewelry to wherever they would bring the best prices. Included were plates, candlesticks, bowls, serving dishes of various sizes and shapes, forks and spoons—many of these items bearing don Diego's coat of arms—as well as two pear-shaped, pendant pearl earrings each with eight fine emeralds (valued at 500 pesos), and two diamond rings (worth 400 and 100 pesos respectively).[185]

In his last will, Diego de Vargas recognized his three illegitimate children: Juan Manuel, twenty-four, and Alonso, twenty-three, with their father in New Mexico; and María Teresa, nineteen, at home in Mexico City with their mother. He bequeathed them 2,000 pesos in cash, to be divided equally among the three. He then began to apportion his personal effects. Each of the young men should have one of his saddles and pairs of pistols, sundry items of his elegant wardrobe, and four mules with gear. In the same clause, Vargas gave his Black slave, Andrés, who had served him loyally since 1691, his freedom, on the condition that he conduct Juan Manuel and Alonso to Mexico City. Antonio Macario Maldonado Zapata was also to go in their company. Supplied for the journey with everything from chocolate to soap, they should leave New Mexico two months after don Diego's death or in the company of the courier who carried the news south.

Because of his great affection for his secretary, Alfonso Rael de Aguilar, who had recovered sufficiently to be present and record the will in his hand, the dying governor canceled his debt and gave him four yards of English cloth, along with buttons and lining, for a suit. To his compadre and lieutenant governor, Juan Páez Hurtado, to whom he entrusted the government of New Mexico until the Duque de Alburquerque might name a successor, Vargas left his black hat with blue and white plumes; his blue, plush-lined cape with silver galloon; a new Vandyke with linen-lace ruff; and his gilded cane.

Regarding the large sums for supply of his government, Vargas referred to the drafts issued in favor of various people against Francisco Díaz de Tagle. He made due provision for continuing the salaries of the one hundred soldiers of the Santa Fe presidio, whose fiscal year had begun on 16 December 1703, designating the inventory of his personal goods, 550 cattle, and the grain he had in storage. He recorded how much he owed two creditors in Mexico City and what Capt. Antonio Valverde of the presidio of El Paso owed him. If the Marqués de Rivas still had the money Vargas had sent to

Don Diego's feeble signature, el Marques de la Naba de Brazinas, on his last will, Bernalillo, New Mexico, 7 April 1704.
New Mexico State Records Center and Archives.

Spain in support of the petition to have El Paso restored to his governorship, don Diego wanted it to go to his second son-in-law, José de Vargas, as partial payment of dowry.

A debt to Capt. Juan de Bazoco would be more than satisfied by what Vargas had paid to facilitate the petition of his younger half-brother, Francisco, for the alcaldía mayor of Guazacualco. As afterthoughts, don Diego forgave whatever Félix Martínez, captain of the Santa Fe presidio, owed him on account, and provided for the future freedom of another mulatto slave, Antonio de la Cruz, when he had served Juan Manuel and Alonso for five years.

The weakened Vargas managed, with great effort, to sign his title, the Marqués de la Nava de Barcinas, across the foot of the document. He could no longer do so later in the day, when he asked that a codicil be appended. Although he had arranged during his years in New Spain for a great many masses to be said for the repose of his soul, he now wanted five hundred more. Two hundred were to be said for him in honor of Our Lady of Remedies, his special intercessor, and three hundred for the souls of the poor who had died to date in the reconquest of New Mexico. [186]

He held on until the following day, but grew weaker. The loyal Juan Páez Hurtado, who had been with the governor for seventeen years, attended him at the head of the bed. Writing to the family in Spain some days later, don Juan described the circumstances. Vargas, when struck by the malady in the field, was reported to have proclaimed, "Where better to lose one's life than in service to God and the king our lord?" His final illness was abdominal, "a severe attack of fever caused by stomach chills," in Páez Hurtado's words. It could have been dysentery. At about five in the afternoon on Tuesday, 8 April 1704, thirty-one years after he had left his beloved Spain, Diego de Vargas died in a faraway, frontier outpost, his honor intact. [187]

———

Still unaware of don Diego's death the following June, Ignacio López de Zárate wrote to him from Madrid. Only part of the letter has survived. The family was concerned. Don Ignacio, who evidently knew that don Diego had his two natural sons with him in New Mexico, seemed at pains to persuade his father-in-law not to make them heirs of his entails in Spain. He had another, sad reason for writing. Gregorio Pimentel de Prado, Vargas's best friend and brother-in-law, who had chosen the life of a gentleman of Torrelaguna, had died earlier in the month.

Politely as always, López de Zárate told his father-in-law what he had been doing at court in his behalf. He had already obtained and sent confirmation of the encomienda for a second generation. Because the king was in Portugal on campaign, don Ignacio had been unable to get action on another of don Diego's petitions. But as soon as his majesty returned, López de Zárate would see to the matter that had exercised Diego de Vargas for so many, many years—securing a better post in the Indies. [188]

Epilog

At the age of twenty-eight, don Diego de Vargas had taken leave of his wife and four children, saying that he would return. Still away in the Indies more than thirty years later, he died at Bernalillo in New Mexico at the age of sixty.

To members of the family, recipients of his letters over the years, it must have appeared that don Diego was chasing what one historian has termed "the huge mirage of the Indies." [189] Success—favorable circumstances and money enough to permit an honorable return home—seemed always to recede before him. He earned promotions in the royal service and gained notable honors, but never enough to satisfy him. Whenever he secured a governorship independent of a viceroy's jurisdiction; as soon as his friend, the Conde de Galve, might recommend him personally to the king; once he had amassed a fortune without having it stolen or lost at sea or consumed in legal fees, then, in due course, he would be free to return to his beloved homeland.

It is possible that he stayed for other reasons as well. On the level of ideals, don Diego de Vargas always presented himself as the Spaniard in America. He wrote to his family in traditional terms of enhancing, through military enterprise and governorship, the honor and nobility of the house of Vargas of Madrid. Yet, at the same time, life in the Indies may have been more agreeable and exciting to him than the prospect of resuming his place in Spain. It is curious that in all his requests for better posts, he never asked for anything closer to home, in Italy, Flanders, or Spain. It was always Guatemala or the Philippines or Chile.

We have no way of knowing to what degree absence in the Indies was for Diego de Vargas an escape from the entanglements of family and property back home. Even he may not have known. The death of his wife, doña Beatriz, so soon after his departure must have had a profound effect on him. We do know that on a practical level don Diego made long-term adjustments to life in New Spain. He learned to deal effectively with peoples of other races, Indians and Blacks, according to the dictates of colonial society. He inured himself to the hardships of travel, prolonged service in far-away places, and military campaign. And, despite his professions that he had not committed himself in the New World, he had a second family.

Once he found the woman who became the mother of his three natural children, he may not have wanted to leave her. We know that Diego de Vargas understood romantic love. He admitted as much to his brother-in-law, Gregorio Pimentel de Prado, when he confided that Juan Manuel had fallen hopelessly in love in Mexico City.[190] And, obviously, he cared about his New World children. He took his two natural sons, by then young men, with him when he went back to New Mexico. The family in Spain, in fact, feared that he might make them heirs.[191]

Whatever the satisfactions and mirages of life in the Indies, one senses in Vargas's letters home that his long absence was not planned; it just happened. Circumstances overseas—disposition of his father's Guatemala estate; anticipated promotions; settling the mercury accounts at Tlalpujahua; the prolonged recolonization of New Mexico; imprisonment, legal defense, and debts; and his vowed return to New Mexico—successively bound him to remain. Once Diego de Vargas had made the break with the land of his birth, the forces drawing him homeward were never strong enough to turn the tide of events, feelings, and relationships that compelled him to remain in the New World. He said he would return, but he never did.

———

In a sense, time and chance have cheated the reconqueror of New Mexico. No monument or shrine marks his grave. His final resting place is unknown. Although we can be reasonably certain that Vargas was buried before the main altar of the parish church in Santa Fe in

April 1704, as he had requested, we do not know where the church stood at that time.[192] A dozen years later, when that temporary building was replaced by a proper, new parish church southeast of the plaza, Juan Páez Hurtado may have seen to the reinterment of Vargas's remains. No record that his bones were exhumed and ceremonially reburied in the larger structure, as we might speculate, has yet come to light.[193] Given the subsequent modifications and rebuilding of the later church, and its eventual supersession by the Santa Fe cathedral, there is little hope that such a reburial has lain undisturbed.[194]

None of don Diego's relatives seems to have stayed to raise a family or be buried with him in New Mexico. Juan Manuel and Alonso, his two natural sons, departed for Mexico City soon after their father's death, presumably in the company of Antonio Macario Maldonado Zapata. In 1706, Vargas's New World companion died in Mexico City, and Juan Manuel, on his own behalf and that of his brother and sister, appealed to Ignacio López de Zárate in Spain for assistance. We know no more about them. Nor do we know the fate of the baby born in the viceregal capital to the lover of Juan Manuel de Vargas Pimentel, the child who resembled Vargas and may have been his grandson.[195]

Don Diego's stepmother, who had remarried, was living in Guatemala. His half-sister, Antonia, had entered the Franciscan Conceptionist convent in the city of Santiago de Guatemala. The two half-brothers he had helped raise, Pedro Alonso and Francisco, were still in New Spain. An attorney, Pedro Alonso represented the Spanish heirs' interests in Mexico City. A lawsuit against don Diego's successor as governor of New Mexico, Francisco Cuervo y Valdés, alleging seizure of Vargas property, and a large, unpaid account with Luis Sáenz de Tagle complicated settlement of the estate.

After Pedro Alonso's death, which had occurred by July 1717, Francisco wrote to Isabel María de Vargas Pimentel from Puebla. It was his suggestion that she not try to have the New Mexico encomienda imposed on the inconstant Pueblo Indians, but instead transferred to a stabler area of New Spain. The grant was eventually converted to a pension and paid to Vargas's heirs for years. As for Francisco, the younger half-brother, we have neither the place nor the date of his death.[196]

Of the interesting artifacts mentioned in don Diego's will of 7 April 1704 and the inventory of his property compiled two weeks later—the silver service bearing his coat of arms; the pearl and emerald earrings; the large, canvas campaign tent; the statue of St. Isidore the Farmer with silver goad and crown; the pair of silver-lined, wooden stirrups—none has been located and positively identified. [197] The large quantities of dry goods and hardware listed on the inventory, evidently intended for the presidial garrison, resembled the stock of a general store. Vargas also had a small library of thirty-three books with him in New Mexico at the time of his death. Nothing light or frivolous was included. Mostly chronicles of kings, noblemen, and the court of Madrid; practical books on politics, law, military science, architecture, and cooking; and devotional works—their titles reflected the tastes of a nostalgic Spanish aristocrat and man of action wholly devoted to his career in the royal service. Not one of these books, with don Diego's name written across the flyleaf, is on display in a New Mexico museum. [198]

Yet even without his bones, or descendants, or an array of his worldly possessions—any one of which could turn up at any time—the posthumous fame of Diego de Vargas in New Mexico seems assured. What has survived, of course, is the historical record, thousands upon thousands of manuscript pages.

―――――

In the great, multivolume *Enciclopedia universal ilustrada*, the most extensive Spanish-language encyclopedia, Diego de Vargas Zapata (1643–1704), midlevel colonial governor and recolonizer, did not merit an entry of his own. He did, however, earn mention in the entry on New Mexico. [199] Whether he is the object of future study in a broader context—perhaps as a representative of Spanish imperial officialdom in the late Habsburg period—Diego de Vargas, by his abundantly recorded acts in New Mexico, has achieved a local prominence transcending changes of sovereignty, perception, and fashion.

For better or for worse, the character of New Mexico was different after Vargas than it was before him. This was not so much because of the man, but because the larger scene was changing. The very reason for the colony's being, as justified at court in Mexico City or Madrid, changed. During most of the seventeenth century, New Mexico had been a government-subsidized, Franciscan ministry to the Pueblo Indians. In the eighteenth, it was a government-subsidized defensive buffer against Apache and Comanche, Frenchman and Englishman. Imperial rivalry had superseded evangelism.

Taos pueblo, by Henry R. Poore.
Kessell, *Kiva, Cross, and Crown.*

The Franciscans, who did not regain the unbridled authority they had exercised before the Pueblo Indians' war for independence in 1680, no longer vied routinely with the governors for economic and political control of the colony. They continued to minister to the Pueblos, but the population and resources of the expanding Hispanic community soon overtook and surpassed those of the missions. Although the friars remained almost the only priests in New Mexico, they saw their spiritual monopoly challenged as three eighteenth-century bishops of Durango made visitations of the distant province.[200]

There was another gradual change, in human relations, from the crusading intolerance of the age of spiritual conquest to pragmatic accommodation. Increasingly beset by Apaches, Navajos, Utes, and Comanches, the Hispanic and Pueblo peoples of the Rio Grande found their best defense in cooperation. Even the friars compromised. Not often in the eighteenth century did they condemn Pueblo Indian kivas as dens of devilish idolatry, as they had in the previous century.[201]

In the words of Fray Angelico Chavez, historian, poet, and twelfth-generation New Mexican, the Vargas reconquest amounted to a "new and distinct colonization."[202] Few survivors of the war of 1680 came back. Those who did found themselves greatly outnumbered by the new settlers of the 1690s and after. Some peninsular Spaniards stayed to found New Mexico families, among them don Diego's second-in-command, Juan Páez Hurtado. Most of the colonists, however, were from New Spain, recruited in and around Mexico City, Zacatecas, and other northern mining districts. A comparison of the muster rolls from the Vargas years and the telephone directories of northern New Mexico today reveals a remarkable historical continuity—the descendants of Vargas's colonists are still here.

Strong-minded, tenacious, and arrogant, Diego de Vargas governed a kingdom he considered remote beyond compare during a pivotal period in its history. The voluminous record he and his contemporaries left—including the journals that contain his official account of these years—remarkably detailed in some areas and frustratingly sparse in others, invites further study. Currently the object of the Vargas Project at the University of New Mexico, it deserves to be made more readily available. By better knowing the times, and the demands they made on those who lived in them, we may better know the man.

Namesake of hotel, savings and loan, and shopping mall; ever-youthful king of the Santa Fe Fiesta; folk hero and secular saint of colonial New Mexico, don Diego de Vargas has been cast in bronze.[203] In the process, the man of flesh and blood has been badly distorted. That is not to say that don Diego is in any way undeserving of the honors bestowed upon him. Yet the image of equestrian reconqueror with sword held high is incomplete.

We should remember don Diego de Vargas also as a lonely grandfather sending hugs to the grandchildren he had never seen and asking for their pictures. He could not pronounce certain words correctly. He knew how to dance. During his long, unintended career in the Indies, he complained monotonously of financial insecurity. As governor of New Mexico, he experienced the extremes of adulation and degradation. He suffered recurring typhus. And he cried out in anguish at the death of his beloved son. By better knowing the man, through his humanness, we may better know the times.

Chronology

1556–98   Reign of Felipe II of Spain

1558–1603   Reign of Elizabeth I of England

1568–1648   Revolt of the Netherlands against Spain

1571   Defeat of Turks at naval battle of Lepanto

1580–1640   Spain assumes control of Portugal

1588   Defeat of Spanish Armada

1589   *Birth of Lorenzo de Vargas in Madrid*

1598   Juan de Oñate founds Spanish colony in New Mexico

1598–1621   Reign of Felipe III of Spain

1600–30   Stagnation of agricultural production and population growth in Castile

1603–25   Reign of James I of England

1605   Publication of *Don Quijote*, part one, by Miguel de Cervantes

1607   Founding of Jamestown

1608   Samuel de Champlain establishes French settlement at Quebec

1609   End of Oñate's proprietorship; New Mexico a royal colony

             Twelve Years' Truce between Spain and the Netherlands

1609–10   Expulsion of Moriscos from Spain

1610–43   Reign of Louis XIII of France

1614   *Lorenzo de Vargas receives knighthood in the military Order of Santiago*

1615	Publication of *Don Quijote,* part two
1618	Outbreak of the Thirty Years' War
1620	Pilgrims found Plymouth Colony under Mayflower Compact
1621	Resumption of hostilities between Spain and the Netherlands
	England attempts to colonize Newfoundland and Nova Scotia
1621–65	Reign of Felipe IV of Spain; ascendency of Conde-duque de Olivares (1621–43)
c. 1622	*Birth of Alonso de Vargas in Lucena (Italy)*
1624	Cardinal Richelieu becomes first minister of France (1624–42)
1625	England declares war on Spain
	First English settlement on Barbados
1625–49	Reign of Charles I of England
1625–64	French settlements in West Indies
1626	Union of Arms proclaimed; all parts of Spanish empire to share costs of defense
	Manhattan Island purchased by Dutch West India Company
1627	Spain declares bankruptcy
1628	Piet Heyn and Dutch capture New Spain's silver fleet
1628–31	Spain battles France in Mantua (Italy); ends with Peace of Cherasco
1629	Colony of Massachusetts Bay given royal charter by England
1630	Publication of *Memorial* by fray Alonso de Benavides, chronicling Franciscan missionary effort in New Mexico
	Spain makes peace with England
1630–60	Fall in American silver revenues to Spain
1630–70	Population and agricultural production reach lowest levels of the century in Castile

1633–41   *Alonso de Vargas a noble page to Spanish Queen Isabel de Borbón*

1635   France declares war on Spain

1636   Spain declares war on France

1637   Anti-Spanish riots in Evora (Portugal)

1639   Destruction of Spanish fleet at the Battle of the Downs

1640   Revolt of the Catalans against Spain; Portuguese revolt

1641   Revolt of Duque de Medina Sidonia and Marqués de Ayamonte in Andalusia

1642   Death of Richelieu; succeeded as first minister by Cardinal Mazarin

Founding of Montreal

1643   Olivares forced to resign

Spain disastrously defeated by French at Rocroi

Death of Louis XIII of France; Louis XIV assumes French throne

Birth of Diego de Vargas in Madrid

1646   England occupies the Bahamas

1647   Beginning of revolt against Spain in Sicily and Naples

Spain declares bankruptcy

1648   Peace of Westphalia ends Thirty Years' War

French support attempted revolt of Duque de Híjar in Aragon

Treaty of Münster; Spain recognizes independence of United Provinces, but retains Catholic provinces of the south

Naples restored to Spanish rule

1649–58   Rule of Oliver Cromwell in England

1650   *Capt. Alonso de Vargas Zapata leaves Madrid to assume post of alcalde mayor of Chiapa (Guatemala)*

1650–54   Devastating plague in Catalonia

1651   Louis XIV attains majority

1651–73	English Navigation Laws
1652	End of revolt of the Catalans
1653	Spain declares bankruptcy
1655	England captures Jamaica
1658–59	Rule of Richard Cromwell in England
1659	Spain signs Peace of the Pyrenees with France
1660	Louis XIV marries María Teresa, Infanta of Spain
1661–85	Reign of Charles II of England
1662	Gov. Bernardo López de Mendizábal arrested in New Mexico on orders of Franciscan agent of Inquisition
1663	New France made a province with Quebec as capital
1664	*Diego de Vargas weds Beatriz Pimentel de Prado in Torrelaguna*
1665	Allied English and Portuguese forces defeat Spanish army at Villaviciosa, securing Portugal's independence
	Succession of Carlos II of Spain under regency of Queen Mariana
	Death of Alonso de Vargas in Santiago de Guatemala
1667	Mexico City cathedral finished (begun 1573)
1668	Treaty of Lisbon; Spain recognizes Portugal's independence
1669	Isaac Newton announces his calculus
1670	Treaty of Madrid; Spain recognizes English possession of Jamaica
1672	Hudson's Bay Company chartered
	Serious drought throughout Spanish peninsula
1673	Founding of Fort Frontenac under the command of Robert de la Salle; French explorers Jacques Marquette and Louis Joliet reach headwaters of Mississippi River and descend to Arkansas
	War between Spain and France
	Diego de Vargas leaves Spain for New Spain; becomes justicia mayor of Teutila by viceregal appointment

1674   *Death of Beatriz Pimentel de Prado at Torrelaguna*

1675   Carlos II attains majority

1675–76   King Philip's War in New England; Bacon's Rebellion in Virginia

1678   Peace of Nijmegen, ending war between Spain and France

1678–79   La Salle explores Great Lakes

1679   Marriage of Carlos II and María Luisa de Orleáns

    Diego de Vargas appointed justicia mayor of Tlalpujahua

1680–92   Pueblo Indians drive Spaniards from New Mexico; colony in exile in El Paso district

1681   Charter of Pennsylvania

1682   La Salle claims Louisiana for France and takes possession of Mississippi Valley

1683   Spain declares war on France; formation of League of The Hague; Emperor Leopold I of Holy Roman Empire and Carlos II join Dutch-Swedish alliance against France

1683–86   Unsuccessful bid by Adm. Isidro de Atondo to occupy Baja California

1683–89   Ill-fated La Salle attempt to found French colony at Fort St. Louis on Texas coast

1685–88   Reign of James II of England

1686   Spain joins League of Augsburg against Louis XIV

    First French settlers in Arkansas

1687–1711   Father Eusebio Francisco Kino, missionary and explorer, in Pimería Alta (Sonora-Arizona)

1688   *Diego de Vargas receives royal appointment as governor of New Mexico*

    Glorious Revolution in England

1688–97   War in Europe; King William's War in the Americas

1689   French explorer Baron de La Hontan visits Great Salt Lake

    Carlos II of Spain marries Mariana de Neoburgo

    Gov. Domingo Jironza of New Mexico wins victory over Pueblo Indians at Zia

1689–1702 Reign of William III and Mary II of England

1690–93 Temporary Spanish occupation of east Texas

1691 *Diego de Vargas accedes at El Paso to governorship of New Mexico*

1692 Salem witchcraft trials (Massachusetts)

Diego de Vargas's first expedition into New Mexico

1693 *Mercurio Volante* by Carlos de Sigüenza y Góngora in praise of Diego de Vargas

1693–96 Recolonization of New Mexico

1695 Death in Mexico City of poet Sor Juana Inés de la Cruz

1696 Pueblo Indians' second war for independence fails

1697 Treaty of Ryswick; Spain cedes western part of Hispaniola to France

1697 Pedro Rodríguez Cubero accedes to governorship of New Mexico

Jesuits begin settlement of Baja California

1697–1700 *Diego de Vargas imprisoned in Santa Fe*

1698 Carlos II's first will, favoring Prince Joseph Ferdinand of Bavaria as successor to Spanish throne

1699 Spaniards occupy Pensacola

Pierre Lemoyne founds first European settlement in Louisiana at Fort Maurepas (present-day Biloxi, Miss.)

Juan Manuel de Vargas arrives in Mexico City

1700 Carlos II's second will, naming Philip of Anjou of France (Felipe V), Louis XIV's grandson, as successor to Spanish throne

1700–1703 *Diego de Vargas defends himself in Mexico City; reappointed governor of New Mexico*

1700–46 Reign of Felipe V of Spain

1701 Spanish treaty of commerce with France, allowing French access to American ports

Felipe V enters Madrid

1701–14 War of the Spanish Succession

1702   French post on Mobile Bay

             *Death of Juan Manuel de Vargas on the return voyage to
                 Spain*

1702–13   Queen Anne's War in the Americas

1702–14   Reign of Anne of England

1703   Methuen Treaty between England and Portugal

             Diego de Vargas reenters Santa Fe

1704   England takes Gibraltar

             Diego de Vargas dies at Bernalillo

             Gregorio Pimentel de Prado dies in Torrelaguna

1705   English navy takes Barcelona

             Edmund Halley's observations on comets

1706   Villa of Alburquerque founded in New Mexico

             *The mother of Diego de Vargas's three natural children dies
                 in Mexico City; they appeal for assistance to the family in
                 Spain*

Abbreviations

AL   Autograph letter
ALS   Autograph letter signed
C   Copy
DS   Document signed
L   Letter
LS   Letter signed
DA   *Diccionario de Autoridades*
EUI   *Enciclopedia universal ilustrada europeo-americana*
NMHR   *New Mexico Historical Review*
RECOP.   *Recopilación de leyes de los reynos de las Indias*
AGI   Archivo General de Indias, Seville, Spain
AGN   Archivo General de la Nación, Mexico City, Mexico
AGNot.   Archivo General de Notarías del Distrito Federal, Mexico
              City, Mexico
AHN   Archivo Histórico de la Nación, Madrid, Spain
AHPM   Archivo Histórico de Protocolos de Madrid, Madrid, Spain
AMNB   Archivo del Marqués de la Nava de Barcinas, Madrid, Spain
ARGD   Archivo de Rafael Gasset Dorado, Madrid, Spain
BNM   Biblioteca Nacional de México, Mexico City, Mexico
SANM I   Spanish Archives of New Mexico, New Mexico State
SANM II   Records Center and Archives, Santa Fe
SRCA   New Mexico State Records Center and Archives, Santa Fe
UNM SC   University of New Mexico, Special Collections,
              Albuquerque, New Mexico

Notes

1. Gonzalo Fernández de Oviedo y Valdés, "Noticias de Madrid y de las familias madrileñas de su tiempo," *Revista de la Biblioteca, Archivo y Museo* 16 (Jan.-July 1947):287–88. A later chronicler of Madrid, whose book would have been available to don Diego, repeated the fable in nearly the same words, expanding on it slightly. Jerónimo de Quintana, *Historia de la antigüedad, nobleza y grandeza de la villa de Madrid* (Madrid, 1954):631.

The antiquity of the Vargases of Madrid was unchallenged. In the prolog to his eighteenth-century work, Joseph Antonio Alvarez y Baena certified that: "The Zapata and Coello families, for example, are very old in Madrid, but they are not native; the Quirogas are from the kingdom of Galicia, although they settled here ages ago; and the same can be said of many others. The Vargases, in contrast—even though they are found scattered all over Europe, and one could even say all over the world—are from Madrid." *Hijos de Madrid, ilustres en santidad, dignidades, armas, ciencias y artes* (Madrid, 1789), 1:[6].

In 1740, chiefly to demonstrate for purposes of litigation that he was the direct heir of the Vargas family, don Diego's grandson, Capt. Diego Joseph López de Zárate Vargas Pimentel Zapata y Luján Ponce de León Cepeda Alvarez Contreras y Salinas, compiled from some thirty sources a *Breve descripción genealógica de la ilustre, quanto antiquíssima Casa de los Vargas de Madrid* (Madrid, 1740), copy in the Real Academia de la Historia, Madrid. Another genealogy, composed by a great-great-great-great-grandson of don Diego to demonstrate the family's link to St. Theresa of Avila, brings one branch down to the 1930s. José Pérez Balsera, *Laudemus viros gloriosos et parentes nostros in generatione sua* (Madrid, 1931). See also J. Manuel Espinosa, "Notes on the Lineage of don Diego de Vargas, Reconqueror of New Mexico," NMHR 10 (Apr. 1935):112–20, and John L. Kessell, "Diego de Vargas: Another Look," NMHR 60 (Jan. 1985):11–28.

2. López de Zárate Vargas, *Breve descripción*, 3–8; Alvarez y Baena, *Hijos de Madrid*, 1:283–84;

Pérez Balsera, *Laudemus*, 99–100. One undated, genealogical table, which listed the Vargases down to don Diego's children, noted whose statues graced the chapel. Descendencia de los Vargas, AMNB. The Vargas chapel was demolished along with the church in 1761 so construction of the present, massive church could begin. Pascual Madoz, *Madrid: Audiencia, provincia, intendencia, vicaria, partido y villa* (Madrid, 1981): 207.

3. Madoz, *Madrid*, 198–200. Alvarez y Baena, *Hijos de Madrid*, 2:78–81, 382–83. For a sketch of Lic. Francisco de Vargas, see Mariano Alcocer and Saturnino Rivera, *Bio-bibliografías de juristas notables*, vol. 5 of *Historia de la Universidad de Valladolid* (Valladolid, 1924):188–90. EUI, 67:2–3.

4. Eleanor B. Adams, "Two Colonial New Mexico Libraries," NMHR 19 (Apr. 1944):151. Quintana, *Historia*, 629. DA.

5. For an idea of what knighthood meant in Spain at this time, see L. P. Wright, "The Military Orders in Sixteenth and Seventeenth Century Spanish Society: The Institutional Embodiment of a Historical Tradition," *Past and Present* 43 (May 1969):34–70.

6. Lorenzo de Vargas, Services, Madrid, 29 Jan. 1638, AHN, Consejos 4.445:39. Lorenzo de Vargas, Petition to the king, 1647, AMNB; Diego de Vargas, Services, Madrid, 30 Apr. 1670, with later note, AGI, Indiferente General 123;

López de Zárate Vargas, *Breve descripción*, 10–11. Alvarez y Baena, in *Hijos de Madrid*, added to the entries of López de Zárate Vargas information from parish records and the files of the Order of Santiago, but later authors simply copied. See, for example, Luis Ballesteros Robles, *Diccionario biográfico matritense* (Madrid, 1912).

7. After his year-long novitiate, during which the marqués attested that don Lorenzo had served the required six months in the royal galleys, he made his profession in the order on 10 April 1615 at the Augustinian convento in Vélez. Felipe III, Title of knighthood to Lorenzo de Vargas, AMNB. Wright, "Military Orders," 43.

8. López de Zárate Vargas, *Breve descripción*, 11. Two of don Lorenzo's appointments survive in the Archivo General de Simancas: to the provinces of Capitanata and the Duchy of Molise, dated 26 July 1621; and to Principato, Citra, and Basilicata, 4 Apr. 1632. Ricardo Magdaleno, *Títulos y privilegios de Nápoles, siglos xvi–xviii: Catálogo 28 del Archivo de Simancas* (Valladolid, 1980), 1:584. Lorenzo de Vargas, Services, 29 Jan. 1638. EUI, 70:1005.

9. Lorenzo de Vargas, Services, 29 Jan. 1638.

10. Trinidad de los Muzos, in the interior of present-day Colombia, was founded in 1560. Manuel Lucena Salmoral, *Nuevo Reino de Granada: Real audiencia y presidentes*, vol. 3, pt. 1 of *Historia extensa de Colombia*, 72.

Antonia's father and mother were Alonso Sánchez de Cepeda y Ayala, a native of Granada in Spain, and Juana Venegas Ponce de León, born in Santa Fe de Bogotá in the Indies. Pérez Balsera, *Laudemus*, 9–47. Felipe III, Permission for Lorenzo de Vargas to wed, Madrid, 26 May 1618, AMNB.

11. Alvarez y Baena, *Hijos de Madrid*, 3:377–78. Alonso de Vargas Zapata y Luján (Madrid, 1636), AHN, Ordenes Militares, Santiago 1.830. Nowhere in the documentation supporting don Alonso's candidacy for membership in the Order of Santiago does his birthdate appear, only the place and the fact that his father was serving in Capitanata and the Duchy of Molise, a post don Lorenzo seems to have assumed late in 1621.

12. Don Alonso's service as a menino to the queen began on 8 May 1633 and ended on 10 January 1641, the day he was knighted. López de Zárate Vargas, *Breve descripción*, 12. Capt. John Stevens, a nearly contemporary Englishman, in *A New Spanish and English Dictionary* (London, 1706), defined a menino as "a very little Page at Court; so call'd, because they are meer Children, kept there only for their Education and for Grandeur. There are bigger Pages, whom they call Pages."

13. Alonso de Vargas Zapata y Luján, AHN, Ordenes Militares, Santiago 1.830. The age of entry into the Order of Santiago had been reduced from the original sixteen to seven, and even that was waived on occasion. Wright, "Military Orders," 52.

14. Antonia Cepeda Ponce de León, Will, Salerno, 11 Jan. 1636, AHPM, P. 5.113. At the time, Lorenzo de Vargas was serving as civil and military governor of Principato, Citra, and Basilicata.

15. Pérez Balsera was unable to locate a copy of the life of don Diego's saintly grandmother. It was through her, however, that he traced the Pérez Balseras back to the family of St. Theresa of Avila. *Laudemus*, 49.

16. A fine characterization of the conde-duque, the king, and the Spanish court at this time is found in J. H. Elliott, *The Count-Duke of Olivares: The Statesman in an Age of Decline* (New Haven, 1986).

17. Juana de Vargas Ponce de León, Petition, Madrid, 1672, AHN, Consejos 4.445:39.

18. Lorenzo de Vargas, Valuation of estate, Madrid, 27–29 Mar. 1642, AHPM, P. 5.113. A remarkably detailed 1656 plan of Madrid shows the Vargas complex, much of the city block numbered 153 on later maps. Pedro Texeira, *Topographía de la Villa de Madrid descrita por don Pedro Texeira, año 1656* (Madrid, 1980); Miguel Molina Campuzano, *Planos de Madrid de los siglos xvii y xviii* (Madrid, 1960). Nineteenth-century buildings occupy the site today. Diego de Vargas, Services, 1670.

19. Documents concerning Alonso de Vargas's renunciation of the inheritance from his mother,

Madrid, 1638, AHPM, P. 5.113.

20. Alonso de Vargas, Will, Santiago de Guatemala, 14 Aug. 1665, photocopy in AMNB. Pérez Balsera includes transcripts of María Margarita's baptismal and marriage entries. *Laudemus*, 59, 61.

21. John Lynch, *Spain under the Habsburgs*, 2 vols. (New York, 1984), 2:125; Wright, "Military Orders," 58–59; López de Zárate Vargas, *Breve descripción*, 12. Felipe IV, Commissions to Alonso de Vargas, Madrid, 27 Apr. 1642, and Huesca (?), 29 May 1642, AMNB. J. H. Elliott, *Revolt of the Catalans: A Study in the Decline of Spain, 1598–1640* (Cambridge, 1963):445–49. One source stated that don Lorenzo paid to equip and arm the company and don Alonso commanded it. Francisco Javier García Rodrigo, *El cuerpo colegiado de la nobleza de Madrid* (Madrid, 1884):332.

22. That don Diego's elder brother was dead by 1660 is evident from Diego de Vargas and José de Castro Castillo, Settling of accounts, Madrid, 29 Aug. 1662, AHPM, P. 10.120. Although the registers of baptisms, marriages, and burials from the parish of San Pedro el Real are preserved today at the parish of Nuestra Señora de la Soledad (la Paloma) in Madrid, the book for the period 1635–79, which likely contains an entry for young Lorenzo de Vargas's death and burial in the Vargas chapel, is missing.

23. The surviving copy of the baptismal entry does not say where the sacrament was administered, only that the ritual was performed by the pastor of the parish church of San Ginés and San Luis. Isabel María de Vargas and Ignacio López de Zárate, 1694, AHN, Ordenes Militares, Casamientos, Santiago 10.461; published in Pérez Balsera, *Laudemus*, 65. The original entry in the San Luis baptismal register seems to have perished during the burning of that church in 1936. *Guía de los archivos de Madrid* (Madrid, 1952):462. On the Calle de la Montera and its church of San Luis, see José Deleito y Piñuela, *Sólo Madrid es corte: La capital de dos mundos bajo Felipe IV* (Madrid, 1968):55–58.

24. Pedro Pérez, Declaration, Madrid, 19 May 1649, Documents relating to certain furnishings of don Lorenzo de Vargas, 1649, AMNB. López de Zárate Vargas says that don Alonso became a captain of heavy cavalry and served in Spain "many years." *Breve descripción*, 12. There are dozens of documents in AHPM, P. 7.213–14 and 7.514–16, detailing don Alonso's economic and legal affairs. It is certain that he was not the lawyer who wrote a treatise on the Duque de Osuna's tax on the people of Messina and left twenty volumes of briefs, a slip by Pérez Balsera (*Laudemus*, 57), who read the entry for the wrong Alonso de Vargas in Alvarez y Baena's *Hijos de Madrid*. The error is perpetuated in the *Diccionario de Historia de España* (Madrid, 1969), 3:901.

25. Division of the estate of Antonia Cepeda Ponce de León, Madrid, 14–18 Apr. 1642, AHPM, P. 5.113.

26. Lorenzo de Vargas, Will, Madrid, 3 Sept. 1643, AHPM, P. 5.113.

27. See Antonio Domínguez Ortiz, *El antiguo régimen: Los Reyes Católicos y los Austrias* (Madrid, 1981):347, 386–98; and Lynch, *Habsburgs*, 2:136–37.

28. Alvarez y Baena (*Hijos de Madrid*, 1:51) says that she died in the parish of Santiago and was buried in the Convento de San Francisco.

29. Lorenzo de Vargas died on 13 November 1649. Documents concerning the expenses of his burial are in AHPM, P. 8.609. Among the furnishings and personal possessions he left were a portrait of Francisco de Vargas, presumably his father, and two portraits of himself. Three additional portraits, of uncles of don Lorenzo, were among the furnishings in don Alonso's apartment mentioned in documents dated 18–21 May 1649, AMNB.

30. A 1672 inventory of don Alonso's entails, inherited by don Diego in 1666, showed the diversity of the family's possessions. Diego de Vargas, Listing of the entire estate, Torrelaguna, 9 Aug. 1672, AMNB.

31. Don Lorenzo's appointment to Zacatecas was dated 27 April 1649. Diego de Vargas, Services, 1670. His petition for the government of Calabria was undated but written on stamped

paper for 1647. Lorenzo de Vargas, Petition, 1647.

32. Alonso de Vargas and Alonso de Santander y Mercado, Contract, Madrid, 2 Apr. 1650, AHPM, P. 7.214.

33. Appointment of tutor and guardian, Madrid, 8 Apr. 1650, AHPM, P. 7.214. By this time, doña Juana must have been at least eighty years old. In case of her death, don Alonso named five more guardians in succession, including his brother, Francisco, and whoever might have married his sister, Antonia.

34. Permission to Alonso de Vargas for passage, Seville, 29 Apr. 1650, AGI, Contratación 5.429.

35. For a lusty picture of Madrid at this time, see Deleito y Piñuela, *Sólo Madrid es corte*. Also Henry Kamen, *Spain in the Later Seventeenth Century, 1665–1700* (London, 1980):45, 51, 154, 167–74, 279–80; and Lynch, *Habsburgs*, 2:149.

36. Diego de Vargas, Petition, Madrid, n.d., and related documents, 24 Sept.-21 Oct. 1660, AHPM, P. 6.587.

37. Diego de Vargas and José de Castro Castillo, Settling of accounts, Madrid, 29 Aug. 1662, AHPM, P. 10.120. The permission to act for himself was dated 8 June 1662. The period covered by the accounting ran from 1 January 1660 to 31 August 1662. A description of family life and the early training of children among the nobility is given by Richard Kagan in *Students and Society in*

Early Modern Spain (Baltimore, 1974):5–30.

38. Kagan, *Students and Society*, 236.

39. Diego de Vargas to Sebastián de Vargas, Power of attorney, Madrid, 4 Nov. 1662, AHPM, P. 10.120. Review of the University of Valladolid's books of incorporation and matriculation for the 1660s, preserved today in the Archivo Histórico Provincial y Universitario de Valladolid, failed to reveal any mention of Diego de Vargas.

40. Diego de Vargas to Conde de Galve, El Paso del Río del Norte, 28 June 1692, BNM 4:4. Sebastián de Vargas, born in Madrid on 12 January 1598, had entered the Society of Jesus on 2 April 1610. José Simón Díaz, *Historia del Colegio Imperial de Madrid* (Madrid, 1952–59), 1:535, 575. Kagan, *Students and Society*, 38–39.

41. Lorenzo Pimentel de Prado, the eldest of the three sons, had been killed during the relief of the fortress of Valenciennes in Flanders. Pimentel de Prado, Services, Madrid, 26 Jan. 1715, AGI, Indiferente General 162. In his will, Lorenzo de Vargas had left Juan Pimentel de Prado a chestnut stallion. He also owed him a debt of 1,480 reales. Lorenzo de Vargas, Will, 3 Sept. 1643. Diputación Provincial de Madrid, *Guía a la provincia de Madrid: Torrelaguna* (Madrid, n.d.).

42. Matrimonios, Libro 3 (1628–66), Parroquia de Santa

María Magdalena, Torrelaguna. Pérez Balsera, *Laudemus*, 71. Diego de Vargas and Beatriz Pimentel de Prado, Marriage contract, Torrelaguna, 1 Apr. 1664, Archivo de Notarías, Torrelaguna.

43. Diego de Vargas, Services, 1670. Fray Francisco Ximénez, *Historia de la Provincia de San Vicente de Chiapa y Guatemala de la Orden de Predicadores* (Guatemala City, 1929), lib. 5, cap. 2:255. Murdo J. MacLeod, *Spanish Central America: A Socioeconomic History, 1520–1720* (Berkeley, 1973):289, 306, 356–57, 391. MacLeod's work provides a context for Alonso de Vargas's service in Guatemala, even though he does not mention Vargas specifically.

44. Alonso de Vargas, Will, 14 Aug. 1665. MacLeod (*Spanish Central America*, 318–20) discusses the efforts in Guatemala of officeholders from Spain to rapidly accumulate wealth for a return to Madrid or for a comfortable, upper-class life in the colony.

45. Lynch, *Habsburgs*, 2:134.

46. Bautismos, Libro 4 (1638–66) and 5 (1667–1701), Parroquia de Santa María Magdalena, Torrelaguna.

47. Documents dealing with these and other legal actions are in AMNB and ARGD.

48. Sancho de Guinea Bracamonte to Lorenzo de Alvarado, n.p., 12 Nov. 1665, AHPM, P. 9.012. Alonso de Vargas, Will, 14 Aug. 1665. Don Diego took formal possession of his

inheritance in Spain in July 1666. Diego de Vargas, Listing of the entire estate, 1672.

49. Detailed estimates of the work to be done are among the documents in AHPM, P. 9.012. Diego de Vargas, Listing of the entire estate, 1672. It would seem that the Madrid and Torrelaguna properties were perennially in need of repair. As early as 1627, Lorenzo de Vargas had claimed that the walls of the houses on the Calle del Almendro were threatening to collapse. AHN, Consejos 4.424, 1627:126. Later, in his 1643 will, he complained of the ruinous state of the Torrelaguna place and admitted borrowing 1,500 ducados for repairs from his son's father-in-law, Diego de Contreras. Lorenzo de Vargas, Will, 3 Sept. 1643.

50. Diego de Vargas and Francisco de Herrera, Contract, Madrid, 31 July 1670, AHPM, P. 11.431. A native of Seville trained in Italy, the exuberant Herrera, whose best-known surviving work is *El triunfo de San Hermenegildo* (c. 1660), had come to Madrid about 1660 and been named court painter by Felipe IV. Reappointed in 1672 by Carlos II, he later became Assistant Keeper of the Palace Keys and Royal Architect. He died in Madrid in 1685, leaving a vibrant, theatrical legacy of works, and an unpaid note receivable for 137 1/2 doblones from don Diego de Vargas. Jonathan M. Brown, "Herrera the Younger: Baroque Artist and Personality," *Apollo* 84 (July 1966):34–43. Ignacio López

de Zárate to Angela Jacinta de Robles, Transfer of debt, Madrid, 5 Oct. 1690, AHPM, P. 13.146.

51. Diego de Vargas, Services, 1670. Kamen, *Spain*, 245. Kagan, *Students and Society*, 81–105.

52. Diego de Vargas, Will, Mexico City, 1 June 1703, AGNot. 692.

53. Don Diego was authorizing his Jesuit great-uncle to act in his stead as patron of several pious endowments. Diego de Vargas to Sebastián de Vargas, Power of attorney, Madrid, 21 June 1672, AHPM, P. 10.125. Domínguez Ortiz, *Antiguo régimen*, 431.

54. Diego de Vargas, Proof of legitimacy, Madrid, 21 June 1672, AHPM, P. 10.956. The only known portrait of don Diego, a full-length representation of him as a young man, corresponds well enough to this description. The painting hangs today in the chapel of San Isidro at Pretil de Santisteban, 3, in Madrid, and bears a posthumous inscription. It may be a copy of a work now lost. Whether it was painted from life is unclear at the present time.

55. Diego de Vargas, Will, Madrid, 21 June 1672, AHPM, P. 10.125.

56. It is impossible to tell from the document just how encumbered the estate was. Diego de Vargas, Listing of the entire estate, 1672. Diego de Vargas, Will, 1 June 1703.

57. Don Gregorio was born on 22 February 1638. Gregorio Pimentel de Prado, AHN, Ordenes

Militares, Santiago 6.471.

58. Kamen, *Spain*, 91, 100–103.

59. Lynch, *Habsburgs*, 2:258–64. Diego de Vargas, Services, 1670.

60. Ramón de Mesonero Romanos, *El antiguo Madrid* (Madrid, 1881), 1:277; Gabriel Maura y Gamazo, *Carlos II y su corte* (Madrid, 1911–15), 2:150–52. Diego de Vargas, Listing of the entire estate, 1672.

61. Diego de Vargas, Petition, Cadiz, n.d., Proceedings in council, Madrid, 21 Jan. 1673, AGI, México 276. In November 1672, while he waited in Cadiz, Vargas executed a general power of attorney in favor of his wife. Diego de Vargas to Beatriz Pimentel de Prado, Power of attorney, Cadiz, 26 Nov. 1672, Archivo Histórico Provincial, Cadiz, Protocolos de Cádiz 5.299.

62. On 28 April 1673, news reached Mexico City that the packet boat had made Veracruz. The chest with the official mail arrived in the capital on 4 May. Antonio de Robles, *Diario de sucesos notables, 1665–1703*, ed. Antonio Castro Leal (Mexico City, 1946), 1:124–28. The 1673 flota did not sail from Cadiz until 13 July, by which time Vargas was already in New Spain. Kamen, *Spain*, 132–33.

63. Irving A. Leonard, in *Baroque Times in Old Mexico: Seventeenth-Century Persons, Places, and Practices* (Ann Arbor, 1959), offers graphic descriptions of the different world don Diego was entering.

64. On the tenure of the Marqués de Mancera, see Hubert Howe Bancroft, *History of Mexico: Vol. III, 1600–1803*, vol. 11 of *The Works of Hubert Howe Bancroft* (San Francisco, 1883):169–81; Lewis Hanke, ed., in collaboration with Celso Rodríguez, *Los virreyes españoles en América durante el gobierno de la Casa de Austria: México* (Madrid, 1978):9–82; and Manuel Rivera Cambas, *Los gobernantes de México: Galería de biografías y retratos de los virreyes, emperadores, presidentes y otros gobernantes que ha tenido México, desde don Hernando Cortés hasta el C. Benito Juárez* (Mexico City, 1872), 1:214–37.

65. Leonard, *Baroque Times*, 172–214.

66. The *Gran Enciclopedia Larousse en veinte volúmenes* (Paris, 1962), 12:897, gives 1608 as the year of Mancera's birth, and the EUI, 62:490, says he died in Madrid on 13 February 1715. Rivera Cambas, *Gobernantes*, 1:237. Diego de Vargas, Services, 1670.

67. Diego de Vargas and José de Alcocer, Promissory note, Mexico City, 17 July 1673, AGNot. 687.

68. Peter Gerhard, *A Guide to the Historical Geography of New Spain* (Cambridge, 1972):300–305; *Diccionario Porrúa de historia, biografía y geografía de México* (Mexico City, 1976), 2:1903.

69. Vargas's salary is found in AGI, Contaduría 776. Diego de Vargas and José de Alcocer, Promissory notes, Mexico City, 17 July 1673 and 23 Sept. 1674,

AGNot. 687. The title *justicia mayor* in this sense is explained by Guillermo Lohmann Villena, *El corregidor de indios en el Perú bajo los Austrias* (Madrid, 1957):123.

70. The laws pertaining to *alcaldías mayores* appear in the *Recop.*, Lib. 5, tít. 2, leyes 1–52. For a commentary on them, see Juan de Solórzano Pereira, *Política indiana* (Madrid, 1972), lib. 5, cap. 2:1–53. See also Charles Gibson, *The Aztecs under Spanish Rule: A History of the Indians of the Valley of Mexico, 1519–1810* (Stanford, 1964):82, 90–94; C. H. Haring, *The Spanish Empire in America* (New York, 1963):132–33; John Leddy Phelan, *The Kingdom of Quito in the Seventeenth Century: Bureaucratic Politics in the Spanish Empire* (Madison, 1967):147–76. The most extensive treatment to date of corregimientos, the Peruvian equivalent of New Spain's *alcaldías mayores*, is Lohmann Villena's *Corregidor de indios*.

71. Letter 1 below. The burial entry for doña Beatriz gave no hint of the cause of her sudden death. Difuntos, Libro 2 (1664–1712), Parroquia de Santa María Magdalena, Torrelaguna. Dating from the 1530s and attributed to architect Rodrigo Gil de Hontañón, the Vélez family chapel of San Gregorio, "because of its perfection of design, is one of the church's most interesting architectural elements." Antonio Momplet Míguez and María Victoria Chico Picaza, *El arte religioso en Torrelaguna* (Madrid, 1979):22–23.

72. Diego de Vargas, Services, 1670.

73. Payo de Rivera Enríquez, Exemption from tribute, Mexico City, 6 Mar. 1677, AGN, Indios 25:232.

74. The legend on the Vargas portrait errs further by attributing to don Diego membership in the Order of Santiago.

75. Conde de Paredes to the king, Mexico City, 3 Apr. 1685, AGI, Guadalajara 141:20. Don Diego said he was appointed *justicia mayor* of Tlalpujahua on 28 April 1679. Diego de Vargas, Services, 1670. Gerhard, *Historical Geography*, 318–20. P. J. Bakewell, *Silver Mining and Society in Colonial Mexico: Zacatecas, 1546–1700* (Cambridge, 1971):139.

76. Leonard, *Baroque Times*, 158. Parroquia de la Asunción, Sagrario, Mexico City, Padrones, Volumen 7 (1670–1824), Genealogical Library, Church of Jesus Christ of Latter-Day Saints, Salt Lake City, Utah, LDS microfilm 036,415. In Letter 64 below, Vargas's natural son, Juan Manuel, wrote that his mother had died in Mexico City on 11 September 1706. The Sagrario parish burial register contains only one entry for a person who died that day, Nicolasa Rincón, described as an unmarried woman, living at the time on the Calle de San Felipe Neri. Death came suddenly, and she did not receive

the sacraments. AGN, Genealogía y Heráldica, Difunciones de españoles (1671–1820), Parroquia de la Asunción, Sagrario, Mexico City, Volumen 5, LDS microfilm 035,750, rollo 32, 5–9.

77. Diego de Vargas (Marqués de la Nava de Barcinas), Will, Bernalillo, 7 Apr. 1704, SANM I:1027. A translation appears in Ralph Emerson Twitchell, comp., *The Spanish Archives of New Mexico* (Cedar Rapids, 1914), 1:301–10.

78. Pedro and Francisco de Vargas, Appointment of curador ad litem, Mexico City, 17 Dec. 1682, AGNot. 379. MacLeod, *Spanish Central America*, 148. Pedro Alonso received his bachelor's degree in 1682 and much later, after don Diego's death, acted in Mexico City as an attorney for the Spanish branch of the family, until he himself died in 1717. Lansing B. Bloom, "Vargas Encomienda," NMHR 14 (Oct. 1939):398–410. Bachelor of arts to Pedro de Vargas, Mexico City, 8 Apr. 1682, AGN, Universidades 148:221.

79. Paredes (1638–92) and Vargas may have been neighbors in Madrid at some point. When don Diego's grandson took possession of the family properties in 1719, the houses on the Calle del Almendro were described as bordering or abutting those owned by the Conde de Paredes. Pérez Balsera, *Laudemus*, 91. Paredes had been appointed to the Council of the Indies on 31 October 1675, a position reserved for him during his term as viceroy. Upon his return to Spain, and even after his appointment as the queen's chief mayordomo, he continued to receive his salary as councilor of the Indies. Ernesto Schäfer, *El Consejo Real y Supremo de las Indias: Su historia, organización y labor administrativa hasta la terminación de la casa de Austria* (Seville, 1935, 1947), 1:271, 278–83, 364; 2:440.

80. Conde de Paredes to the king, Mexico City, 3 Apr. 1685, AGI, Guadalajara 141:20.

81. Silvestre Vélez de Escalante, Extracto de noticias, 1777–78, BNM, 3:1.

82. Conde de Paredes to the king, 3 Apr. 1685. The average price of the mercury Vargas distributed between 1679 and 1684, which Paredes said came from Spain and Peru, was approximately 140 pesos a hundredweight. This is somewhat higher than the price at Zacatecas, which during the 1680s fluctuated between 90 and 100 pesos a hundredweight. On the use, supply, and distribution of mercury, see Bakewell, *Silver Mining*, 150–80. On 8 August 1680, don Diego routinely initiated a request for fifty hundredweight of mercury for the mines at Tlalpujahua. Diego de Vargas to Juan López Pareja, Power of attorney, Mexico City, 8 Aug. 1680, AGNot. 379.

83. Exemption, Mexico City, 25 May 1684, AGN, Indios 28:79. The newly arrived *Recopilación de leyes*

de los reynos de las Indias (Lib. 6, tít. 5, ley 9) stated that Indians employed in the mines should pay tribute.

84. Bakewell, *Silver Mining*, 213. Diego de Vargas to Luis Sáenz de Tagle, Promissory note, Mexico City, 21 Mar. 1680, AGNot. 11. See also Letter 24 below.

85. Conde de Monclova to Diego de Vargas, Commission, Mexico City, 1 Jan. 1687, AGN, General de Partes 16:10. On 10 October 1662, the crown decreed that death penalties imposed on Spaniards or Indians had to be reported to the appropriate audiencia, which would review the case and specify how the sentence was to be carried out. Lohmann Villena, *Corregidor de indios*, 258.

86. Juan González Calderón and Juan Manuel Francisco de Lira, Petition to the king, n.p., n.d., and related documents, Madrid, 20 May–10 June 1688, AGI, Guadalajara 3; Carlos II, Title of governor of New Mexico to Diego de Vargas, Madrid, 18 June 1688, AGI, México 1216. Diego de Vargas to Juan González Calderón, Power of attorney, Mexico City, 14 Aug. 1684, AGNot. 379.

87. J. H. Parry, *The Sale of Public Office in the Spanish Indies under the Habsburgs* (Berkeley, 1953):1–73; Phelan, *The Kingdom of Quito*, 143–45; Solórzano Pereira, *Política indiana*, lib. 6, cap. 13:1–47; Antonio Domínguez Ortiz, "Un virreynato en venta,"

Mercurio Peruano 453 (Jan.-Feb. 1965):43–51.

88. Juan González Calderón and Juan Manuel Francisco de Lira, Petition, 1688; Title of governor of New Mexico to Diego de Vargas, 1688. The allegation in the petition and title that Vargas came to New Spain as royal courier in 1678 with a recommendation to the viceroy, fray Payo de Rivera Enríquez, is almost certainly an error. To reconcile this statement with don Diego's known arrival in 1673, Lansing B. Bloom, in "Vargas Encomienda," 373, surmised that Vargas returned to Spain in the mid-1670s. From the letters published here, and from other documents placing him in New Spain during this period, a trip home appears most unlikely.

89. Letter 24 below. Galve was a member of one of Spain's most prominent families, the Casa del Infantado, with its ancestral home in Pastrana. His older brother, to whom he wrote frequently from New Spain, was the Duque del Infantado. From 1657, after the death of their father, don Rodrigo de Sandoval y Mendoza, Galve and his mother had resided at the family's principal residence in Madrid, the Palacio de Vistillas, within a few blocks of the Vargas complex. Cristina Arteaga y Falguera, *La Casa del Infantado: Cabeza de los Mendoza* (Madrid, 1944), 2:24, 83. Diego Gutiérrez Coronel, *Historia genealógica de la Casa de Mendoza* (Cuenca, 1946),

1:406. Robles, *Diario*, 2:168. Rivera Cambas, *Gobernantes*, 1:265–78.

90. Letters 4–6 below.

91. Letter 48. Pérez Balsera, *Laudemus*, 68–83, includes the baptismal entries for Isabel María and Ignacio, their marriage entry, and biographical sketches of don Iñigo (1605–69), don Juan Antonio (1646–98), and don Ignacio López de Zárate (1647–1707), quoting Alvarez Baena, *Hijos de Madrid*, and the EUI. All three were knights of the Order of Santiago. The Vargas and López de Zárate families had been acquainted for several generations. It was don Iñigo who, as secretary of the Council of Italy, had signed the service record of don Lorenzo de Vargas in 1638. Lorenzo de Vargas, Services, 29 Jan. 1638. Curiously, one Diego López de Zárate had received an appointment as alcalde mayor of Tlalpujahua forty-three years before Diego de Vargas served there. Felipe IV, Appointment of Diego López de Zárate, Mexico City, 6 Mar. 1636, AGN, Civil 77:3.

92. Ignacio López de Zárate and Isabel María de Vargas Pimentel, Marriage contract, Madrid, 15 Nov. 1688, AHPM, P. 13.142. Diego de Vargas's power of attorney to doña Juana, dated in Mexico City on 1 October 1685, and Gregorio Pimentel de Prado's compliance, Madrid, 29 March 1686, were incorporated in the marriage contract.

93. Juana de Vargas Ponce de León to Ignacio López de Zárate, Receipt, Madrid, 20 Nov. 1688, and Ignacio López de Zárate to Marqués de Villanueva de la Sagra, Loan, Madrid, 7 Dec. 1688, AHPM, P. 13.142.

94. Pérez Balsera, *Laudemus*, 73–83. For a discussion of the special relationship between the universities and office holding, see Kagan, *Students and Society*, 109–58, 201–202. Don Ignacio was back in Madrid from Italy by late 1685. Ignacio López de Zárate, Receipt, Madrid, 29 Dec. 1685, AHPM, P. 12.779.

95. Letters 2, 4, and 5 below.

96. When don Diego wrote from Teutila in 1675 (Letter 1), both his sons were alive. In 1689, he referred routinely to Juan Manuel as his only son and heir, as if Francisco Iván had been dead for some time. Diego de Vargas to Juan González Calderón, Power of attorney, 1689.

97. Letter 48 below.

98. Rivera Cambas, *Gobernantes*, 1:260.

99. Kamen, *Spain*, 374–75. R. Trevor Davies, *Spain in Decline, 1621–1700* (London, 1970):135–36.

100. Letter 48 below. Juan Manuel's family said only that he was a noble page of both the queens of Carlos II. He may also have served the queen mother, Mariana. The king, in 1699, recalled Juan Manuel as "having been a menino of my lady the queen, my mother." The king to Conde de Moctezuma, Madrid, 21

Feb. 1699, AGI, México 1102, Registro de Partes, lib. 44.

101. Raimundo de Lantéry, quoted by Kamen, *Spain*, 271.

102. Letter 7 below.

103. Letter 9 below. Disbursements, Mexico City, 1690, AGI, Contaduría 780. Espinosa, *Crusaders*, 32 n. 23. Letters 4–6 below. Conde de Paredes to the king, Mexico City, 3 Apr. 1685, AGI, Guadalajara 141:20.

104. Charles Wilson Hackett, ed., and Charmion Clair Shelby, trans., *Revolt of the Pueblo Indians of New Mexico and Otermín's Attempted Reconquest, 1680–1682* (Albuquerque, 1942); and Vina Walz, "History of the El Paso Area, 1680–1692" (Ph.D. diss., Univ. of New Mexico, 1951):1–72. Robles, *Diario*, 1:295.

105. Rivera Cambas, *Gobernantes*, 1:252–53.

106. Herbert Eugene Bolton, *Rim of Christendom: A Biography of Eusebio Francisco Kino, Pacific Coast Pioneer* (Tucson, 1984):87–228. Rivera Cambas, *Gobernantes*, 1:253–60. Bancroft, *History of Mexico*, 189–207.

107. For the Spanish response to the La Salle colony, that "thorn in America's heart," see Robert S. Weddle, *Wilderness Manhunt: The Spanish Search for La Salle* (Austin, 1973).

108. The king to Conde de Paredes, Cedula, Madrid, 4 Sept. 1683, AGI, Guadalajara 138:22; translated in Charles Wilson Hackett, ed., *Historical Documents relating to New Mexico, Nueva Vizcaya, and Approaches thereto,*

to 1773 (Washington, D.C., 1923–37), 3:349–50.

109. According to a nearly contemporary document, Jironza led 80 armed Spaniards and 120 Indian allies on this campaign, which, as with eleven other campaigns, he provisioned and paid for himself. The dramatic battle at Zia took place in 1689 on the feast day of the beheading of St. John the Baptist, 29 August, and lasted from daybreak until eight o'clock that evening. The pueblo was "devastated and burned." More than 600 of the defenders died, many, according to the account, choosing death amid the flames instead of surrender. The victorious Spanish force returned to El Paso with more than 70 captives. Cabildo of Santa Fe, Certification of the services of Domingo Jironza Petrís de Cruzate, El Paso del Río del Norte, 25 Nov. 1690, AGN, Civil 1743. Walz, "El Paso Area," 246–52, 254–57. The number of natives killed at Zia and certain details of the assault are so similar to what was recorded at Acoma in 1599 that one suspects Jironza may have read the description of that earlier battle published in Spain in 1610. See Gaspar Pérez de Villagrá, *History of New Mexico*, trans. Gilberto Espinosa, ed. F. W. Hodge (Los Angeles, 1933):219–67.

110. Arteaga y Falguera, *La Casa del Infantado*, 2:139; Lillian Estelle Fisher, *Viceregal Administration in the Spanish American Colonies* (Berkeley, 1926):272–73;

Carlos de Sigüenza y Góngora, *Relaciones históricas* (Mexico City, 1940):xvi-xvii.

111. Diego de Vargas to Conde de Galve, El Paso del Río del Norte, 16 Apr. 1691, AGN, Historia 37:2; and AGI, Guadalajara 139:4; printed with omissions in Otto Maas, ed., *Misiones de Nuevo Méjico: Documentos del Archivo General de Indias (Sevilla) publicados por primera vez y anotados* (Madrid, 1929):122–23. The best source for the history of the New Mexico colony in exile from 1680 to 1692 is Walz, "El Paso Area." The several censuses compiled during this period convey the wretchedness of the colonists, many of whom deserted. See Ernest J. Burrus, "A Tragic Interlude in the Reconquest of New Mexico," *Manuscripta* 29 (1985):154–65; and J. Manuel Espinosa, "Population of the El Paso District in 1692," *Mid-America* 23 (Jan. 1941):61–84. A useful summary of the Vargas years in New Mexico, from the point of view of an informed, eighteenth-century Franciscan missionary, is contained in fray Silvestre Vélez de Escalante's unfinished Extracto de noticias, 1777–78, BNM, 3:1. Regarding the circumstances of its compilation, see Eleanor B. Adams, "Fray Silvestre and the Obstinate Hopi," NMHR 38 (Apr. 1963):115–18.

112. The most complete reference work on the Pueblo Indians is Alfonso Ortiz, ed., *Southwest*, vol. 9 of *Handbook of North American Indians* (Wash-ington, D.C., 1979). In the present book, we have used Pueblos (uppercase) for the Pueblo Indians and pueblos (lowercase) for the towns in which they lived. For a characterization of the seventeenth-century, Hispanic colony, see France V. Scholes, "Civil Government and Society in New Mexico in the Seventeenth Century," NMHR 10 (Apr. 1935):71–111, as well as other works by Scholes in the same journal.

113. The non-Pueblo peoples of the region are the subject of Alfonso Ortiz, ed., *Southwest*, vol. 10 of *Handbook of North American Indians* (Washington, D.C., 1983).

114. Walz, "El Paso Area," 264–322.

115. Diego de Vargas to Juan Isidro de Pardiñas, El Paso del Río del Norte, 9 Apr. 1692, AGN, Historia 37:3.

116. EUI, 53:1034.

117. For a more detailed account of the 1692 reconnaissance, see Espinosa's *Crusaders*, 49–113, as well as his *First Expedition of Vargas into New Mexico, 1692* (Albuquerque, 1940), which includes a translation of the daily campaign journal.

118. Diego de Vargas, Journal, Santa Fe, 14 Sept. 1692, AGN, Historia 37:6. The Indian occupants of Santa Fe had built additional stories on the Spanish government complex and further fortified the site. See Bruce T. Ellis, "Santa Fe's Seventeenth Century Plaza, Parish Church,

and Convent Reconsidered," in *Collected Papers in Honor of Marjorie Ferguson Lambert* (Albuquerque, 1976):183–85; and Christopher M. Wilson, "The Santa Fe, New Mexico Plaza: An Architectural and Cultural History, 1610–1921" (M.A. thesis, Univ. of New Mexico, 1981).

119. Diego de Vargas to Conde de Galve, Santa Fe, 16 Oct. 1692, AGN, Historia 37:6.

120. Letter 1 below.

121. Diego de Vargas to Conde de Galve, Santa Fe, 16 Oct. 1692, AGN, Historia 37:6.

122. Cabildo of Santa Fe, Certification of the services of Domingo Jironza Petrís de Cruzate, El Paso del Río del Norte, 25 Nov. 1690, AGN, Civil 1743. *Recop.*, Lib. 4, tít. 1, ley 17.

123. Espinosa, *First Expedition of Vargas*, 103, 107. On Pueblo Indians as auxiliaries, see Oakah L. Jones, Jr., *Pueblo Warriors and Spanish Conquest* (Norman, 1966). Clevy Lloyd Strout, ed. and trans., "Santa Fe Rediviva: The Muster Roll of the Juan Páez Hurtado Expedition of 1695," (c. 1978):doc. 215. The historical evolution of the presidial system is the subject of Thomas H. Naylor and Charles W. Polzer, S.J., comps. and eds., *The Presidio and Militia on the Northern Frontier of New Spain: A Documentary History, 1500–1700* (Tucson, 1986). This impressive bilingual compilation of primary sources was produced at the University of Arizona by the Documentary Relations of the Southwest, a project supported in part by the National Historical Publications and Records Commission and the National Endowment for the Humanities.

124. Robles, *Diario*, 2:276. Carlos de Sigüenza y Góngora, *Mercurio volante con la noticia de la recuperación de las provincias del Nuevo México conseguida por d. Diego de Vargas, Zapata, y Luján Ponze de León, gobernador y capitán general de aquel reyno* (Mexico City, 1693):12; and *The Mercurio Volante of don Carlos de Sigüenza y Góngora: An Account of the First Expedition of don Diego de Vargas into New Mexico in 1692,* trans. Irving A. Leonard (Los Angeles, 1932), which includes a facsimile of the original.

125. Conde de Galve to Diego de Vargas, Mexico City, 24 Nov. 1692, AGI, Guadalajara 139:6. Conde de Galve to the reconquerors of New Mexico, Mexico City, 24 Nov. 1692, SRCA, Alice Scoville Barry Collection.

126. Sigüenza y Góngora, *Mercurio volante*, 18v.

127. Diego de Vargas to the king, Zacatecas, 16 May 1693, AGI, Guadalajara 139:5. Espinosa, *Crusaders*, 112–35.

128. The best summary of the recolonization of New Mexico during these years, 1693–96, is found in Espinosa, *Crusaders*, 112–243.

129. Carlos II, Title of governor of New Mexico to Pedro Rodríguez Cubero, Madrid, 24 June 1692, AGI, México 1216. Espinosa,

Crusaders, 308–10, 318–19. Letter 16 below.

130. On Saturday, 13 March 1694, after news of the Spanish victory at Santa Fe reached Mexico City, the cathedral was again the scene of a service of thanksgiving for the restoration of New Mexico. Robles, *Diario*, 2:302.

131. During the entire Spanish colonial period in New Mexico, only four settlements were designated villas: Santa Fe (1610), El Paso (1683), Santa Cruz de la Cañada (1695), and Alburquerque (1706).

132. Throughout the recolonization, Vargas suffered recurrent bouts of tabardillo, the "spotted fever," or typhus. In December 1695, he was so indisposed that he had a will drawn up. Pedro Rodríguez Cubero, Proceedings against Diego de Vargas, June 1698, UNM, SC, Thomas Benton Catron Collection, PC 29, 803, box 1, folder 1. Espinosa, *Crusaders*, 257 n. 30, 358–59 n. 25.

133. Diego de Vargas to Juan de Ortega Montañés, Santa Fe, 28 Mar. 1696, SANM II:59.

134. Conde de Galve to Diego de Vargas, Veracruz, 20 July 1696, AGI, Guadalajara 141:20. Galve had turned over his office to the audiencia on 21 January 1696. When the bishop of Puebla declined the interim appointment, Ortega Montañés, bishop of Michoacán, accepted, acceding on 27 February 1696. Rivera Cambas, *Gobernantes*, 1:278–80.

135. Espinosa, *Crusaders*, 244–306.

136. Juan de Ortega Montañés to Diego de Vargas, Mexico City, 4 July 1696, AGI, Guadalajara 141:20. In his report to his successor, Ortega Montañés praised Vargas for his noble and exemplary efforts in New Mexico, at the same time pointing out that not even these had prevented the death of several missionaries and other Spaniards. Juan de Ortega Montañés, Report on the Government and Viceroyalty of Mexico, Mexico City, 3 Mar. 1697, New York Public Library, Rich Collection, vol. 39; published as *Instrucción reservada que el Obispo-Virrey Juan de Ortega Montañés dió a su sucesor en el mando el Conde de Moctezuma*, ed. Norman F. Martin (Mexico City, 1965), with a biographical sketch of Ortega Montañés.

137. Francisco Díaz de Tagle was the nephew and son-in-law of Vargas's friend and principal financial backer, Luis Sáenz de Tagle. Documents concerning Vargas's protest, Mexico City, 1697, AGI, Guadalajara 141:22. Having learned the identity of the next royal appointee as viceroy of New Spain, Vargas directed his initial letters to the Conde de Moctezuma even before the latter had formally acceded to office. Diego de Vargas to Conde de Moctezuma, Santa Fe, 28 Nov. 1696, AGI, Guadalajara 141:20. Evidently, Moctezuma took office on 18 December 1696, but delayed his ceremonial entrance into the city until 2 February 1697. As a result, some sources have taken

erroneously the latter as the date of his accession. See, for example, EUI, 54:612. Robles, *Diario*, 3:54, 58.

138. Pedro Rodríguez Cubero to Juan de Saldúa and Francisco de Morales, Power of attorney to make a will, Mexico City, 14 Apr. 1704, AGNot. 692. There has been some confusion of Pedro Rodríguez Cubero with a more famous contemporary, Pedro Cubero y Sebastián (c. 1640–95), missionary, world traveler, and author, who was born at El Fresno, near Calatayud in Zaragoza. EUI, 16:869. Espinosa, *Crusaders*, 311; *Dictionary of American Biography* (New York, 1928–), 4:584. Registro de bautismos, Parroquia de Santa María de la Encarnación, Huéscar (Granada), Spain. Rick Hendricks, Assistant Editor of The Vargas Project, is currently at work on a study of Rodríguez Cubero.

139. A more detailed account of the Vargas-Rodríguez Cubero struggle appears in Espinosa, *Crusaders*, 307–40.

140. Vélez de Escalante, Extracto de noticias. Although it is referred to in other documents, the record of Vargas's residencia has not yet turned up.

141. Espinosa, *Crusaders*, 324–32. Proceedings against Diego de Vargas, Santa Fe, 28 Nov. 1699–1 Apr. 1700, AGN, Vínculos 14. Letters 20–23 below.

142. Diego de Vargas to the king, n.p., 1698, AGI, Guadalajara 141:25; Diego de Vargas to Conde

de Moctezuma, 28 Nov. 1696; Letter 48 below.

143. Letters 48 and 50 below.

144. Valverde had left New Mexico before Rodríguez Cubero ordered his exile from the colony. Espinosa, *Crusaders*, 313 n. 16, 315–24. Letter 20 below.

145. Cámara of the Council of the Indies, Madrid, 7 Jan. 1699, AGI, Guadalajara 141:24. Letter 21 below.

146. Opinion of the fiscal of the Council of the Indies, Madrid, 8 Jan. 1697, AGI, Guadalajara 141:26.

147. Council of the Indies, Madrid, 1 Aug. 1698, AGI, Guadalajara 141:23.

148. The king also waived the media anata regularly collected on a title with annual revenue, in Vargas's case the 4,000-peso encomienda. The king to Conde de Moctezuma, Madrid, 21 Feb. 1699, AGI, México 1102, Registro de partes, lib. 44. Council of the Indies, Madrid, 21 Aug. 1698, AGI, Guadalajara 141:27. Diego de Vargas to the king, n.p., 1698, AGI, Guadalajara 141:25.

149. Letters 20–23 below.

150. Letters 17, 24, and 48 below.

151. Juan Manuel de Vargas Pimentel, Passage to the Indies, 1699, AGI, Contratación 5.459:20.

152. Antonio Valverde y Cosío, Passage to the Indies, 1699, AGI, Contractación 5459:97.

153. Letters 24 and 25 below. The flota had sailed from Cadiz on 19 July. Kamen, *Spain*, 133. The

nineteen ships, under the command of Gen. Manuel de Velasco y Tejada, brought to New Spain not only 2,500 hundredweight of mercury, but also the appointment of Juan de Ortega Montañés as archbishop of Mexico. Robles, *Diario*, 3:83.

154. Letters 28 and 36 below. Diego de Vargas to Juan Manuel de Vargas Pimentel, Santa Fe, 23 Dec. 1699, in Criminal proceedings against Alfonso Rael de Aguilar, Santa Fe, 20 Dec. 1699–5 Jan. 1700, AGN, Vínculos 14.

155. Robles, *Diario*, 3:129. Letters 27 and 28 below.

156. Rivera Cambas, *Gobernantes*, 1:292–93. Letters 27 and 28 below.

157. Robles, *Diario*, 3:142–47, 167–68. Letter 27 below.

158. Vargas had been signing documents with his title, Marqués de la Nava de Barcinas, since November 1700, even though the Conde de Moctezuma did not convey the title formally until 18 December. Conde de Moctezuma, Decree, Mexico City, 18 Dec. 1700, AMNB. Diego de Vargas to Juan Manuel de Vargas Pimentel, Transfer of encomienda, Mexico City, 8 Nov. 1700, AGNot. 7. Regarding the "inflation of honors" under Carlos II, see Kamen, *Spain*, 249; and Antonio Domínguez Ortiz, *Las clases privilegiadas en la España del antiguo régimen* (Madrid, 1973):71.

159. Letters 17, 33, and 36 below. Pérez Balsera, *Laudemus*,

genealogical tree. In 1671, the year before don Diego sailed for the New World, his widowed aunt, doña Juana de Vargas Ponce de León, had petitioned the crown for an annual pension of 1,000 ducados and knighthood in the Order of Santiago for the nephew of her choice. She based her case on the services of her deceased husband, don Alonso de Anaya y Toledo, and father, don Lorenzo de Vargas Zapata, both of whom had been knights of Santiago. In due course, she was granted a pension of 300 ducados and informed that the king would consider her nephews on the basis of their own services. Juana de Vargas Ponce de León, Petition and related documents, AHN, Consejos 4.445:39.

160. See Wright, "Military Orders," 52; and Domínguez Ortiz, *La sociedad española*, 1:203–205.

161. Alonso de Buendía y Ortega and Pedro de Buendía y Ortega, AHN, Ordenes Militares, Santiago 1.267 and 1.268. Evidently, Alonso de Buendía's influence grew during the years that Diego de Vargas sought knighthood in the Order of Santiago. By 1705, for example, he was described as a city councilor of Madrid. Alonso de Buendía, Grant of knighthood for a son, Madrid, 14 Apr. 1705, AHN, Ordenes Militares, Consejo, Santiago 146. A somewhat cursory search of Ordenes Militares in June 1987 failed to turn up any

evidence that Ignacio López de Zárate entered a petition for Vargas. Such evidence may still come to light during the cataloging currently under way.

162. Letter 33 below. Espinosa, *Crusaders*, 333–36.

163. Diego de Vargas to Juan Manuel de Vargas Pimentel, Power of attorney, Mexico City, 12 July 1701, AGNot. 7. Diego de Vargas to Juan Manuel de Vargas Pimentel, Transfer of encomienda, 8 Nov. 1700, AGNot. 7. Juan Manuel, anticipating his return to Spain, empowered his father's attorney, José de Ledesma, to administer the encomienda whenever it might be put into effect. Juan Manuel de Vargas Pimentel to José de Ledesma, Power of attorney, Mexico City, 11 July 1701, AGNot. 7.

164. Letter 30 below. Diego de Vargas to Ignacio López de Zárate, Marqués de la Florida, and Conde de Puebla de los Valles, Power of attorney, Mexico City, 13 July 1701, AGNot. 7.

165. Letter 53 below.

166. Letter 58 below. Robles, *Diario*, 3:214, 216–17, 221.

167. Letter 63 below. Robles, *Diario*, 3:221–22, 227–28. The escorted flota departed Havana on 24 July, bound for Spain. In response to news that a combined English and Dutch armada was besieging Cadiz, the flota's course was changed for Vigo on the Atlantic coast north of Portugal. There, on 22–24 October, the enemy caught the Spanish and French vessels at anchor and inflicted a resounding defeat. Henry Kamen, "The Destruction of the Spanish Silver Fleet at Vigo in 1702," *Bulletin of the Institute of Historical Research* 39 (1966):165–73.

168. Letter 36 below. Documents concerning Vargas's protest, Mexico City, 1697, AGI, Guadalajara 141:22.

169. Letters 36 and 39 below. The Duque de Alburquerque acceded on 27 November 1702 and ruled until the end of 1710. Early in 1703, he ordered the uniforms of the palace guard changed to the French style, including tricorns, which gave impetus to a change in fashion in New Spain. In part because of his success in raising money in the viceroyalty for the war effort, Alburquerque was continued in office for a third three-year term. Concerning his administration, see Rivera Cambas, *Gobernantes*, 1:300–309.

170. Espinosa, *Crusaders*, 336–40.

171. Audiencia of Mexico to the king, Mexico City, 30 Mar. 1703, AGI, Guadalajara 142:20. Diego de Vargas, Will, Bernalillo, 7 Apr. 1704, SANM I1027.

172. Letters 36, 40, 41, 46, and 47 below.

173. Diego de Vargas, Will, Mexico City, 1 June 1703, AGNot. 692.

174. Rivera Cambas, *Gobernantes*, 1:307. Francisco Díaz de Tagle to Luis Sáenz de Tagle, Promissory note, Mexico City, 4 July 1703, AGNot. 692. Diego de

Vargas to Francisco Díaz de Tagle, Power of attorney, Mexico City, 5 June 1703, AGNot. 692. Diego de Vargas to Luis Sáenz de Tagle, Promissory note, Mexico City, 5 June 1703, AGNot. 692. Late in 1704, Felipe V granted to Luis Sáenz de Tagle the noble title Marqués de Altamira. Title of Marqués de Altamira, Madrid, 23 Dec. 1704, AHN, Consejos 8.976:167. Alonso-Cadenas, *Elenco*, 58.

175. Letter 44 below. Diego de Vargas, Will, 1 June 1703.

176. Letters 38, 44, and 45 below.

177. Letters 47 and 48 below. Evidently, don Diego did not receive the news before his death that the Marqués de Vargas, the Conde de Puebla de los Valles, and Sancho Bullón Chacón had refused to accept his power of attorney, dated in Mexico City on 31 December 1702–1 January 1703, for the administration of the Vargas entails of Madrid and Torrelaguna in lieu of López de Zárate. Letters 39, 50, and 56 below.

178. Ill in bed in Mexico City, the forty-seven-year-old Pedro Rodríguez Cubero, son of Antonio Rodríguez Cubero and María González, both deceased, executed on 14 April 1704 a power of attorney in favor of Juan de Saldúa and Francisco de Morales to make his will. Because he had no children, he named Saldúa his heir. He provided that his body be buried in the church of the Franciscan convento. By 31 July,

when Saldúa had an official copy of the document made, evidently don Pedro had died. Coincidentally, the same notary who drew up the power of attorney for Rodríguez Cubero had also done Vargas's will the year before. Pedro Rodríguez Cubero to Juan de Saldúa and Francisco de Morales, Power of attorney to make a will, Mexico City, 14 Apr. 1704, AGNot. 692. Copy of royal approval of the appointment of Juan de Saldúa as captain of El Paso presidio, Mexico City, AGI, Guadalajara 142:16. Vélez de Escalante, Extracto de noticias.

179. Diego de Vargas to the Cabildo of Santa Fe, Santa Fe, 1 Dec. 1703, and Certification by the Cabildo, Santa Fe, 2 Dec. 1703, SANM II:94a; translated in Twitchell, *Spanish Archives of New Mexico*, 2:117–26, and "The Justification of Don Diego de Vargas, 1704," *Old Santa Fe* 2 (July 1915):57–65. Espinosa's account of Rodríguez Cubero's administration and Vargas's return (*Crusaders*, 341–56) is patently pro-Vargas.

180. Letters 53–60 below.

181. Letter 61 below. Diego de Vargas, Journal, 27 Mar.-2 Apr. 1704, SANM II:99; translated in Twitchell, *Spanish Archives of New Mexico*, 2:127–33, and "The Last Campaign of General de Vargas, 1704," *Old Santa Fe* 1 (July 1914):66–72. Diego de Vargas, Will, 7 Apr. 1704.

182. Diego de Vargas, Will, 7 Apr. 1704. He had made wills on at least three previous occasions:

on 21 June 1672 (AHPM, P. 10.125), in December 1695 (mentioned in Proceedings, June 1698, UNM, SC, Catron, PC 29, 803, box 1, folder 1), and on 1 June 1703 (AGNot. 692).

183. Little is known of the Santa Fe church in 1704. The cabildo, in certifying Vargas's self-serving report to the viceroy late in 1703, had written of the structure being used as a parish church, built at Vargas's expense during his first administration (SANM II:94a). It, along with the rest of the villa, the cabildo alleged, had suffered deterioration under Rodríguez Cubero. This interim church seems to have adjoined or been part of the palace complex, perhaps the southeast "tower-chapel" referred to by some writers. See Fray Angelico Chavez, "Santa Fe Church and Convent Sites in the Seventeenth and Eighteenth Centuries," NMHR 24 (Apr. 1949):90. Even less is known of the church at Bernalillo in 1704.

184. Vargas had bought Juana de la Cruz from the estate of Cristóbal de Palma y Mesa in 1703 for 300 pesos. Antonio de Villaseñor y Monroy, Sale of slave, Mexico City, 6 Mar. 1703, AGNot. 13. Other documents from the same archive show that don Diego bought and sold domestic slaves routinely.

185. These items of jewelry and silverware were listed again a few days later, with minor variations. The earrings then, for example,

were said to contain four emeralds each. Juan Páez Hurtado, Inventory and receipt of property belonging to the Marqués de la Nava de Barcinas, Santa Fe, 20 Apr. 1704, SANM II:100.

186. The body of the will, signed by Vargas and his secretary, Alfonso Rael de Aguilar, was witnessed by Juan de Ulibarrí, Antonio Macario Maldonado Zapata, and Félix Martínez, each of whom also signed. Ulibarrí, at Vargas's request, and Rael de Aguilar signed the codicil, along with three other witnesses: Fernando Durán y Chaves, Tomás Holguín, and Bernardo Durán y Chaves. Diego de Vargas, Will, 7 Apr. 1704.

187. Letter 61 below. Local tradition had it that Vargas died after suffering indigestion from eating eggs. "Information Communicated by Juan Candelaria, Resident of this Villa de San Francisco Xavier de Alburquerque, Born 1692—Age 84," NMHR 4 (July 1929):289–90.

188. Letter 62 below.

189. Pierre Vilar, "The Age of Don Quixote," trans. Richard Morris, in *Essays in European Economic History, 1500–1800*, ed. Peter Earle (Oxford, 1974):109.

190. Letter 53 below.

191. Letter 62 below.

192. Writing in Santa Fe in the 1770s, a Franciscan friar who had access to the archives stated that Vargas "is buried in the parish church of the villa of Santa Fe, where they brought his body

immediately after he died." Vélez de Escalante, *Extracto de noticias.*

193. The earliest, extant burial register for the Santa Fe parish church was begun in 1726. "Lost older books," in the opinion of Fray Angelico Chavez, "would likely show Vargas's burial in 1705 [1704] and transfer of remains in 1714–1717." Fray Angelico Chavez, *Archives of the Archdiocese of Santa Fe, 1678–1900* (Washington, D.C., 1957):237.

194. On the parish church and cathedral of Santa Fe, see John L. Kessell, *The Missions of New Mexico since 1776* (Albuquerque, 1980):36–43; and Bruce Ellis, *Bishop Lamy's Santa Fe Cathedral* (Albuquerque, 1985).

195. Letters 53 and 64 below.

196. Francisco de Vargas to Isabel María de Vargas, Puebla de los Angeles, 8 Apr. 1718, ARGD. Bloom, "The Vargas Encomienda," 398–417. Bloom thought that Pedro Alonso was a brother of don Diego who came out from Spain to settle matters in Mexico City.

197. One vaguely possible exception to this statement is a plain, silver tankard, with a single handle and no lid, in the Mary Lester and Neill B. Field Collection, University Art Museum, University of New Mexico, Albuquerque. It has been suggested as the tembladera listed in the will. Leona Davis Boylan, *Spanish Colonial Silver* (Santa Fe, 1974):14–15. The earliest dictionary of the Real Academia Española (1726–37) defined a tembladera as

a wide, rounded, two-handled, silver, gold, or glass drinking vessel with a small base. Regularly made of a very thin sheet, such vessels appeared to tremble. John Stevens's *Spanish and English Dictionary* (1706) gave as the meaning "a Drinking-cup with a round bottom, so call'd, because it shakes and does not stand fast."

198. Juan Páez Hurtado, Inventory and receipt of property belonging to the Marqués de la Nava de Barcinas, 20 Apr. 1704. Adams, "Two Colonial New Mexico Libraries," 135–39, 149–51.

199. EUI, 38:470.

200. Relations between the bishops of Durango and the Franciscans of New Mexico are discussed by Eleanor B. Adams in *Bishop Tamarón's Visitation of New Mexico, 1760* (Albuquerque, 1954).

201. For a telling comparison of the spirit of seventeenth-century New Mexico and that of the colony in the eighteenth century, see Frederick Webb Hodge, George P. Hammond, and Agapito Rey, *Fray Alonso de Benavides' Revised Memorial of 1634* (Albuquerque, 1945); and Adams and Chavez, *The Missions of New Mexico, 1776.*

202. Fray Angelico Chavez, *The Origins of New Mexico Families in the Spanish Colonial Period in Two Parts: The Seventeenth (1598–1693) and the Eighteenth (1693–1821) Centuries* (Santa Fe, 1975):x.

203. On the 1712 proclamation

of an observance marking the twentieth anniversary of Vargas's 1692 entrada and the subsequent evolution of the Santa Fe Fiesta, featuring an annual reenactment, see Donna Pierce, ed., *Vivan las Fiestas* (Santa Fe, 1985); and Ronald L. Grimes, *Symbol and Conquest: Public Ritual and Drama in Santa Fe, New Mexico* (Ithaca, 1976).

Part 2

Facade of the Vargas mansion at Torrelaguna, known today as the Palacio de Salinas.
    Maria Carmen Gambliel.

The Sixty-four Letters

Teutila and Tlalpujahua, 1675, 1686

1. Diego de Vargas to Gregorio Pimentel de Prado, Teutila, 22 October 1675.*

[. . .] the aid referred to here. I left her clothed and all my children and servants as well, the fruit of the vineyards to be sold, and wheat and barley in the house.

All these details oblige me to write you because of the heavy burden you lay upon me in your letter about the concern my house and affairs are causing you. I do not think that I am so far out of the picture that I do not remember my debts very well, for they are pressing, though they should be diminishing each year. The revenue keeps coming in, and its owner is not spending it.

I am writing you now in this letter concerning my young and beloved children. I repeat that you please place my two daughters in the convent of Torrelaguna at once. There, with 2,000 reales, they will be fed and clothed very decently.[1] It seems to me my two sons can get along very well on a similar sum with their grandmother.[2] This should be my entire estate's expense. Since it does not amount to more than 4,000 reales, the vineyards and the revenue from grain are bound to yield enough for this and to pay the memorias of San Francisco.[3] In addition, there is the revenue from the pastures and enclosures at Miraflores de la Sierra, Chozas, and Guadalix, and from the dehesa of Las Gariñas.[4] In Madrid, there is the revenue from the houses, the censo that is to be disencumbered with the money I shall send, the juro of Ocaña, the patronages, the revenue from Granada and Las Camarmas del Caño—all these fincas and possessions are paid up, even though the revenue from Granada, Gariñas, and Camarma has been less.[5] From this year, 1675, everything is free of debt, and the owner is not there to spend the revenue.

So, my brother, I ask that you do as I request, paying in full what I owe to each and every one, and repairing my houses. It would not be proper for me to find my estate as I left it when God sees fit to grant my wish to return to Madrid, having been in this kingdom, missing my homeland and toiling continually over alien lands and roads, whose ruggedness it is not easy to convey to you, and living among Indians, which is the same thing as being in a wilderness.

I trust that you shall live up to your nobility and Christian virtue, not failing in anything, and look after the children, who are as much yours as they are mine. You are their guardian, and they your sister's children.[6] I know I do not deserve that you favor me so. I shall serve you, my brother and friend, in every way that I am able.

I appreciate the help you have been in sending me the letters of recommendation and that you do not tire of doing so. If a new lord viceroy comes with the flota, I shall write to you about whatever the outcome of my Guatemala business may be.[7] I have had neither a real nor a word in more than six months and am resolved to go there once I leave this post. I have received neither the letters from my uncles nor the one from don Agustín Ponce de León.[8] He was to send me the packet in Guatemala, as I am writing him. As you ask, I shall look into the matter of the rubies and send a letter by the flota to don Cristóbal de Aguirre.[9]

Farewell, dear friend and brother. May God keep you the many years I wish and let me see you. Teutila, 22 October 1675.

Your brother and best friend
who loves you from the heart
and kisses your hand,

Don Diego de Vargas
Zapata Luján [rubrica]

To my brother-in-law and friend, don Gregorio Pimentel de Prado

*ARGD. ALS, inc. Two folios, four written pages. Two-thirds of the original letter is missing (the fragment begins with folio 5r and ends at the letter's closing on folio 6v). Vargas addressed don Gregorio in the familiar "tú" form in Spanish, as he did his children, retaining the more formal "Ud." form in correspondence with almost everyone else, including his sons-in-law.

1. The Franciscan Conceptionist convent at Torrelaguna was founded by don Fernando Bernaldo de Quirós and doña Guiomar de Verzosa, his wife, in the second half of the sixteenth century (its altar screen bore the date 1572). Momplet Míguez and Chico Picaza, *Arte religioso*, 63–64. Vargas's sister, doña Antonia de Vargas, was a nun there in 1675.

2. The boys' maternal grandmother, doña Isabel de Olazábal Vélez de Guevara, had been a lifelong resident of Torrelaguna, born there to Domingo de Olazábal and María Sánchez. Gregorio Pimentel (Torrelaguna, 1654), AHN, Ordenes Militares, Santiago 6.471; and Alberto García Carraffa and Arturo García Carraffa, *Diccionario heráldico y genealógico de apellidos españoles y americanos* (Madrid, 1943), 70:22–23.

3. Memorias were pious works, ecclesiastical endowments to commemorate deceased persons, set up to finance such things as masses and dowries. The memorias mentioned here, instituted by Vargas's "aunts," doña Aldonza and doña Antonia Luján, at the Convento de San Francisco in Madrid, provided for the marriage of orphan girls. Diego de Vargas, Listing of the entire estate, Torrelaguna, 9 Aug. 1672, AMNB.

4. Near the village of Buitrago, some twenty miles north of Torrelaguna, the dehesa known as Las Gariñas had been rented for many years by the Duques del Infantado at 2,000 reales a year. In the vicinity of the towns of Miraflores, Chozas, and Guadalix, lying west in the foothills of the Sierra de Guadarrama, Vargas holdings amounted to three enclosures in the first, one pasture in the second, and another enclosure in the third. Diego de Vargas, Listing of the entire estate, 1672.

5. Six miles north of Alcalá de Henares, at Las Camarmas, the family owned tumbledown houses, an enclosure, dovecote, olive orchard, and land, all rented by Juan Sanz, a citizen of that place. The Vargas entail of Granada included two large rural properties near Iznalloz, one called La Nava and the other Barcinas, that later inspired don Diego to choose the title Marqués de la Nava de Barcinas. The juro of Ocaña, in the province of Toledo, was an annuity assigned upon the town's revenue from the sales tax on salt and amounted to 99,707 maravedis (some 2,993 vellon reales) yearly. Diego de Vargas, Listing of the entire estate, 1672. Elsewhere, don Diego placed the value of the juro of Ocaña at 300 ducados a year. Diego de Vargas to Juan González Calderón, Power of attorney, Mexico City, 23 June 1689, AHPM, p. 13.146.

6. Eleven days after doña Beatriz died, the local magistrate, in accordance with what don Diego had provided, appointed don Gregorio guardian of the four

children and their property. Still acting in the same capacity five years later, Pimentel took measures to have the Vargas complex on the Calle del Almendro in Madrid repaired. Again, he claimed, these buildings were badly deteriorated. Gregorio Pimentel de Prado to Diego de Olvera, Power of attorney, Torrelaguna, 5 Aug. 1679, AMNB.

7. Despite the persistent rumors, a new viceroy did not come with the flota, and the viceroy-archbishop, fray Payo de Rivera Enríquez (1673–80), continued in office. Rivera Cambas, *Gobernantes,* 1:241–51. Bancroft, *History of Mexico,* 186 n. 65.

8. A citizen of Madrid who lived on the Calle de la Cruz and a close associate of Vargas, don Agustín Ponce de León was a business agent for the Council of the Indies. Along with three others, he testified in 1672 that don Diego was indeed the son of don Alonso. Diego de Vargas, Proof of legitimacy, Madrid, 21 June 1672, AHPM, P. 10.956.

9. The matter of the rubies remains a mystery.

---

2. Diego de Vargas to Mariana Villalba, Tlalpujahua, 22 March 1686.*

Dear madam,[1]

God Our Lord knows well your troubles and ailments. I see you as another Job, confined to your bed, praising the Infinite Creator. If only I could be of some relief to you, providing the comfort I wish for you. I should like to do everything for you, but my obligations are many. I am forced to live with this affliction. Though I cannot do it all, I shall do what I can, assisting you with a small gratuity for linens. Thus, excuse me till then.

My parents left me no treasures other than my entails. God Our Lord is my witness of how little they have been worth to me and how little I have enjoyed their fruits. After a few days administering them, I discovered that they were burdened with debts, repairs, and a thousand encumbrances. Please give spiritual guidance to my children so that they scrupulously honor their obligations. The mother I gave them was the only dowry I sought, that of her gifts and no other.

So I say in all this that Spain was but a stepmother to me, for she banished me to seek my fortune in strange lands, passing through varied climes. Here, I do what I could not do there, despite my inclination. I have asked for nothing more since I left my homeland. The truth is, there are plenty of things made in this land that can be sent as gifts.

I have gone on at length regarding this point so that the encumbrance of my entails not be attributed to my poor judgment. All that amounted to nothing. If I had had help in that land as I do in this, then I would have done better for myself there with my entails as a foundation, but not as well as I am doing here without them. This is not because one plucks money from trees or rivers. He who has honor but does not work goes about without it and without credit, just as in Spain. May God keep you many years. Please advise me of the condition of your health whenever you have the opportunity. Done in this real, 22 March 1686.

> Your most affectionate and
> considerate servant kisses your hand,
>
> > Don Diego de Vargas Zapata
> > Luján [rubrica]

To my lady, doña Mariana Villalba

*AMNB. ALS. One folio, two written pages.

1. In 1659, when don Diego was only fifteen, his uncle, don Francisco de Vargas, had provided in his will that his heir and sister, doña Juana de Vargas, care for an unnamed female dependent. The latter was to receive a dowry and 50 ducados a year if she chose to enter a convent or 100 if she did not. He further stated that doña Juana and Fathers Cosme Zapata and Sebastián de Vargas, both Jesuits, knew who this person was. Later the same year, in a legal certification, the three disclosed that she was doña Mariana de Villalba, daughter of Diego de Villalba and doña Ana Patiño, of the villa of Alcocer and a resident of Madrid. Juana de Vargas, Cosme de Zapata, and Sebastián de Vargas, Certification, Madrid, 9 Sept. 1659, AHPM, P. 10.118.

3. Diego de Vargas to Isabel María de Vargas Pimentel, Tlalpujahua, 22 March 1686.*

My dearest daughter,[1]

I was very pleased to receive your letter. It was a great comfort to me to see the love and protection all of you find in my lady and aunt, doña Juana de Vargas.[2] While fulfilling her own duties, she attends to mine. Hence, I shall write her with every consideration.

I had to remit the draft for 200 pesos to the Marqués de Yebra by his son.[3] If my wish is fulfilled, I shall be grateful. Since my friend, don Juan de Alvarado, is not in the Indies, I have no one else I trust.[4]

With your good judgment and breeding, my daughter, you will, as the eldest, know how to correct your siblings in whatever you may consider not particularly pleasing to my aunt. You should regard and revere her as the mother she is to you all. I ask you all to take heed not to give her the least displeasure. You will know protection in the form of my continuing aid.

By the flota, I trust that I shall be able to write to you in more detail (if my petition has succeeded) about the settling of certain business affairs and discuss them with greater certainty. Therefore, I do not go on, except to tell you that you will always find in me the love of a father who loves you more than himself and wishes to provide for you in the way that best serves Our Lord. May He keep and favor you in everything, as is my heartfelt wish. Tlalpujahua, 22 March 1686.

Your father who loves and
esteems you from the heart kisses
your hand,

Don Diego de Vargas Zapata
Luján [rubrica]

To my daughter, doña Isabel María de Vargas

*AMNB. ALS. One folio, two written pages.

1. It had now been almost fourteen years since Vargas had seen his family in Spain. Isabel María, the eldest of his children, had just turned twenty-one. His letters to her were always loving, short, and

often simple, as though to a child.

2. Don Alonso de Vargas's sister and don Diego's aunt, doña Juana de Vargas Ponce de León, widow of don Alonso de Anaya y Toledo, was an active, devout, and enterprising woman who had assumed responsibility for the family side of her nephew's affairs in Madrid. In the 1670s, she had rented her house on the Plaza Mayor, retaining only the use of half a balcony on the fifth floor from which to watch the bullfights and other festivities. Juana de Vargas Ponce de León, Rental agreement, Madrid, 2 Nov. 1673, AHPM, P. 10.126.

3. The title of Marqués de Yebra was conferred on don Francisco Vela y López de Castillo on 2 August 1693, with the previous viscountcy of Yebra. Julio de Atienza, *Nobiliario español: Diccionario heráldico de apellidos españoles y de títulos nobiliarios*, (Madrid, 1959):1019.

4. Don Diego dealt with merchant and banking families who had members residing in Mexico City, Cadiz, Seville, and Madrid, or some similar combination. Capt. Juan de Alvarado, along with Pedro, Tomás, and Diego Manuel, seems to have represented such a family.

Mexico City, 1690

4. *Diego de Vargas to Ignacio López de Zárate, Mexico City, 8 February 1690.**

Son and dear sir,

It is certain that I am filled with pride and, at the same time, well pleased now that the turn of fortune's wheel has made me deserving of you as my son-in-law and lord. I attribute my happiness to the merit that my beloved daughter Isabel earned by her virtue. I am most eager to have the chance soon to enjoy your company and serve you.

It is certain, too, that I curse the straits in which the news finds me at present, unable to make the gestures corresponding to Your Lordship's esteem and to your having assumed my duties. Such are the qualities of your illustrious lineage. I assure you that by the flota, though I be stripped of everything I have, I shall remit to you as much as I am able for the settlement of the debt that was made possible through the generosity of the lord marqués, Your Lordship's brother.[1] To him, I humbly offer myself, and whatever may be of value, in his service. I am closely tied to him by a bond of consideration. It is solid, constant, and stripped of flattery, reciprocating the earnestness with which he interceded and took upon himself to favor my children. May time give me the pleasure of elaborating, to show my consideration and affection, which his full demonstration of these qualities merits in return.

I beg you now to take charge of the administration of the revenue from my entails. To this end, I am writing to Juan González Calderón that he transfer to you the power of attorney I sent him by the storeships at the end of June of last year.[2] I am at present petitioning that the most excellent lord viceroy put into effect the royal cedula appointing me governor and captain general in New Mexico, so that I may make arrangements for such a long journey. I cannot help but be greatly perturbed by the alcalde mayor taking over from me inopportunely, after only ten months, the post in which I was employed by the Conde de Galve. Because his majesty had given it to the above-mentioned person, his excellency put the appointment into effect, forcing me out in such a way that for two months I have been collecting for the mercury that was in my charge. Therefore, until the month of May—even though his excellency may put my appointment into effect at once—I shall be detained.

By the flota, I shall write to Your Lordship about whatever happens. In the meantime, no matter where I am, I am most sincerely yours. Likewise, I ask you to look after my beloved son and give my cherished Isabel my constant embraces. May God keep Your Lordship many happy years in her company. I am concerned about whether my daughter will have had a successful delivery and thus withhold my congratulations on the long line of succession I wish for Your Lordship until word of the birth reaches me. I await this news with the arrival of the earliest packet boat. Mexico City, 8 February 1690.

Your most affectionate father, friend, and servant kisses Your Lordship's hand,

Don Diego de Vargas Zapata Luján [rubrica]

To lord Dr. don Ignacio López de Zárate, my son-in-law and lord[3]

*AMNB. LS. Two folios, three written pages.

1. Don Ignacio's older brother, don Juan Antonio López de Zárate y Alvarez de Medina, received the title Marqués de Villanueva de la Sagra on 7 January 1686. Alonso-Cadenas, *Elenco*, 699.

2. Diego de Vargas to Juan González Calderón, Power of attorney, Mexico City, 23 June 1689, AHPM, P. 13.146.

3. Vargas's use of doctor in his early letters to his son-in-law reflected courteous respect. Don Ignacio had a law degree, but not a doctorate.

---

5. *Diego de Vargas to Juan González Calderón, Mexico City, 8 February 1690.*

Dear sir,[1]

I appreciate the congratulations you extend to me on the happy marriage of my daughter, doña Isabel. She has had the good fortune of finding a gentleman of such eminent qualities as those that come together in lord don Ignacio, who is from such an illustrious family— one I know very well.

The news reached me in the alcaldía mayor of Tlalpujahua, which the viceroy, Conde de Galve, granted to me. His majesty was pleased to send the cedula for me in the packet boat preceding the flota. Then, the holder of another royal cedula, a grant for that same alcaldía mayor, presented himself, asking that it be put into effect. His excellency did so, just as he did for the rest. This turn of events perturbed me greatly. Even though at the time I had explained to his excellency that this alcaldía mayor required the distribution of mercury and I had been given a hundred quintals for its miners, I had no way to make his excellency order the alcalde mayor's journey suspended until I had at least completed the year. This was all I was asking, but he went inopportunely to accede to the office.

At present, I have no information at all, since I have been engaged solely in collecting for his majesty's mercury for going on three months. Tomorrow (by the grace of God) I shall submit a report, presenting the title and royal cedula for the government of New Mexico, even though I have misgivings. His excellency has to defer its execution, which would allow me to finish removing any obstacles.

I hope, therefore, that by means of the proposal I sent to his majesty by the mercury ships that sailed in the month of July last year,[2] you will have helped me so that I might obtain most of what I ask of his majesty. The text of the proposal will show how important it would be to the service of God and king for the king our lord to dispatch to me a cedula, definitively ordering that I be provided with effective means for the conquest. Anticipating the arrival of the cedula by the packet boat I await, I shall be able to petition the lord viceroy both for the execution and conveyance of the office by the first cedula and for help in achieving the goal of that conquest.[3]

When you receive this letter, please transfer the power of attorney I sent to you by the storeships for administration of my entails (following the long life of my aunt and lady, doña Juana de Vargas) to my son-in-law, lord don Ignacio López de Zárate. Only the stroke of luck that he is my son-in-law can serve as my excuse to you. I make this change, steadfast and ever attentive to serve you as I shall always demonstrate, and grateful for your many favors.

May God keep you many years. Mexico City, 8 February 1690.

Your affectionate and indebted
servant kisses your hand,

    Don Diego de Vargas Zapata
    Luján [rubrica]

To don Juan González Calderón

*AHPM, P. 13.146. LS. Two folios, three written pages. There are three additional copies of this letter in AMNB.

1. Describing himself as governor-elect of New Mexico, current alcalde mayor of Tlalpujahua, and resident of Mexico City, Capt. Diego de Vargas had executed on 23 June 1689 a general power of attorney in favor of don Juan González Calderón, his agent at court in Madrid. It authorized don Juan, upon the death of Vargas's elderly aunt, doña Juana de Vargas Ponce de León, to manage the Vargas entails. Don Diego reserved to don Juan Manuel de Vargas, his surviving eighteen-year-old heir, the patronages at the Franciscan convento and the parish church of San Pedro el Real, which provided for the marriage of orphan girls, support of widows, and naming of

chaplains. Diego de Vargas to Juan González Calderón, Power of attorney, Mexico City, 23 June 1689, AHMP, P. 13.146.

2. Mercury from the mines of Almadén in south central Spain, shipped in leather bags packed inside wooden casks or boxes, usually reached New Spain on the annual flota. In years when the flota did not sail, it was transported on packet boats or by the royal armada to Portobelo for transshipment in the Caribbean to New Spain. On rare occasions, special ships were outfitted to deliver the mercury. Bakewell, *Silver Mining*, 170–71. In July 1689, mercury ships returned to Spain under the command of the Marqués de Brenas. Lutgardo García Fuentes, *El comercio español con América 1650–1700* (Seville, 1980):396.

3. Apparently written in 1689, don Diego's proposal for the reconquest of New Mexico has not turned up in the archives.

---

6. *Diego de Vargas to Ignacio López de Zárate, Mexico City, 14 June 1690.*[*]

Son and dear sir,

I write this in a letter to lord don Amadeo.[1] I shall be delighted that Your Lordship is very well, that my beloved daughter, doña Isabel María, is also, and that Your Lordship has the heir of whom I wish definite news. I shall happily call myself grandfather of such a father's son. Would that I had a kingdom to give you out of my esteem, love, and duty. But for now, I give to you what my parents and grandparents left to me, all my entails. For this, I am sending you a general power of attorney in order that by virtue of it you may enjoy, manage, administer, and govern them with the obligation of paying any encumbrance they may have. You will please take into your charge the support of your brother-in-law, my oldest son and successor in them, don Juan Manuel de Vargas Zapata Luján.

I answer by telling you in this letter how much I regret the state of fortune in which I am caught. As of the date of this letter, the most excellent lord viceroy, Conde de Galve, granted me the decree for the alcaldía mayor of the real of Tlalpujahua. I obtained one hundred quintals of mercury for this real, taking them with me when I went to accede to office on 20 February 1689. The office had been conferred by his majesty, and, because it was for the lords viceroy to confer, was awaiting the resolution on the report made by the previous lord viceroy, who suspended its execution. His majesty's decision on the report came by the packet boat that arrived in this kingdom at the end of August 1689. It directed his excellency to order that, as soon as they might be presented together with their titles and royal cedulas, the grants his majesty had made should be obeyed. They should be put into effect at once and without excuse and the necessary dispatches issued with the cedula.[2]

Agustín de Hierro, who had been granted that real, presented himself, and his excellency ordered that he be given the dispatches.[3] Hierro came inopportunely to succeed me after only nine months, even though I had been allotted the portion of mercury with a large sum against my credit. This has caused me very serious injury, for I was already prepared to make my journey at the time the most excellent lord viceroy favored me. I assure Your Lordship that were I not so well liked and my reputation so good, I would have lost it, because the people have known that this turn of events could have covered me with disgrace.

From this misfortune, it follows that I neither remit by this flota nor am able to find a peso to risk to help Your Lordship. I give you my word and promise that, because I am most grateful, I shall remit to you by the storeships next year as much as I am able.

In the coming month of July, I shall make ready to leave for my government of New Mexico, for which his excellency has already done me the favor of giving me his decree so that the necessary dispatches be issued to me. I shall assign my salary to whoever provisions me so that he may advance me most of it this coming year. Moreover, I shall not neglect in the least to take every possible measure, hoping that fortune may attend me and give me success, not only with that small amount, but also with the larger, so that my wish may correspond to the fulfillment of my humble duty.

Thus, I repeat to Your Lordship that you need not have the slightest worry that I shall fail you, which would offend me and deny me the esteem my paternal love deserves from you. Your wish is my command, and, with everything I am able to earn, I shall see to paying you. I shall take care to send remittances frequently.

May God keep Your Lordship many happy years in the company of my beloved daughter, whom you will please embrace. Mexico City, 14 June 1690.

Your Lordship's most affectionate
father and servant kisses your hand,

    Don Diego de Vargas Zapata
    y Luján [rubrica]

To lord Dr. don Ignacio López de Zárate

*AMNB. ALS. Two folios, four written pages.

1. Amadeo Isidro Zeyol, mayor-domo of the Conde de Galve's household.

2. The crown, seeking for itself the revenue from sale of these offices, had taken back from its viceroys, presidents of audiencias, and governors, by cedulas of 28 February and 24 May 1678, the privilege of making appointments to all alcaldías mayores and corregimientos, thus eliminating a major source of viceregal patronage. It was also unfair to American candidates, the descendants of conquerors and original settlers. As a result of the protest, Carlos II, on 29 February 1680, restored the former arrangement. As we see here, however, the crown continued to make such appointments. The 1680 cedula is published in Antonio Muro Orejón, *Cedulario americano del siglo xviii* (Seville, 1956), 1:77–79. Lohmann Villena, *Corregidor de indios*, 126, 128.

3. Appointment as alcalde mayor of Tlalpujahua to Agustín de Hierro, Mexico City, 12 Oct. 1689, AGN, Reales Cédulas 34:181. An earlier Agustín de Hierro had been appointed visitador of the Audiencia of Mexico. Ten years later, on 2 March 1651, Felipe IV made him a member of the Council of Castile. EUI, 28:1566; Janine Fayard, *Les membres du Conseil de Castille a l'époque moderne, 1621–1746* (Geneva, 1979):76, 90.

———

7. *Ignacio López de Zárate to Diego de Vargas, Madrid, 6 August 1690.* *

My lord and father,

I reply to Your Lordship's very kind letter of 8 February this year. After celebrating the good news Your Lordship conveys to me, let me emphasize the pleasure and comfort I take in knowing that your health remains as perfect as I wish and need. In such happy circumstances, I am able to bear patiently the affliction and sorrow caused by not seeing Your Lordship and enjoying the good fortune of serving you personally. Yet, I trust in Our Lord that it will be accorded me as soon as possible so that in this way I may have my greatest wish fulfilled.

All in Your Lordship's house are well (thank God), though at present we suffer the displeasure of Mariquita having smallpox. It is of the false variety and of no risk or danger, but, as Your Lordship can imagine, it has us somewhat concerned. We hope to have her up and around by the feast of Our Lady in September. We trust in God that by then she will be well on her way to recovery from her indisposition.[1]

Each day, more and more, as Your Lordship can understand, we miss my aunt and lady doña Juana (may she be in heaven).[2] I, in particular, miss her because of how greatly she loved and showed me favor. As yet, the business affairs of her estate have not been concluded. I assure Your Lordship I am aiding don Manuel Osorio, the executor, as much as I can in order that they be concluded as soon as possible. Having reported to Your Lordship separately on their condition and the decision I made to support all your family, I refrain from repeating myself now. I only add that, with the greatest pleasure in the world, I seek to assist the family. I shall continue always to fulfill my obligation to my aunt with all my will and love. I shall recognize this duty all my life.

I thank Your Lordship countless times for the special favor your great affection and courtesy bestow upon me. You have assured me that with the coming of the flota you will be glad to send me most, if not all, of the dowry offered by my aunt.[3] I am very much obliged and grateful to Your Lordship for the opportunity to extricate myself in this way from the debts caused by the continuing expenses that have plagued me. Relieved of them, I shall more easily be able to attend to all that is my imperative duty, seeing that the great good fortune of my marriage is so warmly applauded and approved by Your Lordship. I offer Your Lordship countless thanks, assuring you that my mother; my brother, the marqués; and all my relatives hold you in the esteem that corresponds to Your Lordship's demonstrations of affection, for which we shall always be greatly obliged.

Your Lordship saw fit to order don Juan González Calderón to transfer to me immediately the power of attorney he held from Your Lordship for the administration of your estate and entails. I requested that don Juan comply with the order, only to devote myself to obeying and serving Your Lordship in this matter. I did so last month on 11 July.[4]

Since then, with all diligence and care, I have sought to dedicate myself to examining the papers that my aunt had brought from Torrelaguna last year and those that were in her possession in order to see what the estate is composed of, what its encumbrances and debts are, and its present condition.

I believed that the latter would correspond to the estate's production from the time Your Lordship went to the Indies, but I found that was not so. The debts were greater, at which I confess to Your Lordship I was profoundly astonished. If due care had been taken each year to settle up and pay off part of the debts, they would be almost paid in full today, and it would not have been possible for the interest to have increased so much. I neither grasp nor is it my nature or disposition to want to investigate the causes and reasons for this. Because of my constant concern, however, it has seemed appropriate to me, and my duty, to speak to Your Lordship in all frankness without dissembling in any way, reporting to you on this estate's present condition. For this purpose, I have prepared the enclosed summary. From it, Your Lordship will see what has been collected and paid for so many years and the true, certain, and actual condition that the estate is in today.

I promise Your Lordship that it is with the greatest affliction that I give you such news. Yet the responsibility of Your Lordship's confidence in me obliges me to do so. I must not fail in this regard, so that Your Lordship may have the information on the condition of your entails. With it, you may take measures you consider most likely to succeed.

As I have assured Your Lordship, in my opinion, what is called for is to pay off the censos promptly. Because this has not been done, excessive arrears and damage have resulted. Likewise, I shall endeavor to have the principal of all the debts settled and paid off in the best way possible, that the interest not increase. This has not been the least of the damage. Seeing how much those interests have climbed and that most of them are unjust, I shall arrange, even though unwillingly, with the creditors whatever the magistrate decides.

Upon the death of my aunt and lady, doña Juana, and having

examined the papers showing that Your Lordship inherited the house she had on the Plaza Mayor, I petitioned that legal possession of it be given to me. I hasten to inform Your Lordship that this has been done. Likewise, about next month (God willing), I have decided to go to Torrelaguna and all the other neighboring places, inspecting this entire estate and trying to put it in suitable condition.

I find in the papers that there are many other assets, such as lands. There is no information about what has become of these lands or who has usurped them. In order to find out, I shall arrange, if the survey that I shall make of them is not sufficient, for the usurpers to be soundly reprimanded. In this way, they will be exposed. In all this, there is no reason whatsoever that the necessary expedients and measures not be brought to bear.

I shall keep Your Lordship advised of whatever may result so that you are informed of everything and recognize the pleasure, care, and diligence with which I have devoted myself to serving you in this administration. In all modesty, I trust that this will be adequate to restore what was usurped and to keep the estate current in the best way possible.

I have no doubt that Your Lordship was inconvenienced by the news that the lord viceroy had put into effect the grant that the alcalde mayor had from his majesty for the office Your Lordship occupied. I trust that his excellency will have immediately given Your Lordship the post of governor and captain general in New Mexico. I shall be immensely pleased if Your Lordship has already acceded to it and that you will have had a very good journey, which you told me was to be a long one. I shall be very concerned until I have this news.

Among the papers I mentioned, I find that in 1681 my aunt and lady, doña Juana (may she be in heaven), made a claim on the estate of San Vicente. After a very long litigation, a writ was obtained to hold the trial in Madrid. The opposing party's claim was that it should be litigated in Valladolid, since he was an inhabitant of that city. In the brief time available, I have tried to gather and assemble certain of Your Lordship's papers, reports, and other documents I have been informed of. To prove in court Your Lordship's just claim, I shall try to press the suit diligently and carefully so that it may be heard and so succeed in having the estate found to belong to Your Lordship. Considering this estate's great value, because of the special circumstances surrounding it and the prerogatives it has, I am surprised that no one has done more.[5]

I have also learned from the documents that in the year 1682 my lady, doña Josefa de Vargas, died.[6] By her death, she left the two entails founded by Gabriel de Vivero and his wife, doña Elena de León, whose heir was doña Francisca de Vargas, from whom the Condesa de Casarrubios is descended. Therefore, the latter claimed for herself the entail founded by Diego de Vargas and his wife, doña Elvira Bernardo de Quirós.[7]

My aunt opposed this, bringing suit. She was the first to take possession of the estate, alleging that it belonged to Your Lordship. An agreement and settlement was made to avoid the many expenses. Namely, my aunt was to take possession of the entail don Diego de Vargas founded and the Condesa de Casarrubios the one Gabriel de Vivero founded. This was understood to be without prejudice to any legal claims the parties might have.

Since I now have Your Lordship's power of attorney and seeing that your right is clear, I shall try to have an interview with my lady, the condesa, in order to demonstrate this to her. First, I shall use every show of urbanity and attention with her ladyship. Should I fail to convince her ladyship to give up the claim to the entail, it will be necessary for me to avail myself of judicial means. It also seemed to me that I should inform Your Lordship of this.

In fulfillment of my duty and love, I should also tell Your Lordship that my aunt and lady, doña Juana (may she be in heaven), informed me two months after I was married that my wife had a married sister in Torrelaguna. This news took me very much by surprise, as Your Lordship can appreciate, since I had not been informed before my marriage. I told her ladyship I was immensely astonished that she should make it known to me when she did. Moreover, had she shared it with my mother, brothers, and me, it would not have been any reason to stop my marriage. Today it would be, because of the great care that was taken that all of us should have the proper feeling, I in particular. I understand that all my family would have had good cause not to accept her, which was surely their duty since she is my wife's sister. So as not to tire Your Lordship, I refrain from repeating the many things I said to her ladyship. She sought to satisfy me by telling me that her pretext for not having revealed this was that her niece had married without Your Lordship's consent and blessing and without awaiting such a necessary detail. At last, my aunt and I were of one mind. After many days she informed me that she had written to Your Lordship asking you to forgive her niece's decision, considering that she had married such a renowned gentleman.

This is borne out by the fact that he is a first cousin of my lady, doña Antonia Bernardo, wife of my uncle, lord don Gregorio Pimentel. This is reason enough to satisfy her ladyship completely that I should receive lord don José de Vargas.[8]

Once this detail was taken care of, I arranged for her to come to Madrid so that all my relatives could know, attend, and esteem my sister and lady, doña Juana. I have had José and Juana in Your Lordship's house for nearly two months. I shall keep them here until they see the bullfights a week from Thursday. In this way, I have renewed the bond forged in the beginning and fulfilled my wish. Confident of how much favor Your Lordship shows me, I must fervently entreat you to please receive, with the paternal love and affection corresponding to all the reasons and circumstances expressed therein, the letter my sister-in-law has given me. I shall be singularly appreciative if Your Lordship sends me the response so that my sister-in-law may have the great comfort and relief she needs, wishing so much to see herself in your good graces. For this favor, I shall be grateful to Your Lordship all my life.

Since nothing else comes to mind regarding these matters, I again render my obedience to Your Lordship, seeking many opportunities to demonstrate it. My wife and Juanico are writing to Your Lordship. I need not say more than that they are well and share my wish to see you. May God grant us this favor and keep you, my lord and father, the many years that only He can, and that are so necessary to us.

Madrid, 6 August 1690.

To lord don Diego de Vargas Zapata y Luján, my lord and my father-in-law

*AMNB. Unsigned c. Eight folios, fourteen written pages.

1. The indisposition may have been cowpox or chicken pox. The Nativity of the Blessed Virgin Mary is celebrated on 8 September. If Mariquita was Ignacio and Isabel María's first child, born late in 1689 or early in 1690 and acknowledged by don Diego in Letter 9 (4 November 1690), she must have died in infancy. In Letter 63 (14 April 1705), Isabel María wrote that Rosalea, the eldest of their four children, was then thirteen, which meant that she was not born until 1692 or 1693. The other three were Diego,

eleven; Frazquita, five; and Mariquita, two and a half.

2. Doña Juana de Vargas Ponce de León had died in March 1690. Juan González Calderón, Petition, Madrid, 21 June 1690, AHPM, P. 13.146. As was customary, don Ignacio referred to her as his aunt. In our strict usage, she was not. She was don Diego's aunt and doña Isabel's great-aunt.

3. In don Diego's absence, doña Juana had set Isabel María's dowry for her marriage to don Ignacio at 10,000 pesos. The marriage contract provided that don Ignacio receive an additional 500 pesos annually until the full amount was paid. Letter 47 below.

4. Juan González Calderón to Ignacio López de Zárate, Transfer, Madrid, 22 June 1690, AHPM, P. 13.146. Less than two months later, López de Zárate divided management of the Vargas estate into three parts, giving powers of attorney to others to administer, respectively, the entails of Torrelaguna, Madrid, and Granada. Ignacio López de Zárate to José de Vargas, Diego de Olvera, and Fernando García Bazán, Powers of attorney, Madrid, 14 Aug. 1690, AHPM, P. 13.146.

5. Fadrique de Vargas Carvajal y Manrique de Valencia, an uncle of don Diego three generations back, was created first Marqués de San Vicente del Barco on 30 March 1629. Alonso-Cadenas, *Elenco*, 541. His daughter had inherited the title and properties. When she died in 1680 without succession, doña Juana had informed don Diego, and he had authorized that a claim be entered in his name, forwarding a legal opinion prepared in Mexico City, money, and chocolate. Letters 9 and 12.

6. According to don Diego's grandson, Diego José López de Zárate Vargas (*Breve descripción*, 10, and family tree), Josefa de Vargas Portocarrero y Negrón, widow of Martín Pérez de Peñalosa and citizen of Móstoles, near Madrid, died on 30 January 1681, the end of her line. She named as heir her cousin, doña Juana de Vargas Ponce de León.

7. Gabriel de Vivero, Francisca de Vargas, Francisco de Vargas, and Lic. Diego de Vargas, corregidor in Biscay, were four of the seven children of Diego de Vargas, "the Lame," and Constanza de Vivero, don Diego's great-great-great-great-grandparents. He and his aunt, Juana, were descended directly from Lic. Diego; Josefa from Francisco; and the Condesa de Casarrubios, Isabel Chacón, from Francisca. The Diego de Vargas mentioned here as founder of the entail was the son and heir of Francisco. He had served as a page to the emperor, Charles V, and later as corregidor of Valladolid. López de Zárate Vargas, *Breve descripción*, 9–11, and family tree. Again, don Ignacio extended the use of uncle to his wife's maternal uncle, Gregorio Pimentel.

8. Without waiting for don

Diego's blessing on the marriage of his younger daughter, Juana Viviana, to José de Vargas, a gentleman from Nava del Rey in the province of Toledo, don Ignacio gave don José a power of attorney to manage the entail of Torrelaguna. Ignacio López de Zárate to José de Vargas, Power of attorney, 14 Aug. 1690. Later, long after his reconciliation with Juana Viviana, don Diego would do the same. Letter 56 below.

———

8. *Diego de Vargas to Isabel María de Vargas Pimentel, Mexico City, 4 November 1690.**

My dearly beloved daughter,

My heart will rejoice to know that you and my beloved grand-daughter are well. I send her lots of kisses and my blessing. My precious, I leave at this moment to take up my government and captaincy general of New Mexico. I go content, having settled up with the person who gave me what I needed. He will remit the dowry to my son-in-law, lord don Ignacio, in two flotas. I write to him and to the marqués, his brother and my friend. Hence, I go, not heeding a journey of five hundred leagues through the land of infidel, heathen, and barbarous Indians, one continually in a state of open warfare. May Our Lord give me life to see my son-in-law, lord don Ignacio, served. May he be assured that my good will and esteem for you are even greater than he can presume. It may be that time will change my luck, and I can better demonstrate my wish.

Please let me know whatever news there may be. Rest assured that I am yours and that your husband will get out of debt handily. Do not doubt this truth. Don Amadeo Zeyol will write him the very same thing.

May God keep you and let me see you, which for me would be the greatest joy I could have. Mexico City, 4 November 1690.

Your father who esteems you
and loves you from the heart,

Don Diego de Vargas Zapata
Luján Ponce de León [rubrica][1]

To my beloved daughter, doña Isabel María de Vargas

*AMNB. ALS. One folio, two written pages.

1. From this letter on, until he began to sign himself the Marqués de la Nava de Barcinas, Vargas added Ponce de León to his signature, seemingly in memory of his deceased aunt, Juana de Vargas Ponce de León.

———

9. Diego de Vargas to Ignacio López de Zárate, n.d., n.p. (c. late fall 1690).*

Son and dear sir,

With the general power of attorney I am sending to Your Lordship in don Amadeo Zeyol's packet, I have enclosed a letter from Mexico City dated in June, informing you of my status and fortune. At present, the evil that pursues me increases. My aunt's goodness, which was lost to me upon her death, was my defense and my only relief. This was such bitter news, and I did not need more to bear. In my aunt I have lost everything, since she alone sustained the luster and memory of my house. Only through her could my actions have possibly resulted in the good fortune I enjoy at present, having Your Lordship as my son-in-law. I entrust everything to you and commit to you the care of my beloved son, don Juan Manuel. I charge him as my son and ask him to treat you not as his brother-in-law, but as the one who is to correct him and take charge of directing his actions.

Your Lordship tells me that my son would like to join me. To this I respond that not even were I at death's door would I entertain the thought of him doing such a thing. Instead, he should serve at the palace and gain the experience of dutifully attending to the exercise of his position. From this, he can in time go on to serve his majesty with a cavalry unit and be a man.

The Indies are fine for those who sell in a store, but not for men of honor who flee the trades. This is a dangerous land. There are many humiliated nobles, for the lords viceroy suffer such an accu-

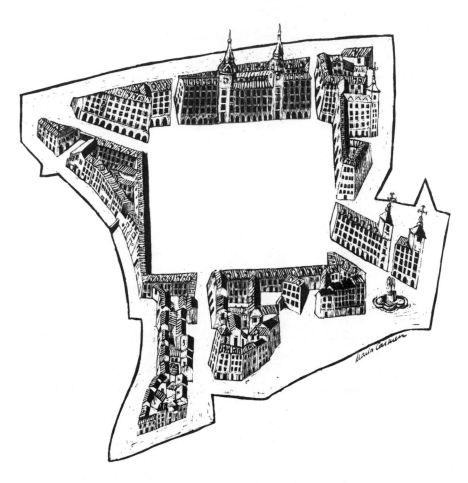

The Plaza Mayor, Madrid.
 After the 1656 Texeira map. Maria Carmen Gambliel.

mulation of recommendations that they set them aside and proceed as they see fit.

I pledge to Your Lordship that I shall provide for the decency of my son. He will not lack aid, either regularly or in the event of a special occasion, and he will have the payments I furnish for his good appearance. I shall remit by special mail a draft for 200 pesos to Capt. don Pedro Martínez de Murguía. He will then remit them to Your Lordship so that two winter suits may be made for my son.

When I gave the power of attorney to Juan González Calderón in June 1689, I did not know, as I do now, of my beloved daughter's marriage and good fortune. Hence, as I am writing to her, it will be evident that I have taken it from him and transferred it to Your Lordship. You will see that I also sent on that occasion a power of attorney for the arrangement and pledge of my daughter's dowry.

By virtue of the general power of attorney, Your Lordship may enjoy, rule, and administer the house on the Plaza Mayor, and take possession of it in my name, if you wish.[1] Likewise, you will please take measures to pursue the lawsuit I have filed against the estate of San Vicente.[2] Please act in everything as if it were yours. Whenever the person, whoever he may be, goes to Spain (God willing), he will make it known everywhere that I am more generous than one who has not met me can judge.

My affectionate wish, as I repeat to you, is that my son, don Juan Manuel, not quit the palace and that he remain in their majesties' service. To this end, I shall strip myself of all that I have and do everything I can to devise a way to send relief in full.

I am beside myself. Eighteen years ago I left Spain with only the salary his majesty gave me for the journey to this kingdom of New Spain. Today, my entails may be in ruin. My beloved wife lived a year and a half, and I made two payments to her, one from Cadiz and the other from the same ship I came over on. I also paid my friend, don José de Liñán, more than 7,500 vellon reales, remitting them from this kingdom. He wrote to me that he had advanced the money to her.[3] In addition, I left her provided with everything at home so that she did not have to buy even a ribbon. On the contrary, the tenants of the house on the Calle del Almendro, the duquesa, Cayetano, and Juan de Yuste, owed me a sizeable sum. I made several payments to my aunt (may she be in heaven) while fortune's wheel was turning.

I am confused by the sorry arrangement of my affairs. Of the debts

I left, the greatest was to don Felipe de Elmas, 1,500 ducados. I do not remember if that to Herrera amounted to 1,000 ducados for the suite in the house on the exchange contract.[4] To don Alonso Fajardo, 1,000 ducados . . .

*AMNB. AL, inc. Two folios, four written pages.

1. The house on the Plaza Mayor was on the south side toward the east end of the building labeled on the 1656 Texeira map El Rastro y Carnicería Mayor, the main meat market, in the section known as the Portal de las Pellas. One contemporary meaning of the word pella was pork lard. From the south the short Calle Imperial (today Botoneras) intersected this row of houses at an angle, precisely where the Vargas house stood and where the entrance was. Diego de Vargas to Juan González Calderón, Power of attorney, Mexico City, 23 June 1689, AGNot. 379; Ignacio López de Zárate to Diego de Olvera, Power of attorney, Madrid, 17 July 1690, AHPM, P. 13.146; Diego de Vargas, Will, Mexico City, 1 June 1703, AGNot. 692. DA. Texeira, *Topographía.*

2. On 10 August 1680—the day of the Pueblo Revolt in New Mexico—don Diego in Mexico City, having learned of the death of the Marquesa de San Vicente del Barco without immediate heirs, had executed a power of attorney in favor of Gregorio Pimentel, Antonio Mejía, S.J., and Juana de Vargas Ponce de León to press his claim to the marquisate and its properties. Diego de Vargas, Power

of attorney, Mexico City, 10 Aug. 1680, AGNot. 379. Six months later, he had another similar instrument drawn up. Diego de Vargas, Power of attorney, 29 Jan. 1681, AMNB, and AGNot. 379.

3. Vargas's friend and neighbor from Torrelaguna, José de Liñán y Cisneros was a descendant of the family that produced the villa's most famous deceased churchman, fray Francisco Cardinal Jiménez de Cisneros (1436–1517), and the brother of its most famous living churchman, don Melchor de Liñán y Cisneros (1629–1708), archbishop of Lima and viceroy of Peru. Don José had acted as a witness to the baptism of doña Isabel María, don Diego's first child, in 1665. Two years later, when he testified regarding don Diego's loan to repair the Vargas houses, José de Liñán was described as a citizen of Torrelaguna, residing at the time in Madrid at the inn of María Hidalgo on the Calle de los Tudescos. José de Liñán, Declaration, Madrid, 30 July 1667, AHPM, P. 9.012. Bautismos, Libro 4 (1638–66), Parroquia de Santa María Magdalena, Torrelaguna. Lewis Hanke, ed., in collaboration with Celso Rodríguez, *Perú*, vol. 5 of *Los virreyes*

españoles en América durante el
gobierno de la casa de Austria
(Madrid, 1979):181.

4. On 31 July 1670, Vargas had
entered into a contract with court
painter Francisco de Herrera as
security on a debt of 11,000 vellon
reales, or 1,000 ducados. Herrera
died in 1685, and the debt had
never been paid. On 5 October
1690, don Ignacio López de Zárate
reached an agreement with
Herrera's widow, doña Angela
Jacinta de Robles Gijón y
Villoslada. Beginning 1 January

1691, she was to receive the
proceeds from Vargas's juro at
Ocaña and the rent from a
downstairs apartment, then
occupied by the ecclesiastical judge
of the papal nuncio's court, in the
complex on the Calle del
Almendro. The arrangement,
which nullified the old contract,
was to run until the entire sum,
plus 3 percent annual interest, was
paid off. Ignacio López de Zárate
to Angela Jacinta de Robles,
Cession, Madrid, 5 Oct. 1690,
AHPM, P. 13.146.

Recolonizing New Mexico:
El Paso and Santa Fe,
1691–93, 1696–97

10. *Diego de Vargas to Ignacio López de Zárate,*
El Paso del Río del Norte, 20 April 1691. *

Son and dear sir,

I assure Your Lordship that I am concerned. I write because I
found myself unable to remit to you in this packet boat the payment
I would have liked to on my beloved daughter's dowry. I can do no
more than to have bound myself, as though I were a slave. In order
to serve his majesty, I came happily to this presidio in the kingdom
of New Mexico, which is in open warfare, for the sole purpose of
paying Your Lordship the dowry. I hope (Our Lord granting me life)
to be applauded for the achievement of what I so wish. To my mind,
this is my foremost duty.

I reached this kingdom and acceded to its government and captaincy general on 22 February of this year. I spent ninety-five days

on the road from Mexico City, a distance of 450 leagues, passing through the territory of warring enemy Indians for more than 350. Our Lord was pleased that I should arrive safely, well after so long and arduous a journey through wastelands, most nights sleeping with my boots on, horse saddled, and weapons at the ready.

I left a general power of attorney with the person who provisioned me for this government, so that when the flota that is expected arrives, he might seek a sizeable sum for Your Lordship. As soon as the flota comes, I shall send a dispatch and at the same time reiterate that I shall be relieved only in proportion to whatever funds he may remit to you. My friend, don Amadeo Zeyol, will attend to this matter, having that person notify me that he has not failed me in extricating Your Lordship from debt. You can rest assured that I shall relieve you of your obligation.

I am sending by this packet boat the title of accession to this government and captaincy general. Your Lordship will please have a copy sent to me after the title is received in the Secretariat for New Spain.[1] This information is necessary so that whoever succeeds me must wait the five years his majesty granted me from the day I might accede. Your Lordship will please pay particular attention to this clarification: see whoever is secretary for New Spain so that, in the event someone seeks this futura, the title, if given, stipulates that it is to take full effect upon accession to this government on such and such a date of the month when the five years his majesty granted to don Diego de Vargas Zapata Luján are up. The date of my accession will be of record in the copy. Your Lordship will handle this matter with greater love than my agent.[2] You will assume a valued role that is not easy for an agent to fill. I am writing to Capt. don Luis Sáenz de Tagle, knight of the Order of Alcántara and citizen of Mexico City. I request him to kindly remit a draft for 400 pesos in favor of my beloved son, don Juan Manuel de Vargas. With this money, he can pay Your Lordship the debt you must have incurred for the welcoming of our lady the queen, whom he serves.[3] I write on this occasion so that the money will arrive in good time.

I am leaving on campaign around June and shall be gone six months. I am going to reconnoiter the enemy, to the villa of Santa Fe, which was the court of the kingdom and province of New Mexico. I shall go on to reconnoiter their condition, in order to make a proposal to his excellency and to his majesty, whom I had written in Your Lordship's packet when I left Mexico City.[4]

May God keep you many years in the company of my beloved

daughter, Isabel, to whom I am writing, and my granddaughter. Done at this presidio and plaza de armas of El Paso del Río del Norte, 20 April 1691.

> Your most affectionate father
> and servant, who esteems you,
> kisses Your Lordship's hand,

> > Don Diego de Vargas Zapata
> > Luján Ponce de León [rubrica]

To Dr. don Ignacio López de Zárate, my son-in-law

*ARGD. ALS. Two folios, four written pages.

1. In 1604, the number of secretaries of the Council of the Indies had been increased from one to four. Two worked for the Cámara of the Council, and the others handled the affairs of the viceroyalties of New Spain and Peru respectively. Among the responsibilities of the Secretariat for New Spain were all matters pertaining to government, war, and the treasury within the viceroyalty and its five audiencias (Mexico City, Guadalajara, Guatemala, Santo Domingo, and the Philippines) and the dispatch of flotas to Veracruz and the ports of Central America. Schäfer, *Consejo Real*, 1:198–99.

2. Vargas retained the services of agent Juan González Calderón at least as late as 1696. Espinosa, *Crusaders*, 318; Letter 16 below.

3. Carlos II had entered Madrid with his second wife, Mariana de Neoburgo, on 20 May 1690. Kamen, *Spain*, 374.

4. Because of a series of local emergencies and shortages, Vargas did not get away on the reconnaissance he hoped to begin in June 1691 until more than a year later.

---

11. *Diego de Vargas to Isabel María de Vargas Pimentel, El Paso del Río del Norte, 23 September 1691.**

My daughter,

I write you, having just arrived from a campaign, victorious (thanks be to God), bringing in as spoils 130 heathen Apache captives.[1] I leave on campaign in October by order of the most excellent lord viceroy to make war in the provinces of Sonora and Sinaloa. At present, they are infested by the enemy, and the men-at-arms of the presidios of those provinces have been united. I go with the men from this presidio as captain general of all the forces because I am governor and captain general of this frontier and kingdom of New Mexico.[2]

I am writing my son-in-law about the disposition of my entails that seems to me to be in his best interest. I also tell him the means by which, I am certain, he will be furnished assistance when the flota arrives. I am putting myself at risk so that he will be cleared of debt and recognize my honor and how much I esteem you. The enclosed letter is for my daughter, Juana, to whom I give my blessing. I wrote when I departed for this government the coming, I mean, last year.

I repeat to you my affection and esteem for my son-in-law, your husband. It pleases and relieves me to have the good fortune of your happy fate and that of your brother, my son, don Juan Manuel. Because of your ability to reason, it is unnecessary to repeat to you both that you please him in everything and serve him as is your duty, for he is there in your father's stead. I can do no more in life than to have given up my country, my entails, and the love of your company, all of which I left on 10 August 1672.

I do not know whether my estates are mere gratuities. I see from the papers and accounting my son-in-law, lord don Ignacio, sends me that there has been bad management and that the estate is more encumbered than when I left it. To cover my sundry debts, I left many rentals due on the house. I also left the lawsuit over the woodland of the dehesa of Viñaderos, which was sold. With these combined proceeds, the debt to don Felipe de Elmas was paid off. Immediately after saving 3,000 reales of interest a year, the revenue from Granada was given and ceded to him, squandering two-thirds of its value. Everything has been mishandled, as I see from the accounts.

All I have to say is that for now I shall leave it to the good management and disposition of my son-in-law, lord don Ignacio, who will attend to everything because he is so close to me and favors me with such generosity. Therefore, I have decided to serve his majesty in one of the posts I am submitting to the lord marqués, his brother, who is surely the person to whom I should entrust my petitions. Should I attain one of these posts, the revenue would be greatly improved and the censos on my entail, which consume and encumber it, would be removed. This is my way of leaving something over and above the entail for the education of my successor's second son.

God be with you and keep you, my daughter. You can expect considerable assistance by the flota so that your husband, my beloved son-in-law, lord don Ignacio, will have relief by the grace of God, who gives me life. I shall come to his aid in every way. Done in this post of El Paso del Río del Norte and its presidio, 23 September 1691.

To my beloved granddaughter many hugs and kisses. I am asking my son-in-law that all of you give me the pleasure of having your portraits. Please send them to me, and I shall pay the cost out of my esteem, with which nothing can compare.

Your father who respects you
and loves you dearly,

Don Diego de Vargas Zapata
Luján Ponce de León [rubrica]

To my beloved daughter, doña Isabel María

*AMNB. ALS. Two folios, four written pages.

1. Given the mobility of the enemy, and the little time Vargas took from his other documented duties, this campaign would have to have been a sudden, surprise attack on Apaches not far from El Paso. The number of captives, dead, and wounded (Letter 12 below) is remarkable. Even more remarkable, considering the magnitude of the victory, is that nowhere in the extant official record are these figures corroborated. The campaign would have had to have taken place between 30 August, when Vargas certified in El Paso the amount of land belonging to each of the several missions, and 23 September, the date of this letter. Walz, "El Paso Area," 289–90. He wrote to the captain of the presidio of Janos on 9 September, acknowledging his participation in the upcoming Sonora campaign, but he did not say where he was on that date. Diego de Vargas to Juan Fernández de la Fuente, n.p., 9 Sept. 1691, AGN, Historia 37:2.

2. Documents about mounting this fall campaign are in AGN, Historia 37:2, with copies in AGI, Guadalajara 139:4. Walz sums them up in "El Paso Area,"

266–81. See also Jack D. Forbes, *Apache, Navaho, and Spaniard* (Norman, 1960):225–31. Vargas claimed that he sent the journal and summary of this joint campaign to the viceroy in January of 1692. Since they have not come to light, details are sketchy. Evidently, the combined force under don Diego left the presidio of Janos, 120 miles southwest of El Paso, on 22 October 1691; rode, according to Vargas, a thousand miles through what is today northern Sonora and southern Arizona, the enemies' country, some of it previously unexplored; and returned in December. The expedition suffered through rain and cold, ran low on provisions, and had trouble finding water holes. The biggest problem, however, reported Capt. Juan Fernández de la Fuente of the Janos presidio, was the wretched condition of the horses ridden by the New Mexico contingent, which slowed everyone. In a fight with Apaches, the Spaniards managed to take alive twenty-three women and children, as well as two young males (whom they shot), and to kill sixteen other people. Because of the ineffectiveness of this joint campaign, the Conde de Galve forbade another. Guillermo Porras Muñoz, *La frontera con los indios de Nueva Vizcaya en el siglo xvii* (Mexico City, 1980):328–29. Diego de Vargas to Conde de Moctezuma, Santa Fe, 28 Nov. 1696, AGI, Guadalajara 141:20. Juan Fernández de la Fuente to Juan Isidro de Pardiñas, Janos, 12 Dec. 1691, AGN, Provincias Internas 30:8

---

12. *Diego de Vargas to Ignacio López de Zárate, El Paso del Río del Norte, 25 September 1691.* *

Son and dear sir,

I was pleased to receive Your Lordship's letter in this government and kingdom of New Mexico with the news I wished for of your good health and that of my beloved children. It was a great comfort to me in this my place of exile, which is the farthest and vastest, as those in Madrid who have experience in this kingdom will inform Your Lordship.

Though I am writing to my children, I repeat my blessing to you. May I tell you how comforted I am that they have Your Lordship's protection and favor. Only with the assurance of their having such a father could I dare to forsake duties so singular in my affection and esteem. But His Divine Majesty willed through His divine providence that I be given a substitute of such character as Your Lordship, in whom I might have relief and confidence. Thus, I shall remain in this kingdom in the royal service, as I hope, long enough to see my plans realized.

As I write, I am about to leave on campaign against the barbarous, rebel nations of this kingdom. I shall continue until the rigor of the season and the snow force me to withdraw again with my army to this presidio and plaza de armas. I dispatch this letter in the hope of receiving Your Lordship's, which may come for me by the flota. I trust that my letter will reach and be taken by the packet boat bringing news of the flota's arrival. I shall be grateful if Your Lordship repeats to me that my beloved children and granddaughter—she must be very grown-up by now—are in good health.

I also hope that in Torrelaguna Your Lordship finds the house repaired, which was the concern expressed by my brother-in-law, don Gregorio Pimentel, who lives in it. I expect that Your Lordship will have inspected the vineyards, lands, and other property. To obtain their fruits and see that they render what profit they may, it is necessary first for Your Lordship to appoint a good mayordomo, completely faithful, knowledgeable, and attentive.

Since don Diego is an old servant and was a gentleman dear to my aunt and lady, doña Juana de Vargas (may she be in glory), Your Lordship can employ him in this service.[1] I advised you of this in the letter I wrote you with the power of attorney.

Four hundred ducados should be more than enough to till the vineyards and hoe them twice, along with the olive orchard on the irrigated land and the others in the vineyards, which are very good and bear well. The lands of Torrelaguna, Torremocha, Talamanca, and Valdepiélagos are rented, most very favorably.[2] The mayordomo will collect their rent, according to the legal instruments, on the day of St. James in July, which is the date the farmers designate to make payment.[3]

There are also the pastures and enclosures of Miraflores de la Sierra, Chozas, and Guadalix, and the dehesa of Las Gariñas in Buitrago. Of these revenues, only the most excellent lord Duque del Infantado pays, and that amounts to 2,000 reales annually.[4] There is in the villa of Buitrago half the dehesa of Viñaderos, whose rent the heirs of Martín de Ahedo should pay. In addition, there is the woodland cut on the enclosures, pastures, and the dehesa of Viñaderos. Before Torrelaguna is a village called El Molar, where they pay a censo of sixteen or twenty fanegas of wheat.[5] In another village called El Espartal (to one side of Talamanca before reaching another called El Bellón) there are very choice wheat fields that used to be rented and were coveted by the citizens.

Many parcels of the Torrelaguna lands border on those of the entail held by my lady and aunt, doña Isabel de Olazábal Vélez de Guevara. From a look at the papers and an examination of the boundaries, my brother-in-law, don Gregorio, will see that many of my lands are usurped. The farmers to whom my lord and uncle, don Juan Pimentel (may he be in heaven), rented have encroached upon them.[6] As such a right-minded gentleman, he will realize this and restore the losses to my entail. The vineyards can be worked, even wastefully, for 400 ducados de vellon. A harvest of from one thousand to twelve hundred arrobas of wine can be brought in.[7] The mayordomo has as profit the best of the second pressing and the excess corn. I know that the olive trees are harvested and that the irrigated land can be sown in barley. There will also be abundant forage for the mules of Your Lordship's coach.

I left the holdings and entail of Camarma del Caño and Camarma de Esteruela in fine shape. Everything is surveyed, with clear boundaries, as will be found in the survey among the papers of my entail. These lands, as well as the dovecote in Camarma del Caño, and a very large and plenteous olive grove, are very much sought after by the citizens of those places. It was thought that for their most advantageous rental, because of their proximity to the villa of Alcalá de Henares, papers should be posted to make it known, so that someone might be found to make a good rental agreement with.[8]

I tell Your Lordship that with these lands, the olive grove, and the dovecote my great-great-grandfather, Pedro Ruiz de Alarcón Sotomayor, knight of the Order of Calatrava, who was alferez mayor of the city of Guadalajara, and his wife, my lady, doña Isabel de Salinas y Guevara, founded an entail.[9] With this estate, they maintained themselves splendidly, in accord with the nobility of their persons. This was related to me by the old people of those villages. When I was granted permission to administer and manage the entails, I found the houses fallen down.

I am telling Your Lordship all this so that you may be informed and obtain a good rental on the entail of Madrid. It would be a good idea to restore in its entirety the entail that became vacant on the death and demise of my aunt and lady, doña Josefa de Vargas. My aunt and lady, the Condesa de Casarrubios, should better recognize my right, since the very designations of succession by the entail's founders clarify to whom it belongs in truth. So as not to appear rude and discourteous, I did not oppose the friendly agreement and solemn contract by my aunt and lady, doña Juana de Vargas, since it was based on close friendship and family ties with those people.[10] I assure Your Lordship that neither I nor anyone in my family have done anything to burden them.

Though my fortune is limited, I have sought to be appreciative, kind, and a good friend. As I was leaving for this kingdom, I went to Móstoles to bid farewell to my aunt and lady, doña Josefa de Vargas (may she be in glory), and her husband.[11] She told me and repeated several times that I and my children were the sole heirs of her entails. Because my uncle, lord don Francisco Zapata, Conde de Casarrubios, of the Royal Council and Cámara of Castile, was a great and powerful man, one might have suspected and feared that in my absence the family would have entered a claim to harm me, to confuse and hide the fact that I am the legitimate heir, alleging that this entail belonged to it.[12] This entail is composed of the houses that are on the corner down from the parish church of San Justo on the Calle de la Puente Segoviana, the revenue from the tercias of the villages of Los Caramancheles, and I do not know what censos.[13]

By virtue of the general power of attorney, Your Lordship can make the proposal to my lady, the condesa, attending to considerations of courtesy and civility, not because my aunt, doña Josefa (may she be in glory), would have permitted it. In this way, you will not damage my claim and right, because this will not be done by special legal instrument that, were it necessary, could confirm it. The possession thus acquired by her ladyship is null, inasmuch as it is prejudicial to third parties, me, my children, and those who may succeed them in the entail of my lady, the condesa. This is of record in the Vargas family papers and agrees with what my uncle, lord don Francisco Zapata, Conde de Casarrubios (may he be in glory), told me is in the genealogical tree of don What's his name Ortiz de Vargas. I offer all this information for Your Lordship's consideration so that you may be better able to counter the lady's charges and so that the two of us do not go to the next life without lifting this burden from our children. In any case, I am always her ladyship's humble servant.

With regard to the entail of Granada, I tell Your Lordship, in the first place, do not rent it. Find a reliable person of good credit in that city to whom its administration may be entrusted. By offering 10 percent, this administration will appeal to someone who is very dependable. Allow me to demonstrate to Your Lordship the quality of this entail. In the year 1669, I mean 1667, Gabriel Ruiz, treasurer of the Santa Cruzada of that kingdom, executed an instrument in my favor, giving 1,000 reales at the end of each month.[14] The first four months of the year, January, February, March, and April, the agreement was for him to advance them to me. At the end of the year, the account was to be liquidated, settling the 12,000 reales of disbursement for the twelve months, paying the balance of the revenue after collecting the 10 percent due the administrator.

This revenue comes from many shops and houses in the best places of Granada, on its public thoroughfares and best business streets. When I was there for the sole purpose of inspecting the entail, I saw everything. I was at the farm called Barcinas that is part of the entail. It was very well stocked, with its very good, fortified house and many fields bordering on the lands belonging to the canons of El Monte Santo. Water for irrigation of these lands legally belongs to the farm. I left an affidavit to this effect, because the canons claimed it was theirs.[15]

Because it was necessary to increase the revenue from these lands, to assure their yield, and to rebuild (at a cost of more that 1,000 ducados) the dam on the small river that passes through them, a finca incorporated in the entail was sold, with an affidavit of public interest by authority of the royal magistrate. The holding was called Horno de la Haza, which rented for more than 200 ducados a year. It was exempt from entail, because a citizen of that city held a perpetual censo on it. As an interested party, he would collect interest every time it sold, assuming it was free and clear according to royal law. It was assigned to him and arranged by a legal acknowledgement of perpetual censo, because he was the owner. Such a sale occurred with the purchaser's legal acknowledgment of the censos it had in addition to this principal one. This holding was mortgaged as security for the fincas of the entail. This purchaser obligated himself to redeem the censos within a year. It is necessary to see whether this has been done. If not, it should be done immediately so that the entail will not be stolen away. If this finca is lost and its value diminished, the interested parties in the censos may have claims and receipts against the entail's fincas and holdings.

The second point is that I do not remember if what he paid for Horno de la Haza was 16,800 or 17,500 reales in cash. He was issued the deed in accord with the auction the civil magistrate held. Out of the auction price, he made an oblation and royal payment before the magistrate. He deposited the remainder so that it would be available to pay for the dam's repair, which was put up for public bid at that time. The money was deposited with Gabriel Ruiz, treasurer of the Santa Cruzada. He, or his heirs, will have had it since 1668. The auction and sale were held around September by authority and order of the teniente de corregidor, don What's his name Pallares, before Andrés de Escos, escribano público del número, who had his office on the Plaza de Bibarrambla of that city. Once the dam was finished, well then, the magistrate was to have ordered that whatever amount remained be applied as a finca to increase the entail or that the censos be partially redeemed.

With this information, Your Lordship should write to my cousin in Granada, don Fernando de Teruel y Quesada, knight of the Order of Santiago.[16] He is my cousin because he is married to my lady, doña Luisa de Cepeda y Ayala, niece (related by blood) of my great-uncle, don Alonso de Cepeda y Ayala, descendants of my great-grandfather, Capt. don Alonso de Cepeda y Ayala, and of my great-grandmother and lady, doña Juana Venegas Ponce de León.

Your Lordship should first have the dam put in operation. From what remains, whatever censos the estate and entail have can be redeemed so that they will be free and clear. Also, the interest can be requested from the depositary, don Gabriel Ruiz, for as many years as he has had the money. Surely a man of personal and business dealings is trustworthy. I advise Your Lordship that the rent the farmers were paying was one-fifth of all the seed, wheat as well as barley and cane. With the dam finished, they said they will pay regularly one-third of the seed, because with irrigation their harvests are assured.

There is also another farm called La Nava de Antonia Gil. Because it has extensive woodlands, this one is rented for the acorns, for which people who have swine willingly pay. Your Lordship will reap the benefit of increased annual revenue, by placing this and the entail in administration. Revenue from the principal houses is collected monthly and from the shops four times a year. The administrator Your Lordship appoints can remit a forty-day draft every three months, saving the exchange fee of one-fourth of 1 percent collected on a sight draft. The seeds and grains are sold in that city of Granada at

The fortified house on the farm of Barcinas, north of Granada.
Maria Carmen Gambliel.

the end of the year, and if they are kept until the following March or
April, then they will sell at the best price.

As I repeat to Your Lordship, you are to administer the revenues
of those entails so as to realize whatever they may yield. They will
not be subject to the waste, failure, and loss they would if rented at a
fixed amount on account. In the event of bad weather, there is the
risk of poor harvests, and one fanega of each commodity is worth
four times more than in an abundant year. In the end, it is better to
accept even difficulties from God's hand than prosperity from those
profiteers.

With respect to the lawsuit against the Marqués de San Vicente
and to the patronage of the chapel of San Andrés (founded therein
by my uncle, the most illustrious lord don Gutierre de Vargas Carvajal,
former bishop of Plasencia, who was a younger brother of the marqués), I sent to my aunt, doña Josefa (may she be in glory), the powers of attorney and the legal opinions of one of this kingdom's best
lawyers, together with money and chocolate. I did this in an effort

to see that the suit is prepared in such a way that there is a good prospect of a favorable decision. I trust in His Divine Majesty that the law is on my side. My great-uncle, Father Sebastián de Vargas of the Society of Jesus, told me as much several times.

Upon notification of the censuras, the papers and instruments of the entail will be produced, as will those of the foundation of the patronage of the chapel, its revenues, the lord bishop's testament, and the grant of the title that his majesty, the king our lord, Felipe IV, made to the Marqués de San Vicente, my uncle. His testament and grant of title will shed light on the justice of my cause.

The lord marqués, my uncle, left no legitimate successor other than his daughter, the marquesa, who succeeded to these entails, the patronage, and the estate of the title and marquisate. Since she died without succession, they pass to me, the legitimate heir, as descendant of the grandparents' eldest brother. They were the younger brothers of my uncle, the Marqués de San Vicente. My great-uncle, Father Sebastián de Vargas, related to me that the latter had also left an illegitimate daughter who had married in Old Castile a gentleman named Villaroel or Villaseca, of whom the present marqués is son or grandson.

In any case, although he may be legitimate, he is excluded by being of a bastard line. The above-mentioned documents will best clarify this matter. I have no doubt about what my great-uncle told me on various occasions. If the marqués were not excluded by descent from that line, as soon as the claim was entered, he would have presented himself with these papers to settle it, requesting the right to legitimate and exclusive possession for him and any children he may have. Not responding, he tried to have the trial take place in the royal Chancillería of Valladolid. All these arguments better prove his malice in usurping my right.

I know that since Your Lordship is in Madrid, you will pursue the lawsuit and clear this matter up, relying on your authority and position, and your intelligence and energy. Hence, I am leaving to Your Lordship the disposition and maintenance of the revenues and entails I have in those kingdoms. I trust you will attend to everything because of your many outstanding honorable qualities. If I am employed in his majesty's service in a good governorship (Our Lord giving me life), everything will be put in order.

As for my petition for a better governorship, I refer to the letter I am writing to the lord marqués, Your Lordship's brother and my friend. I am telling him what, out of his concern, will fulfill my wish. In everything, it will always be my wish to serve Your Lordship, ever obliged for your great concern and many kindnesses. I ask you not as the father-in-law I am so happy to consider myself; rather I ask you as my lord and the gentleman you are to take good care of my beloved son, don Juan Manuel, and see that he does not fail to attend his majesty, the king our lord (may God keep him), and serve the queen, our lady. I shall put myself at risk in this kingdom and serve in this government to settle what I owe you and assist you in such a way that you may be free of your debts. After all, this is what you deserve and what I must do for you.

I hope that my agent and aviador will supply by the flota an amount that will relieve Your Lordship in large part. He promised to do so at the time I left the city of Mexico for this government, and, based on my experience with his word, he will. In order to better see that Your Lordship is aided and assisted, I left him a power of attorney so that I am obligated and the largest amount possible is withdrawn and acquired for the term of eight months. It will be repaid with the rescate and premium of silver according to the standard fineness of the real of Parral.[17] I give Your Lordship this information in advance and am repeating it at present to my agent so that he will be ready. Your Lordship will please send me an account of the sum remitted by the flota.

I repeat to Your Lordship that, with all that I am and all that I have, I am yours from the heart. May God, as only He can, keep Your Lordship the many happy years I wish, in the company of my beloved daughter and granddaughter. I ask that you do me the favor of sending me portraits, including one of my son, don Juan Manuel, so that I may have the pleasure of seeing them. Done at this Paso del Río del Norte, kingdom of New Mexico, 25 September 1691.

Your most affectionate father
who esteems you from the heart kisses
Your Lordship's hand,

Don Diego de Vargas Zapata
Luján Ponce de León [rubrica]

To lord Dr. don Ignacio López de Zárate, my son-in-law

I inform Your Lordship that I have just arrived from a victorious campaign, having captured 130 prisoners and left dead more than forty, not counting many who escaped because of the denseness of the bosque where the wounded enemy was. By his excellency's order, I am leaving for the provinces of Sonora and Sinaloa where the enemy is to be found. I shall have overall command of the armed forces inasmuch as the companies from those presidios and this one are united. I shall advise Your Lordship by the flota of the outcome of the offensive carried to the enemy.

Vargas [rubrica][18]

---

*AMNB. LS. Ten folios, twenty written pages. The body of this letter is written by a scribe, but the postscript, about the otherwise undocumented victory over Apaches, don Diego added in his own hand.

1. This may be a reference to Diego de Olvera, a long-time family employee, about whom there will be more in subsequent letters.

2. The villa of Torrelaguna and the villages of Torremocha, Talamanca, and Valdepiélagos lie north of Madrid in the watershed of the Río Jarama.

3. The feast day of St. James the Greater, patron saint of all Spain, is celebrated on 25 July.

4. Don Gregorio de Silva y Mendoza, who died in 1693, was the ninth Duque del Infantado, the fifth Duque de Pastrana, and Marqués de Cenete. His family's possessions and authority extended throughout Spain. Since July 1661, however, this vast estate had been subject to a creditors' agreement, whereby the government appointed someone to supervise payment of creditors. Kamen,

Spain, 232. The duque's younger brother, the Conde de Galve, was serving at this time as viceroy of New Spain.

5. El Molar is just to the east of the main highway some twenty-five miles north of Madrid in mountainous terrain.

6. Here Vargas was using aunt and uncle to refer to his mother- and father-in-law, Isabel de Olazábal and Juan Pimentel, the parents of his wife, Beatriz, and his brother-in-law, Gregorio.

7. Don Diego's estimate of annual wine production at 1,000 to 1,200 arrobas was far too high. It should be compared with the figures, reported by don Ignacio in Letter 48 below, for 1692 through 1698, which varied from 300 to 756 arrobas.

8. Alcalá de Henares, the walled city where fray Francisco Jiménez de Cisneros founded a university in

1508, is located some twenty miles more east than north of Madrid on an extensive plain.

9. Pedro Ruiz de Alarcón Mata y Sotomayor was the son of the Bernal de Mata and Catalina de Alarcón "branch of the illustrious tree of the Alarcones, Condes de Valverde." Don Pedro married Isabel de Salinas y Guevara, and their third child, Juana, was wed to don Diego's great-grandfather, Francisco de Vargas y Salinas. Alonso Núñez de Castro, *Historia eclesiástica y seglar de la muy noble y muy leal ciudad de Guadalaxara* (Madrid, 1653):302. Núñez de Castro makes Ruiz de Alarcón a knight of the Order of Santiago, not Calatrava.

10. Don Diego's customary, broad use of aunt and uncle to include cousins of all degrees is confusing to readers so far removed from the people mentioned. Only Juana de Vargas Ponce de León was his aunt in the strict sense. She was a cousin of both Josefa de Vargas and Isabel Chacón Cárdenas, the Condesa de Casarrubios. The latter inherited the title from her first husband, Melchor de Chávez. López de Zárate Vargas, *Breve descripción*, 38, and family tree.

11. Josefa de Vargas, who died on 30 January 1681 without heirs, had been married to Martín Pérez de Peñalosa, citizen of Móstoles, who predeceased her. Alvarez y Baena, *Hijos de Madrid*, 1:311.

12. Francisco Zapata, the Conde de Casarrubios by marriage to Isabel Chacón Cárdenas, the Condesa de Casarrubios, was not don Diego's uncle in the narrow sense; instead, he was the second husband of a cousin of Vargas's aunt, Juana. Born in Madrid, the second son of Diego Zapata, the Conde de Barajas, and María Sidonia Riederer de Paar, Francisco was admitted in 1631 to the Colegio Mayor de San Bartolomé at the University of Salamanca, studied law, and two years later became the comptroller of the Chancillería of Granada. He had been named to the Council of Castile in 1653 and died late in 1672, having requested that his widow continue to receive his councilor's salary as a pension because of their straitened circumstances. Fayard, *Membres*, 51, 173, 223, 248, 416, 418, 555; and Gutiérrez Coronel, *Historia genealógica*, 322.

13. The two Caramancheles, or Carabancheles, Alto, or de Arriba, and Bajo, lay just south of Madrid. They are today within the city.

14. As a treasurer of the Santa Cruzada, Ruiz received and forwarded to Madrid the considerable revenue from what C. H. Haring has called "the queerest of all taxes, the *cruzada*." This medieval church tax, the proceeds of which went into the royal treasury, derived from papal bulls of crusade authorizing the sale of indulgences in Spain and later the New World. See Haring, *Spanish Empire*, 267–68.

15. The Monte Santo of

Granada, a mile northeast of the city's center, famous today for its Gypsy caves and panoramic vista, was the site of a center of religious studies founded at the beginning of the seventeenth century. Evidently the Canons of Monte Santo had a house and lands adjacent to don Diego's property. *Diccionario enciclopédico Espasa* (Madrid, 1978), 11:70.

16. A native of Granada, Fernando Alfonso de Teruel y Quesada was Conde de Villamena and Señor de Cosbijar by marriage to don Diego's cousin, Luisa Teresa de Cepeda. She was a daughter of Luis de Cepeda y Ayala, city councilor of Granada, chief constable of the Inquisition, and member of the family of Vargas's paternal grandmother. García Carraffa, *Diccionario heráldico*, 84:162. Don Diego used the term cousin for everyone related to him by blood or marriage in his own generation, except his siblings and his wife and her siblings.

17. On the real de minas of San José del Parral, founded in 1631 and, in Vargas's day, the residence of the governors of New Biscay, see Robert C. West, *The Mining Community in Northern New Spain: The Parral Mining District* (Berkeley, 1949).

18. When don Diego wrote his surname only, Vargas, he followed standard Spanish practice. Since the late nineteenth century, however, De Vargas has been common in local usage in New Mexico. See John L. Kessell, "Vargas or De Vargas: A Modest Justification of Both Forms," in Anne V. Poore, ed., *Collected Papers in Honor of Charles H. Lange* (Santa Fe, 1988).

------

13. *Diego de Vargas to Ignacio López de Zárate, El Paso del Río del Norte, 9 April 1692.* *

Son and dear sir,

I wrote to Your Lordship at great length last September. Because there has not been a good opportunity for the letter to reach you, I am obliged to write another, which I think will arrive at almost the same time. How pleasant to write again of the constant affection I owe you. I contemplate the comfort of having my heart's treasures, my beloved children, protected. Not only is Your Lordship their brother-in-law, but also their true father. They live very securely under your wing. You can be certain that you will always find in me attention and ready affection for all that is dear to me. I wish I had the good fortune of showing you their depth.

Out of such consideration, I could have done no more than to have exiled myself to this kingdom, at the ends of the earth and remote beyond compare. From its distance, I seek the means to fulfill my wish of paying Your Lordship the dowry once and for all. By the flota expected this year, I shall remit (with God's help) money to assist with the disencumbrance. I am enclosing a letter to my son, don Juan Manuel, with my agent's so that the latter will remit a draft for 400 pesos to him. Last year, I had him send one. I assume he will have received my letter. I am awaiting acknowledgement of it (as well as of this one I am writing today). I am dispatching it by courier to Mexico City with the proposal to his excellency for conquest of the kingdom of New Mexico. I am prepared to carry out the invasion this summer on the feast day of St. Lawrence, the same day the kingdom was lost in 1680.[1]

I wrote to my daughter, Juana, last year and I trust that the letter is in my packet. I shall be happy if she is in good health, and I give her my blessing. May God keep Your Lordship many years, sharing in the life of my beloved daughter, Isabel, and my granddaughter, and may He allow me to see them. El Paso del Río del Norte, 9 April 1692.

Your most affectionate father who
esteems and loves you from the heart
kisses Your Lordship's hand,

Don Diego de Vargas Zapata
Luján Ponce de León [rubrica]

To lord Dr. don Ignacio López de Zárate, my son-in-law and friend

*AMNB. ALS. Two folios, three written pages.

1. 10 August.

———

14. Diego de Vargas to Ignacio López de Zárate, Santa Fe, 12 October 1692.*

Son and dear sir,

I have written to Your Lordship on every occasion offered by the mail dispatched to Mexico City. I have apprised you of my progress in this government and of the fortunate results, which are to the satisfaction of the most excellent lord viceroy, the Conde de Galve, and the ministers of the Junta of the Royal Treasury.

I have no doubt that they will inform his majesty of these results in his Royal and Supreme Council of the Indies and of the present success, because it is such a triumph and glory to God and king. I decided to conquer and restore at my own expense this villa of Santa Fe, capital of the kingdom of New Mexico. It seemed appropriate to me to write, though briefly, to the king our lord.[1] Because I was appointed by his majesty, it would not be good to neglect to inform his Royal and Supreme Council of the Indies of this victory. I therefore give him the news of this conquest, of the pueblos and districts I have restored to his royal crown, and the number of people baptized. During the twelve years since the Indians of this kingdom rose up and separated themselves from Our Holy Faith, they have been living as apostates in their idolatry.

Finally, I want Your Lordship to be aware of how important this news will be to his majesty. In 1681, the Rev. Father fray Francisco de Ayeta (who resides at the Convento Grande in Mexico City), procurator general of the Holy Gospel Province of Our Father St. Francis for the entire kingdom of New Spain, left for Santa Fe in the governor's company. At that time, the most excellent lord Conde de Paredes, Marqués de la Laguna, was governing the kingdom of New Spain. He gave Father Ayeta 95,000 pesos for this conquest. I could wish for no better chronicler of this important undertaking than this father, who came in that capacity. As I have said, he came with the then governor, but they did not succeed. They returned in despair after having restored to the faith only 385 people from the pueblo of Isleta, at such a high cost.[2]

Though it was considered a desperate situation, with divine favor and at my own expense, I have now achieved the unexpected. As I write, I am dispatching a courier to the most excellent lord viceroy, the Conde de Galve, from this villa. I have just arrived from the pueblos and nations of the interior as far as the Taos, the most distant.

I am writing this father, although briefly, so that he will be informed of everything and because he will rejoice. I shall send the copy of the military proceedings of the conquest by the flota so that his majesty will be informed in the royal council. Now, don Toribio de la Huerta need not weary himself in this conquest. His majesty can only reward him for his wish, favoring him with the title of marqués of this kingdom and the many other grants he was seeking. He even received on account an ayuda de costa. [3] This is not meant to reproach his majesty for anything, but only to advise Your Lordship on this point. By the flota (if God Our Lord gives me life), I shall send the copy of the proceeding to date and whatever else I do here in the service of God and king.

Please do me the favor of inquiring whether by this packet boat the most excellent lord viceroy and the lords of the royal junta report to his majesty about what I am relating in this letter. It will be easy for Your Lordship to find out in the office of the Secretary of the Indies. Please advise me with all care of the particulars they may tell you and of the report on my services. Once I know with certainty what they tell Your Lordship, I can consider my possibilities for advancement. I long to see letters from Your Lordship and my beloved children. I have remitted to my son, Juan Manuel, two drafts, each in the amount of 400 pesos of 8 reales, free of conveyance charge and placed on deposit in Madrid. I trust that my correspondent, Capt. don Luis Sáenz de Tagle, knight of the Order of Alcántara and silver merchant in Mexico City, will have issued these drafts on don Enrique de la Rosa, with whom he has business dealings in Cadiz. [4]

I shall redouble my effort (Our Lord giving me life), undertaking to remit part of the dowry to Your Lordship by the flota. No reason or cause other than paying what is due you could keep me exiled here. Be assured, therefore, that I shall not fail you, but serve you with the earnestness of a friend and father-in-law who esteems you. I have no doubt that you will be very considerate in your duties to my beloved daughter, Isabel, and my grandchildren. I imagine that by now you will have had more children. To everyone, I give my blessing and ask Your Lordship to embrace them in my name as I would like to personally. I hope that His Divine Majesty will grant me this wish. May He keep Your Lordship many happy years.

Will Your Lordship please hand deliver my letters to the lord Marqués de Villanueva, your brother and my friend, and to my children. Please send to Torrelaguna the packet from this villa of Santa Fe, capital of the kingdom of New Mexico, newly restored to and conquered for the royal crown. 12 October 1692.

He who esteems and loves you
as father and friend
kisses Your Lordship's hand,

Don Diego de Vargas Zapata
Luján Ponce de León [rubrica]

To lord don Ignacio López de Zárate, my son-in-law

After having written this, it occurred to me that to save time, it would be good to ask his majesty for the favor when the report comes from the lord viceroy and the royal junta. Your Lordship will please have this letter presented and advise me, taking it upon yourself to reply. The letter is unsealed so that Your Lordship can read it and understand my just petition.

*ARGD. LS. Four folios, seven written pages. If don Diego wrote this letter from Santa Fe, it probably should have been dated 16 October, the day he also wrote to the viceroy and dispatched a courier to Mexico City. According to his journal, he was in the vicinity of San Juan pueblo on 12 October. The postscript, in the scribe's hand, was written vertically in the left margin of the first page.

1. Don Diego's letter to the king on this date, which he later remembered writing, has not turned up. Letter 20 below.

2. The unsuccessful effort to restore New Mexico in 1681, and Father Ayeta's part in it, are detailed in Hackett and Shelby, *Revolt of the Pueblo Indians*. Francisco de Ayeta, born in Pamplona, Spain, entered the Franciscan order in 1659 in Mexico City. Elected custos, or superior, of the Franciscans in New Mexico in 1676 and procurator general of New Spain three years later, he had petitioned the viceroy for, and conveyed to New Mexico in 1677, badly needed men, arms, munitions, and horses. In 1680, he arrived a second time from Mexico City with the mission supply caravan just in time to succor the governor and refugees fleeing the Pueblo Revolt. During Gov. Antonio de Otermín's restoration attempt in 1681–82, Father Ayeta, who previously

blamed the uprising on the Pueblo leaders, convinced himself that the revolt had the support of the Pueblo peoples in general. As procurator general of the Franciscans in New Spain, he traveled to Madrid where he served effectively at court as advocate for the friars. Adams and Chavez, *Missions of New Mexico,* 329–30. While in Spain, Ayeta recruited for the missions of New Mexico and Tampico a body of thirty-three friars, who arrived in New Spain in 1687. A complete listing of this contingent is in AGI, Contratación 5.546. Father Ayeta returned to New Spain in 1689. Robles, *Diario,* 2:178. He seems to have been in Madrid in 1701 and died soon after. AGI, Indiferente General 3.054.

3. Toribio de la Huerta, who styled himself "one of the principal conquerors of the kingdoms of New Mexico, Sinaloa, and Sonora and discoverer of the kingdom of Gran Quivira, composed of four kings and an emperor, the end in that region of all Christendom," proposed to the crown in Madrid in 1689 a grand plan to restore New Mexico. Moreover, he would develop the allegedly rich silver mines of the Sierra Azul and Cerro Colorado, as well as a mercury mine he claimed to have discovered between the provinces of the Zuñis and the Hopis that would supply the demand of all New Spain. That the plan was seriously considered by the

Council of the Indies was a credit to Huerta's skill as a promoter. The government had little to lose, since none of the grandiose concessions he asked for was to be granted until after he had carried out the plan. Huerta spoke of spending 300,000 pesos on the endeavor, yet "because of his lack of means at present," the king provided 200 pesos to be paid to him in Spain and 400 in New Spain to cover the expenses of his return passage. In a cedula of 13 September 1689, the Conde de Galve was ordered to listen to Huerta's plan and judge its merits. Since Huerta evidently did not follow through, Galve asked Vargas to make an investigation of the purported mercury mine. Vargas did so in August 1691, and the findings proved negative. The pertinent documents are in AGN, Historia 37:3. See also José Manuel Espinosa, "The Legend of the Sierra Azul, with Special Emphasis upon the Part It Played in the Reconquest of New Mexico," NMHR 9 (Apr. 1934):113–58. As for Huerta, who boasted of forty years of experience in New Mexico, Sonora, and Sinaloa, surviving records do not confirm the major role he claimed for himself.

4. Perhaps Enrique de la Rosa was the same person, given the possibility of copyists' errors, as Enrique Varbosso or Balbossa, the agent in Cadiz who four years earlier, acting for Sáenz de Tagle, handled financial details of

Vargas's appointment as governor
of New Mexico. Title of governor
of New Mexico to Diego de

Vargas, Madrid, 18 June 1688,
AGI, México 1216.

———

15. *Diego de Vargas to Ignacio López de Zárate,*
El Paso del Río del Norte, 7 ——— 1693.*

Son and dear sir,

Although I am writing to my son, don Juan, I repeat my decision
to Your Lordship so that you may act on it, since this is all that we
can hope for. Your Lordship will be relieved and on your own to
assist whoever may enjoy the entails, assuming they have no encumbrance, and, with their own revenue, gradually redeem their censos.
Please observe the law and duties of a gentleman, thereby reciprocating the love and esteem I show you. I shall persevere in this government in service to the king our lord. I trust that, because of his
royal lineage, he will remunerate me in accord with the most excellent lord viceroy's report.

I am sending to Your Lordship the letter for my son so that you
may be informed of the position I have negotiated and arranged for
him. It seems to me that it will be most decorous, with the assurance of having what he needs to attend to his affairs. [1]

I am writing to my friend, the lord Marqués de Villanueva, so
that he may be informed and I may demonstrate how greatly I esteem
him. I shall also write to all my relatives by the flota (Our Lord giving me life). May God keep Your Lordship many years. El Paso del
Río del Norte, 7 ——— 1693.

Your most ——— father,
friend, and servant kisses Your
Lordship's hand,

Don Diego de Vargas Zapata
Luján Ponce de León [rubrica]

To lord Dr. don Ignacio López de Zárate, my son-in-law

*ARGD. ALS. One folio, two written pages. Apparently in haste, don Diego forgot to include not only the month, but also the adjective in the letter's closing. Given his travels in 1693, 7 January and 7 October are the most likely dates.

1. After long service as a page to both queens of Carlos II, Juan Manuel de Vargas Pimentel was named captain of heavy cavalry in 1695. Late that year, he set out for the Catalonian frontier. Letter 48 below.

---

16. *Diego de Vargas to Martín de Solís y Miranda, Santa Fe, 25 February 1696.**

My dear sir,[1]

I have had news from my son-in-law, don Ignacio López de Zárate. How important it would be to me, as Your Lordship's loyal servant and constant friend, to humbly esteem you in Mexico City with a personal show of affection. Because mine is a military government, I do not know whether it falls within Your Lordship's jurisdiction, which is over different matters. It seems to me that it comes under the legitimate jurisdiction of the lord fiscal of the Cámara of the Junta of War for the Indies. I know that both civil and military matters pertain to Your Lordship. This gives me great hope for my advancement. Your Lordship has recognized my undertakings and the services I have performed for his majesty in the restoration of this kingdom, which the royal crown possesses now as before the general uprising of 1680.

I shall summarize in a few points the value of my services, since Your Lordship is to compile the report that will bring them to the attention of the lords of the Cámara of the Royal and Supreme Council of the Indies. The first point records for you the expenditures for 1681, made with your approval when you were serving as lord fiscal for civil cases of the Royal Audiencia of Mexico City. In response to the news his majesty, the king our lord (may God keep him), had of the uprising of this kingdom in the previous year, 1680, he dispatched in 1681 his royal cedula to the most excellent lord Conde de Paredes, who was then viceroy. It directed him to put all the crown's resources into the restoration of this kingdom to his majesty and to the fold of Our Holy Faith.

Your Lordship is aware of this because it concurred with the opinions expressed in the Royal Treasury juntas that a draft be made. It was issued on the Royal Treasury office of Mexico City to the Rev. Father fray Francisco de Ayeta. He was going as procurator general to transport alms and friars in his majesty's wagons to this custody, which was in the pueblo of El Paso del Río del Norte, with the citizens and their governor, Gen. don Antonio de Otermín. This was done so that Father Ayeta might hand over the 90,000 pesos to the governor to pay the costs of the men-at-arms and assist the citizens. Thus, the conquest and restoration of this kingdom might begin.[2]

They did not succeed, finding the pueblos from Senecú on deserted. Only at Isleta, thirty leagues short of this villa, did they come to a pueblo inhabited by the Indians of the Tiwa nation. The Indians surrendered, and the general removed them. He resettled them in the district of the pueblo of El Paso.[3]

On this expedition alone, he spent the entire 90,000 pesos. He withdrew because of the protests of the men-at-arms and citizens. The reasons they presented to him were the rigor of the winter, the death of horses and draft mules, and other difficulties. Your Lordship will have better information about this than I, since necessarily the copy of the military proceedings of the expedition will have reached your hands.

I relate this only to prove how much it cost his majesty. In addition, an auxiliary payment of 30,000 pesos was requested. Taken together, the two amounted to 120,000, as is of record in the books of the Royal Treasury office in Mexico City.

Second, the expenditures of 1691 are of record as well, not only in the Royal Treasury office, but also, probably, in the Office of the Secretary for New Spain. They amounted to about 4,000 pesos and were confirmed by the Royal and Supreme Council of the Indies for the expedition Gen. don Domingo Jironza made to the pueblo of Zia when he was governor and captain general of this kingdom. Moreover, he obtained the grant his majesty the king (may God keep him) made to him, a robe of a military order for having conquered by fire and sword the Indians he encountered. Furthermore, the king ordered the most excellent lord viceroy that, in the event I had not already taken up this government, I should be provided for first and don Domingo should be reappointed. He was to be thanked in the king's name, as was done, and to be kept in mind for a better post.[4]

Third, in 1691 his majesty received and approved the memorial don Toribio de la Huerta presented. Huerta was entering into a contract with his majesty, as is of record. [note in left margin in different hand: This contract states the favors they were requesting for conquering New Mexico.] The text relates that he had been in this kingdom and had military experience and knowledge of the land and Indians. Thus, he was promising to conquer this kingdom, if his majesty gave him the following. First, he was to grant him of a title of Castile, marqués of all this kingdom and the provinces of Zuñi and Moqui; the mines of red ocher or vermilion ore, which yields mercury; and the riches of the Sierra Azul silver mine. [5]

In order to carry out this conquest, he was to be given: ten thousand head of cattle, five hundred armed men, the necessary wagons, munitions, supplies, and this government in perpetuity, along with the alcaldías mayores of Sonora and Sinaloa for three generations for his children, grandchildren, and successors. He was to appoint and install judges in the province of Moqui for the collection of royal revenue and mercury from the red-ocher mine. The privileges and asiento enjoyed by the miners of Huancavelica in the kingdom of Peru were to be reserved for him. [6]

His majesty sent this proposal to his Royal Council of the Indies, ordering that a dispatch be sent to his viceroy upon the first sailing of a packet boat for the kingdom of New Spain. He was to order the governor and captain general of this kingdom of New Mexico, who was in the pueblo of El Paso, to inquire and investigate not only whether it was true that there were red ocher, vermilion ore, and mines from which mercury might be extracted, but also the probable cost of an expedition to the province. By the packet boat in 1691, the most excellent lord viceroy, Conde de Galve, received the royal cedula and dispatched the order to me. Having made the investigation, I reported to his excellency that there is mercury ore, as is of record. I estimated what the expedition, survey, and sending the ore might cost, which proves the fourth point about the expense. [7]

Thus, in 1692, I carried out the general conquest of all this kingdom at my own expense. I could not go on to the province of Moqui without having conquered this kingdom first. Its natives and nations, as rebellious and bellicose Indians, would have united and made the expedition impossible by their resistance. This would have been even truer had the people of Acoma, learning of the expedition, come down from the mesa and joined with those of the Zuñi and Moqui provinces.

I faced, overcame, and conquered all this at my own expense, retaking possession on his majesty's behalf. I made the inquiry about the red ocher or vermilion ore, which is the mercury from the mine. I sent some with the copy of the military proceedings of the conquest to the most excellent lord viceroy, Conde de Galve. Having borne this expense, I placed it as a gift for his majesty at his royal feet, offering at the same time the triumph of so glorious an enterprise.

A summary of the points expressed in this letter should demonstrate the value, attention, and consideration that should be given them by Your Lordship and the lords minister serving on the Cámara of the Royal and Supreme Council of the Indies, so that you can report to his majesty. The reconquest of this kingdom doubled the value of my services. It was restored by force of arms, resulting in the settlement of eighteen missions, together with three Spanish villas. This included Santa Fe, with its fortress and presidio of one hundred mounted soldiers for the security and defense of all.

By means of the letters from the most excellent lord viceroy, Conde de Galve, and the lords of the Junta of the Royal Treasury of Mexico City reporting to his majesty in my favor, Your Lordship will recognize the proven nobility of it all. This will also be of record for the lords of the royal council in the recommendation and advice they give to his majesty. They have evidence of the magnitude of my services—the adversities and obstacles—from the reports and opinions the most excellent lord viceroy prepared from the earlier proceedings.

The greater the risks and obstacles contemplated, the more my spirit was kindled, moving me to carry out the conquest at my own expense, not risking anything of his majesty's royal wealth. And so, I can speak with the respect and attentiveness of his humble and loyal vassal, with the liberty of asking that he honor me and grant what I am asking my agent, Juan González Calderón, and my son-in-law, don Ignacio, to seek most persistently.

Heretofore, I have acted with restraint and modesty, as can be seen from the justness with which I prove the request I humbly make to Your Lordship. It is fitting for a gentleman of such illustrious lineage to favor someone who, by risking himself, seeks rewards and promotions. For some, it is necessary to request them, even after having earned them with fortune undone, because wealth is necessary for those who would be at his majesty's side.

I am shipping to Your Lordship a hundred cakes of chocolate that my son-in-law, don Ignacio, will send with the letter. I am at your service, ready in whatever way I may be of use, hoping that Our Lord will keep you many happy years. Done in this villa of Santa Fe, 25 February 1696.

To lord don Martín de Solís y Miranda

*ARGD. Unsigned C. Four folios, eight written pages. Another copy, incomplete, has four folios, seven written pages.

1. Lic. Martín de Solís y Miranda had been criminal fiscal (1671–72), civil fiscal (1672–81), and oidor (1681–86) in the Audiencia of Mexico. Returning to Spain, he had served as a judge in the Chancillería of Granada. Solís was promoted from Granada to the position of fiscal of the Council of the Indies on 22 April 1690, at which time he donated 5,000 doblones to the crown. On 22 June 1696, he was again promoted, now to the position of councilor. He died in office in 1706. Schäfer, *Consejo Real,* 1:365, 369; 2:457–58, 464, 466.

2. Before becoming governor of New Mexico in 1677, Antonio de Otermín had served as a captain in Sonora. Otermín was in office when the Pueblo Indians united in revolt in 1680. After resisting their siege of Santa Fe for nine days, he led the survivors in a retreat to the El Paso area. In November 1681, the governor led an expedition, numbering some 150 men, upriver to attempt the reconquest of the province. On 5 December, Otermín's force surprised the inhabitants of Isleta, easily taking the pueblo. Otermín then divided his command, sending Juan Domínguez de Mendoza north with half the force. Domínguez advanced as far as Cochití, where on 17 September the enemy's superior numbers and the danger of entrapment caused him to retreat. The advancing Otermín met the retreating Domínguez at Sandia pueblo. On 23–24 December, the governor held a junta de guerra. The horses were weak, provisions low, and the weather bad. It was decided to return to Isleta. On 1 January 1682, Otermín announced the removal of the inhabitants of Isleta to the El Paso area. Of 511 Indians captured in early December, 385 were relocated. The others had joined the rebels. This failed attempt at reconquest demonstrated the seriousness of the Pueblo Indians' bid for independence and the need for a large and well-equipped force to bring them back under Spanish control. Hackett and Shelby, *Revolt of the Pueblo Indians,* 1:cxi–ccix. DRSW, Biofile. Late in 1691, Otermín, the former governor, testified in Mexico City regarding the proposed reconquest of New Mexico, suggesting that the alleged mines in the province of Moqui be

secured first. Antonio de Otermín to Conde de Galve, Mexico City, 11 Dec. 1691, AGN, Historia 37:3. Espinosa, "Sierra Azul," 144.

In 1616, the Franciscans raised the mission field in New Mexico to the status of custody. The custody of La Conversión de San Pablo thus became a semiautonomous administrative body within the province of El Santo Evangelio, based in Mexico City. It remained so during the entire colonial period, and its superior, or custos, was elected by the authorities of the province. France V. Scholes, "Problems in the Early Ecclesiastical History of New Mexico," NMHR 7 (Jan. 1932):32–74. Scholes and Lansing B. Bloom, "Friar Personnel and Mission Chronology, 1598–1629," NMHR 19 (Oct. 1944):319–36.

3. Otermín and Ayeta resettled the Tiwa-speaking Pueblo Indians of Isleta at Corpus Christi de la Isleta, known as Ysleta del Sur, between Senecú del Sur and Socorro del Sur. The latter two communities had been formed by Piros and Tiwas who accompanied retreating Spaniards in 1680. The three pueblos were located downriver from El Paso del Norte. Ortiz, *Southwest*, 9:336–39.

4. Partly as a result of Jironza's Zia expedition, the crown recommended that he be continued in office, despite the fact that Vargas already was in possession of an appointment to the same post. Vargas, aware of the possibility of Jironza's reappoint-

ment, successfully petitioned the viceregal authorities in Mexico City to block Jironza. The king to Conde de Galve, Madrid, 21 July 1692, AGI, Guadalajara 73. Walz, "El Paso Area," 261–63.

5. Vermilion, a bright red pigment of mercuric sulfide, is obtained from the mineral cinnabar, the only important mercury-bearing ore. The presence of cinnabar would have indicated an exploitable source of mercury, indispensible for refining silver by the amalgamation process. Red ocher, however, was easily mistaken for vermilion. It is also red, but of an earthy shade, and consists of ferric oxide.

6. The mercury mines at Huancavelica, Peru, were a royal monopoly. Exploitation was leased to the mining guild through contract (asiento), whereby the miners pledged to produce a specified amount of mercury during a specified time, in return for the crown's provision of Indian labor and cash advances and its promise to buy the mercury at a predetermined price. Arthur Preston Whitaker, *The Huancavelica Mercury Mine: A Contribution to the History of the Bourbon Renaissance in the Spanish Empire* (Cambridge, Mass., 1941):9–12; and Guillermo Lohmann Villena, *Las minas de Huancavelica en los siglos xvi y xvii* (Seville, 1949).

7. The investigation lasted from 3 to 12 August 1691. Documents concerning the Sierra Azul, AGN, Historia 37:3.

17. *Diego de Vargas to Ignacio López de Zárate, Santa Fe, 4 January 1697.*[*]

Son and dear sir,

This will serve to inform Your Lordship that I am well, thanks to Our Lord, and trusting in His Divine Majesty that the most excellent lord, Conde de Galve, has arrived in Madrid. For with a prince so great (second only to God Our Lord), I hope that in his munificence he will report to his majesty so that it may move his royal will to reward me for my continued services.

Because of my wish to disencumber my entails, I am remitting to Your Lordship those 10,000 pesos. Four thousand will go by my dear friend, don Juan de Alvarado. I asked my agent, Mre. de campo don Luis Sáenz de Tagle, to hand over 6,000 to his nephew, don Francisco Díaz de Tagle, for him to remit to Cadiz.[1] From Cadiz, the person to whom they are given in Mexico City can put them in a draft in Your Lordship's favor in Madrid, together with the expense of their conveyance by sea and land. It may be that the person to whom don Juan de Alvarado delivers the money will have more than enough for the costs. Hence, the amount may be more than 10,000 pesos.

With this amount, Your Lordship will please disencumber immediately all my entails and redeem their censos, including the one of 100 ducados paid to Lic. Juan Díaz. Please send me a certified copy of this disencumbrance. With it, I shall arrange something to my advantage in this kingdom. I want to have security against any unexpected event or mishap and always have this credit against these entails. I am thinking of unforeseen events, put on my guard by so many difficulties during my prolonged absence. Your Lordship, as so experienced an investor, will appreciate my precaution. Therefore, I place the matter in your hands as I have done with all my entails.

It also occurs to me to tell Your Lordship that should his majesty, the king our lord (may God keep him), honor me, among the favors I hope for from his royal hand is a robe of one of the three military orders, that of Santiago. I have attained such good results through prayer on this glorious saint's day. As soon as I am granted this, Your Lordship will please take whatever may be necessary from the money for the cost of my pruebas.[2]

My father, don Alonso de Vargas, belonged to the Order of Santiago. My paternal grandfather, don Lorenzo de Vargas, also belonged. The brother of my grandmother, my lady doña Antonia Ponce de León, wore the robe of Calatrava. My maternal grandfather, don Diego de Contreras, was a familiar of the Inquisition for the Supreme Council and inspector and paymaster of the army of Catalonia when the king our lord, Felipe IV, went to visit the Catalonian expeditionary army. In addition, my mother, doña María Margarita de Contreras, was the daughter of don Diego de Contreras and doña Beatriz de Arráiz Berrasueta.

This information complements the testimony I gave of being the legitimate son of the above in order to take control of my entails. This document was executed in the presence of Vicente Suárez, escribano del número of that villa of Madrid, in 1666 and was valid until 1672.[3] Because I am in this kingdom, the last on earth, I choose to put on the robe myself. May the cedula be issued, and may Your Lordship send it to me, so that any knight of that order may give me the robe and invest me in the nearest church and place. May it permit me to be away from my government to put on this robe, leaving a lieutenant in my stead and at my risk. May my leave of absence be understood to be for a hundred days and no more.[4] I have come to this decision, because in two years, on the feast day of St. James, I have had at great risk two victories of the utmost importance and I attribute them to miracles from heaven.[5] I want to wear that robe and have made a vow to St. James: if I return to Spain, I shall visit his holy shrine.[6]

Having seen this letter—since it will arrive after his majesty will have already favored me—Your Lordship will please request this grant. Then, request the documentation at once in order to send me the dispatches, I mean, the royal cedula, on the earliest packet boat. Your Lordship will please send me the chapter cloak made in Madrid and a dozen insignia, both large ones for long capes and small ones to put on cassocks. Please have everything ready and waiting at Cadiz for shipment by the first packet boat.

To my beloved daughter, Isabel, and grandchildren I give my blessing. May God keep Your Lordship in their company many years. Done in this villa of Santa Fe, 4 January 1691.

Your most affectionate father
who esteems you from the heart
kisses Your Lordship's hand,

Don Diego de Vargas Zapata
Luján Ponce de León [rubrica]

To my son-in-law, lord don Ignacio López de Zárate

*AMNB. ALS. Three folios, six written pages. The text of folio 2v is contin-
ued, written vertically, in the left-hand margin of the same folio and is
then carried over to folio 3r.

1. Francisco Díaz de Tagle regularly handled the provision and
conveyance of supplies to Vargas
in New Mexico. Pedro Rodríguez
Cubero, Proceedings against Diego
de Vargas, Santa Fe, June 1698,
UNM, SC, Thomas Benton Catron
Collection, PC 29, 803, Box 1,
Folder 1.

2. During the seventeenth
century, entry into one of the three
military orders of Santiago,
Calatrava, and Alcántara was an
obsession among the middling
nobility, primarily for the prestige
it conferred. Before receiving
knighthood in an order, the
aspirant had to undergo the
pruebas in order to prove his
nobility. These were written
testimonials expressed in formulaic
language. Early in the century,
standards for proof of nobility had
become lax, mainly because of
complaints about the slowness of
the prueba process. The situation
deteriorated until, by the 1640s,
knighthood was being sold. This
provoked a meeting of the three
orders in 1652, the express purpose
of which was to reestablish esteem
for membership and to raise
standards for proof of nobility and

purity of blood. In the reign of
Carlos II, the sale of knighthood
ceased altogether. In the actual
prueba process, witnesses answered
a customary list of questions about
the aspirant. This testimony,
authenticated by three escribanos,
was then presented to the Council
of the Orders. It had to show that
the petitioner was legitimate; a
noble by birth, and not by royal
concession; had no admixture of
Moorish or Jewish blood; and had
never been charged by the
Inquisition. Papal dispensations
were possible except in the case of
Jewish blood. Antonio Domínguez
Ortiz, *La sociedad española en el
siglo xvii* (Madrid, 1963),
1:198–209; Guillermo Lohmann
Villena, *Los americanos en las
órdenes militares*, 1529–1900
(Madrid, 1947), 1:lx-lxii; and
Wright, "Military Orders," 34–43.

3. Diego de Vargas, Proof of
Legitimacy, Madrid, 21 June
1672, AHPM, P. 10.956.

4. Among the books in don
Diego's possession in New Mexico
when he died in 1704 was a
manual on the military orders,
*Tesoro militar de cavallería.
Antiguo y moderno modo de armar*

cavalleros, y professar, según las
ceremonias de qualquier orden
militar. . . (Madrid, 1642), by José
Micheli y Márquez. Cited in
Adams, "Two Colonial New
Mexico Libraries," 150.

5. The two victories Vargas

referred to were at Jemez in 1694
and near Santa Clara in 1696.

6. The most famous objective of
pilgrims in Spain was Santiago de
Compostela in Galicia, in the
extreme northwest.

---

18. *Diego de Vargas to Juan Antonio López de Zárate, Marqués de Villanueva de la Sagra, Santa Fe, 4 January 1697.**

Friend and dear sir,

I am writing without having had letters from Your Lordship up to today's date, on which I am dispatching a second courier to Mexico City. I shall be delighted to receive your letters, because I can have no greater pleasure than news of your good health.

In view of the fact that time is passing, I do not want to delay my decisions, but to undertake the remittance of 10,000 pesos by the ships returning to Spain. I am writing the same thing to my son-in-law, lord don Ignacio. I am remitting 4,000 pesos by the hand and agency of my friend, don Juan de Alvarado, and 6,000 pesos with Afz. don Francisco Díaz de Tagle, and his uncle, Mre. de Campo don Luis Sáenz de Tagle, knight of the Order of Alcántara, all citizens of Mexico City. With the 10,000 pesos, lord don Ignacio will disencumber my entails, censos, and charges. I am advising you that I want to have credit against my entails.

I trust that with the arrival of the most excellent lord Conde de Galve my petitions will be fulfilled as is my wish.[1] I am telling my son-in-law, lord don Ignacio, everything that occurs to me, which is why I refer to that letter. In the second place, I am sending this to Your Lordship so that the letter's contents will be carried out. I am directing this letter to Your Lordship early in case there may be a packet boat leaving. If not, the remittance I am entrusting to my friend, don Juan de Alvarado, in this packet and dispatch will be ready. I shall be delighted if Your Lordship and my son-in-law, lord don Ignacio, are satisfied with the remittance I made in the previous flota of 1696; that everything arrived in good condition and on time, as I trust, since I was so determined to get out of debt; and that from this, one can see the esteem I have for my children.

If I wish for another post, it is because I see my children so burdened with their children. The court provides one enough to live on, but not enough to become rich. We see want, and the greatest scarcity is among the sought-after nobility. Everything is an illusion, depending on many people for any advantage. Therefore, my disillusionment makes me ever mindful of acquiring what I need to fulfill my duties.

May God keep Your Lordship the happy years I wish. In this letter, I am not trying to do more than to give notice of the remittance. I am sending it early so that the conveyance to Veracruz will be made in time. Done in this villa of Santa Fe, 4 January 1697.

Your most affectionate friend and
servant kisses Your Lordship's hand,

Don Diego de Vargas Zapata
Luján Ponce de León [rubrica]

To lord Marqués de Villanueva

*AMNB. ALS. Two folios, four written pages.

1. The Conde de Galve was in poor health throughout the later years of his time in New Spain. He died either on the return voyage or shortly after arriving in Spain in March 1697. Arteaga y Falguera, *La Casa del Infantado*, 152. J. Ignacio, *Introducción al estudio de los virreyes de Nueva España, 1535–1746* (Mexico City, 1955), Rubio Mañé, 1:259, writes that Galve died soon after disembarking on 12 March 1697. According to Pierre, Marquis de Villars, *Mémoires de la cour d'Espagne de 1679 à 1681* (Paris, 1893):224, death occurred on 11 March while the former viceroy was still on the vessel. The most authoritative source states that he saw Galve's lifeless body shortly after the ringing of the bells for evening prayer on 12 March. Galve had been taken to the home of his friend, the Duque de Alburquerque, in Puerto de Santa María. Antonio Felipe de Mora, Certification of death, Puerto de Santa María, 12 Mar. 1697, AHPM, P. 12.118.

19. *Diego de Vargas to Isabel María de Vargas Pimentel, Santa Fe, 17 April 1697.**

My darling daughter,

I am writing to you in haste, so that my letter may overtake the packet for the flota. It only amounts to asking out of love and duty after your health and that of my beloved grandchildren, for I hope that you are all well. I remain (thanks be to God) in this government, which is what I am writing to my son-in-law, lord don Ignacio, although in passing, informing him of my wishes. He will carry out in full the content of the letters I wrote him during the month of January.

May God keep you, my beloved daughter, the many years I wish for you. Done in this villa of Santa Fe, 17 April 1697.

Your father who esteems
and loves you from the heart,

Don Diego de Vargas Zapata
Luján Ponce de León [rubrica]

To my daughter, doña Isabel de Vargas Pimentel

*ARGD. LS. One folio, two written pages.

Confinement in Santa Fe, 1698–99

20. *Diego de Vargas to Ignacio López de Zárate, Santa Fe, 30 September 1698.**

Son and dear sir,

I am writing to Your Lordship principally to extend to you condolences on the death of the lord Marqués de Villanueva, your brother.[1] In this villa of Santa Fe, I received the news from my brother-in-law, don Gregorio Pimentel, dated at Torrelaguna, 4 April this year. I have not received a letter from Your Lordship, but I realize that your preoccupations are considerable because of this sad event. I know how much this will have hurt you, just as it did me. It caused me as much grief as it did Your Lordship, and were I to say greater, it would be believable because of your favorable opinion of him, given that I had never met him. He engendered so much affection by letter that I wish I had known him personally. My good fortune in enjoying his friendship through correspondence was the result of the marriage of my daughter, Isabel, to Your Lordship.

You will know by now of my dire misfortune, having been told by Capt. don Antonio Valverde, who was captain of this presidio and went to Spain by the flota that set sail at the end of May.[2] Having enjoyed good fortune in everything, thanks to Our Lord, it was then His will to cast me into this purgatory of imprisonment where I have been since 2 October 1697.

Because of the news Your Lordship intended for me of the grants his majesty, the king our lord (may God keep him), had made to me in recognition of my services, he who now governs was able to prolong his absolute power over me. I wish to God that Your Lordship had sent me the royal cedula reappointing me to this government and that you had not written me that letter, or that it had been lost rather than reach my hands. It became the instrument of the present governor, don Pedro Rodríguez Cubero, whose cousin and agent, don Alonso de Buendía, is comptroller general of the Council of the Indies.[3] With this news, he insisted that the cabildo of this kingdom file claims against me. Its members are compliant, and as people who come to settle such remote lands where recourse is so distant, they did as he wished, induced and prevailed upon, some out of terror, some out of self-interest, and still others because of their evil nature.

Although most of them do not know how to read or even sign their names, the secretary and the governor made them sign and testify to the most malicious and perverse things, making false accusations, calumnies, and very serious charges against me. All this was done with the aim of delaying me during the time required for his review by whoever may come to govern the kingdom once his grant is put into effect.

The present governor made these efforts on his own authority by means of a writ of 23 September 1697. I appealed to his excellency and the Royal Audiencia, presenting several petitions, maintaining that he was not my competent judge and that his jurisdiction had expired 11 August, when the thirty-day term of my residencia was up.[4]

Nevertheless, I find myself a prisoner of absolute power since 2 October 1697. My slaves, mules, and clothing, and even that of the members of my household, have been sold. Because of this, they were providing for me from outside, but were prevented from seeing or visiting me, even the friars. The governor writes to the provincial about those who manage to see me, asking that they be removed and made to leave the kingdom. For this reason, three are leaving this month, aware of wrong, tyranny, and injustice. Hence, I am totally lost, without anyone knowing anything of me, because it is impossible for me to be sure that they will carry a letter for me.

I was notified on the 23rd of the present month of a directive from the most excellent lord viceroy with the opinion by the lord fiscal. I was ordered to post bond as a result of the accusations and charges that could be brought against me in the Royal Treasury. I was also to post a surety bond in the amount of 13,500 pesos with the governor, don Pedro Cubero. The directive came, commissioning an alcalde to notify me. I replied that I was challenging his jurisdiction because I had been honored by his majesty with reappointment to this government and captaincy general and granted a title of Castile. I was insisting on and reintroducing my appeals presented before the most excellent lord viceroy, the lords of the Royal Junta and Acuerdo of the Audiencia of Mexico City, and the lord fiscal.

I am preparing a report of my services, citing the certifications also in the directives. I conclude that though I was not asked to post bond for the conquest I made at my own expense of this entire kingdom and its provinces, I am now being asked to do so in order to leave. With regard to the debt of the surety bond, under the challenge of jurisdiction I was calling into question the competence of the alcalde ordinario as judge. I appealed to the most excellent lord viceroy, the lord fiscal, and Royal Junta and Acuerdo. Once my objections are presented and I am given a fair hearing as one without defense in these parts, I shall be ready as a loyal vassal of his majesty to give an accounting, because I had an interest in it. I recognized as my competent judges, entirely and exclusively, the most excellent lord viceroy and the lords of the Tribunal of Accounts, to whom alone by royal law of the *Nueva Recopilación* I must give an accounting and the lords must accept it from me.[5]

I have made this brief report to Your Lordship so that you may have this information should the party, out of malice, resort to writing and giving his account in the Council of the Indies to assure his continuation in office, as I expect he will. I shall regret my loss of continuation in this government not because of its advantages, but because of the loss of an honor appreciated by any man of my station. It is not right that with baseless, paper charges obtained by such malevolent means I should be injured and imprisoned, when I am so deserving because of my services and when the hearing of the case by the most excellent lord viceroy and royal junta is pending. The party has proceeded with such malice that he himself retains the residencia he took of me—whose term ran out on 28 August 1697—and that of the justicia mayor of El Paso. Neither residencia contained a valid claim or charge against either of us, since everything said in censure was null because, in addition to being false, the term of the residencia had passed.[6]

I reiterate to Your Lordship that the governor can avail himself of his cousin, don Alonso de Buendía. He says that with a gift and a few false charges, he will see if he can obtain his continuation and have mine understood to come after his term of government has expired, which is what his cousin has written.

I am not writing to Your Lordship about anything regarding the disposition of my property, except that Your Lordship should assist my daughter, Juana, with the 2,000 reales of revenue from the dehesa of Las Gariñas. I am writing to you that it weighs heavily upon me to be in this prison and not able to lovingly assist her as I would like.

May God keep Your Lordship in the company of my beloved daughter, Isabel, and my grandchildren the many happy years I wish for you. Our Lord giving me life, wherever He wills me to be and whatever my circumstances, I shall write to Your Lordship by the flota. The present is for me more grievous than if I were captive in Algiers. Done in this villa of Santa Fe, 30 September 1698.

As I have not received a letter from Your Lordship in the packet boat that arrived in New Spain on 11 July, I do not know the status of the grants; of the decision regarding the selection I have sent to Your Lordship of the name of the title, the Conde de Barcinas; or whether his majesty's grant is of conde or marqués. In the letter I wrote to his majesty from this villa on 16 October 1692, I asked that he favor me, giving me lordship over the villages of Los Caramancheles. Therefore, even if Your Lordship has not acted on my petition, please begin first, to find out if it can be obtained and to see whether those villages will pay his majesty a pledge. If so, it must be with the alcabalas, lordship, and complete authority.

Your Lordship will please advise me regarding this point. With the information you have, and now with the honors of royal councilor who enjoys seniority (for which I congratulate you), you can easily find out. You will also please advise me about: the packet I entrusted to don Juan de Alvarado; the marriages I was suggesting, according to my wishes, for my son don Juan Manuel; and the other favor for my robe of Santiago. In case the encomienda for 6,000 pesos is not obtained, the grant might be exchanged for an encomienda of the Order of Santiago, even though of less revenue.[7]

My detention and the misfortune of my imprisonment in this kingdom have hindered me in the arrangement and sending of what I proposed. Either I would have sent it by the flota or I would have brought it myself. For the moment, I must delay. I ask Your Lordship that in my name you kiss the hand of your cousin, lord don Antonio de Ubilla, and that you give him the letter in which I congratulate him, offering my services.[8]

Your father, who esteems and
loves you from the heart and wishes
to serve you, kisses Your
Lordship's hand,

Don Diego de Vargas Zapata
Luján Ponce de León [rubrica]

To lord don Ignacio López de Zárate, my son-in-law and lord

*ARGD. LS. Two folios, four written pages. Folio 2v contains in the left margin the following notations of material to be inserted " + Jurisdicion alta y/baja mero y mixto/Ymperio;" " + de mi *h*avito de/Santiago en Caso/de que no se llogre/la encomienda y/se permite en Una/encomienda de la/orden de Santiago aun/que sea de Corta Renta y no de/la *d*icha de los seys mil."

1. The Marqués de Villanueva de la Sagra, Juan Antonio López de Zárate y Alvarez de Medina, Ignacio López de Zárate's brother and a member of the Order of Santiago, received his title on 7 January 1686. Alonso-Cadenas, *Elenco*, 699. From 1697 to 1698, don Juan Antonio held the position of Secretario del Despacho

Universal. This post, created in 1621, was particularly prestigious and important by the late seventeenth century. The secretario's job was to transmit the orders of the king (or his chief minister) and to present affairs of state to the monarch. Juan Antonio López de Zárate died in Madrid in 1698, leaving no heirs. As a result, his brother, Ignacio, inherited the title. José Antonio Escudero, *Los secretarios de estado y del despacho, 1474–1724* (Madrid, 1969), 2: "Cuadros sinópticos de los secretarios de Estado y del Despacho"; Kamen, *Spain*, 28–29.

2. Antonio Valverde had left New Mexico in the summer of 1697 and sailed for Spain the following year, both to defend Vargas in Madrid and to seek for himself the captaincy of the El Paso presidio and the alcaldía mayor of its district. Having been appointed captain, he returned to New Spain in 1699, where he found himself involved in a dispute with Rodríguez Cubero's appointee to the same post. Valverde won viceregal approval to assume the captaincy in 1700 and, later the same year, also became alcalde mayor of the El Paso district, subordinate to the governor of New Mexico. Espinosa, *Crusaders*, 331.

In 1716, Antonio Valverde was appointed interim governor of New Mexico, a position conferred upon him in his own right in 1718. His term, which lasted until 1722, saw active efforts to ascertain and oppose French intrusion into Spanish territory across the Great Plains. Valverde himself reconnoitered as far as the Arkansas River in late 1719 and the following year dispatched the expedition under Capt. Pedro de Villasur, massacred near the North Platte River by Pawnees inspired by Frenchmen. Addison E. Sheldon, "The Massacre of the Villasur Expedition at the Forks of the Platte River, August 12, 1720," *Nebraska History* 7 (July-Sept. 1924):68–81; and Alfred Barnaby Thomas, ed. and trans., *After Coronado: Spanish Exploration Northeast of New Mexico, 1696–1727* (Norman, 1935):26–42, 110–37, 219–45.

When Valverde's governorship ended in 1722, he returned to El Paso and resumed his post as captain. He died there on 15 December 1728. Chavez, *Origins*, 304. Hubert Howe Bancroft, *History of Arizona and New Mexico, 1530–1888* (Albuquerque, 1962):238 n. 29.

3. Alonso de Buendía was comptroller of the Council of the Indies from 7 December 1689 to 26 January 1723, when he died in office. His father-in-law, Luis Antonio Daza, originally purchased the post for him for 1,000 doblones. As comptroller, he was responsible for reviewing royal accounts sent from the Indies, particularly those from the Tribunals of Accounts, and taking the accounts of the treasurer of the Council of the Indies every two years. Schäfer, *Consejo Real*, 1:373; *Recop.*, Lib. 2, tít. 11, leyes 1–8.

4. A competent judge was one who heard only those cases that fell legitimately within his jurisdiction. Joaquín Escriche, *Diccionario razonado de legislación y jurisprudencia* (Bogotá, 1977), 3:242.

5. *Recop.*, Lib. 5, tít. 15, ley 34.

6. The residencia was a judicial review of an official's conduct at the end of his term. The purpose was to take testimony and to determine whether the official had performed satisfactorily and honestly during his administration. *Recop.*, Lib. 5, tít. 15, leyes 1–45. A querella was a criminal complaint between parties. Escriche, *Diccionario razonado*, 4:420–21. It would appear that Vargas was purposely confusing the two, because if the charges brought against him, after the thirty-day period of his residencia had run, were taken as a continuation of those proceedings, and not as a separate querella, they would not have been allowed under the law.

7. The military orders possessed encomiendas, revenues produced on lands under their jurisdiction. Individuals who were assigned to oversee such encomiendas were known as comendadores. Valentín Vázquez de Prada, ed. *Historia económica y social de España* (Madrid, 1978), 3:165.

8. Antonio de Ubilla y Medina served as the Secretario del Perú on the Council of the Indies from 13 July 1695 to 1699; from January 1698, he simultaneously held the post of Secretario del Despacho Universal. In the latter position, he succeeded the Marqués de Villanueva de la Sagra. Schäfer, *Consejo Real*, 1:371, 430; Gabriel Maura Gamazo, *Vida y reinado de Carlos II* (Madrid, 1954), 1:181; Kamen, *Spain*, 29.

---

21. *Diego de Vargas to Isabel María de Vargas Pimentel, Santa Fe, 30 September 1698.**

My darling daughter,

Although I am writing condolences to my son-in-law, lord don Ignacio, on the death of the lord Marqués de Villanueva, his brother, my friend and lord (may he be in glory), I am also telling you. I recognize among your duties the expression of proper sentiment at such a loss. If by chance my lady, the marquesa, is still living, you will please express my condolences to her, whose feet I kiss many times, assuring her that I am humbly, though uselessly, at her service, for I esteemed the lord marqués with special affection.[1]

As I said, I am writing to you only so that you may express my condolences. You and my beloved son-in-law, lord don Ignacio, and my grandchildren can be certain of my benevolence. Our Lord giving me life, I shall write to you at greater length by the flota concerning the state of my fortune. May God keep you, my beloved daughter, the happy years I wish for you. Santa Fe, 30 September 1698.

Your father who loves you with
every consideration of the heart
and who wishes for your well-being
and to serve you,

Don Diego de Vargas Zapata
Luján Ponce de León [rubrica]

To my beloved daughter, doña Isabel María de Vargas

I am writing to your brother and my son, don Juan, in the packet for my brother-in-law, don Gregorio, believing that he is in Flanders.[2] If I should be able to do something for you, I shall do so. Though I suffer misfortunes and hardships, they are borne in the interest of all of you. For this reason, I regret that the royal cedula was not dispatched to me. Don Alonso de Buendía wrote in the letter to his cousin, my successor, that my son-in-law, lord don Ignacio, had written to him 29 January that he had not had the royal cedula copied. He had obtained from his majesty the assurance that it would be understood that I would begin my term once his cousin, don Pedro Rodríguez Cubero, completed his five years.[3]

*AMNB. LS. One folio, one written page. Two postscripts are written vertically in the left-hand margin, the second in Vargas's hand.

1. Doña Luisa de Loyola. Letter 36 below.

2. Evidently Juan Manuel de Vargas Pimentel was not in Flanders. By this time, unknown to his father, he must have been planning to come to the Indies.

3. As late as January 1699, don Ignacio still had not had the cedula copied. Cámara of the Council of the Indies, Madrid, 7 Jan. 1699, AGI, Guadalajara 141:24.

22. *Diego de Vargas to Ignacio López de Zárate, Santa Fe, 9 October 1698.* *

Son and dear sir,

I have already written to Your Lordship this month regarding the attempt on the part of don Pedro Rodríguez Cubero, present governor of this kingdom, to ignore the continuation in office that his majesty, the king our lord (may God keep him), has granted to me. A letter from the governor's cousin, don Alonso de Buendía, comptroller of the Royal Council of the Indies, was passed along to me. If what he advises is true (that only after the governor has completed his five years would I begin the exercise of this government and that Your Lordship, as of 29 January 1698, had not yet made the legal copies of my appointment), then I am compelled to doubt Your Lordship's affection.

I am asking you to earnestly seek a better post for me, advancing my petition for the government and captaincy general of Buenos Aires, which they call the Río de la Plata; in second place, for Panama; in third place, for Concepción, in Chile, which is a government equivalent to this kingdom; and in fourth place, for the island of Havana, governed by don Diego de Córdoba. Your Lordship can intercede for the favor of my lady, the Condesa de Galve—because of the great help I received from his excellency (may he be in glory)—and of don Juan Manuel de Vargas Lodeña, who was his secretary when his excellency was viceroy. [1] Please have lord don Antonio de Ubilla use whatever influence he can regarding my petition.

For my part, I shall repay Your Lordship in every way for any debt you may incur. I aspire to governments independent of the jurisdiction of a lord viceroy. I could go and have no superior, of course, and would not need a new appointment, as do those subject to such supervision. They need to petition again, and at times their appointments are delayed.

Therefore, I am asking Your Lordship again to please address my complaint and the just resentment I feel over your sending me news of the grant but not the cedula in your letter of April 1697. Following this news, everything has happened to me that I related to you in my letter of the first of this month from this villa, where I am still imprisoned by the governor's absolute power.

May God keep Your Lordship the many happy years I wish for you. Santa Fe, 9 October 1698.

Your father who esteems you
from the heart and wishes for your
well-being kisses Your Lordship's hand,

Don Diego de Vargas Zapata
Luján Ponce de León [rubrica]

To lord don Ignacio López de Zárate, my son-in-law

I forgot to ask Your Lordship in the first place to make every effort in
my petition for the presidency of Guatemala. Please intercede for
me with the two former most excellent ladies vicereine of the kingdom of New Spain, the Condesa de Paredes,[2] whom Your Lordship
can ask very candidly, assuring her that with my zeal I shall know
how to return her largess, and likewise the Condesa de Galve. If
lord don Pedro de la Bastida, who was promoted from the Audiencia
of Mexico to Granada, should be in Madrid, he can make a specific
report about me because he knows me.[3]

*ARGD. LS. One folio, two written pages. The postscript regarding the gov-
ernorship of Guatemala is written vertically in the left-hand margin of folio
1r.

1. Galve's secretary signed his name Juan Francisco de Vargas Manuel de Lodeña. Sailing clearance, Cadiz, 30 June 1688, AGI, Contratación 5.450:47. In 1698, the Condesa de Galve was Gelvira María de Toledo. Arteaga y Falguera, *La Casa del Infantado*, 2:138.

2. Doña María Luisa Manrique de Lara y Gonzaga was the Condesa de Paredes in 1698. Rivera Cambas, *Gobernantes*, 1:252. When the Conde de Paredes died in 1692, his son, don José Francisco de la Cerda Manrique de Lara, was appointed to his father's seat on the Council of the Indies, despite the fact that he was only nine years old at the time. Schäfer, *Consejo Real*, 1:278–83, 364; 2:440.

3. Lic. Pedro de la Bastida was a member of the Council of the Indies from 16 December 1697 to 24 August 1699; he died in office. He had previously served as oidor on the Chancillería at Granada, fiscal for civil proceedings for the Audiencia of Mexico (24 July 1681–21 December 1686), and oidor on the Audiencia of Guadalajara (6 April 1680–24 July 1681). Schäfer, *Consejo Real*, 1:366; 2:458, 464, 496.

23. Diego de Vargas to Ignacio López de Zárate, Santa Fe, 11 March 1699.*

Son and dear sir,

As long ago as 1 October 1698, I had written to Your Lordship about the wretched state of my fortune. I am not repeating to you that the cause was your omission, not sending to me the official copy of the grant that his majesty (may God keep him) had made to me for this government, though you did send me the news. Had this letter been lost, it would have been better for me.

Because of this news, the present governor, don Pedro Rodríguez Cubero, prevailed upon the cabildo, justicia, and regimiento, insisting that it keep my grant from being put into effect. On his own, with absolute power, he first made me a prisoner on 2 October 1697. I do not know when my redemption from this vile captivity will come. May God pardon Your Lordship, for I suffer and do not know whether I shall lose my life. God Our Lord has favored me with his infinite mercy so that I may resist such persecution and the very real danger of being lost. I am already as good as dead, seeing myself so unprotected and defenseless.

With me in these straits, Your Lordship has not sent the official copies by the frequent packet boats and flotas. Instead, the governor received a letter, dated Madrid, 29 January 1698, from his cousin, don Alonso de Buendía. He said that Your Lordship had not had the legal copies made. From this, I came to know more fully how ill-starred I am, and, because of your great omission, how poorly my esteem and affection for Your Lordship were returned. Moreover, don Alonso wrote to the governor that his majesty had made the grant with the understanding that mine should begin after the five years of don Pedro Rodríguez Cubero's government.

At present, the governor, having recourse to his cousin, requests that he seek from his majesty the favor of continuation in office for another five years, using the letters in which the cabildo of this kingdom speaks for him. In them, I am slandered. He is sending the certified copy of the proceedings and case maliciously brought against me, taking advantage of the fact that a decision has not been handed down by the superior government of Mexico City. He does not expect that it will be rendered for a long time.

All this was done so that the case might be heard by the Supreme Council of the Indies, its review delayed, time wasted, and my services obscured. He also tried to show that my reports to his majesty of what I have performed in his royal service were perverse and not the truth.

The governor has given 2,000 pesos to the cabildo, which is remitting the money to don Alonso, together with unsigned papers, so that he can choose the attorney he thinks best and give him power of attorney to pursue the case until the 2,000 pesos are spent.

When I received this news, I wrote to Mexico City to his highness in the person of his viceroy and his Royal Acuerdo. I am asking him to provide me with his letter or an official copy of a preliminary judgment, so that with it Your Lordship can challenge the validity of those papers, demonstrating their perverseness and maliciousness. I have established beyond a doubt the truth of my services rendered on behalf of his majesty and carried out for his highness.

I write to Mre. de Campo don Luis Sáenz de Tagle, requesting him to get the official copy and a report from my lawyer, in which he may make whatever points of law occur to him. It is to be sent along with this letter to Your Lordship.

I beg you to come to my defense. In the first place, I advise Your Lordship above all that you are to ask for a fianza de calumnia from the agent who may have the cabildo's power of attorney and likewise, from don Alonso de Buendía, acting for the cabildo and the governor who influences it. Should the opportunity present itself, ask for 1,500 doblas for the appeal and make it on the grounds of the perverse report and the fact that the hearing of the superior government and Tribunal of Accounts of Mexico City is pending.

Likewise, Your Lordship will please ask that they post bond for the costs, damages, and losses of my long, drawn-out imprisonment and detention; my financial affairs; and the offenses against me, my credit, and reputation. What they are asking is for the governor's malicious purpose of keeping me from the government, thereby achieving his goals, gaining the advantage, and obscuring my services. He and the cabildo have neither assets nor equivalent known property to lose or to pay as the law demands.

Those who have brought this lawsuit should pay the costs, damages, and the rest, as required by royal law and because the case is pending before the superior government and Royal Junta in Mexico City, where all the directives and the orders contained therein originate. Commendations of me and my services to his majesty, not only in this government, but also in the alcaldía mayor of Tlalpujahua, have been repeated in his supreme council. This is of record in a letter dated 1685 from the former lord viceroy, the most excellent Conde de Paredes, and in letters of the subsequent viceroy, the most excellent lord Conde de Galve. The cabildo's malicious letter establishes nothing.

It is not of record that Gov. don Pedro Rodríguez Cubero has served his majesty well in this kingdom. On the contrary, in January and September 1698, the Indians were on the verge of rebelling. The Apache nation has, at different times, stolen more than 460 mules and horses. In addition, there have been many deaths and injuries among our people, and the governor has neither gone out nor sent his soldiers, as he should have, to make war.

The cabildo is composed of people of very low class and menial offices—tailors, a shoemaker, and a lackey—poor and base people. By bribes, gifts, and promises, and having been rechosen for their posts for a third year, they, induced by the governor, drew up and sent the letters composed by him and his secretary (who also bears the mark of a lawbreaker).[1] These two do not even have the approval of the citizenry, who seemingly petition and send the letters.

Father Ayeta, procurator general of the entire Franciscan province of El Santo Evangelio, is in Mexico City and will affirm the lowly character of these people. They are given to swear falsely, perjuring themselves in exchange for a young goat, and are of very bad qualities and worse behavior.

May God keep Your Lordship and my daughter, Isabel, and grandchildren, to whom I give my blessing, for I do not know if I shall see them again. The unhappy turn of my fortune and my sad lot have placed me in this wretched state, without the grant of which Your Lordship so vaingloriously gave me news that was of no advantage and only ruin to me. May this serve as a letter to my beloved son, don Juan Manuel, and to all the others, for even paper has been taken from me, and these pages were in a book.

I made my will in Madrid in June 1672 before Mateo de Malabear, escribano real, who had his place of business on the Calle de Toledo and was escribano for the Colegio Imperial of the Society of Jesus.[2] I inform Your Lordship of this in case God should call me, for I am in a land without remedy and have suffered many attacks, though His divine mercy has granted me life but not healed me. May God keep Your Lordship many happy years. Santa Fe, 11 March 1699.

Your father, although unhappy,
esteems you and kisses Your Lordship's
hand,

>   Don Diego de Vargas Zapata
>   Luján Ponce de León [rubrica]

To lord don Ignacio López de Zárate

Lord don Pedro de la Bastida is probably in Madrid. He went there with the lord Conde de Galve and his secretary, don Juan Manuel de Vargas Lodeña. They know of my disinterestedness in the conquest I financed and of my departure and travel to the kingdoms of New Galicia and New Biscay. I was given neither financial assistance (though I did not ask, it was offered) nor any favor. No complaint of any kind was made against me.

*ARGD. ALS. Two folios, four written pages. Postscript written vertically in the left-hand margin of folio 2v.

1. Domingo de la Barreda (or Barrera), a native of Zamora in Spain and thirty years old in 1694, was Rodríguez Cubero's secretary. He had served Vargas in the same capacity during the difficult winter of 1695–96. During proceedings in the summer of 1698, he recorded testimony against the imprisoned former governor, all too readily, according to the latter. Diego de Vargas to the Cabildo of Santa Fe, Santa Fe, 1 Dec. 1703, and Certification by the Cabildo of Santa Fe, Santa Fe, 2 Dec. 1703, SANM II:94a; translated in Twitchell, *Spanish Archives of New Mexico*, 2:117–26, and "The Justification of Don Diego de Vargas, 1704," *Old Santa Fe* 2 (July 1915):57–65. Pedro Rodríguez Cubero, Proceedings against Diego de Vargas, Santa Fe, June 1698, UNM, SC, Thomas Benton Catron Col., PC 29, 803, box 1, folder 1. Chavez, *Origins*, 146.

2. Diego de Vargas, Will, Madrid, 21 June 1672, AHPM, P. 10.125.

24. *Luis Sáenz de Tagle to Ignacio López de Zárate, Mexico City, 11 July 1699.* *

My dear sir, [1]

I wrote to Your Lordship by the flota under the command of don Juan de la Calzadilla and sent you certain proceedings regarding lord don Diego de Vargas, your father-in-law. [2] I ordered don Fausto Bustamante, citizen of Cadiz, to remit 4,000 pesos to Your Lordship. [3] For conveyance by the flota that sailed in 1696, I had 6,000 pesos delivered to don Amadeo Isidro Zeyol, mayordomo of the lord Conde de Galve, by virtue of the power of attorney Your Lordship had given him.

I have not had the favor of a reply from Your Lordship, either by the flota that arrived in New Spain around September 1698 or by the packet boat of 22 June. So as not to betray my long-standing friendship with lord don Diego de Vargas, I inform Your Lordship that he is at present in New Mexico, having undergone his residencia, detained by the governor. This whole story has come down to the same thing that has happened for many years—let those who conquer reap this reward.

Because the governor found out or had news that lord don Diego was to succeed him, he demanded that everyone who had taken the oath recant and say that their sworn testimony had resulted from the knowledge that lord don Diego was to return to the government. Everyone then made perverse claims. Most of these people who had taken the oath many years ago had been declared false witnesses, according to word from those provinces. Seeing that things had come to this, I was obliged to enter a report requesting that lord don Diego de Vargas be allowed to appear in Mexico City to defend himself against the calumnies. I also offered to post bond. Neither the lord viceroy nor the lord fiscal was willing, demanding instead that I put up bond on each one of the calumnies and falsehoods. I am, of course, in no position to provide such bond.

To find a solution to this and get him out of trouble, Your Lordship needs to send a cedula allowing lord don Diego de Vargas to appear in Mexico City. It can state the amount of personal bond. [4] If only Your Lordship had sent the continuation in office three years ago, it might have given him and all his children new hope. This failure was a grave omission, and the faithful knight is paying the price.

I have suffered, breaking with everyone, and I shall continue doing so, to defend lord don Diego. It is the misfortune of all who do their jobs well in these times that God wills it to be this way. May His will be done in all things. We are so defenseless in our situation, because there is no one of confidence by whom we can write to lord don Diego. Not even I dare to, because don Pedro Rodríguez Cubero has all the passes covered. He is even exiling from that kingdom the Franciscan friars who are not of his party, directing vicious reports to their commissary general. This don Pedro Rodríguez Cubero has been very much in favor around here.

This is as much news as I can report. Seeing that this matter is of such great interest to you, I am mindful of keeping Your Lordship informed.

Meantime, I am at your service. I ask God to keep you for me many years. Mexico City, 11 July 1699.

The least of your servants
kisses Your Lordship's hand,

Luis Sáenz de Tagle [rubrica]

To lord don Ignacio López de Zárate

*AMNB. LS. Two folios, three written pages.

1. Luis Sáenz de Tagle, a native of Santillana del Mar in Santander, was a silver merchant, banker, and financier in Mexico City. He rose to prominence in the 1670s and from the 1680s to the end of the century served twice as first consul, and then as prior, of the Mexico City Consulado. His economic success brought a correspondingly conspicuous social role. In 1690, he became a member of the Order of Alcántara and in 1692, was named capitán de caballo during the riots in Mexico City. In 1704, he acquired the noble title of Marqués de Altamira.

Sáenz de Tagle had begun his business relationship with Vargas at least as early as 1680, when he and Capt. Juan de Urrutia lent don Diego 10,311 pesos, which were to be repaid in three months. It continued at least as late as 1703 when Sáenz de Tagle loaned Vargas 12,354 pesos. Apparently business dealings developed into friendship, for after Vargas's arrest in Santa Fe in 1697, Sáenz de Tagle offered to support him for as long as he might be incarcerated. When don Diego died in 1704, he left an outstanding account with Sáenz de Tagle, who tried to collect with the help of Francisco Cuervo y Valdés, Vargas's successor as governor of New Mexico. On the basis of information provided by Vargas's natural sons, Sáenz de Tagle was convinced that Juan Páez Hurtado had managed to hide much of the late governor's wealth and prevent collection of the debt. After Sáenz's death, Pedro Sánchez de Tagle, his nephew, son-in-law, and heir, pursued the claims for repayment against Vargas's estate, an action lasting until at least 1713. Pedro Alonso de Vargas to Isabel María de Vargas Pimentel, Mexico City, 3 Jan. 1713, AGI, México 379. Luis Sáenz de Tagle to Francisco Cuervo y Valdés, Mexico City, 24 Oct. 1704 and 17 Mar. 1706, AGN, Vínculos 125. Proceedings in the criminal case against Diego de Vargas, Santa Fe, 28 Nov. 1699–1 Apr. 1700, AGN, Vínculos 14. Diego de Vargas to Luis Sáenz de Tagle and Juan de Urrutia, Promissory note, Mexico City, 21 Mar. 1680, AGNot. 11. Diego de Vargas to Luis Sáenz de Tagle, Promissory note, Mexico City, 5 June 1703, AGNot. 692. Alonso-Cadenas, *Elenco*, 58. Leopoldo Martínez Cosío, *Los caballeros de las órdenes militares en México: Catálogo biográfico y genealógico* (Mexico City, 1946):309. Robles, *Diario*, 2:112, 134, 238; 3:75. Bakewell, *Silver Mining*, 213. D. A. Brading, *Miners and Merchants in Bourbon Mexico, 1763–1810* (Cambridge, 1971):105, 172, 263.

2. The fleet under the command of Gen. don Juan Gutiérrez de la Calzadilla sailed for Spain on 19 May 1698. Robles, *Diario*, 3:64.

3. Don Fausto de Bustamante y Díaz, born near Torrelavega in northern Santander, later resided in Cadiz, where he married Eusebia de la Torre y Martínez. He was probably related to Luis Sáenz de Tagle, since both the Bustamante and Tagle families came from the same area and intermarried extensively. Don Fausto entered the Order of Santiago on 7 February 1698. As a merchant, Bustamante sometimes accompanied his goods from Spain to Mexico City. He maintained business dealings in New Spain and Guatemala with Juan Ruiz de Bustamante and Antonio Ruiz de Bustamante. Fausto de Bustamante, Declaration, Mexico City, 21 Mar. 1701, AGNot. 7. Escriche, *Diccionario razonado*, 2:67. García Carraffa, *Diccionario heráldico*, 19:172, 80:208.

4. Early in 1698, fray Francisco de Vargas, having left New Mexico, petitioned the viceroy in Mexico City for don Diego's release, so that he could present his case to the authorities. Vélez de Escalante, Extracto de noticias.

25. *Juan Manuel de Vargas Pimentel to Ignacio López de Zárate, Mexico City, 2 November 1699.* *

Brother and dearest friend,

Although in haste, I cannot fail to wish you the very best of health. I shall be happy if it is perfect and if the same is true of my beloved sister and nieces and nephew, whom you will please embrace again and again. My health is good and at your service, which you cannot doubt from my love for you.

After having had a very bad journey from Veracruz to Mexico City, I entered this city to the tolling of bells.[1] This is how things are going. Most important, my father is well, though imprisoned a year ago and mightily abused, for which I must exact ample satisfaction from don Pedro Cubero. All this is happening to my father because of your omission in not having sent in time the legal copies of the continuation in that government. Everyone blames you, principally don Luis Sáenz de Tagle, who is full of complaints that you have not replied to him. In sum, my brother, I find my father poor and imprisoned.

Since no decision was made to get legal copies of his majesty's grant, what I beg of you is that the continuation apply to me in recognition of our services, in the event of my father's death before entering that government. This is not with a view to my staying, but only because we do not know what may happen in the three years remaining. With the grant, I shall be able to work the government to acquire some advantages. I charge you not to fail and to send me the legal copies by the earliest packet boat.

I shall see the lord Conde de Moctezuma tomorrow. The reason for not having done so today is that he has been busy with the crates of correspondence.

A student, my father's son, as big as I am and very like me in appearance, came to see me. There is another young one. Their mother sent to welcome me and to offer her home, but I shall not see her.

You will please give my considerate regards to all the relatives. I do not write to them because there is no time. To all your family, as well as to mine, my greetings. I have it that García is very ill.

To my sister and nieces and nephew many embraces. I hope that Our Lord will keep you in their company, brother and dearest friend, the many years He may and are so necessary to me. Mexico City, 2 November 1699.

Your brother and friend
from the heart till death,

Vargas [rubrica]

To my brother-in-law, don Ignacio

*ARGD. ALS. Two folios, three written pages.

1. According to Robles, *Diario*, 3:83, the bells were ringing on 9 October 1699 because news had arrived in Mexico City that the flota had reached Veracruz.

Mexico City, 1701–3

26. *Diego de Vargas to Isabel María de Vargas Pimentel, Mexico City, 20 March 1701.*

My dearest daughter,

I received your letter of last November and was pleased to know of your good health and the happy event of your having given birth, though I mourn the death of my grandson.[1] Thanks to Our Lord, I have been in this city of Mexico since the end of last October, occupied with settling my accounts and other business affairs. This long, drawn-out process has caused me considerable hardship. You cannot even conceive of what I have suffered. Because I shall send my son with the flota and he will explain to you, I am omitting further details and leave them to his telling.

I received the letter from your husband, my son-in-law, lord don Ignacio. I am amazed that he does not remember from one letter to the next what he writes. Nevertheless, I put my feelings aside and go on only to tell you that I am yours truly. I shall serve you in whatever way I can, wishing that God Our Lord keep you in the company of my beloved grandchildren many happy years. Mexico City, 20 March 1701.

Your father who loves you
from the heart and esteems you as well,

The Marqués de la Nava de
Barcinas [rubrica]²

To my beloved daughter and lady, doña Isabel María de Vargas

*AMNB. LS. One folio, two written pages.

1. About October 1700, Isabel María de Vargas Pimentel must have given birth to a son who died. Writing on 14 April 1705, she stated that her only son, Diego, was then eleven years old. Letter 63 below.

2. From the time the grant of his title was presented to him on 18 December 1700, don Diego signed invariably as the Marqués de la Nava de Barcinas. Letter 29 below. Although he had spelled Barcinas correctly before he left Spain, in the Indies he consistently misspelled the name Bracinas. We have rendered it Barcinas throughout.

———

27. Diego de Vargas to Ignacio López de Zárate, Mexico City, 25 March 1701.*

Son and dear sir,

I received Your Lordship's letter of last November and the one from my beloved daughter. I am in this city of Mexico; it was God's will that I arrive on 30 October 1700. I went immediately to see his excellency, who received me with esteem, promising he would favor me in everything.¹ I shall consider myself most fortunate if I am vindicated in a court of law with regard to the declaration of damages. I am asking Your Lordship to assist me, using the copy of the report I shall present, which I am sending you.

My residencia was reviewed by the lord fiscal and the asesor general. Both state that his excellency should declare me a fair judge, pronouncing null and void the malicious charges brought through my successor's absolute power. Moreover, the term of the residencia had expired.[2] By the flota, I shall dispatch the copy I have asked for.

I am sending to Your Lordship with this first duplicate, which the captain of this packet boat is taking, the duplicate I requested of the selection of my title. This was in response to the presentation of my cedula of a grant for marqués or conde in Castile. In view of the fact that his majesty left the selection up to me, I made it, as Your Lordship will see from the copy of the report I presented to the most excellent lord viceroy. I was declared Marqués de la Nava de Barcinas, as you will see, by his decree of 18 December.[3]

In keeping with your duties, Your Lordship should have sent the legal copies to me by your brother-in-law, my beloved son, don Juan Manuel, paying the media anata. Having served his majesty in this government and captaincy general, I am exempt, as they will exempt me, from paying the lanzas. Furthermore, he also honors me by declaring that I be called conqueror and pacificator.

Your Lordship could have paid the media anata with less than half of the sums you received from me and sent me the royal title of the grant and the other legal copies, leaving my choice blank. Moreover, I have already advised Your Lordship that the name was to be La Nava de Barcinas, only if the means from two villages of Caramancheles were insufficient for that arrangement, which was my intention. So handsome and timely a sum, in addition to the interest that so increased my remittance, was dissipated and came to naught.

Your Lordship gives me no good explanation. You act as though you do not understand what I specifically requested you to send me, when you promised in your letter of April 1700 to send it. Such an omission astonishes me, Your Lordship, for if I were some little gadfly who went around showing off letters, I would understandably have exposed myself to scorn. It would be better for Your Lordship to speak plainly to me in response to this, so you can disabuse yourself of the notion that you are not implicated.

In addition, it was thoughtless of you to allow my son to outfit himself by committing me to encumber the revenue from Los Caramancheles when Your Lordship had already received my remittance. It was also an ill-advised and unwarranted decision for my son to come without bringing a grant. You should have realized that I was not in Mexico City, but imprisoned and detained in a kingdom so distant, a land of danger and war, five hundred leagues in the interior. I was detained there by its governor, my mortal enemy. Since I had nothing more than the wretched state of my misfortune, it was heedless for my son to come, as I repeat, without a grant for himself.

The one he brought to me for the 4,000-peso encomienda I have transferred to him for the term of my life, according to the way in which his majesty favored me.[4] His majesty directed that the royal cedula be presented, for reasons of state, lest my successor seize the opportunity to stir up the Indians against me and say that they have risen in rebellion. Therefore, I would have preferred to take this loss rather than run the risk of any eventuality that the governor's malevolence might bring to pass.

With my credit (thanks be to Our Lord), I have been able to see to the debts my son contracted from the time he left Spain until 30 October 1700 when I arrived, as I am relating. He has presented himself well. I do not know what will become of me, since my decision to send him with the flota is firm.

I am continuing to present my accounts and to pursue my claims. May Our Lord favor me, for in this kingdom any business depends on many people.

It seems to me that his majesty, lord Felipe V (may God keep him), will confirm the grants that lord don Carlos II, our former king (may he be in heavenly glory), had made.[5] It will not be necessary to reapply; I trust that this will be the interpretation of his general royal cedula on advice of his Supreme and Royal Cámara of the Council of the Indies. It occurs to me that I should not fail to ask Your Lordship to please present a report in my name if, by the time you receive this, the decision has not been made and sent by the expected packet boat. Have the legal copy of the royal cedula of the grant made, if necessary, asking his majesty to confirm his royal will as expressed in the cedula of the original grant. In the cedula, the former king our lord (may he be in heavenly glory) favored me, as is of record in the legal copy of 18 June 1688.[6]

One can see that the grant was for all the kingdom and provinces of New Mexico. The company of the presidio of El Paso, with its civil and military government, was not separated as it is at present. This is a great disadvantage and presents many difficulties by not keeping it with the company of the government of New Mexico, at its disposition and under its administration. With the forces divided, those of New Mexico will not be of use to El Paso when they are requested, nor will those of El Paso be of use to New Mexico, whose forces will be immobilized without them. Without the arms and personnel of both presidios under the command of the captain general of New Mexico, there will be no operations in the royal service to meet the great need there is for continuous movement on campaign in so vast a kingdom.[7]

I am advising Your Lordship about the legal copy in particular and earnestly charging you to send it to me, given that in the one I have from his majesty he favored me, reinstating and continuing me in office. As I am relating, please request it in its entirety, having it state that he is granting it to me for the presidio of the pueblo of El Paso del Río del Norte, its pueblos and frontiers, and its political and military government, with power to appoint both the justicia, military officers, and captain of its presidio, and in the villa of Santa Fe. This was the situation when I governed and when I turned it over on 2 July 1697 to my successor, don Pedro Rodríguez Cubero, upon his accession.

The royal cedula should come in this form so that the present or future most excellent lord viceroy of this kingdom of New Spain will put it into effect without imposing obstacles, with the understanding that it commits the company of the presidio of the pueblo of El Paso to the charge of the governor of New Mexico. On his account and at his risk, he will, on his own authority, appoint whoever seems best.

Regarding this point, I trust Your Lordship will have made the request. My son prudently sent by the flota the one that was asked for and newly presented to his majesty. This was done without the precaution of the grant being made in its entirety, as is stated and of record in the royal cedula my brother-in-law, the Marqués de la Florida, kindly sent me, along with the other cedulas, and last, that of the royal provision charging me to conduct my successor's residencia.[8] Your Lordship will know whether another legal copy will be necessary, getting me several, with the stipulation that its fulfillment not be delayed for any reason by the present or future viceroy.

I refer you to the letter my son wrote by the flota. I shall be lost if I am prevented from immediately entering upon the exercise of the government, after having departed from it and from my imprisonment under the oath I took. I swore fealty, promising not to leave the kingdom of New Spain without first having settled and paid off any balances due his majesty from the account in my charge. Thus prevented from availing myself of what I needed to settle up, and having now spent four years without a post and with the expenses of the lawsuit, Your Lordship can imagine the wretched state in which I find myself.

Your Lordship will please act upon everything I relate in this letter, as your honor requires. Please know how much my love has served you and lament my state, binding yourself to the terms of my just reproach. Take heart in the discharge of your proper duty in the fulfillment of my wishes. I ask why the aid was remitted and why, when you received it, you spent it, when Your Lordship's fortune and position were improving—for which I congratulate you. It will be easy for you to use your office for what I wish; you know my mind. I trust, therefore, at the first opportunity I shall receive the dispatches from you. I shall not refuse to serve Your Lordship should my fortune be restored.

It pleases me, Your Lordship, that my brother-in-law and friend, the Marqués de la Florida, is living in the apartments and that you have accommodated him so well. I regret that his salary is somewhat in arrears. I trust in Our Lord that his services may be deserving of every attention from the king our lord (may God keep him).

The packet boat carries the bearer of this letter. He is the brother of a member of his excellency's household, among those who attend his lordship. Should he have recourse to Your Lordship with his petitions, you will please see to him with all courtesy. Please do not forget the petition for a canonry for don Sebastián Altamirano de Castilla, whose 500 pesos Your Lordship received. I remind you of this because it has been so long and because I am not as informed about it as I am about the rest.

Your Lordship's sister-in-law, my daughter Juana, may collect for herself the revenue of 2,000 reales from the dehesa of Las Gariñas. Your Lordship wrote to me that this was being kept from her or being delayed. Her necessity demands great promptness.

Your Lordship will also please give to my sister, doña Antonia de Vargas, 500 reales to meet her needs at once. Our Lord gives me life to shelter all my family, not to dwell on my woes.

May God keep Your Lordship in the company of my beloved daughter, Isabel, and grandchildren, to whom I give my blessing, the happy years I wish for you. Mexico City, 25 March 1701.

I repeat to Your Lordship that I shall appreciate your sending me the legal copies so that I may put on the robe of Santiago. I await the copy of the grant of title in response to the copy I am sending of my selection. It could be that my fortune will be restored. Your Lordship will find in me the consideration with which I have always lovingly esteemed you.

> Your father and faithful
> servant who esteems you and
> kisses your hand, kisses
> Your Lordship's hand,

> The Marqués de la Nava de
> Barcinas [rubrica]

To my son-in-law and lord, don Ignacio López de Zárate

*AMNB. LS. Six folios, twelve written pages. The postscript, on folio 6v, is in Vargas's hand.

1. José Sarmiento y Valladares, Conde de Moctezuma y de Tula (1643–?) was named the thirty-second viceroy of New Spain on 9 April 1696. His title of nobility was obtained by marriage to a descendant of Moctezuma II. He took possession of the government on either 18 December 1696 or 2 February 1697 and served until he was requested to leave on 4 November 1701. Porrúa, *Diccionario*, 2:1957; Rubio Mañé, *Virreyes*, 1:295; Robles, *Diario*, 3:54; EUI, 54:612.

2. Vargas chose to present the criminal complaint brought against him by the Villa of Santa Fe as an illegal extension of his residencia, which it was not. Letter 20 above.

3. Conde de Moctezuma, Decree, Mexico City, 18 Dec. 1700, and the king to Diego de Vargas, Title of marqués or conde, Madrid, 15 June 1697, AMNB.

4. Diego de Vargas to Juan Manuel de Vargas Pimentel, Transfer of encomienda, Mexico City, 8 Nov. 1700, AGNot. 7. In 1695, don Diego had requested, in addition to the title of nobility, an encomienda of 6,000 pesos for two generations, to be collected annually from the subjugated Pueblo Indians, despite the fact that encomiendas in the Indies by this time were mostly extinct. The 1680 Pueblo Revolt had put an end to the encomiendas that had previously existed in New Mexico. Not until January 1697 did the Council of the Indies recommend approval of Vargas's requests. The title of nobility was granted by the king, but not the encomienda. Finally, on 21 August 1698, after

receipt of further reports, the king did grant to don Diego a 4,000-peso encomienda. But the accession of Governor Rodríguez Cubero, Vargas's "six lost years," and the unsettled conditions in New Mexico upon his return in 1703, all combined to prevent him from implementing the grant. After his death in 1704, his heirs eventually succeeded in having the encomienda converted to a pension. See Bloom, "The Vargas Encomienda."

5. Carlos II died on 1 November 1700. Felipe V, the Duke of Anjou, named as his successor, entered Madrid on 17 or 18 February 1701. Janine Fayard, "La Guerra de Sucesión (1700–1714)," in Manuel Tuñón de Lara, ed., *La frustración de un imperio, 1476–1714*, vol. 5 of *Historia de España* (Barcelona, 1982):427; and Henry Kamen, *The War of Succession in Spain, 1700–15* (Bloomington, 1969):4, 9.

6. The king, Title of governor of New Mexico to Diego de Vargas, Madrid, 18 June 1688, AGI, México 1216.

7. Antonio Valverde requested that Carlos II appoint him captain of the El Paso presidio and alcalde mayor of the El Paso district. In 1699, based on the recommendation of the Junta of War, the crown granted the captaincy, but not royal appointment as alcalde mayor, which would have placed the El Paso district outside the jurisdiction of the governor of New Mexico. Only after months of litigation in Mexico City with Juan Bautista Saldúa, Rodríguez Cubero's appointee as captain of the El Paso presidio, did Valverde win viceregal approval in 1700, first as captain and then as alcalde mayor subject to the governor of New Mexico. Proceedings in the matter of Antonio Valverde's claims to the captaincy and alcaldía mayor of El Paso, AGI, Guadalajara 142:16.

8. Juan Antonio Pimentel de Prado, brother of Gregorio, Lorenzo, and Beatriz, was given the title Marqués de la Florida (-Pimentel) by Carlos II on an unspecified date. Atienza, *Nobiliario*, 865. When admitted to the Order of Santiago on 22 August 1658, don Juan Antonio had been a captain of the Spanish infantry in the tercio of his uncle, Mre. de Campo Antonio Pimentel de Prado. Juan Antonio Pimentel de Prado, AHN, Ordenes Militares, Santiago 6.472; Pimentel de Prado, Services, Madrid, 26 Jan. 1715, AGI, Indiferente General 162.

28. *Juan Manuel de Vargas Pimentel to Ignacio López de Zárate, Mexico City, 7 April 1701.**

Brother and dearest friend,

I am replying to your two letters, dated 17 November and 3 December, which I received by the packet boat that reached this kingdom on 8 March, and another that arrived by the Campeche registro on 22 April. In all of them, I find the good news that you continue in the perfect health my love wishes for you; my health remains good and ready to serve you. I am impatient to depart from this kingdom as soon as possible, though (thank God) I did achieve the much-desired end for which I came, to know my father.

He reached this city on 29 October, so fit that those who had known him were amazed, for the hardships he has undergone were enough to have put him in his grave. Our first sight of each other was three leagues from here. He was so astonished to see me that for a long time he did not say a word. The next day he went to see the viceroy, who received him with many false courtesies, as is his custom. I do not dwell on this, for the captain in charge of the mail packet, don Juan Díaz del Campo, by whose hand this goes, is in a hurry.

I shall say only that our king's death caused great sorrow, but then came the consolation of learning how well everything had been worked out. On the 4th of the current month, the swearing of allegiance to the new king was held with even greater splendor and solemnity than in Madrid. First, the condolences were proclaimed, and then the honors were done. Because of these events, nothing is said about the departure of the flota, by which (if it pleases God) I hope to return to Spain. Although the worse for having come, I am consoled by having finally known my father.

The reason he is not coming with me is that he must return to his government for the sake of his honor. That so-called gentleman, Pedro Rodríguez Cubero, has been the source of so many evils, known to all the ministers but not remedied, because all-powerful private interest intervenes.

Please give my considerate remembrances to all the relatives, and many embraces to my beloved sister and nieces and nephew, and to all the family, regards in my behalf. Also, when you write to Torrelaguna, please send my regards. Tell each and every one of my friends that I am in fine fettle, although I trust in Our Lord that I shall be able to do so in person one day. In the meantime, I beseech His Divine Majesty to keep you, brother and dearest friend, the many years He can, and I wish and need so much. Mexico City, 7 April 1701.

Your brother and best friend
from the heart until death,

Don Juan Manuel de Vargas
Pimentel [rubrica]

To my brother-in-law and friend, don Ignacio López de Zárate

*ARGD. LS. Two folios, three written pages.

—————

29. *Diego de Vargas to Ignacio López de Zárate,
Mexico City, 3 May 1701.*

Son and dear sir,

They tell me that the mail the packet boat is taking will be sealed today. Although I have written to Your Lordship in duplicate, my affection for you keeps me from repeating myself and telling you what is in the two I have written you. I hope they reach Your Lordship's hands, finding you in the good health I wish for you; my beloved daughter, Isabel; and my grandchildren. I continue in good health (thanks to Our Lord) as does my son, Your Lordship's brother-in-law. We are eager for the expected packet boat to arrive with news of the entrada of the most serene lord, our king Felipe V (may God keep him), and his happy accession to the throne.[1]

I trust that Your Lordship, despite your considerable duties, will send me legal copies of the appointments about which you have been advising me since April 1700. With them, I may fulfill my wish. I do not doubt that you will also send me those that it may be necessary to resubmit in order to assume (if it pleases Our Lord) the office of government with which our former king, lord Carlos II (of glorious memory), favored me. I hope Your Lordship will send me confirmation, if necessary, of these legal copies and those of the royal provision to conduct the residencia of my successor, don Pedro Rodríguez Cubero. This is necessary because of the recent entrada of the king our lord and his succession to the crown. In this kingdom, even with all these precautions, other extraordinary steps and exertions are necessary, which I leave to Your Lordship's imagination.

I have also written to you that my residencia has been reviewed. I have been declared a fair judge, as was the consensus of the two lords fiscal and this kingdom's asesor general. Also, I am continuing to present my accounts in the Royal Audiencia and Tribunal of Accounts.

I am sending to Your Lordship the first duplicate of the copy of the selection I am making regarding the grant of a title of Castile. I do so, having presented the royal cedula to his excellency with the report. He had previously ordered his secretario de cámara to inform me of his majesty's cedula, in which he gave this notice.

I selected Marqués de la Nava de Barcinas from the entail I have in Granada. I suppose that don Diego de Olvera will have put this entail in order with the 1,000 pesos my son gave him in Seville. I paid it in Mexico City to the person in whose favor he gave his note. I judge that the property's business will run more smoothly with this repair and that of its dam. This should have been accomplished by means of the sum, which amounted to more than 17,000 vellon reales, in the possession of Gabriel Ruiz, former treasurer of the Santa Cruzada in that kingdom. Your Lordship will please give me a report of the state of this property.

Returning to the matter of the copy, I am sending to Your Lordship the selection of title and the decree of 18 December of his excellency, the most excellent viceroy, Conde de Moctezuma, in accord with what relates to declaring me by such title. Your Lordship will please present the rest of what is of record immediately upon seeing the copy and arrange payment of the media anata. Please pay this royal fee, whatever it may be, out of the goods and sum you received on my account in 1699. With regard to what is paid in lanzas, I am exempt because of my employ, serving in the office of governor and captain general.

You will please do me the special favor of sending to me the royal title and the cedula of title with the royal seal in the customary form. At the first opportunity, please acknowledge receipt of this letter along with those, as I repeat, that I am sending to you. I hope at the same time that Our Lord will keep Your Lordship many happy years in the company of my beloved daughter, Isabel, and grandchildren, to whom I give my blessing. Please give them many embraces and heartfelt remembrances. Done in Mexico City, 3 May 1701.

I kiss the hand of my brother-in-law and friend, the Marqués de la Florida, with all my affection. I have written to him twice in duplicate, as I have mentioned, and I hope they will reach his hands and find him in good health.

Your most affectionate father
and servant who esteems you
kisses Your Lordship's hand,

The Marqués de la Nava de
Barcinas [rubrica]

To my son-in-law and lord, don Ignacio López de Zárate

*ARGD. LS. Three folios, five written pages.

1. Word that the new king had taken possession of the realm on 26 February 1701 did not reach Mexico City until 11 June, five and a half weeks after Vargas wrote this letter. Robles, *Diario,* 3:157.

———

30. *Diego de Vargas to Ignacio López de Zárate, Mexico City, 23 July 1701.**

Son and dear sir,

I shall be pleased if the packet boat has reached Spain. Your Lordship will have realized from the letter I wrote what my feelings have been about everything. In this letter, I repeat to Your Lordship my reprimand. I trust that out of your honorable qualities, such just reasons will impel you to expedite the legal copies of the grant of the title. I sent you the copy of its selection, including the royal cedula, so that, upon seeing it, you might arrange payment of the media anata, which was to have been paid in Madrid. I have asked Your

Lordship about the rest, and you advised me by letter of April 1699.

I am writing to my beloved daughter, doña Isabel. Your Lordship will not fail to understand the contents of the letter, which will also serve as notice of the three cases of chocolate I am sending. Please deliver one to my daughter, so that you may drink it with her and my beloved grandchildren. Your Lordship will please deliver another case to my brother-in-law, the Marqués de la Florida. Please send the last with the packet to Torrelaguna for my daughter, doña Juana de Vargas, so that she can carry out what I am ordering her to do in the letter I am writing to her. Capt. don Fausto de Bustamante, knight of the Order of Santiago and citizen of the city of Cadiz, will store and send all three of these cases, after having paid all the duties and transportation costs as far as Madrid. Your Lordship needs to do no more than receive them. Likewise, he will give you a draft for 50 pesos that you will remit to my sister, doña Antonia de Vargas, or deliver to whomever she may designate in the letter she will write to you.

I am sending to Your Lordship by don Fausto the power of attorney for my petition and the second duplicate of the copy of the selection of title. He will mail the packet as soon as he arrives home in Cadiz.

With this information, Your Lordship can anticipate how long it will take for the power of attorney to arrive. Petition should be made for the following offices:

First, the government and captaincy general of the kingdom of Guatemala and presidency of its royal audiencia;

In second place, the government and captaincy general of Santa Fe de Bogotá and presidency of its royal audiencia of the kingdom of New Granada;

In third, the government and captaincy general of the kingdom of Chile and presidency of its royal audiencia;

The government and captaincy general of the kingdom of Buenos Aires and Río de la Plata;

And the government and captaincy general of the kingdom and islands of the Philippines and presidency of its royal audiencia.

Not obtaining one of the five, petition should be made for either the government and captaincy general of the island of Havana or that of the kingdom of Tucumán. Surely if Your Lordship makes this petition with every consideration, it will result in my being able (Our Lord seeing fit to give me life) to lessen your obligations somewhat.

I close, trusting in your effort, wishing that Our Lord keep Your Lordship in the company of my beloved daughter and grandchildren, to whom I give my blessing. Done in Mexico City, 23 July 1701.

> Your most affectionate father who
> esteems you and wishes for your well-being
> kisses Your Lordship's hand,
>
> > The Marqués de la Nava de
> > Barcinas [rubrica]

The letter for my lady, the Condesa de Lemos, is from a person I esteem, and therefore I beg Your Lordship to send it to her excellency.[1]

To lord don Ignacio López de Zárate, my son-in-law

*AMNB. LS. Two folios, four written pages. A note regarding the delivery of an enclosed letter is written vertically in the left-hand margin of folio 2v. The date is repeated, written vertically at the bottom of the right-hand margin.

1. The Condesa de Lemos, Ana de Borja, was a daughter of the most influential and prestigious family of Granada. In 1664, she married the tenth Conde de Lemos, Pedro Antonio Fernández de Castro, who was appointed viceroy of Peru on 21 October 1666 and served until 6 December 1672, when he died in office. She was related by marriage to the Duques de Alburquerque. Carlos A. Romero, "La virreina gobernadora," *Revista Histórica* 1 (Mar. 1906):39–59; Schäfer, *Consejo Real*, 2:442.

---

31. *Diego de Vargas to Ignacio López de Zárate, Mexico City, 25 October 1701.**

Son and dear sir,

With this letter, I am sending to Your Lordship the certification of the payment I made pertaining to the fee of the media anata for the honorific of the title of captain general.[1] I also send the copy of the proceedings by which, as Your Lordship will see, I demonstrated to the lord juez privativo that, because it was given for open warfare, I am exempt from paying any fee.

In consideration of this, he ordered by writ that I make payment in the form of a deposit; that the copy and its certification be given to me; and that I apply to the Council of the Treasury, asking its lords to declare, upon review, that I should not pay and directing that the deposit I had made be returned to me from the Royal Treasury office. Your Lordship will please tend to this matter and send me the lords' dispatch.

Wishing that Our Lord may keep Your Lordship for many happy years. Mexico City, 25 October 1701.

Your most affectionate father
and faithful servant kisses
Your Lordship's hand,

The Marqués de la Nava de
Barcinas [rubrica]

To lord don Ignacio López de Zárate, my son-in-law

*ARGD. LS. One folio, two written pages.

1. Although don Diego claimed exemption from payment of the media anata, by virtue of appointment to a post in a region of open warfare, the *Recopilación* did not seem to exempt captains general from payment. Rather, the passage that dealt with "guerra viva" appeared to refer only to soldiers and other officials below the rank of captain general. See *Recop.*, Lib. 8, tít. 19, ley 4.

---

32. *Diego de Vargas to Isabel María de Vargas Pimentel, Mexico City, 14 March 1702.*

My beloved daughter,

By the storeships that brought the mercury and arrived at the end of last October, I received your letter and with it the pleasure of knowing you are in good health. I am distressed by the ingratitude of your husband, my son-in-law, lord don Ignacio, in not sending a letter by the packet boat that sailed at the beginning of December and arrived on 15 February this year. I do not blame you for your omission, rather your husband, who failed both to write and to inform you of the opportunity to write me. I attribute this to his probably not having had time and being hindered by his concerns.

I am not a little involved in my business matters and am informing my son-in-law and lord, don Ignacio, about them. I refer only to this and to the delay of your brother, my son, because the flota has not sailed. By the letters you receive, you will know that, on the certain assumption that the flota would sail, I wrote you and later wrote again around October, when a decision had been made for the packet boat to sail. Since neither sailed, my care and attention came to nothing. Out of my love, I repeat my wishes for you and inform you of the state of my business affairs, which are long and drawn-out.

It is a great burden to find myself without resources, destroyed and consumed. I do not know how I shall be able to assist your brother, my son, in his voyage, when the day to send him arrives.

I now consider impossible my hope of seeing you and leave it completely to His Divine Majesty. May He keep you many happy years in the company of my beloved grandchildren, to whom I give my blessing. You will please give them many embraces. Mexico City, 14 March 1702.

Your father who esteems you
from the heart and who leaves seeing
you only to the will of God Our Lord,

The Marqués de la Nava de
Barcinas [rubrica]

To my dear daughter, doña Isabel María de Vargas

*ARGD. LS. Two folios, three written pages.

———

33. Diego de Vargas to Ignacio López de Zárate, Mexico City, 15 March 1702.*

Son and dear sir,

By the mercury ships that arrived at the port of New Veracruz at the end of October last year, I received Your Lordship's letter. I was sorry not to have been worthy of another from you by the packet boat that was sent at the beginning of December, the news of which reached this kingdom and city of Mexico on 15 February this year. I judge that the performance of Your Lordship's duties must have prevented you. Whatever the circumstances, I will always be steadfast in my duty.

To give you an idea of my responsibilities, the settlement of my affairs, despite all my personal attention, has been complicated and drawn-out for the following reasons. The process of review, report, and advisement depends on so many people. Also, in view of the royal cedula (done in Barcelona on 16 October 1701)[1] that the opposing party obtained through a perverse report, I had to present the two that Your Lordship sent to me that year. This was necessary to avoid delays. Time was saved by citing in the royal cedula and presenting them in the Royal Acuerdo, where the hearing is set. This was necessary to avoid delays.

I cannot deny to Your Lordship that my own objections were the reason I refused to settle. Only the circumstance of his majesty citing the two earlier cedulas in the above-mentioned royal cedula to the villa could have obliged me. For one thing, in the cedula of April 1700, his majesty, our lord the king Carlos II (may he be in glory), was not aware of two specific points that should have been made.[2]

The first point is the restoration of my honor. The former lord viceroy, Conde de Galve, by resolution of the lords minister who make up a plenary session of the Junta of Royal Treasury and War of this entire kingdom of New Spain, entrusted to me not only the matter of undertaking the conquest of the whole kingdom of New Mexico, which I carried out at my own cost in 1692, but also its colonizing expedition at his majesty's expense in the following year.

For its settlement, I recruited families in the kingdoms of New Galicia and New Biscay, a hundred soldiers for the founding of the new presidio in the villa of Santa Fe, and the original families of the kingdom. The support of all of them fell to me personally, without the cabildo's participation. For this I was given full and complete authority to draw on the Royal Treasury offices of the three kingdoms.[3]

Thus, by the directives and orders I had received and have presented, all this was entirely up to me. This authority was given to me without bond, for I was unable to post it, for whatever I might consider necessary. Much less could my honor admit of such an order with that stipulation and obligation. Assuming this, it is improper and incongruous for the royal cedula to order that only under bond would I be allowed to leave prison and go to render my accounts.

The second point, which is omitted both in this cedula and in the second one from our lord the king, Felipe V (may God keep him), is the request made by the cabildo and the attorney on its behalf. This supposes that he is not directed to post bond for libel, as I advised Your Lordship and Gov. don Pedro Rodríguez Cubero, who was the origin and instrument of the lawsuit brought not out of zeal for the royal service, but out of malice and for his own interest. A review of the many proceedings requires a very long time; inasmuch as they go and have gone to various places, the long delay is unavoidable. As a result, don Pedro succeeds in his wish of preventing me from assuming this government.

I do not know when my account will be settled. I have lost five years—wasted and misspent—so that to send my son with the flota, I shall be hard put to find even what is needed for his voyage.

This is the wretched state I am in, bound by an oath of allegiance, having lost the most precious thing, liberty. I swore, as I was ordered, not to leave this kingdom of New Spain without first paying the balances of my account that might result in favor of the Royal Treasury.

By this packet boat (God willing that it arrives safely), Your Lordship will receive two packets from me. The one of September 1701 I gave to don Fausto de Bustamante, who is responsible for the chocolate and its costs. By the flota that did not sail, I intended to send it to Your Lordship, and with this packet, the copy of the review of my residencia. It is of record that I have been declared a fair judge and that all the charges were held to be null and void.

From the second duplicate of the copy I sent to Your Lordship upon the coronation of the king our lord (may God keep him), news of which arrived on 15 August last year, Your Lordship will have realized that I have selected the title Marqués de la Nava de Barcinas by virtue of the royal cedula of his majesty (may he be in heavenly glory). I am again entrusting to you settlement of the fee that is owed and payment of the media anata, as I sought to repeat to you in the second packet of last October by the packet boat that did not sail. I was sending to Your Lordship the copy of the receipt for also having paid, by means of deposit in this Royal Treasury office, the fee of the media anata because as governor I also had the honorific of captain general.

In order to settle the media anata out of my salary, it was charged against me, even though I made an objection before the juez privativo. Several writs and petitions were presented, showing that my governorship was a war zone and his majesty was exempting all who command in those presidios from payment of this royal fee. I referred the matter to Your Lordship, making this report, so that my payment would be ordered returned to me and I might have recourse to the Royal Council of the Treasury. I do so again, having written to the people in Veracruz who have the packets so that they will address and send them by the packet boat. Since I have the utmost confidence in these people, I trust that they will do this with the necessary security. Likewise, I am depending on Your Lordship to attain everything I request of you. I also sent you a power of attorney for my petitions and, in order to facilitate them, the copy of the statement of my account. According to it, there is a balance in my favor.

By this packet boat, I am sending to don Diego de Olvera a power of attorney for the business of Granada. Because he will show it to Your Lordship, I shall refrain from relating its contents to you.

I remain at your service with the same love and esteem that you will find and command, come what may, wishing that Our Lord keep Your Lordship for many happy years in the company of my beloved daughter, doña Isabel, and grandchildren, to whom I give my blessing and many embraces. Mexico City, 15 March 1702.

Your father, always your surest
servant, who esteems you from
the heart, kisses Your Lordship's
hand,

The Marqués de la Nava de
Barcinas [rubrica]

I await the grant of the robe by the first packet boat, in case the dispatch for me to don it is sent.

To lord don Ignacio López de Zárate

*ARGD. LS. Five folios, nine written pages. The postscript, in Vargas's hand, appears as a note in the left-hand margin of folio 5v. The date 15 March 1702 is also written on folio 5v.

1. According to correspondence of the Audiencia with the king, the date of this cedula was 10 October 1701. Royal Audiencia to the king, Mexico City, 30 Mar. 1703, AGI, Guadalajara 142:20.

2. The date of the cedula was 22 April 1700. Royal Audiencia to the king, Mexico City, 30 Mar. 1703, AGI, Guadalajara 142:20.

3. Vargas had the authority to draw 40,000 pesos on the treasury offices of Guadiana, Zacatecas, and Sombrerete during the 1693 recolonizing effort. The money was to be used to enlist soldiers and help finance the expedition. Espinosa, *First Expedition*, 33; and *Crusaders*, 339 n.79.

---

34. *Diego de Vargas to Ignacio López de Zárate, Mexico City, 29 May 1702.* *

Son and dear sir,

I have written to Your Lordship by my son, don Juan Manuel. This letter is only to give you the news that he sails with this flota, hoping to arrive safely in Your Lordship's presence.¹ He will explain the other legal instruments I am sending by him and likewise what I refer to in them.

I am making a report to Your Lordship reflecting my intention and wish that on the occasion of its presentation, his majesty should be asked to better my post, since my services in the restoration and conquest of the kingdom of New Mexico have been meritorious.

They have also been the cause of my suffering in the delay of five years, three of them in prison, with the indignity of five months in shackles. From these instruments, one can see the injustice and malice with which Gov. don Pedro Rodríguez Cubero proceeded against me for the purpose of preventing my continuation in the government and not out of zeal for his majesty's service. The redress of my injury—the loss of my property and the frustration of my advancement—can only be given by the Cámara of the Supreme Council of the Indies. Therefore, I am pointing out to Your Lordship that by virtue of the power of attorney I am sending to you for my petition and the posts I am asking of his majesty as a favor, it devolves upon you to see that the grant takes effect in any one of the six posts I am asking for.

This I must owe to Your Lordship as one last favor, for which I shall always be grateful, during the time Our Lord may see fit to give me life. Your Lordship's knowledge of my words and generosity may be my only way of repaying you.

You yourself will please work persistently to improve my post so that I may live more happily, unburdened and without anguish, and so that I may have the gain without the adversities and perils of that government of New Mexico. Please reply as soon as possible, without losing the opportunity to obtain what I want.

Also I ask that you do not forget, as I have repeated, Lic. don Sebastián de Altamirano's petition. He is a person I esteem very highly and in whom many merits and nobility concur so that any favor is justified. Moreover, securing for him the grant he may deserve from those lords will reflect well on Your Lordship.

May God keep Your Lordship many happy years, as I wish. Mexico City, 29 May 1702.

I repeat my tender embraces to my beloved daughter, doña Isabel, and my grandchildren and give them my blessing with the heartfelt love in which I hold them.

Your most affectionate father
and ever-faithful servant who
esteems you from the heart
kisses Your Lordship's hand,

The Marqués de la Nava de
Barcinas [rubrica]

To lord don Ignacio López de Zárate, my son-in-law

*AMNB. LS. Two folios, four written pages.

1. The flota sailed from Veracruz on 11 and 12 June 1702. The departure had been delayed because the Junta General in Mexico City refused to entrust the silver fleet to the French admiral, Count Chateaurenaud, until he showed his orders from the king. When finally it did sail, escorted by French warships, there were more French vessels than Spanish. Kamen, "Destruction of the Spanish Silver Fleet," 165–66. Robles, *Diario*, 3:214, 221.

———

35. *Diego de Vargas to Isabel María de Vargas Pimentel, Mexico City, 31 December 1702.* *

My beloved darling daughter,

From the letter I write to my son-in-law, don Ignacio, you will see that I am still in this city of Mexico. I am impatient for the review of the proceedings in the Royal Audiencia so that I can emerge from the ignominy of being lost in this kingdom, my wealth encumbered and consumed. For this reason, I am sending the power of attorney with the clauses contained therein to see whether I may receive any assistance out of what God Our Lord saw fit to give me in revenue from those entails. Though I may not be supported wholly from them, they will relieve me in part by what they may yield.

I am well aware that it is difficult for my son-in-law to take up his pen. In your letter, delivered to me by the page of my lady, the duquesa, you tell me he is writing. [1] Even having had such sure bearers, he was not about to do it, which completely convinces me of his intention.

May Our Lord sustain me and give grace and long life to you and my beloved grandchildren, to whom I give my blessing. May God keep you for many happy years. Mexico City, 31 December 1702.

Your father who esteems you from the heart and wishes for your well-being,

The Marqués de la Nava de Barcinas [rubrica]

To my beloved daughter, doña Isabel María de Vargas Pimentel

*AMNB. LS. One folio, two written pages.

1. Doña Juana de la Cerda y de Aragón, daughter of the eighth Duque de Medinaceli. She accompanied her husband, the viceroy, Francisco Fernández de la Cueva Enríquez, Duque de Alburquerque, Marqués de Cuéllar, Conde de Ledesma y de Huelma, during his term from 1702 to 1711. García Carraffa, *Diccionario heráldico*, 25:308. *Diccionario Porrúa*, 1:760.

————

36. Diego de Vargas to Ignacio López de Zárate, Mexico City, 31 December 1702–4 April 1703.*

Son and dear sir,

As soon as the flota safely reaches that kingdom of Spain (as I trust in Our Lord it will), Your Lordship will have the news and the letter of Capt. don Francisco Marcos López de Villamil, citizen of Cadiz, by which you will know of the early death of my dear son, don Juan Manuel de Vargas Pimentel. I received news of this from Havana, and I assure Your Lordship that my heart was broken by the pain.[1] It was only by chance that this gentleman and others, with whom my son had a close friendship in this city, went with him. Given the untimely death of your brother-in-law, my dear son, and the sorrow it will have caused my beloved daughter, doña Isabel, I know from Your Lordship's honorable qualities that you will have been with her. I avoid dwelling on this point, being unable to repress my feelings. I go on only to inform Your Lordship of the present state of my business affairs.

On 17 August, Our Lord saw fit that the papers concerning the consistency of the gloss of my accounts and their settlement were presented. Immediately I proceeded to ask in the Tribunal of Accounts and the Audiencia that I be given the certification I am sending to Your Lordship, along with the certification that the decision in the matter is pending in the Royal Audiencia, by virtue of the royal cedula entrusting jurisdiction to it. The perverseness of the report by

LA Villa de Santa Feé,

Cabeçera de las Provincias de la Nueva Mexico, informa à V. S. en el pleito que figue contra Don DIEGO DE VARGAS, ZAPATA, Y LVJAN, Governador que fue de aquel Reyno, y Provincias, fobre diferentes exceffos que el fufo-dicho, fus Miniftros, y Criados executaron en el tiempo de fu govierno, cantidades que percibiô para fu manutencion, y no convirtiô en el fin â que fe deftinaron, que deve reftituir á fu Mageftad, é interefados, y fobre que no buelva à governar dicho Reyno; proponiendo fu informe en cinco puntos, que fe expreffaràn.

A   Exem

Charges against don Diego de Vargas brought by the villa of Santa Fe, Mexico City, 1703.
Courtesy of The Huntington Library, San Marino, California.

which the villa attained the cedula from his majesty has been established. It is of record in the certification not only that I owe nothing to the Royal Treasury, but also that it has been ordered to draw and pay me the balance that resulted in my favor.[2] With this, I can pay in part the people who provided for me out of their wealth during the delay of five years—going on six—that I have been waiting to assume office.

Without any information at all, Your Lordship will realize how much in debt I would be as a result of such a serious lawsuit and the expenses and obligations caused by the coming of my beloved, deceased son. I regret only the loss of his life. In my estimation, there is no way I can express to you the happiness I had found in him. From the papers that will have been sent to Your Lordship, you will know of the general power of attorney for all my entails that I executed in his favor, without excepting or reserving anything, and with my full consent and pleasure. The power of attorney will affirm the esteem and affection with which I tenderly loved him.

Likewise, in this kingdom I had ceded to him for his lifetime, in place of mine, the 4,000-peso encomienda granted by his majesty, so that during his lifetime it would have devolved upon the son Our Lord might have seen fit to give him. I had assured my son of assistance in whatever pledge he might make for the best possible marriage.

These were my thoughts. I did not consent to having him come, nor did I imagine that in any way he would trap himself here. Out of esteem and goodwill, a place was made for him, and it might have worked for the best. Yet, it never occurred to me that he would not be present in Madrid or that he would not be the representative of my ancestors' memory, maintaining the luster of my house, when I myself had bestowed upon it a title of Castile.

I hope and trust that Your Lordship will have paid the media anata. Since so important a request of Your Lordship required my attention, I have repeated it in all the letters I have written to you since I entered this city of Mexico at the end of 1700. Having no doubt that you will have carried it out, I trust I shall receive the royal cedula of the selection I made of the title Marqués de la Nava de Barcinas, in accord with the copy (for which I have Your Lordship's reply) I sent to Your Lordship in the packet boat that arrived in Spain at the end of August 1701.

As a result of Your Lordship's reply and the death of my beloved son, it has been necessary for me to make the decision, in accor-

dance with the present state of my fortune and the debts I have contracted, to recover my losses. I must guard my honor, so that it does
not wane and I come to see myself disgraced, lacking what is needed
for proper appearances to keep and support myself for as long as I
have to delay in this kingdom.

Now Our Lord has seen fit to take unto Himself my beloved son,
who was the reason for setting aside this very just consideration.
Because of the love I blindly felt for him, I dispossessed myself of
everything while still alive. His life was my only life. As the idol of
my love, he could not object to what I must do in his absence now
that I have returned to my senses. I need to prepare all that is required
to remedy my situation and avoid the ruin of dishonor and disre-
spect, and at the same time, that of exposing myself to perpetual
captivity, lost in this kingdom, unable to leave and impeded by debt.

Therefore, having considered and weighed these questions of hon-
or, and the hardship, injury, and irreparable damage, it is well that I
open my eyes to the thought of thirty years lost, from 11 August
1672, when I left Spain, my beloved homeland—that delightful villa of Madrid, crown of all the world. I am reflecting on debts in
place of payments on my entails, which might have supported me
comfortably during my last days and the time Our Lord saw fit to
give me. I would have enjoyed my family, without having the additional burden of the whole labyrinth and abyss necessary for human
life in these parts.

Not only did I find myself on the parallel of fortune, my retirement delayed by virtue of the length of my absence, but also on the
parallel of experiencing again the bitterness of so harsh a life. The
unburdening of my heart is very necessary so that, in its grief, it will
not be so completely without vigor that it lacks the life force when
all courage is necessary to revive it and not let it be faint. Its noble
spirit and valor give it the courage to put aside such well founded
reasons for depriving it of life.[3] The lengthiness of this digression has
been to satisfy Your Lordship and to assure your spirit so that mine
may continue.

With these affairs and considerations, putting aside the matter of
my son and looking to that of your position in the family, you should
respect me for having made the decision to execute the powers of
attorney, relieving you of the care of administering my entails. Reflecting upon the causes of my present fortune and state, you will have
seen that instead of making you secure, it is more legitimate that I

avail myself of what God Our Lord gave me than to incur scorn by asking for what another needs. Hence, I have treated Your Lordship with all courtesy. Despite this, I do not want to use this motive to reduce what you need for attention to your duties to your mother and siblings, which is most just and born of your honorable qualities, in addition to those to your children and wife, my beloved daughter.

I am sending a general power of attorney to the city of Granada for my cousin, don Fernando de Teruel, Conde de Villamena and knight of the Order of Santiago. He can transfer it to whoever may be most worthy of his trust and request don Diego de Olvera's accounting (from 1 January 1700 to whenever that person may receive the power of attorney) of everything the entail may have yielded during that time.[4] It should also show what is on hand and what has been paid out, as well as how the 1,000 pesos were spent that my beloved son (may he be with God) left with Olvera in June 1699 when he traveled to New Spain. I paid this amount in this city of Mexico to don Miguel Vélez de la Rea, knight of the Order of Santiago.

I am giving this general power of attorney independently so that no one may receive the revenue of the entail. This should instead only be applied to its censos and other charges; the necessary repairs to its holdings; its fincas; and what is needed to pursue its lawsuits and the claims that may arise for its maintenance, increase, and security. My lord and cousin, the Conde de Villamena, will hold for me all profits it may yield, which will be used for punctual payment of drafts I may issue against him.

I now consider the entails of Madrid, Torrelaguna, Los Caramancheles, and the other holdings; the juro of Ocaña; the censo of 100 ducados of perpetual revenue from Lic. don Juan Díaz, imposed on the house on the Calle del Almendro; the house I own on the Plaza Mayor of Madrid at the corner of Carnicería and Portal de las Pellas; the estate of the villages of Camarma del Caño and Camarma de Esteruela, called del Cristo; the dehesa of Las Gariñas and half the dehesa of Viñaderos at the villa of Buitrago; the pastures and enclosures of the villa of Porquerizas, Miraflores de la Sierra, Chozas, and Guadalix; the farmlands of the villages of Talamanca, Valdepiélagos, and the others that belong to the entail of Torrelaguna; Torremocha; the patronages that pertain to the entail of Madrid, such as the one my aunts, doña Aldonza and doña Antonia Luján, founded at the Convento de Nuestro Padre San Francisco, whose copatrons are the guardian of the convento and the curate of Villaverde; the patronage that María Suárez founded in the parish of San Pedro, whose copatrons are the curate of that parish and whomever the regidor of the villa of Madrid names to attend on the feast day of Our Lady of the Immaculate Conception in the afternoon in that curate's chamber for the selection of the three orphan girls each patron chooses and the dowries designated for them from the revenue; and the chaplaincy that provides for saying the masses.

Since I cannot be present, I am separating from the general power of attorney another I am giving in absentia to Your Lordship for your eldest son. You will recognize that my only consideration is to relieve you of the administration of the entails for the causes stated. I cannot fail in the responsibilities of my honor and duties. Only attention to them and to the wretched state of my fortune could bring about changes in that of the power of attorney, looking to secure my resources against decline, as I repeat. This is not a minor point but my principal consideration, justified by such weighty experiences that burden those who depend on a lord viceroy's will. The higher one's position, the more this follows and to the greatest degree.

I do not dwell on this but only make this brief note, since the arrival of the most excellent lord Duque de Alburquerque gives me occasion.[5] My consideration will be to serve him, though I recognize the strong competition. I am spent from a lawsuit still pending after five years, pursuing my just case, while my opponent governs with the interests that support him and pay his costs. This is the difference between one who fights with weapons and one who lacks them.

Your Lordship can see how saddened I would be by so inopportune and drastic a change. The most excellent lord archbishop and viceroy was in the process of rendering me justice, and I could have been assured of a prompt decision.[6] Now I must delay while the new lord viceroy decides. From this will follow doubt and injury, though I thought I was safe from the past.

I went out fifteen leagues from this city to receive his excellency and my lady the duquesa. He honored me greatly, and both of their excellencies spoke to me highly of Your Lordship and my daughter. Don Diego de Molina gave me the letter my daughter, doña Isabel, gave him, dated 12 May. She told me about herself and the four children Our Lord has seen fit to give you, one boy and three girls. He spoke highly to me of your nephew, don Diego de Olvera, who also was a page of Your Lordship's cousin, don Antonio de Ubilla. I have attended and shall attend him in whatever way I may be of use.

I have not received Your Lordship's letters. Don José de Uribe Castrejón, having come as a lord oidor of this Royal Audiencia, brought me a letter from my cousin, don Sancho Bullón Chacón. He assures me of your favor, which I may know (Our Lord seeing fit) at the end of January this coming new year, 1703. I was sorry that Your Lordship did not give the packets my daughter informs me you are writing to me to don Diego de Molina, who brought her letter. Regardless, God wants to punish me, and God's will be done.

I am writing to my brother, the Marqués de la Florida, by the French captain under whose command this armada sails for France. I hope the letter reaches his hands. To assure that he does get a letter from me, I am sending you a duplicate, so that you can forward it to him.

I do not have to advise Your Lordship to see to the grant of the robe my son (may he be with God) received from his majesty. It was in his papers, which don Francisco Marcos López de Villamil sent to Your Lordship from Cadiz. He left the copy of it with me, and it reads as follows:

Don Bernardino Antonio de Pardiñas Villar de
Francos, knight of the Order of Santiago,
perpetual regidor of Madrid, of his majesty's
Council, his secretary in the Royal Council of
the Three Military Orders of Santiago,
Calatrava, and Alcántara, and their Junta of
Knighthood:

I certify that the king our lord (may God
keep him) by his royal decree of the 11th
of the current month has seen fit to
make to don Juan Manuel de Vargas Pimentel,
who is on the register as noble page
of the queen our lady, the grant of a robe
of the military orders, for which the
necessary appointment will be given to him
by this office of the secretary, upon return
of this certification. Madrid, 13 February
1694.

In view of this, Your Lordship may petition so that the grant will devolve upon me or whomever I choose of proper honorable qualities. Through your ability to reason, you will see that my wish is fulfilled. I also hope that Our Lord keeps Your Lordship many happy years. Mexico City, 31 December 1702.[7]

I am sending this certification to Your Lordship in case you think it appropriate to present it in the Royal and Supreme Council of the Indies, so that his majesty might know from his council the perverseness with which the royal cedula that I cite to Your Lordship in this letter, dated ———— , was obtained by the villa of Santa Fe as plaintiff.[8]

Taking advantage of the sailing of the packet boat, I am again sending to Your Lordship the duplicate I refer to as well as the one relating the state of the case. Judgment having been rendered in my favor in the hearing and review on the 9th of the current month, I send the copy of this so that Your Lordship can present it with the second duplicate of the tribunal's certification that I am sending again with the instruction for whoever the lawyer will be. By this method, I know that this will come before the council where the plaintiff may apply. This being so, the Royal Audiencia will report with the proceedings, sending the original documents of my residencia.[9] In this, Your Lordship will please assign a wholly trustworthy person to challenge any perverse report, although I think that the Royal Council will attend to the matter with a review of the documents I cite and the report of the Royal Audiencia. I am preparing to leave for my government with dispatch. I shall try to set out from this city during the month of May.[10]

It has occurred to me to send the report to Your Lordship to show his majesty that I should be given a salary equal to that which the governor and captain general of the kingdom of New Biscay enjoys. No one enjoys the salary of captain general of New Mexico, only that of civil and military governor. It is not right that I silently pass over an issue founded on such justified reasons.[11]

I am also sending again to Your Lordship that other draft of the second report so that the cedula of royal favor can be shown to his majesty. It was made to me by royal cedula of 15 June 1699 (on advice of the council in 1697) for the continuation in office of the government and provinces of New Mexico (I was first appointed on 18 June 1688). In addition, the grant of the presidial company of El Paso del Río del Norte and its frontiers was made. In compliance with it, the most excellent former lord viceroy, Conde de Moctezuma, was directed to appoint its captain, don Antonio Valverde, and give him its civil government with the title of justicia mayor. Having removed from the government of New Mexico the presidial company of fifty soldiers and its jurisdiction, the grant made to me is diminished by half, when his majesty's will was to make it to me in its entirety in remuneration for my services, without removing anything from me. The royal cedula begins, "Whereas on 18 June 1688, I granted you the civil and military government, etc., I now do so according to and in the same form, etc."[12]

In view of this, I am showing and reminding his majesty, and requesting of him, what is referred to in the report. With the news I am providing Your Lordship, you will please make the effort and petition, should you see fit to favor me, not neglecting to do so when my purpose is to preserve what is honorable, corresponding to the qualities of my lineage, merits, and services. Though I may live on, Your Lordship, my beloved daughter, and my grandchildren will have a greater share of the benefits God may see fit to give me through good fortune than the next man.

I have told Your Lordship in this letter all that occurs to me, adding and repeating that you give my humble thanks to the most excellent lord viceroy, the Duque de Alburquerque, and my lady the duquesa for the favor they have shown me through the ample protection I have found in their greatness. Please have my beloved daughter, doña Isabel, do so as well. It has occurred to me to write my lady, doña Luisa de Loyola, Marquesa de Villanueva, thanking her. The most excellent lord viceroy told don Miguel de Ubilla that I was highly spoken of by this lady, by Your Lordship, by my daughter, and by my lady the duquesa.[13]

I am at Your Lordship's service in consideration of my honorable qualities and the love with which I hope that God will keep Your Lordship the many happy years I wish for you in the company of my beloved daughter and grandchildren. Mexico City, 4 April 1703.

Your Lordship's father
and faithful servant who
esteems you from the heart,

The Marqués de la Nava de
Barcinas [rubrica]

Please write to thank the lords of this Royal Audiencia: don Miguel Calderón de la Barca, senior oidor and president;[14] Dr. don Juan de

Escalante y Mendoza, knight of the Order of Santiago; don Francisco Valenzuela Venegas, knight of the Order of Santiago; don José de Luna; don José de Uribe Castrejón; and don José de Espinosa Ocampo y Cornejo, fiscal of civil and criminal affairs, etc.

To lord don Ignacio López de Zárate, my dear son-in-law

*AMNB. C. inc. Four folios, eight written pages. ARGD. LS. Seven folios, fourteen written pages. Both copies are in the hand of the same scribe. The AMNB fragment, judging from a copying error, was written first.

1. News that Juan Manuel de Vargas Pimentel had died on the voyage from Veracruz to Havana had reached Mexico City in September. Robles, *Diario*, 3:227–28. Letter 63 below.

2. The balance owed to Vargas was 17,619 pesos, 2 tomines, and 6 granos. José de Contreras and Isidoro Ruano de Arista, Tribunal of Accounts, Mexico City, 18 Aug. 1702, AGN, Vínculos 14.

3. The phrase, "para quitarle la vida," was omitted in the later, ARGD copy.

4. Diego de Vargas to Fernando de Teruel, Power of attorney, Mexico City, 12 Nov. 1702, AGNot. 692.

5. The Duque de Alburquerque entered Mexico City on 27 November 1702, when he acceded to his post. Robles, *Diario*, 3:239–40.

6. Juan de Ortega Montañés (1627–1708) served, at different times in his career, as inquisitor, bishop, archbishop, and viceroy of New Spain. He acted in this latter capacity from 27 February to 18 December 1696 and from 4

November 1701 to 17 November 1702. Rivera Cambas, *Gobernantes*, 1:279–83, 292–300; Rubio Mañé, *Virreyes*, 1:296; *Diccionario Porrúa*, 2:1533.

7. It would appear that Diego de Vargas had a part of this letter written on 31 December 1702, on which date he had also written to Isabel María (Letter 35 above) and to other members of the family.

8. The cedula the cabildo obtained was dated 10 October 1701. Royal Audiencia to the king, Mexico City, 3 Mar. 1703, AGI, Guadalajara 142:20.

9. Because of the bulk of the proceedings, which included don Diego's residencia, officials in Mexico City requested and received permission to forward only a brief summary to Spain. The residencia has not yet come to light. See Bloom, "Vargas Encomienda," for details.

10. Vargas did not in fact leave Mexico City until 8 June 1703. Diego de Vargas, Will, Bernalillo, 7 Apr. 1704, SANM I:1027.

11. The salary of the governor of New Biscay was 3,614 pesos, 2

tomines, while that of the governor of New Mexico was 2,000 pesos. *Planta de las pensiones y cargas anuales que tienen las reales cajas de Nueva España, Galicia y Nueba Viscaya, y del producto de los ramos de hacienda afectos a su satisfacción*, Mexico City, 1697, The John Carter Brown Library.

12. This royal cedula of 15 June 1699 continued don Diego in office, extending the appointment made in the cedula of 18 June 1688. The king, *Title reappointing Diego de Vargas governor of New Mexico*, Madrid, 15 June 1699, AGI, México 1216.

13. Brother of Antonio de Ubilla, Miguel de Ubilla, a resident of Mexico City, was a member of the Order of Santiago, a gentleman of his majesty's table, and retired comptroller of the Royal Tribunal of Accounts in New Spain. He also served as an executor of Vargas's 1703 will. Diego de Vargas, *Will*, Mexico City, 1 June 1703, AGNot. 692. Diego de Vargas, *Codicil*, Mexico City, 1 June 1703, AGNot. 692.

14. Miguel Calderón de la Barca had been, according to Schäfer, a supernumerary in 1689. Vargas was imprecise when he identified him as president of the Audiencia. Since 1535, the viceroy of New Spain had served as the Audiencia's president. Schäfer, *Consejo Real*, 2:451, 458; *Recop.*, Lib. 2, tít. 16, ley 1. In 1697, when torrential rains caused serious flooding in the capital, the Conde de Moctezuma had put Oidor Calderón de la Barca in charge of relief measures. Rivera Cambas, *Gobernantes*, 1:288.

---

37. *Lawyer's advice [Mexico City, c. 1703].* *

Lawyer's counsel for the defense that may be necessary in case the villa, as plaintiff, has recourse to the supreme council with some perverse claim based on the report that had been examined by the lord oidor semanero to see if it was in decent and honest terms.[1] Though it was only a matter of his review, the party claims that this was his judgment.

According to the information from the lord marqués, I find little need of preparations for Madrid, if neither a copy of the proceedings nor the originals are being sent and if the Audiencia's report is as favorable as it should be in view of its decisions. Preparations have already been made should the proceedings be sent, repeating that they are all a fabrication and despotic contrivance, wholly the creation of don Pedro Rodríguez Cubero. He has put in writing all he has imagined and invented, and those unfortunates of the villa and its environs have signed—those who knew how.

As a remedy for this damage, we are taking care to present an allegation so that the proceedings will be turned over to the judge of don Pedro Rodríguez Cubero's residencia. The former will proceed to take the statements of those who signed and made depositions under duress, compelled by the rigor of the latter's well-known self-interest. Such fictions will vanish, thus strengthening the case against don Pedro, both in Madrid and in this city.

In the proceedings of the residencia, it is noteworthy that to color them, the first edict containing the proclamation was removed, so as to obscure the fact that they were null and void. This deceit is proven by the rest of the edicts in which the proclamation appears and by the interrogatory don Pedro composed, where the edicts proclaimed are written at the end. The numbers of the folios are altered without explanation.

One of the charges states that no charges were made against him during the term of the residencia, because the members of his household had let it be known that he would return as governor. Under these circumstances, the residencia was proclaimed. It is very much of note that they did not make depositions for fear of his return. Once the cedula of continuation in office had come, they made charges against him, because don Pedro saw as his successor the person from whom he had, according to that person's reckoning, taken 22,500 pesos. Therefore, all his plans and actions have been to prevent the lord marqués's return, so that his stratagems might not be brought to light and his fictions vanish. By divine favor, as a result of don Pedro's residencia, he will be punished and disqualified from any other office or employment.[2]

The very clear proceedings regarding the 22,500 pesos are being sent. The reserve for the soldiers has already vanished for the most part, because, as has been declared, they were paid their salaries when Cubero acceded.[3]

A report is being printed, as is within his rights, based wholly upon a so-called fact.[4] It is so poorly prepared that for full proof of it, and of all the complaints, we must await don Pedro Cubero's residencia. Once we have it, we shall prepare a legal, public declaration both of the deceit of this whole issue and its propositions, and of the ones that are legitimate, resulting from the truth about what happened.

We shall then request that both original proceedings be sent to the royal council. In every case, any defense that requires the arguments and opposing claims should be addressed solely to the council, with the assurance that all would be sent by the earliest flota.

This is done to please the lord marqués, and only to prepare for what is provided herein.

*ARGD. C. Two folios, three written pages.

1. Vargas's abogado in Mexico City was Lic. Manuel de Figueroa. Diego de Vargas to Juan Manuel de Vargas Pimentel, Santa Fe, 23 Dec. 1699, AGN, Vínculos 14. His procurador in 1703 was José de Ledesma. Diego de Vargas to José de Ledesma, Power of attorney, Mexico City, 30 May 1703, AGNot. 692.

2. Pedro Rodríguez Cubero had already received another appointment, but died in 1704 before taking office.

3. The expediente regarding this money and payment of the presidial soldiers is AGN, Historia 37:1.

4. The printed indictment, prepared by Lic. Cristóbal Moreno Avalos, ran to twenty-nine numbered pages. The document contained the charges leveled by the villa of Santa Fe against Vargas, his appointees, and members of his household for alleged excesses committed during his administration. *La Villa de Santa Feé, Cabecera de las Provincias de la Nueva Mexico, informa á V. S.a en el pleito que sigue contra Don Diego de Vargas, Zapata, y Lujan . . .,* Huntington Library, Rare Book 70361.

---

38. *Diego de Vargas to King Felipe V [Mexico City, c. 1703].*

Your Majesty:

Don Diego de Vargas Zapata Luján Ponce de León, Marqués de la Nava de Barcinas, conqueror and pacificator of the kingdom and provinces of New Mexico, governor and captain general and castellan of its fortress and presidio, who is newly appointed, restored, and continued in office by your majesty, states that it seems proper to him to demonstrate, repeat, seek, and ask the following with all due respect at your royal feet.

Since he is dispatched to proceed to that government, what is most important is that he enjoys only the 2,000-peso salary he earns annually while serving your majesty in the civil and military government of these posts in that kingdom and provinces, and that no further salary has been assigned, and he does not enjoy one for the post of captain general equal to what the present governor of the kingdom of New Biscay and the real of Parral receives.

This being the case, it should be justly considered that the governor of New Mexico is on the frontier, opposed on all sides by enemies from the far-flung Apache nation, at distances of five, ten, fifteen, or twenty leagues. The governor of Parral is in the interior at a distance of three hundred leagues across uninhabited territory, the only intermediate place being the presidio of El Paso del Río del Norte. It is in a constant state of warfare because it is very open and far from the jurisdiction and settlement of that kingdom, and its defense is in his charge. This is so, even though he does not have for this purpose, as the above-mentioned governor of New Biscay does, on the one hand, the subsidy in addition to his salary for aid to the peaceful Indian allies and warriors; and, on the other, recourse to haciendas and presidios, in addition to the settlements and camps in its jurisdiction, for the provision of meat, maize and wheat, and horses and mules, at much less expense than at a distance of three hundred leagues.

The governor of New Mexico does not have these advantages, much less what is most important: men he can avail himself of. It follows from this that he must leave behind, out of the one hundred soldiers of the presidio of the villa of Santa Fe, a sufficient number for its defense. He must also assign enough to several frontiers as escort for the protection and security of the lives and haciendas of the citizens settled there, and on ranchos and farms. He can go out with only a few men on campaign for the operations necessary because of continuous enemy incursions.

All this he places before your majesty's royal sovereignty, seeking of you as he hopes, humbly at your royal feet, that you grant to him the same salary the governor of New Biscay and the real of Parral enjoys. Please direct that your royal cedula favoring him be dispatched, should your majesty see fit to make it to him, and that it state this to be so. May it direct your viceroy of this kingdom of New Spain, whoever he may be, and the royal officials of your Treasury office in Mexico City to pay and direct that he be paid from the Royal Treasury office, from the day he accedes to the government, the salary that corresponds to him as captain general, equal to that of the civil and military government paid to him from the Royal Treasury office, just as that of the governor of your kingdom of New Biscay is paid from Guadiana.[1] May he thereby receive a grant from your majesty, as he hopes, in view of the justness of the account and presentation of his request, etc.

*ARGD. C. Two folios, three written pages. A scribal insertion is indicated near the top of the left-hand margin on folio 1r: "And Castellan of its fortress and presidio."

1. The northernmost royal treasury in New Spain was located at the villa of Guadiana, present-day Durango. Bakewell, *Silver Mining*, 184.

---

39. *Diego de Vargas to Isabel María de Vargas Pimentel, Mexico City, 28 March 1703.**

My dearest daughter,

I trust in Our Lord that this finds you in the good health I wish for you. May His Divine Majesty give me the same, after the misfortunes and cares I have had during the lengthy six years of my lawsuit, three years in prison, and another three in Mexico City. I was delayed in coming here by all the malice of the governor, who put me in this wretched state. Our Lord has seen fit that the sentence of the hearing and review turned out in my favor, declaring that I should be permitted to proceed to my government by order of the most excellent lord viceroy, the Duque de Alburquerque. To this prince I owe the honor of his having attended the hearing of the lawsuit that took place on 13 February and the review on 9 March.

Because the plaintiff, who was condemned to costs, has appealed, I do not doubt that the Royal Audiencia is reporting to his majesty on the proceedings by this packet boat, sending the originals of my residencia. This is according to his royal cedula of 10 October 1701, obtained at Barcelona on behalf of the villa, insisted upon and encouraged by its governor to prevent me from acceding to that government, for which I am preparing to leave with dispatch, in the month of May, with burdens I do not know how to explain to you. They and the question of my honor are the shackles that detain me and will delay me in this kingdom for as long as God Our Lord sees fit to give me life for me to free myself from my debts. In the meantime, also by His mediation, my wish to put those entails in order may be realized, so that they may help me get out of my captivity. The only thing that could delay me would be paying whomever I owe.

For this reason, I have decided to divide the administration of the entails into two parts. I am sending a separate power of attorney for the one of Granada[1] and another for those of Madrid, Torrelaguna, and the rest of the revenue to the lords Marqués de Vargas,[2] Conde de Puebla de los Valles,[3] and my cousin, don Sancho Bullón, so that they can transfer it to business agents.[4] I have sent the duplicate of the powers of attorney and letters with the mail by the French ships that sailed about January.

When these lords have put this into effect, I shall have the report and know the truth about the state of my entails and have hope for my prompt relief. In this, I am aided by whatever fortune gives me in that government of New Mexico (Our Lord seeing fit). I am counting on something to ease and support me there.

I shall not dwell any longer on explaining this to you. I am hoping to have a letter from you, now that your husband, my son-in-law, refuses to write. I have not received a letter from him since 1701. May God give him good health and keep him in your company and that of my beloved grandchildren, to whom I give my blessing, the many years I wish. Mexico City, 28 March 1703.

Your father who loves and esteems
you from the heart and wishes for
your well-being,

The Marqués de la Nava de
Barcinas [rubrica]

To my dear daughter, doña Isabel María de Vargas

*AMNB. LS. Two folios, four written pages. The end of the text and the closing appear vertically in the left-hand margin of folio 2v.

1. Diego de Vargas to Fernando de Teruel, Power of attorney, Mexico City, 12 Nov. 1702, AGNot. 692.

2. Francisco Antolín de Vargas y Lezama Arteaga y Ochoa de Jugo, a noble from Bilbao, was given the title Marqués de Vargas in the year 1700. He left no succession. Alonso-Cadenas, *Elenco,* 658. García Carraffa, *Diccionario heráldico,* 48:167.

3. Conde de Puebla de los Angeles or de los Valles was a title granted by Carlos II by decree of 18 June 1690 and royal cedula of 30 September 1691 to the Vizconde de Liñán, José de Liñán y Cisneros. He was a member of the Order of Alcántara. He received the title in recognition of his services and those of his brother, Melchor de Liñán y Cisneros, who was bishop of Santa Marta, Popayán, archbishop of Charcas and Lima, and viceroy of Peru. Both were from Torrelaguna. EUI, 48:70.

4. Diego de Vargas executed his power of attorney to the Marqués de Vargas, the Conde de Puebla de los Valles, and Sancho Bullón Chacón on 31 December 1702, but the document was voided and drawn up again the following day. Diego de Vargas to the Marqués de Vargas, the Conde de Puebla de los Valles, and Sancho de Bullón Chacón, Power of attorney, Mexico City, 31 Dec. 1702 and 1 Jan. 1703, AGNot. 692.

―――――

40. *Diego de Vargas to Isabel María de Vargas Pimentel, Mexico City, 12 April 1703.**

My beloved daughter,

Because the packet boat has been delayed, I again inform you that I am preparing to set out with dispatch for my government at the end of this month. This is because the sentence on hearing and review of the proceedings by the lords of the Royal Audiencia came out in my favor. The most excellent lord Duque de Alburquerque, to whom I owe all honor and favor, concurred. Therefore, you and my son-in-law, lord don Ignacio, will please write to him, thanking him and my lady the duquesa. Your husband should also write to all the lords of this Royal Audiencia, as well as to the lord fiscal. I include their names in the letter to him so that he can write to each one. They condemned the present governor to costs.

I presented to his excellency the royal cedula of the grant of encomienda so that he might direct that I be given the dispatches. Yesterday, I made the payment of 1,200 pesos in the Royal Treasury office for the royal tax of the media anata. I drew up a contract with a guarantor of good credit to hand over a like amount at the beginning of the second year.

For the second generation, his excellency has directed me to seek recourse from his majesty in his supreme council. This is so that he can confirm the grant, since by his royal cedula of 1701, he instituted the reform that persons living in Spain could enjoy for only one generation the grants that were made for two.[1] He declared that this did not apply to those living and having their residence in these kingdoms of the Indies. For this reason, his majesty may confirm whoever succeeds me in the second generation in the grant made to me in consideration of my services and conquest of the kingdom of New Mexico, and whether he would have to reside in these kingdoms to enjoy the encomienda. I shall leave this in writing for you and your husband, my son-in-law, sending the copy so that the confirmation of the second generation will be assured for whoever inherits my entails.

This letter will serve my son-in-law and the other relatives as news that I am in good health (thanks to Our Lord), hoping that His Divine Majesty keeps you for many years in the company of your beloved husband and my beloved grandchildren, to whom I give my blessing. Mexico City, 12 April 1703.

> Your father who loves and
> esteems you from the heart and
> who, if it is the will of God
> Our Lord, will see you again,
>
> The Marqués de la Nava de
> Barcinas [rubrica]

To my beloved daughter, doña Isabel María de Vargas Pimentel

*AMNB. LS. Two folios, three written pages.

1. In 1701, the crown decreed that encomiendas granted to residents of Spain could only be held for the lifetime of the actual possessor. At the end of that time, the encomienda reverted to the crown. Silvio A. Zavala, *La encomienda indiana* (Mexico City, 1973):246–47.

---

41. *Diego de Vargas to Ignacio López de Zárate, Mexico City, 16 April 1703.* *

Son and dear sir,

Because of the delay in closing the chests this packet boat carries, I saw to the encomienda's disposition, the copy of which I am sending to Your Lordship enclosed in this letter. When you have seen it, please seek in the Cámara of the Supreme and Royal Council of the Indies confirmation of the second generation, as expressed in the royal cedula giving it.

Your Lordship will please send it to me in duplicate, retaining the triplicate in your possession for safekeeping to send to me if the first two are lost. I would give you news in case of such misfortune. I shall continue to send, whenever possible, the copy in duplicate until such time as Your Lordship acknowledges receipt.

I repeat what I am asking of you about writing at every opportunity to their most excellent lordships, the viceroy and vicereine, the Duque and my lady the Duquesa de Alburquerque, to thank them for the honor they do me. Your Lordship may be sure they will continue, as the princes they are in every way. Also, please write to the lords of this Royal Audiencia; I have provided Your Lordship with their names. Please convey to my lady the Marquesa de Villanueva, Your Lordship's sister-in-law, my readiness to serve her. Offer her that, as is my duty. The memory of her deceased husband, my friend the lord marqués, is everlasting. I feel his loss at present, because he had offered to favor me with his influence, energy, and effectiveness.

I must also remind Your Lordship to take every care you deem appropriate to assure, in my behalf, that my household rests on a firm foundation, now that my fortune is again taking me to so distant a place, Our Lord giving me life. Your Lordship will therefore please pay close attention to all the letters you may receive from me.

May God keep Your Lordship many happy years, as I wish, in the company of my beloved daughter and grandchildren, to whom Your Lordship will please give my embraces and to whom I give my blessing. Mexico City, 16 April 1703.

Your father and most
affectionate servant
who loves you from the
heart kisses Your Lordship's hand,

The Marqués de la Nava
de Barcinas [rubrica]

To my dear son-in-law, don Ignacio López de Zárate

*AMNB. LS. Two folios, four written pages.

---

42. *Diego de Vargas to Ignacio López de Zárate, Mexico City, 27 April 1703.* *

Son and dear sir,

I have written to Your Lordship during the present month and sent the copy of the grant assigning me 4,000 pesos of revenue from an encomienda that our majesty, King Carlos II (may he be in holy glory), gave me for two generations. In this letter I am again requesting that Your Lordship will please present it in the Cámara of the Royal and Supreme Council of the Indies, seeking its confirmation as stated in the copy.

Please try to secure the revenue, bearing in mind the distance the kingdom of New Mexico is from this city. Consequently, the only recourse to secure collection of the revenue independent of whoever may be governor of that kingdom is to ask his majesty for a royal cedula. It should limit jurisdiction over cases that may arise with regard to collection and impede whoever has the power of attorney, thus reducing the revenue. Also, this person or persons should not fail to do their duty, without bothering the Indian tributaries, who are to pay only in kind and at the rate customary in that kingdom. They should not ask them for more than what is indicated and what each tributary, such as single males and females of sufficient age, widowers, and widows, should pay, preserving their custom in every detail and the way they paid former encomenderos of that kingdom, as is expressed in the copy.[1]

Also, the person who, by virtue of the power of attorney, is charged with collection of revenue should be allowed to live either in the villa of Santa Fe (or in any other villa) or in an Indian pueblo, or on any hacienda, rancho, or estancia that may be convenient and to his advantage, without the governor prohibiting him from doing so. Instead, the person may of his own volition live wherever seems most convenient to assure collection of the revenue of the encomienda and its environs.[2]

Whenever he sees fit, that person may also leave the kingdom of New Mexico for those kingdoms beyond—New Biscay, New Galicia, and Sonora—even for this kingdom of New Spain, to trade and contract to sell the goods he acquires as revenue from the encomienda. The Indians will pay him the tribute in kind, collected according to the custom of that kingdom. They have no other coin than those goods. To convert goods to money, and remit it to Castile, he himself may need to leave without further explanation. This would be neither reason nor motive for whoever may be governor in that kingdom to prevent him. Should the governor do so, the holder of the power of attorney should protest the damage, delay, losses, interest, and reductions in revenue that could result. It is appropriate for him to seek their conversion in those kingdoms. In the event that he is ill, the royal cedula itself should allow him to give authority to whomever he selects, designates, and appoints, someone who will do it in the most effective way, so as not to delay and run the risk of losing the goods.

Your Lordship is to put into effect these dispatches in confirmation and the royal cedulas, sending them to me immediately in duplicate to this city of Mexico, addressed to lord don Miguel Calderón, senior oidor of this Royal Audiencia, and in the second place to lord don Diego de Suazo, archdeacon of the holy metropolitan church of Mexico City.[3]

To my beloved daughter and to the grandchildren countless embrac-

es. I give them my blessing and I wish you all good health. May Our
Lord keep them in Your Lordship's company many happy years. Mexico City, 27 April 1703.

> Your father and servant, who
> esteems you from the heart until
> death, kisses Your Lordship's hand,
>
> The Marqués de la Nava
> de Barcinas [rubrica]

To my son-in-law and lord, don Ignacio López de Zárate

I caution Your Lordship to write me always in duplicate, the first to
lord don Miguel Calderón and the second to lord don Diego de Suazo,
archdeacon of this holy church. The most secure way will always be
in the packet of the lord marqués to his cousin, don Miguel de Ubilla,
knight of the Order of Santiago, gentleman of his majesty's table,
retired comptroller general of the Royal Tribunal and Chief Accounting Office in Mexico City.

*ARGD. LS. AMNB. C. Two folios, four written pages. The postscript is writ-
ten vertically in the left-hand margin of folio 1r. The text of the last folio
continues vertically in the left-hand margin and is followed by the closing.

1. The encomienda, a royal grant, was in theory a reciprocal arrangement whereby the grantee, the encomendero, provided religious instruction and military protection to a group of Indians in exchange for the tribute they owed the crown. In New Mexico, the usual items of tribute were maize, mantas (pieces of cotton or woolen cloth between four and five feet square), and buffalo and other animal hides, supplemented with piñon nuts, salt, and other commodities. Sometimes labor was substituted for items of tribute. The household was the tributary unit, and collection occurred in May and October. Although abuses were recorded, one ethnohistorian has concluded recently that the institution was not as burdensome to the Pueblo Indians, at least initially, as has been generally assumed. David H. Snow, "A Note on Encomienda Economics in Seventeenth-Century New Mexico," in *Hispanic Arts and Ethnohistory in the Southwest: New Papers Inspired by the Work of E. Boyd*, ed. Marta Weigle (Santa Fe, 1983):347–57. See also John

L. Kessell, *Kiva, Cross, and Crown: The Pecos Indians and New Mexico, 1540–1840* (Washington, D.C., 1979):98–99, 187–90.

2. By asking that the revenue collector be allowed to reside in the area where the Indians of the encomienda lived, Vargas was seeking to set aside various laws of the Indies that specifically prohibited such residence. *Recop.*, Lib. 6, tít. 9, leyes 10–12, 14.

3. Diego de Suazo Coscojales also served as an executor of Vargas's 1703 will. Diego de Vargas, Codicil, Mexico City, 1 June 1703, AGNot. 692.

---

43. *Juan Antonio Pimentel de Prado, Marqués de la Florida, to Diego de Vargas, Milan, 17 June 1703.**

My brother and friend,

With particular pleasure, I received your last letter, of 31 December 1702, in which you saw fit to give me favorable news of the state of your health. I hope that it continues many years so that, in whatever may lead to your greater pleasure and service, you can avail yourself of mine, which (thanks be to God) is also good.

After the flota had put into harbor, I had the unhappy news of the premature death of my beloved nephew, Juanito (may he be in holy glory). You must not doubt the deep sorrow that so great a loss causes me, and I offer you my sympathy.

You will have had news of the disaster that befell the flota when it was in the port in Galicia. In the attack by the navies of Holland and England, a great part of the merchandise was lost. This has caused a great setback, affecting me personally with the loss of the chocolate you were sending me. I wrote to Cadiz to inquire of don Fausto de Bustamante. He replied that everything had been lost, and that he was not able to salvage even his clothing.[1]

From the copy of the certification you sent to me, I see the state of your business affairs. I shall be happy if the settlement of your accounts has already come out so favorably, given the setbacks you have been caused while seeking it. I hope that you will have been restored to that government. I do not doubt that, in his justness, the lord viceroy will have harkened to your arguments.

I have seen the copy of the letter that you are writing to your son-in-law, my nephew, don Ignacio. The decision you have made about the general power of attorney that you have given for the administration of your entails in the city of Granada seems wise. Rest assured that I profoundly regret not being at court, where I might see to your business affairs. Yet, you must believe in my consideration and love. Insofar as I might be able to assist you from here, you will find me prompt in my wish to serve you as you have always known. I have wished to serve you to your greater satisfaction, as I shall do, as often as you permit me.

This is all that occurs to me to tell to you. May Our Lord keep you the many years He is able and I wish. The Royal Castle of Milan, 17 June 1703.[2]

My brother and friend, I was most contented awaiting the arrival in Spain of my beloved nephew, Juan de Vargas. I had no doubt that he would come immediately to look for me here, but God saw fit to dispose otherwise. May His holy will be done. I remain well and pleased in this post. I only regret not being able to attend to business as I should like, being so far from Madrid. Yet, I shall do what I am able and press my nephew, don Ignacio, to keep in mind how much he owes you.

Your brother and friend from
the heart kisses your hand,

The Marqués de la Florida [rubrica][3]

My brother-in-law and friend, the Marqués de la Nava de Barcinas

*AMNB. LS. Two folios, four written pages. The postscript is in the hand of the Marqués de la Florida.

1. On 24 July 1702, the Spanish silver and French commercial fleet under the escort of French Admiral Chateaurenaud had sailed from Havana for Spain. Learning of the presence of an allied Dutch and English fleet off Cadiz, the Spaniards and Frenchmen had sought a safe port at Vigo in Galicia, reaching there on 23 September. A defensive position had been established and most of the bullion safely put ashore. On 22 October, the enemy fleet had arrived off Vigo. On the 24th, the allied ships and troops had

attacked, passing barriers in the harbor entrance and overrunning land positions. The Spanish-French fleet had been lost and the ships evacuated and burned, resulting in a great loss of merchandise. This episode has long been considered a signal naval disaster for Spain. Yet most of the seventeen ships lost were French, and most of the merchandise belonged to English and Dutch merchants. Moreover, the silver had already been unloaded and, according to the calculations of one historian, it amounted to the largest shipment that Spain received from the Indies in a single year. Kamen, "Destruction of the Spanish Silver Fleet," 165–73.

2. Because of its strategic location, Milan had often been the scene of struggles between Spain and its European challengers. During the War of the Spanish Succession, the opening battles took place there. Soon after Felipe V was named king of Spain, he acceded to the wishes of his grandfather, Louis XIV, and traveled to Italy to consolidate Spanish holdings there. While in the Duchy of Milan, Felipe V participated in several conflicts, among them the Battle of Luzzara, pitting Spanish, French, and Sardinian forces against Prince Eugene of Savoy. The action, fought on 15 August 1702, was bloody and indecisive. Eight to ten thousand casualties made it the costliest conflict of the long war. All parties claimed victory, and, by the end of 1702, Felipe had returned to Spain. J. S. Bromley, ed., *The Rise of Great Britain and Russia 1688–1715/25*, vol. 6 of *The New Cambridge Modern History* (Cambridge, 1970):557–58; EUI, 23:606–607; Kamen, *War of Succession in Spain*, 10–11; *Enciclopedia italiana di scienze, lettere ed arti* (Rome, 1949), 21:709.

3. After his service in Milan, the Marqués de la Florida returned to Madrid, where he was buried on 7 January 1708 in the chapel of the Hospital de la Venerable Orden Tercera de San Francisco. Pérez Balsera, *Laudemus*, 78.

Return to New Mexico:
El Paso and Santa Fe, 1703

*44. Diego de Vargas to Ignacio López de Zárate,
El Paso del Río del Norte, 16 September 1703.* *

Son and dear sir,

I am sending to Your Lordship the enclosed duplicate of the letter I dispatched to you on 27 April.[1] I do so again from this presidio of El Paso del Río del Norte, four hundred leagues from Mexico City, and one hundred and twenty leagues short of the villa of Santa Fe. I could not fail to give you word that I am in good health after such an extended journey. I am sending a courier to Mexico City to seek news from Your Lordship. I think I shall receive it in the coming month of October, when the ships should have arrived from those ports, now that the ones from France have arrived.[2]

I have not had the good fortune of receiving any news from Your Lordship. Your cousin, the lord Marqués de Rivas,[3] sent a packet he writes to Mexico City to his cousin, don Miguel de Ubilla, to whom this is addressed. Thus, news could have arrived safely in my hands. As far as I am concerned, Your Lordship need offer me no excuse, unless it is the cooling of your good will, or better said, the complete absence of it. So that you will not judge mine lacking (nor could it be, much less my consideration for you), I am giving you word, sending to you in the first place those two reports. Your Lordship may add or delete whatever may occur to you to put them in the proper form and present them in the Council of the Cámara of the Junta of War for the Indies.

I am sending the first to request a salary equal to that which the governor and captain general of New Biscay enjoys. The second is to request that I be promoted to one of the posts I have indicated. For this, I have sent to the lord Marqués de Rivas the power of attorney in duplicate, dating from January of the current year until May. I am repeating the request in this same letter, with the news of my arrival. I sent to Your Lordship the copy of the hearing and review in my favor by the Royal Audiencia, condemning don Pedro Cubero and the cabildo and villa of Santa Fe to costs. Therefore, I am not repeating it here until I have word from Your Lordship. It is necessary for you to inform me about the legal documents I have sent to you, what may have been done regarding the dispatch of the title of Marqués de la Nava de Barcinas, the arrangement of its royal fee of media anata, and the grant of a robe of a military order for my son (may he be with God) about which I have written to Your Lordship. It was in the original papers he was carrying with the record of his service. His friends will have sent them to Your Lordship.

There can be no doubt of the flota's safe arrival in the ports of Galicia, as is everyone's wish, and mine also, for the common good, above and beyond my concern about what I sent. I have written to Your Lordship about the cases of chocolate I sent with don Fausto Bustamante and the case you were to send to my brother-in-law, the Marqués de la Florida.

The points I am relating to Your Lordship are to put you on guard against any perverse report by don Pedro Cubero, who is encouraging and supporting the lawsuit, alleging that the villa requests it. These points are to advise Your Lordship that the Royal Audiencia has made a report on the sentence promulgated in my favor upon hearing and review. It has declared that there is no impediment to transferring the royal cedula to me and that a copy of it should be given to me so that the most excellent lord viceroy, upon review, if he sees fit, may order that I be given the dispatches.

With the report and copies sent to Your Lordship of my having been pronounced a fair judge by the hearing of my residencia, and with the copy from the Tribunal of Accounts stating that I owe nothing to his majesty and ordering that I be paid the balance in my favor, the royal council will recognize the malice of the charges and confirm the sentence as by competent judge by virtue of the royal cedula entrusting cognizance to the Royal Audiencia. I have obtained judgment from those tribunals that all testimony against me is null and void.

I do not need to advise Your Lordship further. With this information and the duplicate of 27 April this year I have written you everything. Your Lordship will please not fail to find someone on the council to give you word. You will also please let me know when you have seen your cousin, the lord Marqués de Rivas, and what may have been set in motion. Do send me a copy of the report presented and of the lords' opinion. I trust always that my wish will be fulfilled, since it should be recognized that what I ask is so just.

Upon accession to my government in the villa of Santa Fe, I shall dispatch the copy to the superior government in Mexico City, as ordered in the royal cedula. I shall repeat this and more for Your Lordship, to which you should reply. As for the letter you may be writing to me (if your concern has moved you to do so), I hope it contains the good news of Your Lordship's good health and that of my daughter and grandchildren. I give my blessing, wishing that Our Lord will keep you in their company many happy years. Your Lordship will please send to Torrelaguna the letters to my children and to my brother-in-law, don Gregorio.

Done in this presidio of El Paso del Río del Norte and kingdom of New Mexico, 16 September 1703.

Your father and servant, who esteems
you only with consideration, kisses Your
Lordship's hand,

The Marqués de la Nava
de Barcinas [rubrica]

To my son-in-law and lord, don Ignacio López de Zárate

*ARGD. LS. Two folios, three written pages.

1. Letter 42 above.

2. On 3 May 1703, news arrived in Mexico City that a heavily armed warship dispatched by the king of France had dropped anchor in Veracruz with word that Chateaurenaud's fleet had safely made the port of Vigo. As don Diego wrote from El Paso, he had not yet learned of the destruction of the fleet in October 1702. This news did not arrive in Mexico City until 19 August 1703. Robles, *Diario*, 3:264–65, 281. For more on the battle of Vigo, see Letter 43 above.

3. The title of Marqués de Rivas de Jarama was granted to Antonio de Ubilla y Medina on 3 January 1702. Alonso-Cadenas, *Elenco*, 495.

45. *Diego de Vargas, Memorial to King Felipe* V
*[El Paso del Río del Norte, c. 16 September 1703].**

Your Majesty,

Don Diego de Vargas Zapata Luján Ponce de León, Marqués de la Nava de Barcinas, placing himself humbly at your majesty's royal feet, would show how, after the general uprising of the Indian nations and pueblos of the kingdom of New Mexico and its provinces, which occurred in 1680, your majesty's dominion was reduced in those regions to only the pueblo of the presidio of El Paso and the surrounding areas since rebels and apostates occupied the rest. The insurgents, having shaken off the yoke of obedience to your majesty, rendered vassalage only to their uncivilized, unbound will. They persisted in this obstinacy for more than twelve years, until (upon the occasion of the grant of governor and captain general of that kingdom your majesty saw fit to make to him in 1688) the supplicant arrived. Encountering this stubbornness, he overcame their disobedience, reconquering them in their rebelliousness and pacifying the unrest. The rebels were returned to their former faith, which was impressed upon spirits until then resistant, and your majesty's crown was restored.

By official cartas consultas from the viceroys of New Spain and from the Junta of Royal Treasury and War of this kingdom, your majesty was informed of these services. Since they merited approval in your royal estimation, you saw fit on the advice of the Royal and Supreme Council of the Indies, its Cámara, and Junta of War to continue don Diego in the government by royal cedula of 1697, accompanying this grant with one for the title reconqueror and pacificator of those provinces, for he had thus served with the success and favorable results recorded for your majesty. [1]

There was no lack of rivals, your majesty, who tried to dissipate the glory that the supplicant was able to attain, at the cost of his own fortune and at the risk of his life. These people declared much more loudly once they sensed that the royal munificence, considering the crown well served by the supplicant's military feats, began to reward him. Then the governor of that kingdom, don Diego's successor, declaring himself opposed and even an enemy, set about encouraging and suggesting complaints and claims against don Diego. These came even to your majesty's royal attention. From your supreme council judgments emanated. As a result, today the false charges, which this successor and others (his ill-willed accomplices) machinated against don Diego's conduct, reputation, fortune, and life, are dissipated and undone. He has been restored to the five-year term of his continuation in office and is about to return to govern the kingdom.

Your majesty granted this to him in the same form as the first time, as stated in the royal dispatch continuing him in office. When the time comes, he will accede to it, though it is now incomplete. The first time he merited it from your majesty, this government included political and military jurisdiction over the presidio of El Paso and its adjoining and outlying areas. Midway through don Pedro Rodríguez Cubero's government, the presidio of El Paso was separated from that of New Mexico, because its company had been given to Capt. don Antonio Valverde, to whom the viceroy, the Conde de Moctezuma, also issued dispatches naming him justicia mayor for political affairs. Today he is in possession of both. Thus, the supplicant will receive the limited government as reward, when his good deeds delayed him. Even before, he had learned from the grant that he merited the whole of it.

The diminution this government suffers today is no less. This is because of the time that has passed since he was continued here and the more than six years his accession has been delayed. During this period, what he has suffered is inconceivable. The whole time has been nothing but litigation, having for a judge (if the incompetent can be considered one) a biased governor, who without listening to the supplicant's defense, offended him in as many arbitrary ways as his whim dictated. He held him prisoner for three years—five months in shackles—embargoing his properties and depriving him of even the holiest and most religious company and communications. He brought suits, stirring up complainants, and bringing out in public unjust claimants. Through them, he gained the destruction of the supplicant's wealth; harming, if not wounding, his reputation; and seeking to despoil him of the grant with which your majesty honored his services. Above all, he tried to ensure that the supplicant would not succeed him. All this was done with no more reason than the supplicant's having acted properly in serving your majesty, pacifying a kingdom to expand your majesty's dominions and don Pedro's government.

This denigration, the poverty, lawsuits, delays, and other aggravations he has suffered the supplicant places on the scale with his merit so that your majesty may consider them as services (for they proceed from the facts) and bear in mind how much this government has been pared down by having the presidio of El Paso, its administration, and military and political jurisdiction removed. This amounts to a reward unequal to his performance, when the compensation for his suffering should have been very generous and ample. Your majesty may deign to better the grant made to him, disposing that it be understood and verified: in the government, captaincy general, and presidency of the kingdom of the Philippines; or in that of the kingdom of Guatemala; or in that of the kingdom of Santa Fe and New Kingdom of Granada; and, if they are not available, that of the government and captaincy general of the kingdom of New Biscay as soon as the one who exercises it, Mre. de Campo don Juan Fernández de Córdoba,[2] completes his term, because its war is similar to that of this kingdom of New Mexico and it borders upon it. In 1691, by order of your most excellent viceroy, the Conde de Galve, by resolution of the General Junta of Royal Treasury and War of the court at Mexico City, the supplicant went in command of the forces. It seemed advisable that those of his presidio and those of Janos, Sinaloa, and the Casas Grandes flying company should be united. This was done, and the war and campaign carried to the frontiers of Sonora, at his expense, which serves him as a recommendation for his petition, either for this post, because of the knowledge and experience he has of that entire land and kingdom, or for wherever your majesty may see fit that he receive a grant.[3]

> The Marqués de la Nava
> de Barcinas [rubrica]

*ARGD. DS. Two folios, four written pages. The last paragraph, in Vargas's hand, begins on folio 2r and ends with the signature on folio 2v. Since don Diego wrote it himself, he may not have wanted the scribe to know his intentions.

1. Council of the Indies, Consultas, Madrid, 28 July and 21 Aug. 1698, AGI, Guadalajara 141:27.

2. Juan Fernández de Córdoba was born in 1653 in La Rambla in the province of Córdoba, Spain. From 1678 to 1693 he served with the Spanish army in Flanders, holding several ranks over the years, including alferez, lieutenant, and captain. He was listed as

maese de campo in Barcelona in 1693. From 1703 until 1708, Fernández de Córdoba was governor and captain general of New Biscay. DRSW, Biofile.

3. Concerning the 1691 Sonora campaign, see Letter 11 above.

————

46. *Gregorio Pimentel de Prado to Diego de Vargas, n.p., n.d. (mid-1703).* *

My brother, lifelong friend, and very dear sir,

I assure you by the truth I profess that my tears, caused by the sad news the last flota brought us of my dearly beloved nephew, don Juan Manuel de Vargas, have not yet dried, and his memory (to commend him to God) will last as long as I may live.[1]

Your letter, friend and brother, written 29 March of this year, greatly elates me. In addition to bringing me the very happy news that you are quite well, it adds the news my duty and friendship were eagerly wishing—thinking of you restored to your government with as good a reputation as your widely known actions merit. For this, I offer you many, many congratulations. Although I ponder the long time that you now must spend before I can hope to see you in Spain, I have heard the reasons, the main one being your honor, that will oblige you to do so. I must reconcile myself to such a long absence, since the Divine Majesty allows it to be so.

As soon as I received your letter, I did what you requested, writing to my niece and nephew. I asked them to write without delay to their most excellent lordships, the Duques de Alburquerque, viceroy and vicereine of that kingdom, thanking their excellencies in response to so great an obligation as that under which they have placed us all by the way they have honored and favored you. My lady the Duquesa de Alburquerque, the elder, and my lady doña María Alvarez, her very close friend, have replied to me that they are very much in agreement and offered to add other letters. I am aware that her ladyship accompanied my niece, my lady doña Isabel de Vargas, when their excellencies left Madrid for New Spain. You can imagine, my brother, how well she would have known how to present your argument and how effectively she would have persisted, so that we all might see such a happy day. You can be sure that their consideration will continue, as their unwavering love and duty bid them.

Although you did not, nor do you, inform me of the new decision you have made for the administration of your entails, because the friendship I profess for you is so loyal, I venture to offer for your consideration the following. Lord don Ignacio López de Zárate, my nephew, of the Councils of Castile and Italy, is representing your house at present with propriety and brilliance, to which is added his large family of such handsome children. I believe that these are reasons, my brother—the great adversity of the times being more serious than you can imagine, despite what may be suffered there, and I imagine your setbacks— for you to delve into your generosity. You may demonstrate it by extending yourself in every way you can for the greater relief of your children and grandchildren.

If you see fit to rightly acknowledge the confidence of one who lives by your many favors, I would venture to propose to you that the Granada estate might continue in the care of the person you have chosen. That of Torrelaguna you may give and entrust to my nephew, don José de Vargas, and my niece, Juanica. I consider it very fitting that my nephew, lord don Ignacio, and niece, my lady doña Isabel, care for and enjoy what remains. This, my brother and friend, is what I would do if your duty were mine.

I have very recent word of the good health of my brother, don Juan, and the little ones, your nephews and nieces.[2] I know what a great pleasure all of them will take in reading everything in the letter you tell me you are writing to my brother. I wrote in the last mail to his grace and do so again in this one, telling him, as so interested a party, to write to the most excellent lord viceroy and lady vicereine. I assume that his grace will not fail in this duty.

I have written thanking you for wishing that I might enjoy the chocolate you were sending by don Fausto de Bustamente. I now thank you again, though, as you must know, don Fausto has not delivered it.

My brother and friend, nothing occurs to me to add to what I have expressed to you, except to repeat the great pleasure I take in thinking of you restored with such renown to your government, where I hope you will have gone with the greatest happiness.

Your brother, friend, and most grateful
servant who wishes for your greatest
pleasures,

Don Gregorio Pimentel [rubrica]

My brother, I do want you to know that your nephew, Sebastián, is now a cavalry captain. My brother writes me that Gregorio will be placed soon.[3]

To lord Marqués de la Nava de Barcinas, my brother-in-law and my best friend and lord

*AMNB. LS. Two folios, four written pages. The last paragraph, closing, and postscript are in don Gregorio's hand.

1. A memorial service had been held in Torrelaguna for Juan Manuel on 23 November 1702. Difuntos, Libro 2 (1664–1712), Parroquia de Santa María Magdalena, Torrelaguna.

2. Juan Antonio Pimentel de Prado, Marqués de la Florida, was then serving in Milan. Letter 63 below.

3. Sebastián and Gregorio, don Gregorio's sons, were with their uncle in Milan. Letter 63 below.

----

47. Ignacio López de Zárate to Diego de Vargas, Madrid, 28 September 1703.*

My father and dear sir,

Since this packet boat is being sent, I am offered the opportunity I so wished for to repeat my humility at Your Lordship's feet and to make known to you the great consolation I received from your letter of 31 December last year with the good news that Your Lordship remains in the perfect health necessary, for which I repeatedly thank Our Lord. I do so in consideration of the pain and grief Your Lordship must have suffered as a result of the news you had from Havana of the untimely, sudden death of my beloved brother-in-law and friend, don Juan Manuel de Vargas Pimentel. Every day, his loss makes me more disconsolate. So as not to deepen the loss I know is Your Lordship's so justifiably, I refer in this particular to one of the paragraphs of the letter I wrote to you on 5 May this year.

I have taken note of all the rest of the content of Your Lordship's letter I refer to and found it repeated and confirmed by another of 4

April this year.[1] Some French captain must have brought it, because of all three of the letters Your Lordship relates to me that you have written and sent by him and other French captains, no other has reached my hands. The contents of both come down to your just decision to entrust the administration of your entails and estate, as regards Madrid, to the Marqués de Vargas, my cousin, or to the Conde de Puebla, or to lord don Sancho Bullón, my friends, and as for what pertains to Granada, to lord don Fernando de Teruel, Conde de Villamena.

It only occurs to me to say to Your Lordship that this was very proper and necessary and in accord with all the reasons Your Lordship relates to me. These are very characteristic of Your Lordship's great understanding and prudence. My respect for and attention to Your Lordship must only contribute to assuring you of how much pleasure and special satisfaction I take in celebrating Your Lordship's decision. I do so by committing myself in such a way that from this day your entails and estate can only acquire assets for your greater security and gain so that Your Lordship may accomplish your just purpose and wish.

My wish can never be other than Your Lordship's best interests, so that those of my wife, your daughter, and those of her children, your grandchildren, are secure. I go on to thank you very much for everything. In prompt fulfillment of my duty, I tell Your Lordship that as a result of what you have arranged, I shall hand over to the above-mentioned lords the new powers of attorney and the papers I have pertaining to Your Lordship's entails and estate, and a separate report of the state they are in today. So informed, they will be able to more easily manage them in administration.

As for what relates to Granada, I shall have don Diego de Olvera do the same so that the lord Conde de Villamena will also be able with the same ease to administer that estate.

Your Lordship did me a special honor by revoking the powers of attorney from don Juan González Calderón, by reason of the news you had of my happy marriage to Isabel, your daughter, and by giving them to me unconditionally. I recognize that in them Your Lordship excused me from rendering accounts. I have endeavored from the time I began to exercise them to continue preparing the accounts, as befits my honor and duty. I did this with the same trust that Your Lordship showed in me, should the occasion have arisen, as it almost did, that my dear brother-in-law, don Juan Manuel de Vargas

Pimentel, might ask me for them. He did not arrive to offer himself for this purpose, however, because of God's just judgment. In the new powers of attorney that Your Lordship has executed, I shall try to assure that whoever exercises them examine and review the accounts so that he may give a precise report of the results to you.

In the interim, it has occurred to me to make, in summary, an abstract to be sent to Your Lordship. I am doing this with the enclosed document, in which three reports are set forth. The first states the components and assets comprising the entails and properties; the second, what they have produced and yielded in profit during the entire time I have administered them; the third, the receipt of everything received and collected.[2] This is all that occurs to me in response to Your Lordship's two letters.

Having received in the special mail dispatched by the lord viceroy another three letters from Your Lordship, dated 7, 16, and 27 April this year, I have learned again that Your Lordship remains in the perfect health that is so necessary.[3] I leave to Your Lordship's consideration how much pleasure such favorable news will have been to your entire household, as was news that the lawsuit, brought against Your Lordship out of malice, temerity, and ambition, has been concluded, with the proceedings of hearing and review by that Royal Audiencia so much in Your Lordship's favor.

We of your household are extremely delighted and comforted to see Your Lordship finally free of persecution and restored to your government, as is just. All of us have offered countless congratulations for this. I repeat them to Your Lordship, hoping that you have reached your residence in very good health and that this happiness continues, as is so necessary to us.

As soon as I received the letters, I went to see my lady, the Duquesa de Alburquerque.[4] My wife did the same, so as not to delay thanking her excellency and making known to her how grateful and obliged we were to the lord duque for how much he has favored Your Lordship. My relatives did the same. We all have again urged her excellency to the end that the lord duque may look after Your Lordship, as he has until now. I do not doubt that her excellency will act accordingly, because of how much she has always favored and honored us.

As soon as I received, with Your Lordship's three letters, copies of the sentences of hearing and review, of the assignment of the encomienda of 4,000 pesos, and of the balance of the 17,000-odd pesos you have with the Royal Treasury from the two accounts that were

in your charge, I presented everything in the Council of the Indies.
I also presented a report for confirmation of the second generation,
in accord with what had been done by that lord viceroy, speaking to
the lord Marqués del Carpio and to all the ministers of which it is
composed to see if I could send the dispatches to Your Lordship in
this packet boat. [5]

But I am getting ahead of myself. I have not been able to achieve
this, given how much there is to do in the expediting of any business
in the Council before a decision is made. Before a report is considered, it is referred to the fiscal, as has been done with the one I presented. Next, it goes to the relator so that he may make a summary.
Once made, a recommendation is agreed upon so that his majesty
can resolve the matter. I surmise that a special mail will be dispatched
and that with it I shall be able to send the dispatches to you. I shall
pursue this request and thereby have the good fortune of serving Your
Lordship. I shall also seek to do so regarding the petition that your
salary be made equal to that enjoyed by the governor and captain
general of the kingdom of New Biscay and the real of Parral. Afterward, I shall take up the petition that they should better Your Lordship's post, which is what you direct me to do.

Because you informed me of the possibility that recourse might
have been had to the Council of the Indies on behalf of the villa of
Santa Fe or of don Pedro Rodríguez Cubero, I would like to assure
Your Lordship that it has not come to that. In case they do try on
the occasion of another packet boat that may come from New Spain,
I am very much on the alert to oppose them, using the lawyer's counsel you sent me for whatever defense may be necessary. I am convinced, however, that the villa and don Pedro Rodríguez will not
commit this second error and blunder.

I shall also obey Your Lordship and write to the lord Duque de
Alburquerque, thanking him. I shall do the same to all the ministers of the Royal Audiencia of Mexico. It also seemed fitting to me
to write to the lord archbishop in the same vein. Henceforth, I shall
direct all the letters for Your Lordship, as you advise me, in two
copies, one to don Miguel Calderón de la Barca and the other to
don Diego de Suazo.

I am sending to Your Lordship the enclosed letters from my uncles,
the Marqués de la Florida[6] and don Gregorio Pimentel,[7] and my aunt
and lady, doña Antonia de Vargas, who are well (thanks be to God),
as are all of us in this Your Lordship's house. We are wholly dedi-

cated to your service, hoping and praying that Our Lord may permit us the chance to see you. May He keep Your Lordship the many and long years He can and we need so much. Madrid, 28 September 1703.

> Your most affectionate, grateful,
> and obliged servant and son
> kisses Your Lordship's feet,

> Don Ignacio López de Zárate [rubrica]

To lord don Diego de Vargas Zapata y Luján Ponce de León, Marqués de la Nava de Barcinas, my lord and my father-in-law

*One part of this letter is in AMNB and the other in ARGD.LS. Five folios, ten written pages.

1. Letter 36 above.
2. Letter 48 below.
3. The letter of 7 April 1703 is missing, but those of 16 and 27 April are included herein as Letters 41 and 42 above.
4. Doña Ana Rosalía Fernández de la Cueva was the daughter of the eighth Duque de Alburquerque, don Francisco Fernández de la Cueva, Marqués de Cuéllar, Conde de Ledesma y de Huelma (1619–76), who was viceroy of New Spain from 1653 to 1660. She married her uncle, don Melchor de la Cueva y Enríquez, ninth Duque de Alburquerque. Their son, don Francisco Fernández de la Cueva, tenth Duque of Alburquerque, was viceroy of New Spain from 1702 to 1710. Rubio Mañé, *Virreyes*, 1:249–52, 294.

5. Don Francisco de Haro Guzmán y Toledo, Marqués del Carpio, was Gran Canciller de las Indias. Before he married Catalina de Haro Guzmán y Enríquez, seventh Marquesa del Carpio y de Eliche, Duquesa de Montoro, Condesa-duquesa de Olivares, and Condesa de Morente, he was known as Francisco de Toledo y Silva. García Carraffa, *Diccionario heráldico*, 40:295. Shäfer, *Consejo Real*, 1:227. Ignacio López de Zárate, Memorial, Madrid, 18 Mar. 1709, AGI, Guadalajara 70; translated in Bloom, "Vargas Encomienda," 394–95.

6. Letter 43 above.
7. Letter 46 above.

48. *Financial statement, Ignacio López de Zárate to Diego de Vargas, Madrid, 6 October 1703.**

Statement of all the various components and assets that make up the entails and properties belonging to lord don Diego de Vargas Zapata y Luján Ponce de León, Marqués de la Nava de Barcinas, in Madrid, the villa of Torrelaguna, and other neighboring villages, as well as in the city of Granada.

In Madrid
Certain large and principal houses on the
    Calle del Almendro.
Other outbuildings on the short, narrow street
    that begins at the parish church of San Pedro.
Other houses on the Plaza Mayor.
A censo paid by don Juan Díaz Mariño, curate
    of the parish church of San Pedro.

In the villages of Los Caramancheles
The tercias.

In the villa of Ocaña
A juro on the alcabalas of that district.

In the villa of Torrelaguna
A large house in an enclosed olive orchard.
Forty-four aranzadas of vineyards composed of:
    7 in the place they call Las Arras
    1 in Los Llanos
    2 in La Lanilla
    3 in Las Presillas
    7 1/2 in Las Cañadas
    4 in Las Vegas
    4 in Mirabueno
    7 1/2 in Las Peñuelas
    8 in El Yrialón.
Forty fanegas of grain-producing fields in that
    district and 80 in the district of
    Torremocha, which make 120 in all.

In Miraflores

The enclosures.

In Buitrago

The dehesas of Las Gariñas and Viñaderos.

In Carmarmas del Caño

An olive orchard, dovecote, and fields.

In Valdepiélagos

Six hundred fanegas of grain-producing fields,
    uncultivated because the village is
    abandoned. For this reason, they were
    rented neither during the tenancy of don
    Gregorio Pimentel, my lady doña Juana
    de Vargas, nor don Ignacio López de Zárate.

In the city of Granada

The farms, houses, and censos.

Statement of all the revenue these entails and properties have produced since 1690, the year don Ignacio López de Zárate began administering them by virtue of a power of attorney from lord don Diego
de Vargas, through this year, 1703, fourteen years in all. From these,
five years are subtracted, because the Granada property, revenue from
Buitrago and the tercias of the two Caramancheles, and don Juan
Díaz Mariño's censo were transferred by legal instrument to lord
don Juan Manuel de Vargas, don Ignacio's brother-in-law. All this,
lord don Juan Manuel encumbered for the five years, which are up
this year. These assets will be free and clear as of 1 January 1704.[1]

Madrid

The large, main houses on the Calle del
    Almendro were rented for 6,600 reales
    a year before lord don Ignacio López
    de Zárate y Luján came to live
    in them. Deducting the five-year
    occupancy provided for in the
    articles of marriage, as is of record in
    the contract, the number of years is

reduced to only nine. At the stated rate
of 6,600 reales, this amounts to   59,400
The outbuildings have been vacant two
    of the fourteen years. Twelve years at the
    rate of 1,950 reales of rent each year
    amounts to   23,400
The houses on the Plaza Mayor rent for 4,200
    reales a year. For the fourteen years, this
    amounts to 58,800 reales, without
    deducting for the vacancy of many of the
    apartments during the stated time.   58,800
The censo paid by don Juan Díaz Mariño is 1,100
    reales a year. Deducting for the five years it
    was transferred to lord don Juan Manuel de
    Vargas (may he be in heaven), and the five
    it was held by José Martínez de Robles,
    escribano del número (as per legal instrument
    from lord don Diego de Vargas because it
    was pledged to him in an exchange contract),
    the number of years don Ignacio
    had charge of it comes to only
    four, which amounts to 4,400 reales.   <u>4,400</u>
                                  146,000

Caramancheles

Their royal tercias, on average, year in and
    year out, came to 4,400 reales, more
    or less. Deducting the five years they
    were transferred to lord don Juan Manuel de
    Vargas, nine years amount to   39,600

Ocaña

The juro paid on the alcabalas of this district
    amounts to 1,300 reales a year. It is
    three years in arrears. The eleven
    collected for amount to   14,300

Torrelaguna

The large house has been occupied during the
    entire time by lord don José de Vargas

and my lady doña Juana de Vargas,
his wife, and for this reason no rent
whatsoever has been collected.   o
                                                         _____
                                                         199,990

The olive orchard. Lord don Ignacio harvested the
    fruit, 8 or 9 arrobas, one year only. At
    a rate of 30 reales each, it amounted to
    270 reales. Two other years he availed himself
    of the ground cover as feed for his mules,
    which amounted to 400 reales. The two items
    together came to 670 reales.   670
The rest of the time, until 1698 when the entire estate
    of Torrelaguna was transferred to lord don José,
    the value of each of those items, 1,050 reales,
    has gone to him. During the five years lord don
    José has had charge of the properties, they
    amounted to 5,250 reales.   5,250
The ground-floor apartment of the house was rented for
    four years to Lic. don Lorenzo Furel at 350
    reales, which amounts to 1,400 reales.   1,400
The vineyards were worked in 1691, and the harvest
    of 1692 was only 300 arrobas of
    wine, which sold at 7 reales each and
    amounted to 2,100 reales.   2,100
In the 1693 harvest, 382 arrobas of wine were
    brought in and sold at 6 1/2 reales,
    which came to 2,483.   2,483
In the 1694 harvest, 446 arrobas of wine were
    brought in and sold at 7 reales.
    This came to 3,122 reales.   3,122
In the 1695 harvest, 516 arrobas of wine were
    brought in and sold at 8 reales.
    This came to   4,128
                                                         _____
                                                         219,053

In the 1696 harvest, 756 arrobas of wine were
    brought in and sold at 5 1/2 reales. This
    came to 4,158 reales.   4,158
In the 1697 harvest, 567 arrobas of wine were
    brought in and sold at 10 reales. This
    came to 5,670 reales.   5,670

In the 1698 harvest, 581 arrobas of wine were
brought in and sold at 7 reales. This
came to 4,067 reales.[2]

4,067
232,948

The 40 fanegas of grain-producing land
in this district and the 80 in
Torremocha, 120 in all, have been rented
for thirteen years at 40 fanegas of grain on the
average. This has been diverted to pay part
of the amount owed for the bread alms given
each year on the three paschal holidays and on
regular holidays, as is of record in the
proceedings of the district inspector and
the certification of the parish priest of
Torrelaguna. This amount is paid up
through the present year, 1703.

Miraflores

The enclosures of Miraflores have rented for all
fourteen years at 450 reales a year,
which altogether amounts to 6,300 reales.

6,300

Buitrago

The dehesas of Las Gariñas and Viñaderos, which
are in this district, have always been rented
by the Duque del Infantado, who pays 2,000
reales for them. Deducting the five years
they were transferred to lord don Juan de
Vargas, the remaining nine years
amount to 18,000 reales.

18,000

Camarmas del Caño

The olive orchard, dovecote, and lands have been
and still are rented for 900 reales a
year, which for the fourteen years
amounts to 12,600 reales.

12,600
269,848

Valdepiélagos

Six hundred fanegas of grain-producing land. Lord
   don Ignacio has not had charge of these for
   the reason mentioned in the first statement
   of the assets and various components of these
   entails and properties.

Granada

The farms, houses, and censos have been rented
   for this entire time by virtue of a legal
   instrument executed by lord don Gregorio
   Pimentel in 1685 in favor of don Francisco
   Molina Matamoros for 5,000 reales a year.
   Lord don Ignacio had had charge of them for
   ten years and has collected this rent
   through 1700, when the transfer to lord
   don Juan Manuel de Vargas took effect.
   For the ten years stated, this amounts to 50,000
   reales.   50,000
The censo on the old public granary of that city,
   amounting to 2,750 reales of revenue a
   year, is under a creditors' agreement
   that includes four debts paid
   off in order to institute it. The debts are
   ranked at second, fifth, eleventh, and
   fourteenth place. Only the second and the
   fifth are paid. From them, 990 reales
   a year are collected, and for the ten years
   stated, this amounts to 9,900 reales.   9,900
                                                                     329,748

The revenue from all these items I have in
   my charge totals 329,748 vellon reales.

Statement of what don Ignacio López de Zárate
has paid out since 1 June 1690, when he began
administering the entails and properties of lord
don Diego de Vargas Zapata y Luján, through the
present year, 1703.

First, a censo of 150 ducados, which was owed
and for which payments continued
to be made for the entire time,
on the entail's principal houses
in Madrid on the Calle del Almendro, 26,400
vellon reales, as is of record in the
receipt.   26,400
For the censo on the fountain of this house paid
to the villa at the rate of 275 reales a
year, which was owed and for which payments
continued to be made for the entire
time, 5,500 vellon reales, as is of
record in the receipts.   5,500
For a censo whose principal is 40,000 silver
reales and the 2,941 vellon reales a year
it yields, imposed on the houses of the Plaza
and paid to the Convento de los Angeles and
don Manuel de Alcedo, which was owed and for
which payments continued to be made for the
entire time stated, 47,056 vellon reales,
as is of record in the receipts.   47,056
                                                                                 78,956

For a one-third share of the payment in lieu
of the huésped de aposento on this house, [3]
at the rate of 39 reales a year, 546 reales,
as is of record in the receipt.   546
To the lord Constable of Castile[4] as per the two legal
instruments his treasurer, don Alonso Fajardo,
had, one from lord don Diego de Vargas for 2,000
ducados and the other from lord don Gregorio
Pimentel for the same amount, both with interest,
55,000 vellon reales, as is of record in
the two redeemed instruments.   55,000
To doña Angela de Robles, widow of don Francisco de
Herrera, 11,000 vellon reales owed as per
a legal instrument from lord don Diego de
Vargas by which don Francisco had two
apartments, upper and lower, in the principal

houses of the entail in Madrid as part of
an exchange contract, as is of record in the
redeemed instrument.   11,000
                                                       145,502

To the heirs of doña Francisca del Castillo,
    10,200 vellon reales lord don
    Diego de Vargas owed as per legal instrument,
    as is of record in the redeemed instrument.   10,200
To doña Margarita and doña Dorotea Gil, former
    members of my lady doña María de Zúñiga's
    household, 96 reales de a ocho, as is of
    record in the document from lord don Diego
    they had in their possession, which comes to
    1,440 vellon reales.   1,440
To the Convento de San Francisco in Torrelaguna,
    for the memoria amounting to 474
    reales a year, 7,500 vellon reales, as
    is of record in the receipts.   7,500
To the Colegio Mayor of Alcalá for the censo of
    4,000 maravedis a year in its favor on the
    properties of Torrelaguna, which was owed
    and for which payments continued to be made
    for the entire time stated, 2,158 vellon
    reales, as is of record in the receipts.   2,158
For the subsidy on the royal tercias of the
    villages of Los Caramancheles, which is
    paid at 276 a year, 3,864 vellon reales,
    as is of record in the receipts.   3,864
                                                       170,664

For the repairs, made during the entire time
    stated, to the principal house and
    outbuildings of the entail, as well as to
    the house on the plaza of this court and villa of
    Madrid, namely, carpentry, locksmithing, a
    plumber, a blacksmith, and masonry.
    So as not to lengthen this statement unduly, no
    itemization in detail of everything done is
    provided. All of it amounted to 24,509 reales,
    as is of record in the master craftsmen's
    receipts.   24,509

For work done in the vineyards of the villa
of Torrelaguna during the eight years lord
don Ignacio had charge of them, for
cultivating, digging, replanting and layering
the vines, and for harvesting during
these eight years from 1691 through 1698
(since 1699 lord don José de Vargas has had
charge). Everything spent in those eight
years amounts to 18,939 reales, as is
recorded by the mayordomos for digging
and pruning. [5]   18,939

                                                                              214,112

To the Convento de Torrelaguna, 1,600 reales,
the cost of repairing and retiling the roof
of the chapel of San Juan and of Nuestra
Señora de los Esclavos, after a bolt of
lightning struck the tower of the convento,
demolishing a part of the chapel, as is
recorded in the receipt.   1,600

For the lawsuit don Manuel Gómez de Rosas,
citizen of the city of Segovia, brought,
and the attachment he obtained of the
houses on the plaza by virtue of his
lawful succession to a censo (whose
principal was 1,500 ducados upon
redemption), imposed on these houses by
lord don Lorenzo de Vargas and acknowledged
by lord don Alonso de Vargas, in favor of
doña Ana de Torres, widow and former
citizen of the city of Segovia. The lawsuit
lasted more than two years, and to pursue it
to its conclusion and favorable judgment,
which declared the houses free of this censo,
cost 2,200 reales.   2,200

                                                                              217,912

For the lawsuit brought by the Premonstratensian
Fathers[6] over a censo whose principal was
8,000 reales with revenue at the rate of 400
a year from 1668 through 1696, which lord
don Lorenzo de Vargas imposed on the

principal house and outbuildings of the
entail by virtue of royal permission
his father, lord don Francisco de Vargas,
obtained to impose a censo of 3,500 silver
ducados on these houses, thereby freeing
them from the huésped de aposento. After
lord don Francisco had freed them in 1630,
lord don Lorenzo proceeded to impose this
censo in 1638. For this reason, the lawsuit
was won, as is of record in the judgment
of the lords of the Royal Council of Castile.
Pursuing this lawsuit, which lasted more
than two years, cost 2,300 reales.   2,300
                                                         ─────────
                                                          220,212

To the heirs of doña María García, the widow who
    lived on the Calle de Silva, 3,500 vellon
    reales of the 1,000 ducados as per the legal
    instrument lord don Diego de Vargas
    executed in her favor, as is of record in
    the endorsement of the mentioned payment
    on this instrument.   3,500
On the censos and capellanía on the properties of
    Torrelaguna during the ten years don
    Ignacio had charge until they were ceded
    to his brother-in-law, lord don Juan Manuel,
    8,000 reales have been paid, as is of record
    in the receipts.   8,000
For repairs and cleaning of the main sewer and
    water pipes of the houses in Granada done
    during these ten years, 7,600 reales have
    been paid. All is of record in the
    statements and receipts don Francisco Molina
    Matamoros, renter of those properties, rendered
    during this time.   7,600
                                                         ─────────
                                                          239,312

For the support and sustenance of lord don Juan
    Manuel de Vargas (may he be in heaven),
    which don Ignacio had charge of from the
    beginning of 1690 through the end of June

1699, when the former left Madrid for
Granada to travel from there to Cadiz and
embark on his voyage to the Indies of New
Spain. It is worthy of note that he had a
valet, a groom, and a horse, so that he
might travel in grand style whenever he chose
not to use his brother-in-law's coach.
Added to this were his personal
expenses in his former office as page to the
queens, lady doña María Luisa de Borbón
and lady doña Mariana de Neoburgo. The
greatest of these was for the latter's
entrance into Madrid. For this and for
the journeys their majesties made to the
royal country places at the Escorial[7] and
Aranjuez,[8] several embroidered suits had to be
made for him, in colors as well as black, with
trimmed waistcoats and doublets, and all his
other suits for the king and queen's birthdays,
and uniforms for the groom. These costs,
which one year exceeded 1,500 ducados,
continued through 1695, when toward the
end of the year he traveled to Barcelona
to serve his majesty in that army with the
rank of captain of heavy cavalry.[9]
For everything stated it cost almost exactly
7,000 ducados—rather more than less—which
comes to 77,000 reales.   77,000
For the journey lord don Juan Manuel made to
    Catalonia, three gold- and silver-trimmed
    suits with their matching waistcoats;
    eighteen sets of linens; lace cravats;
    trimmed handkerchiefs; all the necessary
    accessories, such as hats, socks, stockings,
    and silk ribbons; the groom's uniform
    and the valet's suit that were made, for
    all of which 21,000 reales were spent.   21,000
Another 100 doblones given to him for travel
    expenses, which come to 6,000 reales.   6,000
                                                              343,312

During the entire time he was in Barcelona,
   a number of payments of 25 and 50 doblones
   were sent to him, and likewise a draft for
   9,000 silver reales don Ignacio had from
   his salary when he was serving in the post
   of fiscal of the Council of War, which
   altogether amount to 27,000 vellon
   reales.   27,000
In addition, 100 doblones given to him on the
   first year's account to travel to Granada,
   which he was not to collect because of
   the conveyance of the Granada estate to the
   Constable of Castile's treasurer that same
   year. This comes to 6,000 vellon reales. [10]   6,000
All these items I enter as debits come to
   376,312 vellon reales. Subtracting the
   329,748 reales of credit, there remains a
   balance against don Ignacio López de Zárate
   of 46,564 reales, always excepting
   error.

Total credit	329,748
Total debit	376,312
Balance	46,564

This, sir, is the present condition of Your Lordship's properties and entails as I leave them to you today. I do so with great pleasure, for Your Lordship will see that they are completely disencumbered and that the malicious suspicion reported to Your Lordship that the estate is under a creditors' agreement is shown for what it is. I do not dwell on this point, assuring Your Lordship that it has caused me neither the least discomfort nor affliction that you might have had a similar impression. I recognize that it stemmed more from a lack of information and knowledge than from the will of anyone persuaded by such a false supposition.

I know that it was not necessary to have compiled this accounting summary. It should appear as no more than a wish to give satisfaction to one who has favored me as much as Your Lordship has, especially because of your confidence expressed in the power of attorney exempting me from rendering accounts. Still, I must trust in Your Lordship's great understanding that you will agree to this formality, now that the time has come for me to be asked for so just a review.

In it, the only claim that can be made against me, which has been insinuated so many times, is for the 4,000 pesos Your Lordship sent. Although I thought that another, similar sum would not be sent to me, for the motives and reasons I set forth to Your Lordship when I acknowledged receipt of this sum, I now find myself obliged to say to Your Lordship in addition that had I intended to marry for the base advantage of gain, I would have accepted the many offers made to me when I returned to Madrid from Italy. Since my purpose was no other than to realize my greatest happiness—to join Your Lordship's family—I paid no heed to other circumstances.

The way I calculate it, the dowry I was given amounted to 9,000 pesos. Although Your Lordship sent me 10,000, 1,000 went for payment and satisfaction of what I loaned to my aunt and lady, doña Juana de Vargas (may she be in heaven), before I got married, for the expenditures she wished to make then. Your Lordship is aware of this from the marriage contract itself. Until the 10,000 were paid, the contract provided that I would be paid 500 annually. More than five years had passed before I received the first payment of 5,000 Your Lordship sent to me. You will recognize that precisely 2,500 were owed to me for those five years.

I am greatly troubled that the time has come to relate this to Your Lordship, since I have tried to ignore all that is expressed here. Time, my honor, and my esteem make it necessary to take note. Furthermore, I thought Your Lordship might have considered the heavy expenses I incurred merely to have the wedding with a splendor reflecting my proper consideration and respect upon marrying one of Your Lordship's daughters. The entire court attended the ceremony. The sponsors, in case Your Lordship has not heard, were the lord Duque and lady Duquesa de Fernandina, children of the lord Marqués de Villafranca, and the lord Duque de ———— .[11]

I leave to Your Lordship's imagination how this ceremony would have been celebrated and what expenses there were, with coaches, chairs, liveries, servants' clothes, besides the customary wedding gifts and the groom's gift to the bride and the clothes for my aunt and lady, doña Juana de Vargas, her family, and my beloved brother-in-law and friend, don Juan Manuel de Vargas. There were also the expenses for the entire time that guests were received. On 13 December, I will have borne these expenses for the fifteen years I have been married.

Your Lordship can infer how much in debt I am. Still, I have faith that you will help me extricate myself and, at the same time, make it easier for me to support my family and raise my children in the manner befitting their status as Your Lordship's grandchildren. You will make it possible thereby for me to seek the future most in keeping with the inclinations of my daughter Rosalea, who is the eldest and about to reach her twelfth birthday next 4 April.

Regarding Your Lordship's properties, I shall always feel the satisfaction and pride of having tried to live up to your confidence out of my duty and honor. What weighs heaviest on my mind and what I beg you to pardon me for is having delayed in presenting this statement. Even though Your Lordship may be imprisoned as a result of vicious and false reports, you will sympathize with the reason, motives, and circumstances that have placed me in these straits.

This is all that occurs to me to tell Your Lordship. Let me repeat, as always, my devotion and wish that Our Lord keep you the many and long years He can and I need so much. Madrid, 6 October 1703.

Your most affectionate, grateful,
and obliged servant and son
kisses Your Lordship's feet,

Don Ignacio López de Zárate [rubrica]

*AMNB. DS. Fourteen folios, twenty-four written pages.

1. This document is especially useful because it supplies the equivalents of several major monies of account:

doblon   1:60 vellon reales
ducado   1:11 vellon reales
silver real   1:2.4 vellon reales

A few examples of prices in Castile during this period, from Earl J. Hamilton, *War and Prices in Spain, 1651–1800* (Cambridge, Mass., 1947):234–37, are:

one chicken   5.4   vellon reales

olive oil
  (1/8 arroba) 22.1   vellon reales
beef (1 lb.)   .94 vellon reales
chickpeas (1 lb.) .066 vellon reales
hake (1 lb.)   1.2   vellon reales

2. The graph on page 277 illustrates wine production on the Vargas entail from 1692 through 1698.

3. Huésped or casa de aposento referred to the service the villa of Madrid rendered to the king by reserving a part of all houses for lodging members of the royal

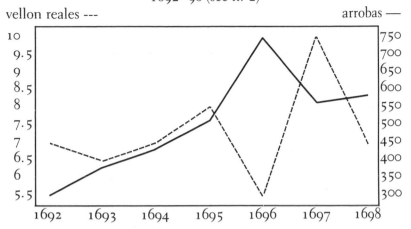

Wine Production, Vargas Mayorazgo
1692–98 (see n. 2)

court. In lieu of providing lodging, a payment could be made.

4. Created in 1382 by Juan I to replace the post of king's standard bearer, the constable of Castile was the highest position in the militia. Over time, the office became an honorific. In 1473, it was granted to the Velasco family. Don Iñigo de Velasco, Duque de Frías, a long-time incumbent, had died in 1696. Kamen, *Spain*, 353 n. 28.

5. Grapes will grow in almost any soil and need little fertilizer, although ashes from prunings will help them greatly. The most important aspect of viticulture is planting the vinestock and getting the plants established. The soil should be loose and well aerated. After planting, the vines take three or four years to mature. Their principal care, aside from adequate irrigation, is annual pruning to establish the height of the vines (important to protect them from rot

in areas of high rainfall or irrigation) and promote vigorous growth. Grafting and earth-layering improve vines and fill in where others have died or been removed because of disease. The vineyard should also be weeded and cultivated several times a year. Pests and diseases such as mildew vie with late frosts and excessive rainfall or drought to lessen or prevent harvests. Joaquín Belda, *Vinos de España* (Madrid, 1929):27–30; José de Bano, *Instrucciones para el cultivo de la vid: Zonas vitícolas del país; ligeras indicaciones sobre el cultivo intensivo de la vid; variedades americanas de esta planta* (Mexico City, 1919):4–7; Ya-hya ibn Mu-hammad, *Libro de Agricultura*, ed. Claudio Boutelou, trans. José Banqueri (Seville, 1878):211–26.

Subtracting the 18,939 vellon reales it cost to produce the wine from the 25,728 reales of income realized showed a profit of 6,789 reales for the seven years.

6. The Premonstratensian Fathers were members of the Order of Canons Regular of Prémontré, also called White Canons or Norbertines, founded by St. Norbert, near Laon, France, in the twelfth century.

7. Felipe II (1527–98) first ordered construction of the Escorial, some twenty miles northwest of Madrid, in 1563 as a mausoleum for the remains of his father, Carlos I (1500–58). Finished twenty-two years later, it came to include a royal residence, monastery, and church. Lynch, *Habsburgs*, 1:183; George Kubler, *Building the Escorial* (Princeton, 1982):12, 17.

8. About twenty-six miles south of Madrid, Aranjuez was known principally as a royal summer retreat. It, like the Escorial, dated from the reign of Felipe II. The same architects who designed the Escorial also drew the plans for the residence at Aranjuez. Elías Tormo y Monzó, *Aranjuez* (Madrid, n.d.):9–11.

9. Louis XIV's French forces had taken a number of cities in Catalonia during the campaign of 1694. In 1695, the Spanish viceroy, the Conde de la Corzana, had abandoned Barcelona. Evidently don Juan Manuel was among the reinforcements sent to the Catalonian front late that year. By the Treaty of Ryswick (1697), France had restored the occupied territory. Fernando Soldevila Zubiburo, *História de Catalunya* (Barcelona, 1963):1091–95.

10. The expenses set forth in this document totaled 376,312 vellon reales. Of that figure, 137,000, or 36 percent, went to support Juan Manuel de Vargas Pimentel.

11. Don Ignacio took obvious pride in the influential aristocrats who served as sponsors of his marriage. The witnesses listed in the entry in the marriage register were the Conde de Benavente, the Duque de Montalto, and Gaspar Girón. Pérez Balsera, *Laudemus*, 87. The twelfth Conde de Benavente, a leading figure at the court of Carlos II, was Francisco Casimiro Antonio Alfonso Pimentel de Quiñones y Benavides. The title Conde-Duque de Benavente had been in the Pimentel family for centuries. García Carraffa, *Diccionario heráldico*, 5:26–31, 70:5–27. The Duque de Montalto also was prominent in the affairs of government. See Kamen, *Spain*, 378 n. 74, 386, 388. Gaspar Cayetano Girón Venegas, a native of Madrid, had entered the Order of Santiago on 8 October 1663. García Carraffa, *Diccionario heráldico*, 37:63.

49. *Ignacio López de Zárate to Diego de Vargas,* n.p., n.d. (mid-late 1703).*

My lord and father,

Since another packet boat leaves for that kingdom, I am availing myself most gladly of the chance to repeat my obeisance at the feet of Your Lordship and to seek the wished-for news that you continue in the perfect health that is so necessary. I also seek news that Your Lordship has concluded your long peregrination, so drawn-out a journey, with all felicity, and arrived at that villa and acceded to the government of that entire province. I do not doubt that you will have been very well received. The frauds and such improper, irregular measures that temerity and maliciousness employed to obscure Your Lordship's just actions, so well known and accredited, have disappeared entirely. God, who is just, has permitted today your greater renown. And at the same time, so great a conspiracy, such audacity and insolence, are completely exposed and shamed.

Now it is appropriate for Your Lordship to try to look after yourself, which is so important to us, and to think of nothing but living. With life, one attains everything, and nothing else matters. Also, please reflect fairly on the fact that it is not just that Your Lordship's outstanding services and your . . .

*AMNB. L. inc. One folio, two written pages.

————

50. *Francisco de Vargas y Lezama, Marqués de Vargas, to Diego de Vargas, n.p., n.d.*

My dear sir,

I am favored by Your Lordship's letters, dated 31 December of last year and 9 April of this year. I am most gratified by your words, which I fully appreciate, celebrating the news you convey to me of your good health and also of your restoration to your government of New Mexico, which greatly pleased me. I offer Your Lordship my congratulations, hoping that many more follow these, as I would wish. I hope I am worthy of the many orders you may be most pleased to have me carry out.[1]

I assure Your Lordship that the news we had of the sudden and untimely death of my friend, lord don Juan Manuel de Vargas, was a crushing blow to my cousin and me and this your house. No other could have surpassed it, because of how deeply we esteemed and loved him with great tenderness. He reciprocated with the confidence and security he felt in our love. I believe that, because of Your Lordship's love, this blow must have been heartbreaking, as much for the loss as for the suddenness of his death. I give you my condolences in the earnestness of my true consideration and love, being able to say that my cousin and I received such great attention from the deceased that in Spain I judge no one owed him more. Your Lordship will appreciate what our sorrow must have been. The only consolation is that he will be with God.

I value, as I must, the confidence and consideration with which Your Lordship favors me by your trust in sending the power of attorney for the administration of your honored entails and the collection of their revenue. I assure you that it is with my greatest respect and equal regret that I am unable to accept. The principal reason is that Your Lordship is very badly informed. You suggest that the entails have been declared insolvent, which is not true. If it were, I would be aware of it. Besides that, how could they be, when my friend, lord don Juan Manuel, left all the revenues encumbered for five years for the expenses of his journey and the debts he had? This is true, as it is that my cousin, lord don Ignacio López de Zárate, has managed the entails with the greatest diligence, for their greatest revenue, through his great love and authority. This will be evident to Your Lordship from the detailed accounting he tells me he is providing you.

To this, one might add that since my cousin, lord don Ignacio, is here, there was no reason for another to have the power of attorney, when none of us knows how to exercise it better or with more love, intelligence, or authority than my cousin, lord don Ignacio. The lords Conde de Puebla and don Sancho de Bullón are explaining the same thing to Your Lordship that I am. They have not accepted the power of attorney either, as they express to you, for the reasons I relate.

In my case, I add what Your Lordship may excuse in me—the obligation I have to my cousins. What would the world say if I were to sit in judgement of my relatives? Especially in view of the fact that those other two lords who follow in the power of attorney, who even without this obligation, are not accepting it? I hope that Your Lordship will understand my excuse. I must tell you I consider it in the best interest of your honor as well as my cousin's not to use this power of attorney, whose terms are unfavorable both to Your Lordship's dignity and esteem and to my cousin's honor. More so, since I know that you are bound by the reports that my friend, lord don Juan Manuel (may he be with God), might have made, motivated more by his generosity and wish to spend than by reason. As I said above, this is true. Regarding what Your Lordship directs me to tell you about whether my cousin, lord don Ignacio, has obtained the title for you and paid its media anata and lanzas (for which purpose Your Lordship had remitted 4,000 pesos), what I have been able to learn is that my cousin, lord don Ignacio, is making the most diligent effort to relieve Your Lordship of this concern as quickly as possible, as with everything else you place in his charge.

Your Lordship should bear in mind that lord don Juan Manuel (may he be with God) needed to spend a great deal in order to comport himself properly as befitted your son. He did so splendidly and spent much, even on what was not necessary. Because of this, it may be that his love was not as great as it should have been for his siblings, who, I know, did everything imaginable for him. Rest assured that my cousin, lord don Ignacio, will return in every way the great love and duty he feels toward you and he owes himself.

If I may be of some service to Your Lordship, you may be very sure of my attention. From the confidence you have placed in me, you will find me obedient to carry out promptly whatever may be to your greatest satisfaction, with my very considerate and certain will, for what it may be worth.

The powers of attorney and the letters that came for the agents remain in my possession for whatever Your Lordship may direct.

*ARGD. L. inc. Two folios, four written pages.

1. The son of don Juan de Vargas y Arteaga, who served the king for forty years in the Basque country, don Francisco de Vargas y Lezama had compiled his own impressive record of civil and fiscal service in Castile, Flanders, and North Africa. He had superintended the quarantine and supply of Málaga during an epidemic of the plague

and, as corregidor of Ubeda and Baeza, pursued don Luis de Peñalosa and his bandits, capturing four of them. He had also been corregidor of Madrid and, in 1700, was contador mayor of the Council of the Treasury. The king, Title of Marqués de Vargas to Francisco de Vargas y Lezama, Madrid, 8 February 1700, AHN, Consejos 8.975:127.

———

51. *Diego de Vargas to Ignacio López de Zárate, Santa Fe, 1 December 1703.*

Son and dear sir,

I am notifying Your Lordship of my accession to this government of New Mexico on 10 November in its villa of Santa Fe. I am sending to Your Lordship the certification of the accession that its illustrious municipal government gave me so that Your Lordship can have it presented in the Cámara of the Royal and Supreme Council of the Indies.[1] Also, this is necessary, because his majesty so orders by his royal cedula.

May the applause and general acclamation with which I was received be of record, contrary to what is reported by the procurator of this villa. Encouraged and supported by Gov. don Pedro Cubero, who pursues his own interests, in addition to the mortal enmity in which he holds me, the procurator has been and is even now at the court of Mexico City on his account. According to the information I have, he is still with don Pedro.[2] From El Paso del Río del Norte in the month of October of this current year of my arrival, I have also informed Your Lordship that the governor, don Pedro, had departed. He left a power of attorney for someone to undergo his residencia, appointing a lieutenant in his place. He did both following his excellency's order.

To terrorize these citizens, his nephew, don Miguel de Solá Cubero, twenty-five years of age, convinced them that don Pedro would go to Madrid to petition for this government, as if he might emerge from the residencia meritoriously. On the contrary, many claims, charges, and accusations are expected to be brought by different people, in addition to my concerns. At the time of the residencia, my right to petition the Royal Acuerdo for an advisory vote was delayed. I am reporting to the most excellent lord viceroy about the condition in which I am receiving the kingdom. One finds from my previous writings that what I wrote may be authenticated by a representation made to this cabildo. It has occurred to me to send to Your Lordship copies, although I am advising my procurator in Mexico City to do so, together with what his excellency may provide. Therefore, with this report, Your Lordship will be fully informed for whatever might arise.

I await the mail from Mexico City in case Your Lordship wrote to me by the packet boat that arrived in the month of July, I mean 15 August, at the port of New Veracruz with news of the five thousand quintals of mercury the storeships and warships from France are bringing. They had orders to go first to the island of Martinique in order to sail with escort from there to this kingdom and the port of Veracruz. They have not arrived, and it is known that they went to Cartagena and that they would not arrive, in any event, until December.[3]

May Our Lord give them a good voyage and me the pleasure of knowing of Your Lordship's good health and that the chocolate I sent to you reached your hands without risk of being destroyed by the enemy, as was the flota a month after dropping anchor in the port of Vigo. I also want to know about the possessions left when my son died, even though the person in charge of them is wholly trustworthy.

In accordance with the powers of attorney I sent by the packet boats of the present year, I trust his possessions will be recovered, according to the arrangements I have made. I think that, as I have told Your Lordship, with the powers of attorney for the entails, it would be good to remedy unforeseen problems, to assure the satisfaction of my obligations, and to see that I am not subject to misfortune. This will not seem bad to Your Lordship, because of your affection for me and my daughter doña Isabel's wish for my alleviation. I am writing to her. May Our Lord keep Your Lordship in the company of my beloved grandchildren many happy years. Santa Fe, 1 December 1703.

Your father and servant who esteems
you from the heart kisses Your
Lordship's hand,

The Marqués de la Nava
de Barcinas [rubrica]

To lord don Ignacio López de Zárate, my son-in-law

I repeat to Your Lordship that for my honor I proceeded to this government. It lacks the presidio of El Paso del Río del Norte, his majesty having granted it for life to Capt. don Antonio Valverde. My obligations will always be the same, if Your Lordship, as a result of my letters, does not better my post and all the rest, seeking it in earnest.

*ARGD. LS. Two folios, four written pages. The postscript is in Vargas's hand.

1. On the same day that he wrote this letter to his son-in-law, don Diego signed a justification of his first administration and a condemnation of his successor's. The next day, the cabildo added its certification and elaborated on the same themes. Diego de Vargas to the Cabildo of Santa Fe, Santa Fe, 1 Dec. 1703, and Certification by the Cabildo of Santa Fe, Santa Fe, 2 Dec. 1703, SANM II:94a.

2. Since 1700, the villa's procurator had been José García Jurado, a native of Mexico City and forty years old in 1693, when he was recruited with his family as a colonist for New Mexico. He had been sent back to the viceregal capital by the cabildo to represent it in actions against Vargas and Antonio Valverde. See Espinosa, *Crusaders*, 336–39; and Chavez, *Origins*, 183.

3. The storeships had reached Veracruz with the mercury and correspondence from Spain on 23 October 1703. Robles, *Diario*, 3:293.

---

52. *Diego de Vargas to Isabel María de Vargas Pimentel, Santa Fe, 2 December 1703.**

My dearest daughter,

Even though I am informing my son-in-law, don Ignacio, about my accession to the government of New Mexico, where I find myself, it is not well that I fail to fulfill the duty of my love, with which I esteem you tenderly, wishing that you and my beloved grandchildren are very well. I hope to have a letter from you to relieve me of this concern. Since October 1701, I have had no other letter than the one his excellency's page, don Diego de Molina, brought, the one from my son remaining unwritten, as well as other packets I did not receive.

Nothing more occurs to me to tell you, since I have already written to you from the presidio of El Paso del Río del Norte. Please write at every opportunity. My son-in-law, don Ignacio, will send the letters I write to my relatives and my beloved children Juana and don José. I remain well (thanks to Our Lord) and disposed to serve you with all my love. To my beloved grandchildren I give my blessing. I hope that God may keep you in their company for many happy years, for above all, Our Lord is master of His will, to which I submit. Santa Fe, 2 December 1703.

Your father and servant from the
heart, until death, kisses your hand,

The Marqués de la Nava
de Barcinas [rubrica]

To my beloved daughter, doña Isabel María de Vargas

*ARGD. LS. One folio, one written page.

Settling Affairs,
Santa Fe, 1704–6

53. *Diego de Vargas to Gregorio Pimentel de Prado,
Santa Fe, 8 January 1704.* *

My brother and lifelong friend,

I have received your letter of last May and am pleased by the good health Our Lord grants you. I am also well, ready to serve you and my beloved nephews and nieces, whose hands I kiss. I hope also that those at the side of our brother, the Marqués de la Florida, are well. I am happy at the news you give me about how well received, pleased, and content he is at the castle in Milan. He would have been worthy of repeated honors and royal favors when his majesty, the king our lord (may God keep him), returned there from campaign.

My very dear brother, I find myself in this government, since Our Lord so disposes. It seems that my misfortunes—these events—are unspeakable. I say only that I have experienced an inconstant fortune, with blows of exceeding grief, since the year 1697, after my well-known injuries and hardships. These can be explained, without deliberation, by the conquest and reconquest of this kingdom, then seeing my wealth and estate lost, consumed in six years of a lawsuit, three of which I spent in prison. Then, there was the misfortune of my son (may he be with God) having foolishly come without my order or permission, which resulted in his death, as well as the losses caused by the bad judgment of the ship's captain. When Our Lord gave the latter the time to save his goods and those of others, he chose instead to see them go up in flames and be lost at sea. Don Fausto did the same, after I had given him the cost of freight and conveyance on the flagship for the cases of chocolate. This was for their delivery in Castile and payment both of duties and of freight to the muleteer until they were delivered in Madrid. Also, by pursuing his foolishness, don Fausto lost and wasted the money. I assure you that this loss has been a source of disgust to me, having been caused by the human error of these individuals. [1]

My son was deceitful. He did not even marry as they told you. The woman they make out to be his wife was the woman he began to live with a few days after he had arrived in Mexico City. This cost me not a little money, because he was hopelessly in love with her. Finally, I gave him the money for her burial. This is what is happening now. She died in childbirth, and I cannot say for sure that her baby boy is his, even though he is the very image of me. Nevertheless, I am keeping him in the custody of a friend my son chose without informing me. When he left in May, he told me nothing. I would not even have known of the mother's death, had I not been asked for money for the burial.

It is certain that had I received news in that land and kingdom of my son's death, I would have chosen to marry in Spain, someone of like temperament and my social equal, though I would not have asked for even a yard of ribbon from her. In Spain, the most impeccable nobility is that which has nothing. Being in this kingdom, and having been in New Spain, has made me not commit myself in order to freely go anywhere (Our Lord seeing fit).[2]

With the news that my children, don José de Vargas and doña Juana, are returning to Torrelaguna, I am sending to them the power of attorney I executed before the justicia of this villa so that they may administer, enjoy, and possess this entail for as long as I shall be delayed and Our Lord sees fit to give me life.[3] It is my wish that they pay whatever is owed: the memorias of its founders; the debt for the repair and maintenance of the house on the Coso, which is the glory of the entail; and the cost of cultivation and increase of its vineyards, land, and olive orchards.

I refer to the contents of the power of attorney I set aside from the inclusive and general one I sent to Madrid. As I have informed you and my sister, doña Antonia, I give it, referring to that letter. I am also assigning her 500 reales a year from the revenue of the pastures and enclosures of Miraflores de la Sierra, Chozas, and Guadalix, so that she may have something to live on. With regard to the revenue from the prebend of the patronage of San Francisco, and so that my son-in-law, don Ignacio, may attend in my place as patron, which I am legitimately named and appointed, I have sent him a power of attorney. With both measures, he may get by more easily. This is all he will receive from me while I am living (Our Lord seeing fit).

I ask you to send the letter to my brother-in-law, the Marqués de la Florida. This fulfills my duty and love, as you will always do in inquiring after his health. May Our Lord give you good health and a happy life for the many years I wish. Please kiss the hand of my friend and lord, don José de Arteaga, and tell him I esteem his affection and memory. Villa of Santa Fe, 8 January 1704.

Your brother and sincere
friend and servant, until death,
kisses your hand,

El Marqués de la Nava
de Barcinas [rubrica]

To my brother-in-law and friend, don Gregorio Pimentel de Prado

*ARGD. LS. Two folios, four written pages. Because of don Gregorio's death the following June, it is unlikely that he saw this letter.

1. Vargas's juxtaposition here of his son's death and the losses suffered in the battle of Vigo caused Kessell ("Vargas: Another Look," 22) to conclude incorrectly that Capt. Juan Manuel de Vargas Pimentel had been killed in action.

2. Thus don Diego justified not marrying the mother of his three children born in Mexico City. Letter 59 below.

3. Letter 56 below.

———

54. *Diego de Vargas to Antonia de Vargas, Santa Fe, 8 January 1704.* *

My dearest sister,

I received your letter of April of last year and am pleased that you are alive, since Our Lord sees fit for you to be indisposed. You tell me of this and of your failing eyesight, which is most troublesome. I know that your prayers can and do have great efficacy with Our Lord and His Most Holy Mother. They give me good health and strength in my peregrinations and inconstant fortune. I have suffered painful blows in a long imprisonment of three years, and in another three to conclude the lawsuit that my predecessor's malice and envy unjustly brought against me in order to consume my assets in defense of my honor.

Then there were the expenses for my beloved son, all of which came to naught. Even his goods and the valuables with which I provided him were burned and lost at sea, along with the papers and the rest of the dispatches. Their loss was not a hindrance to my intentions for the administration of the entails, except for the one of Granada. I had already arranged for and anticipated this in March 1672 with don Diego de Olvera. He could have acted by virtue of the power of attorney he had, without recourse to the one my son (may he be with God) was carrying, since he will have acted upon what I ordered in it. In his letter, he began to exaggerate don Ignacio's difficulties and obligations, saying that any revenue from the entail of Granada must be ordered handed over to him for his aid.

Upon the news of my son's death, to put aside doubts, I executed the new power of attorney in favor of my cousin, the Conde de Villamena, don Fernando de Teruel, knight of the Order of Santiago.[1]

He is heir to an entail and a person of all authority, fine talents, and very Christian and loyal conduct, to such a degree that it does not seem to me that he could act in any other way. Therefore, as a favor, I am asking this gentleman to transfer the power of attorney to a trustworthy person, should it seem to him that don Diego de Olvera is not appropriate. The revenue is to be collected and remitted to Seville to my friend, don Diego Manuel de Alvarado, so that he may carry out my order in full. I sent the details of this arrangement in duplicate in January 1703.

I am informing you of this so that you may tell my children, don José and doña Juana, that I hold don Diego de Olvera suspect. He should be mindful that his master is my son-in-law, don Ignacio, and he has to obey him in everything. I see in his letter that he exaggerates the insufficiency of his means and how much he requires for his appearance and family, reasons that give me this cause for distrust and caution.

With regard to the entails in Madrid, I sent the power of attorney in the first place to the Marqués de Vargas of the Treasury Council; in the second, to the Conde de Puebla de los Valles; and in the third, to my cousin, don Sancho Bullón Chacón. [2] I also included that other power of attorney. Having received the news that my children, don José and doña Juana, write that they are returning from the town of La Nava del Rey to live in Torrelaguna, I am sending a letter to my son, don José. By virtue of it and the power of attorney that I have executed before the justicia of this villa, I am appointing him as administrator of that entail and its revenue. This will be done as expressed in the power of attorney, since I need his assistance, so that during the time that Our Lord sees fit to give me life and that I may be delayed in this government, he may administer and enjoy its revenue. His duty will be the maintenance, cultivation, and working of its vineyards and olive orchards; paying the charges of the founders' memorias; and also the necessary repair that the principal house on the Coso of that entail may demand, for it is its splendor and monument. [3]

My children will thus enjoy considerable relief, since the vineyards are good and the fields many. With the revenue, they can support themselves. This is done out of my love, and so that you may know that I shall protect them in every way. I am stipulating that they are to give you 500 reales of the revenue from the pastures of Chozas, Miraflores, and Guadalix. With the power of attorney I sent to don Ignacio for attending to the patronage of San Francisco, I also charged that he attend to the revenue (as he will designate) you have enjoyed and seek to have you given, in part, the arrears. His administrator can aid you with the revenue, giving it to the person holding your power of attorney or to whomever you send. The merchants of Torrelaguna will take charge, and you can avail yourself of them, since don Ignacio's business affairs do not permit him to assist you.

I have regretted the loss of the chocolate. It was lucky that you received the 50 pesos in aid, considering the bearer's misfortune.

Farewell, my dearest sister. So long as you live, I am more than a father to serve you. I love and esteem you from the heart and in everything submit myself to divine will. May God keep you many happy years. Villa of Santa Fe, 8 January 1704.

> Your brother who loves and esteems you
> from the heart kisses your hand and
> leaves to Our Lord the possibility of
> his seeing you again,

> The Marqués de la Nava
> de Barcinas [rubrica]

To my beloved sister and lady, doña Antonia de Vargas

*ARGD. LS. Two folios, four written pages.

1. Diego de Vargas to Fernando de Teruel, Power of attorney, Mexico City, 12 Nov. 1702, AGNot. 692.

2. Diego de Vargas to the Marqués de Vargas, the Conde de Puebla de los Valles, and Sancho Bullón Chacón, Power of attorney, Mexico City, 31 Dec. 1702 and 1 Jan. 1703, AGNot. 692.

3. Letters 55 and 56 below.

———

55. *Diego de Vargas to José de Vargas, Santa Fe, 9 January 1704.**

My dear son,

I have your letter from La Nava del Rey and am pleased to learn of your good health and that of my beloved daughter, doña Juana, and the grandchildren, to whom I give my blessing. I esteem and love them tenderly.

Although I am writing to my sister, doña Antonia de Vargas, at somewhat greater length, for now this is only to tell you of my affection in the form of my power of attorney. Our Lord has seen fit to take my son, don Juan Manuel de Vargas. While he lived, I could not separate any of my entails (taking into consideration the furthering of his career), since he was to have been provided with their revenue. It was my intention that revenue to you in partial recompense of dowry would be independent of the entail's and that I would remit it in lump sum. Now that fortune has stripped me of my means and Our Lord has taken my beloved son for his own, I want you to realize my love in the power of attorney I send to you so that you may administer the entail I have in Torrelaguna and enjoy its yield and revenue, as set forth in the power of attorney.[1]

By this letter, I charge you earnestly with conservation of its lands through their cultivation, repair of the entail's principal house on the Coso, and punctual payment of whatever charges and pensions it may have from its pious works. Also, please pay to my dear sister, doña Antonia de Vargas, the 500 reales a year that I am assigning to her from the revenue of the pastures and dehesas of Miraflores de la Sierra, Chozas, and Guadalix, as is stated in the power of attorney I am sending to you.

I give it to you, as set forth therein, first in partial recompense of dowry and second for as long as it is my will (and as long as Our Lord sees fit to give me life and I am detained in these kingdoms). I have no other way to convey my affection to you. Quite unexpectedly, this relief will reach your hands. I assure you that time will tell how much I esteem you and love my beloved daughter, doña Juana, in whose company and that of my grandchildren I hope that God may keep you for many years. Villa of Santa Fe, 9 January 1704.

Your father who esteems you
and wishes your well-being
kisses your hand,

The Marqués de la Nava
de Barcinas [rubrica]

To my beloved son-in-law, don José de Vargas

*AMNB. LS. One folio, two written pages.

1. Letter 56 below.

———

56. *Power of attorney, Diego de Vargas to José de Vargas, Santa Fe, 11 January 1704.**

First duplicate.

In the villa of Santa Fe, seat of government and capital of this kingdom and provinces of New Mexico, on 11 January 1704, I, Mre. de campo Lorenzo Madrid, alcalde de primer voto of this said villa,[1] having entered the casas reales and palace wherein resides lord don Diego de Vargas Zapata Luján Ponce de León, Marqués de la Nava de Barcinas, governor and captain general of this newly restored kingdom and its provinces, continued in office by his majesty, its conqueror, pacificator, colonizer, and castellan of its fortresses and presidios, attest that I know His Lordship.

Being in his sala in the presence of the two witnesses in attendance, I, as juez receptor, since there is no escribano, public or royal, in this villa and said kingdom or within 260 leagues, attest that the said lord marqués, governor, and captain general states that it is necessary for him to send a power of attorney to Spain to one of his sons-in-law. Proceeding to do so, he executed it before me, said maestre de campo, completely in the necessary form as required by law, in favor of don José de Vargas, householder of the villa of Torrelaguna and resident in the village of La Nava del Rey in the kingdoms of Castile, married in accordance with the ritual of the holy mother church to doña Juana de Vargas Pimentel, the second daughter.

In favor of his said son-in-law, don José, he executed his said power of attorney in partial recompense of dowry. The said lord Marqués de la Nava de Barcinas has and possesses in the said villa of Torrelaguna the estate Juan de Salinas, the elder, and Juan de Salinas, the younger, and doña Catarina Vélez de Guevara, his wife, founded. It is composed of more than 115 aranzadas of vineyards and extensive croplands, in the said villa and in the villages of Torremocha, Talamanca, Valdepiélagos, El Bellón, El Espartal, and El Molar. This must amount in all to more than seven hundred fanegas of cropland. Also in said villa, there are white poplar groves and some olive trees in the vineyards. There is also the entail's principal house on the Coso, with its kitchen garden, its walls, and within, a large olive grove with more than four hundred trees. There are also the patronages of the two chapels of San Juan and Santiago on the epistle and gospel sides of the principal chapel of the Convento de San Francisco.

There is also the revenue from the four enclosures and pastures in the villages of Miraflores de la Sierra. There is also the revenue of 2,000 vellon reales the most excellent lord Duque del Infantado y Pastrana pays annually for the dehesa of Las Gariñas, which bounds the forest that said lord duque has in his villa of Buitrago. There is also the revenue from the half of the dehesa of Viñaderos that should be paid by any surviving heirs of Martín de Ahedo, householder of the said villa of Buitrago, or the person to whom, in the absence of the said lord marqués and by virtue of his power of attorney, they may have rented it. The other half of the dehesa of Viñaderos, at the time the said lord marqués came to the Indies in the year 1672, was owned by Martín de Ahedo. The revenue from the first half, which belongs to the lord marqués, in the event that it is not of record in letters of payment from those who hold Martín de Ahedo's power of attorney, should have been paid to his heirs and to whoever may have made use of the forage and pasture of the said half dehesa of Viñaderos. There is also the sale of holm oak, which is sold for charcoal, and Pyrenean oak as standing timber, according to custom and manner of cutting so that the trees will grow back.

The yield of said properties, that of the vineyards as well as of the olive orchards, the revenue from the said cultivated grain-producing fields of wheat, rye, and barley; and revenue from the said enclosures and pastures in the said villages of Miraflores de la Sierra,

Chozas, and Guadalix, the said lord marqués cedes and gives to his said son-in-law, don José de Vargas, in whose favor he executes this said power of attorney for as long as Our Lord may see fit to give him life and while he may be detained in this kingdom and so long as it may be His will. This said revenue from the said entail and said principal house is given by limited power of attorney in partial recompense of dowry to don José de Vargas, his son-in-law, as spouse, husband, and consort of the said doña Juana de Vargas Pimentel, the second daughter, with the obligation of having to pay the pension, any charge it may have, and the memorias of the founders of the entail.

Second, said lord marqués assigns to his sister, doña Antonia de Vargas, professed Franciscan Conceptionist nun of said villa of Torrelaguna, 500 reales annually from the revenue of the said pastures and enclosures of Miraflores de la Sierra, Chozas, and Guadalix, and also from the 2,000 reales of revenue from the dehesa of Las Gariñas.

Said don José de Vargas is to spend at least 1,000 reales of said revenue each year for retiling the roof and for whatever other repairs the said houses may require, and more if need be, for their maintenance, since they are the splendor and monument of the founders of said entail. He also is to take great care in the cultivation of said vineyards and of its olive groves, trying to plant and propagate the vines in such a way that they may be filled with vinestocks and its fields cultivated. Let him undertake to survey the croplands by authority of the justicia ordinaria of the districts and jurisdiction where they are located and where it may be necessary. Also, for security, let the boundaries be marked in the presence of said justicia, an escribano, and the eldest, best-informed, most knowledgeable, and conscientious persons, paying the cost of the taxes and what may need doing out of the revenue of said entail, asking that notice of date, time, and place be given to owners adjoining the said lands and properties, and that the farmers who rent be present as well for their information and so they will remember what belongs to and is the property of said entail.

Under the stated conditions, I am executing the power of attorney to the said don José so that he may enjoy the revenue. To this end, I am revoking the general power of attorney that includes this entail, which I executed and gave in the city of Mexico on 31 December 1702 before Juan de Valdés, escribano real y público of said city, in favor of the lords Marqués de Vargas, knight of the Order of Calatrava, of his majesty's Treasury Council; lord Conde de Puebla de los Valles, knight of said order; and my cousin, don Sancho Chacón Bullón, knight of the Order of Santiago, gentleman of his majesty's bed-chamber.[2]

To said lords, I executed, gave, and sent the said general power of attorney that included the entails I have of the Vargases of Madrid; and that of Los Caramancheles; and that of Las Camarmas del Caño, de Esteruela, and Encima, which are two leagues north of the villa of Alcalá de Henares; the juro of Ocaña; in the said villa of Madrid, the patronages my aunts, doña Aldonza and doña Antonia Luján, founded in the parishes of San Pedro and San Francisco; its Vargas chapel on the gospel side of the principal chapel of said church of San Francisco; and the other clauses and points that are stated, and to which I refer in the said power of attorney, including in it that of the said entail of Torrelaguna, which at present I am excluding, revoking, and annulling by virtue of this said power of attorney for the said reason. I beseech and entreat said lords to do so and comply, revoking what they may have given to the persons they may have designated for and to whom they may have transferred the administration of this said entail of Torrelaguna.[3]

If they have rented the said vineyards and olive orchards, the renter may have them only for the term of three years, paying the said rent to my said son-in-law, don José de Vargas, as the person to whom I am ceding completely the administration of the said entail. May he enjoy it in partial recompense of dowry as husband and consort of my said daughter, doña Juana de Vargas Pimentel, as is stated, for as long as it is my will and Our Lord sees fit to give me life and I am delayed in these kingdoms.

For this purpose, according to the necessary form as required by law and as I am able, I execute and give the said power of attorney before said maestre de campo, Lorenzo Madrid, in the form stated and with the expressed obligation.

He so executed it and signed before me, Alc. ordinario Lorenzo Madrid, as juez receptor, and with the witnesses who attend me, Capt. Juan Páez Hurtado, lieutenant of the lord governor and captain general; and Capt. don Félix Martínez, who is captain of the presidio of this villa of Santa Fe;[4] and the witnesses of this instrument, who were the adjutant of the lord governor and captain general, don Antonio Maldonado Zapata; and Capt. don Alfonso Rael de Aguilar, secretary of government and war; and don José Manuel Gil Tomé, soldier of this presidio,[5] whom I attest that I know; and that they signed it in this said villa of Santa Fe on said day, the eleventh of the present month of January 1704.

This is on ordinary blank paper, because stamped paper is not available in these parts. I so certify and attest as juez receptor with said witnesses in attendance, and I signed it. Done ut supra.

El Marqués de la Nava de Barcinas [rubrica]

Witness in attendance: Félix Martínez [rubrica]
Witness in attendance: Juan Páez Hurtado [rubrica]

Before me as juez receptor, to which I attest:
Lorenzo de Madrid [rubrica]

*AMNB. DS. Four folios, seven written pages.

1. Described in 1680 as forty-seven, tall, and swarthy, with black beard and hair and one bad arm, Lorenzo de Madrid had survived the Pueblo Revolt and returned to Santa Fe with Vargas and the colonists in 1693. In 1697, despite or because of his prominence in the community, Madrid was accused of living in concubinage with a widow. He had three legal wives in succession and many children and made his last will and testament in 1715. Chavez, *Origins*, 66, 216.

2. Diego de Vargas to the Marqués de Vargas, the Conde de Puebla de los Valles, and Sancho de Bullón Chacón, Power of attorney, Mexico City, 31 Dec. 1702 and 1 Jan. 1703, ANGot. 692. Vargas incorrectly identified the scribe as Juan when in fact he was Francisco de Valdés.

3. At this point, don Diego did not know that the Marqués de Vargas, the Conde de Puebla de los Valles, and Sancho Bullón Chacón had refused to accept his power of attorney. Letter 50 above.

4. Félix Martínez de Torrelaguna, like Juan Páez Hurtado, Alfonso Rael de Aguilar, and Antonio Valverde, was one of the close circle of don Diego's officers. Born in Alicante, Valencia, Spain, and recruited by Vargas at Zacatecas in 1693, Martínez fought bravely in the reconquest, serving successively as Vargas's adjutant, commander at El Paso, and from 1703 captain of the Santa Fe presidio. From late 1715 until early 1717, he acted as interim governor of New Mexico, after which he found himself beset in Mexico City by legal problems concerning presidio supply. He

wrote in 1717 to Isabel María de Vargas Pimentel, asking her to use her influence with the Council of the Indies to get him reappointed governor so that he could put into effect the Vargas encomienda. In 1726, he came back to New Mexico to defend himself, after which he returned for the last time to Mexico City. Ted J. Warner, "Don Félix Martínez and the Santa Fe Presidio, 1693–1730," NMHR 45 (Oct. 1970):269–310; and Bloom, "Vargas Encomienda," 406–11.

5. José Manuel Gil Tomé, or Giltoméy, who seems to have come to New Mexico as a soldier during the recolonization, owned property in Santa Fe as early as 1696, served as a church notary (which meant he must have been literate), and died at the pueblo of San Juan on 21 April 1727. Chavez, *Origins*, 186.

---

57. *Diego de Vargas to Juana de Vargas Pimentel, Santa Fe, 9 January 1704.**

My dearly beloved daughter,[1]

I have your letter, dated in May of last year, in which you tell me of the decision you have made to return to the villa of Torrelaguna with my son-in-law, don José, and my beloved grandchildren. Because Our Lord has been served by the death of my dear son, your brother, don Juan Manuel de Vargas Pimentel, I sent a power of attorney in January 1703 for the administration of the Granada estate to my cousin, don Fernando de Teruel, Conde de Villamena. This was so that he, considering all objections and cautions, might transfer it to the person most satisfactory to him.

The first thing I told him was that don Diego de Olvera was not appropriate, because he was with his family in Madrid. Every objection I have made has been in response to his letter informing me of his meager means for so large a family and of the obligations of your brother-in-law, don Ignacio. I began to fear that he would scarcely have enough on hand to pay any draft I might remit, thus exposing me to loss. Don Diego might give his master, my son-in-law don Ignacio, whatever he directs, offering me as an excuse that he could neither fail to do this nor do any less. I have considered this objection in this instance, ordering that he not be given the power of attorney and that it not be transferred to him.

I also sent in January 1703 a general power of attorney in favor of the Marqués de Vargas, the Conde de Puebla de los Valles, and my cousin, don Sancho Bullón Chacón, for the administration of the entails of Madrid, those of the villa of Torrelaguna, and of other revenue that belongs to me. I repeat, having learned of your decision, that it has occurred to me (considering that we are mortal) to send the power of attorney to your spouse, my son-in-law, don José de Vargas. This is in partial recompense of dowry, which I offer out of my love for you, assigning to you the revenue from the entail of that villa so that your husband, my son-in-law, don José, by virtue of the power of attorney may administer and enjoy it (for as long as Our Lord sees fit to give me life and I am delayed in these parts).

Also included is the revenue of the 2,000 reales from the dehesa of Las Gariñas, with the obligation to pay all charges and the founders' memorias and to use at least 1,000 reales every year for improvement and repair of the entail's principal houses on the Coso. Because I have every confidence in your spouse, my son-in-law, don José, regarding the maintenance and attention to cultivation of the vineyards and olive orchards and to parcels requiring new plants and shoots, I know he will proceed in such a way that they will bear fruit and yield increased harvests, since it will be to his benefit.

I do not go on at greater length, because I have already written to you the news of my arrival and my accession to this government. I am telling you what I am writing in my letter to your aunt, my sister, doña Antonia de Vargas, about the assignment to her of 500 reales a year from the revenue of the pastures of Miraflores de la Sierra, Chozas, and Guadalix, as I specify in the power of attorney I am sending to my son-in-law, don José. In this way, my sister will have recourse to all of you from her cell now that her ailments keep her so ill. Also, you will take pleasure in the fact that, by means of the revenue from the entail, what I am assigning to you may enable you to stay in that villa.

May God give you the life I wish for you and for my beloved grandchildren, to whom I give my blessing. Done in this villa of Santa Fe, 9 January 1704.

Your father who loves and esteems
you from the heart and wishes for
your well-being,

The Marqués de la Nava
de Barcinas [rubrica]

To my dear daughter, doña Juana de Vargas Pimentel

*ARGD. LS. Two folios, three written pages.

1. Juana Viviana de Vargas Pimentel lived much longer than any of her siblings. At the age of seventy-three or seventy-four, she was still alive in 1740, residing in La Nava del Rey "with many children and grandchildren." López de Zárate Vargas, *Breve descripción*, 15–16.

---

58. *Diego de Vargas to Isabel María de Vargas Pimentel, Santa Fe, 12 January 1704.**

My dearly beloved daughter,

I have your letter brought by the packet boat that arrived on 15 July last year with the news of the unhappy fate of the flota. This was after Our Lord had freed it from the enemy and given time to secure the consignments of goods and property of those who had entrusted them, and despite the eagerness of people in this kingdom to acquire pesos. This is how they demonstrate the character of their generous hearts and the love with which each fulfills his duties.

After the principal loss, that of my dear son, the loss of the goods I had given him and the money, which will have run the same risk, also pains me. I paid the 20-percent interest, not counting the rest of what I furnished him: wrought silver; other valuables and curios from China; a crate containing nine arrobas net of the finest chocolate for him to give to his loved ones; along with bags of polvillo from Oaxaca, linen, and fancy clothes for him and his servant. All this cost me a very considerable sum. I also gave him 1,000 doblones the day he left Mexico City; and I provided all the outfitting, paid as far as Veracruz; my servants, who accompanied him with mules, horses, and the train of pack mules with muleteers; and fine food and drink for land and sea. Not even the son of a grandee of Spain could have gone with more abundance and splendor.

I also gave him drafts, but, knowing his nature, I turned over the money to the person who was to pay them in Cadiz. To don Fausto Bustamante, who would run the same risk, I turned over three crates of chocolate with costs for freight, exemptions, loading and unloading at the ports, and the royal fees for customs until delivery at Madrid into the hands of your husband, my son-in-law, lord don Ignacio, without his having to pay anything.

Consider how much I indebted myself in sending my beloved, now-deceased son, and how much also must have been lost by the carelessness of those upon whom possession of the goods devolved.

I give thanks to Our Lord for all that He permits. I am well (thanks to Our Lord) in this government. He gives my heart the relief it requires amid so much misfortune and adversity. I do not go on at greater length in this letter, inasmuch as I have informed you of my arrival in this government and of the certification of accession given me, a copy of which I sent to your husband, my son-in-law, last December. Therefore, I am referring in everything to it and to previous letters.

I would only add the news of the decision I have made, and about which I am writing to the holders of my power of attorney, regarding the power of attorney that I am sending in partial recompense of dowry to don José de Vargas, my son-in-law, as husband of my daughter, doña Juana de Vargas, your sister, for the entail of Torrelaguna. It includes the revenue of the 2,000 reales from the dehesa of Las Gariñas and that from the pastures of Miraflores, Chozas, and Guadalix, from which I am assigning 500 reales to my sister, doña Antonia de Vargas. I am giving him the power of attorney for as long as it is my will, Our Lord sees fit to give me life, and I am detained in these kingdoms. It was not right for me to ignore so necessary a duty.

We are mortal and not eternal. Though Our Lord was disposed to take my beloved son for Himself, I cannot escape the idea that not having made this decision earlier resulted from my having transferred the estate to my son for his relief from indebtedness and his support. The debts he contracted in order to journey to the Indies come due this year, 1704. They will have to be paid off in order to put into effect my decision and arrangements by virtue of the general power of attorney I am sending along with the news of his death.

Therefore, my son-in-law, don Ignacio, will not have this burden. He wrote me to this effect. With regard to my business affairs and petitions in the council, I leave the decision to him, trusting that he will always live up to his considerable duties. I wish wholeheartedly for his advancement. May Our Lord keep you many happy years in his company and that of my beloved grandchildren, to whom I give my blessing. Santa Fe, 12 January 1704.

Your father who loves and
esteems you from the heart
and wishes to see you,

The Marqués de la Nava
de Barcinas [rubrica]

To my dear daughter, doña Isabel María de Vargas

*ARGD. LS. Two folios, four written pages.

———

59. *Diego de Vargas to Ignacio López de Zárate, Santa Fe, 13 January 1704.* *

Son and dear sir,

I have Your Lordship's letter that came in the packet boat, news of which reached Mexico City on 15 July last year. I see that you are well, as are my beloved daughter, doña Isabel, and my grandchildren, to all of whom I give my blessing. It would be my wish to give them many embraces tenderly and lovingly. I submit myself wholly to divine will. My afflicted heart surely needs His divine assistance. Seeing that my fortune is undone, consumed by a six-year lawsuit and imprisonment, I am left with debts that oblige me to count the worrisome hours, taking from me everything that could have been a relief, an enhancement to my house, and the pleasure of enjoying my land and my beloved children and grandchildren. Furthermore, one-third of this government was removed. His majesty gave away the presidio of El Paso, separating from this one a third of its jurisdiction and frontiers.

These are the arguments I have written to Your Lordship for all your efforts in seeking the recompense I am asking his majesty for. In everything, I refer to the letters I wrote repeatedly in duplicate to Your Lordship last year on the occasions offered by the warships from France and the packet boats that came to the most excellent lord viceroy. I wrote also to the lord Marqués de Rivas with the power of attorney for my petitions and my proposal to better facilitate them. I repeat this here so that he may be informed of everything and Your Lordship as well. I also wrote him to make sure of the grant of the robe of a military order that his majesty, the king our lord (may he be in holy glory), made to my beloved son, now deceased. Therefore, you can rest assured, based on what I have written, that it will devolve upon me or upon whomever I choose.

Your Lordship also informs me in confused terms that I may have some impediment so great that it causes me to long to make my home in this kingdom. With regard to this, thank God, my will has been free. Even during so long a time as my stay in the Indies, I have not pledged it in such a fashion that I am not very much my own absolute master. Only the adversity of the lawsuit unjustly brought could have frustrated my wish. Had I returned to Spain, there is no doubt that in my present status I would have sought to live out my days in the quietude that follows from holy matrimony. Moreover, I would not have asked for even a yard of ribbon from the person I might have chosen. In this eventuality, I could commit myself however I please to someone suitable, regardless of age. I say this to Your Lordship to satisfy your vague thoughts.

I recognize the care you took to inquire about the belongings of my deceased son from the letters Your Lordship sends me. I arranged for the suffrages and masses for his soul in Mexico City upon the news that reached me from Havana. I ordered the money paid on the draft I had given him and on the one he had with him. I sent a power of attorney to the individuals who ended up with his belongings. Until I have word from them, I cannot rest assured. Since they are trustworthy and of good character, my loss, when all is said and done, will be whatever Our Lord sees fit. I am informing my beloved daughter, doña Isabel, concerning this point, as Your Lordship will see.

Regarding the disposition of those entails, since my beloved son has died, I recognize as my duty in partial recompense of dowry to send a power of attorney to my son-in-law, don José de Vargas. This is so that he can enjoy the entail of Torrelaguna in administration. It includes the revenue of 2,000 reales from the dehesa of Las Gariñas, that from half of the dehesa of Viñaderos, and that from the pastures and enclosures of Miraflores de la Sierra, Chozas, and Guadalix. It will be his duty to pay the 500 reales each year I am assigning from this revenue to my sister, doña Antonia de Vargas. He must also spend 1,000 reales annually, and more if it is required, for retiling and improvement of the principal houses on the Coso and for charges the entail may have and the memorias the founders left.

Recognizing that we are mortal, I wish in part to clear my conscience as it requires, paying attention to my just concern and duty to provide recompense of dowry. I had two reasons for not having done so before. First, it was my intention to do so in person in Spain, but at the time, the lawsuit was brought against me and I was prevented from leaving this government. Second, my son, now deceased, to whom I had given the general power of attorney in its entirety, was still alive. With the news of his death and because of the great debts and expenses occasioned by his coming and by my sending him on the return trip (since I am paying such high interests), I find that my presence here and employment in the service of his majesty are absolutely necessary, for whatever the Divine Majesty sees fit that I be given in return.

On this point, I say to Your Lordship only that this pertains to all the letters I have written you during the last year with the memorial and plan for the petition. I am leaving this to the lord Marqués de Rivas, Your Lordship's cousin, having full confidence in him and that he will value the recommendation of don Miguel de Ubilla, knight of the Order of Santiago and retired comptroller of the Tribunal of Accounts, his cousin and my great friend.

I do not doubt that Your Lordship will have conferred with the lord marqués about my petition and that His Lordship will have done the same. The resulting decision will be in my favor. Above all, during this delay please see to the arrangements I have made for the administration of those entails and their disencumbrance. Use what they have according to what is of record in the copy my son, now deceased, brought me for my satisfaction, stating how he left them in 1699. This was so that I might believe that he was not just angry with Your Lordship, and so that, having seen it, I would recognize and apply the measures called for by your failure to pay the censos on the house you have been living in and on the house on the Plaza

Mayor. With the authority of your station and person, you could not be compelled to do so.

I see this from the copy of the creditors' agreement drawn up during my manager's tenure. I did not report that my beloved son, now deceased, spoke to me against Your Lordship, but only the matter of the favor I had requested, which you should not have delayed until he left. He had no record that you had acquired it, as Your Lordship told me. Your omission was in not dispatching the royal cedulas. My brother-in-law, the Marqués de la Florida, negotiated for them and sent them to Cadiz so that my son might bring them to me. From their date, I see the truth of his report, based on the copy, stating the encumbrance the property had from the constant arrears of its censos and other pensions.

Your Lordship should neither complain nor be resentful because you have been the interested party in that property and in what I have sent you. I am the one who with reason could be complaining and resentful. In your complacency, you do not give me a reason that can convince me, since you fail me and have failed me in everything you wrote to me in your letters of 1698 and 1699, which I have. I do not doubt that my letters will reach you together with the instruments of the selection and title of Marqués de la Nava de Barcinas I executed before the then most excellent lord viceroy, the Conde de Moctezuma.

I have sent Your Lordship the copy in duplicate and asked for settlement in full of the media anata and other fees that must be paid to his majesty, requesting his royal cedula in the customary form. My son (may he be with God) also informed me that the collection of the media anata had been attempted by the council, which tried to seize the rentals of that house and other possessions.

I have also sent to Your Lordship in duplicate the certification of my having been declared a fair judge in my residencia and the copy in duplicate from the Tribunal of Accounts stating that I owe nothing to his majesty and that the balance in my favor should be paid to me.

Also, I have sent to Your Lordship the copy in duplicate of the sentence in my favor pronounced on hearing and review of the proceedings in the suit that don Pedro Cubero, my predecessor, brought against me, and the one stating that I had been ordered sent to this government by the royal cedula of the grant.[1]

In addition, I dispatched to Your Lordship a statement in duplicate, which is the one you inform me about, contradicting the judge of the media anata, to the effect that I do not have to pay what I was ordered to pay by deposit in full in the Royal Treasury of Mexico City until, upon review, the president and lords of the Council of the Treasury make a determination. Your Lordship could have sent me their decision, and with it, my petition might have been considered favorably. I am asking Your Lordship to send this to me, whether they grant it or deny it. I base my argument on his majesty's royal cedula and the examples of those who have not paid, even though they were not supported by reasons of such great relevance and justification as attend me. The lord viceroy, Conde de Moctezuma, proposes as much in his decree to the lord judge of the media anata.

Last, I sent to Your Lordship last month, December 1703, the copy in duplicate the most illustrious municipal government gave me, recording my accession to this government and captaincy general in November at this villa of Santa Fe. Reference is made to the acclamation and applause with which I was received and how joyful the kingdom was.

I sent to Your Lordship the news that the most illustrious cabildo had written to his highness in his Royal Audiencia of Mexico, reporting on the proceedings against me by don Pedro Rodríguez Cubero, my predecessor. They are but poor men and fearful of the governor's violent nature, the more so because he pointed out to them that they were going against the Royal Treasury and must sign everything against me. He gave them the documents so that they might do so. Likewise, he was giving 50 pesos a month to the procurator who had been in Mexico City in their name. He was encouraging and paying all the costs of the lawsuit against me through his own arrangement and that of his secretary, Domingo de la Barreda; that of don Juan de Saldúa (holder of don Pedro's power of attorney), who represented him and whose expenses he was paying in Mexico City;[2] and that of the attorney and procurator of the Royal Audiencia and its secretaries.

In all, he was the absolute master who made and unmade. They knew nothing about anything against me. The governor, don Pedro, had made them sign. They testified and made claims, making amends with the report they gave me for the unburdening of their consciences. They appealed to his highness, revoking the power of attorney they had given along with signatures on blank paper to the procurator, José García Jurado, that don Pedro Cubero had made them sign and give to him. The signatures were on blank paper so that, if it were necessary to issue some document against me, the holder of the power of attorney, don Juan de Saldúa; the procurators; attorney; and other people engaged in the lawsuit on don Pedro's account might do whatever occurred to them. This was in his own interest of maintaining himself in this government and hindering me by his arrival from putting my grant into effect, as he succeeded in doing for more than six years with the lawsuit.

For this reason, the cabildo was appealing to his highness, his majesty, the king our lord (may God keep him). They informed him in their name, revoking and annulling the power of attorney and signatures on blank paper given and sent to the holder of don Pedro Cubero's power of attorney and to his cousin, the comptroller of the Royal Council of the Indies, don Alonso de Buendía, for direction of and attention to everything. They asked his majesty in his Secretariats of the Cámara and of the Indies that this be made known so that the power of attorney could be used, nullifying any document and petition that might have been issued in the cabildo's name and presented before or after this letter and its report.

They wrote the same to his excellency, the most excellent lord viceroy, the Duque de Alburquerque, in his Royal Acuerdo and to the lords of the Royal Audiencia so that it would be of record in both tribunals.

They also wrote to the king our lord in his Junta of War and the Cámara of his Supreme and Royal Council of the Indies. I sent this document to Your Lordship so that you might take it in person to the office of the secretary and make sure that it was seen. Regarding what may result and be ordered by his majesty, please see to the matter. Make sure it is sent to Mexico City as his majesty's dispatch, so that coming in the chest addressed to the Royal Audiencia it will reach this kingdom. It should include an order that the copy be sent of its receipt by the escribano of the cabildo of this kingdom.

I do not doubt that Your Lordship, after having seen the dispatch, will ask his majesty for the just satisfaction and recompense that should be given to me. The injury and damage have been so great, with the loss of my fortune; the three-year imprisonment; and what is more, my loss of opportunity for promotion and gain, as I have written to Your Lordship. Because of your great understanding and talent, you will make, with the energy and persuasiveness necessary, a very effective report. This will require proper representation so that the lords of the royal and supreme council, should don Pedro return with his perverse charges, may order that I be granted the satisfaction I seek from his majesty, for only he can give it.

Don Pedro left this kingdom and is going to Spain with the intention of presenting himself. He seeks in the council to be pardoned and excused from having his residencia taken, so that his accusers and aggrieved claimants will be left without the satisfaction due them. More than all of them together, I, with so great a loss, have claims to make. Please have command of this knowledge in every way, so that don Pedro will not be pardoned. Considering the injury to the parties, I know that justice would not be served.[3]

For now, I do not write more to Your Lordship than is necessary, referring to the previous letters and hoping that Our Lord may keep you many happy years in the company of my beloved daughter, doña Isabel, and grandchildren, whom I esteem so much and to whom I give my blessing. Santa Fe, 13 January 1704.

Your father and surest servant
who esteems and loves you from
the heart kisses Your Lordship's
hand,

The Marqués de la Nava
de Barcinas [rubrica]

To lord don Ignacio López de Zárate, my son-in-law

*ARGD. LS. Six folios, eleven written pages.

1. Royal Audiencia to the king, Mexico City, 30 Mar. 1703, AGI, Guadalajara 142:20.

2. After a twenty-year military career, which included distinguished service in the navies of both the Old World and the New, Juan Bautista de Saldúa was appointed to the captaincy of the El Paso presidio by Rodríguez Cubero on 2 July 1697. Although the appointment was confirmed by the crown, Saldúa found himself thwarted by Antonio Valverde (Letter 36 above). He later served as Rodríguez Cubero's agent in Mexico City. Copy of royal approval of the appointment of

Juan de Saldúa as captain of El Paso presidio, Mexico City, AGI, Guadalajara 142:16. Espinosa, *Crusaders*, 327–28.

3. By December 1698, Rodríguez Cubero had already received the futura as governor of Maracaibo, Mérida, and La Grita, but he was to die in 1704 before acceding to the post. Copy of royal approval of the appointment of Juan de Saldúa as captain of El Paso presidio.

---

60. *Diego de Vargas to Diego de Olvera, Santa Fe, 13 January 1704.* *

I am in receipt of your letter. Because of the affection you felt for my son (may he be with God), I realize how grievous his untimely death must have been for you. The news moved me to send the general power of attorney for those entails, unburdening my son-in-law, lord don Ignacio, of this care. For that of Torrelaguna, I am sending one in recompense of dowry (for as long as it is my will) to don José de Vargas, my son-in-law, as husband and consort of my daughter, doña Juana de Vargas. I also sent a power of attorney for the entail of Granada to my cousin, the Conde de Villamena, so that he might transfer it to the person most satisfactory to him and ask of you an accounting for the time you administered it, of the expenditure of the sum my son left you, and of the second sum he remitted to you from Mexico City.

Considering that you are in the service of my son-in-law, don Ignacio, with your family in his house, it is not right that I should separate you from them or deny you this convenience and security. With this in mind, I am sending at present a letter to my cousin, the Conde de Villamena, so that he may transfer the power of attorney to the person he considers most reliable. I am thinking of this person only in terms of assisting him in the collection of the entail's revenue. I am requesting that he give an accounting each year and that my cousin collect and hold the revenue in the amount God Our Lord sees fit to give from the entail. With this security I may be able to pay and satisfy whomever I owe. It would not be right for me to entrust it to someone who would squander it.

I am giving you this explanation so that you will not think that I have any other motive than to promptly attend to the satisfaction of my debts through a person such as my cousin and not another. I shall keep you very much in my memory, submitting my will in everything to the divine, which sustains me in the hope of returning to Spain. May Our Lord keep you many years. Santa Fe, 13 January 1704.

From the one who most esteems you
and wishes for your well-being,

The Marqués de la Nava
de Barcinas [rubrica]

To lord don Diego de Olvera

*ARGD. LS. One folio, two written pages.

---

61. *Juan Páez Hurtado to Ignacio López de Zárate, Santa Fe, 20 April 1704.* *

My dear sir,

Because it is necessary and my principal duty to inform Your Lordship, as one so close to the lord Marqués de la Nava de Barcinas, I advise you of his death. It happened in this way.

The heathen Indians of the Apache nation (who continually commit hostilities in this kingdom, resulting in deaths and robberies) hurled themselves upon the outpost of Bernalillo. They took from the house of Capt. don Fernando Durán y Chaves, citizen of the outpost, about a hundred head of cattle. As soon as he missed them, don Fernando set out with some citizens and seven soldiers who were there. Overtaking the enemy in a sierra, they joined in battle and took back from them about forty head of cattle. [1]

Upon receipt of this news by letter, the lord marqués set out in person, heeding neither the harshness of the weather of this king-

1704

La noticia que me comunica V.m. en su carta d 18 del pasado del fallecim.to del Marq. de la Nava de Ba-zinas Gov.or de este Reyno; me ha ocasionado el sentim.to correspon-diente a lo que le estimaba, asi por sus prendas como por lo que solicitaba el m.or serv.o del Rey en estas Prov.as adonde deseando yo haya Persona que le continue, atendien-do a essos naturales para que logren buen.r satisfas.on y consuelo: he conferido este encargo, y Gov.no de este Reyno, al Gen.l D.n Fran.co Cuervo, y Valdes Cauallero del orden de S.n tiago, con quien no dudo

Letter of condolence by the Duque de Alburquerque on the death of Diego de Vargas, Mexico City, 29 May 1704.
Courtesy of The Huntington Library, San Marino, California.

Salles cn Naturales muy
bien por su azertado prozeder, y lar-
gas Experiencias, que sabran defender, y conservar esa Jurisdiz.on
acuyo fin llevara las ordenes
mas combenientes, y que conduz-
gan al aliuio de Sm. que
gd. Dm. as Ntros. 29 de Mayo

Dot—   M Duq de Alburquerq

Al Cauildo Justizia, y Reximto de la Nueva fee

dom nor his advanced age. Such was his zeal and devotion to the royal service that he neglected no detail, however small, to which he might attend personally and that might contribute to the preservation of what he had conquered and reconquered in this kingdom with such great toil.

In order to punish the enemy's audacity, he set out on 27 March this year from the villa of Santa Fe with part of a column of men-at-arms and Indian auxiliaries.[2] Having marched with the camp about forty leagues from this villa, tracking the enemy, he suffered a severe attack of fever caused by stomach chills. Seeing him so fatigued, the Rev. Father Preacher fray Juan de Garaicoechea, chaplain of the camp,[3] urged him to turn back, because he saw him very fatigued. He answered the father, Where better to lose one's life than in service to God and the king our lord?

Yet, because the attack was so severe, and by dint of urging and begging he was compelled to return on the shoulders of the Indians to the outpost of Bernalillo, about sixteen leagues from this villa, where I was awaiting him with medicines to treat him. They had no effect, because he did not have the strength for them to have any effect.

As I was saying, he arrived on the 5th of the present month. He confessed repeatedly and requested the habit of the Third Order of Penitence, in which he professed.[4] On the 7th, he made a will, which Your Lordship will see.[5] I am sending a legal copy to don Miguel de Ubilla, whom the lord marqués named executor in a will made at Mexico City on 1 June 1703.[6] In the last one, he corroborated and confirmed everything done in the first.

On the 8th of the current month, at about five o'clock in the afternoon, he delivered up his soul to his Maker, leaving this afflicted kingdom orphaned, for he was father to all its residents, and even more so to me. During the seventeen years since I came to this kingdom of New Spain from those of Castile, I knew no other. Thus, I have lost all my consolation and comfort. Although I was at the head of his bed until he expired, he has left me with great consolation, since I believe that, mercifully, he is in heaven because of his readiness to conform to God's will. He would repeat many times *Dominus dedit et Dominus abstulit*,[7] a clear indication of his salvation.

Because it is my duty, I am giving Your Lordship this news so that the suffrages will not delay me in my duty. I hope that Your Lordship, as a good son-in-law, together with my lady, doña Isabel, whose feet I kiss humbly, are in perfect health on the date of this letter. In your service I offer the health I enjoy, humble at your feet. In this kingdom, where the lord marqués left me as executor and lieutenant general until the most excellent lord Duque de Alburquerque sends someone to govern it, I hope to have many orders from you to carry out, with humility and devotion, out of respect for Your Lordship.[8]

Meanwhile, I ask Our Lord to keep Your Lordship for me many years. Villa of Santa Fe, capital of this kingdom of New Mexico, 20 April 1704.

My lord, your most devoted
and grateful servant kisses
Your Lordship's hand,

Juan Páez Hurtado [rubrica]

To lord Dr. don Ignacio López de Zárate, my lord

*AMNB. LS. Two folios, four written pages.

1. Born in New Mexico about 1650, Fernando Durán y Chaves II was descended from the Chaveses who arrived in the colony early in the 1600s. In 1670, he was serving as an alferez. By the time of the 1680 Pueblo Indian war, Chaves was a captain. In 1693, he and his wife, Lucía Hurtado de Salas, and their numerous children returned to New Mexico with Vargas. They were the only branch of the Chaves family to do so. By 1696, don Fernando was alcalde mayor of Bernalillo—a post he held in 1704 at the time of don Diego's death. By 1707, he had moved south to Atrisco, where he died sometime between 1712 and 1716. Chavez, *Origins*, 20–21, 160–61.

Bernalillo was founded in late 1695 by Spanish colonists. They laid out a plaza and built a church and convento dedicated to San Francisco. This settlement, reportedly flourishing by the following year, was located several miles north of present-day Bernalillo, apparently on the west side of the Rio Grande. Marc Simmons, *Albuquerque: A Narrative History* (Albuquerque, 1982):45. David H. Snow, "Santiago to Guache: Notes for a Tale of Two (or More) Bernalillos," *Collected Papers*, 161–81. Espinosa, *Crusaders*, 227, 244.

2. Diego de Vargas, Journal, 27 Mar.-2 Apr. 1704, SANM II:99.

3. Fray Juan de Garaicoechea served at several New Mexico missions, among them Zia and Zuñi. He died at Zuñi on 9 August 1706 and was buried on the epistle side of the sanctuary. Adams and Chavez, *Missions of New Mexico*, 333.

4. The Third Order of St. Francis was established for laypersons who wished to follow the austere precepts of St. Francis, yet still live and work in the secular world. Members wore a modified Franciscan habit either underneath or over their clothing. Adams and Chavez, *Missions of New Mexico*, 363.

5. Diego de Vargas, Will, Bernalillo, 7 Apr. 1704, SANMI:1027.

6. Diego de Vargas, Will, Mexico City, 1 June 1703, AGNot. 692.

7. *Biblia Sacra*, Job 1:21.

8. Juan Páez Hurtado served as acting governor until 10 March 1705 when don Francisco Cuervo y Valdés, named by the Duque de Alburquerque to the post late in 1704, took office. Duque de Alburquerque to the king, Mexico City, 11 Oct. 1704, cited in Bancroft, *Arizona and New Mexico*, 227.

------

62. *Ignacio López de Zárate to Diego de Vargas, Madrid, 26 June 1704.* *

[. . .] person, they may remain forever in that kingdom, when for both, Your Lordship should persuade and assure yourself that in this they must always be well cared for so that you will have all the posts there so rightfully yours.[1] Now more than ever, this consideration is necessary, having lost my beloved brother-in-law, don Juan Manuel de Vargas. In this way, Your Lordship's best interest is served, not only in preserving the splendor of your entails and household, but also in their greatest gain.

May Your Lordship resolve, as I beg of you, to give this consolation to all your children and grandchildren, in whose name I also make this request to you. The long time that Your Lordship has been in that kingdom and the latest outrages you have suffered from the experience of your residencia are enough. In everything referred to, I am moved only by my love, duty, and wish to see Your Lordship enjoying all the pleasures and happiness that I must ask for you.

In all my previous letters, I have informed you separately of every-thing that occurs in a general sense regarding Your Lordship's busi-ness affairs. I shall be glad if all my letters and duplicates have reached you. I should add that efforts are continuing regarding the petition for the governments. I hope to have the good fortune of serving Your Lordship, as when I sent you the dispatches confirming for the sec-ond generation the encomienda of 4,000 pesos of 8 reales.

Surely no one would believe how costly any petition is at present, chiefly because the king (may God keep him) is on campaign in the war in Portugal. Since the climate of Extremadura is hot and the season advanced, it is thought that very soon his majesty will retire to Madrid, until the weather cools off.[2] All here are delighted by this news, since nothing is more important to us than his life. With his majesty here, it will be possible for me to more easily make arrange-ments and obey Your Lordship.

At present, all of us in Your Lordship's household are extremely grief stricken and disconsolate at the news we received last week that our uncle, lord don Gregorio Pimentel, died after a long and pain-ful illness, which was a great pity. For us, it was a great sorrow and affliction, because we esteemed and loved him so much, and because we owed him so much. We have only the consolation that his death was very much in keeping with his exemplary life. He will be with God, which is what is most important.[3]

In everything, I refer to the letters and duplicates I have previous-ly written to Your Lordship. Because nothing particular occurs to me to add, I must tell you that the events of the war in Portugal go very favorably, and that we hope that Our Lord sees fit to continue them and give our king (may God keep him) all the success he mer-its, as befits this monarchy.

May His Divine Majesty make it so and keep Your Lordship, my lord and father, the many and long years that He can and I wish and need so much. Madrid, 26 June 1704.[4]

To lord don Diego de Vargas Zapata y Luján Ponce de León, Marqués de la Nava de Barcinas, my lord and my father-in-law

*AMNB. C. inc. Three folios, five written pages.

1. Here, don Ignacio seems to be referring to don Diego's two natural sons, Juan Manuel and Alonso (or Ildefonso), who were

with him in New Mexico when he died. Diego de Vargas, Will, Bernalillo, 7 Apr. 1704, SANM I:1027.

2. In March 1704, Archduke Charles of Austria embarked in an English squadron and sailed to Portugal. He was received in Lisbon, where he declared himself Carlos III of Spain. In response to this challenge, Felipe V set out from Madrid, leaving the government in the hands of the queen. In Plasencia, he took command of forty thousand troops and launched an invasion, resulting in a series of triumphs over Portuguese, Dutch, and English allies. By July, however, both sides were ready to call a halt to hostilities because of the brutal heat. On 16 July, Felipe returned to a Madrid joyous over events in Portugal. Victor Gebhardt, *Historia general de España y de sus Indias, desde los tiempos más remotos hasta nuestros días* (Madrid, 1863), 6:36–37.

3. Gregorio Pimentel de Prado died in Torrelaguna on 20 June 1704 and was buried in the family chapel of San Gregorio in the parish church. He was survived by his wife, Antonia Bernaldo de

Quirós, and his two sons, Sebastián and Gregorio. In a will dated 7 November 1703, he had named as his executors the Marqués de la Florida, his brother; Ignacio López de Zárate, his nephew by marriage; and Alonso de Valenzuela. Difuntos, Libro 2 (1664–1712), Parroquia de Santa María Magdalena, Torrelaguna.

4. Don Ignacio, who at the time he wrote this letter did not know that don Diego had died more than two months earlier, formally took possession of the Vargas properties in Spain on 21 February 1705. He himself lived only until 1707. After giving to Isabel María, his wife, on 28 October of that year a power of attorney to make his will, Ignacio López de Zárate died two days later. He was buried in the Convento de San Francisco. His heirs were Isabel María and their four children. He had also named his wife as one of his executors, along with the Marqués de la Florida, Gaspar Girón Venegas, Alonso Carnero López de Zárate, Antonio de Ubilla, José Sobremonte, the Marqués de Vargas, Francisco Gómez Lara, and Diego de Olvera. Pérez Balsera, *Laudemus*, 73–74.

63. *Isabel María de Vargas Pimentel to Antonio de León, Madrid, 14 April 1705.*

Most illustrious sir,[1]

Although I have not sought to put myself at Your Lordship's disposal on the most recent occasions, I can assure you that only my concern not to bother you with my letters has been the cause of my silence. Now, however, unable to bear patiently not knowing the state of Your Lordship's health, I proceed in accordance with my duty to express to you my hope that you enjoy the full and perfect health that is so important to me. With my good health (thanks be to God), I repeat that I am as always at Your Lordship's disposal and service as your acknowledged servant because of the particular favors you bestowed upon me when you were in Torrelaguna. You will never find my feeling of obligation and appreciation wanting.

I inform Your Lordship that Our Lord saw fit last year to take to himself my uncle, don Gregorio Pimentel, after a long and painful illness. Since this was preceded by the death of my grandmother, my lady doña Isabel de Olazábal, Your Lordship can imagine the depth of my sorrow and affliction over the two losses. My only consolation on both occasions was that my uncle, the Marqués de la Florida, had decided much earlier to take my cousins, Sebastián and Gregorio, with him when he went to serve as castellan of Milan. If this had not happened, these poor boys would have found themselves lost and utterly forsaken. Today they are on the way to achieving success. Already Sebastián is a cavalry captain in that state, and Gregorito, I hope, will be one very soon. Both have managed to take part in all the campaigns there.

By these last ships, which the Duque de Alburquerque, viceroy of New Spain, outfitted, I received the fateful news of my father's death (may he be in holy glory). Your Lordship will know the special help from Our Lord that I shall have needed to resign myself to His most holy will in this great tragedy. It would appear that God wanted me to experience such heavy blows, to which the following is also added.

My brother, don Juan Manuel, had gone to Mexico City to see if he could persuade our father to return to Spain. Unable to achieve this, he decided to do so himself with the last flota. During the voyage from Veracruz to Havana, he died suddenly from respiratory failure. I tell Your Lordship that I do not know how I shall have the courage to overcome such understandable grief. My only strength is the justifiable confidence I have in Your Lordship that you, because you esteemed, loved, and favored them so, will keep them very much in mind, commending them to Our Lord, as I trust in your great kindness you will and I beg you to.

The arrangement my father made comes down to having declared me, as his eldest child, immediate successor in all his entails.[2] I wanted to tell Your Lordship all of this, adding that don Ignacio; my son Diego, who is now eleven; my three daughters, Rosalea, now thirteen; Frazquita, five; and Mariquita, two and a half, are well (God be praised). They place themselves with all humility at Your Lordship's feet, and I do the same, wishing with all our hearts that Our Lord will keep you the many years He can and we need so much. Madrid, 14 April 1705.[3]

To the most illustrious lord, don Antonio de León, bishop of Arequipa

*AMNB. L. Two folios, four written pages.

1. As parish priest of Torrelaguna in the bishopric of San Lozano, Dr. don Antonio de León, a native of Madrid, had baptized all of Isabel María's children. From Torrelaguna, he was elevated in 1677 to the office of bishop of Trujillo in Peru. In 1679, he took possession of the see of Arequipa, where he served as bishop until his death in 1708. Santiago Martínez, *La diócesis de Arequipa y sus obispos* (Arequipa, 1933):137–50.

2. Diego de Vargas, Will, Mexico City, 1 June 1703, AGNot. 692. Ignacio López de Zárate to Diego de Olvera, Torrelaguna, 21 Feb. 1705, AHPM, P. 14.744.

3. Isabel María de Vargas Pimentel lived until 1718. She made her will on 22 January, died on 1 March, and was buried in the chapel of San Antonio de Padua of the Convento de San Francisco. She had named as her heirs don Diego José López de Zárate Vargas, her son, and her three daughters. As executors, besides Diego José, she had designated Félix de Feloaga, oidor of the Chancillería of Granada, her son-in-law; Gaspar Girón Venegas, chief royal chamberlain; Alonso Carnero López de Zárate of the Council of the Indies; Antonio de Ubilla, Marqués de Rivas—all of the preceding, members of the Order of Santiago; José Carnero, Conde de Villafranca de Gaitán, of the Order of Alcántara; Lic. Francisco Gómez Lara, priest and chaplain of Girón; and Diego de

Olvera, her mayordomo. Don
Diego José, twenty-eight years old,
took possession of the Vargas

family properties on 23 September
1719. Pérez Balsera, *Laudemus*,
85, 91–92.

---

64. *Juan Manuel de Vargas Zapata to Ignacio López de Zárate, Mexico City, 7 October 1706.* *

Lord marqués, my dear sir,

Permit me to tell Your Lordship how my lucky state sought to add joy to my good fortune on receiving the letter you saw fit to honor and favor me with in the packet of the lord archdeacon of this holy church. I believe that these honors and favors will not be the end of Your Lordship's courtesy, as those lines demonstrate. Therefore, I go on by this letter to return Your Lordship's condolences warranted by the magnitude of the grievous death of my father and lord (may he rest in glory). Your Lordship must believe that my tongue has been silenced by my distress and cannot express the pain of so great a loss. The Divine Maker, however, in His infinite wisdom, so disposed, either to reward the eagerness with which he sought to serve both God and king or to punish my sins. For me, this has been my greatest fear.

Yet, it gives some relief, sir, to the source of my sorrow that though I earlier thought myself abandoned because of the loss, I now see myself better aided than before. Although one normally lends more credence to a single word promised by a great person than to the validity of writings that only hint at security, it seems to me that my surest hope is that Your Lordship will aid me. I see that you say you will and sign by your own hand, the more so when the duty of Your Lordship's greatness is incumbent upon you, as are grief and fraternity. Heaven wished that we should be brought together, giving me, my brother, and my sister the same father as you, making us relatives, if not *proxime* to Your Lordship at least *remote*, since you are the spouse of my beloved sister and lady, doña Isabel.[1]

The trust that my father and lord had in the two of you was so great that he told me on several occasions, and on the point of death,

Look to my son, lord don Ignacio, and to doña Isabel, and you will receive from them as much aid as from me. Thus, trusting in this and above all in the majesty of Your Lordship's greatness, prostrate and humble at your feet, I beg you to have compassion for my need and that of my brother and sister. We find ourselves without a single real to get by with in this land.

My brother, Ildefonso, and I sought to avail ourselves of the lord Duque de Alburquerque so that he might accommodate us in some employ in order to maintain ourselves with the honor of sons of such a father and aid our sister, a maiden. This being a case so worthy of compassion, I believe he could have done so. Because we did not have sufficient means for the customary gratuity, he refused to aid us, even though we presented the great merits of my father and lord (not unknown in Madrid or in New Spain) and my minor ones of having served my king and lord with the rank of alferez real. I underwent the severe hardships that New Mexico occasions. Above all merits was the fine character of my father who, seeing himself already weighed down by years and poor health, set out on the campaign on which he died, having no other remedy than the divine, for he lacked the human.

I also inform Your Lordship that God saw fit to take my mother on 11 September this year, leaving me with the family.[2] From this, you can imagine how I see myself weighed down by cares, both my brother and I destitute, without the means to get by and to support and to make arrangements for our sister. Hence, on the advice of several gentlemen of this city and trusting in Your Lordship's word and power, I beg you to secure employ for me in these kingdoms, whether it be a position of comptroller in the Royal Treasury office of this city, or an alcaldía mayor, for example, either Mestitlán de la Sierra or San Miguel el Grande or another in which Your Lordship can find a place where I could be appointed.[3] With Your Lordship's authority interceding, I trust this will be attained. Of course, Your Lordship will also cover for me with the expenses of the dispatches at Madrid. I shall oblige myself to pay for them, because, as soon as I have a grant by Your Lordship's hand (as I trust I shall), there will be someone to give me the money to pay you in Madrid.

I shall continue to be Your Lordship's steadfast slave, remaining in the debt of such character and charity. Please do this to demonstrate your greatness and to aid the helpless. May I say now that, once you have the grant of an employ for me, Your Lordship can issue an order for me to pay the expenses. Something else Your Lordship can do for me as a favor: please have the grant come in triplicate for greater security, and also a letter of recommendation to whoever the lord viceroy of New Spain is at the time of your reply to this letter.

In the meantime, I continue asking God Our Lord to will my happiness and keep Your Lordship in the good health that I wish for you out of my affection and that is so necessary for our aid. I am ready and able to carry out the orders of Your Lordship and my lady, doña Isabel, whose feet I kiss. My sister, loving and humble, dedicates herself to you and my lady, wishing for your health and kissing your hands.

I now cease to tire and bother Your Lordship. From your house. Mexico City, 7 October 1706.

Lord marqués, my dear sir, your
least, surest, and most affectionate
servant and slave kisses Your
Lordship's feet,

Juan Manuel de Vargas
Zapata Luján [rubrica]

*ARGD. ALS. Two folios, four written pages.

1. In his final will in 1704, don Diego gave the names and ages of his three natural children as Juan Manuel, twenty-four; Alonso (here Ildefonso), twenty-three; and María Teresa, nineteen. Diego de Vargas, Will, Bernalillo, 7 Apr. 1704, SANM I:1027.

2. Juan Manuel's mother may have been Nicolasa Rincón, the only burial entry at the Sagrario parish on 11 September 1706. AGN, Sección Genealogía y Heráldica, Difunciones de españoles (1671–1820), Volumen 5 (1704), fol. 365v, Parroquia de la Asunción, Sagrario, Mexico City, LDS microfilm 035,750, rollo 32, 5–9.

3. San Miguel el Grande (since 1862, San Miguel de Allende) is in north-central Guanajuato on the cool, dry plains of the Meseta Central. Mestitlán de la Sierra, in present-day northern Hidalgo, lies in a region that varies from arid valleys to cold, rainy mountains (the Sierra Madre Oriental) and even today is difficult of access. Gerhard, *Historical Geography*, 183–87, 237–39; Bakewell, *Silver Mining*, 22; Francisco de la Maza, *San Miguel de Allende: Su historia, sus monumentos* (Mexico City, 1939).

Glossary

---

acuerdo   Meeting of the audiencia and its president to decide matters of political administration

alcabala   Sales tax, levied on first and subsequent sales

alcalde de primer voto   One of two magistrates chosen yearly by the cabildo

alcalde mayor   In New Spain, a district administrator with extensive political and judicial authority; also known as a corregidor in both New Spain and South America

alcalde ordinario   Civil magistrate elected yearly by the cabildo

alcaldía mayor   District administered by an alcalde mayor

alferez   Field-grade officer in the Spanish army, similar to a colonel

alferez mayor   Cabildo member who carried the royal standard in civic ceremonies

aranceles   Official listings of fees for goods and services

arroba   Measure of weight equivalent to .25 quintal or 25 libras; as a liquid measure, equivalent to 2.5-4 gallons

asesor general   Legal advisor to the viceroy on matters that did not fall within the audiencia's jurisdiction

audiencia   Superior tribunal in the New World, and by extension, the territory it governed

aviador   Agent and outfitter, usually a local merchant, who provided supplies for expeditions; in the mining camps, an aviador advanced cash or goods on credit to miners

ayuda de costa   Per-diem expenses given in addition to a salary

bosque   Dense growth of trees and underbrush, especially in New Mexico, of cottonwoods, frequently found along a river or other body of water

cabildo, justicia y regimiento   Municipal council, also known as ayuntamiento

Cámara of the Council of the Indies   Subcouncil of the Council of the Indies, responsible for making appointments to offices in the Indies

capellanía   Chantry endowed by private individuals

casas reales   Principal government building and residence of president of the audiencia

322

carta consulta   Written recommendation of a royal council, sent to the king

cedula   Decree issued by the king

censo   Long-term financial contract, similar to a mortgage, that was in effect a perpetual loan

censura   Ecclesiastical interdiction

chancillería   Superior tribunal in Spain, located at Granada and Valladolid

conde   Title of nobility equivalent to a marqués in Spanish- and Portuguese-speaking countries; not equivalent to the title of count in the English nobility

Consulado   Merchant guild and court

corregidor   See alcalde mayor

cortijo   House in the country, frequently surrounded by lands used for cultivation or the hunt

coso   Plaza or enclosed place for bullfights and other public celebrations

Council of the Indies   Supreme administrative body that handled the affairs of the New World

Council of War   Administrative body in Spain responsible for military matters throughout the empire

custody   In the Franciscan Order, an administrative unit subordinate to a province and presided over by a custos

dehesa   Area reserved for the exclusive use of flocks belonging to townspeople and formed by enclosing sections of the town commons and set aside, either permanently or for certain months of the year, for nonmigratory animals

duque   Duke in Spanish- and Portuguese-speaking countries; not equivalent to the title of duke in the English nobility

encomienda   Royal grant giving an individual the right to Indian tribute in exchange for his provision of protection and Christian instruction to the Indians

entrada   Formal accession of a ruler; a military expedition into an unconquered area

escribanía   Office or profession of a scribe

escribano real y público del número   Licensed scribe with exclusive right to exercise his post in the town or district in which he had his appointment

escribano real   Scribe allowed to pursue his profession anywhere, except in those areas where an escribano público maintained an escribanía

estancia   Large tract of land used for raising livestock

familiar   Lay official who served as an informer for the Inquisition

fanegas   Dry-weight measure equivalent to approximately 1.5 bushels; also a measure of land equaling 1.59 acres

fianza de calumnia   Bond to be paid to the accused by the accuser if he brought charges out of malice and crime attributed to the accused could not be proved

finca   Right to collect a stipulated revenue in an area

fiscal   Royal prosecutor

flota   One of the two fleets that were customarily sent each year from Cadiz or Sanlúcar de Barrameda, Spain, to Veracruz, New Spain, carrying Spanish products and passengers, and transporting New World products and passengers back to Spain; corresponding fleet for Tierra Firme (Peru) was known as the Galeones

futura   Individual's right of succession in employment at some time in the future

grandee   Member of one of the families comprising the official elite of Spanish society

hacienda   Landed estate, larger than a rancho, that combined stock raising, agriculture, and often mining

Hacienda   Royal Treasury

juez privativo   Judge having jurisdiction over a case to the exclusion of the judge who would normally hear it

juez receptor   Magistrate commissioned to take testimony

junta   Meeting of the viceroy and ministers of an audiencia; meeting of civil or military officials

juro   State-financed annuity, whereby an individual or corporation, upon lending the crown a sum of money, received a government bond in return

justicia   Magistrate

justicia mayor   Lieutenant appointed to serve in the absence of a governor or alcalde mayor

lanzas   Payment made to the crown by Spanish grandees and titled nobles in lieu of providing soldiers for military service

legua   Approximately 2.6 miles

ley   Fineness of metal

libra   Approximately one pound

licenciado   Licentiate

maestre de campo   Field-grade officer

marco   Eight ounces of silver

marqués   Marquess in Spanish- and Portuguese-speaking countries

mayordomo   Chief steward of a great household

media anata   Tax constituting half a recipient's first year's salary and a third of all other financial perquisites from the grant of a public office, favor, or concession, whether permanent or temporary

memorias   Ecclesiastical endowments used to finance memorial masses, dowries, and charitable works

oidor semanero   Rotating on a weekly basis, the audiencia judge who handled petty criminal cases and civil cases involving less than 200 pesos

patronage   Endowment of a pious work

plaza de armas   Site where an army camps and musters in formation when it is on campaign or where garrisoned troops muster and drill

presidio   Garrison of soldiers or the place where they are posted

querella   Criminal complaint

quintal   Hundredweight

rancho   Small, rural landholding that produced much the same sort of products as the hacienda, but on a smaller scale

real   Mining camp

regidor   Member of the cabildo

registro   Ship having special permission to sail apart from the flota

rescate   Refined, but unminted, silver produced from ore that was either bought or received as payment

residencia   Judicial review of a public official at the end of his term of office

servicio   Payment made to the crown

tercias   Payment to the crown of two-ninths of the ecclesiastical tithe

traslado   Copy of a document with the same legal force as the original

Tribunal of Accounts   Audit court responsible for monitoring all public accounts except those for the alcabala, tribute, and mercury

vara   Unit of length equal to between 31 and 34 inches

villa   Chartered municipality superior in size, status, and privileges to a pueblo, but inferior to a ciudad

Part 3

A Note on Symbols

1. Scribal emendations of text are enclosed in pairs of carets (ˆ).
2. A caret (ˆ) followed by a number and text indicates a change to a hand other than the original hand.
3. Editorial emendations and expansion of abbreviations in the original text are indicated by italics.
4. Line lengths correspond to original lengths. Lines exceeding typeset length are indented.

Spanish Text of Letters

---

1. Diego de Vargas to Gregorio Pimentel de Prado,
Teutila, 22 October 1675, ARGD, ALS, LS, inc.

[fol. 1r]
los socorros aqui Referidos Yo la deje Bestida
y a todos Mis Hijos y Criados tambien, y el fru-
cto de las Biñas Por vender, Y trigo y zebada en casa todas estas Menudencias me obligan el escribirte Por el cargo tan grande
que me *hazes* en tu carta delo cuydado q*ue* te
ha costado Mi casa y el q*ue* te cuestan Mis
Cosas Pues no se q*ue* me *halle* tan en la calle q*ue* no tenga Muy en la Memoria Mis
Deudas q*ue* esas esfuerzan, Bayan en
desminuycion cada año. Pues la Renta
Corre, y no la gasta su Dueño, Porque
Mis tiernos y queridos Hijos ya te escribo en esta Y te Repito que es mis dos
Hijas las Ponga luego en el convento
de tordelag*una* que con Dos Mil R*eales* de vellon estan sustentadas, y Bestidas muy
dezentemente, y mis dos Hijos me Pareze
con Otro tanto lo Pueden Passar muy bien
Con su Aguela este es el gasto q*ue* Puede
[fol. 1v]
tener toda mi hazienda pues no llegan mas que
a quatro Mil R*eales* las Biñas *h*An de dar Para
esto, y la Renta de Pan, Y se *han* de Pagar
las Memorias de San fran*ci*sco Y sobra la Renta
de Prados zercas en Miraflores Chochas

Y Guadaliz y la Renta de la Dehesa de las Gariñas, en Madrid la Renta de las Casas
Censo, que se desempaña con el Dinero que embia-
re, Juro ^de ocaña^ Y Patronatos, la Renta de Granada, y Renta de las Camarmas del Caño
todas estas fincas Y Possesiones estan Corrientes y han estado Menos la de Granada Garinas, y Camarma, desde este año de setenta y cinco queda todo llibre de Deuda y sin
tener el Dueño que lo gaste, y asi Hermano
mio te pido, que cumplas, en Satisfazer lo
que yo debo a todos muy Por menor y Reparar-
me mis casas, que no sera Razon que des-
[fol. 2r]
pues de haverme estado en este Reyno carezien-
do de mi Patria, y trabajando continuamente
Por Diferentes tierras Y caminos que no es fazil
Ponderarte su Aspareza Y Bibiendo entre Yndios que es lo mismo que estar uno en un
desierto halle yo quando sea Dios servido
que se me cumpla el deseo de Yr a esa Corte
Mi hazienda como la deje. Me Prometo
que asistiras a tu Nobleza y Christian-
dad No faltando a nada Y atiende a esos
Ninos, que son tuyos, Como mios Pues eres
su curador, demas de ser Hijos de tu Hermana que ya veo que yo no meresco por mi el
que tu Me favorescas Yo te servire en todo
quanto valiere, Hermano Y Amigo mio y te estimo
la asistencia que has tenido de Remitirme las
Cartas de Recomendacion, y no te cansas en
hazerlo. Si Biniere Nuebo Señor Birrey
en la flota te escribire del suceso que tubiere en Mis Negocios de Guatimala
[fol. 2v]
no he tenido un Real Ni Razon mas ha de seys
Messes tengo la Resolucion de Yr en saliendo de
este oficio, las cartas de Mis tios No he rezibido ni la de Don Agustin Ponze de leon que hubo de Remitirme, el Pliego a Guatimala como

se lo escribo *h*are la Dilijencia de los Rubies
q*u*e me Pides y escribire en la flota a D*o*n Chris-
tobal de Aguirre, Y A Dios Amigo Y Her-
m*a*no de mi Bida los m*ucho*s años q*u*e deseo y te
me deje veer. Teutila, Y Octubre 22 de 1675

Tu Herm*a*no Y M*a*yor Amigo que
te quiere de Corazon Y B*esa tu* M*a*no

D*o*n Diego de Vargas
Zapata lujan

Mi Herm*a*no Amigo D*o*n Gregorio Pimentel de Prado

---

2. *Diego de Vargas to Mariana Villalba, Tlalpu-*
jahua, 22 March 1686, AMNB, ALS.

[fol. 1r]
[cross top center]
S*e*ñora mia bien Sabe Dios N*uest*ro Señor sus
trabajos de V*uestra* m*erced* y sus Males que Recognosco a V*uestra* m*erced* otro Job, en esa Cama
Dando Alabanzas al Criador ymmen-
sso Ojala pudiera ser Parte de su
Remedio q*uando* me Corren tantas Obligaziones para Darle a V*uestra* m*erced* los
Alibios que Deseo y quisiera Ser
el todo Me es fuerza que me quede
la Mortificazion para ya que no
sea el todo Sere la Parte que
sirva a V*uestra* m*erced* Con Alguna ayuda
de Costa Para Sabanas Y asy
perdoneme *h*asta entonzes. Y De
los Consejos espirituales A mis Hijos
para que Miren por el pun-
to de sus obligaziones pues a my
mis P*a*dres no Me Dejaron Ningunos

Folio 1r of Diego de Vargas to Mariana Villalba,
Tlalpujahua, 22 March 1686.
     Archivo del Marqués de la Nava de Barcinas,
Madrid.

tesoros mas que esos Mayoras-
gos que pongo a Dios ~~por~~ Nuestro Señor
por testigo De lo poco que me han
Valido y Gozado de sus fructos pues
quatro Dias que los Administre
los Coji Con Deudas Reparos y
[written vertically in left margin] Dos mil pensiones la Madre que
les Dy fue el Dote del de sus prendas
que Solizite y no otro y asy Digo en todo esto que esa tyerra me
    fue
Madrastra pues me Desterro a Buscar por mis Peños en tye-
rras estrañas y Corriendo Diferentes Climas y en ella hago
lo que por mi Affecto No pudia hazer en esa pues Unos Guantes
    no
he pedido desde que sali de mi Patria Verdad es que no me faltan
en esta que se pueden ymbiar De Regalo los que se hazen en esta
[fol. 1v]
Y asi me he dilatado en este punto porque
no se atribuya a mal juizio mio lo empeñado de mis Mayorasgos que todo ello
ymportaba nada y si tubiera ayuda
en esa tyerra Como en esta Mejor con
el fundamento de ellos me hubiera vandea-
do que No en esta tyerra sin ellos pues
no es porque la Plata se coje en los Arboles ny en los Rios que el que no trabaja
y tyene Punto, se anda sin el y sin Credito Como en ese Reyno Guarde Dios a Vuestra merced
muchos años y Aviseme de Su Salud en las
que se ofrezieren Fecha en este Real hoy 22
de Marzo de 1686

Besa la Mano de Vuestra merced su
Mas Affecto y fino Servidor

Don Diego de Vargas
Zapata lujan

Mi señora Doña Mariana Villalba

———

3. *Diego de Vargas to María de Vargas Pimentel, Tlalpujahua, 22 March 1686*, AMNB, ALS.

[fol. 1r]
[cross top center]
^2Padre^
Hija mia, de mi vida mucho gusto tube
con tu Carta y me fue de Mucho consuelo veer el que teneys Con Mi señora
Doña Juana de Vargas Mi tia y que su
merced Con sus Realizadas obligaziones atyenda a las Mias y asy
escrivire a su merced Con toda fineza Remito esa Carta Para el Marques
de Yebra De dozientos pesos por su Hijo si se llograre Mi Deseo lo es-
tymare porque de No estar en las
Yndias Mi Amigo Don Juan de Albarado No tengo Otra persona de
mi Confianza tu Hija mia
Con tu lindo Juizio y Punto de tu
Sangre Sabras Como la Mayor Correjir a tus Hermanos en lo que Recogno-
zieres que no Dan gusto muy
Particular a mi tia a quien de Mirar
y Reverenziar Como a Madre que
os es a todos de amparo de mi parte Recognozereys Continuas asis-
[fol. 1v]
tenzias y os Ruego mucho a todos
que, tengais toda atenzion en no dar
el Menor Disgusto a mi tia y en la flota me prometo si se Consiguio mi
Pretension poder escriviros Con Mas
forma Para el Desahogo de Algunas
Dependenzias y tratar, de mas fundamento Y asy no me Dilato mas que
Dezirte que me hallaras siempre Con
el Amor de Padre que te quiere Mas que
a si y Desea darte el estado mas de el

Servicio de Nuestro Señor que te Guarde Y favo-
resca en todo Como mi fina Voluntad
Desea. Tlalpujagua y Marzo a 22
de 1686 años.

~~Besa la Mano~~
tu Padre que te ama
Y estima de Corazon,

Don Diego de Vargas
Zapata lujan

Mi Hija ~~Mi Señora~~ Doña Ysabel María de Vargas

---

4. *Diego de Vargas to Ignacio López de Zárate,
Mexico City, 8 February 1690, AMNB, LS.*

[fol. 1r]
[cross top center]
hijo Y Señor mio es cierto que desvanecido quedo
Y Ufano a un mesmo Tiempo en la ocasion
que rodada me ofrecio la fortuna en merecer
le por mi hijo Y Señor atribuio mi dicha del
merecimiento que por Su Virtud consiguio mi
querida hija Ysabel en mi queda la ancia
de Ver lograda mi Suerte de que pueda en
breve gosarle Y Servirle Y es cierto que mal
digo la estrechez con que me halla al presente la noticia para no hacer las demostra-
Ciones correspondientes a la estimacion de
Vuestra Señoría Y confiansa de mis obligaciones atribu-
tos de Su illustre Sangre Y le aseguro en la
flota aunque me desnude de quanto tenga
le remitire lo mas que pueda para el desahogo del empeño que Uso la Visarria del
Señor Marques hermano de Vuestra Señoría a quien ren-
    didamente ofresco mi persona Y quanto pueda

Valer a su Servicio *h*aviendo Un Vinculo Y
laso estreço de finesa en mi firme Siempre
Y desnuda de lisonja p*ar*a Corresponderle
[written vertically in left margin] ma
[fol. 1v]
a las Veras Con que Se empeño Y tomo a su
Cargo el favorecer a mis hijos el tiempo
me de felisidad p*ar*a explaiarme a manifes-
tarme en lo fino de mi afecto que resi-
procam*en*te le meresca toda la demostracion
del Suio, Y en la ocasion presente le Suplico tome a Su Cargo la administracion de las rentas de
mis maiorasgos p*ar*a lo qual escrivo a Ju*an* Gonsales
Calderon, Substituia el poder qu*e* le remiti en las
Urcas en fin de Junio del año passado, Yo que-
do al presente pretendiendo el *Excelentísi*mo Se*ñ*or Virrey me
de paso a la R*e*al Cedula de merced de *G*obernad*o*r Y Capitan *Genera*l en el nuebo Mexico p*ar*a disponer Viaje
tan dilatado no dejo de descomponerme mucho
el irme intempestivam*en*te a los dies meses el alcalde m*a*yor
a el ofiscio en que me hallava entretenido por
el Conde de Galve Y respecto de tenerlo dado Su
M*a*gesta*d* al Susodi*c*ho le dio Su *Excelencia* Cumplimiento
a d*i*cha merced Y a mi me desquicio de tal Suerte
que ha dos meses que me hallo recogiendo el
Valor de los asogues que fueron de mi Cargo
Y assi hasta el mes de Maio aunque Su *Excelencia* me
de luego Cumplimiento me detendre d*i*cho tiempo
en la flota escrivire a V*uestra* Se*ñorí*a lo que resultare interin
en qualquiera parte me tiene tan de Coraçon
[fol. 2r]
Suyo quanto igualmente le pido la asistencia
de mi querido hijo Y a mi amada Ysavel
mis repetidos abrasos en cuia compania gu*ar*de
Dios a V*uestra* Se*ñorí*a felises años, Y me asiste el quidado
del felis parto *h*aya tenido mi hija, y reservo
la enorabuena de la dilatada Sucecion que
deseo a V*uestra* Se*ñorí*a Con la noticia de ella que espero
en el primer aviso. Mexico Y febrero
8 de 1690 años

^2*Besa* la *Mano* de *Vuestra Señoría* Su mas
Affecto *P*adre Amigo y *Ser*vidor

Don Diego de Vargas
Zapata lujan^

*Señ*or D*octor* D*on* Ygnacio Lopez de Zarate mi hijo Y *Señ*or

[fol. 2v]
8 feb*r*ero 1690
14 Junio 90
14 el mismo
4 Jullio 90
[upside down at foot of 2v] Dupp*lica*do

---

5. *Diego de Vargas to Juan González Calderón, Mexico City, 8 February 1690,* AHPM, LS.

[fol. 1r]
303
[cross top center]
*Señ*or mio estimo la enorabuena q*ue*
*V*u*estra* m*erced* me da del feliz empleo
de mi hija Doña Ysabel en la
suerte de haber hallado Un Cavallero de tan relevantes prendas como las
que concurren en el *señ*or Don Ygnacio
y una parentela tan Ylustre y q*ue* conos-
co muy bien, a mi me hallo la noticia en la Alcaldia mayor de Tlalpujagua merced q*ue* me hiso el *señ*or Virrey Conde de Galve y con la Cedula q*ue* su Ma-
*ge*sta*d* fue Servido de remitir en el aviso
antecedente a la flota Se presento
la persona q*ue* tenia su real cedula
y merced de d*ic*ha Alcaldia mayor a
pedir su cumplim*ien*to y su *Excelenc*ia se lo dio

asi a este como a los demas de cuyo accidente se me ocasiono grande Vejacion
y aunque en tiempo represente a su Excelencia ser
dicha Alcaldia mayor de repartimiento
de Azogues y haberseme dado cien
quintales para el repartimiento para sus mineros
[fol. 1v]
y no obstante no tube recurso a que
Su Excelencia mandase Suspender el viage
al dicho Alcalde mayor Siquiera hasta
que yo cumpliese el año que era lo que le pedia
no mas y asi intenpestivamente fue
a tomar posesion de dicho officio al presente
me hallo Sin intelignecia ninguna ba
para tres meses Solamente entendi-
endo en la cobransa de los azogues de Su
Magestad y mañana con el fabor de Dios
dare memorial presentando el titulo
y real cedula del Govierno del nuevo
Mexico Si bien me recelo su Excelencia
me ha de dilatar el cumplimiento de donde
se me ocasionara el acabarme de imposibilitar, y assi espero que Vuestra merced mediante la
carta consulta que escrevi a su Magestad en los
azogues que salieron el mes de Julio del
año pasado me habra hecho favor de que
tenga yo alivio en lo que pido a su Magestad
en la mayor parte pues en la nanarrativa
de dicha consulta Se habra conocido
quan importante sera del Servicio de
ambas Magestades el que Se me despache
Cedula del Rey nuestro señor mandando deter-
minadamente Se me asistan con los medios eficazes para dicha Conquista y asi con
la esperansa de la Cedula que aguardo en
el aviso podre hacer ynstancia a dicho
señor Virrey asi para el cumplimiento
[fol. 2r]
304
y paso del officio por la primera Cedula

como para el socorro de conseguir el fin
de dicha Conquista.

El Poder que remiti a Vuestra merced en dichas
Urcas para la administracion de mis
maiorasgos despues de los largos dias
de mi tia mi señora Doña Juana de Vargas
lo sostituira Vuestra merced Vista esta en el
dicho mi hijo el señor Don Ygnacio lopez de Zarate pues solo el accidente de mi fortuna en serlo puede Servirme de disculpa con Vuestra merced
haga yo esta mudansa siendo a-
tentamente siempre mi afecto para
Serville como lo manifestare
siempre y reconocido a sus muchos fabores guarde Dios a Vuestra merced muchos años Mexico
y febrero 8 de 1690.

Besa la Mano de Vuestra merced Su afecto
y obligado Servidor

^2Don Diego de Vargas
Zapata lujan^

[written in left margin] Juan Gonzales Calderon

[fol. 2v]
[written vertically] Mexico Y febrero 8 de 1689

Don diego de bargas
Lujan y çapata

———

6. *Diego de Vargas to Ignacio López de Zárate, Mexico City, 14 June 1690, AMNB, ALS.*

[fol. 1r]
[cross top center]
Hijo y señor mio, esta escribo en Car-

ta de el señor Don Amadeo y me allegrare
se halle Vuestra Señoría Muy bueno y lo este Mi
querida Hija Doña Ysabel María y que llogre Vuestra Señoría la sucession que Deseo tener Notyzia fija pues Dichosamente
Me Nombrare Abuelo de Hijo de tal
padre y para Mi estymazion Cari-
no y obligazion quissiera tener
un Reyno que Darle pero le Doy
al presente lo que me Dejaron mis
Padres y Abuelos que Son todos Mis
Mayorazgos para lo qual le Remito ese Poder General para que
en Virtud los Goze Rija administre
y Govierne con la obligazion
De la asistenzia de la Carga que tu-
bieren y la de tomar a su Cargo
el asistenzia de su Hermano y mi Hijo Mayor y Sucessor en ellos Don
Juan Manuel de Vargas Zapata lujan
y Respondo, y Digo a Vuestra merced en esta Mi Animo y el Paraje de fortu-
[fol. 1v]
na que me Coje a la fecha De esta el
Excelentísimo Señor Birrey Conde de Galbe me hizo Merced del Decreto de la Alcaldia Mayor de el Real de tlalpujagua para cuyo
Real saque 100 quintales de Azogue y Saliendo Con ellos a tomar Possesion a 20 de
febrero de 1689, estando Dicho Ofizio provey-
do por su Magestad y aguardando por ser de la
Provission de los Señores Birreyes la Resoluzion de el Ynforme hecha por el señor Bi-
rey Antezedente que suspendio su Cumplimiento Bino en el avisso que lleguo
a este Reyno en fines de Agosto de dicho año
de 89 la Determinazion de Dicho ynforme De su Magestad Mandando a su Excelencia que
luego que se Presentassen Con sus titulos
y Reales Cedulas de Merced de las que su Magestad

tenia *h*echas las Mandasse luego sin
Pretexto Cumplir y guardar y Dar
los Despachos Necess*arios* con D*i*cha R*ea*l zedula se pres*ent*o el que tenia la De D*i*cho R*ea*l
^D*on* Agustin de el Yerro^ y su E*x*cel*enci*a le mando Dar los
    Despachos
y Me fue a suceder ymtespestivam*ent*e a los
Nueve Messes *h*Allandome Reparty-
do Con la D*i*cha Porzion de Azogue Como
[fol. 2r]
con Caudal crezido a mi Credito que
se me *h*a ocasionado Gravissimo Daño por *h*allarme ya prevenido para hazer Mi Biaje al tyempo
que D*i*cho Se*ñ*or E*x*celent*ísi*mo Birrey me Hizo
D*i*cha M*erc*ed que asseguro a V*uestra* Se*ñorí*a que
a no hallarme tan bien quisto
y assegurado Mi credito le Hubiera perdydo porque las Personas
*h*an Conozido que D*i*cho azidente
lo pudo Rodear Mi Desgrazia
De este Contratyempo Naze la ocasion de que en esta flota no Remita ni *h*ayga podydo *h*allar Un
peso a rriesguo para socorrer a
V*uestra se*ñ*orí*a a quien empeño Mi Pallabra Y la fee que Recognosco
de Muy agradezido de en las urcas del año que Biene Remityr-
le la Mayor porzion que pudiere
pues el Mes que Biene de Julio
Me empiezo a despachar Para
Mi Govierno ^de el Nuevo Mexico^ donde su E*x*celenc*i*a Me
tyene ya *h*echo M*erc*ed de Darme su
Decreto para que se Me Den los
Despachos Necessarios. Y *h*are zesion
[fol. 2v]
a la Persona que me Habiare de my Sueldo para que me antyzipe el año que
Biene la Mayor Porzion De mas

que no Dejare Un punto de hazer todas
las Dilijenzias que Caben en quien
Desea No en esa Minima Porzion
pero aun en la Mayor que la fortuna Me ofreziere y adelantare Para que
Mi Deseo Corresponda a lo executi-
vo de Mi Rendyda Obligazion y asy
Repito a Vuestra Señoría que no tiene que Discurrir el Menor Pensamiento de Cuydado en que le faltare que sera ofender-
me y no darme la estymazion que le
Mereze My Paternal Amor pues
todo y quanto pueda Granjear Mi Deseo
estara a su Rendyda Obedienzia y Manutenenzia pues sere el que Solizite hazerle los embios en las Repetydas ocasio-
nes y A Dios que ~~te~~ guarde a Vuestra Señoría muchos y felizes
    años
en Compañía de My querida Hija a quien Dara
ra muchos abrazos Mexico a 14 de Junio de 1690.

Besa la Mano de Vuestra Señoría su Mas Affecto Padre Y Servidor

Don Diego de Vargas Zapata lujan

[written vertically] Carta de 14 de Junio
de 1690 Con Vienes
de [poder]

Señor Doctor Don Ygnazio lopez de Zarate

————

7. *Ignacio López de Zárate to Diego de Vargas,
Madrid, 6 August 1690, AMNB, L.*

[fol. 1r]
[written vertically on right edge] Aqui se Contienen diferentes
Cartas de Yndias

[fol. 1v]

[cross top center]

Mi Señor Y mi Padre, Respondiendo a la
muy favorecida de Vuestra Señoría de 8 de febrero de
este Año, despues de çelebrar las buenas nue-
vas, que me conduçe de la Salud de Vuestra Señoría devo
ponderar a Vuestra Señoría el gusto Y Consuelo, que me
han occassionado Saviendo se mantiene
tan perfecta, Y cumplida Como desseo, y
tanto he menester, y Con tan alegre Circunstançia podre llevar en paçiencia la mortificazion
y Sentimiento, que me origina la de no Veer
a Vuestra Señoría y lograr la fortuna de Servirle personalmente pero espero en Nuestro Señor
que Me la ha de Conçeder, quanto antes para
que de esta Suerte logre io toda la Satisfazion
de mi mayor desseo; todos en esta de Vuestra Señoría
quedamos a Dios, gracias buenos, y al presente
Con la desazon de hallarse Mariquita Con *las*
Viruelas, que aunque son Vastardas, y de ningun
riesgo y peligro nos tiene Con algun Cuydado
Como Vuestra Señoría puede Considerar; el Dia de Nuestra
señora de Septiembre esperamos el ponerla a Andar
[fol. 2r]
pues para Entonçes Confiamos en Dios,
se hallara muy Conbaleçida de su indiposi-
cion;

Cada dia nos hace mucha mayor falta
mi tia mi señora Doña Juana, que este en el çielo
Como Vuestra Señoría puede reconocer, y a mi en particular me la haçe mucha mayor por lo
mucho, que me queria, y favorecia; hasta ahora
no se han Concluydo las dependençias de su testa-
mentaria Sobre, que puedo asegurar a Vuestra Señoría
asisto Con quantto es posible, a Don Manuel
osorio, que es el testamentario para, que
quantto antes se logre su Conclussion, y
haviendo dado a Vuestra Señoría distinta relazion
del estado en que, quedaron, y de la resoluzion

que tome manteniendo a toda su familia escusso
el hacerlo ahora añadiendo Solo, que Con el
mayor gusto del Mundo procuro asistir
a la dicha familia, y que lo continuare siempre Con toda Voluntad, Y cariño en Cumplimiento de la obligazion, que devo reconocer
toda mi Vida a mi tia.

Doy a Vuestra Señoría infinitas, gracias por el particular
favor, que me dispenssa Su gran Cariño,
[fol. 2v]
y fineza asegurandome, que con la venida
de la flota se servira de embiarme
quando no el todo de la Dotte ofre-
çida por mi tia, la mayor parte de ella,
de que, quedo Summamente reconocido y
agradecido a Vuestra Señoría por la çircunstançia de
poder de esta Suerte Salir de los em-
peños en que me han constituydo los gastos
Continuados, que se me han seguido, y aliviado
de ellos podre Con mayor façilidad atender a todo lo que es de tan de mi preçissa
obligazion mayormente Viendo tan
aplaudida, y aprovada de Vuestra Señoría la dichosa
Suerte de mi feliz Empleo porque rindo
a Vuestra Señoría infinitas, graçias asegurandole
quedamos mi, Madre, mi hermano el
Marques Y todos mis parientes Con la
estimazion, que Corresponde a las demos-
traciones de Vuestra Señoría a que estaremos Siempre
muy reconoçidos;

hAviendose servido Vuestra Señoría de tomar la resoluzion
de mandar a Don Juan Gonzalez Calderon
Sostituyese en mi luego el Poder Con que
[fol. 3r]
se hallava de Vuestra Señoría para la administrazion
de su Hazienda, Y mayorazgo solo por
Sacrificarme a obedeçer, y servir a Vuestra Señoría en
esto Solicite, que el dicho Don Juan diese

Cumplimiento a la dicha orden, y haviendolo
executado en esta Conformidad el dia 11
de Jullio proximo passado procure desde entonces de-
dicarme con toda aplicazion Y cuydado a reconocer los papeles que mi tia hizo traher
de Torrelaguna el Año passado, y los que
estavan en poder de su señoria para reconoçer
de que se Compone la dicha hazienda, que
Cargas, y deudas tiene, y que estado tiene
al presente, y Juzgando fuese el correspondiente al producto de la dicha hazienda, y al
tiempo, que ha que *Vuestra Señoría* paso a Yndias
hallo no ser en esta Conformidad antes Vien
ser mayores las deudas de que Confiesso
a *Vuestra Señoría* me he admirado infinito pues Si se
huviese puesto el devido Cuydado Cada
Año en ir satisfaçiendo, y pagando partte
de las dichas deudas se hallaran hoy Cassi sa-
tisfechas, y no se huviera dado lugar a que
los intereses huviesen Crecido tanto, los motivos, y raçones, que ha havido para esto ni los
[fol. 3v]
alcanzo ni es de mi genio, y natural el
querer haçer estudio para Comprehender-
los; Y porque mi puntualidad no puede
dejar de que se reconozca en todos tiempos
me ha parecido ser muy de ella y de mi obli-
igaçion hablar a *Vuestra Señoría* con toda Claridad, y sin
revoço ninguno informandole del estado pre-
sente en que hoy se halla esta hazienda
y para este efecto, he dispuesto el resumen
adjunto por donde Vera *Vuestra Señoría* lo que se ha
cobrado, y pagado en tantos Años, y el estado
Verdadero çierto, y fisico, que hoy tiene dicha
hazienda, prometo a *Vuestra Señoría* me sirve de Summa
Mortificazion el dar a *Vuestra Señoría* semejante
noticia pero la precission de la confianza
que *Vuestra Señoría* ha hecho de mi me obliga a ello
assi por no faltar io en esta parte a ella, Como
porque *Vuestra Señoría* se halle en la inteligençia, que

Conviene, y es Justo del estado, que tienen Sus
mayorazgos para que con ella pueda dar la
providençia, que Juzgare ser mas acertada,
y la que por mi parte Se dara Como se lo aseguro a *Vuestra Señoría* sera el pagarse Con toda puntua-
[fol. 4r]
lidad los Censsos, que por no haverse hecho
en esta Conformidad se ha seguido Summo
atrasso, y perjuicio, y assi mismo procurarse
se bayan Satisfaçiendo y pagando los princi-
pales de todas las deudas en la mejor forma, que se pudiere en considerazion de que no se
aumenten los intereses, que no ha sido el
menor perjuicio, y reconoçiendo lo mucho,
que dichos intereses han subido, y que la mayor
parte de ellos son injustos dispondre quando no Sea de Vien a Vien con los acrehedores
el que por Justicia assi se declare;

Con motivo de la muerte de mi tia mi *señora*
Doña Juana haviendo Visto por los Papeles, que
Subçedia *Vuestra Señoría* en la Cassa de la plaza que gozava
Solicite Judicialmente se me diese la Posesion
de ella Y haviendose hecho en esta Conformidad passo a dar a *Vuestra Señoría* esta noticia
y assi mismo Como para el Mes, que Viene Siendo
Dios Servido tengo tomada la resoluzion
de yr a Torrelaguna Y a todos los demas
lugares circunbeçinos ha rreconocer toda
esta hazienda para procurar ponerla en
el estado, que conviene pues enquentro
[fol. 4v]
en los papeles hay otros muchos efectos
Como Son tierras, y de estas ni hay
noticia, que se han hecho, quienes las
han Usurpado, Y quando para descubrir-
las no sea Vastante el apeo que hare de ellas
dispondre se pongan excomuniones para
que de esta suerte se descubran, pues no
hay razon ninguna para que sobre esto y todo

lo demas no se apliquen los medios, y diligençias q*ue* se requieren, y de lo que fuere
resultando ire dando avisso a V*uestra Señoría*
para que se halle noticioso de todo
y reconozca el gusto, Cuydado, Y aplicazion
Con que me he dedicado a servir a V*uestra Señoría*
en esta administrazion Y espero sin Vanidad ninguna sera la que Conviene para
restaurar lo Usurpado de esta hazienda
y q*ue* quede Corriente en la mejor forma, q*ue* fuere posible;

No dudo la mala obra q*ue* se le *h*abra Seguido
a V*uestra Señoría* Con la novedad de *h*aver dado el
se*ñ*or Virrey Cumplim*ien*to al Alcalde Mayor
[fol. 5r]
de la m*er*ced q*ue* tenia p*or* su Magesta*d* del
oficio en que se hallava V*uestra Señoría* entretenido
y espero, q*ue Su* excelenci*a* se le daria a V*uestra Señoría* luego
al puntto del puesto de Governad*or* y Cappi*t*an
General en el nuevo Mexico, me ale-
grare infinito se halle V*uestra Señoría* ia en posession de el, y q*ue h*aya tenido muy buen Viaje, q*ue por* decirme V*uestra Señoría* era tan dilatado
*h*asta lograr esta noticia me tendra muy Cuydadoso.

Entre los Papeles referidos enquentro, que
en el Año de 81 se pusso p*or* mi tia mi
se*ñ*ora Doña Juana q*ue* este en el cielo la demanda al estado de s*a*n Vicente, y que
despues de muy largo pleytto se consiguio
el ganarse Autto para q*ue* se radicase
el Juicio en esta Cortte no obstante
la pretenssion de la parte Contraria, que
se redu*ç*ia a que se *h*avia de litigar en
Valladolid p*or* razon de ser Domiciliario
de aquella Ciudad, y Con esta occassion
*h*e procurado en el breve tiempo, que
he tenido recojer algunos papeles, y
[fol. 5v]

otras memorias de V*uestra Señoría* y quedo ha-
çiendo diligencia de otros muchos
papeles de que se me ha dado noticia p*ara*
Juntarlos todos, y Justificando el gran
derecho, q*ue* asiste a V*uestra Señoría* al dicho
estado procurare, Seguir el pleytto Con
Toda aplicaz*ion* Y cuydado para q*ue*
se vea, y se logre de esta Suerte el que, quede
declarado pertenezerle a V*uestra Señoría* y siendo este
estado de tan grande estimazion por las par-
ticulares çircunstancias, y prerrogativas
de que se compone devo estrañar el que
no se *h*ayan passado a haçer mas diligençias.

Tambien p*or* d*ich*os papeles *h*e rreconoçido, que en
el Año de 82 Murio mi *se*ñora Doña Josepha
de Vargas, Y que p*or* su muerte, quedaron
los dos Mayorazgos, q*ue* fundaron Gabriel
de Vivero, y Do*ña* Elena de Leoz Su
muger a que *e*s llamada Do*ña* francisca de
Vargas de quien deçiende la Conde-
sa de Cassarrubios, Con cuyo motivo, pre-
[fol. 6r]
tendia Tocarle el Mayorazgo, que
fundaron Diego de Vargas, y do*ña*
elvira Ber*n*ardo de Quiros su muger, Y
*h*aviendose opuesto a esta pretenssion
mi tia, q*ue* fue q*uie*n tomo primero la posesion de la hazienda Con el pretesto de tocarle a V*uestra Señoría* se siguio Pleyto, Y por escusar los Muchos, gastos, q*ue* *h*avia se hizo
Un Convenio, y ajuste en la forma sig*uie*nte
q*ue* fue, q*ue* mi tia tomase la posesion
del Mayorazgo, q*ue* fundo Don Diego
de Vargas, Y la Condessa de Cassarrubios
del que fundo Gabriel de Vivero, y
esto, se entendiese sin perjuicio del
derecho, q*ue* las partes tuviesen, y Viendo, q*ue* el derecho de V*uestra Señoría* es claro procurare, Veerme Con mi *se*ñora la Condessa

para representarselo Con el motivo de hallarme *hoy* Con los Poderes, de *Vuestra Señoría* Y
Ussando primero Con su *señoria* todos los
actos de urbanidad, y atencion si no Con-
siguiere el que su *señoria* diponga el apar-
tarse del *dic*ho Mayorazgo Sera preçisso
[fol. 6v]
prevalerme de lo Judicial de que me
ha pareçido noticiar tambien a *Vuestra Señoría*

Devo tambien en Cumplim*ient*o de mi obligacion
y Cariño deçir a *Vuestra Señoría* Como *h*aviendo mi
tia mi *señora* Doña Juana q*ue* este en el çielo
Comunicadome despues de dos Meses, que
me Casse Como mi Muger tenia Una
hermana Cassada en Torrelaguna, Cojie-
ndome esta noticia tan de improvisso Como
Vuestra Señoría puede Considerar *por* razon de no *h*averse
me dado antes de Cassarme passe a decir a su
señoria estrañava infinito me la diese entonces
y mas quando de *h*averla participado a
mi Madre, hermanos, y a mi no podia ser
motivo paraq*ue* se dejase de haçer mi
Matrimonio, y q*ue hoy* lo seria *por* el grande
Cuydado, que se pusso en esto, para que
todos estuviesemos Con el Justo Sentim*ient*o
y io en particular *por* reconoçer la mucha razon, q*ue* tendrian todos mis Parientes, para
no estimar, como era tan de su atencion
Una hermana de mi muger, Y despues
[fol. 7r]
de otras muchas Cossas, q*ue* dixe a su *señoria*
q*ue por* no Cansar a *Vuestra Señoría* dejo de referir,
me procuro Satisfaçer Con decirme, que
el pretesto, q*ue* tuvo *p*ara no *h*aver reve-
lado esto, fue *por* q*ue* su sobrina se casso sin
gusto, y Voluntad de *Vuestra Señoría* y sin esperar
precediese tan precissa çircunstançia, por
Ultimo fuimos Corriendo Con grande Union
mi tia y io y despues de muchos dias

me significo *h*aver escripto a V*uestra Señoría* discul-
passe la resolucion de su sobrina en considerazion de *h*averse Cassado Con un Cavallero
tan Conocido Como lo acreditava el ser
Primo herm*a*no de mi *señora* Doña Antonia Anton*i*a
Bern*a*r*d*o Muger de mi tio el *señor* Don Gregorio
Pimentel lo qual fue motivo Por comp-
laçer en todo a su *señor*ia para q*ue* io me
dejasse Veer del *señor* Don Joseph
de Vargas, y *h*aviendo preçedido ia esta
Circunstançia, p*or* q*ue* todos mis Parientes
Conoçiesen, assistiesen, y estimasen, a mi hermana mi *señora* Doña Juana, dispuse
se viniese a Madrid, Y *h*aviendo tenido
[fol. 7v]
a mis hermanos Cassi dos Meses en esta
Su Cassa de V*uestra Señoría* los detendre en ella
*h*asta q*ue* bean los toros, q*ue* son del Juebes
en ocho dias, Con que *h*aviendose enmendado
de esta suerte el hierro, q*ue* al prinçipio se
hizo, y logrado io la satisfaçion de mi desseo,
con la Confianza de lo mucho, q*ue* V*uestra Señoría* me
favoreçe no escusso Supp*l*icar a V*uestra Señoría* con mi mayor encareçim*i*e*n*to se sirva V*uestra Señoría* de reçivir essa
Carta, q*ue* mi hermana me ha dado Con a-
quel paternal amor, y Cariño, q*ue* corresponde
a todos los motivos, y Circunstançias, que
llevo expressadas, que sera para mi de singu-
lar estimazion Y rreconocimiento Como q*ue* V*uestra Señoría* me
embie la respuesta para, q*ue* mi hermana
Consiga el grande Consuelo, y alivio, q*ue* tanto
necesita, y dessea de Veerse en la grazia
de V*uestra Señoría* y io este favor q*ue* reconoçere toda mi
Vida a V*uestra Señoría* Y no ofreçiendose otra Cossa
particular repito mi ob*ed*iencia a V*uestra Señoría*
   dess*ea*ndo
mereçer a V*uestra Señoría* muchas occassiones en
q*ue* poderla manifestar; Mi muger, Y
[fol. 8r]
Juanico escriben a V*uestra Señoría* Con que no tengo,

que deçir de uno y otro, mas, que
el quedar buenos, y con los mismos desseos
que io de Veer a *Vuestra Señoría* Dios nos conceda
esta fortuna, Y nos guarde a *Vuestra Señoría* mi señor Y mi
Padre los muchos, y dilatados Años, que
puede Y tanto hemos menester, Madrid
y Agosto 6 de 1690 [unsigned]

señor Don Diego de Vargas Zapata Y luxan mi señor Y mi Padre

———

8. *Diego de Vargas to Isabel María de Vargas Pimentel, Mexico City, 4 November 1690,* AMNB, ALS.

[fol. 1r]
[cross top center]
Hija y querida Mia de mis Ojos
Muy de mi Corazon sera el que te
halles Muy buena y lo este Mi querida Nieta a quien Beso Muchas Vezes
y echo Mi Bendyzion. Yo mis
ojos salgo a la hora de esta para exerzer Mi Govierno y Cappitania General de la Nueva Mexico
y Boy Gustosso por haver ajustado con el que me havia ya dado lo que he menester el que en
Dos flotas Remityra el Dote
a my Hijo el señor Don Ygnazio
a quien se lo escribo y al señor Marques su Hermano y mi Amigo que
Boy Por dicha Razon sin atender a un Biaje de quinientas
leguas de tyerra de Ynfieles y
Jentyles, Yndios Barbaros
que se esta Continuamente en
Guerra Biba. Nuestro Señor me

De Bida para *h*aver sirvido a
mi Hijo el *seño*r D*on* Ygnazio y que
[fol. 1v]
este assegurado que mi Voluntad es
mas de la puede Presumir y lo mucho que te estymo Puede ser el tyempo
Mude la fortuna y que Con ella te
Pueda aun Mejor Manifestar my
Deseo De todo q*uan*to Hubiere de Novedad Me avysaras y estaras Zierta
que Soy tuyo Y que tu Marido
saldra de su empeño Muy bien
y no Dudes De esta Verdad que D*on*
Amadeo Zeyol le escribira esto Mes-
mo y A Dios que te *guar*de y te Me deje Veer q*ue*
sera para My el Mayor Gusto que Pueda
tener Mexico y N*ov*iem*b*re a 4 de 1690.

tu Padre que te estyma
y quiere de Corazon

D*on* Diego de Vargas
Zapata lujan Ponze de leon

Mi querida Hija D*oña* Ysabel M*arí*a de Vargas.

———

9. *Diego de Vargas to Ignacio López de Zárate, np,*
c. late fall 1690, AMNB, L, *inc.*

[fol. 1r]
[cross top center]
Hijo y *seño*r mio en Pliego de d*on* Amadeo
Zeyol con el Poder General que re-
mito a V*uestra Señorí*a tengo escrito Desde Mexico
su *fe*cha el Mes de Junio en que por ella
le aviso el estado y fortuna Mia
y al pres*ent*e se me augmenta la Ma-

la que Me presigue pues era el Reparo y todo mi alibio el Bien que *he* perdydo Con la Muerte de mi querida tia
Notyzia para Mi tan Amarga que
no me faltaba otra que Passar pues en Mi tia me *ha* faltado el todo
pues era la que Mantenia el Ilustre y mem*oria* de mi Casa y en quien
Mis *acz*iones pudieran *h*aver tenido
la suerte que al pres*ente* Gozo en tener
a V*uestra* Señor*ía* por mi Hijo pues todo lo fio Y encargo el asistenzia de mi querido Hijo
d*on* Juan Man*uel* a quien le encargo
a mi Hijo y le pido No le tenga por su
Herm*ano* sino como tal pues el que
le *h*a de Correjir y tomar a su Cargo la
Direction de sus Actiones Dizeme V*uestra* Señor*ía*
que queria Venir a mi lado a lo qual
Respondo que ny por pienso, Ni yma-
[fol. 1v]
jinacion se pueda tener el que hiziesse
tal pues fuera en mi Punto caerme
Muerto, sino que asista en Palazio y
tenga el exerzicio de no faltar a la asistenzia de su Plaza pues de ella puede Con
el tyempo Salir a servir a su Mag*esta*d con
Una Comp*añía* de Cavallos y ser Hombre que las
Yndias son buenas para los que venden en
Una tyenda pero no para Hombres que
tyenen el Punto, de, ^Huir^ la mecanica y asy es tierra
Pelligrossa pues *h*ay Mucha Nobleza a-
jada pues los *se*ñores Birreyes Biben con la
concurrenzia de Recomendaziones tan de-
sabridos que estas Dan de Mano Y
ban a su Convenienzia. Yo empeño a V*uestra* señor*ía*
My Pallabra de que le asistire Para la
Dezencia de mi Hijo y que no le faltara
socorro, Ni en aviso, Ni en ocasion q*ue*
Hubiere De suerte que tenga para su luzim*ien*to mis Socorros Y Remityre en Alca-

nze De este Correo una llibranza De Dozientos pesos al Cappitan don Pedro Martinez de Murguia
para que se los Remita a Vuestra Señoría para que a mi
Hijo se le hagan un Par de Bestydos el Hibierno. en quanto al Poder que tenia Juan
Gonzalez Como escribo a mi querida Hija
lo de el Mes de Junio pasado de 89 que yo no
[fol. 2r]
sabia el feliz estado que Gozaba Ny
su Dichosa suerte pues en el se Recog-
nozera le Revoco por dicha Razon y
se lo Doy a Vuestra Señoría quien Vera que en Dicha
ocasion Remitia Poder Para La Disposicion y Promessa de Dote De la dicha
Mi Hija y asy segun el Poder General
y su amplititud puede Vuestra señoría Gozar Rejir y administrar la Casa de la Plaza Mayor
y tomar la Possesion en Mi Nombre
si le Pareze y asi Mesmo hara las Dilijenzias de seguir el Pleyto que tengo Puesto a el estado de San Bizente
y en todo Obrara De suerte que puede
hazer quenta es suyo pues quando Nuestro Señor
Permita el que Baya a ese Reyno
Passare por todo, que soy mas libe-
ral de lo que puede juzgar que no me tyene esperimentado lo que le Repite my
Affecto y Deseo es que mi Hijo don Juan
Manuel No falte de Palazio que este
en el Servicio de sus Magestades que para ello
Me Desnudare de quanto tengo y hare
quanto pueda por Discurrir y Descubrir
Rumbo para la Remision de el alibio
en el todo que me tyene fuera de my
el que a 18 años que Sali de ese Reyno
[fol. 2v]
Con Solo el Sueldo que su Magestad me Daba hasta que llegue a este Reyno y que se
esten en tanta Ruyna Mis Mayorazgos pues Mi querida Esposa bibio

año y Medio y en ella Hize Dos socorros uno desde Cadiz y otro en el Mesmo
Navio que Bine y Mas pague a mi Am-
igo d*on* Joseph de liñan Mas de Siete Mil y quinientos *Reales* de Vellon que me escribio *haver*-
la Dado y Socorrido y se los Remity desde
este Reyno. Y asy mesmo la Deje prevenida de todo en Casa de suerte que No
tenia que comprar una Zinta Y Antes by-
en Me Debian los Ynquilinos de la Cassa de la Calle de el Almendro, la Duquessa Cayetano y Juan de Yuste una Porzion crezida a mi tia que este en Gloria
la Hize Diferentes socorros en Medio de Andar Rodando fortuna y asy
Me Deja Confusso Beer la Mala Disposicion pues Mis Deudas, que Dezir
la Mayor era A d*on* felipe de elazas
de Un Mil y quinientos Ducados 1500 Ducados
que no Me acuerdo si llegaban
A Herrera Mil Ducados de el quarto de la Casa a Gozar y Gozar 1000
A d*on* Alonso fajardo Mil Ducados 1000

---

10. *Diego de Vargas to Ignacio López de Zárate,
El Paso del Río del Norte, 20 April 1691,* ARGD,
ALS.

[fol. 1r]
[cross top center]
Hijo y S*eñor* mio, asseguro a V*uestra Señoría* que
escribo esta Con el Cuydado de que
me *h*alle sin poderle en este aviso
Remitir la Porzion que quisie-
ra de q*uen*ta de la Dote de mi querida
Hija No puedo *h*azer mas que es
el *h*averme puesto a empeñarme

Como si fuera un esclavo Y Gustosso vine a este presidio a servir a su Magestad en Guerra Biba
en este Reyno de la Nuevo Mexico
Solo a fin de Poder cumplirle a Vuestra Señoría
su Dote espero en Nuestro Señor que Con-
zediendome la Bida llograre
Con aplauso lo que tanto Deseo
y Es la primera obligazion de my
estimazion llegue a este Reyno
y tome Possesion de su Govierno
y Cappitania General el Dia 22 de febrero
De este presente año de 91. y tarde
en su Camino Desde Mexico que
son 450 leguas 95 Dias Pasan-
[fol. 1v]
do por tierra De Yndios de Guerra enemigos Mas de 350 leguas fue Nuestro
Señor Servido el que arribasse a Sal-
vamiento Con Salud Pues en tan Dilatado y Penoso Biaje De Despoblado
quedando las mas de las Noches
Vestido Con Botas Y Con el cavallo
ensillado Con las Armas para estar
Prompto. Deje a la Persona que me
Avio Para este dicho Govierno Poder
General Para la flota que se espera le Bus-
case a Vuestra Señoría Una buena Porzion y luego que Benga dicha flota hare Correo para ello y Juntamente le Bolbere hazer Yns-
tanzia que segun los effectos le Remitiere, Me Sacara de dicho Cuydado
y el Amigo Don Amadeo Zeyol asistyra a
dicha Dilijenzia haziendo que el dicho que me
avice No me falta a Desahogar a Vuestra Señoría quien
puede Bibir zierto le sacare de su empeño
Y Vuestra Señoría me hara favor de que se Remita el testimonio
Del titulo Rezibido en la secretaría de Yndias de
la Parte de Nueva españa que Remito en este
[fol. 2r]

aviso de *h*aver tomado la Possesion
De este *d*icho Govierno y Cappitania *G*enera*l*
para que se tenga *d*icha Notyzia y
Yntelijenzia en ella de que la persona que Me sucediere *ha* de
aguardar cinco a*ñ*os que Son los
que su Mage*sta*d me *h*Yzo Mer*ce*d desde el
Dia que tomasse *d*icha Possesi-
on y Para esta Declarazion esta-
ra *V*u*estra* Se*ñoría* A la mira y *V*era a *d*icho Secre*tario* que fuere de *d*icha Parte
de Nueva España por si algu-
no pretendiere esta futura y asy
*d*icho su titulo que se la Diere que
Distinga *h*ayga de tomar toda
a la posesion de *d*icho Govie*r*no
a tantos de tal mes que es
q*uan*do Cumple Dichos cinco a*ñ*os que
su Mage*sta*d le Hizo Mer*ce*d a D*on* Diego
de Vargas zapata lujan Segun Cons-
ta por el testim*onio* de el tyempo que
tomo *d*icha possesion esta Dilijenzia Con Mas Amor la *h*ara
*V*u*estra* Se*ñoría* que no el Ajente y Su persona supondra aquella parte
que no es fazil el ajente ocupe de
[fol. 2v]
De estymazion escribo en esta ocasion al Capp*itán* D*on* luis
Saenz de tagle *Cavallero* del orden de
Alcantara y Vez*ino* De Mexico
Me *h*Yziesse, Gusto de Remi-
tyr una llibranza de quatrozientos *p*esos a favor de mi querido Hijo D*on* Juan Man*ue*l de Vargas para que pague a *V*u*estra* Se*ñoría* el
empeño que hubiere *h*echo en
el Rezivim*iento* de su Ama la
Reyna N*uestra* Se*ñora* y asy llegaran a buen tyempo Yo sal-

go a Campaña Para Junio
Y estare en el seys Messes
Boy a Recognozer al ene-
migo A la villa de *S*anta fee
que era la Corte de el Reyno y Prov*inc*ia de la Nuevo Mexico y Passar a Recogno-
zer el estado en que se *h*allan
Para *h*azer Consulta a Su
ex*celenci*a y a su Mage*sta*d a quien
Deje escrito q*uando* sali de Mexico
en Pliego de V*uestra* Señoría Y A dios
que le *g*uar*d*e *M*uc*h*os años en comp*añí*a
de mi Hija querida Ysabel
[written vertically] y Nieta a quien escribo. *f*echa en este Presidio y
Plaza de Armas De el Paso
De el Rio de el Norte, a 20 de Abril de 1691.

*B*esa *l*a *M*ano de V*uestra* Señoría su Mas
Affecto *P*adre y *S*er*v*i*d*or que le estima

*D*o*n* Diego de Vargas
Zapata lujan Ponze de leon

*Doct*or *D*o*n* Ygnazio lopez de Zarate
*M*i Hijo.

[written in left margin] Abril de 91 en que *h*abla de la dote

———

11. *Diego de Vargas to Isabel María de Vargas Pimentel, El Paso del Río del Norte, 23 September 1691, AMNB, ALS.*

[fol. 1r]
[cross top center]
Hija mia te escribo esta acabado de llegar de Campaña Con victoria Grazias

a Dios y *h*aver traydo una Pressa
de 130 captivos Jentiles Apaches.
Salgo el Mes de Octubre de orden
De el ex*celentís*imo *señor* Birrey a Campaña
y Hazer Guerra a las Provinzias
de Sonora y Zinalao Donde se *ha*-
llan ynfestadas de el enemigo y
se *h*an Yncorporado la jente de Guerra de los Presidios de *D*ichas
Provinzias Yo Voy con la de este
y Por Cappit*án* G*eneral* de toda Como G*overna*dor
y Cappit*án* G*eneral* de esta frontera y
Reyno de la Nueva Mexico es-
crivo a mi Hijo la Disposicion
de la administrazion de los Mayorasgos que me Pareze la
Mejor en q*uan*to a Socorrerle tambien le Digo los Medios que tengo por firme y Seg*ur*o Se *h*allara
en flota Socorrido Yo me tengo
[written in left margin] Mi Hija de Mis Ojos
Doña Ysabel Maria de
Vargas
[fol. 1v]
de Vender para que quede enterado y Desempeñado y Recognosca mi Punto
y lo Mucho que te estimo, la que estaba ynclusa es para Mi Hija Juana
a quien echo mi Bendicion y la Deje escrito quando sali para este Govierno el a*ño* ~~que Biene~~ pasado digo: te
Repito Mi Affecto Y estimazion a
Mi Hijo y tu Marido y me sirve de
Gusto y Alibio tener tal suerte de tu bu-
en Empleo Y de la d*ic*ha de tu Herm*an*o y
mi Hijo D*on* Juan Man*ue*l V*uest*ra Capazidad
y Discurso No Necesita de Repetiros
le Deys en todo el Gusto y sirvays
Como es de V*uest*ra Obligazion pues esta
en lugar de B*uest*ro Padre yo no puedo mas

que en Vida *h*averme Desapropriado de
mi Patria Mayorazgos y el amor
de estar en V*uestr*a Comp*añía* pues sali
el dia 10 de Agosto de 72, y no se que sea
unos Guantes de mis Haziendas y Recognosco por los papeles y q*uen*ta que me
[fol. 2r]
Remite Mi Hijo el s*eño*r D*on* Ygnazio
la Mala forma que se *h*a tenido
Y que esta la Haz*iend*a Mas empe-
nada que la deje pues yo Para Mis Deudas Sueltas Deje
Muchos Alquileres de la Casa
Caydos Y Deje el Pleyto de
el Monte de la dehessa de Biñaderos que se Vendio y Con la Par-
tyda Junta *h*aver Desempe-
nado la Deuda de D*on* felipe de el
mas luego Y *h*Aver a*h*orrado
tres Mil R*eale*s de Reditos al año
*h*Averle Dado Y zedido la Renta de Granada Quemandola y
perdiendola Dos partes de su
Valor todo se *h*a errado Segun
Veo de Di*ch*as quentas. Y no tengo que Dezir Sino Dejarlo al pre-
*sent*e al Buen expediente y Disposicion de mi Hijo el s*eño*r D*on* Ygnazio
que atendera en todo Como Ymmediato que es y lo mas el favo-
[fol. 2v]
rezerme Con tanta Galanteria y a-
sy yo Determino el Servir a su Mag*esta*d
en Uno de los puestos que Refiero al
s*eño*r Marques su Herm*an*o que *h*a de ser
la Persona a quien tengo de fiar mis
Pretensiones pues llogrado Uno de
di*ch*os Puestos se Pondra en Gran
Corri*ent*e esa Renta y se le quitaran
sus zensos que Son los que Se Comen

y las Cargas que tiene que es my
Manera Para Dejar Sobre el Mayorasgo para el Hijo *Segun*do que tubiere el sucessor en el Mayorasgo
Para sus estudios quedate Con Dios
Hija mia que te *guar*de y espera en flota
Un buen socorro para que tenga tu Marido y mi querido Hijo el *seño*r *D*on Ygnazio
el alibio que tendra Con el favor de Dios que me De Bida pues le asistyre
en todo *F*echa en este Puesto de el Paso
de el Rio de el Norte y su Presidio a 23
de Sep*tiem*bre de 1691, a mi querida Nieta
*Mucho*s Besos y abrazos y Pido a mi Hijo tenga-
ys el Gusto de *B*ues*t*ros Retratos y asy
[written vertically in left margin] tu Me los Remite que te Pagare
    el
Costo de mi estymazion que esta
no tyene Comparazion.

Tu *P*adre que te estima y quiere de Corazon

*D*on Diego de Vargas
Zapata lujan Ponze de leon

———

12. *Diego de Vargas to Ignacio López de Zárate, El Paso del Río del Norte, 25 September 1691,* AMNB, LS.

[fol. 1r]
1
[cross top center]
Hijo, Y ss*eñor* mio, Resivo, la de V*uestra Señoría*
en este *Govie*rno Y *R*eino de la nueba mexico Con
mucho gusto por la notizia q*u*e deseo de Su buena
Salud, Y mis queridos hijos a q*uie*n escribo
Y no, obstante, en esta le *D*uplico mi bendizion

Y me Sirve de grande Consuelo, en este destierro
donde me hallo que es lo ultimo, Y dilatado
Como informaran, a Vuestra Señoría las personas que
tienen experiençia de este Reino Y Se hallan, en
esa Corte, Y assi me Consuela Como digo la
dicha mia en tener mis hijos el amparo, y Sombra, de Vuestra Señoría que Con ella Solo asegurados
en tener tal padre podia yo tener osadia, a, a-
lejarme de tales obligaziones, tan unicas de
todas maneras de mi Cariño, y eStimazion
pero Su Divina Magestad quiso Con Su Divina
Providenzia, darme Un Sobstituto, Como, Vuestra Señoría
en quien pudiera yo tener tal desahogo, Y Confianza, de tales prendas, para que pudiera
asistir en este Reino en el Real Servicio, Co-
[fol. 1v]
2
mo, lo eSpero, en el tiempo que Sera el que acredite
mis pensamientos; al tiempo que eScribo, esta
estoy para Salir a Campaña Contra, las naziones
barbaras, alzadas deste Reino me dilatare, en
ella hasta que el rigor del tiempo de las niebes
me haga Volver, a Retirar, Con mi Campo, a
este prezidio, Y plaza de armas, Y despacho
esta para que tenga el gusto de Resevir, las
que me pueden Venir, en flota de Vuestra Señoría y que
alcansen el aviso de Su llegada para que las
llebe, Y assi estimare me Repita Vuestra Señoría quedar, Con Salud, Y mis queridos hijos, Y nieta se halle ya muy Crezida, Y que en tordelaguna hallase, Vuestra Señoría la Casa Repara-
da Segun el Cuydado me eScribe, mi hermano
don Gregorio pimentel que es el que la habita
Y que las Viñas, tierras, y demas hazien-
da, haya Reconosido, Vuestra Señoría el fuste, de ella
Y que para lograr Sus frutos, Y Rindan
el interes que pueden fructificar, es nesesario
lo primero, que Vuestra Señoría ponga Un buen mayordomo de toda fidelidad, inteligenzia, Y
Cuydado, Y Supuesto que don Diego, es Cri-

ado, antiguo, Y fue Gentil hombre, del Cariño
de mi tia, mi *Señora Doña* Juana de Vargas
[fol. 2r]
3
que este en gloria puede encargarle, *Vuestra Señoría* la dicha
   asistencia que asi Se lo previne en la Car-
ta que le eScribi, Juntamente Con el poder, y assi
Con quatro Cientos ducados Se puede desenvol-
ber, Cabar, Y Vinar, las Viñas muy bien
a todo Su Costo, Y Juntamente el olivar de la guerta, Y los demas que hay en las Viñas, que Son
muy buenas, Y de lindo llebar, las tierras
de tordelaguna torremocha, talamanca
Y Valdepielagos, se ariendan, muy bien
las mas de ellas, Y esas por las dichas eScripturas Cobrara el dicho mayordomo, la Renta desde el dia de Santiago, de Julio, que
es el plazo que los dichos labradores, Se-
ñalan, haser la dicha paga, y assi mesmo, hay los prados, Sercas, de miraflores, de
la Sierra, chosas, y guadalix, hay, la dehesa, de las gariñas, en buytrago, Cuyas
Rentas de ellas Solamente paga el excelentísimo sseñor
Duque, del infantado que Son dos mill *Reales*
Cada año, hay en dicha Villa de buytrago
la mitad de la dehesa de biñaderos, Cuya
Renta deve pagar de ella, los herederos
de martin de hahero, Y assi mesmo
el monte que Se Corta en dichas Sercas, prados, Y dehesa de Viñaderos,
[fol. 2v]
hay delante de tordelaguna, Un lugar, que
llaman, el molar, donde pagan, Un Senso, de
beinte, o dies y Seis hanegas de trigo, hay en otro
lugar, a un lado de talamanca llamado, el
espartal, antes de llegar, a otro que llaman, el
Vellon, tierras, de pan llevar, muy eScojidas
que Se arendaban, Y las Codiciaban dichos Vezinos
las tierras de tordelaguna, alindan, muchos
pedazos, Con las de el Mayorasgo, que

posee, mi sSeñora Doña Ysabel de, olaza-
bal, Velez, de guevara, mi sSeñora y mi tia
Y mi hermano don Gregorio Con Vista de
los papeles, y Cotejo de los linderos, y de
los Suyos, Reconosera, muchas de las dichas tierras de las mias, muy defraudadas
por haver intrometidose, los labradores, a
quien arendo don Juan pimentel, mi sseñor
que este en el zielo, y mi tio, Y assi como, Cavallero tan ajustado lo Reconosera, Y entera-
ra, al dicho Mi mayorasgo, dicha hazienda
la de Viñas, Se labrara Con todo desperdiçio
con 400 ducados de Vellon, Y Se Coje, Una
Cosecha de mill, y mil, y dozientas arrobas
de Vino, Y tiene el mayordomo, la grangeria
de los aguapies, de yema, demas elote
Y Se que Se Coge de los olivos, y la guerta
[fol. 3r]
5
la puede sembrar de Zebada, y tener,
muy abundantemente Con que dar Verde, las
mulas de la Carroza de Vuestra sSeñoría en quanto a la
hazienda y mayorasgo de Camarmas, del Ca-
ño, y de eSteruela, Yo dexe en lindo Corriente, Y de mucha apetenzia las tierras entre los Vezinos de dichos lugares, Y
apeado todo Con los linderos Claros
que Se hallaran dicho apeo, en los papeles, de dicho
mi mayorasgo, tanbien el palomar, en
dicho lugar, de Camarma del Cano, y Un
olivar, muy poblado, Y grande, Y asi, para Su mejor logro de Su arrendamiento
era de parezer por lo Sercano que esta, a la
Villa de alcala, de henares, se pusiesen
Seulas, para que llegase, a notizia de las personas que podia Ser, Se hallase alguna
Con quien haser, un buen arrendamiento y Con
dezir a Vuestra sSeñoría que Con dichas tierras, olivar, y palomar, instituyo mayorasgo
mi Revisabuelo, el alferez, mayor

que fue de la Ziudad, de guadalajara
llamado pedro Ruiz, de alarcon, Sotomayor, Cavallero de la horden, de Calatraba, Y Su muger mi Señora, Doña Y-
[fol. 3v]
6
sabel, de Salinas, y guevara, Y con dicha
hazienda Se mantenian Con todo luzimiento
Segun la Calidad de Sus personas, y esto, me
lo contaron los Viejos de dichos lugares, Cuyas Casas, halle Caydas, quando me dieron
la Venia, para administrar, y Rejir los
dichos mayorasgos, digo, a Vuestra sSeñoría todo esto
para que Se halle enterado, y se logre Un buen
arrendamiento en el mayorasgo de Madrid,
me parese muy bien el que por mayor, Se Re-
integre, el mayorasgo que Vaco, por fin y muerte de mi tia mi sSeñora Doña Josepha, de Vargas, Y para mas bien Reconosca mi Señora, la Condesa, de Casas Rubios mi ti-
a el derecho que me asiste, los mesmos
llamamientos de los fundadores de dicho
mayorasgo, aclaran mas Vien, a quien
le pertenese en Consiençia, y io por no pa-
reser grosero, Y desatento no Contradixe
el pacto, amistoso, Y Convenio politico, Y Reveren-
te que la dicha mi tia mi sSeñora Doña Juana de
Vargas, mediante la estrecha amistad, y cores-
pondencia que Se ha tenido por el deudo, Con esos
Señores a quienes, aseguro, a Vuestra sSeñoría que ni a Sus
Señorias Cosas mias, ni yo, Como a todos
[fol. 4r]
7
los demas de mi linage, les he enbarazado
en nada, Y en medio de mi Corta fortuna, he procurado la estimazion, atenzion, y buena Co-
Respondenzia, de mi parte, Y mi tia, mi sSeñora
Doña Joseph, de Vargas, que este en gloria, Yendo
me a despedir de Su merced, Y de Su marido
a mostoles, quando pase, a este Reino y dicha sSeñora

me Refirio, y Repitio diferentes Vezes que
los dichos mayorasgos que poseya, era yo, el unico heredero de ellos, Y mis hijos, y que no por
hallarse el Señor don Francisco Zapata, Conde
de Casas Rubios, mi tio, del Conzejo Real
y Camara de Castilla Su mucha Suposisi-
on, Y autoridad Se Rezelaba, Y temia
Con dicha mi ausensia havian dichos Señores
introduzir derecho Suponiendo perteneserles para perjudicarme, desvaneser,
Y Confundir, el Ser yo, el ligitimo heredero
Como lo Soy de dicho mayorasgo que Se Conpone
de las Casas que estan, a la esquina que baja
de la parrochia, de San Justo, a la Calle, de
la puente Segoviana, Y no Se que Sensos, Y la
Renta de las terçias de los lugares, de los Caramancheles, Y assi, *Vuestra sSeñoría* puede en Virtud, del
poder General haser la proposision, a dicha, mi
[fol. 4v]
8
sSeñora la Condesa que no porque tolerase, la Suso, dicha
mi tia que este en gloria atendiendo a los motivos
Y Respectos de Urbanidad, y buena politica, no por
eso, perjudica la aczion, y derecho mio, quando
no, ha Sido por, instrumento, Juridico, espezial
que lo pueda rebalidar, Y assi la posesion, adqui-
rida que Su Señoria haya aprehendido, es nula, por
quanto es Con perjuizio de terçero, que Soy, io, Y terse-
ros que Son mis hijos, Y los que Susedieren, en, a-
delante en Su lugar, en dicho mayorasgo, en
poder, de dicha sSeñora mi sSeñora la Condeza, en Sus papeles
    para los de los Vargas, Y el arbor, ge-
nealogico, de don fulano, ortiz, de Vargas, Segun me lo dixo mi tio, el Señor don Francisco Zapata que este en gloria Conde, de Casas, Rubios, todas estas noticias pongo en la Considerazion de *Vuestra Señoría* para mas bien pueda Recon-
venir a dicha sSeñora Y que no nos vamos los dos
a la otra Vida Sin dejar a nuestros hijos
Sin este gravamen, pues Sienpre Soy de qual-

quiera Suerte Rendido Criado, de Su
sSeñoría. en quanto al mayorasgo de granada
le digo a V*uestra* sSeñoría lo primero el que no lo tenga en arrendam*ien*to Sino q*u*e adquiera, en
d*i*cha Ciudad Una persona, fide, digna, Y
[fol. 5r]

9

abonada, a q*uie*n darselo en administrazion dandole Un dies por Ciento q*u*e *h*avra persona muy Segura q*u*e apetesca la d*i*cha administrazion, Y para q*u*e Vea, V*uestra* sSeñoría de la Calidad q*u*e es d*i*cho mayorasgo; en el año de Sesenta, y nuebe, digo; 67 me otorgo, *e*Scriptu-
ra gabriel Ruiz thesorero de la Sancta
Cruzada de d*i*cho R*e*ino de darme mill
~~pesos~~ Reales ^1000 R*eales* ^ en fin de Cada mes, Y los quatro
meses primeros del año, henero, feb*re*ro marzo,
Y abril, era el Conchabo me los *h*avia de dar
adelantados, Y al fin del año, ajustando
los doze mil R*eales* del desenbolso de los
doze messes Se *h*avia de liquidar la q*uen*ta Con
pago, pagando, Cobrado, el dies por Ciento
de la d*i*cha administrazion, el resto, y alcanse q*u*e la d*i*cha renta hisiese al d*i*cho administrador, la d*i*cha Renta, Se Conpone
que estube en granada solo por rreconoserlo
Y la Vi toda q*u*e Son, muchas tiendas, y
Casas en los mejores puestos de la d*i*cha
Ciudad, en las Calles publicas, y mejores
del Comercio de ella, estube en el Cortijo
que tiene d*i*cho mayorasgo, q*u*e llaman
el de brasinas muy bien poblado, y Su
[fol. 5v]

10

Casafuerte muy buena, Y Sus tierras de
labor, q*u*e Son muchas q*u*e alindan Con las tie*r*ras
de los Canonigos del monte Sancto, Cuyas, agu-
as para el riego de d*i*chas tierras pertenesen
a d*i*cho Cortijo, ligitimam*en*te de q*u*e deje dada
informasion por q*uan*to pretendian d*i*chos Cano-

nigos, tocarles, y perteneserles, Y Respecto
de Ser nesesario para aumentar, la Renta de
di*c*has tierras, Y asegurar Sus frutos, Redifi-
car, la presa del di*c*ho Rio, pequeño, que
pasa, por di*c*has tierras, Y Ser menester para Su Costo mas de mil ducados, Se vendio
Con informazion de Utilidad, por autoridad
de la R*eal* Justicia, Una finca q*ue* estaba en-
corporada en di*c*ho mayorasgo, Y possesion
q*ue* era, el horno q*ue* llamaban, del *hass*a, q*ue* Ren-
taba, mas de dozientos ducados Cada año
esta di*c*ha possesion, era ezenpta de poder, Ser
Vinculada por tener, Un Vezino de di*c*ha Ciudad, Un Senso perpetuo, Sobre ella, y Como
interesado en las mas Vezes q*ue* Se pueda
Vender Siendo libre percibiendo el interes
Segun ley R*eal* q*ue* le esta Señalada, Y dis-
puesta por el reconosimi*en*to de di*c*ho Senso
perpetuo, Y Como a S*eño*r del, Y tubo efecto
la di*c*ha Venta Con Reconosimiento que hiso, la
[fol. 6r]

11

parte, a los Sensos q*ue* tenia de mas de *e*ste
principal, Y a los demas q*ue* estaba, *h*ypote-
cada, esta di*c*ha posesion Con obligazion, de
la Seguridad, de las fincas de di*c*ho mayorasgo, Se obligo el tal Comprador, a Redimir-
los dentro de un año, lo qual es menester, Reconoser, Si lo *h*a hecho, haziendo q*ue* lo haga
luego, porq*ue* no quede defraudado, el
di*c*ho mayorasgo, Y perdiendose la
di*c*ha finca, Y pasando en menoscabo
tengan, la aczion, Y lasto los di*c*hos
interesados de di*c*hos Sensos por di*c*ha razon Contra las possesiones, y fincas
de di*c*ho mayorasgo, el Segundo puncto
es, q*ue* la Cantidad, q*ue* dio por di*c*ha posesion, Y horno, del *h*asa no me acuerdo
Si fueron dies, y Siete mil, y quinientos
R*eal*es de Contado, o dies, y Seis mil, Y ocho-

sientos, los quales para otorgalle, la
eScriptura Segun el remate que en el Se hiso, por dicha Justiçia hordinaria dicha
Cantidad, en que Se le remato, hiso, obla-
zion, Y paga Real ante, dicha Justiçia
la qual Deposito, para que estubiese
[fol. 6v]

12

de pronpto, para pagar, el Costo de dicha presa, que en dicho tiempo Se puso en pregon
Su obra, a quien Se deposito, dicho dinero, fue
a gabriel Ruiz thesorero de la dicha Sancta
Cruzada, Y lo tiene o tendran Sus herederos, desde, el año de Sesenta y ocho, por
el mes de Septiembre fue quando Se hiso el remate, Y Venta de la dicha possesion, Con
autoridad, y mandado, del theniente de
Corregidor, don fulano pallares, Ante
andres, de escos, eScribano publico, de
los del numero que tenia Su oficio en la Plaza de Viva Ranbla de dicha Ciudad, y
hecha Como digo la presa mando, dicho Juez
la Cantidad que Sobrase Se aplicase, en finca para el aumento de dicho ayorasgo
o Se Redimiesen los Sensos, hasta, donde
alcansase, Y assi *Vuestra sSeñoría* mediante esta
noticia eScriba, a granada a mi primo
don fernando de teruel, y quesada, Cavallero de la horden de Santiago, Y es mi
primo por estar Casado Con mi Señora Doña
Luisa de Zepeda, Y ayala Sobrina
Carnal de mi tio Don alonso de Zepeda
Y ayala, desendientes de mis abue-
[fol. 7r]

13

lo el CCappitán don alonso de Zepeda, y
ayala, y de mi Visabuela mi sSeñora Doña
Juana, Venegas, ponze, de leon, Y asi *Vuestra Señoría*
deve, lo primero, haser, Se ponga en execuzion, la dicha presa, Y de lo que Sobrare Se

pueden Redimir los Sensos que tiene la dicha
hazienda, Y mayorasgo para que quede libre, y tanbien Se le pueden pedir los Reditos al dicho de-
positario, don Gabriel Ruiz de tantos años Como
ha gosado, el tener dicho dinero, y en un honbre
de trato, Y Contrato, Como el Susodicho tiene
estimazion, advierto, a Vuestra sSeñoría que la rrenta que
pagaban, los dichos labradores de dicho Cortijo
era el quinto de todas las Semillas, asi, trigo
Como Sebada, y Caña, Y hecha la dicha pressa
dixeren, y pagaran, Corrientemente el terzio, de
dichas Semillas porque Con el Riego aseguran
las dichas Cosechas tanbien, hay otro Cortijo
que llaman de la naba de antonia gil; este
Se arienda para la bellota por tener mucho
monte, Y asi lo pagan de buena gana, los que
tienen ganado de Zerda, Y teniendo Vuestra sSeñoría
la dicha Renta, Y mayorasgo, en administrazion Se lograra mas bien el gosar, Un
[fol. 7v]

14

Crezido pedaso de Renta, Cada año pues
las Casas prinzipales, Y tiendas Se Cobran
por meses, Y por tercios, Y asi el administrador que Vuestra sSeñoría pusiere Cada tres messes Se puede
Remitir libranza en letras de a quarenta
dias Vista pues Se ahorrara el premio del
Cambio, del quarto por Ciento que lleban quando es
a letra Vista; las Semillas, y granos Se Venden en dicha Ciudad de granada; en fin del
año, Y Si Se guardan para el mes de marzo
o abril el Siguiente Se Venden Con rreputazion
que es quando la tienen, los granos en dicho Reyno
en la forma que Repito, a Vuestra sSeñoría ha de, administrar, las dichas Rentas de dichos mayo-
rasgos, para lograr lo que pueden dar, pues
no tendran el desperdizio, malogro, y perdida que dando las en arrendamiento
por Un tanto por quenta Y Riesgo de los acziden-
tes del tiempo que estos Si los hay en la Corte-

dad, de las Cosechas tiene de estimazion
una hanega de Cada genero quatro Veses, mas
que en el año abundante, Y por ultimo, mas
Vale, Resevir lo que Dios diere, aunque Sean
trabajos de la mano de Dios que no de
[fol. 8r]

15

esos logreros, la Salud, en quanto al pleyto del
Marquez de San Visente, y patronato de
la Capilla de San Andres que fundo en ella
el Yllustrísimo sSeñor Don gutierre de Vargas, Ca-
rabajal mi tio, obispo, que fue de plazensia
hermano Segundo que fue de dicho marquez
a mi tia que este en gloria le enbie los poderes, los punctos, de Uno de los mejores, a-
bogados deste Reino Y Juntamente dinero
Y chocolate para la Solicitud, de poder
poner, el pleyto de Calidad de la buena, esperanza de Su Sentencia, Como lo fio en Su divina Magestad el que en el derecho que me asiste
que este me lo dijo diversas Vezes, mi tio, el
Padre Sebastian de Vargas de la Compañía de Jesus
hermano de mi abuelo, Y Respecto de que
a la notificazion de las Sensuras, Se haran
manifestazion de los papeles, y instrumentos del dicho mayorasgo la fundazion
del dicho patronato, de la dicha Capilla, Sus
Rentas, el testamento, del dicho Señor obispo
la merced, del dicho titulo, que la Magestad
del Rey Nuestro Señor felipe quarto, hisso
al dicho Marquez de San Vizente
[fol. 8v]

16

mi tio Cuyo testamento, y fundazion de la
dicha merced, de titulo, dara luz de dicha
Justicia que me asiste pues de dicho Señor marquéz
mi tio no quedo mas Susesion ligitima
que la dicha marqueza Su hija que Susedio
en los dichos mayorasgos patronato, y
estado de dicho titulo, y marquesado, y havien-

do muerto Sin Susesion Como murio
pasa a la linea, ligitima que Soy io, Como
dessendiente de hermano, mayor de los
abuelos, hermanos Segundos que fueron, del
dicho marquez de San Vizente mi tio, quien
me Conto, el dicho mi tio, el Padre Sebastian de
Vargas que havia dexado tanbien, Una hija, bas-
tarda que esta havia Casado en Castilla, la Vie-
ja Con Un Caballero, llamado Villa, Roel
o Villaseca, de quien es hijo, el dicho marquez
o Nieto, que de qualquiera Suerte, aunque el
Sea ligitimo es escluydo por Ser de linea
de bastardia, Y dichos instrumentos Seran
los que mas bien, asi nos Saquen de la duda
pues yo no la tengo de que me lo Conto, diferentes Vezes el dicho mi tio, y Si, el dicho marquez no fuera, escluydo, por rrazon, de
[fol. 9r]
17
Venir de dicha linea, desde luego que pusieron
la dicha demanda Se hubiera presentado Con
dichos papeles a Su Satisfaczion, Y pedir
la possesion ligitima Y exclutoria del
dicho derecho Ser Suyo, Y de Sus hijos en
Caso de tenerlos, y no Responder, intentando, Radicar, el juizio en la Real chan-
silleria de Valladolid, Razones todas
que mas bien acreditan la maliçia de
no tener el derecho el qual me tiene, Usurpado, Yo Reconosco que Vuestra sSeñoría estando, en
esa Corte Con la autoridad de Su persona, y puesto inteligenzia, y actividad,
Sacara esto en limpio Siguiendo dicho pley-
to para lo qual le dejo a Vuestra sSeñoría en la dispossision, y manutenenzia de las dichas Ren-
tas, y mayorasgos, que tengo en esos Reinos
para que asista, Como me prometo de Sus muchas, Y Relevantes, obligaziones, a
todo pues de estarme, yo empleado, en
Servizio de Su Magestad en algun buen
Govierno dandome, Nuestro sSeñor Vida, Se

podra poner todo en grande Corriente
Y dispossision, Y en quanto a la pretenzion
[fol. 9v]
18
de dicho Govierno me remito en todo, a la Carta que escribo, al sSeñor marquéz hermano de Vuestra
  sSeñoría
Y mi amigo a quien mediante Sus afectos
le digo lo que Conduze a mi deseo, Y
en todo Sera Siempre el mio en Servir a
Vuestra sSeñoría Y Vivirle, obligado, a Sus muchos afectos
Y atenziones, Y le pido no Como Su padre
de que tan dichoso me Reconosco, Sino, Como a Señor mio, y Cavallero que es, me Cuyde
mucho de mi querido, hijo don Juan manuel el que no falte de la asistencia de
Su Magestad el Rey Nuestro sSeñor que Dios guarde
Y del Servicio de la Reina Nuestra sSeñora
pues, Yo me Vendere en este Reino Y asistire
en este Govierno donde me hallo para Satisfaser
a Vuestra sSeñoría tanto, Como le devo, Socorrello, de
Suerte que Salga de las empeñoz, y que Corresponda no Solamente Vuestra sSeñoría Sino, mi devida, atenzion, y en flota espero, mi Correspondiente, Y aviador me Supla, Como, me
dio palabra de haserlo, al tiempo que sali de la Ciudad, de mexico para este, dicho
Govierno Una porzion que aliviase a Vuestra sSeñoría Ya
que no en el todo en la mayor parte, y asi
lo executara Segun tengo experienzia
[fol. 10r]
de su palabra, Y para mas bien Con Seguro Se asistiese a Vuestra sSeñoría Y Socorriesse
le deje poder, para que me pudiese obligar
Y Sacar la mayor Cantidad, que pudiese, haber
Y adquirir, por el termino de ocho messes
pagandola Con el Rescate, y premio de
la plata Conforme, a la ley del real, del
parral, antisipo, a Vuestra sSeñoría esta notiçia la
qual Repito, al presente al dicho mi encomendero, para que Se halle prevenido, y de la

Cantidad que entregare, y Remitiere, en
dicha flota me enbiara Razon Vuestra sSeñoría
a quien Repito quanto Soy, y quanto Valgo Soy Suyo
de Corazon, Y a Dios que guarde a Vuestra sSeñoría los
muchos y felizes años que puede, y io deseo, en
Compañía de mi querida hija y nieta, Y le
pido me haga el gusto de enbiarme los Retratos, Y de mi hijo, Don Juan manuel para que tenga el gusto de Verlos, fecha en este
passo, del Rio del norte, Reino de la nueba
mexico a 25 de Septiembre, de 1691.

^2Besa la Mano de Vuestra Señoría su
mas Afecto Padre que le estima De Corazon

Don Diego de Vargas
Zapata lujan Ponze de leon^

sSeñor Doctor, Don ygnacio
Lopez, de zarate mi hijo.

[fol. 10v]
^2Doy Notycia a Vuestra Señoría acabo de llegar de
Campaña Victoriosso Con Una Pressa
de 130 captivos y dejado Muerto en la
Campaña Mas de quarenta sin Muchos que
se escaparon Por la espesura del Bosque
Donde se hallaban dichos enemigos Heri-
dos Salgo de orden de su excelencia a las Provincias
De Sonora y Zinaloa Donde se halla el
enemigo llevo la Superyntendenzia
De las Armas por quanto se Juntan
las Compañías de dichos Presidios y la de
este avisare a Vuestra Señoría en la flota de la
fortuna que se adquiriere en la Guerra
ofensiva que se Ba hazer al enemigo.

Vargas^

13. *Diego de Vargas to Ignacio López de Zárate,*
El Paso del Río del Norte, 25 September 1692,
AMNB, ALS.

[fol. 1r]
[cross top center]
Hijo y señor mio muy largo tengo escrito
a Vuestra Señoria Desde Septiembre de el año pasado y por
no haver havido ocasion zierta Me pare-
ze llegara esta casi al Mesmo tiempo que Me obliga hazerlo lo Gustosso
que es para Mi Repetir la Pluma
Mis firmes y Devidos affectos alibios que Considero en tener Afianzado
las Prendas de mi Corazon de Mis
queridos Hijos pues No Solo es
Vuestra Señoría su Hermano Sino su lijitimo
Padre pues Biben a su Sombra Muy
Seguros es Zierto que en Mi estara
siempre la atenzion y Affecto tan
Ymmediato en el todo de el cariño que
es Zierto quisiera tener fortuna para Manifestar Algo de su Ynterior
No puede Obrar Mas mi fineza
que es el haverme Desterrado a este Reyno Ultimo de el Mundo
Y Remoto Sin Ygual Para
en su Retiro Solizitar Medios
Para de Una Vez quedar alibiado
en el Deseo de Cumplirle a Vuestra Señoría
[fol. 1v]
su Dote y asy en la flota que se Juz-
gua llegue este año Remityre Dandome Nuestro Señor algun Socorro Para
Ayuda del Desempeño A Mi Hijo Don
Juan Manuel le escrivo en Carta
de Mi encomendero Para que le Remita una llibranza de quatrozientos
pesos y otra Hize el año pasado le Remi-
tyesse y Carta Mia Juzguo la havra

Rezibido y asy aguardo la Razon
Como de esta de la fecha de esta que
Despacho Correo a Mexico a su *excelencia* para el Ynforme de la Conquista de el
Reyno de la Nueva Mexico quedo prevenido para en este Verano hazer dicha
Ynvasion el Dia de San Lorenzo que fue
el Mesmo Dia en el año de 1680 quando
se Perdio. a mi Hija Juana escrivy
el año pasado que juzguo esta la Carta Con
mi Pliego Me allegrare este Con Salud
y la echo Mi Bendizion y a Dios que Guarde
a Vuestra Señoría en Bida de my querida Hija Ysabel y Nieta Muchos Años y me los
Deje Beer Paso de el Rio de el
[fol. 2r]
Norte y Abril 9 de 1692

Besa la Mano de Vuestra señoría su
Mas Affecto Padre que le estima y quiere de Corazon

Don Diego de Vargas
Zapata lujan Ponze de leon

señor Doctor Don Ygnazio lopez de Zarate
Mi Hijo y Amigo

———

14. *Diego de Vargas to Ignacio López de Zárate, Santa Fe, 12 October 1692,* ARGD, LS.

[fol. 1r]
[written in left margin] ^hAviendo escrito esta me pa-
resio no perder el tienpo
pues Sera bien pedirle a Su magestad
la merced en ocazion que ba el informe del Señor birrey, y la real

Junta, y asi Vuestra Señoría hagase de
dicha Carta y me avise, y tome a
Su Cargo la respuesta de ella
ba abierta la Carta para que la lea
Vuestra sSeñoría y este en la inteligencia de
mi justificada pretenzionˆ
[cross top center]
Hijo, Y Señor mio, tengo escrito a Vuestra sSeñoría
en todas las ocasiones de Correo que se han
ofresido despachar a la Corte de mexico
Y en ellas le he dado parte de mis progre-
ssos en este govierno Con felizes Susesos, y a
Satisfaczion del excelentísimo sseñor Virrey Conde
de Galve, Y de la Junta de real hazienda
Y Señores ministros de ella tengo por
Sin duda que los participaran a Su magestad
en Su real Y Supremo Consejo de las
Yndias Juntamente Con el presente Siendo
de tanto triunpho Y gloria de ambas magestades pues me determine a mi Costa
a reduzir Y Conquistar esta Villa de
Santa fee reyno Y Cabezera de la
[fol. 1v]
nuebo mexico Y me ha paresido el escribir aunque Corto al Rey Nuestrro Señor
pues no Sera bien estando puesto por
Su magestad dexar de partizipar dicha Victoria, a Su real Y Supremo Consejo de
las Yndias, Y asi le doy noticia de dicha
Conquista pueblos, Y partidos que le
tengo reduczidos a su real Corona
Y las almas que Se han baptizado pues, en el discurso de doze años que
ha que se alzaron los Yndios de este
Reino Y apartados de Nuestra Sancta
fee, Viviendo Apostatas en Su Y-
dolatria Y por ultimo para que Vuestra sSeñoría
se halle Capaz de quanta estimazion
Sera para Su magestad dicha noticia el año
de 81 paso a ella en Compañía de su

Governador governando el reyno de la
nueba eSpaña el excelentísimo Señor Conde
de paredes marquez de la Laguna
Y dio, Y resivio para dicha Conquista
[fol. 2r]
nobenta Y Sinco mil pesos al Padre
Reverendo fray francisco de Ayeta procurador general de la religion del Sancto
Evangelio de Nuestro Padre San francisco de todo el Reino de la nueba eSpaña el qual
Vive en su Convento grande de esa Corte
Y no quiero mas Coronista de la in-
portancia de dicha enpresa que el dicho
Padre en medio de que Vino Como digo
Con dicho Governador que era en dicho tiempo
a ella Y no la logro, Y desesperadamente
Se Volvieron haviendo reduzido Solo, 385
personas del pueblo de la isleta Con dicho
gasto, Y io a mi Costa he logrado mediante el favor Divino lo que no se esperaba
Y Se tenia Ya por materia desespera-
da al tiempo que escribo esta despacho
Correo al excelentísimo Señor Virey Conde de
Galve desde esta dicha Villa haviendo
acavado de llegar de los pueblos Y naziones de tierra adentro hasta los taos, que es la ultima, Y para que dicho
[fol. 2v]
Padre este Sabedor de todo le escribo aunque Corto porque Se alegrara
mucho, Y los autos de dicha Conquista
de guerra remitire Su testimonio en la
flota para que Se halle Su magestad enterado en dicho real Consejo que Ba dicho
Don toribio de la guerta no tiene que
Cansarse en esta Conquista que Solo le
puede premiar Su magestad el deseo Con la
merced de titulo de Marquez de este reyno
Y otras muchas que le pedia Y aun resivio a quenta tanbien un socorro de
ayuda de Costa; no es esto para reconve-

nir a Su mag*esta*d Con nada Sino por*que*
Se halle V*uestra* sSeñor*ía* noticiado de este puncto
Y en flota Si Dios N*uest*ro Señor me da
Vida remitire d*ic*ho testimonio de
d*ic*hos autos Con lo demas q*ue* Se ofresi-
ere Y executare en Servicio de
la Divina, y humana mag*esta*d en estas
[fol. 3r]
partes, Y me hara favor de Ynquirir Si Con este aviso d*ic*ho Señor
ex*celentísi*mo Virrey, Y d*ic*hos Señores de la
re*a*l Junta dan quenta a Su mag*esta*d
de lo q*ue* refiero en esta pues le Sera
fazil a V*uestra* sSeñor*ía* Se lo digan en la Secretaria de Yndias Y me avise, V*uestra* sSeñor*ía*
Con todo Cuydado Segun las Sir-
cunstancias le dixeren, Y informe
de mis Servicios para q*ue* noticiado
Con Sertesa de lo que a V*uestra* sSeñor*ía* le dixeren pueda yo deliberar mis pre-
tenciones harto deseo, Ver, Cartas
de V*uestra* sSeñor*ía* Y de mis queridos hijos, Y a
mi hijo, Ju*an* Man*u*el le he remitido
dos libranzas de a 400 pessos en
Reales de a ocho libres del premio
de Su Conduzion Sino puestos en esa
Corte me prometo de q*ue* mi Correspondiente el Capp*itá*n Don Luiz Saens,
[fol. 3v]
de tagle Cavallero del Orden de
alcantara Y mercader de plata en
mexico h*a*vra dado d*ic*ha libranza
Sobre Don enrique de la Rossa Con q*u*ien
tiene Correspondencia en Cadiz, Y
en la flota dandome N*uest*ro Señor Vida
hare aprieto Y empeño para remitir
a V*uestra* sSeñor*ía* parte de Su dote pues no me tiene ni me tendra en estas partes otra
razon ni Causa desterrado Sino
el Coresponderle Y asi se halle asegurado no le faltare Y a Servirle Con

las Veras de amigo, Y padre que le estima Y en Sus obligaziones no dudo
Sera muy fino Con mi hija Y querida Ysabel, y nietos que le Jusgo
Ya tener los hijos duplicados a todos echo mi bendizion, Y pido, a
Vuestra sSeñoría les de en mi nombre los abrasos que quisiera darles personalmente
Su Divina magestad espero me Cumpla
[fol. 4r]
este deseo Y guarde a Vuestra sSeñoría felizes años
Y esas Cartas dara Vuestra sSeñoría en mano propia al Señor Marquéz de Villanueba Su
hermano Y mi amigo, Y a mis hijos Y
remitira a tordelaguna ese pliego
de esta Villa de Santa fee Reyno
Y Cavezera de la nueba mexico nuebamente reduzida, Y Conquistada, a
la real Corona a 12 de octubre de 1692 años.

^2Besa la Mano de Vuestra Señoría su Hijo
que le estima y quiere Como
padre y Amigo

Don Diego de Vargas
Zapata lujan Ponze de leon^

Señor Doctor Don Ygnacio Lopez
de zarate mi hijo

————

15. *Diego de Vargas to Ignacio López de Zárate, El Paso del Río del Norte, 7 ——— 1693,* ARGD, ALS.

[fol. 1r]
Hijo y señor mio aunque escribo a mi Hijo Don Juan Mi Resoluzion se la Repito a Vuestra Señoría para

que la execute pues es lo que
podemos desear y *Vuestra Señorí*a quedara Alibiado y solo para asis-
tyr el que los Mayorazgos
No teniendo empeño los Goze y Reduzga a con sus mes-
mas Rentas yr Redimien-
dos sus Zensos pues asistyra
a la ley de *Cavallero* y obligaziones
en corresponder a mi Cariño
y estymazion Con que le amo
pues yo en *Servicio* de el Rey
N*uestro* Señor me Mantendre
en el Govi*erno* que me prometo
de su Real Sangre Asisty-
ra a darme Remunera-
zion a lo que se hallara por
Ynforme de el *excelentísi*mo *señor* Birrey
[fol. 1v]
y Remito a *Vuestra señorí*a la Carta de my
Hijo para que se *h*alle entera-
do de el empleo que le tengo
tratado y ajustado que me pareze sera el Mas decoroso y Con
el Seg*uro* de llevar Con que asistir a sus obligaziones y al *señor*
Marques de Billanueba Mi Amigo le escrivo para que se *h*alle
enterado y Cumplir Con lo
mucho que le estimo y en la flota lo Hare Dandome N*uestro* Señor ^vida^ a todos los Parientes y a
Dios que *Guard*e a *Vuestra Señorí*a *muchos* años Paso del Rio de el Norte a 7 de 1693

Besa la *M*ano de *Vuestra señorí*a su mas
*P*adre Amigo y *S*ervidor

D*on* Diego de Vargas
Zapata lujan Ponze de leon

señor Doctor Don Ygnazio
Lopez de Zarate Mi Hijo

---

16. *Diego de Vargas to Martín Solis y Miranda, Santa Fe, 25 February 1696, ARGD, C.*

[fol. 1r]
[cross top center]
Mui *señor* mio por mi hijo Don Ygnaçio
lopez de Zaratte he tenido notiçia lo interesado que soy Siendo Tan Servidor
de V*uestra señorí*a Y su seguro amigo de que tan in-
mediattamentte partiçipa mi afectto Con q*ue*
rendidamentte esttime a V*uestra señorí*a en Mexico
Y por Ser mi gobierno de guerra Careçia
de Saber si incumbia a su conozimien-
tto a V*uestra señorí*a que estte estava en intelligençia
diversa pareçiendome que al señor fis-
cal de la camara de Juntta de guerra
de Yndias era su legitima Conozimien-
tto Y reconozco En V*uestra señorí*a asistte, asi por lo
que mira a lo zivil, como a lo de guerra
de que me sirbe de mucha esperanza de
mis prettensiones haviendo sido
reconozidas de V*uestra señorí*a mis empresas como
los Serv*icio*s que en la restauraçion de este
R*ein*o ttengo *h*echas a su Ma*gestad* poseyen-
dolo su Real corona como anttes de la
Sublebaçion general del año de 80. Y
a quattro punttos hago el resumen
de la estimacion de *d*ichos mis Servizios
para benir en conozimientto los Señores
de ese R*ea*l Supremo Consejo de camara de Yndias como V*uestra señorí*a que ha
de hazer el imforme Y relaçion
[fol. 1v]
de sus puntos, el primero el que le

Constta el gastto *h*echo en el año de 81
pues fue Con su parezer hallandose
exerçiendo la plaza de Señor fiscal
de lo zivil de la real audiençia de
Mexico pues en Virtud de la nottiçia
que su Mag*esta*d el rey n*uest*ro Señor que
Dios guarde ttubo de la susod*i*cha Sublebaçion de este d*i*cho reino en el Año
antezedentte de 80. despacho
en d*i*cho año de 81 su real zedula
al ex*celentísi*mo Señor Virrey que lo era el
Señor Conde de Paredes para que
pusiese ttodos los medios de su real
*h*Aver para la restauraçion de este
d*i*cho reino a su real Corona Y al Yugo
de n*uest*ra Santta fee, Y le consta a V*uestra señoría*
pues concurria Con sus parezeres Y
en la asistençia de las reales Junttas de
Haçienda a que se librasen como
Se libraron en la real Caxa de d*i*cha
Cortte de Mexico al re*verend*o Padre
Fray Françisco de Aietta para que
Como procurador g*ener*al que pasaba
a la conduzion de limosnas, religiosos, Con los Carros de su Mag*esta*d a esta
Custodia que se Hallava en el pueblo
del Paso del rio del nortte con los
Vezinos Y su go*vernad*or el g*ener*al Don Anttonio
de Ottermin le enttregase d*i*chos no-
ventta mil pesos Y con ellos Costease
la genttе de guerra Y socorriese a d*i*chos
Vezinos en la mesma forma Y
entrasen los Unos Y los ottros
[fol. 2r]
a Hazer la d*i*cha Conquista Y restaura-
zion de este d*i*cho reino lo qual no con-
siguieron hallando los pueblos despo-
blados que estan desde Senecu, Y solo
el de la Ysleta a 30 leguas anttes de
entrar en esta d*i*cha Villa en el ha-

llaron se Hallava poblado con los Yndios de nazion Tiguas, que se rindie-
ron Y el dicho general saco y poblo en el
districtto del dicho pueblo del Paso
Y en dicha entrada ttan solamente hizo
Y Consumio los dichos nobenta mil pesos
haviendose retirado por protestas de la dicha
gentte de guerra y Vecinos por causas que
le representaron de ser el rigor del Hibierno
Morirsele la cavallada Y mulada de dichos
Carros Y ottros incombenienttes de que Vuestra señoría
tendra mejor notiçia que Yo pues precisa-
mentte Yria el ttestimonio de auttos de Guerra de dicha entrada a sus manos, esto
que refiero es solo por probar el gasto
hecho a su Magestad Y mas el adminiculo
Segundo que se le pidio de Treinta mill
pesos que ambos a dos fueron de çien-
tto y Veintte mil como consta en los li-
bros reales de la Real caxa de Mexico.

El segundo en el año de 91 consta tanbien no
Solo en dicha real Caxa, sino Constara
en la secrettaría de Yndias de partte del
reino de la nueva españa el gasto que hizo
y se le comfirmo por ese real y dicho Supremo
Consejo de Yndias el general Don Domingo
Gironza Siendo governador Y capittan general
de este dicho reino para la entrada que
Hizo al pueblo de Zia que fue de çerca
[fol. 2v]
de quatro mil pesos Y mas Consiguio
la merced que su Magestad el rei nuestro Señor
que Dios guarde le hizo por haberle ganado
a Sangre Y fuego de los Yndios que
en el hallo de Un habitto, Y mas man-
daba al Señor excelentísimo Virrey que en caso
de no haber yo entrado en este govierno
Se me acomodase primero Y se le conti-
nuase en el al dicho Don Domingo dan-

dole las graçias como se las dio en dicho
Su real nombre Y prometiendole le
tendria presentte para acomodarle
en mayores puesttos.

El Terzero fue el de ser admitido Y oido
Con aceptaçion por su Magestad en dicho año
de 91, el memorial que le presentto Don
thorivio de la Huertta en que por el
Consta Capitulaba con su Magestad
en su relaçion de el que Haviendo
estado en este reino se hallava con las
esperiencias de la Guerra Conozimiento
de la Tierra Y de los Yndios Y asi se
promettia a dar dicho reino Conquistado
dandole su Magestad lo siguientte, lo primero
le havia de Hazer merced de Tittulo
de Castilla de Marques de todo
este dicho reino sus provincias de Zuni Y
Moqui Y minerales de la Tierra del
almagre O mermellon que es el mettal del azogue Y el de la riqueza
del mineral de platta de la sierra azul
Y le havia de dar para hazer dicha
Conquista diez mill reses, quinien-
ttos hOmbres de armas Y mas los Carros
armas Y muniziones Y los pertrechos
[fol. 3r]
de guerra nezessarios Y estte govierno per-
pettuo con mas las alcaldias mayores
de Sonora Y Zinaloa por ttres Vidas
en sus hijos niettos y subzesores que havia de poner Y ser de su nombradia
los Juezes en la dicha provincia de Moqui para la recaudaçion de los reales haberes
Y de la dicha mina del almagre de dicho
mettal de azogue Se le havian de guardar los previlegios Y asientto que gozan
y tienen los de la mina de fuencabilica
en el reyno del Peru, Y estte dicho memorial

remittio Su Magestad a dicho su real Consejo
de Yndias mandando en la primera
Ocasion de aviso para el reino de la nueva
españa se le despachase a su Virrey de el
para que mandase al governador Y Capittan general
de este reino de la nueva Mexico que se Hallava
en el pueblo del Paso hiziese la deligencia
e Ymformazion no solo de si era Ziertto
Haber el dicho almagre Y tierra del mermellon Y mina que de el Se sacase sino
tanbien el costo que podia tener la enttrada
a dicha provincia Y en dicho año de 91 en el aviso
que llego rezivio dicha real Zedula el excelentísimo
Señor Virrey Conde de Galve Y me despacho
dicho Orden Y rezivida la informazion consta
de ella que le remitti a su excelencia haver la dicha
tierra Y mettal de azogue Y el costo que
podia tener la dicha entrada Su recono-
zimientto Y remision de donde Se prueba
el quartto puntto de dicho Costo Y asi
el año de 92 executte a mi Costa la conquista general de todo estte dicho reino
que sin ella no podia pasar a entrar
a dicha provincia de Moqui pues no hallan-
[fol. 3v]
dose Conquistado estte dicho reino
primero, Sus natturales Y naciones
de que se compone como Yndios al-
zados Y ttan belicosos se havian de
Unir e Ymposibilittar resistiendo
la dicha entrada y mas Con dicha notticia
bajando los de el Peñol de Acoma
provincia de Zuni Y la dicha de Moqui
todo lo qual Contrastte benzi Y con-
quiste a mi costa ttomando de nuebo
la posession a favor de su Magestad Y hize
la diligencia de la dicha tierra almagre
O mermellon que es el metal de azogue de la dicha mina de que hize
remision Con el ttestimonio de auttos de

guerra de dicha Conquista a dicho Señor
excelentísimo Virrey Conde de Galve haziendo
obsequio a su Magestad a sus reales plantas
del dicho Costo ofreziendole juntta
mentte a ellas el triumpho de tan
gloriosa empresa Y con los quatro
punttos expresados en esta se reconoze por su resumen la estimaçion atten-
cion Y Consideraçion que se deve tener
por V*uestra señoría* como por esos señores ministros
que asisten en dicho real Y supremo
Consejo de Camara de Yndias para
Hazer el imforme a su Magestad haviendose duplicado a dichos mis Servicios los de
la reconquista de este dicho reino Siendo
por fuerza de armas su restauraçion y
quedando diez y ocho missiones pobladas
como mas Junttamentte tres Villas
de españoles Con esta de Santta fee
y en ella en su fuerza su presidio de
los cien Soldados de a caballo
[fol. 4r]
para seguridad Y resguardo de todo
y por las carttas de imforme a su Magestad
a mi favor del excelentísimo Señor Virrey Conde de
Galve Y Señores de la real Juntta de Hazienda
de Mexico reconozera V*uestra señoría* la calificaçion
de todo Como asimesmo Constara a dichos
Señores de ese dicho real Consejo los dichos
mis Servicios recomendaçion Y encargo
que Hazen a su Magestad por constarles
la magnitud de ellos dificultades e Yn-
posibles por los imformes Y parezeres
que de las diligençias que prezedieron
Hizo dicho Señor excelentísimo Virrey Y quantto mayores riesgos ponderaron e Ympo-
sibles mas enzendieron mi animo
Y fue la razon que tube Y militto en
mi p*ara* Hazer a mi costa la dicha Conquista
no arresgando nada a su Magestad de su real

Haver Y asi puedo *h*ablar debajo de
el respectto Y atençion de su rendido
Y leal Vasallo con el desa*h*ogo de pedirle
me Honrre Y haga la m*erced* que le escribo
a mi agentte Juan gonzalez Calderon
Y a *d*icho mi Hijo Don Ygnaçio solizitte
Con toda instançia pues anttes me mido
y proporçiono con modestia como se reconoze por lo Justificado con que pruebo
la *d*icha mi suplica para lo qual a V*uestra señoría*
Se la hago rendidamentte pues en caba-
lleros de su illustre Sangre es el favorezer el que Con los riesgos solizitan los pre-
mios Y aszensos Y para pedir los
en Unos son menestter aun despues
de Haverlos Conseguido con fortuna
des*h*echa tenerla para los que se hallan
al lado de su Mag*estad*

Remitto a V*uestra señoría* esos çien ladrillos de choco-
[fol. 4v]
late que Con ella remittira el *d*icho
mi hijo Don Ygnaçio Y me tiene a su
Servic*io* con llaneza en quantto Valiere
deseando *g*uar*d*e n*u*estro Señor la persona de
V*uestra señoría* felizes años. F*echa* en esta Villa
de Santta fee en 25 de feb*r*ero de 1696.

Señor Don Mart*í*n de Solis Y Miranda.

————

17. *Diego de Vargas to Ignacio López de Zárate,*
Santa Fe, 4 January 1697, AMNB, ALS.

[fol. 1r]
[cross top center]
Hijo y s*e*ñor mio esta sirve de
dar aviso a V*uestra Señoría* me *h*allo con sa-

lud grazias a Nuestro Señor y esperando en su Divina Magestad
llegaria el *excelentísimo* Señor Conde
de Galbe a esa Corte que en
Prinzipe tan grande Despues
de Dios Nuestro señor espero en su
Grandeza *hara* tal Ynforme
a su Magestad que le Mueva su
Real animo a darme el premio en Parte de mis repety-
dos Servicios y por el Deseo
que tengo de que se Desem-
peñen esos Mayorasgos
Remito a Vuestra Señoría esos Diez
mil pesos quatro mil por
Mano de mi querido Ami-
go Don Juan de Albarado y
Seys mil pesos que escribi
a mi encomendero el Maestre
[fol. 1v]
de Campo Don Luis Saenz de
tagle entregasse a su sobrino Don Francisco Diaz de tagle para
que los Remittyesse a Cadiz
y desde Cadiz los Pusiesse
en libranza a poder de Vuestra Señoría en
esa Corte la Persona que se
los entregasse en la Corte de
Mexico Con mas los Costos
de Mar y tyerra de su Conduzion Y asy puede ser le sobren
de Dichos Costos a la Persona
que entregare Dicho Don Juan
de Albarado y asy sera esa
Cantidad mas de Dichos Dyes
Diez mil pesos y con dicha Cantydad
luego me Desempeñara Vuestra Señoría
todos Mis Mayorasgos y qui-
tara sus Zensos y Desempeñara el Zenso de los Zien Ducados

de Renta que Paga el liz*enci*ado
D*on* Juan Diaz y me Remity-
[fol. 2r]
ra testim*oni*o de D*ic*ho Desempeño
pues Con el ajustare en este
Reyno alguna Convenienzia
y quiero tener Resguardo para qualquier azidente o Contratyempo y que tenga siempre D*ic*ho Credito Contra D*ic*hos
Mayorasgos y asy Miro los
futuros Contin*g*entes acu-
chillado de tantos trabajos
en Mi Dilatada ausenzia
y V*uestra Señoría* Como tan jurista le
asentara bien d*ic*ha Mi Preven-
zion y asy la Pongo fio y Con-
fio en su Mano Como lo *he hec*c-
ho de todos Mis Mayorasgos
tambien se me ofreze Desir a V*uestra señoría*
que si ˆsuˆ Ma*g*es*ta*d el Rey N*uest*ro Señor
que Dios *gua*r*de* entre las M*erc*edes que
espero de su Real Mano me
Honrrare Con Alguna M*erc*ed
de *h*Abito de las tres ordenes
Milytares sea la de Santia-
[fol. 2v]
go Por *h*aver Merezido tan buenos Sucesos por Ynterzesion
Y en el Glorioso ˆdiaˆ de este Santo
y asy luego que se me *haga d*icha
M*erc*ed De D*ic*ho Dinero Saque
V*uestra Señoría* el que fuere Menester
para el Costo de mis pruevas
pues mi P*ad*re D*on* Alonso de Vargas
fue de el orden de Santiago
Mi Aguel*o* Paterno D*on* Lorenzo
de Bargas fue de d*ic*ha Orden
y mi Abuela Mi *s*eñora Doña Anton*i*a
Ponze de leon Su Herm*ano* fue
del *h*Abito de Calatrava Mi Ague-

lo Materno D*on* Diego de Contreras fue familiar del *S*anto Ofizio
por la suprema Y Beedor Y Pa-
gador de el exerzito de Cataluna
quando el Rey N*uestr*o Señor felipe
quarto fue al exerzito y Jornada
de Cataluna Y Asy Mi M*a*dre
Doña M*ar*ía Margarita de Contreras
es Hija del D*i*cho D*on* Diego de Contreras y de Doña Beatriz de Araez Berrasueta Y asy V*uestr*a Se*ñorí*a Debajo de
[written vertically in left margin] esta Notyzia y de mi
    Ynformazion que Di Para tomar Posesion de mis
Mayorazgos de ser Hijo lejitimo de ^los^ D*i*chos que paso ante
    Vizente
Suarez escriv*a*no de l*a* Num*e*ro de esa Villa en el año de 66 se
    Reco-
nozera D*i*cho Ynstrum*e*nto *h*asta el año de 72. y *h*allandome en
    estos Reynos
Determino ponerme d*i*cha Ynsignia por serlo Ultimo de el Mundo
    y Venga
Y me Remita V*uestr*a Se*ñorí*a la zedula de suerte que me Pueda
    Dar o poner D*i*cho
*h*Abito qualquier Cavallero de d*i*cha orden en la Yglesia Y lugar
    Mas Ym-
[fol. 3r]
ymmediato y pueda Salir de mi Gobierno Dejando teniente por mi q*ue*nta
Y Riesguo a Ponerme D*i*cho *h*avito
Y d*i*cha ausenzia que Hiziere se en-
tyenda *h*a de ser por el term*i*no de zien
Dias y no mas y asy tomado
esta Resoluzion por *h*aver tenido en Dos a*ño*s D*i*cho dia de Santiago Dos victorias de la M*a*yor
ymportanzia y Riesguo que lo
atribuy a Millagro del zielo
y quiero traer D*i*cho *h*avito y le tengo Promessa Sy Voy a ese Reyno
el Yr a visitar su *S*anto templo
Y asy V*uestr*a Se*ñorí*a vista esta pues llegara

a tyempo que ya su Magestad me hay-
ga hecho Merced le Pedira dicha
Merced y luego al punto pedira los
Ymformantes para En la Primera
ocasion de aviso Despacharme
Dichos Despachos Digo Dicha Real
zedula y me Remityra el Manto
Capitular hecho en esa Corte y Una
[fol. 3v]
Dozena de hAbitos asy Grandes
para los capotes Como peque-
nos para Poner en las cham-
bergas Y tendra en Cadiz
Vuestra Señoría Prevenido Y Puesto todo
lo Dicho Para en la Primera ocasion de Aviso Remytyrmelos y
a mi Hija querida Ysabel y
mis queridos Nietos BEcho mi
bendyzion y a Dios que Guarde a Vuestra Señoría
en su Compañía muchos años fecha en esta
Villa de Santa fee en 4 de Henero de 1697.

Besa la Mano dè Vuestra Señoría Su Mas
Affecto Padre que le estima
de Corazon

Don Diego de Vargas
Zapata lujan Ponze de leon

Mi Hijo señor Don Ygnazio lopez
de Zarate.

———

18. *Diego de Vargas to Juan Antonio López de
Zárate, Marqués de Villanueva de la Sagra, Santa Fe, 4 January 1697, AMNB, ALS.*

[fol. 1r]
[cross top center]
Amigo y Señor mio esta escribo

sin tener Cartas de Vuestra señoría a la fecha
de esta que Despacho Segundo Correo
a Mexico y me allegrare el Re-
zibirlas quando no tengo Mayor
Gusto que rezivir Notyzias
de su Salud y atendyendo a que
el tyempo se Pasa no quiero
Dilatar mis Resoluziones
y sea Dando Prinzipios de
hazer la Remision que
hago de los Diez mil pesos segun
escrivo a mi Hijo el Señor Don
Ygnazio en estas Naos que
se buelben a esos Reynos y
asy los quatro mil pesos Remito por Mano y Direccion
de mi Amigo don Juan de Albarado y los seys mil pesos
Por Mano de el Alferez don francisco
Diaz de tagle y de su tio el Maestre
de Campo don luis Saenz de ta-
[fol. 1v]
gle Cavallero del orden de Alcantara
y Vezinos de Mexico y con Dichos Dies
mil pesos me Desempene Mis Mayorasgos y zensos y Cargas que
se Pagan y le hago la adbertenzia que quiero tener Contra ellos
Dicho Credito. me prometo Con la
llegada de el señor excelentísimo Conde de Galbe
tendran el Complimiento de mi Deseo
Mis Pretensiones Y Digo a Dicho
Mi Hijo ~~de~~ Señor don Ygnazio todo lo que
se me ofreze y asy me Remito
a Dicha Carta y en segundo lugar
hAgo a Vuestra señoría la Dicha Remision
Para que execute el Conteni-
do de Dicha Carta Y asy anti-
zipo esta a Vuestra señoría por si Hubiere ocasion de Aviso y de no se
halle prevenida la Dicha Remi-

sion que fio este Pliego y Despacho de el Dicho Mi Amigo
don Juan de Albarado y me a-
llegrare se halle Vuestra señoría y mi Hijo el
[fol. 2r]
Señor don Ygnazio Satisfechos
Con la Remision que le Hize en la flota pasada de 96,
y que llegasse todo Muy bueno y a tyempo Segun me prometo de mi Voluntad Con que
saly de Dicho empeño y que se
Recognoziesse la estimazion
Justa que Hazia de Dichos mis
Hijos. Y si Deseo los Puestos
es por Recognozerlos tan
cargados de Hijos y que la
Corte Da para Mantenerse
pero no para acaudalar pues Vemos la Cortedad que
hay y que en la Nobleza que
se busca es Donde hay mas
escazes Y todo es una pres-
pectiva y Pender de muchos
Para qualquier Convenien-
zia Y asy este Desengaño me
haze tener siempre en que
quiero por my adquirir para
[fol. 2v]
mis obligaziones y a Dios que
Guarde a Vuestra señoría los felizes años que
Deseo No trato en esta mas
que Dar aviso de Dicha Remision
pues la antyzipo para que
en tyempo se hAga Dicha Conduzion a la Veracruz. fecha en
esta Villa de Santa fee en 4 de
Henero de 1697.

Besa la Mano de Vuestra señoría su
Mas Affecto Amigo y servidor

d*on* Diego de Vargas Zapata
Lujan Ponze de leon

Se*ñor* Marques de Villanueva

---

19. *Diego de Vargas to Isabel María de Vargas Pimentel, Santa Fe, 17 April 1697, ARGD, LS.*

[fol. 1r]
[cross top center]
Hija mia de mis ojos
esta te escrivo aselerada-
mente Porque alcanse
al Pliego de flota Y
Solo Se rreduze a la de-
bida obligazion de mi
cariño de solisitar de tu
Salud, Y de mis queridos
nietos que deseo esteis,
todos Vuenos yo quedo
a dios grazias en este gobierno Como escribo a mi
hijo, el Señor don ygna-
zio, a quien le doi aun-
que de pazo la notizia
de mi deseo Y las que le
escribi en el mes de he-
nero executara en todo
Su contenido Y a dios
que te *guar*de mi querida *h*yja
los muchos años que de-
[fol. 1v]
seo fecha en esta Villa
de Santa fee en 17 de a-
bril de 1697 años

^2Tu Padre que te es-
tima y quiere de Corazon

Don Diego de Vargas Zapata
lujan Ponze de leon^

Mi hija Doña Ysabel de Vargas
Pimentel

———

20. *Diego de Vargas to Ignacio López de Zárate, Santa Fe, 30 September 1698, ARGD, LS.*

[fol. 1r]

[cross top center]

Hyjo y señor mio. Esta escrivo a *Vuestra Señoría* mas por darle el
pe-
same de la muerte del *señor* Marquez de *Vi*lla Nue*v*a su herm*a*no
cuya noticia *R*ecivi en esta *Vi*lla de *Sa*nta fee de mi herm*a*no Don
Gregorio Pimentel su *f*echa en Tordelaguna en qu*a*tro de
Abril de este presente año de la *f*echa que Carta de
*V*uestra Señoría no he re*ci*bido reconozco seran sus ocupaciones
ta-
les mediante *di*cho suseso de que le reconozco muy las-
timado; Yo lo quedo, y me causso tanto sentim*ie*nto como
a *V*uestra Señoría y aunq*ue* dixera m*a*yor podia Creerse de su
consepto qu*a*ndo
en mi faltaba el conocim*ie*nto y si por carta engendro
tanto cariño, este deseava el logro de la comunicaçi-
on, Ya que el de la Correspondença se la devia mi suerte
a la de mi hija Ysabel en haverse empleado con *V*uestra Señoría

Ya tendra por el Cappit*á*n Don Antonio Valverde que lo fue
de este Presidio, y Paso a esse *R*eino en la flota que en
fines de Mayo se dio a la Vela de mi infausta fortu-
na pues haviendola tenido en todo graçias a n*u*estro *señor* quisso
darme el purgatorio desta prission en que me hallo
desde dos de octubre del año passado de 97 y el havermela
dilatado el absoluto poder del que go*v*ierna fue la noticia que *V*uestra Señoría me dio de las m*e*rcedes que su
Magesta*d* el Rey n*u*estro *señor* que

Dios *guarde* me havia hecho en atençion de los *d*ichos mis serviçios, publera a Dios para no remitirme *Vuestra Señoría* la Real
Cedula de la Prorrogaçion de *d*icha me*rc*ed deste Govierno *d*icha
    carta
no me hubiera escripto y antes se hubiera perdido q*u*e
llegado a mis manos pues fue instrum*en*to para que el
Governad*o*r actual Don Pedro Rodriguez Cubero, Cuyo Primo
y agente tiene por Contador m*a*yor del Consejo de Yndias, y
se llama Don Alphonso de Buendia, y assi mediante
*d*icha notiçia Ynsistio a el Cavildo de este *Reino* pidiesen
contra mi, y la gente de el façil, y como gente que
Viene a poblar a tierras tan remotas y el recurso
tan lejos, unos de terror, otros de Ynteres, y otros de
su mal natural, inducidos, y incistidos, y sin saber
firmar los mas ni leer les hizieron que firma-
sen, y declarasen todo q*u*a*n*to la industria, y maliçia assi
[fol. 1v]
del Secretario Como del *d*icho Governad*o*r pudo
    lebantandome fal-
ças acusaçiones Calunias, y Capitulos de mu*ch*o Volumen todo a
fin de embarazarme para el tiempo, que se requiere de su Vista
el que en casso que entre a governar el *Reino* sea haviendo logrado
    el
de *d*icha Su me*rc*ed *d*ichas diligençias hizo por si, por auto de
23 de 7setiemb*r*e del año passado de 1697 del qual apele ante Su
Ex*celencia* y *Real* Audiençia dando diferentes petiçiones, y
    alegando no
ser mi Juez Competente, y haver expirado su Jurisdiçion
desde el dia onçe de Agosto que se havia Cumplido el termino
de los treinta dias de mi reçidençia, y no obstante de poder
    absoluto
me hallo presso desde dos de Octub*r*e passado de *d*icho año de 97
    ha-
viendome Vendido mis esclavos, mulas, ropa de mi vestuario,
y de la de mi familia con que me socorrian de afuera pribando
me de que me vean, y vissiten aun hasta los Religiosos y con los
que lo hazen escribe contra ellos a su Provinçial para que los
quite y haga salir de el *Reino* como salen en este mes tres por
*d*icha Razon de conoçer la sinraçon, tirania, y Ynjuztiçia
y assi quedo totalm*en*te perdido sin saver de mi pues una car-

ta me es Ymposible asegurar me lleben, y un mandam*ien*to que
se me notifico en 23 del presente mes del Ex*celentísi*mo se*ño*r
    Virrey
con par*eç*er del *señor* fizcal fue el que diesse fiança por ra-
con de los d*i*chos Capitulos y cargo que podia resultar contra mi de la R*eal* Haz*ien*da y assi mesmo pagase a el d*i*cho
    Govern*ad*or
D*on* Pedro Cubero una escriptura de compromiso de 13500 p*es*os
y d*i*cho mandam*ien*to Vino cometido me lo notificara Un alcalde a lo qual respondi que declinava Jurisdi*ç*ion por hallarme honrrado por Su Mag*es*ta*d* Con las M*e*rc*ed*es de la
    prorroga*ç*ion
deste Gov*ie*rno y Cap*itaní*a Gen*era*l y mas la de Titulo de Castilla
    que Yn-
sitia y reprodu*çi*a las apela*ç*iones por mi hechas e inter-
puestas ante d*i*cho *señor* Ex*celentísi*mo Virrey y d*i*chos
    *señor*es de la Real
junta, y acuerdo de la Audiencia de Mexico, y *señor* fizcal, y hago R*e*la*ç*ion de los d*i*chos mis servicios citando
la Certifica*ç*iones mas en los mandam*ien*tos y Concluyendo que
no se me pidio fiança para la conqu*is*ta que hize a mi costa de
este R*ein*o Gen*era*lm*en*te y sus Pro*vincia*s y se me pide para salir
    del
y por lo que mira al d*i*cho devito de d*i*cha escriptura de compromiso debajo de la d*i*cha declina*ç*ion de Jurisdi*ç*ion recusaba
por Juez a d*i*cho Alcalde ordinario apelando a d*i*cho *señor*
    Ex*celentísi*mo
Virrey y R*eal* Junta, y acuerdo y a el *señor* fizcal donde
oydas mis esepciones, y oydo en Juz*ti*çia como yndefenso en
estas partes estaba prompto como leal vasallo de su Mag*es*ta*d*
[fol. 2r]
a dar la d*i*cha q*uen*ta pues era Ynteresado en ella y recono-
çia a mis Juezes competentes onmnimoda y pribatibam*en*te
a d*i*cho *señor* Ex*celentísi*mo Virrey y d*i*chos *señor*es de
    Tribunal de q*uen*tas Ser so-
lo a quien por la Ley Real de la nueba Recopila*ç*ion
la devia yo dar y d*i*chos *señor*es tomarmela. He hecho
a V*uestra Señorí*a esta vreve rela*ç*ion para que se halle en d*i*cha
Ynteligen*ç*ia por si la parte segun Juzgo de Su
mali*ç*ia se baliere de escribir y dar q*uen*ta en el consejo

para asegurar dicha su Prorrogaçion, y Yo no sentire la
de perder la de este Govierno por su interes sino por el
punto que es el que deve estimar qualquier hombre
de mis obligaciones, y no sera razon que por papelones Sin fundamento y adquiridos con tan siniestros
medios se me perjudiqo y se me haga reo quando
me hallo tan venemerito por dichos mis servicios y
hallarse pendiente el conocimiento de dicha Caussa de dicho
señor Excelentísimo Virrey, y dicha Real Junta, y dicha Parte
haver obrado Con tanta maliçia que retiene en si
la dicha Recidençia que me tomo y a el Justiçia
mayor del Passo que Se cumplio su termino en 28
de Agosto del año passado dicho de 97 ni en una ni
en otra hubo demanda ni Capitulo contra el ni
contra mi, y todo lo dicho y fulminado es nulo por haver sido demas de ser falço passado el
termino de la dicha residençia.

Y bueblo a Repetir a Vuestra Señoría puede Valerse dicho
   Governador de
dicho Su primo Don Alphonso de Buendia para con
un Regalo como el dize, y algunos papelones
ver si puede lograr la dicha Su prorrogaçion
y que la mia se entienda Como la escrito el dicho
su primo ser despues de cumplido dicho tiempo
de dicho Govierno

No escribo a Vuestra Señoría tocante a nada a disposiçion
de mi hazienda sino que socorra Vuestra Señoría a mi hija
Juana Con los dos mil Reales de la renta de
la dehessa de las Gariñas y assi se lo escribo y
me pesa harto el hallarme en esta presion por
no socorrella Como mi amor quisiera y a Dios que
guarde a Vuestra Señoría en Compañía de mi querida hija Ysabel y Nietos por felizes años que deseo
[fol. 2v]
En la flota dandome nuestro señor Vida y a donde fuere su
santissima Voluntad me halle escribire a Vuestra Señoría en la
   fortuna
que me hallare siendo para mi la presente de mas sentimiento

que si me hallara Cautibo en Argel fecha en esta Villa de
Santa fee en 30 de Septiembre de 1698 años

Como no he recibido Carta de Vuestra Señoría en el avisso que
    lle-
go en 11 de Jullio a la Nueva España no se el estado
de dichas mercedes como la resoluçion de la Demominacion
del titulo que tengo escripto a Vuestra sSeñoría de Conde de
Vraçinas Si es la merced de su Magestad de Conde y si es de
Marques de la mesma manera y en la carta que le escribi
a su Magestad desde esta Villa en 16 de octubre del año de 1692
le pido me la haga dandome el señorio de los lugares
de los Caramancheles y assi no obstante que Vuestra Señoría no
    haya he-
cho la pretençion la pondra empractica primero para reconoçer si se podra conseguir y de dezir que solo pagan-
dole a su Magestad dichos lugares la hara y asi ha de ser con
las alcavalas señorio
^Jurisdicion alta y baja^
^2mero y mixto Ymperio^ y mero misto imperio y me abisa-
ra Vuestra Señoría tocante a este punto pues Con la Ynteligençia
    que
le assiste y ya Con los honores de Consejero Real y que goze
de la antiguedad de que le doy la enhorabuena tendra fa-
cilidad el adquirir dicha notiçia avisandome tambien
del pliego que tenia empoder de Don Juan de Albarado ca-
samentos que en el proponia ser de mi deseo para mi hijo
Don Juan Manuel y tambien la otra merced ^2de mi havito de
Santiago en Caso de que no se llogre y la encomienda se permute
    en Una
encomienda de la orden de Santiago aunque sea de Corta Renta y
    no de la
Dicha de los seys mil pesos ^ y Con mi detençion y des-
grasia de mi prision en este Reino me ha embaraçado el ajuste
y remiçion que de lo propuesto o hubiera hecho en la flota, o em persona hubiera sido el portador lo qual a el
presente se me dilatara su execuçion Y le pido a Vuestra Señoría
    en
mi nombre Bese La Mano a su Primo el señor Don Antonio de
    Ubilla y le de la
que le escribo la enhorabuena ofresiendome a su Servicio:

^2B*esa* l*a* M*a*no de V*uestra señoría* su P*a*dre que le estima
y quiere de Corazon y desea servir

D*on* Diego de Vargas Zapata
lujan Ponze de leon^

D*on* Ygnaçio lopez de Zarate
mi hijo y *señor*

---

21. *Diego de Vargas to Isabel María de Vargas*
Pimentel, Santa Fe, 30 September 1698, AMNB, LS.

[fol. 1r]
[cross top center]
Hija mia de mis ojos aunque escribo el
pesame a mi hijo el *señor* D*on* Ygnaçio de la
muerte de el *señor* Marquez de V*illa* Nueva su hermano mi amigo y señor que santa gloria
haya, te la doy a ti pues Reconozco en tus
obligaçiones el Juzto sentim*ien*to de tal
perdida y si acaso vivia mi *señora* la Marqueza en mi nombre y a sus plantas
le Vesso muchas Vezes la daras a su
Señoría el pessame asegurandose me tiene
rendido aunque innutil a su serviçio
que estimava con especial cariño a d*ich*o
señor Marquez, y esta te escribo solo para que en mi nombre des como te repito d*ich*o pessame y me tienes asy tu como
mi querido hijo el *señor* D*on* Ygnaçio y nietos Con Muy Segura Voluntad, y en
la flota dandome N*uestro señor* Vida te escribire mas largo del estado de mi
fortuna y a Dios que te *guarde* hija y
querida mia de mis ojos los feli-
çes años que deseo S*anta* fee y Septiembre 30
de 1698 años

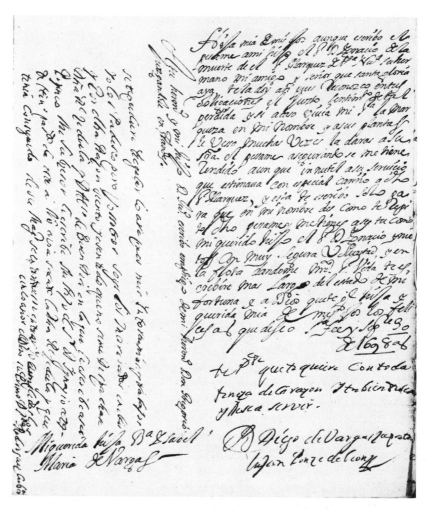

Diego de Vargas to Isabel María de Vargas Pimentel, Santa Fe, 30
September 1698.
 Archivo del Marqués de la Nava de Barcinas, Madrid.

^2tu Padre que te quiere Con toda
fineza de Corazon Y tu bien desea
y Desea servir.

Don Diego de Vargas Zapata
lujan Ponze de leon^

[written vertically in left margin] A tu hermano y mi hijo Don
Juan escribo em pliego de mi hermano Don Gregorio
juzgandole en Flandes.
^2si te pudiere Regalar lo hare pues mis Ynfortunios y trabajos
Yo los Padesco pero Vossotros soys los Interesados en ellos
y Por dicha Razon siento y he sentido que no se me Despachase
dicha Real zedula y Don Alonso de Buen Dia en la que le
   escribe a su
Prymo Mi Subzesor le escribe Mi Hijo el señor Don Ygnazio a 24
de henero pasado de este año No havia sacado la dicha Real zedula
   y que
tenia Conseguido de su Magestad se entendiesse entrar Yo
   Cumplidos los
cinco años el dicho su Primo Don Pedro Rodriguez Cubero^

Mi querida hija Doña Ysabel
Maria de Vargas

---

22. *Diego de Vargas to Ignacio López de Zárate, Santa Fe, 9 October 1698, ARGD, LS.*

[fol. 1r]
[cross top center]
Hyjo y señor mio aunque tengo escripto a Vuestra Señoría
en este mes tocante a que se intenta de parte
de Don Pedro Rodriguez Cubero actual governador deste
Reino desvaneçer la Merced que su Magestad el Rey
nuestro señor que Dios guarde me tiene hecha de su prorrogaçion y si es zierta la Calidad con que su pri-
mo Don Alonso de Buendia Contador del Real

Consejo de Yndias le avissa cuya carta me
remitio ser despues de haver cumplido sus
çinco años entrar Yo al exerçiçio de dicho
govierno y que *Vuestra Señoría* en Veinte y nuebe de henero de
este Año de 98 no tenia aun Sacados mis
despachos me haze fuerça y lo dudo
de Su Cariño de *Vuestra Señoría* a quien pido me
solicite Con empeño mejorarme de
puesto haziendo pretençion en el *govierno* y
Capitania *general* de Buenos ayres que llaman
el Rio de la Plata y en segundo lugar
en el de Panama, y en tercero lugar en
el de la Consepçion del Chile que es *govierno* Ygual a el deste *Reino* y en *quarto* lugar al de la
Ysla de la Habana que esta en el Don Diego de Cordoba y puede *Vuestra Señoría* empeñarse de
el fabor de mi *señora* la Condeza de galbe
por el grande que le mereçi a su *Excelencia* que
este en gloria, y de *Don Juan Manuel* de Vargas
Lodeña Su secre*tario* que fue siendo Virrey
Su *Excelencia* y que el *señor Don* Antonio de Ubilla
Ynfluya Como puede a dicha pretençion
[written vertically in left margin] Se me olvido de pedir a *Vuestra*
   Señoría en primer lugar haga todo empeño en mi pretençion
de la presidencia de Guatimala y empeñe para ello a las dos
   Excelentísimas señoras Virreynas que
han sido del *Reino* de la Nueba España assi mi señora la Condeza
   de paredes que puede *Vuestra Señoría*
con mucha llaneza pedirselo asegurandose de mi selo sabre a su
   grandeza correspon-
der y assimesmo a la dicha mi *señora* Condeza de galbe y si se
   hallare en essa Corte el Señor
Don Pedro de la Vastida que paso de la audiençia de Mexico a la
   de Granada puede dicho
señor haçer espesial informe de mi porque me conoçe
[fol. 1v]
y de mi parte desempeñare a *Vuestra Señoría* de todas maneras en qualquier empeño que hiziere que
pretendo *govier*nos yndependentes de Jurisdiçion de
Un *señor* Virrey Sino de ir a ser absoluto desde

luego sin necesitar de nuebo despacho como
lo nessecitan los que estan debajo de dicha in-
terbençion y nessecitan de nueba pretençion y dilatarles a Vezes el paso de Su
despacho y assi a *Vuestra Señoría* le repito haga dicho
empeño para quitarme la quexa y sentim*ie*nto
Justo que me assiste de remitirme la Noticia de la *Merce*d Sin la Cedula que me escribe
en la de Abril passado de 97 y de dicha notiçia
se me *ha* seguido todo lo que le refiero en la
que escribi en Primero de la *fe*cha desta *Vi*lla a donde Me hallo aun preso en su fuerça del
poder avsoluto del que *govie*rna *guar*de Dios a *Vuestra Señoría*
los felizes a*ño*s que deseo Santa fee y octu*b*re
9 de 1698 años

^2*Besa* l*a* M*an*o de *Vuestra Señoría* su *P*adre que le estima
de Corazon y su bien Desea

*D*on Diego de Vargas Zapata
lujan Ponze de leon^

*se*ñor *D*on Ygnaçio lopez de Zarate Mi hijo.

———

23. *Diego de Vargas to Ignacio López de Zárate, Santa Fe, 11 March 1699,* ARGD, ALS.

[fol. 1r]
[cross top center]
Hijo y S*eño*r mio desde prim*er*o de octubre Pasado de 98 tengo
   escrito a *Vuestra Señoría* el
misero estado de mi fortuna; No le repito *h*a sido la causa Como lo
   fue
su omision de no Remitirme el Despacho de la *Merce*d que su
   Magesta*d* que Di-
os *guar*de me tenia *h*echa de este Govierno; Y Remitirme la
   Notizia, que

Dicha Carta se hubiera perdido fuera para mi y Hubiera sido
   Mejor,
pues mediante de la Dicha Notizia, el Governador actual Don
   Pedro Rodriguez
Cuvero por embarazarme la Dicha Merced Movio, Ynduzio, Y
   Ynsis-
tio, a este Cavildo, Justicia y Rejimento Y el Por si Primero de
   Poder Ab-
soluto me puso Presso en 2 de octubre de 97 y me halle sin saver
quando sera el de mi Redempzion de este Vil Captiverio Dios
se lo perdone a Vuestra Señoría pues he padezido y me hallo
   padeziendo; Y
no se si perdere la Vida, pues Dios Nuestro Señor me ha
   favorezido
Con su Misericordia Ynfinita para Resistir tanta ocasion de
   Perder-
me, Y Presequuzion, Y me hallo ya, Como un Cuerpo Muerto,
   de
Veerme tan sin Amparo Y ni defenssa. y que a ese Passo Vuestra
   Señoría
en los Repetidos avissos Y flota no ha remitido Dicho Despacho;
   An-
tes bien, tubo carta Dicho Governador su fecha en esa Corte de 29
   de he-
nero de 98 de su Primo Don Alonso de Buendia diziendo Vuestra
   Señoría No havia
sacado los Despachos en que acabe de Cognozer Mas bien
mi Corta estrella y mal correspondido mi estimazion Y Affecto
de Vuestra Señoría por su Gran Omission; y Mas Vale Dicho Don
   Alonso le escrivio
que tubo lugar de que su Magestad le Hiziesse la Merced de que se
   entendie-
sse la que a mi me tenia hecha fuesse Despues de Cumplidos
los 5 años, ~~Mediante las Cartas~~ de su Govierno, Dicho Don
   Pedro
Rodriguez Cubero. Y Al presente el Dicho Remite y ocurre a que
su Primo le solizite de su Magestad la Merced de la Prorrogazion
de otros cinco años Mediante las Cartas que Pide por el
a su Magestad el Dicho Cavildo de este Reyno Y a mi me
   calumnia

en ellas Y Remite el testim*oni*o el testim*oni*o de los Autos, y
  Causa
[fol. 1v]
contra mi fulminada valiendose que no se le *h*a dado
  cumplim*ient*o de
Just*ici*a por el Superior G*ovi*erno de Mexico y lo dilatado y que no
  espera en
mucho tiempo se l*e*o den. Y Para que passe D*i*cho Cognozim*ient*o
  a ese
Supremo Consejo de Yndias y la Dilazion de su vista embarazar el tyempo, Y obscurezer mis Serv*ici*os y dar los D*i*chos
  Ynformes
por my *h*echos a su M*ag*esta*d* por siniestros Ynformes Y no por lo
veridico de lo por mi obrado en su R*e*al serv*ici*o. el D*i*cho
  G*o*vern*a*dor
le *h*a dado al D*i*cho cavildo Dos mil p*e*sos que remite por su M*a*no
al D*i*cho D*o*n Al*o*nso y D*i*chos Ynstrumentos, Y mas la firma en
Blanco Para que elija el Procurador que le Pareziere y le de el
Poder y sigua la D*i*cha causa *h*asta que Consigua Y consu-
ma D*i*chos Dos mil p*e*sos. Con D*i*cha Notizia que tube escrivi a Mexico a su Alteza en su Virrey y R*e*al acuerdo y le Pido
me provea de su carta, o Despacho en Preparatorio Juizi-
o, para que Con ella pueda V*uestra* Señor*í*a Pedir y *h*Azer la
  oposizion
a lo siniestro, Nullo Y Malizia de los D*i*chos Ynstrum*ent*os
y que yo tengo executoriados mis serv*ici*os *h*echos a favor de
su M*ag*esta*d* y en Desempeño de su Alteza, escrivo al M*a*estr*e* de
Campo D*o*n luis Saenz de tagle que Solizite D*i*cho Despacho
Y Asimesmo un Ynforme de mi Abogado para que De en
el los Puntos que le Pareziere Y Con esta Carta se la
remita a V*uestra* Señor*í*a a quien Pido saque la Cara; Y lo Prim*e*ro
advierto a V*uestra* Señor*í*a que ante todas Cosas *h*a de Pedir
  afianze
la Calumnia el D*i*cho Procur*a*dor a quien Dieren el Poder Y asimesmo el D*i*cho Al*o*nso de Buendia por D*i*cho cavildo y
G*o*vern*a*dor que lo Ynduze. Y asimesmo las Mil y quinientas Doblas Para la apellazion si se ofreziere *h*azerla Por la Causa
de la Relazion siniestra Y estar Pendiente su Cognozi-
m*ient*o de el Superior Govierno Y tribunal de q*u*entas de la corte de Mexico Asimesmo *h*a de Pedir V*uestra* Señor*í*a Afianzen
  las Costas

[fol. 2r]

Danos Menoscavos de mi Dilatada Prission Y Detenzion Ynteresses Y Agravios en la de mi Persona Creditos Y estimazion; pues los que piden, el Dicho Governador lo haze Por Dicha Malizia de embarazarme el Dicho Govierno Y llograr el fin de sus
Ynteresses Y Convenienzias y la de obscurezer los Dichos
Mis Servicios y el Dicho Cavildo Y el No tyenen bienes Ni
Hazienda Cognozida^equivalente^ que Perder Ni con que Pagar Segun
Derecho Y segun la ley Real deben Dar asi los Unos Como
los otros que Mueben y han Movido Dicho Pleyto las Costas y Daños Y lo demas segun lo Dispuesto Por las Dichas
leyes Reales y estando pendiente de el Superior Govierno y
Real Junta de Mexico de Donde Dimanaron todos los Mandamientos y ordenes que en ellos Consta Y estas Repetidas a su Magestad en su Supremo Consejo las Recomendaziones de mi Persona y tenerse las experienzias de lo que Yo le he servido No
solo en este Govierno sino en la Alcaldia Mayor de tlalpujagua Como consta por carta de el año de 85 de el excelentísimo señor
Virrey que fue Conde de Paredes y las de el excelentísimo Señor Virrey
que fue Conde de Galve y que no supone la de la Mali-
zia de Dicho Cavildo pues No consta Dicho Governador Don Pedro
Rodriguez Cuvero a su Magestad servido en este Reyno que Antes ha estado en henero de 98, y en Septiembre de Dicho año de
98, Para los Yndios Alzarse Y la Nazion Apache hA-
verla en Diferentes lunas Rovado mas de 460 Bestias Mulares y Cavallares Y Demas las Muertes Y Heri-
dos en los Nuestros sin haver Dicho Governador salido ni Remitido
a sus Soldados Como Debia hazerles Guerra; Que el Dicho
Cavildo se Compone de Una Jente de unas obligaziones muy
viles Y ofizios Mecanicos de Sastres Zapatero Y lacayo Jente

[fol. 2v]

Pobre y Ynfirma. Y Por Coechos Dadivas y Promessas Y
haverles en terzero años Reelecto en sus ofizios Ynduzidos de Dicho

Governador haze y Remite Dichas Cartas escriptas por el y su secretario que tambien tiene las tachas De Delinquente sin que
ellos Ni con Consentimiento de la Vezindad, que suponen Pedir las Remitan y que el Padre Ayeta Procurador General de toda
la Provincia de el Santo evanjelio de Mexico de Nuestro
    Padre San francisco que
asiste en el de esa Corte Dira la Calidad, Baja de esta
jente Y hechos A jurar falsso Y Prejurarsse por Un cabrito
y de Muy Malas Calidades y Peores Prozederes, Y A Dios que Guarde a Vuestra Señoría y a mi Hija Ysabel Y Nietos
    echo Mi Ben-
dizion que no se si los vere Ya que la fortuna Y Ynfeliz de mi Suerte me ha puesto en este Misero estado
sin haverme sido de Provecho la Merced que Vuestra Señoría tan
    Ufano
me Dio Notizia para perderme. A mi querido Hijo
Don Juan Manuel que tengan esta por suya Y a todos los Demas
que hasta el Papel me han quitado Y este tenia un libro. My tes-
    ˆ72ˆ tamento otorgue en esa Corte el Mes De Junio de 72, Ante
    Matheo
de Malavear escrivano Real que tenia su ofizio en la Calle
de toledo Y lo era del Colejio Ymperial de la Compañía de Jesus
Aviso a Vuestra Señoría, esto por sy Dios Dispusiere de my que
    estoy
en tyerra Sin Remedio y he tenido Muchos achaques que su
    Divina
Misericordia Me ha dado salud sin Curazion Guarde Dios a
    Vuestra Señoría
felizes años Santa fee y Marzo 11 de 1699 años

Besa la Mano de Vuestra Señoría Su Padre aunque Ynfeliz
que le estima

Don Diego de Vargas Zapata lujan
Ponze de leon

[written vertically in left margin] En esa Corte estara el señor
    Don Pedro de la Bastida que Paso Con el señor Conde de Galve
    y su Secretario Don Juan Manuel de

Vargas lodena que saben Mi Desinteres que la Conquista a mi
    Costa la Salida y el Salir a los Reynos de la
Galizia y Viscaya Y no se me Dio ayuda de Costa ni la pedi
    aunque se me ofrezio ni Merced Ninguna,
y que no se Dio queja de mi Ninguna

Señor Don Ygnazio lopez de Zarate

———

24. *Luis Sáenz de Tagle to Ignacio López de Zárate, Mexico City, 11 July 1699, AMNB, LS.*

[fol. 1r]
Señor mio En la flota de Don Juan
de la calzadilla escrevi a *V*uestra señoría Y le
Remiti Unos autos Pertenezientes al Señor
Don Diego de Bargas Su Suegro Y di
orden a Don Fausto de Busttamante Vezino
de la Çiudad de cadiz Remitiera A *V*uestra Señoría
quatro mil pesos Y en la flota que salio el año
de 96 entregue a Don Amadeo Ysidro Seol
Maiordomo del Señor Conde de Galves
Seis mil pesos en Birtud del Poder
que *V*uestra señoría le dio Y con *h*aver benido a este
Reino flota por Septiembre de 98 Y *h*aver entrado
En este Reino aviso a 22 de Junio no le
*h*e merezido A *V*uestra señoría Respuesta Y por no
faltar a la antigua amistad que *h*e tenido
Con El señor Don Diego de Bargas
le Partizipo A *V*uestra señoría que se halla *h*oy En
El nuebo Mexico detenido por El Governador
*h*abiendo dado Residenzia Y todo este quento se
*h*a Reduzido a lo que Subzede muchos años a
a que ttengan este Pago Los que conquistan.

El Governador Como bio o tubo notizia que le *h*avia de
Subzeder dicho señor Don Diego Conmobio
a que todos los que *h*abran Jurado Se desdigeran

diziendo que lo que Constava por Su Juramento
habia sido por que habia de Volver al
[fol. 1v]
Govierno Y pusieron demandas Sinies-
tras Y todos Los mas que han Jurado a
muchos años que estan declarados por
testigos falsos Segun Las bozes de
aquellas Provinzias Y biendo este negozio
En este estado me preziso a meter Un
Memorial pidiendo Se le conzediera que
dicho Don Diego de Bargas Compa-
deziese En esa Corte a defenderse de
las Calunias Y ofrezi fianza no quiso El
Señor Birrey ni El señor fiscal Sino
que havra de Afianzar todas Las Calunias
y todos los enRedos no me hallo En
Paraje de Poder hazer esta fianza
Y para que esto pueda tener Remedio Y
Se salga de estos Cuidados es nezesario que
Vuestra señoría Enbie Una Zedula para que El
Señor Don Diego de Bargas Compadezca
En esta Corte Y puede traer Exspresa-
do que de fianza de su Persona que
Si Vuestra señoría hubiera Enbiado hoy haze tres
años La Prorrogazión le hubiera Sido
de Nueba Combenienzia Y a todos
Sus hijos Este ha sido desCuydo Y
El buen Caballero esta Padeziendo Y yo he pasado mis Sinsavores Ron-
piendo Con todos Y los pasare por
defender al señor Don Diego
Es Ynfelizidad de todos los que
obran bien en estos tiempos quiere
lo Dios asi Cumplase Su
boluntad En Todo y estamos
[fol. 2r]
tan Yndefensos de Papeles por que
no hay Persona Segura Con quien poder
Escribir El señor Don Diego ni yo me
atrevo por que Don Pedro Rodriguez Cu-

bero tiene Cogido todo Los Puertos y los
Religiosos de San francisco que no son de
Su Sequito Los ba destterrando de aquel
Reino Con Ynformes Siniestros al comisario
General dicho Don Pedro Rodriguez Cubero
ha sido por aca muy favorezido esta es
la notizia que puedo dar Y Respecto de Ser
Este negozio tan Propio tengo presente
la memoria Vuestra señoría asi Y quedo a Su serbizio
Y pido a Dios me le guarde muchos años
Mexico Y Julio 11 de 1699 años

Vesa la mano de Vuestra Señoría su menor servidor

Luis Saenz de tagle

Señor Don Ygnazio Lopez de Zarate

---

25. *Juan Manuel de Vargas Pimentel to Ignacio López de Zárate, Mexico City, 2 November 1699, ARGD, ALS.*

[fol. 1r]
[cross top center]
Hermano Y Amigo de mi Vida. aunque de
priesa no puedo dejar de Solicitarte muy
buena Salud, que me alegrare sea muy
Cumplida, y que le suceda lo mismo a mi
querida, Hermana y sovrinos a quienes habra-
Caras mucho. la mia es buena para Ser-
virte Como no puedes dudar de mi Cariño.
Despues de haver tenido muy mal via-
je desde la Veracruz a Mexico entre
Con Clamores en dicha ziudad y asi Son los
Sucesos. aunque lo principal es que mi
Padre esta bueno, preso un año ha

y muy atropellado, de lo que *ha* de ser
preciso tomar yo una gran Satisfazion
del G*overnad*or Don Pedro Cubero. Todo esto le
Suzede a mi Padre p*o*r tu omision, de
no *h*aver ymbiado Con tiempo los des-
pachos de la Prorrog*ac*ion del G*o*vi*er*no y a q*u*ie*n*
te Culpan todos y principalm*ent*e Don
Luys Saenz de tagle que esta muy quejoso de que no le *h*as Respondido en fin
Herm*an*o mio yo *h*allo a mi Padre Pov*r*e
[fol. 1v]
y Preso, lo que te Sup*l*ico es que ya que no se dis-
currio en Sacar M*er*ced de su M*a*gestad que en
caso de faltar mi Padre antes de entrar
en el G*o*vi*er*no Sirva p*ar*a mi la Prorrog*ac*ion
en aten*ç*ion de los Ser*v*i*c*ios de uno, y otro esto no es Con la mira de quedarme Si Solo
de que en tres a*ñ*os que faltan no savemos
lo que puede Suceder, y teniendo yo esa m*er*c*e*d
podre beneficiar el G*o*vi*er*no p*ar*a adquirir
algunas Comb*en*i*en*cias te encargo no lo dejes
de *h*a*ç*er, y Remitir los Despachos en el primer aviso

Al S*eñ*or Conde de Montezuma le bere ma-
ñana, y el no *h*averlo *h*echo *h*oy *h*a sido el motivo de estar ocupado en el Despacho
de los Cajones.

Un Colejial Hijo de mi Padre me vino
a ver, tan grande, Como yo y muy pare-
*ç*ido, *h*ay otro pequeño, y su Madre me ymbio la vien Venida y a ofre*ç*er su Casa pero yo no la Vere.

A todos los Parientes daras mis finas
mem*or*ias que el no escrivir es p*o*r no
*h*aver lugar, y a toda la familia m*i*s
Recados y la mia supone a t:? P:? y Gar-
cia le tengo vien malo.

A mi Herm*a*na y Sovrinos m*u*ch*o*s abrazos
[fol. 2r]
y en Comp*añía* de todos deseo te g*uar*de n*u*est*ro*
S*eñor* Herm*a*no y Amigo de mi vida los m*u*ch*o*s
a*ño*s que puede y he m*e*n*e*st*e*r Mexico y N*o*v*i*emb*re*
2 de 99
Su Herm*a*no y Amigo de
Corazon *h*asta morir

Vargas

Mi Herm*a*no Don Y*gnacio*

---

26. *Diego de Vargas to Isabel María de Vargas
Pimentel, Mexico City, 20 March 1701, AMNB, LS.*

[fol. 1r]
Hija mia de mi Corazon Rez*i*bo
la tuya de nov*i*emb*re* pasado y Con ella
el gusto de saver de tu salud Y
del feliz Suzeso de tu Parto sintiendo la muerte de mi Nieto Yo
quedo gracias a n*u*est*ro* Señor en
esta Ciudad de Mexico
desde fin de Oct*u*b*re* pasado en
en el ajuste de mis quentas y demas dependen*zi*as cuyo dilatado
t*i*empo i interbalo me *h*a tenido
Con bastante penalidad cuya ponderazion no cabe lo que *h*e padezido Y por que en la Flota remitire a mi Hijo Y con el te
regalare omito, y lo dejo a su
[fol. 1v]
relazion, Rezibo la de tu Esposo
el Señor Don Y*gnacio* y mi Hijo que me admira de que no se acuer-

de de Carta a carta lo que Escribe Escuso mi sentimiento, y
solo paso a dezirte me tienes de
Corazon para servirte en quanto Valiere deseando te Guarde
Nuestro Señor en compañia de
mis queridos Nietos Felizes
años Mexico y Marzo 20 de 1701 años

^2tu Padre que te quiere
de Corazon Y mas te estima

el Marques de la Naba
de Brazinas^

Mi querida Hija y Señora doña Ysabel
Maria de Vargas

---

27. *Diego de Vargas to Ignacio López de Zárate, Mexico City, 25 March 1701, AMNB, LS.*

[fol. 1r]
[cross top center]
Hijo Y Señor mio Rezibo Su carta
de Vuestra Señoría de 9 noviembre del año pasado Y la de
mi querida Hija hallandome en esta
Ciudad de Mexico que fue nuestro Señor
Servido entrase en ella el dia 30 de octubre del dicho ano de 700 Y luego pase
a la presenzia de su Excelencia quien me rezibio
Con estimazion prometiendome favore-
zeria en todo Y me tendre por muy
dichoso Se me de Satisfazion en Justizia al manifiesto de agrabios
que por el traslado del Memorial
que presento Y remito a Vuestra Señoría
pido Se me asista.

Mi Residencia se vio por el Señor Fiscal
y Asessor General y ambos dizen me
debe Su Excelencia declarar por buen
Juez dando por nulos los Capitulos
[fol. 1v]
Puestos por la malizia Y poder
adsoluto de mi Subzesor Y ser demas de eso pasado el termino de la dicha
residencia Y en la flota despachare el
testimonio que tengo pedido y se me diere.

Remito a Vuestra Señoría (con este primer duplicado que lleba el Capitán de este aviso) el
que pedi de la eleccion que hize de titulo en atenzion de haver presentado
mi Zedula de merced de Marqués
o conde en castilla, Y en atenzion de
dejar su Magestad a mi deliberazion
la que eligiese lo hize Como Vera
Vuestra Señoría por dicho Testimonio del Memorial que
para ello presente a dicho Señor Excelentísimo
Virrey declarandome como vera
Vuestra Señoría por su decreto de 18 de diziembre
pasado por tal Titulo de Mar-
ques de la Nava de Brazinas
que Vuestra Señoría debiera a fuer de sus o-
bligaciones con su hermano Y mi querido
hijo don Juan Manuel haverme remitido los despaços pagando la media anata
[fol. 2r]
haviendo Servido yo a su Magestad
en dicho Govierno y Capitania General de donde me haze asimesmo merced me deno-
mine Conquistador Y pazificador me hallo
relebado como me relebaran de pagar
las lanzas, y con los medios que
rezivio mios para ello Vuestra Señoría pudo
Con menos de la mitad que rezibio
haver pagado la dicha media anata
y haverme remitido el Real titulo

de merced Y demas despachos y dejar en blanco el que yo eligiese demas que ya tenia adbertido a *Vuestra Señoria*
fuese la denominazion de la Naba
de Brazinas en caso de no haver ni
alcanzar con dichos medios para el
ajuste Y valor de los dos lugares
de los Caramancheles donde era
mi intenzion haviendoseme frustrado
y desvanezido una porzion tan luzi-
da y tan a tiempo malogrado demas los intereses que me tubieron
tan crezido la dicha remision

Asimesmo menos *Vuestra Señoria* me da razon Y
se da por desentendido de la que le pedi
[fol. 2v]
Y Señale me remitiese Siendo así
que me la promete me la remitiria
por la Carta de Abril y año pas-
ado de 700 admirandome conmigo *Vuestra señoria*
tal falta pues si yo fuera algun ta-
banito que andubiera enseñando Cartas me ponia a la Zensura y irri-
sion que se deja entender Y mas
bale que *Vuestra Señoria* me hable claro en respuesta de esta para Vivir con el
desengaño de hallarse *Vuestra Señoria* embarazado.

No menos fue de poca Considerazion el
dejar que para aviarse mi hijo
haverme hiziese el empeño de la
renta de los Caramancheles quando se
hallaba haver rezivido *Vuestra Señoria* dicha porzion

Tanbien fue sobrada resoluzion la de que mi
hijo Se viniese Sin traher algu-
na merced pues se debia reconozer me
hallaba, no en Mexico, Sino
preso Y detenido en un Reino tan

distante de 500 leguas adentro, de
tierra de riesgo Y de Guerra, de
[fol. 3r]
detenido en el por su Governador mi
enemigo Capital y sin tener mas
que el miserable estado de mi mala
fortuna fue inadbertenzia Se viniese
Como repito dicho mi hijo Sin alguna
merced la que me trujo de la encomienda
de los 4000 pesos le tengo hecha la Zesion
del tiempo. de mi vida Segun Su Magestad
me la conzedio, Comitido la presentazion
de la Real çedula de razon de Estado
por que no con dicha Ocasion mi subzesor no me inquietase los Yndios Y
digan Se han alzado y asi mas he querido perder que no ponerme al riesgo
del accidente que la Malignidad del que
Govierna podia influyr.

Mediante los Creditos que tengo Grazias
a nuestro Señor, hE podido asistir a los enpeños que el dicho mi hijo contrajo desde
España hasta el dia 30 que entre como
refiero Y no le ha faltado el porte dezente
de su persona no se lo que sera de la mia
siendo fija de mi parte la resoluzion de
remitirle en la flota.

Yo quedo dando mis quentas Y siguiendo
mis demandas nuestro Senor me favorezca
[fol. 3v]
que En este Reino pende de muchos
qualquiera negozio.

Me pareze su Magestad que Dios guarde
el Señor Phelipe quinto confirmara las
Mercedes que dejo hechas el Señor don Carlos segundo nuestro Rey que Santa Gloria
haya y que no sera menester hazer pa-

ra ello representazion quando ese Juzgo sera su declarazion por su Real Cedula General a consulta de su Suppremo Y
Real Consejo de Camara de Yndias
pero no me pareze dejar de pedir
a Vuestra Señoría que si al tiempo que rezibe esta no se ha tomado dicha resoluzion Y con-
siguientemente remision de ella en el
aviso que se espera se presente Memorial en mi nombre sacando el testimonio de dicha Real Cedula de merced
en caso nezesario Y pidiendo en el a su
Magestad la confirmazion de su Real voluntad según se expresa en la de la su-
sodicha merced en que el Rey nuestro
Señor que fue y Santa Gloria haya
me la hizo según el despacho de diez y o-
cho de Junio del año de 88 Y asi
se reconoze fue integramente de todo el
Reino Y Provincias de la nueba Mexico
[fol. 4r]
Y no haviendo dibidido como al presente
lo esta la Compania del Presidio del Paso
y el de su Govierno politico Y militar Cuyos in-
convenientes Son de mucho reparo por no
tenerlos a la de dicho Govierno de la nueba Mexico
a su disposizion Y manejo pues dibididas dichas
Fuerzas no serviran las del Paso al tiempo
de la Ocasion que lo pidiere al Nuebo
Mexico ni las del Nuebo Mexico
sin estas tendran mobimento Y asi Sus
armas de uno y otro Presidio y sus
Gentes no hallandose debajo del mando
y Capitán General de la Nueba Mexico Seran
sus operaziones ningunas en el Real servicio
sin adelantar lo mucho que en dicho Reino tan dilatado se nezesita Continuo mobimiento en
Campaña, otras muchas razones hay que
omito por no ser molesto Y asi dicho
Despacho adbierto a Vuestra Señoría y le

Encargo mucho Se me remita con distin-
zion supuesto que en el que tengo su
Magestad me hizo la merced de restituyrme
y prorrogarme Según refiero integramente
se pida se declare me haze la dicha merced
asi del Presidio del Pueblo del Paso
del Rio del Norte la de sus Pueblos y Fronteras Su Govierno politico Y militar que pueda
[fol. 4v]
Nombrar en ellos Su Justizia offiziales de
Guerra y Capitán de su Presidio Como asimesmo en dicha Villa de santa fee Y en la
forma del tiempo que la governe Y se
la entregue a don Pedro Rodriguez
Cubero mi subzesor en dos de Julio del
año de 97 que tomo posesion, Y dicha Real
cedula venga en dicha forma para que
la Execute sin poner embarazo el Excelentísimo
Señor virrey que es o fuere de este Reino
de la Nueba España entendiendose que
dar dicha Compañia de dicho Presidio
del Pueblo del Paso en el todo a carga
y del cargo de dicho Governador de la Nueba
Mexico para poner por si El que le pareziere por su quenta Y riesgo.

Me prometo que tocante a este Punto habra
hecho Vuestra Señoría dicha pretension pues mi hijo adbertidamente en la flota hizo la de
que se pidiese Y representase nuebamente
a su Magestad aun sin el reparo de ser
integramente la merced hecha Según Se expresa y consta por dicha Real Zedula
que me hizo favor de remitirme mi
Hermano el Marqués de la florida Y asimesmo las demas ultimamente la de la
Real Provision en que se me comete tome la
residencia a mi subzesor que reconozera tanbien
[fol. 5r]
Vuestra Señoría Si sera menester nuebo despacho
sacandome repetidos Y con el encargo

por ninguna razon por dicho Señor Excelentísimo
Virrey que es o fuere Se le retarde su
cumplimiento pues me remito a la que
El dicho mi hijo Escribio en dicha flota
pues me hallare perdido de ponerme
embarazo de entrar luego al Exerzi-
zio de dicho Govierno haviendo salido de el Y
de mi Prision debajo del Juramento que
se me rezibio y hize el pleyto home-
naje de no salir de todo el Reino de la
nueba España Sin primero haber ajustado Y dado satisfazion de qualesquiera
alcanzes que podian resultar a favor de su Magestad de la quenta que
fue de mi Cargo teniendo embarazado por esta razon de lo que pudiera valerme Sin poder darseme satisfazion haviendo pasado ya quatro
años de vacante Y con los gastos del
pleyto dejo al discurso de Vuestra Señoría
El misero Estado en que me puedo
hallar.

Vuestra Señoría Obre en todo lo que le refiero en esta lo
que mas su punto le hiziere fuerza
y reconozca quanto mi cariño le ha serbido
[fol. 5v]
Sintiendo el estado en que me hallo para Estreçharlo a los terminos de
esta justa recombenzion mia, Y se ali-
ente al desempeño que pide Su debida
Obligacion en el cumplimiento Y fin de mi deseo Y voluntad de lo que le tengo
pedido, Y pido que fue la Causa de la
remision de dicho Socorro que si quando
le rezibio Se valio de el, hallandose
Vuestra Señoría en la mejora de fortuna Y puesto de que le doy la enhorabuena le sera
fazil el executar Su empleo En lo que
deseo Y sabe mi intenzion Y asi me prometo en la primera Ocasion merezerle

en el todo dichos despaços pues no
me negare a servir a *Vuestra Señoría* si
Volbiere a restaurarme En mi fortuna.

Doy por bien a *Vuestra Señoría* el que mi Hermano y
amigo el Marques de la florida viva
el quarto según *Vuestra Señoría* le tiene acomodado
y he sentido el que no tenga muy corriente
Su sueldo espero en nuestro Señor le
merezeran al Rey nuestro Señor que dios
guarde toda atenzion Sus Servicios

El dador de esta que lleba El aviso
Es hermano de un Criado de su
Excelencia
[fol. 6r]
de los que asisten e su Señoría Y asi en sus
pretensiones Si ocurriere a *Vuestra Señoría* le atendera Con toda Estimazion no olbidando
la pretension de la Canongia de don Sebastian Altamirano de Castilla
cuyos quinientos pesos rezibio *Vuestra Señoría*
y asi le hago este recuerdo por el
mucho tiempo Y no darseme por
Entendido Como en lo demas.

A Su Hermana de *Vuestra Señoría* mi Hija
doña Joana se le deje Cobre por si la
renta de los dos mill *Reales* de la *d*Edhesa
de las Gariñas que me escribio *Vuestra Señoría*
se la embarazaba o dilataban Y
su nezesidad pide mucha puntualidad

Tambien le dara *Vuestra Señoría* luego a mi hermana Doña Antonia de Vargas qui-
nientos *Reales* para socorro de sus
nezesidades Y nuestro Señor
me da Vida para amparar a todos los mios pues el no reparar

en trabajos es esa la Causa
y a Dios que *Guar*de a V*uestra Señoría*
en compañia de mi querida Hija
Ysabel Y nietos a q*ui*e*n*es heçho
[fol. 6v]
mi Vendi*z*ion los Felizes años
que deseo Mexico Y Marzo
25 de 1701 años

^2Repito a V*uestra señoría* le estimare me Remita
los Despachos *p*ara Ponerme el *h*Avito
y el de la m*er*c*e*d de titulo en Virtud
de el testim*on*io que Remito de su eleccion que Puede ser Mi fortuna
la Restaure Y me *h*alle V*uestra Señoría* Con la
fineza que siempre Con Cariño le
*h*e estimado y le estimo.

B*e*sa l*a* M*an*o de V*uestra señoría* Su P*a*dre que
le estima y Besa su M*an*o
y Seguro S*er*vidor

el Marques de la Naba
de Brazinas ^

Mi Hijo Y S*eñ*or don Y*gn*a*c*io Lopez de Zarate

_____

28. *Juan Manuel de Vargas Pimentel to Ignacio*
López de Zárate, Mexico City, 7 April 1701, AMNB,
ALS.

[fol. 1r]
Herm*an*o y Amigo de mi Vida doi respuesta a dos tuias que recivi en el aviso
que llego a este Reyno a 8 de Marzo
Su fecha de 17 de n*ov*iemb*r*e y 3 de X*diciemb*re y a otra
que llego por el registro de Campeche

de 22 de Avril y en todas enquentro
las favorables notiçias de mantener-
te Con la Caval Salud que mi Cariño te desea, quedando la mia para
Servirte buena y Con la ympaçien-
cia de no Salir quanto antes de este
reyno, y aunque gracias a Dios logre
el fin tan deseado, a que pase de
Conoçer a mi Padre, que llego a esta Ziudad el dia 29 de octubre tan bueno que se quedaron admirados
los que le Conoçian pues los trabajos que ha pasado eran motivo para
haverlo echado a la Sepoltura, nuestra
primer vista fue a 3 leguas de
aqui y se quedo tan absorto al
verme que en mucho rato no
me hablo palavra, a otro dia fue
a ver al Virrey quien le hyço muchos
agasajos falsos como acostumbra
no me dilato en esta por estar
de prisa el Capitán del Pliego
[fol. 1v]
Don Juan Diaz del Campo, por Cuia mano
ba; Solo dire que la muerte de
nuestro Rey Causo gran dolor pero
despues entro el Consuelo Savien-
dolo vien dispuesto que quedo todo, el dia 4 del Corriente se hyzo
la funzion de la Jura Con la mayor
Grandeza y Solemnidad; que
aun en esa Corte; primero se
Publicaron los lutos y ahora se
hazen las honrras, y Con estos Cuidados no se habla, de que se baya
esta flota, en la qual Siendo Dios
Servido espero Volver a España
aunque peor que vine llevo el
Consuelo de haver Conozido a mi
Padre, y el no pasar Su merced Conmigo es la razon hallarse precisa-

do a Volver a Su Govierno por Su
Punto, ya que este Cavallero ha dado
lugar a tantas maldades Cono-
zidas de todos los ministros y no
remediadas, por que terçia el ynteres, que es quien lo puede todo.

A todos los Parientes daras mis
finas memorias y a mi querida Hermana y Sovrinos muchos avrazos y
a toda la familia recados de
mi Parte y tambien quando
escrivas a torrelaguna se los ym-
[fol. 2r]
biaras, y a todos los Amigos que de cada uno de por Si quisiera Signifi-
car mi buena Ley, espero en nuestro
Señor lo hare en persona, y en el ynterin ruego a Su Divina Magestad te guarde
Hermano y Amigo de mi vida los muchos
años que puede deseo y he menester Mexico
y Avril 7 de 1701

Tu Hermano y mayor Amigo
de Corazon hasta morir

Don Juan Manuel de
Vargas Pimentel

Mi Hermano y Amigo Don Ygnacio Lopez de Zarate.

---

29. *Diego de Vargas to Ignacio López de Zárate,
Mexico City, 3 May 1701, ARGD, LS.*

[fol. 1r]
[cross top center]
Hijo Y señor mio hoy me dizen se zierra
el pliego que lleba este aviso y aunque

tengo escrito a V*uestra Señoría* por duplicado
no permite mi afecto El repetirlo
y darle la notizia de las dos que le tengo Escritas deseando que lleguen
a manos de V*uestra Señoría* Y le hallen Con la
Salud que le deseo Y a mi querida
Hija Ysabel Y Nietos quedando
Con ella *Gracias* a n*uestro* se*ñor* Y mi Hijo
Y Herm*ano* de V*uestra Señoría* y Con vivos deseos
llegue el aviso que se Espera con las
notiz*ias* de la entrada y feliz Posesion del serenisimo Senor n*uestro*
Rey Phelipe quinto que Dios
gu*ar*de Me prometo V*uestra Señoría* con sus Grandes oblig*aciones* me remitira los despachos q*ue* me tiene avisado desde
Abril pasado de 700 Y con ellos
logre El de mi deseo y no dudo tanbien me remitira los que nuebamente fueren prezisos para En-
[fol. 1v]
trar Siendo n*uestro* Se*ñor* Servido en el empleo del Gov*ierno* de q*ue*
me dejo heçha M*erced* El se*ñor* n*uestro*
Rey que fue Carlos Segundo de
Gloriosa memoria Y asi de ellos
como de los de la R*eal* Provis*ion* para
tomar la Resid*encia* a mi Subzesor
don Pedro Rodriguez Cubero Es-
pero me remita V*uestra Señoría* confirmazion
en caso que fuere nezesario por el nuebo accidente Y entrada del Rey
n*uestro* Senor en la subzesion de la
Corona que en este R*eino* aun con
todas estas prebenz*iones* son menester las de otros pasos particula-
res y pensiones que dejo al dis-
curso de V*uestra Señoría* a q*uie*n tambien tengo escripto *h*aberse visto mi
Resid*encia* Y declaradome por buen

Juez *h*aviendose conformado
con los dos Parezeres de los dos
Se*ñ*ores fiscales Y el de su Asesor G*e*ner*a*l
tambien quedo dando mis qu*e*ntas
En su R*ea*l Tribunal Y audi-
enzia de ellas, remito a V*uestra Señoría*
En el primer duplicado El testimonio de la Elec*ci*on que hize de
[fol. 2r]
la M*e*rc*e*d de Titulo de castilla *h*aviendo presentado la R*ea*l
çedula a su Ex*celenci*a con Memori*a*l
mediante el *h*aver prezedido
*h*aver mandado a su S*e*cret*a*rio de
Camara me hiziese notoria
con la que se hallaba de su
Ma*g*esta*d* en que le daba d*i*cha
not*ici*a Y asi hize Y eligi la
de Marques de la Naba
de Brazinas del Mayo-
razgo que poseo en Granada
que me pareze don Diego de
Oblera, *h*abra dejado compuesto
Con los un mill p*e*sos que mi hijo
le dio En Sevilla los quales
pague En esta Ciud*a*d a la persona a cuyo fabor otorgo su
Escriptura Juzgo tendra me-
jor Corri*e*nte con d*i*cho reparo d*i*cha
Haz*i*enda Y si se consiguio el de
su Presa mediante la Porzion
que estaba en poder de Gabriel
Ruyz thesorero que fue de la
Cruzada de d*i*cho R*ei*no que era
de mas de diez y siete mill
R*ea*l*es* de Vellon Y asi V*uestra Señoría* me
[fol. 2v]
dara razon de el estado en que
se hallare esta Haz*i*enda Y prosigu*i*endo
a la del testim*o*nio que remito a V*uestra Señoría*

de dicha Eleccion de Titulo Y su Excelencia
dicho señor Excelentísimo Virrey Conde de Montezuma por su decrepto de 18 de
diziembre pasado por lo que asi toca
declararme por tal titulo Y lo
demas que Consta se servira
Vuestra Señoría con vista de dicho testimonio
presentarlo luego Y ajustar
El entero de la media anata
cuyo Real derecho el que fuere
satisfara Vuestra Señoría de los efectos Y porzion que rezivio de mi quenta
En el ano de 99 Y por lo que mira
a lo que se paga de Lanzas
me hallo libre por el empleo servido
de Governador Y Capitán General Y me hara
Expezial favor Y gusto en remitirme El Real titulo Y Cedula de tal titulo con el Sello Real
y en la forma que se acostumbra
en la primera ocasion avisando-
me Vuestra Señoría de la del rezivo de esta
con las que En ella repito le remito
[fol. 3r]
Y deseo Juntamente nuestro señor guarde la persona de Vuestra Señoría felizes años en compañia de mi querida Hija Ysabel
y Nietos a quien hecho mi vendizion
y dara Vuestra Señoría muchos Abrazos y memorias de Corazon fecha en Mexico
En 3 de Mayo de 1701 años
A mi Hermano Y amigo El Marqués de la florida
beso la mano Con todo afecto y le tengo
Escripto por duplicado en los dos que refiero En esta que deseare lleguen a sus
manos, Y le hallen Con buena Salud

Besa la Mano de Vuestra Señoría su Mas
Affecto Padre y Servidor
que le estima

^2el Marques de la Naba
de Brazinas^

Mi Hijo Y señor don Ygnacio Lopez de Zarate.

———

30. *Diego de Vargas to Ignacio López de Zárate,*
Mexico City, 23 July 1701, AMNB, LS.

[fol. 1r]
[cross top center]
Hijo Y Señor mio estimare que el aviso
llegase a ese Reino y por la que en el Escribi a *Vuestra Señoría h*abra reconozido lo que me *ha*
parezido sentir En el todo que en esta
a *Vuestra Señoría* repito la de su recombenzión prometiendome de sus obligaz*iones* le ha-
ran fuerza las razones de tanta
Justificaz*ión* para haver puesto su
desempeño En Execuz*ión* los despaç*h*os
de la merced de titulo Cuyo testim*onio*
de su Eleccion incluso en el la *R*eal
çedula le remiti para que con su
Vista ajustase el entero de la
media anata que pretendieron se
le pagase En esa Corte y de lo demas
que a *Vuestra Señoría* tengo pedido y me aviso
en Carta de Abril del año de 99.

Escribo a mi querida Hija Doña Ysabel a cuyo contesto Entendido por
[fol. 1v]
Vuestra Señoría no faltara sirviendo esta de aviso
Juntamente de la remision de tres Caxo-
nes de chocolate que el uno entregara a *Vuestra Señoría*
a la d*i*cha mi Hija para que En su compa-
ñia y la de mis queridos nietos beba y el
Otro entregara *Vuestra Señoría* a mi Herm*a*no el Marqués

de la florida y el otro remitira *Vuestra Señoría* con ese
pliego a torrelaguna a mi Hija Doña Juana
de Vargas para que Execute lo que la
ordeno En la que le Escribo, todos dichos
tres Caxones pondra El *Capitán* don fausto de Bustamante *Cavallero* del orden
de Santiago y *Vezino* de la Ciudad de
Cadiz que pondra y remitira haviendo pagado todos sus *derechos* y el
de su conduccion hasta Esa Corte
de suerte que no tenga a *Vuestra Señoría* mas
que la de mandar rezivirlos y asimesmo le pondra una libranza de
cinquenta pesos que remitira o entregara a la Persona que mi Hermana Doña Antonia de Vargas di-
jiere En la que le Escribo.

El Poder que remito para mi pretension y el segundo duplicado del testimonio de la Eleccion de titulo
[fol. 2r]
Con *dicho* don Fausto remito a *Vuestra Señoría*
que despachara *dicho* pliego luego
que llegue a *dicha* su Casa En *dicha* Ciudad de Cadiz y los offizios que se *ha* de
hazer pretension son los *siguientes* para
que *Vuestra Señoría* con su notizia adelante
el *tiempo* En el que se dilatare En llegar *dicho* Poder.

Primera*mente* el Govie*rno* y Capitania gene*ral* del *Reino* de Guatemala y Presidente de su *Real* Aud*iencia*.

En segu*ndo* lugar el Govie*rno* y Capitania gene*ral* de *Santa*
fee de gogotan y Presidente de su *Real* Aud*iencia*
del Nuebo *Reino* de Granada.

En terzero el Govie*rno* y Capitania gene*ral*

del Reino de chile y Presidente de su Real
Audiencia.

El Govierno Y Capitania general del Reino de
buenos Ayres y Rio de la Plata.
El govierno y Capitania general del Reino y Ys-
las Philipinas y Presidente de su Real Audiencia

Y de no conseguirse uno de los Cinco
se hara pretension o del Govierno y Capitania general de la Ysla de la Habana, o del Reino del tucuman
y desde luego haziendo Vuestra Señoría dicha
Pretension con fineza pues de
[fol. 2v]
Ella redundara siendo Nuestro Señor
servido de darme Vida el poder ali-
biarle en parte a sus obligaziones y ze-
so prometiendome su empeño de-
seando Guarde nuestro Señor a Vuestra Señoría en su
compañia de mi querida Hija
y Nietos a quien hecho mi Vendizion
fecha En Mexico En 23 de Julio
de 1701 años

^2Besa la Mano de Vuestra Señoría su Mas
Affecto Y Padre que le estima
y su Bien Desea

el Marques de la Naba
de Brazinas^

[written vertically in left margin] Esa Carta para mi Señora la
condesa de lemos Es de persona de mi
Estimazión y asi suplico a Vuestra Señoría se la remita a su
Excelencia
[vertically on lower right side] 23 de Jullio 1701

señor don Ygnacio Lopez de Zarate mi Hijo

---

31. *Diego de Vargas to Ignacio López de Zárate,* *Mexico City, 25 October 1701, ARGD, LS.*

[fol. 1r]
[cross top center]
Hijo y señor mio remito a Vuestra Señoría juntamente la zertificazión de el entero que hize
perteneziente al del derecho de media
anata por lo honorifico del titulo de
Capitán General que este esta dado por de Guerra viva y asi remito el testimonio
de los autos que con el señor Juez pribatibo represente como lo vera Vuestra Señoría estar Esento por la dicha razón de pagar
ningún derecho y en dicha atenzión por su
auto Mando hiziese el entero por
via de deposito se me diese el dicho testimonio y zertificazión de el y ocurriese
al consejo de Hazienda para pedir
con su vista los señores de el declarasen no deberlo pagar y mandasen
se me volbiesen de dicha Real caxa
la Cantidad que debajo de dicha Calidad
[fol. 1v]
havia Enterado y asi Vuestra Señoría haga la dicha diligenzia y me remita el despacho de dichos
señores deseando Guarde nuestro señor a Vuestra Señoría felizes años Mexico y octubre 25 de 1701

^2Besa la Mano de Vuestra Señoria su
mas Affecto Padre y Seguro Servidor

el Marques de la Naba
de Brazinas^

señor don Ignacio Lopez de Zarate mi Hijo.

———

32. *Diego de Vargas to Isabel María de Vargas Pimentel, Mexico City, 14 March 1702, ARGD, LS.*

[fol. 1r]

[cross top center]

Hija querida mia de mis ojos con las
Urcas que trujeron los azogues y llegaron
a fines de octubre pasado rezivi la tuya
Y con ella el Gusto de saber de tu salud
sintiendo a ingratitud, me faltase, Carta, de
tu esposo, y mi Hijo el señor don Ygnacio
con el aviso, que salio, en prinzipios de diziembre, y llego a 15 de febrero de este año
de 702 que a ti no te culpo tu omision,
Sino a tu marido, que dejo de hazerlo y de darte a ti la razon, de la ocasión
para escribirme, atribuyolo, no tendria
tiempo y hallarse embarazado en lo que le
importa, bastantemente me hallo yo
En mis dependenzias y porque de el
las doy notizia a dicho mi hijo y señor

[fol. 1v]

don Ygnazio me remito En todo a ella
y a la detenzión de tu Hermano y mi Hijo
por no haver salido la flota pues por
las que reziviras que en suposizión zierta
de que salia te escribi y despues dupli-
que por octubre que en el aviso se havia tomado resoluzion saliese y no haviendo tenido Execuzión en la una ni en la
otra no sirvio la de mi Cuydado Y a-
tenzión con que mi Cariño te repite
la de mis deseos Y te da razon de el
estado de mis negozios que Caminan
por sus pasos muy dilatados, Y para mi
de muçho grabamen hallandome sin fundamentos destruydo y consumido pues
no se de que forma podre Aun dar para
su Viaje a tu hermano y mi hijo quando llegue el de su despaço y la de veer-

te ya lo tengo por imposible y solo
en todo lo dejo a su Divina Magestad
[fol. 2r]
que te Guarde felizes años en compañia de mis queridos nietos a quien
eçho mi bendizión Y daras muchos abrazos Mexico Y Marzo 14
de 1702

^2tu Padre que te estima de
Corazon y Deja Solo a la
Voluntad de Dios Nuestro Señor
el Veerte

el Marques de la Naba
de Brazinas ^

Mi querida Hija Doña Ysabel Maria de Vargas.

---

33. *Diego de Vargas to Ignacio López de Zárate, Mexico City, 15 March 1702, ARGD, LS.*

[fol. 1r]
[cross top center]
Hijo y señor mio En las Naos de Azogues que llegaron al Puerto de la Nueva
Vera cruz En fines de octubre del Año
pasado rezivi la de Vuestra Señoría y senti no
haverle merezido lo repitiese En el
aviso que se despacho en prinzipios
de Diziembre y llego a este Reino Y Ciudad
de Mexico su notizia en 15 de febrero
de este año de la fecha Juzgo tendria
Vuestra Señoría el despacho de su obligación que le En-
barazase la que en mi sera fija siem-
pre en qualquier fortuna

Y haziendo relazión a V*uestra Señoría* de la mia
aun con toda mi asistenzia me *ha* Embarazado y dilatado el fenezim*iento* de mis
dependenzias de pender de tantos la
de su Vista ynforme y parezer y con
la R*eal* Cedula que la parte Contraria gano su *fe*cha En barzelona En 16 de oct*ub*re pas*a*do
de 701 con siniestra relazión haviendo sido
[fol. 1v]
forzoso el presentar, las dos que
V*uestra Señoría* me remitio en *d*icho año que por
zitarlas en *d*icha R*ea*l Cedula para la
brevedad Y que en el rr*eal* Acuerdo
donde se halla radicado su conozim*iento*
me fue forzoso para Escusar dila*zio*nes
el presentarlas; no puedo de dezir
a V*uestra Señoría* los reparos que hize en ellas fueron el motibo para haver Escusado
el hazerlo que solo la *d*icha Circunst*a*ncia
de Zitarlas su M*a*g*es*t*ad* en la susod*i*cha
R*ea*l Cedula a *d*icha V*illa* me pudiera haver
prezisado pues lo uno en la de Abril
de el año de 1700 que su M*a*g*es*t*ad* que este En
Gloria el s*eñ*or Rey Carlos Seg*un*do En
ella no se adbirtio para que la diese
dos puntos que en ella se havian de
espezificar; el primero de mi punto
su reparo pues no era bien que haviendo confiado de mi el s*eñ*or Virrey
que fue conde de Galbe con resoluzion
de s*eñ*ores Minis*tros* de Una Junta plena
[fol. 2r]
de los que se Compone serlo de R*ea*l
Hazi*en*da Y Guerra de todo Este R*ein*o de
la nueba España no solo la de la enpresa de la Conq*uis*ta del R*ein*o de la N*uev*a
Mexico que a mi Costa consegui ge-
neralm*en*te de todo el en el año de 92
sino la de su entrada por quenta de
S*u* M*a*g*es*tad en el subseq*uen*te de 93 a su Pobla-

zon con las familias que reculte
en los Reinos de la Galizia Y Vizcaya
y los 100 soldados para la ereccion
del Nuebo Presidio en su Villa de santa
fee y las familias originarias de el
Reino cuyos socorros de toda dicha Gente corrio por mi pribatibamente sin in-
terbenzión de el Cabildo y para Ello
dandoseme plena y onimoda autoridad de poder librar en las tres Reales
Caxas de dichos Reinos Y siendo asi
que de dichos Mandamientos y ordenes
que tube Y tengo presentados se fue
de mi en el todo y lo que hallare Y
tubiere por preziso Se me da dicha
[fol. 2v]
Facultad Y esto Sin fianza que
no era Capaz de darla ni menos mi punto admitir tal orden debajo de dicha
Calidad y obligación y esto Supuesto
es incompatible se mande por dicha
Real Cedula debajo de fianza se me deje venir a dar mis quentas Y salir de la prision lo segundo que se omita
asi en esta Zedula como en la segunda
de dicho señor Rey, y Nuestro Phelipe quinto que Dios guarde el pedir la parte de
dicho Cabildo Y procurador En su nombre que asimesmo de el de dicha Villa
supone no se le mande afianzar la
Calunia como a Vuestra Señoría prebine ya
Don Pedro Rodriguez Cubero su Governador
como instrumento Y origen de dicha causa no llebado de el Zelo de el Real
Servizio, Si de el de su malizia a fin
de sus intereses pues pide tan
dilatado Tiempo la Vista de el bo-
[fol. 3r]
lumen de sus autos que estos como pasan a diferentes partes y

*h*an pasado es preziso de dilatado
*tie*mpo y con el logra el de su deseo
*d*icho *D*on Pedro para embarazarme de entrar en *d*icho Govi*er*no lo q*ua*l
no se quando se hallara En estado
de el fenezimi*en*to de mi q*uen*ta haviendo
perdido Cinco años consumido
Y Gastado de suerte que para haver de remitir a mi Hijo en la flota aun para lo preziso de su Viaje
me hallare confuso a hallarle; Este Es el estado misero en que quedo
y debajo de la fianza de el pleyto
*h*omenaje perdido lo mas prezioso
que es la libertad pues lo hize
según se me mando de no salir de
este *R*eino de la nueba España
Sin dar prim*er*o satisfazion de los
alcanzes que pudiesen resul-
[fol. 3v]
tar Y Resultaran Contra mi de
*d*ic*h*a q*uen*ta a favor de la *Rea*l Hazienda—

En este aviso siendo *N*uestro s*e*ñor Servido llegue a salbami*en*to rezivira
*V*uestra S*e*ñor*ía* dos pliegos mios el Uno de
Sep*tie*mbr*e* de 701 que entregue a Don Fausto
de Bustam*an*te en cuyo poder Esta
el chocolate y sus costos que en la flo-
ta que dejo de salir remitia a *V*uestra S*e*ñor*ía*
y con *d*icho pliego el testim*o*nio de la Vista de mi resid*en*cia Y en el Consta
haverseme declarado por buen Juez
y dados por nulos todos los Capitulos
tambien El seg*un*do duplicado del test*imo*nio
que remiti a *V*uestra S*e*ñor*ía* con el aviso de
la Coronazión del Rey n*ue*stro señor q*u*e
Dios *G*uar*d*e que se tubo notizia de su llegada a 15 de Agosto de el año pasado
y por el *h*abra reconozido *V*uestra S*e*ñor*ía h*aber

hecho la elección de titulo de
Marqués de la Naba de Brazinas
en Virtud de la Real Cedula
[fol. 4r]
de su Magestad que santa Gloria haya
y le repito el encargo de el ajuste
de el derecho que se debe y entero de
la media anata como se lo repe-
ti en el Segundo pliego de octubre pasado
de dicho año con el aviso que dejo
de salir y en el remitia a Vuestra Señoría El
testimonio también de haver enterado
por via de deposito en esta Real
Caxa el derecho de la media anata
por razon de el Titulo honorifico
que tube de Governador Y Capitán general y para
ajustarme la de mi sueldo Se me
Cargo y aunque hize la contradizión
con su Juez pribatibo y pasaron
diferentes autos y pedimentos no
obstante haver representado
por ser de Guerra viva su Magestad
daba por esentos de la paga de
dicho Real derecho a todos los que Exerzie-
sen en dichos presidios dichos Cargos y
para que se me mande debolber
[fol. 4v]
y que ocurriese al consejo
Real de Hazienda se lo remitia
Vuestra señoría haziendole Esta relazión
que le repito haviendo a las
personas En cuyo poder paran
dichos pliegos Escrito a la Vera
Cruz los dirijan En dicho aviso
y por ser de toda mi confianza
me prometo lo haran con la seguridad que se requiere encargan-
do asimesmo a Vuestra Señoría se logre
mi deseo en el todo de lo que le pido pues también le remiti po-

der para mis pretens*io*nes y p*a*ra fa-
zilitarlas el testim*o*nio de el estado
de mi q*ue*nta Y de ella resulta a mi
favor alcanze

En este aviso remito Poder
a Don Diego de olbera para lo
de Granada y porque hara a V*uestra Señorí*a
demostraz*ió*n Escuso El referirle
[fol. 5r]
la de su Contenido

Y quedo a su servizio con igual
cariño Y estimaz*ió*n con que me hallara Y tendra en todas fortunas
deseando *Guard*e N*ue*stro *se*ñor a V*uestra Señorí*a En
compañia de mi querida Hija
do*ñ*a Ysabel Y nietos a q*uie*nes hecho mi
bendiz*ió*n y doy repetidos abrazos fe-
lizissimos años. Mexic*o* Y Marzo
15 de 1702
^2La M*erc*ed del *h*Avito
aguardo el Primer
aviso p*a*ra se me Re-
mite el Despacho
p*a*ra Ponermelo^

^2*Besa L*a *M*ano de V*uestra señorí*a su *P*adre
que le estima de Corazon
y S*ervi*dor
Mas s*egur*o siempre

el Marques de la Naba
de Brazinas^

*se*ñor Don Ygnazio Lopez de Zarate mi Hijo,

[fol. 5v]
Mexico 15 de Marzo 1702

34. *Diego de Vargas to Ignacio López de Zárate, Mexico City, 29 May 1702, AMNB, LS.*

[fol. 1r]
[cross top center]
Hijo y señor mio tengo escrito a
Vuestra Señoría con mi hijo don Juan Manuel y esta sirve solo de darle la notizia pasa
en esta Flota deseando llegue con sa-
lud a la Vista de Vuestra Señoría quien dara razón
demas de los instrumentos Que con el remito y la que asimesmo refiero con e-
llos hago relación a Vuestra Señoría como de la
de mi intenzión Y deseo de que con el
motibo de su presentazión se pida a su
Magestad me mejore de Puesto haviendo sido de merito mis servicios en la
restaurazión Y conquista del Reino de la
Nueva Mexico haviendo sido la
Causa de mi padezer en la demora
de Cinco años y los tres en una prision con el vilipendio de Cinco
Meses
[fol. 1v]
Con Grillos, y de dichos, Ynstrumentos,
se reconozera la Ynjustizia Y malizia con que el Governador don Pedro
Rodriguez Cubero prozedio contra
mi a fin de embarazarme la prorrogazion del Govierno y no al Zelo
del servicio de su Magestad Cuya satisfazión del dicho mi agrabio y perdida
de mi Caudal atraso de mis aszensos incumbe solo el darmela a ese
Suppremo Consejo de Camara de Yndias y asi a Vuestra Señoría señalo En virtud
del poder que le remito para mi
pretensión y puestos que pido por merced
a su Magestad Senalando seis para
que tenga efecto recayga la merced

que le pido en qualquiera de los
que refiero esto tengo de deber
a V*uestra Señoría* por ultima dadiba en el *tiem*po
que n*uest*ro *señ*or fuere Servido de
darme de vida que sera para
[fol. 2r]
mi siempre de reconozim*ien*to tal
q*ue* solo sea mi desempeño la experienzia que a V*uestra Señoría* le asiste de mi
palabra y galanteria y asi en si
mesmo hara En con empeño
mejorarme de puesto para
poder pasar con mas gusto
alibio y sin zozobra y pueda
tener el Ynteres sin los
Contra *tiem*pos que se ofrezen y
Riesgos de el *d*icho govi*er*no de la nueba Mexico Y me responda V*uestra Señoría*
a este con la brebedad que se ofreziere sin perder ocas*ión* del fin que
deseo.

Tamb*ién* le pido no olbide la pretens*ión*
que le tengo repetida del Liz*enc*ia*d*o Don
Sebastian de Altamirano perso-
na tan de mi estimaz*ión* Y q*ue*
concurren tantos meritos y
nobleza de suerte que qualquiera m*erced* es de justizia
[fol. 2v]
demas que de todas ma-
neras quedara V*uestra Señoría* con
el luzim*ien*to en el desempeño
de el favor que mereziere
a esos *señ*ores y a Dios que gua*r*de
a V*uestra Señoría* felizes años como deseo Mexico Y Mayo 29 de 1702

A mi querida Hija do*ñ*a Ysabel Y nietos
repito mis tiernos abrazos y hecho

mi bendizión con el cordial cariño
con que los Estimo.

^2Besa la Mano su
Mas affecto Padre que de
Corazon le estima Y Servidor siempre

el Marques de la Naba
de Brazinas ^

Señor Don Ygnacio Lopez de Zarate mi Hijo

———

35. *Diego de Vargas to Isabel María de Vargas Pimentel, Mexico City, 31 December 1702, AMNB, LS.*

[fol. 1r]
[cross top center]
Hija Y querida mia de mis ojos
por la que escribo a mi hijo Don Ygnazio
reconozeras hallarme en esta Ziudad
de Mexico aun con la inpazienzia para
que se vean los autos en la Real Audiencia y
Salga de la confusión de hallarme perdido en este Reino empeñado y consumido mi Caudal motibo para dar
el poder que remito con las clausulas que se Expresan y veer si puedo
tener algun socorro de lo que Dios
nuestro señor fue servido de darme en la renta de esos Mayorazgos y ya que de ellos
no me mantenga en el todo me ali-
biaran enparte de lo que produ-
[fol. 1v]
jeren bien Veo que embaraza
mucho a mi hijo el tomar la pluma pues por la que rezivi tuya

con el paje de mi *señora* la Duquesa me
dizes me escribe y haviendo
havido tan seguro portador y por-
tadores no fue para hazer lo de donde q*ue*do muy satisfecho de su
Voluntad y que no me falte n*ue*stro
señor y su grazia y a ti te la de
Con larga Vida y a mis queridos nietos que echo mi Vendizión y te *guar*de felizes años Mexico Y
Diziemb*re* 31 de 1702

^2tu Padre que te estima
de Corazon y tu bien Desea

el Marques de la Naba
de Brazinas ^

Mi querida hija Doña Ysabel María de Vargas Pimentel

---

36. *Diego de Vargas to Ignacio López de Zárate,* *Mexico City, 31 December 1702–4 April 1703,* AMNB, C, *inc.,* ARGD, LS.

[fol. 1r]
[cross top center]
Hijo y *señor* mio luego que llegase a salbame*n*to a ese
*R*eino de españa la flota que se espera En n*ue*stro *señor* tendria V*ue*stra *Señoría* la notizia y carta ^2de don^ del
Capit*án* Don fra*n*cisco Mar-
cos lopez de Villamil vezino de Cadiz en que recono-
zeria la temprana muerte de mi querido Hijo don J*ua*n
Man*ue*l de Vargas Pimentel cuya notizia tube desde
la Havana que aseguro a V*ue*stra *Señoría* mi corazon me tras-
paso de dolor haviendo solo tenido la suerte de que fue-
sen en su Compañia este Cavallero y otros con quienes en esta Ziudad tenia y tubo estrecha amistad juz-

go en las oblig*aciones* de V*uestra Señoría* biendo el malogro de
  d*i*cho
su Herm*ano* y mi querido Hijo con la ternura q*ue* causaria a mi querida hija D*oña* Ysabel la *ha*bra asistido
igualm*ente* escuso dilatarme en este punto no pudiendo reprimir mi sentim*iento* y paso solo a dar no-
tizia a V*uestra Señoría* del estado pres*ente* de mis dependen*zi*as.
En 17 de Agosto fue n*uest*ro *señ*or servido se presentasen los
pliegos del fenezim*ien*to y consist*en*cia de la Glosa de mis quentas
  y luego pase a pedir en su tribun*al*
y Aud*iencia* de qu*en*tas se me diese la Zertifi*ca*z*ión* que remito a
V*uestra Señoría* con mas la de hallarse pendiente la determin*a*z*ión* del Punto en la R*e*al Audienzia por la R*e*al Cedula cometida su co-
[fol. 1v]
Conozim*iento* a ella haviendo executoreado lo siniles-
tro de la relaz*ión* con que la gano la parte de la Villa
de su Mag*es*t*ad* quando de d*i*cha Zertifi*ca*z*ión* no solo consta deber yo nada a su R*e*al Hazienda˄2su Mag*es*t*ad*˄ si antes bien
haverseme mandado librar y pagar el alcanze q*ue*
a mi favor resulto para que yo pueda hazerlo
enparte a las personas que me supliern su caudal en medio de que la dilaz*ión* de Cinco años
y que van corriendo Seis que a que me hallo de vacante y sin tener ninguna intelig*encia* puede reconozer V*uestra Señoría* quan empeñado me hallare con un
pleyto de tanta Grabedad y los gastos y empeños q*ue*
me ocasionaron y se me siguieron de la venida del
d*i*cho mi querido Hijo difunto que solo siendo˄2Siento˄ la
de la perdida de su Vida quando en mi estimaz*ión*
no *ha*y con que pueda explicar a V*uestra Señoría* la
  feliz*idad*
que en el solo tenia Zifrada y por los papeles
que a V*uestra Señoría ha*bran remitido reconoz*e*ra el poder
Gen*e*r*al* que sin exzeptuar ni reservar nada
le havia otorgado con tan plena Voluntad
y gusto mio de todos mis mayorazgos que el
d*i*cho Poder sera el que acredite la de mi Estimaz*ión* Y cariño con que tiernam*ente* le amaba

asimesmo en este Reino le havia Zedido la Encomienda de los 4U pesos en virtud de la encomienda de su Magestad en su Vida por la mia para que
recayese en la suya el hijo que nuestro señor fuese servido de darle haviendole asegurado de mi parte
asistirle para el empeño que hiziese casando En ˆ2conˆ
el enpleo mas superior que hallase estos eran
mis pensamientos no consintiendo nunca lo tubiese
[fol. 2r]
ni Ymaginase por ninguna manera Se cauˆ2tibaˆ-
Se en estas partes que aunque por la estimazión Y Voluntad que se hizo lugar huviera fazilitado lo mejor
nunca se me puso faltase la asistencia de su Persona En esa
Corte y que fuese la que representase la memoria de
mis pasados manteniendo el lustre de mi Casa
haviendola yo por mi condecorado con la de titulo de Castilla; Para lo qual espero y me prometo
Vuestra Señoría habra pagado la media anata pues con tanta
recomendazión a Vuestra Señoría se la pidio mi atenzión y
repetido ˆ2repitoˆ en todas las que le tengo escrito desde que entre en esta Ziudad de Mexico en fines del
año de 700 no dudando lo habra executado prometiendome rezivir la Real cedula de la elección del titulo de Marqués de la Naba de Brazinas que hize segun el testimonio remiti a Vuestra Señoría en el haviso
que llego a ese Reino en fines de Agosto del año
de 701 de que tube respuesta de Vuestra Señoría.
Y mediante a la muerte de ˆ2del dichoˆ mi querido hijo
Y la suso dicha respuesta de Vuestra Señoría me ha sido forzoso
    tomar
la resoluzión según el presente estado de mi fortuna y
empeños que he contrahido volber sobre mi mirando por el punto de mi Persona y que este
no descaezca y llegue a veerme en el Vilipendio
me falte el del porte dezente para Conservarme
y mantenerme el tiempo que me sea forzoso dilatarme en este Reino para lo qual ya que nuestro señor fue
servido de llebarse para si a mi querido hijo
que era el motibo de apartar esta tan justa considerazión Y el amor Ziegamente que le tenia despo-

seerme en Vida de todo solo la suya siendo la un^2ica^
[fol. 2v]
mia y el Ydolo de mi Cariño podia no reparar
a lo que con su falta vuelto en mi ser y sentido
me es fuerza prebenga todos los requisitos y reparos para no experimentar una ruyna en mi
desdoro y desestimazión y juntamente la de que mi
imposibilidad no me Exponga a la del perpetuo
Cautiberio de quedarme en este Reino perdido
por no poder salir de el y me lo impidan las deudas y asi Consideradas y premeditadas Estas Causas de tanto punto y grabamen perjuyzio y daño irreparable es bien que abra los ojos
a la considerazión de 30 años perdidos desde 11 de
Agosto del de 72 que sali de ese Reino y mi querida
patria Esa deleytosa Villa de Madrid corona de todo el mundo para que en mi esta reflex-
sion de veer empeños en lugar de desempeños En
mis mayorazgos y con que dichosamente me pudiesen
mantener en los Ultimos de mis dias y *tiempo* de
Vida q*ue* n*ue*stro señor fuese ^2fuere^ servido de darme gozando
de los mios y sin tener el subsidio de los Cuydados
Con que para pasar la Vida humana En estas partes es fuerza todo Un laberinto y abismo de ellos me
halle no solo en el paralelo de la fortuna de tener el retiro
al descanso mediante el dilatado de mi ausenzia
sino antes bien el de nuebo Experimentar lo amar-
go de tan aspera Vida Vien es menester lo dilatado
de mi Corazon para no con su Pena quedar En
el todo tan sin aliento que le falte el Vital
quando todo Espiritu^2y animo para apartar
razones de tanto fundam*en*to es menester reviva
y no desmaye dandole esfuerzo el de su Generoso
espiritu^ es menester reviva y no
desmaye dandole esfuerzo el de su generoso espi-
ritu
[fol. 3r]
Y animo para Apartar razones de tanto fun-
dam*en*to para quitarle la vida y asi *todo* lo dilatado
de esta digresion *ha* sido para satisfazer a V*uestra* Señor*í*a y con-

benzerle su animo para que el mio pase debajo
de estas atenziones y respectos que apartando lo de hijo y mirando la de su Gerarquia debe hazer mi
respecto para haver tomado la resoluzión de otor-
gar los poderes para exonerarle El del cuydado
de la administrazión de mis Mayorazgos y discu-
rridas las Causas de mi fortuna y estado presente
haya reconozido afianzando en ellos la de su
recurso siendo mas legitimo Valerme de lo que Dios nuestro señor me hizo dueño que no llegar al de-
sayre de pedir lo que otro nezesita y asi a *Vuestra Señoría*
he servido con toda Galanteria y en medio de eso
no quiero Valerme de ese motibo para Estre-
charle a lo que nezesita y la de la asistencia de sus
obligaciones de Madre y hermanos que es muy justo y hija de sus obligaciones esa atenzión demas de la de sus
hijos y esposa mi querida Hija; Y asi remita
a la Ciudad de Granada poder General a mi Primo
Don fernando de teruel Cavallero del orden de santiago y Conde de Villamena para que lo sostituya en la Persona que fuere mas de su
confianza pida y tome la quenta a Don Diego
de olbeda desde primero de henero del año de 700
hasta el del dia del año que reziviere el dicho
Poder de todo lo que huviere en dicho tiempo ren-
tado dicho Mayorazgo Y lo que tubiere en
[fol. 3v]
ser y le huviere quedado liquido; como asi mesmo del Consumo y enpleo de un mill pesos que mi querido hijo que goze de Dios le entrego en Junio
del año de 99 que paso a este Reino y yo pague En
esta Ciudad de Mexico a Don Miguel Velez de la Rea
Cavallero del orden de santiago y dicho Poder
General se lo doy independiente para que reconozca a nayde con sus rentas sino que tan solamente
de ellas pagados sus Zensos y demas Cargas que
tubiere y los reparos prezisos en las Posesiones de el y
sus fincas y la de seguir Sus pleytos y demandas
que se ofrezieren para su conserbazión y mayor
aumento Y seguridad todo lo que rediturare me lo

retenga en si el dicho mi Primo para la paga
y satisfazión puntualmente de las libranzas que
diere sobre dicho señor y mi Primo el conde del Villamena

En quanto a esos Mayorazgos de Madrid torrelaguna los Caramancheles y las demas Posesiones
del juro de Ocaña Zenso de Cien ducados de renta perpetua del Lizenciado Don Juan Diaz impuesto
sobre su Casa de la Calle del Almendro la casa
que poseo de la Plaza mayor de esa Corte a la
esquina de la Carnenzeria y Portal de las
Pellas la hazienda de los lugares de Camarmas
del Caño y de esteruela que dizen del xpisto
la Dehesa de las Gariñas y la mitad de la Dehesa de Viñaderos en la Villa de Butrago ˆ2Buytragoˆ
[fol. 4r]
Prados Y Zercas de la Villa de Porquerizas Miraflores de la Sierra Chozas y Guadalix; las tierras de labor de los lugares de talamanca Valdepielagos y demas que pertenezen al
y mayorazgo del torre laguna torre mocha;
ˆ2yˆ los Patronatos que tocan al de Madrid como son
el que fundaron mis tias Doña Aldonsa y Doña Antonia lujan en el convento de nuestro Padre San
francisco
Cuyos compatronos son de el el Guardián que
fuere de dicho Convento Y el cura de Villaver ˆ2deˆ
y el Patronato que fundo y dejo Maria
Suarez en la Parroquia de san Pedro cuyos
Compatronos son el cura que fuere de dicha
Parroquia y el Regidor que nombra asista
(la Villa de madrid) [ARGD omits parentheses] el dia de Nuestra
    Señora
de la conzepzión en la tarde en la sala del dicho
Cura para la elección de las tres Guerfanas
que cada uno nombra y dotes que se le señala
en su Renta y la de el Capellan que sirve
a dezir las Misas.
Separo del dicho Poder el que doy a Vuestra Señoría para
su hijo mayor por ausenzia de no poder asistir

por*que* reconozca que en mi solo esta la atenzión de [four slashes
   to NB]
relebarle de la administrazión de d*i*chos mayorazgos por las Causas d*i*chas; Y no falta como
no puede faltar en mi las debidas de mi punto
y obligazión Y solo el atender a el y a ellas y el
[fol. 4v]
misero estado de mi fortuna puede innobar
la de el d*i*cho Poder mirando a tener Como repito asegurado el recurso para no descaezer de
el no siendo menos Sino la mayor de mi considerazión Justa (mediante las experienzias) [ARGD omits
parentheses]
que sirven de tanto grabamen y contrapeso
los que pendemos de la Voluntad de un señor
Virrey y quanto mas superior su Gerarquia
lo es correspondiente en superlatibo grado
no me dilato sino Solo hago este brebe apun-
te Cuya nobed*a*d me da motibo con la llegada
del E*x*celentísi*m*o Se*ñ*or Duque de Arburquerque que de
mi parte estara la atenzión de servirle si bi-
en reconozco la oposizión grande que tengo quando yo me hallo gastado y empeñado de cinco años de un pleyto y pendiente aun pro-
siguiendo el de mi jus*ti*cia Y mi Contrario
exerziendo el Govi*erno* con los interes ^2intereses^ que
lo mantiene y costea que es la diferenzia del
que pelea con armas al que careze de ellas
Vea V*u*estra Se*ñ*oría quan contristado me hallare con esta
mudanza tan intempestiba y distinta pu-
es el E*x*celentísi*m*o se*ñ*or Arzobispo Virrey se hallaba En el
heçho de mi justizia y asi podia en brebe ase-
gurarme el Expediente conforme a ella y p*ara*
que d*i*cho se*ñ*or nuebo Virrey le tenga *h*abre menes*te*r se me dilate
   y seguirseme de esta la duda y el
perjuyzio que de ambas Causas me hallaba asegur*a*do
del pasado [AMNB incomplete, ARGD continues]
Sali a rezivir a *su* E*x*celencia 15 leguas de esta Ziud*a*d y me
*h*onnro mucho y mi se*ñ*ora la duquesa dandome notizia los dos Se*ñ*ores E*x*celentísi*m*os lo muy recomendado
de V*u*estra Se*ñ*oría y de mi hija y dandome Don Diego de

Molina la carta que le dio mi hija Doña Ysabel
su fecha de 12 de mayo en que me da notizia de si
[fol. 5r]
y de los quatro hijos que nuestro señor es servido goze
el Uno Varon y las tres hembras y de re-
comendarme por su sobrino Don Diego
de olbeda y paje que fue asimesmo de su primo
de Vuestra Señoría Don Antonio de Ubilla y asi le he asistido
y asistire en lo que se valiere de mi y pudiere
las Cartas de Vuestra Señoría no he rezivido haviendo
Venido por oydor de esta Real Audiencia un señor oydor llamado
   Don Joseph de Uribe Castrejon quien
me trajo Carta de mi Primo Don Sancho Bullon chacon asegurandome el de su favor
que Experimentare Siendo nuestro señor servido a fines de Henero de este año nuebo
de 703 que entra y he sentido Viniendo el dicho
Don Diego de Molina quien trajo la de mi hija
Vuestra Señoría no le entregase los pliegos de que me da
razon Vuestra Señoría me escribe de todas maneras
Dios me quiere mortificar y asi venga
lo que fuere servido.
A mi hermano el Marques de la florida le
escribo con el Capitán franzes a cuyo Cargo
va esta armada a franzia y asi espero
llegue a su mano y por asegurar no le falte
carta mia le remito duplicado para que
Vuestra Señoría se lo remita.

No tengo que adbertir a Vuestra Señoría asegure la merced
del havito que mi hijo que goze de Dios
tenia de su Magestad pues en sus Papeles que le
harian a Vuestra Señoría remisión desde Cadiz don francisco
[fol. 5v]
Marcos lopez de Villamil y a mi me dejo
el traslado de ella que es el siguiente.

Don Bernardino Antonio de Pardinas Villar de francos
Cavallero del orden de santiago regidor Perpetuo de Madrid del
Consejo de su Magestad su secretario en el Real de las tres ordenes

Militares de Santt*iago* Calatraba y alcantara y junta de la Cavalleria de ellas:

Zerttifico que el Rey n*ues*tro se*ñor* Dios
le G*uard*e por el R*ea*l decreto de 11 del pres*en*te mes
*h*a sido Servido hazer mer*ce*d a Don J*ua*n Man*ue*l de Vargas
    Pimentel que sirve en el asiento
de menino de la Reyna n*ues*tra Se*ñor*a de havito de las ordenes militares de q*ue* se le dara
el despacho nezes*ari*o por esta secret*ari*a Vol-
biendo esta Zertificazión Madrid a 13
de febrero de 1694.

Y en cuya atenzión V*uest*ra Se*ñor*ía puede hazer la supl*i*ca
para que recaya la d*i*cha mer*ce*d en mi o En
la persona que fuere de mi Voluntad y prezisa oblig*ació*n pues tendra en su discurso
la fazilidad de q*ue* se logre la de mi deseo sien-
do el q*ue* n*ues*tro se*ñor* G*uard*e a V*uest*ra Se*ñor*ía felizes años
Mexico Y diz*iemb*re 31 de 1702

remito a V*uest*ra Se*ñor*ía esa Zertificazión por si
a V*uest*ra Se*ñor*ía le parez*i*ere presentarla en el R*ea*l
Y Supp*re*mo Consejo de Yndias para que
conozca en el Su Mag*esta*d lo siniestro con q*ue*
[fol. 6r]
Su R*ea*l Zedula la parte de la Villa
de Santa fee que zito a V*uest*ra Se*ñor*ía en esta Carta
Su *f*echa.
Repito a V*uest*ra Se*ñor*ía el dupl*i*ca*d*o que refiero proseguien-
do Con la ocasion del abiso la de el es-
tado de haverse dado a mi favor En vista Y rebista de 9 de el pres*en*te Mes de
la *f*echa la sentenzia Cuyo testimonio
para que V*uest*ra Se*ñor*ía lo presente con la Zertificazión del tribunal que repito por
Segundo duplicado y la instruzion
del Abbogado que sera por Cuyo me-
todo se este para en el cons*e*jo donde la
parte puede ocurrir siendo asi q*ue*

la Real Audiencia Ynformara con autos remitiendo los originales de mi residencia
Y asi En esto Vuestra Señoría ponga persona de toda
Confianza para que se repare qual-
quier relazión Siniestra Si bien Considero que el Real consejo atendera
con Vista de los Ynstrumentos
[written in left margin] Señor Ygnacio Lopez de Zarate mi
hijo.
[fol. 6v]
que zito y mas con el Ynforme de
la Real Audiencia; Yo me hallo despa-
chandome a mi Govierno que procurare
Salir de esta Ciudad el Mes de Mayo

Y me ha parezido el remitir a Vuestra Señoría Ese memorial
para representar a su Magestad Se me de igual
Sueldo al que goza el Governador y Capitán General
del Reino de la Vizcaya por no gozar ninguno por Capitán general de la Nueva Mexico y solo tenerle por Governador de lo politico y militar y no es bien
pase en silenzio el hazer dicha representazión
fundada Con tan justificadas Causas.

tambien repito a Vuestra Señoría ese otro borrador del segundo
Memorial para que se represente a su Magestad
la de su Real merced haviendomela hecho por su Real
Cedula de 15 de Junio del año de 99 por con-
Sulta del Consejo del año de 97 de la prorrogacion
del Govierno y provincias de la Nueba Mexico
Segun me la hizo en 18 de Junio del año
de 88 y haviendo hecho la merced de la compañia del presidio del paso del rio del norte y sus fronteras y en su Cumplimiento
El excelentísimo señor Virrey que fue conde de montezuma mandadole dar los despaçhos
[fol. 7r]
a su Capitán don Antonio Balberde y tambien el de su Govierno de lo politico con titulo
de justizia mayor haviendo separado

de dicho Govierno de la Nueba Mexico la dicha
Compañia Presidio de 50 soldados y la de su
Jurisdizión queda la dicha merced a mi hecha
diminuta en la mitad quando a mi
integramente la Voluntad de su Magestad
fue hazermela en remunerazión de mis
Servicios Sin separarme nada quando la
dicha Su Real Cedula enpieza por quanto
en 18 de Junio de 1688 os hize merced del
Govierno politico y militar &etcétera al presente os la hago
segun y en la mesma forma &etcétera en cuya
atenzión hago a su Magestad la representazión recombenzión Y Suplica que se refiere en dicho
Memorial y debajo de esta notizia que a Vuestra Señoria
doy siendo Servido por hazerme favor
hara la dicha diligenzia y pretensión no escusan-
dose de ella quando mi fin Es atendiendo
al punto y lo pundonoroso que corresponda
a las obligaciones de mi Sangre meritos y servizios y aunque duro mas parte tendra
[fol. 7v]
Vuestra Señoría mi querida hija y nietos en los Vienes que dios fuere servido de darme de
fortuna que no el Vezino y con esto hE dicho
a Vuestra Señoría en esta lo que se me ofreze añadiendo
y repitiendo a Vuestra Señoría de las gracias muy
rendidas a dicho señor Excelentísimo Virrey duque
de Alburquerque y a mi Señora la duquesa
del favor que me ha hecho del mucho amparo que en su Grandeza he hallado
Y tambien lo haga mi querida Hija
Doña Ysabel y mi Señora Doña luisa de Loyola Marquesa de Villanueba que me ha
parezido escribia dandole las gracias
a esta señora pues dicho señor Excelentísimo Virrey
dijo a Don Miguel de Ubilla Venia
muy recomendado de parte
de esta Señora y tambien de
Vuestra Señoría y de dicha mi Hija mi Señora la duquesa y estoy para Ser-

vir a V*uestra* S*eñoría* con la fineza de mi
oblig*aci*on Y cariño con el que deseo
[fol. 8r]
G*uard*e Dios a V*uestra* S*eñoría* los felizes años q*u*e
deseo en compañia de mi queri-
da Hija y nie*t*os Mexico y
Abril 4 de 1703.

^3Su P*a*dre de V*uestra* S*eñoría* Y S*eguro*
S*ervi*dor que le estima de Cora-
zon

el Marques de la Naba
de Brazinas ^

V*uestra* S*eñoría* Escriba las Grazias a los se*ñ*ores de esta R*ea*l
    Aud*ienci*a don Mig*u*el Cal-
deron de la Barca oydor mas antiguo y pres*id*en*t*e de la R*ea*l
    Aud*ienci*a, al
se*ñ*or don Juan de Escalante y Mendoza Ca*vall*e*r*o del orden
de santiago, al se*ñ*or don franz*i*sco Balenzuela Benegas
    Ca*vall*e*r*o
del orden de santiago, al se*ñ*or don Joseph de luna al se*ñ*or don
Joseph de Uribe Castrejon, y al se*ñ*or Don Joseph de Espinosa Ocampo y cornejo fiscal de lo Zibil y Criminal
&*etcétera*

se*ñ*or don Ygn*aci*o Lopez de Zarate mi q*u*erido Hijo.

———

37. *Lawyer's advice, [Mexico City, c. 1703],*
ARGD, C, *inc.*

[fol. 1r]
[cross top center]
Adbertenzia del Abb*o*g*ad*o para la defensa que fuere prezisa en
    caso que la
parte de la Villa ocurra en el sup*r*emo consejo con algun siniestro
    pedim*e*nto

con el Ynforme siniestro que este por haver pasado su
 reconozim*ien*to del
Señor oydor Semanero para si estaba en terminos dezentes y
 *h*ones-
tos fue solo la de su Vista y la p*a*rte da a entender su calificazión
 por ella

Segun lo Ynformado por el señor Marques ha-
llo poca nezesidad de prebenz*ion*es para Madrid porq*ue*
no yendo Copia de los Autos o los originales y solo si el Ynforme de la Aud*ienci*a este *h*a de ser tan pro-
pizio como es preziso en consequenzia de sus de-
terminaziones

Y Si fueran los autos ya se *h*a prebenido y se repitiera
que todos ellos son una fabrica y dispotica ordena-
cion y absoluta hechura de don Pedro Rodriguez
Cubero quien *h*a reduzido a escripto quanto *h*a i-
maginado y arbitrado y los desdichados de la
Villa y defuera de ella *h*an firmado los que *h*an sabi-
do

Para reparo de este daño Estamos con el Cuydado de
presentar Escrito para que los autos se entreguen
a el Juez de resid*enci*a de d*i*cho Don Pedro Rodriguez
Cubero y que este prozeda a rezivir sus declara-
ciones a los que violentam*en*te *h*an firmado y depuesto compelidos Con los rigores que sabemos por su
Ynteres particular y se desbanezeran tales maquinas Y aun daran nuebo poder contra d*i*cho
[fol. 1v]
don Pedro asi para la Corte como p*a*ra Esta Ciud*a*d

En los autos residenzia es de notar que para dar
algun color se quito el primer edicto en que
estaba su publicazión para tomar de aqui asumpto
a nulidad y esta falsedad se halla Combenzida por los
demas edictos en que pareze la publicazión y en el
interrogatorio que hizo don Pedro a el final de el
se refieren los Edictos publicados y se hallan
enmendados los numeros de los folios sin

alcanzar la Causa y en uno de los Capitulos se
expresa que no le capitularon en la residenzia
por haver dado a entender los Criados volberia
por Governador Con que la residencia se publico y es muy de
notable que no depusiesen por el rezelo de volber y que haviendo Venido la Zedula de prorrogazión le capitulasen porque vio Don Pedro por
su zuzesor a quien le havia sacado En su sentir Veynte y dos mill y quinientos pesos y a-
si todas sus disposiziones y maximas han sido
imposibilitar la nueba entrada del señor Marqués
porque sus ardides no lleguen a aclararse y a
desbanezerse sus maquinas pues con el favor
divino quedara de su residencia para ser Castigado
y inabilitado para otro algun ofizio o exer-
zizio
[fol. 2r]
Los autos de los Veynte y dos mill y quinientos
pesos Van, muy claros y la reserva que se hizo a los soldados en la mayor parte esta ya des-
banezida por haver declarado les estaban
pagados sus sueldos quando entro Cubero

Haze Ympreso un Ynforme en derecho todo con
Un hecho supuesto y tan mal guisado
que para su total combenzimiento y de todas
las quexas dadas Esperamos la residencia
de Don Pedro Cubero para con ella hazer
Un manifiesto Juridico de la falsedad de
todo el hecho y sus proposiziones y de las le-
xitimas y consequentes a la Verdad de lo
suzedido y entonzes pediremos se remitan
Unos y otros autos originales a el Real consejo
a que se ha de dirigir Unicamente en todo Caso
qualquier defensa a que prezise las Yns-
tanzias o pretensiones contrarias con la
seguridad de que ira todo en la primera flota. Esto es por dar gusto al señor Marques
y solo por prebenir lo que aca se dispone

———

38. *Diego de Vargas to King Felipe* V, *[Mexico City, c. 1703]*, ARGD, C.

[fol. 1r]
[cross top center]
Señor
Don Diego de Vargas Zapata lujan Ponze de
leon Marques de la Naba de Brazinas Conquistador y Pazificador
del Reino y provincias de la Nueba Mexico Governador y capitán
   general ^Y Castellaño de su fuersa y presidio^
nuebamente electo restituydo y prorrogado por
su Magestad: dize y se le ofreze representar repetir su-
plicar y pedir con la benerazión que debe puesto a sus
Reales pies que en atenzión de hallarse despachado para
pasar a dicho Govierno lo primero y a que tan solamente
goza el sueldo de dos mill pesos en cada Un año que
debengare y sirviere a Vuestra Magestad por el Govierno politico
Y militar que Exerziere en el empleo de dichos Puestos en dicho Reino y provinzias y no tener señalado sueldo ni gozar por el de Capitán general igualmente que goza
el Governador que lo es del Reino de la Vizcaya y Real del Parral siendo asi que se debe considerar justamente
que hallandose el de la nueba Mejico tierra dentro de los Enemigos por todas partes fronterizos a
distanzia de Cinco diez quinze Veynte leguas que llaman de la Nazion muy dilatada
de Apaches hallandose del Parral a distanzia
tierra dentro despoblado solo el intermedio
la del Presidio del Paso de su rio del norte 300 leguas
[fol. 1v]
estando en un Continuo mobimiento de Guerra por ser
muy abierta y distante la de la jurisdizión poblazon de dicho
Reino y de mi Cargo la de su defensa y esto sin tener para
ello lo uno como tiene el suso dicho Governador de la Vizcaya
la Situazión fuera de su sueldo por lo que mira a la asistenzia
de los Yndios de paz y guerra y lo otro la del recurso de
haziendas y Presidios demas de las poblazones que hay
en su jurisdizión y parajes para adquirir para mantener y mantenerse de los Vastimentos de Carne Mayz
y harina bestias Cavallares y mulares con el costo mucho menos al que en la dicha distanzia de 300 leguas no

tiene el del Nuebo Mexico ni menos que es lo mas el
de la dicha Gente con que se puede favorezer de donde se
sigue serle forzoso con los 100 soldados del Presidio de la
Villa de santa fee dejar el numero Competente para la
defensa de ella regulando tambien el de algunas fronteras para la escolta en el resguardo y seguridad de
las Vidas y haziendas de sus Vezinos poblados En
ellas y ranchos y labores salir con el corto numero
a la Campaña para las operaziones que son prezisas
por las continuas Entradas de los enemigos lo qual todo
pone y representa a su Real soberania de Vuestra Magestad su-
plicandole Como lo espera asi rendido a sus Reales pies le con-
Ceda igual sueldo que el que goza el suso dicho Governador de la
    vizca-
ya y Real del parral mandandole Despachar Siendo
servido Vuestra Magestad de conzederle dicha Merced su Real
    cedu-
[fol. 2r]
la que lo declare asi y mande a Vuestro Virrey
que es o fuere de este Reino de la Nueva españa y a sus
ofiziales Reales de su Real Caxa en su corte de Mexico
le paguen y manden pagar desde el dia de la Posesion que tomare de dicho Govierno en dicha Real Caxa el sueldo
    que le corresponde a capitán general igual con
el del Govierno politico y militar con el que se le paga
en dicha Real Caxa al que en la de Guadiana se le paga al del suso dicho Governador de su Reino de la Vizcaya
que en ello rezivira merced como lo espera de Vuestra Magestad
atendiendo a lo justificado de la relazión y representacion
de su pedimento &etcétera.

———

39. *Diego de Vargas to Isabel María de Vargas Pimentel, Mexico City, 28 March 1703, AMNB, LS.*

[fol. 1r]
[cross top center]
Hija de mi Vida Espero En Nuestro señor

te halle esta con la salud que te deseo
dandomela su divina Magestad despues
de mis ynfortunios y Cuydados que he tenido En lo dilatado de mi pleyto
de 6 años los tres en una prision y los
otros tres en esta Corte y lo que me dilate En pasar a ella de toda la malizia
Con que el Governador me puso en este miserable Estado ha sido nuestro señor servido de que salga a mi favor la sentenzia
de Vista y rebista declarando de-
berseme dar el paso a mi Govierno por el
Excelentísimo Señor Virrey duque de Alburquerque
debiendo a este prinzipe la honrra
[fol. 1v]
de asistir a la Vista de dicho pleyto
que fue el dia 13 de febrero y el dia 9 de
Marzo el de la rebista por razon de
haver Suplicado la parte a quien Condenaron
en costas tengo por sin duda la Real
Audiencia haze informe a su Magestad con este
abiso de los autos remitiendo los originales de mi residencia según por su Real
Cedula ganada en Varzelona de
10 de Octubre pasado de 701 por parte
de la Villa insistida y con fomento de su Governador por Embarazarmela
de la Entrada a dicho Govierno para donde
me hallo despachando para salir
el Mes de Mayo con los Empeños
que no te sabre Esplicar que son asi
ellos Como la de mi punto los Grillos
que me detienen y me dilataran En este Reino El tiempo que dios nuestro señor fuere
Servido de darme de Vida para mi
[fol. 2r]
desempeño Y en el Ynterin tambien de su intermedio se logre la de
mi deseo de poner En corriente Esos
Mayorazgos, y tambien puedan ayu-

darme a sacarme del Cautiberio q*ue*
paso quando solo lo que me dilata-
re Sera la de dar satisfazión a q*uien* debo
motibo para haver determinado di-
bidir en dos Cuerpos la administrazión
de d*i*chos Mayorazgos remitiendo
para el de granada poder aparte y p*ar*a
Esos de Madrid torrelaguna y demas
rentas a los se*ñor*es Marques de Vargas Conde de la Puebla de los Valles
y mi primo Don Sancho Bullon
para que los sostituyan En los
Ag*ent*es de Negozios haviendo remitido el duplicado de los poderes
Y Cartas en el haviso que salio
por henero por Nabios de fran-
[fol. 2v]
zia Con cuya razon de ha-
verse puesto En execuzión por
d*i*chos se*ñor*es tendre la relazión si es
Zierta del estado en q*ue* se hallare
para estar en el conozimi*ent*o de
mi deseo poder Esperar el brebe desempeño mio en q*ue* quedo
ayudado con lo q*ue* la fortuna
Siendo n*uest*ro señor Servido
Solizite darme En el d*i*cho Govi*er*no
en q*ue* fundo tener tambien algun desenbaraza~~deo~~ para mantenerme y asi no me dilato mas
en esta quedarte Esta razon
deseando tener Carta tuya, ya q*ue*
tu esposo y mi hijo se Estrañale
hazerlo no haviendo rezivido
letra suya desde el año de 701 dios
le de salud Y le Guard*e* en tu compañia Y a mis queridos nie-
[written vertically in left margin] tos a q*uien*es hecho mi
Vendizión los mu*ch*os años que deseo Mexico Y Marzo
28 de 1703

^2tu Padre que te quiere y estima
de Corazon y tu bien Desea

el Marques de la Naba
de Brazinas^

Mi querida Hija doña Ysabel
Maria de Vargas.

———

40. *Diego de Vargas to Isabel María de Vargas Pimentel, Mexico City, 12 April 1703, AMNB, LS.*

[fol. 1r]
[cross top center]
Hija querida mia de mis ojos haviendose dilatado el abiso repito el darte la notizia en esta de hallarme despachado para salir a mi Govierno a fin
de este Mes en atenzión de haver salido a mi favor en vista y rebista la
Sentenzia de los autos por los señores
de la Real Audiencia haviendo Concurrido
a ella el excelentísimo señor Duque de Alburquerque a quien debo toda honrra
y favor y asi mi hijo el señor Don Ygnacio
Y tu Escribiras dandole las gracias
y a mi señora la duquesa y dicho tu Esposo lo hara tambien a todos los
Señores de esta Real Audiencia como al señor fiscal Cuyos nombres para que lo
haga de Cada uno lo pongo En su
[fol. 1v]
Carta Condenaron en costas al governador
actual presente ante su Excelencia la Real
Cedula de merced de la encomienda para
que mandase Se me diesen los despachos
y ayer hize el entero de un mill y
duzientos pesos En la Real Caxa y por

el Real derecho de la media anata y asimesmo otorgue Escritura de fiador a-
bonado de entregar Otra ^mesma^ cantidad
al prinzipio del segundo año y a-
si Su Excelencia me ha mandado que para la segunda
Vida ocurra a su Magestad en su suppremo
Consejo para que confirme la dicha merced mediante a que por su Real cedula del año de
701 hizo la reforma para que no goza-
Sen sino por Una Vida las mercedes que
estaban hechas de dos a las personas que
Vivian en esos Reinos declarando no se
entendia con los que Vivian En estos de las Yndias y residian En ellos
Y por dicha razon su Magestad hiziese y die-
[fol. 2r]
Se la confirmazión para la persona
que me Subzediere en la segunda Vida
atento a haverseme hecho dicha merced
En atenzión de mis servicios Y conquista de
dicho Reino de la Nueba Mexico y si
por dicha razon no debia residir para el gozo de dicha encomienda En estos Reinos y asi te dejare Escrito y a
tu esposo y mi Hijo remitiendo El
testimonio para que se asegure la confirmazión de dicha Segunda Vida en la per-
Sona que subzediere en mis Mayorazgos y esta Carta Sirve para mi
Hijo y los demas parientes de notizia de hallarme con salud gracias
a nuestro Señor deseando su divina Magestad te
guarde muchos años en compañía de tu querido Esposo y mis
queridos nietos a quienes hecho mi bendizión Mexico y Abril 12 de 1703

^2tu Padre que te quiere y estima de Corazon Y Ve-
erte Deja a la Voluntad
de Dios Nuestro señor

el Marques de la Naba
de Brazinas ˆ

Mi querida Hija doña Ysabel María de Vargas Pimentel

———

41. *Diego de Vargas to Ignacio López de Zárate, Mexico City, 16 April 1703, AMNB, LS.*

[fol. 1r]
[cross top center]
Hijo y señor mio Haviendose dilatado el Zerrar los Cajones que lleba Este abiso puse el cuydado de la situazión de la encomienda Cuyo testimonio
remito a Vuestra Señoría incluso En esta para
que con su Vista Solizite la confirma-
cion de la segunda Vida en el Suppremo Y Real
Consejo de Camara de Yndias
Segun se expresa y se refiere de la Real
Cedula de Merced y asi Vuestra Señoría me lo remitira por duplicado quedandose con
el triplicado en su poder para
el resguardo de remitirmelo En
caso del mal suzeso de perderse
los dos Cuya notizia le dare a Vuestra Señoría
[fol. 1v]
Y repetire en las ocasiones que se
ofrezieren con el segundo testimonio
hasta tanto que tenga de Vuestra Señoría asimesmo rezivo en que me lo abise
repito a Vuestra Señoría la que le pido en la de
escribir asimesmo en todas
las ocasiones a los Excelentísimos Señores Virrey
Y Virreyna duque y Mi señora
la duquesa de Alburquerque
las gracias de la honrra que me
hazen y que se promete Vuestra Señoría me

la continuaran Como prinzi-
pes que son En todo y asi mes-
mo a los *Señores* de esta *Real* Aud*iencia*
que tengo Escrito a V*uestra Señoría* Sus
nombres; a mi *Señora* la Marquesa
de Villanueba su cuñada de
V*uestra Señoría* me pondra a sus plantas
y le dara Esa pues En mi oblig*ación*
[fol. 2r]
Esta *Siem*pre Viva la memoria
de la persona de su difunto
esposo el *señor* Marq*ués* y mi amigo
reconoziendo Su falta En la
ocasion pres*ente* por su gran palabra actibidad y eficazia
con q*ue* se me havia ofrezido
a favorezerme y tambien
me es forzoso representar a V*uestra Señoría*
que no omita diligenzia nin-
guna que se ofreziere por asegurar de mi parte el dejar mi ca-
Sa fundamentada dandome n*uest*ro
Señor Vida ya que mi fortuna
me lleba de nuebo a tanta distanzia y asi atienda V*uestra Señoría* con
Cuydado a todas las que re-
zivira mias y a dios que
G*uarde* la Persona de V*uestra Señoría* felizes
[fol. 2v]
años como deseo en com-
pañia de mi querida Hija
y nietos que dara V*uestra Señoría* mis
abrazos y hecho mi bendiz*ión*
Mexico Y Abril 16 de 1703

^2*Besa* L*a* M*ano* de V*uestra Señoría* su
P*adre* y su Mas Affecto Y de
Corazon q*ue* le ama

el Marques de la Naba
de Brazinas ^

Mi querido Hijo don Ygnacio Lopez de Zarate

----

42. *Diego de Vargas to Ignacio López de Zárate, Mexico City, 27 April 1703, ARGD, LS.*

[fol. 1r]
[cross top center]
Hijo y señor mio tengo Escrito a Vuestra Señoría En
este Mes de la fecha con el testimonio de haverseme asituado los 4000 pesos de renta que
por via de encomienda me hizo la merced
la Magestad de nuestro Rey Carlos Segundo que
Santa gloria haya por dos Vidas y por esta
le repito a Vuestra Señoría lo presente En el Real Y suppremo
Consejo de Camara de Yndias pidiendo la
Confirmazión Como asi se refiere en dicho
testimonio y tambien para asegurar la
dicha renta respecto de lo lejos que se
halla el Reino de la Nueva Mexico de Esta Ciudad
y por consiguiente su recurso para asegurar la cobranza de dicha renta
Yndependente de los Governadores que fueren
de dicho Reino pedir a su Magestad Su Real
Cedula Ynibiendo del conozimiento
[written vertically in left margin] adbierto a Vuestra señoría que
    me Escriba siempre por duplicado el primero al señor Don
    Miguel Calderon
Y el segundo a dicho señor Don Diego de suazo Arzediano de esta
    Santa Yglesia,
^2y lo mas seguro siempre en pliego del Señor Marques a su Primo
    Don Miguel de
Ubilla Cavallero de el orden de Santiago JentilHombre de la Boca
    de su Magestad

Contador Mayor Jubilado del Real Tribunal Y Contaduria Mayor
    de quentas ~~el~~
en Mexico.^
[fol. 1v]
de las Causas Que se puedan ofrezer
en atenzión de la dicha cobranza por via de
agrabio a dicha renta para impedir
a la persona o personas a quien se le
diere el poder como asimesmo que
estas no faltando a lo que es de su
obligación sin hazer molestia a los Yndios tributarios pagando estos tan
Solamente en los generos y a la tasa de
el Valor que tienen en dicho Reino como
tambien Sin pedirles mas de lo que
Se les señalare y debiere pagar cada
tributario como el soltero soltera
de edad competente Viudo y Viuda
guardando En todo el estilo que tubieron y pagaron a los encomenderos
que fueron de dicho Reino como En dicho
testimonio se Expresa.

Asimesmo que la dicha Persona que Em
Virtud de dicho poder entendiere en la
Cobranza de dicha renta pueda vivir
o dentro de la Villa de santa fee o en
otra qualquiera, o pueblo de dichos
[fol. 2r]
Yndios Hazienda rancho, o estan-
zia que fuere de su utilidad y combenienzia sin prohivirselo el dicho
Governador sino que la dicha Persona pueda a su voluntad vivir en las partes o lugares donde le pareziere mas
Combeniente para el Seguro de la
Cobranza de la renta de dicha Encomienda
e inmediazión.

Asimesmo que la dicha Persona pueda sa-

lir en las ocasiones Que le pareziere y *tiempos*
de dicho Reino y lugares de la Nueva Mexico
a los de afuera de los Reinos de la Vizcaya Galizia, y Sonora y aun a este
tambien de la nueba España si se
le ofreziere para tratar y contratar
Vender los dichos Generos que adquiriere de la renta de dicha Encomienda
pues en su espezie de los que le pagan
el tributo los dichos Indios es la de la
Cobranza Según el estilo de dicho Reino por
no tener moneda mas que la de los
[fol. 2v]
dichos generos que asi para redu-
zirlos a ella como para la de la remisión a los Reinos de Castilla neze-
Sitare salir En persona lo pueda
Sin pretesto Causa ni motibo el Governador
que fuere de dicho Reino embarazar protestan-
do en caso que lo hiziere el daño atraso
perdidas Yntereses que se le puede seguir
y menoscabos de dicha renta por dicha razon y ser de Justizia la de buscar la de
su reduzión en dichos Reinos por su persona
mesma y en caso de que se halle enfermo
pueda asimesmo la dicha Real Cedula darle la facultad para la persona que eli-
giere señalare y nombrare, que sera
Siempre en la que lo hiziere mas de su satisfazión por no dilatar y poner la perdida En riesgo que pueden tener los
dichos Generos estos Despachos de confirmazión Y Reales Cedulas Son los que
Vuestra Señoría ha de poner en Execución luego remitiendome por duplicado a esta Ciudad
de
[written vertically in left margin] Mexico con el sobre Escrito al
   señor Don Miguel Calderon oydor mas antiguo desta Real
   Audiencia y en segundo
lugar al señor Don Diego de suazo Arzediano de esta santa
   Yglesia Metropolitana de Mexico. a mi querida

hija mill abrazos y nietos y a todos echo mi bendizion y deseo su
    salud que n*ue*stro *se*ñor g*uar*de en compania
de V*uestra* *Señoría* felizes años Mexico y abril 27 de 1703

^2Besa l*a* M*a*no de V*uestra* *se*ñor*í*a su P*a*dre y S*er*vidor
qu*e* le estima de corazon ˄ 3y seguro servidor ˄ *h*asta Morir

el Marques de la Naba
de Brazinas ˄

Mi hijo y *se*ñor Don Yg*nacio*
lopez de Zarate.

―――――

43. *Juan Antonio Pimentel de Prado Olazábal,*
Marqués de la Florida, to Diego de Vargas, Milan,
17 June 1703, AMNB, LS.

[fol. 1r]
[cross top center]
Hermano Y Amigo mio: Con particular
gusto rezivo su ultima Carta de 31 de Diz*iembr*e
De 1702 En que te sirves darme favorables
notizias de El Estado de tu salud, que deseo te se
frequente por dilatados años para que la mia
(que gracias a Dios) logra de este veneficio
la Exerzites En quanto Condujere a tu mayor agrado y servicio.

Despues de haver arrivado la flota, tube
la Ynfausta nueba de la temprana muerte de
mi Querido sobrino Juanito que s*an*ta gloria
*h*aya En que no deves dudar El gran sentim*ient*o
que me motivaria tan gran perdida, porque paso a darte el pesame.

Ya habras tenido notizia del frangente que ha subce-
dido a la flota, estando en El Puerto de Galizia

[fol. 1v]
Por la Ymbasion que En Ella hizieron las
Armadas de *h*Olanda y Ynglaterra En q*ue*
se perdio gran parte de Mercadurias, que
ha Causado g mucho atraso, haviendome toca-
do a mi tambien de perdida El Chocolate que
me remitias, pues haviendo escrito a Cadiz para que se Ynformaran de D*o*n Fausto
De Bustamente respondio que todo se
habia perdido y que ni aun su ropa
Pudo salvar:

Por la Copia de la Zertificazion que me re-
mites veo el estado de tus dependenzias
que me alegro *h*aya llegado ya El caso de Su
fenezimiento tan a tu favor En medio
de los atrasos que te se han Ocasionado para solizitarlo, Y Espero que te hayas
restituido a ese Govierno, pues no dudo de la
Justificazion de ese *se*ñor Virey habra atendido a tus razones,

He Visto la Copia de la Carta que escrives
[fol. 2r]
a tu hijo y mi sobrino D*o*n Ygnacio
Y me pareze bien la determinazion que
has t*h*omado En El Poder G*e*n*e*ral que has
dado a Granada para la Administrazion de tus Mayorazgos En aquella
Ciudad Y deves asegurarte sien*d*to yn-
finto no hallarme en la corte, donde pu-
dieras atender a tus dependenzias, pero
deves Creer de mi fineza y cariño, que En
quanto pudiere contribuir a Ellas desde aqui
me hallaras con la promptitud, que en todas ocasiones has Experimentado
he deseado servirte, como lo executare en
quantas me facilitares nuebamente de tu
mayor satisfacion, que Es quanto se me
ofreze dezirte N*ue*st*r*o senor te guarde
los m*u*ch*o*s años que puede y deseo Real Casti-

llo de Milan Y Junio 17 de 1703.

^2hermano y Amigo, mio yo estaba gusto-
sisimo aguardando la llegada a espana^

Mi hermano Y Amigo el Marqués de la Nava de Brazinas

[fol. 2v]

^2de mi querido Sobrino Juan de Vargas
no dudando me bendria luego a buscar aqui, pero dios fue serbido de
disponer otra Cosa Cumplase su
Santa boluntad, yo quedo bueno y
gustoso en este empleo y Solo Siento el no poder asistir a las dependençias Como quisiera por estar tan
apartado de Madrid pero hare lo que
pudiere y apretare a mi sobrino
Don ygnaçio para que atienda a lo
mucho que te debe;

Te Besa la mano tu hermano y
Amigo de Coraçon

el Marqués de la florida^

---

44. *Diego de Vargas to Ignacio López de Zárate, El Paso del Río del Norte, 16 September 1703, ARGD, LS.*

[fol. 1r]

[cross top center]

Hijo Y Señor mio remito a Vuestra Señoría el duplicado adjunto
    de la que en

27 de Abril pasado de este año le hise despacho y lo repito desde este presidio del Paso del rio del norte a distancia de 400 leguas de mexiCo para pasar a la Villa de Santa Fee 120 leguas, no
    de-

xando de dar a Vuestra Señoría esta razon de hallarme con salud
    despues de t-

an dilatado Viaje porque por solizitar notizias de V*uestra* S*eñoría*
    remito

Correo a Mex*i*Co pareziendome el mes que biene de octubre
    pueda

adquirirlas, *h*aviendo llegado naos de esos puertos ya que las

qu*e h*an, llegado de la Franzia i no tengo fortuna de resibir de

V*uestra* S*eñoría* ninguna en medio de tener al Primo el S*eñor*
    Mar*qué*s de

Ribas y en el pliego que escribe a mex*i*Co a su primo Don Mig-

uel de Ubilla por cuya direczion ba esta, biniera Segura a

mis manos, y asi V*uestra* S*eñoría* para mi no tiene que darme
    disculpa si

no es, la del resfrio de su Volumtad, o por mejor dezir ninguna

y porque no jusgue faltar la mia ni poder faltar ni menos

la de mi atenzion le doy razon remitiendole en el primer lu-

gar esos dos memoriales para que en el Consejo de camara de

Junta de guerra de Yndias añadiendo, o quitando lo que a

V*uestra* S*eñoría* le paresiere para ponerlos en el estilo que se deba
    darselos

remito.

El primero de pedir ygual Sueldo del que gosa el gobernador

y Cap*itán* Gene*ra*l de la nueba Viscaya,

y el Segundo el pedir se me mejore en uno de los puestos que e-

n, el Señalo para lo qual tengo remitido el poder al S*eñor* Mar*qué*s
    de

Ribas por duplicado desde Enero pasado deste presente a*ñ*o a *h*as-

[fol. 1v]

ta Mayo; y lo repito en esta mesma la suplica con la notizia

de mi entrada haviendole remitido a V*uestra* S*eñoría* el testimonio
    de la vis-

ta y revista a mi fabor de la R*ea*l Audienzia condenando en cos-

tas a D*on* P*edr*o Cubero, al cabildo y Villa de S*an*ta Fee y asi no
    lo repito

en esta hasta tener notizia de V*uestra* S*eñoría* pues es fuerza me la
    de de los

instrumentos que le tengo remitidos; como tambien de lo que

*h*ubiere exe executado en el despacho de Mar*qué*s de la Naba de
    B-

razinas; y ajuste de su R*ea*l derecho de la media *a*nata; y de la mersed del *h*abito de mi hijo que gose de D*ios* como le tengo escrito y

por sus papeles que llebaba originales con los de sus Serbizios; que *h*ari-

an remision a V*uestra Señoría* sus Amigos: de cuya llegada de flota aunque

se tiene por sin duda de su Salbamento a los puertos de Galizia se de-

sea, y yo tambien por el bien Comun, demas de saber de lo que remiti

y tengo escrito a V*uestra Señoría* de los cajones de chocolate que remiti con Don

Fausto Justamante y el que a V*uestra Señoría* le escribi remitiese a mi herm-

ano el Mar*qués* de la Florida.

Los puntos que remito a V*uestra Señoría* para estar a la defenza de qualquie-

ra informe Siniestro de parte de Don P*edro* Cubero que es que fomenta y

*h*a mantenido el pleito suponiendo la Villa pide. estos son para que V*uestra Señoría* se halle en la adbertenzia de *h*aber hecho ynforme la R*ea*l A-

udiencia de la Sentencia a mi fabor promulgada en Vista y re-

Vista; y declarar no tener embarazo paraque se me de paso a la R*ea*l Cedula, y que se me de por testimonio paraque el Excelent*ísimo* Señor Virei

Con su Vista me mande dar los despachos si fuere servido; y asi

Con dicho ynforme y los testimonios remitidos a V*uestra Señoría* de *h*ab-

erme declarado por buen Jues con vista de la Residenzia; y con el del tribunal de cuentas de no deber nada a su Ma*gestad* y man-

dado se me pagar lo que a mi fabor alcanzo; se reconosera la malizia en el R*ea*l Consejo Confirmando la d*i*cha Sentenzia c*omo* de

Juez Competente en birtud de la R*ea*l Cedula Cometiendo el Conosi-

[fol. 2r]

~~si~~miento a d*i*cha R*ea*l Audien*ç*ia haviendo executoriado: por

d*i*chos Tribunales todo lo Contra mi depuesto por nulo: y no nesesito

a V*uestra* S*eñorí*a demas adbentenzia quando todo se lo tengo
    escrito; con es-
ta notizia con el duplicado del mes de Abril de 27 de este año
y no dexara V*uestra* S*eñorí*a de tener persona en el Consejo que le
    de razon,
dandomela V*uestra* S*eñorí*a tanbien de *h*aber visto a *d*icho S*eñor*
    Su Primo el
M*arqué*s de Ribas y de la que se *h*ubiere, puesto en execusion,
    remi-
tiendome V*uestra* S*eñorí*a el traslado del memorial q*u*e se *h*ubiere
    presen-
tado; y lo que *h*ubiere parezido a esos ss*eño*res prometiendome
Siempre tendra logro mi deseo, quando tan en justicia se debe
reconoser lo que pido.

En tomando possezion de mi Gobierno en la Villa de S*anta* Fee
    des-
pachare el testimonio que se me manda en la R*eal* Cedula a
    Mexico
al superior Gobierno: y repetire a V*uestra* S*eñorí*a esta y mas a lo
    que debiere
responder: segun la que V*uestra* S*eñorí*a me escribiere si es que *h*a
    solizita-
do su cuidado el hazerlo deseando sea con la buena notisia
de la Salud de V*uestra* S*eñorí*a y de mi Hija y nietos y echo mi
    bendizion de-
seando N*uestro* S*eñor* guar*d*e a V*uestra* S*eñorí*a en su Compañia
    felizes años; y remitira V*uestra* S*eñorí*a
esas Cartas a mis hijos; y a mi hermano Don Gregorio a tordelaguna. *f*echa en este presidio del passo del Rio del norte, y Reyno de
la Nueba Mexi*C*o y septiembre 16 de este año de 1703

^2B*esa* l*a* M*ano* de V*uestra* s*eñorí*a su Padre y s*ervid*or
que Solo le estima Con fineza

el Marques de la Naba
de Brazinas ^

Mi Hijo y s*eño*r Don Ygnasio Lopes Zarate.

———

45. *Diego de Vargas to King Felipe V, El Paso del Río del Norte, c. 16 September 1703*, ARGD, LS.

[fol. 1r]
[cross top center]
Señor
Don Diego de Vargas Zapata luxan Ponze de leon; Marques de la naba de brazinas, puesto rendidamente a los Reales pies
de Vuestra Magestad le representa como despues de la sublebasion
    general
de las naziones indios y pueblos del Reino de la Nueba Mexico y
    sus
probincias que acesio por el año pasado de 680 quedo solo redu-
çido el dominio de Vuestra Magestad; en aquellos territorios al
    Pueblo del pre-
sidio del passo, y los demas de sus fronteras porque el resto de ello
lo ocupaban rebeldes y apostatas, los sublebados que sacudido
el Yugo de la obedienzia de Vuestra Magestad solo rendian
    Vasallage, a la ba-
rbaridad de su arbitrio; en cuya terquedad, se mantubieron por
mas tiempo de 12 años hasta que con ocazion de la merzed que
    Vuestra Magestad
fue serbido de hazerle al suplicante de Gobernador i Capitan
    General
de aquel Reino por el año pasado de 88 entro hallando su indozi-
lidad; redusiendo su inobedienzia, reconquistando su rebe-
ldia; y pasificando su inquietud; y puesto en su antigua de-
bozion los alterados, se restituyo la Corona de Vuestra Magestad
    ynprimio en
los animos hasta entonses resistentes de estos Servicios fue informado Vuestra Magestad por cartas consultas de los Virreyes de
    esta Nue-
ba España i de la Junta de Real hazienda y guerra de este Reino i
mereziendo en su Real aprezio, aseptazion fue serbido a consulta del Real y supremo consejo, Camara y Junta de Guerra de Yndias de prorrongarle a dicho Don Diego dicho gobierno por Real
    çedu-
la del año de 697 acompañando esta mersed con la del titulo
de reconquistador y pasificador de aquellas Probinzias, por ha-
berlo sido con la felizidad i buen efecto que a Vuestra Magestad
    Consta.

No faltaron Señor emulos que procuraron desbanezer la Gloria
[fol. 1v]
que el Suplicante a costa de su proprio caudal, y a rriesgo de su
    Vida supo
adquirir y estos se declararon mucho mas luego que sintieron que
    la Real
manifizensia dandose por bien servido de sus facsiones Comenzo a
galardonarlas pues el Gobernador de aquel Reino subsesor de Don
    Diego de-
clarandose desafecto, y aun enemigo dio en fomentar y aun en
Sugerir quexas i demandas Contra Don Diego que hasta los Reales
    Oi-
dos de Vuestra Magestad llegaron de cuyo Supremo Consejo
    emanaron rescriptos en
cuya Virtud; se hallan hoy desbanezidas y deshechas las ynpostu-
ras, que este i otros Sus malquerientes maquinaron Contra su
    proze-
der, Creditos Caudal i Vida, y Don Diego restituido al quinquenio
    de
su prorogazion, e inmediato a bolber a gobernar dicho Reino.

Esta merzed se la hizo Vuestra Magestad segun i Como la gozo la
    primera vez, que asi
lo expreza el Real despacho en que se la prorrogo; Y llegando el
    caso de su
obtension la habra de pozer diminuta respecto de que la primera
    oca-
zion, que se la merezio a Vuestra Magestad incluya este gobierno
    el politico y mi-
litar del prezidio del passo y sus addiasenzias i agregaziones; y en el
medio tiempo del Gobierno de Don Pedro Rodrigues Cubero se
    separo de
el de la Nueba MexiCo dicho prezidio del paso por haberle dado
    la Com-
pañia del al Capitán Don Antonio Valberde a quien tanbien
    expedio
el Virrey Conde Montesuma despachos de Justizia Mayor en lo
politico y esta hoi en posezión de uno, i otro; Con que bendra el
    suplicante
a conseguir por premio el gobierno lymitado, quando sus buenas
    oper-

aziones le supieron dilatar, y antes de ellas lo supo merezer integro por
merzed.

No es menos diminusion la que *h*oy padeze este Gobierno, por razon
del *ti*empo que aqui se le prorrogo i el de mas de 6 años que *h*a que se le dilata
Su yngrezo; en cuyo espazio no es ponderable lo que *h*a padezido; todo
el *h*a sido un puro pleitear, teniendo por Jues (si lo es el inCompetente)
un Gobernador apazionado que sin darle oidos a su defensa; execu-
taba en su ofenza quantos arbitrios le dictaba su antojo; teniendole
preso tres años los 5 meses de ellos Con grillos, enbargandole vienes; i prib-
andole aun las mas santas i religiosas Combersaziones, i comuni-
caziones prose*s*a*n*do causas inquietando querellosos i sacando a plaza
[fol. 2r]
Ynjustos demandantes; y logrando con ellos el destruir el
Caudal del Suplicante lastimar ya q*u*e no herir en sus Creditos Solizitando degradarle de la mersed con que V*uestra* M*agestad* honrro
Sus Serbizios, y Sobre todo intentando que el suplicante no
le susediera y todo esto Sin mas razon que la de haber aser-
tado a serbir a V*uestra* M*agestad* y pasificado un R*ein*o para q*u*e fuese aumento de los dominios de V*uestra* M*agestad* i Gobierno de Don P*edr*o

Este, axamiento, Pobreza, Pleytos, dilaziones, y demas molestias
padezidas por el suplicante las pone en la balanza de su merito para que atendiendolas V*uestra* M*agestad* Como Servizios (pues de los
hechos dimanaron) y teniendo prezente quanto se le *h*a zerze-
nado d*i*cho Gov*iern*o Con *h*aberle desmenbrado el prezidio del passo, y su direccion y Jurisdiccion militar y politica y que biene a ser desygual premio a su obrar quando havia de ser
mui larga y ampla la Compensazi*ó*n de su padezer; se dig-

ne de mejorarle la mersed hecha disponiendo se entienda
y berifique. ^2En el Govierno y Capitania General
y Presidenzia de el Reyno de filipinas,
O en la del Reyno de Guatimala, O en
la del Reyno de Santa fee Y Nuevo Reyno
de Granada; Y de no tener lugar la del
Govierno y Capitania General de el Reyno de
la Vizcaya, para quando Cumpla el
que lo exerze que es el Maestre de Campo
Don Juan fernández de Cordoba por ser Ygual
su Guerra de la de este de la Nueva
Mexico, y Confinar Con el; Y el Suplicante en el año de 1691, por Manda-
miento de Vuestro excelentísimo Virrey que fue
Conde de Galbe Con Resoluzión de junta^
[fol. 2v]
^2General de Real Hazienda y Guerra de su Corte de Mexico
le Mando yr al suplicante Governando
las Armas que Parezio se Uniesen Con las
de su Presidio las del de Janos, y de Zinaloa y las de la Compañía Volante de Ca-
asas Grandes Como fue y siguio la Guerra y Campaña a las fronteras de Sonora a su Costa, lo qual le serbe de Mery-
to Para esta Pretension de este empleo
por el Cognozimiento y esperienzia que tiene
de toda la tyerra y Reyno, O en la que
Vuestra Magestad fuere servido en que Rezivira Merced.

el Marques de la Naba
de Brazinas^

———

46. *Gregorio Pimentel de Prado to Diego de Vargas, np, nd [mid-late 1703],* AMNB, LS.

[fol. 1r]
[cross top center]
Mi Hermano, Amigo, Y señor mio de mi Vida

te aseguro por la Verdad que professo Que aunque
no se me han enJugado las Lagrimas de la triste
noticia que nos trajo la flota passada de mi Muy
querido Sobrino Don Juan Manuel de Bargas
CuYa memoria (para EnComendarle a Dios) du-
rara mentras Viviere. Tu Carta amigo Y Hermano mio escrita En 29 de Marzo deste pressente
año me tiene alborozadissimo porque ademas
de traerme la mas alegre noticia que es hallarte
Muy bueno la hallo aCompañada Con la que anhe-
laba Con ansia mi Obligacion y amistad: Con-
siderandote rrestituido Con tanto Credito Como
te tiene merecido tu tan notorio proceder a Regen-
tar tu Govierno, de que te doy muchissimas enhorabuenas. Y aunque Considero el Largo tiempo que
ahora tienes que passar para poder esperar Verte
En este Reyno Como tengo por oidos los motivos
que te obligaran a ello, y el principal que es tu puntto
habre de Conformarme Con tanta ausencia, pues
la permite asi la Divina Magestad.

Luego que Recivi tu Carta eJecute lo que me Man-
das en ella escriviendo a mis Sobrinos pidien-
doles que sin perder ocassion escriviessen a los
excelentísimos Señores Duques de Alburquerque, ViRe-
[fol. 1v]
yes de esse ReYno, dando a Sus excelencias las gracias, de
tanta obligazion, Como en la que a todos nos han
puesto, Con lo que te han honrrado, Y favorezido. a que me han rrespondido, estan muy En esso,
y ofreciendo aCompañar Otras Cartas de mi
señora La Duquessa de Alburquerque la maior Y
mi señora Doña Maria Alvarez Que es muy su estrecha; Constandome que su sseñoria aCompaño a mi
Sobrina mi señora Doña Yssavel de Bargas, quando Sus excelencias Salieron de Madrid para esse Reyno, Y deJo a tu Consideracion Hermano mio Como Sabria rrepresentar tu rrazon, Y Con que
eficazia se empeñaria para que todos hayamos
logrado tan alegre dia. Y asi deves estar Cierto de

q*ue* Continuaran Sus finezas, Como lo piden Su
immutable Cariño, Y obligazion.

Y aunq*ue* no me *h*as dado, ni das parte de la nueva rresoluz*ión* q*ue h*as tomado para la administracion de tus mayorazgos, Siendo tan fiel la
amistad que te professo me atrevo a poner En
tu Consideracion Que atendiendo a q*ue* tu Cassa *h*oy la esta rrepresentando Con tanta de-
cenzia y lustre, El *señor* Don Ygnazio de zarate
mi Sobrino de los ConseJos de Castilla, Y ytal-
lia a q*ue* se añade Su larga familia Con tan Ve-
llissimos Hijos, tenia Yo estos por motivos Her-
[fol. 2r]
mano mio, para q*ue* atendiendo a q*ue* la grande
YnJuria de los tiempos es mayor que lo que
podras Considerar no obstante q*ue* por alla se
padezca, Y q*ue* supongo tus atrassos, Cave
en tu generossidad, q*ue* la manifiestes alargan-
dote en todo quanto pudieres para el maYor
alivio de tus Hijos Y nietos, Y si la Confianza Con q*ue* Vivo de tus muchos favores, te sirves
de admitirla, Como ella es, me atreviera a pro-
ponerte, que el Cuidado de la hacienda de
Granada, Corriese por el Cuidado de la Persona que has elegido; Y la de Torrelaguna
la diesses y en Cargasses a mis Sobrinos, Don
Joseph de Bargas, Y Juanica; Y lo demas Considero por muy proporcionado, Que lo Cuiden
y gozen mis Sobrinos, el *señor* Don Ygnazio, y mi *señora*
Do*ña* Ysavel, Y esto Hermano y amigo mio, es lo q*ue*
yo eJecutara asistiendome tu obligazion.

De mi Hermano Don Juan, Y de los Hijitos tus
Sobrinos tengo muy frescas noticias de Su
buena Salud, Y Considero el grande gusto q*ue*
todos tendran Con leer la Carta que me dices escrives a mi Hermano por todo su Contenido: yo
escrivi el Correo passado a su M*erced*, Y lo rrepito
En este diciendole que Como tan Ynteressado

escriva a los ex*celentísi*mos se*ñ*ores Virreyes, Y supongo, no
[fol. 2v]
faltara a esta obligacion. Y aunque
te tengo Escrito dandote gracias porque
gustavas gozase Yo el chocolate q*ue* embiabas
Con D*on* fausto de Bustamante, te las rrepito ahora, Si bien Como Sabras no lo *h*a entre-
gado d*i*cho D*on* fausto:

^2her*m*ano mio y mi Amigo, no se me ofreze q*ue* añadir
a lo q*ue* te llebo expressado, sino es rrepetir
el gran gusto Con q*ue* me hallo Conssiderandote
Ya restituido y con tanto Credito a tu Go*vie*rno
donde desseo *h*ayas passado Con la m*a*yor felisidad.

tu her*m*ano Amigo y mas reconozido
Serv*i*dor q*ue* desea tus m*a*yores gustos.
D*on* Gregorio Pimentel

no quiero her*m*ano mio Carezcas de la no*ti*cia de hallarsse ya tu
Sobrino Sebastian Cap*itá*n de Caballos, y de G*re*gorio me escribe
mi her*m*ano le acomodara presto.^

Se*ñ*or Marques de la nava de Bracinas mi Her*m*ano y mi m*e*jor
    amigo y se*ñ*or

————

47. *Ignacio López de Zárate to Diego de Vargas, Madrid, 28 September 1703*, AMNB, C.

[fol. 1r]
[cross top center]
Mi se*ñ*or y mi Padre Con la Occassion
de este avisso q*ue* se despacha se me ofrece
la q*ue* tanto desseava de repetir mi rendimiento a los pies de V*uestra* Se*ñor*ía y manifestar
a V*uestra* Se*ñor*ía el summo Consuelo q*ue* reçivi Con
su Carta de V*uestra* Se*ñor*ía de 31 de Diziembre

del año proximo passado por las buenas nue-
bas de Mantenerse Vuestra Señoría en la perfecta
salud que tanto he menester, porque doy muchas graçias a Nuestro señor mayormente por la
conçiderazion de la pena y dolor que Causaria
a Vuestra Señoría la notiçia que tubo desde la Habana de la trempana y açelerada muerte
de mi querido Hermano y amigo Don Juan
Manuel de Vargas y Pimentel Cuya perdida me tiene Cada dia Summamente descon-
solado, y por no agravar mas la que reconozco
[fol. 1v]
asiste tan Justamente a Vuestra Señoría me remito
en este particular a Uno de los Capitulos de la Carta que escrivi a Vuestra Señoría en 5
de Mayo de este presente año

hAviendo Observado todo el demas contheni-
do de la referida Carta de Vuestra señoría y
hallandole repetido, y confirmado por
otra de Vuestra Señoría de 4 de Abrill de este
presente año, (que devio de traher algun
Capitan françes porque de todas las Otras
tres Cartas, que Con el y otros Capitanes
françeses me refiere Vuestra Señoría haverme escripto no ha llegado Otra ninguna a mis ma-
nos) Y reduçiendose Uno, y otro conthe-
nido a la Justa resoluçion que Vuestra Señoría ha tomado en encargar la Administrazion de
sus Mayorazgos, y Haçienda por lo res-
pectivo a esta Corte al Marques de
Bargas, mi Primo, O, Al conde de la
Puebla, O, al señor Don sancho Bullon
mis amigos, Y por lo perteneçiente a
Granada al señor don fernando teruel, conde
[fol. 2r]
de Villamena; Solo se me ofreçe deçir
a Vuestra Señoría ha sido tan Combeniente, y preçissa,
Como Correspondiente a todos los motivos,
que Vuestra Señoría me refiere, que son muy propios
de la gran Comprehenssion, y prudençia de

Vuestra Señoría Con que mi respecto y atençion a Vuestra
  Señoría
solo deve Contribuir en asegurar a Vuestra Señoría
Con quanto gusto, y expeçial Complasencia
quedo çelebrando la determinazion de
Vuestra Señoría por Comprometerme de esta suertte
que dichos Mayorazgos y haçienda de Vuestra Señoría
han de Experimentar de hoy mas los efectos
de su mayor resguardo, y aumento, para
que Vuestra Señoría Consiga su Justo fin y desseo, pues
el mio nunca puede ser otro que el de sus mayores Yntereses de Vuestra Señoría porque queden en
el todo afianzados los de mi muger hija
de Vuestra Señoría y los de sus hijos, Nietos de Vuestra Señoría
y por todo passo a dar a Vuestra Señoría muchas graçias, Y en Cumplimiento puntual Obedien-
çia a deçir a Vuestra Señoría que En Consequencia de lo dispuesto por Vuestra Señoría Entregare a los señores referidos
[fol. 2v]
nuebos Poderes Abientes los papeles que
tengo perteneçientes a dichos Mayorazgos
y haçienda de Vuestra Señoría y Una relaçion Yndivi-
dual del estado en que hoy dia se halla
por que instruidos de Uno y otro puedan Go-
bernarse Con mayor façilidad en su Admi-
nistraçion, y por lo que toca a Granada, hare
execute lo mismo don diego de olvera, para
que el señor Conde de Villamena pueda Con
la misma façilidad Administrar tambien
aquella Hacienda;

Y aunque en la expeçial honrra que Vuestra Señoría me hizo
en Rebocar los Poderes a don Juan Gon-
zalez Calderon, por el motivo de la notiçia que tubo Vuestra Señoría de mi dichoso empleo
Con Ysabel hija de Vuestra Señoría por darmelos
a mi tan absolutos reconozco que en ellos
me eximia Vuestra Señoría de dar quentas, procure desde que empeçe a Ussar de ellos
yr previniendo las que eran tan Correspondientes a mi punto, y Obligacion, por la

misma Confianza, que Vuestra Señoría ^haçia^ de mi por si lle-
gava el casso (Como estava ya tan proximo)
[fol. 3r]
de que me las pidiese mi querido Hermano
Don Juan Manuel de Vargas, y Pimentel
y no haviendo llegado este por los Justos Jui-
çios de Dios Y ofreçiendose para el
efecto el mismo en los nuebos Poderes que
Vuestra Señoría ha dado soliçitare, que quien Ussare
de ellos las reconozca, çensure, y Vea
para que de su Resulta de quenta a Vuestra Señoría
Con toda distinçion, y en el ynter me ha
pareçido haçer por mayor Un extracto
de ellas para remitirsele a Vuestra Señoría como
lo executo en el papel adjunto, en que
ban expressadas tres Relaçiones la primera de los efectos, Y Cuerpos, de que se
Componen dichos Mayorazgos, y haçienda
la Segunda de lo que han produçido y ree-
dituado todo el tiempo, que las he Administrado, y la terçera se Reduçe al descargo
de todo lo perçivido, y Cobrado, que es
quanto a sus dos Zitadas Cartas de Vuestra Señoría
[fol. 3v]
se me ofreçe Satisfaçer

Y haviendo Reçivido Con el Alcançe, que despacho
esse señor Virrey Otras tres de Vuestra Señoría de 7 16 y
27 de Abril de este presente año, en que
he logrado la repetiçion de mantenerse
Vuestra Señoría en la perfecta Salud que tanto he
menester, dejo a la Considerazion de Vuestra Señoría
de quanto gusto habra sido para toda
esta su Cassa tan favorable notiçia, y
añadiendose la de haverse feneçido la Caussa, que la maliçia temeridad, y ambiçion
fulmino a Vuestra Señoría Con los autos de Vista y
rebista, que por essa Real Audiençia
se dieron tan en favor de Vuestra Señoría que
damos todos los de ella Summamente
Alborozados, y Consolados de Veer ya a

Vuestra Señoría libre de semejante persecuzion y restituydo Como era tan Justo a su Go-
bierno de que nos hemos dado todos mill
enhorabuenas y io se las repito a *Vuestra Señoría*
desseando *h*aya llegado *Vuestra Señoría* a su residençia muy bueno, y que se Continue esta
[fol. 4r]
feliçidad Como tanto hemos menester

Luego q*ue* Reçivi dichas Cartas fui a Veer a mi
se*ñ*ora la Duquessa de Alburquerque, y mi
muger Executo lo propio p*or* no dilatar
el dar a *su excelencia* las graçias y manifestarla
lo reconoçidos, y obligados, q*ue* nos hallava-
mos al se*ñ*or Duque por lo mucho, q*ue* ha
favoreçido a *Vuestra Señoría* y mis parientes hiçieron
lo mismo y todos hemos buelto a haçer
nueba Ynstancia a *su excelencia* en Orden
a que el se*ñ*or Duque atienda Como *h*asta
aqui a *Vuestra Señoría* y no dudo q*ue su excelencia* lo executara en esta misma Conformidad, por
lo mucho, q*ue* siempre nos ha favoreçido,
y honrrado

Ynmediatamente q*ue* Reçivi Con las tres referidas de
Vuestra Señoría el testimonio de las dichas senten-
çias de Vista y rebista y el de la situazion
de la encomienda de 4U pessos, y el de el
Alcançe de los 17U y tantos pessos, q*ue Vuestra Señoría* haçe
a la R*e*al Haçienda p*or* las dos quentas que
estubieron a Su Cargo, lo presente todo Con
[fol. 4v]
Un Memorial q*ue* hiçe p*ar*a la Confirmaçion
de la Segunda Vida en Conformidad de lo
executado p*or* esse se*ñ*or Virrey en el Consejo
de Yndias *h*ablando al se*ñ*or Marqués del
Carpio y a todos los M*i*nistros de que se compone p*or* si podia en este avisso remitir
a *Vuestra Señoría* los Despachos pero *h*aviendole an-
tiçipado no se ha podido Conseguir respecto de lo

mucho que *h*ay que haçer en la expediçion
de qualquier negoçio en dicho Conssejo antes
de tomarse en el resolucion alguna, pues
primero se vee el Memorial se remite
al fiscal, Como se ha executado, con el que
yo presente se passa luego al Relator p*ara*
q*ue* haga relaçion y hecha se aquerda Consulta para que su M*agesta*d resuelva pero dis-
curro se despachara Alcançe y que podre
Con el remitir dichos despachos a V*uestra Señoría* Cuya
soliçitud no dejare de la mano, p*or* lograr
la fortuna de servir a V*uestra Señoría* Como lo
procurare tambien en la pretenssion
de que se le Yguale a V*uestra Señoría* el Sueldo
del que goza el Govern*ado*r y Capitan general
del Reyno de la Vizcaya y Real del
Parral y despues Entrare en la pretension
de que a V*uestra señoría* mejoren de puesto, que es
quanto V*uestra señoría* me manda,

Y *h*aviendome informado si p*or* parte de la Villa
de s*an*ta fee, o, de Don Pedro Rodriguez
Cubero se *h*avia acudido en dicho Consejo
de Yndias, devo asegurar a V*uestra señoría* no
se *h*a hecho tal recursso, y q*ue* en Casso
de que Con la Occassion de Otro avisso
que Venga de esse Reyno le quieran
haçer, quedo Con el Cuydado de estar
muy a la Vista para Oponerme Con las
advertençias, que V*uestra señoría* me embia del
Abogado, para la defenssa, q*ue* fuere
preçisso haçer, pero me persuado, q*ue* la dicha,
Villa, y don Pedro Rodriguez Cubero
no Cometeran este Segundo Yerro, y dis-
parate;

tambien Obedeçere a V*uestra señoría* escribiendo al *señ*or
Duque de Alburquerque, dandole las graçias,
y lo mismo execute Con todos los Ministros
[fol. 5r]

de essa Real Audiencia, y me ha pareçido tambien escrivir al *señor* Arzobispo
en la misma Conformidad,

Y todas las Cartas para V*uestra señoría* encaminare en
adelante, Como V*uestra señoría* me previene por
duplicados a don Miguel Calderon de la
Varca, y a don Diego de Suazo;

Remito a V*uestra señoría* las adjuntas de los tios Marqués
de la Florida, y don Gregorio Pimentel,
y de la tia mi *señora* Doña Antonia de
Vargas, qu*ie*nes a Dios gracias se hallan
buenos, Como lo estamos todos en esta
de V*uestra señoría* y Siempre a sus pies Con toda
resignaçion, desseando, qu*e* N*uestro* señor nos permita la fortuna de Veer a V*uestra señoría* Como
se lo suplicamos, Y que gu*ard*e a V*uestra señoría* los
Muchos, y dilatados años, que puede
y tanto hemos menester; Madrid, y sep*tiemb*re 28
de 1703

^2B*esa* los p*ie*s de V*uestra Señoría* Su Mas affecto
Reconocido y Obligado servido*r* y hijo

Don Ygnaçio Lopez
de Zarate^

señor don diego de Bar*ga*s Zapata Y Luxan,
Ponçe de Leon Marqués de la Naba de Bar-
çinas mi *señor* y mi Padre;

————

48. *Ignacio López de Zárate to Diego de Vargas,*
Madrid, 6 October 1703, AMNB, DS.

[fol. 1r]
Relazion de todos Los Cuerpos y efectos de que se componen

los mayorazgos y hazienda que posee el *señor* Don Diego de
   Vargas
Zapata y luxan Ponze de leon Marques de la Nava de
Barzinas asi en esta corte Villa de Torrelaguna y otros
Lugares a ella ZircumVecinos como en la Ziu*da*d de Granada

[centered and underlined] En Madrid
Unas casas grandes Prinzipales que es-
tan en la Calle del Almendro;
Otras Acesorias que estan a la callexuela
que sale a la Parroquia de *sa*n Pedro;
Otras Casas q*ue* estan en la plaza ma-
yor;
Un Zenso que paga D*o*n Juan Diaz
Marino Venefiziado de la d*i*cha Parro-
chia de *sa*n Pedro;

[centered and underlined] En los Lug*ar*es de los Carabancheles:
Las terzias;

[centered and underlined] En la Villa de Ocaña
Un juro en las alcavalas de aquel
Partido;
[fol. 1v]
[centered and underlined] En la villa de torrelag*un*a
Una Casa Grande en que Un olivar
Zercado;
Quarenta y quatro Aranzadas de Viñas
que se componen en la forma sig*uien*te;
Siete en las Arzas que llaman;
Una en los llanos;
Dos en la lomilla;
Tres en las Presillas;
Siete y media en las Cañadas
Quatro en las Vegas;
Quatro en mirabueno;
Siete y media en las Peñuelas
ocho en el Yrialion,
Quarenta fanegas de tierras de pan
llebar, que *h*ay en aquel termino

Y ochenta en el de Torremocha que
hazen todas Ziento y Veinte;

[centered and underlined] En Mira Flores
Las Zercas;

[centered and underlined] En Buitrago
Las dehesas de las Gariñas y
Viñaderos;

[fol. 2r]
[centered and underlined] En Camarmas del Caño
Un olivas Palomar y tierras;

[centered and underlined] En Valdepielagos
Seisçientas fanegas de Tierras de
pan llevar que Estan Valdias por
hallarse despoblado el lugar por cuya
Causa ni se aREndaron en tiempo
del señor Don Gregorio Pimentel ni en
el de mi señora Doña Juana de Bargas
ni en el de Don Ygnazio Lopez de Zarate;

[centered and underlined] En la Ziudad de Granada
Los Cortixos Casas y Zensos que hay
en ella;
[fol. 2v]
[fol. 3r]
Relazion de todo lo que ha Ymportado dichos mayorazgos
Y Hazienda desde el año de 1690, que fue quando Empezo a
    Administrarlos
Don Ygnazio Lopez de Zarate, En Virtud de
Poder de dicho señor don Diego de Vargas hasta todo Este
    año
Corriente
de 1703; que son En todo Catorze de que sevaxan los Zinco; por
    que Zedio en
virtud de Ynstrumento al señor don Juan Manuel de Vargas
su hermano la referida Hazienda de Granada la renta de Buy-

trago; la de las terzias de los dos Carabancheles, y el Zenso de
 Don Juan Diaz Mariño, que todo lo qual dicho señor don Juan Empeño
Y obligo por el dicho termino de los Zinco años que Cumplen en
 este
presente de 703; y Vienen a quedar desenbarazados y Libres
estos efectos desde Primero de henero del año proximo Venturo de
 1704;

[centered and underlined] Madrid
Las Casas grandes Prinzipales que Estan en la calle del Almendro se
Arrendarian en 6U600 Reales cada año
antes que pasasen a vivirlas los señores
Don Ygnazio Lopez de Zarate Y
Doña Ysavel Maria de Vargas
Zapata y luxan, y Revaxando
los çinco de habitazion, que se le ofrezei-
eron en las Capitulaziones como
Consta de su Escritura, bienen
[fol. 3v]
A quedar solo nueve años que a la
dicha Razon de 6U600 Reales Ympor-
tan 59U400   59U400

Las Casas Acesorias han tenido de hueco
en los dichos Catorze años dos, y los doze
a Razon de 1U950 Reales que ymporta
su Alquiler cada año hazen 23U400   23U400

Las Casas de la plaza mayor Rentan
cada año 4U200 Reales que en los dichos
Catorze años ymportan 58U800 Reales
sin hazer desquento de los huecos
que han tenido muchos de los quar-
tos de dicha casa en el Referido tiempo   58U800

El Zenso que paga Don Juan Diaz Mariño es de 1U100 Reales al año y Re-

vaxando los Zinco de la Zesion q*ue*
se hizo al *señor* Don Juan Manuel
de Vargas que este en el Zielo y
çinco que le gozo Joseph M*artínez* de
Robles *esscriva*no del Numero en Virtud
de Escritura del *señor* Don Diego de
Bargas, por que se le Empeño a
gozar y gozar Vienen a quedar
solo a cargo de d*icho señor* Don Ygnacio
quatro años que ymportan 4U400 R*eales*   4U400

[centered and underlined] Carabancheles
Sus terzias Reales p*or* mitad se Repittan

                                                                        146U000
[fol. 4r]
Un año con otro poco mas o menos   146U
por 4U400 R*eales* y Revaxando los
çinco de la Zesion que se hizo a d*icho*
señor don Juan Manuel de Vargas Ym-
portan los nueve años 39U600   39U600

[centered and underlined] Ocaña
El Juro que en las Alcavalas de aquel
partido se paga Ymporta cada año
1U300 R*eales* de que se Estan deviendo
tres Cumplidos y los onze cobrados
Ymportan 14U300   14U300

[centered and underlined] Tordelaguna
La Casa grande la han vivido
todo el Referido tiempo los *señores* Don
Joseph de Vargas y mi *señora* Doña Juana
de Vargas su muger y por Esta Raçon no se se ha cobrado de sus m*ercedes*
alquiler alguno   o

El olivar solo un año coxio el *señor* Don
Ygnaçio su fruto que llego a ocho
o nueve a*rrobas* de azeite q*ue* a Razon

de 30 R*eale*s cada una ymporta 270 R*eale*s
Y otros dos años el sembrado de la
tierra que fue Verde para sus
Mulas, que Ymportaron 400 R*eale*s y

199U900

[fol. 4v]
Ambas partidas hazen 670 R*eale*s y
todo El demas tiempo *h*asta el
año de 98 En que se le zedio a di*ch*o se*ñor*
don Joseph toda la ha*zien*da de Torrelaguna En precio cada una de 1U050
R*eale*s ha corrido a Venefizio del
di*ch*o se*ñor* don Joseph

199U900
U670

De los çinco años q*ue* di*ch*o se*ñor* don Joseph
ha corrido con di*ch*a hazienda Ymportan 5U250 R*eale*s

5U250

El quarto vajo de la casa estubo arrendado quatro años al Li*zenzia*do don Lorenço furel En precio de 350 R*eale*s q*ue* Ymportan 1U400 R*eale*s

1U400

Las Viñas se labraron el año de 91 y
la cosecha de 92 fue solo de 300 *arrobas*
de Vino que se Vendieron a siete
R*eale*s q*ue* Ymportan 2U100 R*eale*s

2U100

En la Cosecha del año de 93 se cojieron
382 *arrobas* de vino que se vendieron
a seis R*eale*s Y medio q*ue* montan
2U483 R*eale*s

2U483

En la cosecha del año de 94 se cojieron
446 *arrobas* de vino q*ue* se Vendieron
a siete R*eale*s montan 3U122 R*eale*s

3U122

En la cosecha del año de 95 se cojieron
516 *arrobas* de vino q*ue* se vendieron
a 8 R*eales* montan 4U128   4U128
                                                                                219U053

[fol. 5r]
En la cosecha del año de 96 se cojieron   219U053
756 *arrobas* de vino que se Vendieron
a çinco R*eales* y me*di*o montan 4U158 R*eales*   4U158

En la cosecha del año de 97 se cojieron
567 *arrobas* de vino q*ue* se Vendieron a 10
R*eales* montan 5U670 R*eales*   5U670

En la Cosecha del año de 98 se cojieron
581 *arrobas* de vino que se Vendieron
a siete R*eales* montan 4U067 R*eales*   4U067

Las quarenta fanegas de Tierras de
pan llevar que *h*ay en aquel termino y ochenta en el de torremocha q*ue* hazen todas Ziento
y Veinte han estado arrendadas
los *di*chos treze años en quarenta
fanegas de Pan por mitad las
quales se *h*an Convertido en pagar
parte de la Cantidad que se estava
deviendo de la Limosna de pan
Cozido que se da en las tres Pasq*ua*s
de cada año y las de los Corrientes
como consta por los autos de Visita*d*or
del Partido y de la Zertificazion del
Cura de la *di*cha Parroquia de Torrelaguna de estar Cumplidas *h*asta
el Corri*ent*e año de 1703

[centered and underlined] Miraflores
Las Zercas de miraflores han estado

                                                                232U948

[fol. 5v]
Arrendadas todos los dichos 14 años   232U948
en 450 Reales cada uno que en todo Yn-
porta 6U300 Reales   6U300

[centered and underlined] Buytrago
Las dehessas de Gariñas y Viñaderos que estan en su termino las ha
tenido siempre arendadas el
Duque del Ynfantado y paga
2U Reales por Ellas y descontados
los Zinco de la Zesion del señor
Don Juan de Vargas ymportan
los nueve años que quedan 18U Reales   18U

[centered and underlined] Camarmas del Caño
El olivar palomar y tierras ha
estado y esta arrendado en
900 Reales cada año que Ymportan
los 14 años 12U600 Reales   12U600

[centered and underlined] Baldepielagos
De las 600 fanegas de tierras de pan
llevar no haze cargo el señor don Ygnacio
por lo que ba referido en la
Primera relazion de los efectos
Y Cuerpos de dichos Mayorazgos
Y hazienda

[centered and underlined] Granada
Los Cortixos Casas y Zensos
                                                        269U848

[fol. 6r]
Han estado arendados todo   269U848
este tiempo por Escriptura que otorgo
El señor don Gregorio Pimentel año
de 85 a favor de don Francisco Molina Matamoros en 5U Reales ca-

da año y haze cargo El señor don Ygnaçio de Diez años que ha cobrado
esta rrenta hasta el año de 1700
que enpezo a correr la Zesion del
señor don Juan Manuel de Vargas
conque los Diez Referidos ym-
portan 50U Reales   50U

El Zenso sobre el posito antiguo de dicha
Ziudad de 2U750 Reales de rrenta
cada año se halla en concurso y
se compone de quatro que se Re-
dimieron para ymponerle y
estan Graduados en segundo
quinto, onze; y Catorze lugar
Y solo tienen Cavimiento el segundo y quinto de que se cobran
cada año 990 Reales que en los Refe-
ridos diez años ymportan 9U900 Reales   9U900

Suman y Montan todas Estas Partidas de
que me hago Cargo trezientos y Veinte y nueve   329U748
mill setezientos y quarenta y ocho Reales Vellon;
[fol. 6v]
[fol. 7r]
Relacion de lo que Don Ygnacio Lopez de Zarate ha pagado desde
Primero de Junio del año de 1690 que fue quando Empezo a
    admi-
nistrar los Mayorazgos y hazienda del señor don Diego de Vargas
Zapata y luxan mi señor hasta todo este presente año de 1703

Primeramente por lo que se estava deviendo, y ha corrido todo el referido
tiempo de Zenso de 150 ducados
que se paga de las Casas prinzipales
del Mayorazgo que estan en esta Corte en la Calle del Almendro Veinte Y seis mill y quatrozientos Reales
de vellon como consta de la Carta de pago   26U400

Por el Zenso de la fuente de dicha Casa
que se paga a la Villa a Razon

de 275 R*eales* cada año de lo que se Estaba devie*n*do y ha corrido todo el Referido tiempo cinco mill y quinientos R*eales* de *vell*on como consta de
las Cartas de pago   5U500

Por el Zenso de 40U Reales de plata
de Prinzipal y 2U941 de *vell*on q*ue*
rrentan cada año que estan Yn-
puestos sobre las casas de la plaza q*ue*
se pagan al convento de los Anxeles
y don Manuel de Alcedo de lo que
se estava deviendo, y *ha* corrido todo
el Referido tiempo quarenta y
siete mill y cinquenta y seis R*eales*
de *vell*on como consta de cartas de pago   47U056
                                                                         78U956

[fol. 7v]
Por la tercera parte de Yncorri-   78U956
da Particion de huespede de a-
posento que tiene la d*ic*ha casa a
Razon de 39 R*eales* cada ano quinientos Y quarenta y seis R*eales* como
consta de Carta de pago   U546

Al se*ñor* Condestable de Castilla por dos Es-
crituras que tenia Don Alonso faxar-
do su Thesorero Una del se*ñor* Don
Diego de Vargas de 2U du-
cados, y otra del se*ñor* Don Gregorio
Pimentel de la misma Cantidad
con sus Yntereses Zinquenta y
çinco mill R*eales* de *vell*on como consta por
Ambas Escripturas Recuperadas   55U

A Do*ñ*a Angela de Robles Viuda de Don
Francisco de Herrera onze mill
R*eales* de *vell*on por los mismos q*ue* por
Escritura del Se*ñor* Don Diego de Var-
gas que se le devian y por ellos tenia
en las casas Prinzipales del mayo-

razgo de esta corte dos quartos
alto y vaxo a gozar Y gozar como
consta por la misma Escritura
Recuperada   11U

A los herederos de Doña Françisca del
Castillo diez mill y duzientos Reales de vellon
Por los mismos que devia dicho señor

                                                    145U502
[fol. 8r]
Don Diego por Escritura como   145U502
consta de la misma Recuperada   10U200

A Doña Margarita y Doña Dorotea Gil
Criadas que fueron de mi señora Doña
Maria de Zuñiga Noventa y
seis Reales de a ocho como consta del
papel que tenian en su poder de dicho
señor don Diego que hazen de vellon mill
quatrozientos y quarenta Reales   1U440

Al Convento de san Francisco de Torrelaguna
por la memoria de 474 Reales que
se paga en cada año siete mill y
quatrozientos Reales de vellon como cons-
ta de sus Rezivos   7U500

Al Colexio mayor de Alcala por el Çenso
de 4U maravedís que tiene a su favor
cada año sobre la hazienda de torrelaguna asi por lo que se le estava deviendo como por lo Corrido en el
Referido tiempo dos mill Ziento
Y Cinquenta y ocho Reales de vellon como
consta de sus Rezivos   2U158

Por el Subsidio de las terzias Reales de los
lugares de los Carabancheles por
que se pagan cada año 276 Reales tres

mill ochozientos y sesenta y quatro
Reales de *vell*on como consta de los Rezivos   3U864

170U664

[fol. 8v]
Por los Reparos que se han hEcho   170U664
en todo el Referido tiempo asi
en las casas Prinzipales Y Açeso-
rias del Mayorazgo como en las
de la plaça de esta Corte y Villa de
Madrid de obras de Carpinteria
Zerrajeria fontanero y herrero
y Albañileria que por no dilatar
esta Relaçion no se Yidividu-
aliçan pormenor todos los que se
han Executado, Ymportan Veinte Y quatro mill quinientos y nueve *Reales* como consta de
los Rezivos de los maestros   24U509

Por las lavores que se han hEcho en las
viñas de la villa de Torrelagu*n*a en los
ocho años q*ue* han corrido a cargo del
se*ñ*or Don Ygnaçio labrarlas Cavarlas
Replantarlas aMogrunarlas
Y en las Vendimias q*ue* en d*i*chos ocho
años hizo que son desde el año de 91
*h*asta el de 98 por que desde el de 99
han corrido y corren p*or* todo el
presente a cargo del se*ñ*or d*o*n Joseph
de Vargas y lo gastado en d*i*chos
ocho años Ymportan diez y ocho
mill Novezientos y treinta y nueve
Reales como consta de los mayordomos
de Cava y Poda   18U939

214U112

[fol. 9r]
Al convento de Torrelaguna mill y   214U112
Seisçientos *Reales* por los mismos que
tubo de costa El Reparo y tras-

tejo de la capilla de san Juan y
la de Nuestra señora de los Esclavos por
haver Caido un Rayo en la Torre
de dicho convento que arruino y deRuco
Un Pedaço de dicha Capilla como cons-
ta del Rezivo   1U600

Por el pleito que Don Manuel Gomez
de Rozas Vezino de la Ziudad de
Segovia puso y enVargo que consiguio sobre las Casas de la plaza
con motivo de haver subçedido en el
derecho de Un Zenso de mill y quinientos ducados de prinzipal al-
quitar Ympuesto en ellas por el
señor don Lorenço de Vargas Y Reconozido por el señor don Alonso de Vargas a favor de doña Ana de Torres
Viuda Vezina que fue de dicha Ziudad
de Segovia, que duro mas de dos
años se gastaron en seguir dicho
pleito hasta su conclusion y executoria que se gano declarando
el ser libres dichas Casas de dicho
Zenso dos Mill y Duzientos Reales   2U200

Por el pleito que pusieron los Padres
Mostenses sobre un Zenso de 8U Reales
                                                               217U912

[fol. 9v]
de Prinzipal y sus Reditos   217U912
a Raçon de 400 Reales cada año
desde el de 68 hasta el de 96 que
Ympuso el señor don Lorenso de Vargas sobre las casas Prinzipales Y
Acesorias del Mayorazgo en Virtud de la facultad Real que su Padre el señor don francisco de Vargas
obtubo para Ymponer 3U500
Ducados de plata a Zenso sobre

dichas Casas para livertarlas de
huesped de aposento Y haviendolas
dicho Señor Libertado El año de 630
paso dicho señor Don Lorenzo a Ymponer
dicho Zenso el año de 38 por cuyo
motibo se gano dicho pleito como
consta de su Executoria de los señores
del consejo Real de Castilla y en el
seguimiento de dicho pleito que duro
mas de dos años se gastaron dos
mill y trezientos Reales   2U300

A los herederos de Doña Maria Garzia que
hera la viuda que vivia en la calle
de Silva tres mill y quinientos Reales
de vellon por quenta de la Escritura
de mill ducados que el señor Don Diego
de Vargas la hizo como consta
del Respaldo de la referida
                                                           220U212

[fol. 10r]
Paga que se hizo en dicha Escriptura   220U212

De los Zensos y Capellania de la   3U500
Hazienda de torrelaguna en los
diez años que corrio a cargo de don
Ignacio hasta que se la Zedio a su
Hermano El señor Don Juan Manuel
se han pagado ocho mill Reales como
consta de los Recivos   8U

De Reparos limpias de Madres Y
encanados de las casas de Granada
que en dichos diez años se han hecho
se han pagado siete mill y seis
çientos Reales como todo consta de
Relaziones y cartas de pago que dio
en dicho tiempo don Francisco
Molina Matamoros Arrendador
de dicha hazienda   7U600

Por las asistenzias y alimentos del *señor*
Don Manuel de Vargas
q*ue* este en el Zielo que estubieron
a cargo de don Ignaçio desde prinzipio del año de 90 *h*asta Ultimos
de junio de 99 que salio de esta
Corte para Granada para En-
Caminarse desde alli a Cadiz a
enVarcarse para pasar a las
Yndias de Nueva España

239U312

[fol. 10v]

Es de ad*e*vertir se le tubo Una   239U312
ayuda de Camara un lacayo,
y un Cavallo, por que andubie-
se desenzia, quando no quisiese
usar del coche de su hermano, Y a-
nadiendose a d*i*cha desenzia el por*te*
de su Propia Persona en el Empleo de Menino, que fue de la
*señ*ora Reina Do*ñ*a Maria Luisa
de Borvon y de la *señ*ora Reina Do*ñ*a
Mariana de Neymburg Y el
mayor en la entrada que hizo
en esta corte La Ultima en que
fue Preziso que en lo Referido
Y en las Jornadas que sus M*a*ges*ta*des executaron a los sitios R*eale*s del Es-
curial y Aranjuez se hiziesen
diversos Vestidos Bordados asi
de color como de negro en las chupas y Jubones guarnezidos, Y
en todos los demas Vestidos, que
en dias de años de Rey Y Reina
se le hazian y libreas para el
lacayo hubo año q*ue* paso de mill
y quinientos ducados que *h*asta
el año de 95 que paso al fin
de el; a Barzelona a servir

239U312

[fol. 11r]
a su Magestad en aquel Exerzito   239U312
en el empleo de Capitan de Cavallos
Corazas;
a su Magestad en aquel Exerzito 239U312
en el empleo de Capitan de Cavallos
Corazas, se gasto en todo lo Referido hasta siete mill Ducados
con poca diferienzia antes mas
que menos que hazen setenta y
siete mill Reales   77U

Para la Jornada que Executo dicho señor
don Juan a Cataluña se le hizieron tres Vestidos Guarnezidos
de oro y plata con sus chupas Correspondientes, diez y ocho aderezos
de Ropa blanca, Corvatas de En-
caxes, Pañuelos Guarnezidos
con todos los demas Recados Y ade-
rentes nezesarios de sonbreros Me-
dias Calzetas y colonias con librea
de lacayo y vestido del ayuda
de Camara en que se Gastaron Veinte y Un mill Reales   21U

Ottros Zien doblones que se le dieron
para el Gasto de dicha Jornada
que hazen seis mill Reales   6U

En Todo el tiempo que estubo en Bar-
çelona se le Ymbiaron diferentes
de a Veinte y çinco y Zinquenta
doblones y asimismo Una librança
     343U312
[fol. 11v]
de nueve mill Reales de plata que   343U312
tenia don Ignaçio de sus Gaxes de
la plata de fiscal de Guerra que
servia entonzes que Junto todo

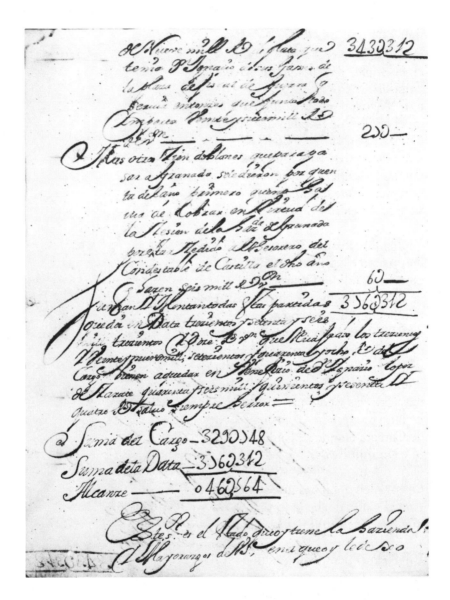

Folio 11v of Ignacio López de Zárate to Diego de Vargas, Madrid, 28 September 1703.

Archivo del Marqués de la Nava de Barcinas, Madrid.

502

Ymporta Veinte y siete mill R*eale*s
de v*ell*on   27U

Mas otros Zien doblones que para pasar a Granada se le dieron por quenta del año primero que no havia otra de Cobrar en Virtud de
la Zesion de la ha*zien*da de Granada
por estar Zedido al thesorero del
Condestable de Castilla el d*ic*ho año
q*ue* hazen seis mill R*eale*s de v*ell*on   6U

Suman Y Montan todas estas partidas 376U312
que doi en Data trezientos y setenta y seis
mill trezientos Y doze R*eale*s V*ell*on que Revajados los trezientos
Y Veinte y nueve mill; setezientos y quarenta y ocho R*eale*s del
Cargo bienen a quedar en Venefizio de don Ygnazio lopez
de Zarate quarenta y seis mill; quinientos y sesenta Y
quatro R*eale*s salvo siempre herror;

Suma del Cargo   329U748
Suma de la data   176U312
Alcanze   046U564
Este, s*eñor* es el estado que *hoy* tiene la hazienda
Y Mayorazgos de V*uestra Señorí*a en el que *hoy* le dexo
[fol. 12r]
Mui gustoso porque conozera V*uestra Señorí*a queda en el
todo desempeñado Y la mali*çi*a Convenzida
de lo que Ynformo a V*uestra Señorí*a de hallarse d*ic*ha
hazienda concursada; no me detengo en este Punto aseguarando a V*uestra Señorí*a no me ha causado la menor
novedad y mortificazion se hiziese a V*uestra Señorí*a Semejante Ynpression por Reconozer fue mas Ori-
jinada de la falta de Yntelixenzia y conozim*ien*to
que de Propia Voluntad de quien persuadio *sobre*
tan falsso supuesto;

Aunque Reconozco por superfluo el *haver* Exercitado
este estracto de quenta por que pareze que es querer dar satisfazion a quien tanto me ha favorezido

como V*uestra* Señoría mayormente quando la confianza ??
en el poder que me ymbio me eximia el darlas
devo Prometerme de la gran Comprehension de V*uestra* Señoría
Compadecera esta formalidad por *h*aver llegado
el caso de que se me pida tan justa Residenzia
en ella solo se me puede hazer el cargo que tantas
Vezes se me ha insignuado de los 4U pesos
Que V*uestra* Señoría Embio, Y quando Jusgue no se me
hubiese Repetidos por los motivos y Raziones
que Represente a V*uestra* Señoría quando avise el Rezivo
de d*i*cha Cantidad, me beo Prezisado a añadir
ahora a V*uestra* Señoría que si Yo hubiese atendido
[fol. 12v]
A acasarme con la convenienzia mecanica
de Yntereses hubiera logrado los muchos que
se me ofrezieron luego que Volvi de Ytalia a esta
corte, pero como mi fin no fue otro que lograr la
fortuna de mi mayor dicha que fue la de En-
troncar con la casa de V*uestra* Señoría no atendi a otras
Zircunstanzias como lo Califico la Dote que se
me dio de 9U pesos pues aunque V*uestra* Señoría me Enbio Diez, los mill fueron por paga y satisfazion
de los que preste a mi *s*eñora Y mi tia Doña Juana de
Bargas que este en Zielo antes de Casarme
para los gastos que quiso hazer entonzes como
Es notorio a V*uestra* Señoría por la misma Escrip*t*ura de
Capitulaz*i*ones Y estando Prevenido en la d*i*cha Escritura
que se me havian de dar quinientos pesos cada año
en el Ynterim que se me pagarian efectibamente
los diez mill Y *h*aviendo pasado mas de Zinco quando Rezivi el primer Socorro de los 5U—que V*uestra* Señoría
me Enbio Reconoçera V*uestra* Señoría quien justamente
se me devian los 2500 pesos de d*i*chos çinco años
Corridos, mortificome mucho *h*aya llegado el
tiempo de hazer a V*uestra* Señoría esta Narrativa, quando
he procurado no hazer caso de todo lo Referido
Pero me Preziza ̶h̶a̶ hazerla el mismo tiempo;
Mi punto Y mi estimazion y el añadir a V*uestra* Señoría
[fol. 13r]
Juzgue hubiese tenido Presente V*uestra* Señoría los Crecidos
gastos que me ocasiono la Boda solo por

Executarla Con el Lustre Correspondiente a *mi*
Prezisa atençion y Respecto de Casarme con
Una hija de *Vuestra Señoría* a cuya funzion asistio toda
la Corte siendo los Padrinos por si *Vuestra Señoría* no lo *havia*
savido los *señores* Duques de Fernandina hixos *??*
señor Marques de Villafranca y *señor* Duque de *??*
con que dexo a la Considerazion de *Vuestra Señoría* como se
Executaría esta funzion, que gastos Ocasion*aría ??*
con coches silla libreas Vestidos de Criados y *??*
das, fuera de las Prezisas galas y Vistas de *??*
Y de los Vestidos a mi tia mi *señora* Doña Juana de
Vargas a su familia y a mi querido hermano
Y amigo don ^Juan^ Manuel de Vargas los gastos ^que^
se hicieron todo el tiempo que duro Rez*ivir*
las Visitas, los que me *habran* orijinado en
quinze años que cumplen a 1 3 de Diziembre
Proximo Venturo que ha que me caso lo qu*e*
podra Ynferir *Vuestra Señoría* lo empeñado que m*??*
pero fio en *Nuestro señor* me ayudara para *poder*
yr desaogando y me dara fazilidad para
asimismo pueda mantener mi Crezida *fami*-
lia Criar mis hijos con la desenzia Correspondiente a ser Nietos de *Vuestra Señoría* y que abrira Con
[fol. 1 3v]
no para que pueda yo por Cumplir ^mi^ hija
Rosolea (que es la mayor) el dia 4 de Abril proximo Venturo doze años solizitarla el Estado
mas proporzionado a su ynclinazion; Y en lo
Tocante a la hazienda de *Vuestra Señoría* tendre siempre la satisfazion y Vanidad de que procurado Cumplir con la confianza de *Vuestra Señoría* con
mi obligazion y punto y sobretodo con el
prinzipal de mi Conzienzia, por mas Ym-
prisionado que se *halle Vuestra Señoría*, de siniestros y falsos
Ynformes, suplico a *Vuestra Señoría* disculpe *haver* me
dilatado en todo lo Espresado compadeziendo
la Razon motivos Y Zircustanzias
que me han puesto en estos terminos que de quanto
se me ofreze dezir a *Vuestra Señoría* Repitiendo mi Rendim*iento* siempre Y deseando que *Nuestro señor guar*de a
Vuestra Señoría

los muchos y dilatados años que puede y tanto he
menester Madrid y octubre 6 de 1703

^2Besa los pies de Vuestra Señoría Su mas affecto reconocido y Obligado Servidor y hijo

Don Ygnaçio Lopez
de Zarate^

———

49. *Ignacio López de Zárate to Diego de Vargas, np, mid-late 1703, AMNB, C, inc.*

[fol. 1r]
[cross top center]
Mi señor y mi Padre, despachandose
nuebo avisso a Esse Reyno, logro
muy gustosso la fortuna de repetir
mi rendimiento a los pies de Vuestra Señoría
y Solicitar Las desseadas notiçias
de mantenerse Vuestra Señoría En la perfecta
Salud, que tanto he menester, y assi mismo las de haver Concluydo Vuestra Señoría su
larga Peregrinazión y tan dilatado
Viage Con toda feliçidad, y haver
llegado a essa Villa, y tomado la
Possession del Govierno de toda
Essa Provinçia En la misma, En donde
no dudo habra sido Vuestra Señoría muy Vien
reçivido, por haversse desvaneçido En el
[fol. 1v]
todo las Ymposturas, y medios tan
Ympropios, y Estraños, de que se Valio
la temeridad, y Maliçia para os-
Cureçer las Justas operaçiones,
y tan Conoçidas, y acreditadas de
Vuestra Señoría y dios, Como Es Justo, ha
permitido el dia de hoy su mayor
realçe, y Juntamente que tan gran

Conjuraçion, Arrojo, y desverguen-
Za, quede En El todo Combençida,
y avergonzada, Lo que ahora Combiene Es que *Vuestra Señoría* trate de mirar
mucho por si, que Es lo que tanto
nos Ymporta, y no penssar En
otra Cossa, que Vivir, pues Con la Vida
todo se Consigue, y nada Es primero, Como
tan Vien, el que *Vuestra Señoría* haga la Justa
reflexion de no ser Justo, que los re-
lebantes Serviçios de *Vuestra Señoría* y su

---

50. *Francisco Vargas y Lezama, Marqués de Vargas,
to Diego de Vargas, np, [10 December 1703?],
ARGD, L, inc.*

[fol. 1r]
[cross top center]
Muy Señor mio Hallome favorezido, con sus Car-
tas de *Vuestra Señoría* sus fechas de 31 de Diziembre de el año
    passado
Y de nueve de Abril de este quedando con summo
reconocimiento a sus expressiones que son de toda mi estimazion Celebrando las noticias, que me comunica de
su buena Salud, como tambien de hallarse restituydo a su govierno de el nuevo Mejico, de que quedo summamente gustosso, Y doy a *Vuestra Señoría* la enhorabuena desseosso
    de
que a esta se sigan muchas, como las solicita mi atenzion
y el merecer muchas, Ordenes de el mayor agrado de
Vuestra Señoría en que exercitarme,

Aseguro a *Vuestra Señoría* que la noticia que tubimos de la
    azelerada
Y temprana muerte de mi amigo El sseñor Don Juan Manuel
de Vargas, fue de tanto quebranto para mi Prima Y
para mi, y toda esta su Cassa que no pudo excedernos
ningunos Otros, por lo que le estimavamos, y amavamos

q*ue* era con gran ternura, y nos lo correspondia en la
confianza, y seguridad, q*ue* tenia de nuestro cariño y considero, que en el de V*uestra Señoría* este golpe, habra sido de gran
      que-
branto a su Corazon assi por la perdida como por lo acele-
rada q*ue* fue su muerte de que doy, a V*uestra Señoría* El pessame
      con
[fol. 1v]
Las Veras de mi Verdadera atencion y cariño pudiendo decir a V*uestra Señoría* que mereciamos, mi prima y yo tan
gran fineza al difunto, q*ue* en España, juzgo, ninguno se
la devia mas con que acreditara V*uestra Señoría* qual, *h*abra sido
nuestro sentimiento, siendo el unico consuelo El que
estara gozando de la divina presencia.

Estimo a V*uestra Señoría* como devo la confianza y fineza, con
      que me
favorece, con su satisfazion en la remission de el poder para la Administrazion, y cobranza de sus honrra-
dos Mayorazgos asegurando, a V*uestra Señoría* es de mi mayor
      Venera-
cion e ygual sentimiento, el no poderle admitir; lo principal por que V*uestra Señoría* esta muy mal ynformado, pues asien-
ta estar concurssados los Mayorazgos q*ue* no es cierto pues
si lo fuesse, no lo ygnorara yo ademas de que como pudieran estarlo, quando mi amigo El señor don Ju*an* Manuel
dejo empeñadas todas la rentas por cinco años para
los gastos de su Viage, y empeños que tenia q*ue* esto es cierto
como tambien el que mi primo, El ss*e*ñor don Ygnazio Lopez de Zarate, *h*a cuydado, de los Mayorazgos, con la mayor aplicacion, a su mejor Cobro, con su gran cariño, y autoridad, como se lo manifestara a V*uestra Señoría* en la quenta
      que
por menor me dice, da a V*uestra Señoría* a que se añade q*ue*
      estando
aca mi primo el ss*e*ñor Don Ygnacio, no era razon el que
Otro tubiesse El poder quando ninguno no lo supiera-
mos hacer mejor ni con mas Cariño inteligencia
[fol. 2r]
ni autoridad, que mi primo El ss*e*ñor don Ygnazio y lo
mesmo que yo representan, a V*uestra Señoría* los Señores Conde

de la Puebla, y Don Sancho de Bullon, que tampoco
*h*an admitido el poder como se lo expressan a V*uestra Señoría* por
las razones que yo refiero, añadiendose en mi lo que discul-
para, V*uestra Señoría* a la obligacion q*ue* tengo a mis primos que
    que
diria El Mundo, de que yo pudiesse executar actos Judiciales, con mis parientes y mas a la bista de
q*ue* los Otros dos Señores, que se siguen, en El poder, no teniendo estas obligaciones, no lo *h*admiten con que espero
merecer a V*uestra Señoría* tenga a bien mi escussa debiendo decir,
    a
V*uestra Señoría* q*ue* la tengo por del mayor punto de V*uestra*
    Señoría como tambien
de el de mi primo El que no se usse de este poder cuyas expressiones no son nada, favorables, para el garbo, y estimacion de V*uestra Señoría* ni punto de mi Primo, y mas
    conociendose
q*ue* V*uestra Señoría* esta ymprisionado de los ynformes que pudo
    haver
hecho mi amigo El sse*ñ*or Don Juan Manuel que goce
de Dios Con mas motivo de su Vizarria, y desseo de
gastar, que con la razon y como digo arriva, esto es lo
cierto.

En lo q*ue* V*uestra Señoría* me manda le diga de si mi Primo El
    sse*ñ*or don Ygnacio
le ha sacado a V*uestra Señoría* el Titulo, y pagado la media
annatta, y lanzas de el, para cuyo efecto havia
V*uestra Señoría* remitido quatro mill pessos, lo que he podido
[fol. 2v]
Saver Es que mi primo El señor don Ygnazio, esta
en la mayor aplicazion para sacar a V*uestra Señoría* de este
cuydado, en la mayor brevedad, como de todo lo demas q*ue* V*uestra Señoría* le encarga debiendo V*uestra Señoría*
    tener presen-
te, que el sse*ñ*or Don Juan Manuel que dios *h*aya
fue precisso gastase mucho p*a*ra portarse con la decencia
q*ue* Correspondia como hijo de V*uestra Señoría* que assi lo lucio,
y gasto mucho aun en lo que no era necessario
que por esto puede ser que no fuesse su cariño, tan
grande como devia con sus hermanos, quienes

me consta hacian con El quanto era Y-
maginable, y asi *Vuestra Señoría* este cierto q*ue* mi primo El
   ss*eñ*or
Don Ygnacio correspondera en todo al gran
Cariño y obligazion q*ue* tiene a *Vuestra Señoría* y se deve assi
propio, y si yo pudiere ser de algun pro-
becho En El servizio de *Vuestra Señoría* puede estar muy
cierto de mi atencion y por la confianza
q*ue* he merecido a *Vuestra Señoría* q*ue* en quanto fuere de su
mayor Satisfaccion hallara, promtamente mi
Obediencia para exercitarla, con muy fina
Y segura Voluntad en quanto Valiere,

Los poderes y las Cartas que Venian para los agentes,
quedan en mi poder para lo que *Vuestra Señoría* mandare.

------

51. *Diego de Vargas to Ignacio López de Zárate, Santa Fe, 1 December 1703*, ARGD, LS.

[fol. 1r]
[cross top center]
HyJo y *señ*or mio notizio a *Vuestra Señoría* mi entrada en este govi*er*no de la Nueba Mexico en su Villa
de S*an*ta fee el dia diez de Novi*em*br*e* de Cuya Pose-
zion Remito a *Vuestra Señoría* la zertifiçaçion que me
dio el Yllus*tr*e Cavildo Justiçia y Reximi*en*to para que
Vuestra Señoría La mande presentar en el R*e*al y Supremo
Consejo de Camara Yndias, Y tambien por q*ue*
es pressizo por que assi lo ordena Su Magestad
por su R*e*al zedula, y Conste Con el aplaus-
sso, y aclamazion gen*er*al que fui reçivido y al
contrario de lo ynformado por el Procurador
de esta Villa, que este fomentado mantenido por el Govern*ad*or D*on* Pedro Cubero a fin
de sus ynterezes de mas de la enemiga Capital que me tiene *h*a estado y esta aun actu-
alm*en*te en la Corte de Mexico por Su quenta
aun Con el d*ic*ho D*on* Pedro Segun noticia ten-

go Como tambien a V*uestra* Señor*ía* se la tengo dada
desde el Passo del Rio del Norte en el
mes de octu*b*re deste año de la *f*echa de mi
llegada haver d*i*cho governad*o*r D*o*n Pedro en Virtud de mandam*i*ento de Su E*x*celenci*a* haver salido
dejando poder para dar la Recidenzia
y teniente en su Lugar nombrado como
lo executo lo uno, y otro, y para aterro-
[fol. 1v]
rizar a estos Vez*inos* les persuade su Sobrino Don
Miguel de Sola Cubero de edad de Veinte y Zin-
co años que passara a essa Corte a pretender este govi*erno*
Como si de la recidenzia Saliesse en esse merito
Sino al Contrario Segun Sus muchas demandas
Capitulos, y Cargos, que se le esperan por diferentes personas pedir de mas de lo que a mi
me assiste haviendoseme reservado al tiempo de
la recidenzia pedir por Voto conzultivo en
el R*eal* Acuerdo, y a d*i*cho señ*or* E*x*celentís*i*mo Virrey lo
hago La relazion del estado en que R*e*civo
el Reyno, y Se halla por mis escritos que
*h*an pressedido passen autenticos Con representazion hecha a este d*i*cho Cavi*l*do y me ha
parezido a V*uestra* Señor*ía* remitir Sus trasLados aunq*ue*
a mi Procurador en Mexico le prevengo lo
haga juntam*e*nte Con lo q*ue* Su E*x*celenci*a* probeyere
y assi devajo desta Razon se hallara V*uestra* Señor*ía* en
todo para Lo que se ofreziere.

Aguardo de Mexico el Correo para si V*uestra* Señor*ía*
me escribio en el avisso que entro el mes de
Jullio en el Puerto de la Nueba VeraCruz
digo en quinçe de Agosto Con la notizia de
los 5000 quin*tales* de Aazogue que traen las
urcas y navios de franzia Con orden de pasar primero a la Ysla de la Martinica para
con escolta desde ella passar a este Reyno
y puerto d*i*cho de la Veracruz Las quales no
[fol. 2r]
no *h*an llegado, y se save fueron a Cartaxena
y que no llegarian hasta en todo Diz*i*embre n*u*estro señor

Folio 2r of Diego de Vargas to Ignacio López de
Zárate, Santa Fe, 1 December 1703.
Archivo de Rafael Gasset Dorado, Madrid.

512

Las de buen biage y a mi el gusto de Sa-
ber de la Salud de *Vuestra Señoría* y de que llegase
a sus Manos el Chocolate que le remiti
Sin que tubiesse el riezgo del destrozo que
el enemigo hizo en la flota despues de
Un mes dado fondo en el puerto de Vigo
tieneme tambien Con cuidado el saver de
los Vienes que quedaron por muerte de mi
hijo, si vien es persona de toda Satisfazion en cuyo poder Yban y por los poderes que remiti en los avissos de este pressente año me prometo su recaudazion segun la dispossizion tengo remitida y tambien los poderes para essos Mayorasgos
pues Yo Como tengo dicho a *Vuestra Señoría* es bien
que repare Los accidentes y asegure mis
desempeños, y no me Vea Suxeto a un Ynfortunio lo qual a *Vuestra Señoría* no le paresera
mal Segun el afecto me tiene y el de-
seo mi hija Doña Ysabel de mis alibios *que*
escribo y deseo a *Vuestra Señoría* en Compañia de mis
queridos nietos *nuestro señor guarde* felizes años *Santa* fee
y Di*ziembre* 1 de 1703 años.

^2*Besa* la *Mano* de *Vuestra señoría* su *Padre* y *servidor*
que lo estima de Corazon

el Marques de la Naba
de Brazinas ^

[written vertically in left margin] ^2Repito a *Vuestra señoría*
que a este Gov*iern*o Pase por mi Punto y que tiene
Menos el Pre*sidio* del Paso de el Rio de el Norte *haviendo*
Su Mages*tad* por su vida *hecha* la M*erced* de el Al Cap*itán* Don
An*tonio* Balberde Y que mis empeños seran siempre
Unos si *Vuestra señoría* Mediante mis Cartas no Me Mejora De
Puesto Y de todo lo demas Con empeño lo Solizita ^

Señor Don Ygnaçio lopez de Zarate
mi hijo.

———

52. *Diego de Vargas to Isabel María de Vargas Pimentel, Santa Fe, 2 December 1703, ARGD, LS.*

[fol. 1r]
[cross top center]
HyJa querida de mi Corazon aunque doy notiçia
a mi hijo Don Ygnaçio de la posseçion de este govierno
en que me hallo de la Nueva Mexico no es bien dexe el Cumplir Con la obligaçion de mi cariño
con que tiernamente te estimo deseando te halles
muy buena y lo esten mis queridos nietos deseando tener carta tuya que me saque de este
cuidado pues desde Octubre del año de 701 no
he tenido mas que la que trujo el Paxe de
Su Excelencia Don Diego de Molina quedando en
blanco la de mi hijo y demas pliegos que
no recibi no se me ofreze que deçir mas pues
te tengo escripto desde el Presidio del Passo del
rio del Norte y tu en todas las ocasiones
no omitas el hazerlo y a los Parientes y
mis queridos hijos Juana y Don Joseph remitira mi hijo Don Ygnaçio las que les escribo
quedando bueno grasias a nuestro señor y para ser-
birte Con todo amor a mis querido nietos
hecho Mi Vendizion y a ti en su Compañia
y nuestro Sobre todo es dueño de su Voluntad
en la qual me resigno, y deseo te guarde felizes
años Santa fee y Diziembre 2 de 1703

^2tu Padre Y Servidor de Corazon
hasta Morir que tu Mano Besa

el Marques de la Naba
de Brazinas^

Mi querida hija Doña Ysabel
Maria de Vargas.

———

53. *Diego de Vargas to Gregorio Pimentel de Prado,*
Santa Fe, 8 January 1704, ARGD, LS.

[fol. 1r]
[cross top center]
Hermano mio y amigo de mi Vida rezivo la
tuya de Mayo passado con el gusto de la salud
que nuestro señor te Conzede hallandome ygualmente
con ella para Servirte a ti y a mis queridos sobrinos que Beso Su Mano deseando tambien lo esten
los que estan al Lado de nuestro hermano el Marqués
de la florida de quien me alegro las noti-
sias que me das de lo Vien rezivido gustoso y hallado que se halla en su Castillo
de Milan a donde Su Magestad el Rey nuestro
señor que Dios guarde haviendo buelto de la Campaña lo havra merezido sus repetidas honrras y Reales mercedes yo hermano de mi Vida me
hallo en este govierno Ya que nuestro señor assi lo
dispone pues pareze que mis Contratiempos
es indezible sus susezos sino en mi haver
experimentado una varia fortuna y con golpes de bastante pessar desde el ano de
Noventa y Siete despues de mis riezgos noto-
rios y travajos Sin ponderazion que los puedan explicar en la Conquista y reconquista de
este Reino y Ver por ultimo hallarme haver perdido y Consumido mi Caudal y
hazienda en Seis años de Un pleito y presion de
tres en ellos, y despues el contratiempo de
[fol. 1v]
mi hijo que goze de Dios cuya Venida dispa-
ratada Sin orden ni Voluntad mia le ocasiono la de su muerte y por Ultimo la perdida por mal Juizio del Capitán del Navio pues
dandole nuestro señor tiempo para librar Su hazienda Y
la agena la quiso ver en el fuego y en
el agua y assiMesmo el Don Fausto dandole el flete y Conduczion en Capitana
y almeranta de los Caxones de Chocolate

que havian de Servir su entrega en Castilla
y mas la paga de los derechos y flete de
el harriero hasta *h*aser su entrega en Madrid
tambien por seguir Sus disparates Se pierde y ma-
logra *d*icho gasto y Costo te asseguro me
*h*a servido de mohina la *d*icha perdida haviendo sido ocasionada en lo humano por *d*ichos
Suxetos.

Mi hijo es falso que ni se casso Como te
dixeron la que hazen su muger tubo en
ella y Contrajo amistad desde pocos dias de
entrado en Mexico que me gasto Vastante
plata por hallarse perdido y enamorado de
ella y por ultimo le di para su entierro esto es
lo que passa y haver muerto de sobreparto
cuyo niño no puedo asegurar ser suyo en
medio de Ser todo mi retrato y no obstante
le tengo empoder de un amigo de quien el
*d*icho mi hijo hizo eleczion sin darse conmigo por entendido pues en *d*icho mes de
mayo que Salio no me dio razon de nada
[fol. 2r]
ni menos la hubiera tenido de la muerte
de Su Madre Sino se me hubiera pedido
para el entierro es zierto que haverme
Coxido la Notizia de la muerte de mi
querido hijo en essa Tierra y *Reino* hubiera elixido persona Con quien tomar
estado y hubiera hallado Segun mi
natural mi ygual quando no pidiera
ni Una Vara de sinta Con ella y en
esse *Reino* la mas asendrada nobleza es
la que no la tiene esso el hallarme en este *Reino* y el haver estado en el de la nueba
españa me *h*a hecho no cautivarme pa-
ra libre*me*nte Siendo n*ue*stro se*ño*r servido correr
a qualquiera parte.

Con la notizia de Volverse a tordelaguna
mis hijos D*on* Joseph de Vargas y Doña Juana

les remito el poder que otorgue ante la
justizia de esta Villa para que administren
gozen y posean esse Mayorazgo Durante el
tiempo que me dilatare y n*uestro señor* fuere
Servido de darme de Vida y de mi Voluntad fuere con la penzion de pagar
las que tiene Sobre Si y memorias de Sus
fundadores y Con la obligazion del reparo
Conservazion de la Cassa del cosso que es
el Lustre de d*ic*ho Mayorazgo lavor y au-
g*m*e*nto* de Sus Viñas tierras y olibares y me
remito al Contenido de d*ic*ho poder que Separo del que inclusibe y g*eneral* remiti a Madrid
[fol. 2v]
Como te *he* dado notizia y a mi hermana Doña
Antonia Se la doy remitiendome a d*ic*ha Carta
tambien la Señalo quinientos R*eales* a el año en
la renta de los prados y sercas de miraflores
de la Sierra Chosas y Guadalix para que passe
su vida y Con la renta de la prevenda del patronato de San fran*cis*co y para que asista en mi lugar Como patron que Soy lexitimo llamado y
nombrado le tengo remitido poder a mi hijo
D*on* Ygnazio y assi Con uno y otro medio lo
puede passar Con algun alibio que es el que
hallara en mi mientras Viva siendo n*uestro señor*
servido en todo. Te pido a mi herm*ano* el Marqu*és*
de la florida le remitas essa Carta pues cumple mi obligazion y Cariño Como lo haras
siempre en Solizitar su salud y asi te la de
n*uestro señor* Con feliz Vida los mu*chos* años que deseo
al amigo y *señor* D*on* Joseph de Arteaga B*eso* L*a Mano* y
que estimo su afecto y memoria Villa de
S*an*ta fee y Henero 8 de 1704 años

^2tu Herm*ano* Y Amigo Muy
de Corazon y *serv*i*dor hasta* Morir
que tu M*ano* Besa

el Marques de la Naba
de Brazinas^

Mi hermano y amigo *D*on Gregorio
Pimentel de Prado.

————

54. *Diego de Vargas to Antonia de Vargas, Santa Fe, 8 January 1704,* ARGD, LS.

[fol. 1r]
[cross top center]
Hermana mia de mis ojos rezivo la tuya
del mes de Abril de el año passado con el gusto
de que estes Viva ya que *nuestro señor* es servido tenerte
con los achaques que me dizes, y lo corto de Vista
que es lo mas penoso; Vien reconosco tus oraziones
pueden y Valen mu*cho* Con *nuestro señor* y su *Madre* ss*antísi*ma
dan-
dome Salud y fuerzas en mis peregrinaziones
y baria fortuna Con los golpes tan sensibles
que *he* padezido en una dilatada presion de tres
años, y otros tres para Concluir el pleito que la
malizia, y emulazion de mi antesezor ynjusta-
m*ente* me mobio para Consumirme mi ha*zie*nda en defenssa de mi pundonor, y despues el gasto de mi
querido hijo malogrado todo pues hasta sus
Vienes, y alajas Con que lo havie se perdio y que-
maron en la mar con los papeles y demas despachos que estos para mis pretenziones no em-
barazavan su falta para la administrazion
si de los Mayorazgos si bien para el de granada
Ya tenia prevenido y antizipado por Marzo del
año de setezientos y dos a *D*on Diego de Obleda y podia em Virtud del haver obrado sin que le sirviese
de perdida el que llevava mi hijo que goze de Dios pues habra obrado lo que en el *di*cho poder
le ordeno y Segun su carta entro en desconfianza por ponderarme ahogos, y empeños de Don
[fol. 1v]
Ygnazio, y que qualquiera renta que el Ma-

yorazgo de granada le *h*a de assistir con ella
y se le *h*a de entregar y mandar se le de y assi para
apartar Yo de dudas otorgue el nuebo poder
Con la notizia y motivo de la muerte del di*c*ho
mi hijo a mi primo el Conde de Villamena
Don fernando de teruel Ca*vallero* del orden de Santiago mayorazgo, y persona de toda autoridad de lindas prendas, y proseder muy Xpistí-
ano, y legal, de tal Suerte que no me pareze
tiene otro, y assi a este Cavallero le pido por
m*erced* sostituya el poder empersona de Su
Satisfazion en casso de parezerle el di*c*ho Don
Diego de Oblera no lo es al propozito, y la
renta se recaude y se remita a Sevilla a mi
amigo D*on* Diego M*igue*l de Alvarado para q*ue* execute mi orden en todo esta dispossizion tengo
remitida desde henero del año passado de setezi*ento*s y tres por Duplicado assi te doy esta
razon para que se la des a mis hijos Don
Joseph, y Do*ñ*a Juana, de tener Yo por sospechoso al
di*c*ho D*on* Diego de Oblera para atender que siendo
su amo mi hijo D*on* Ygnazio le *h*a de obedezer
en todo pues ~~no~~ veo en Su carta me pondera
lo corto de Sus medios, y los mu*c*hos que requiere
para Su Luzim*ient*o y familia razones que
me dan este Motivo de desconfianza y rezelo.

En q*uan*to a los Mayorazgos de Madrid remiti el poder
en primer Lugar al Marq*ué*s de Vargas del consejo de Hazi*en*da y en Segundo a el Conde de la
[fol. 2r]
Puebla de los Valles, y en terzero a mi Primo Don
Sancho Bullon Chacon, y tambien incluye
el poder esse y Con la notizia que me escriben
mis hijos D*on* Joseph y Do*ñ*a Juana, de Volverse
a Vivir a essa Villa desde el lugar de la Nava del Rey remito Carta al di*c*ho mi hijo
D*on* Joseph para que en Virtud de ella y de
el poder que ante la Justizia desta Villa *he*
otorgado le nombro por administrador de esse

mayorazgo y Su renta en la forma que
Contiene el dicho poder para que en el tiempo que nuestro señor fuere Servido de darme
de Vida Y me dilatare en este govierno que me
es forzossa su assistenzia lo administre
y goze su renta Con la obligazion de Su
Conzerbazion Cultivo y lavor de Sus Viñas
y olivares y pagar las cargas que tienen sobre si
de las memorias de los fundadores y assi mesmo el reparo forssozo que pidiere la cassa
del Cozo grande de esse Mayorazgo pues es
la memoria Ylustre de el y assi tendran grande
alibio los dichos mis hijos pues las Viñas son
buenas y las tierras muchas para Con su renta poder mantenerse esto obra mi Cariño
y que reconoscas tienen en mi todo amparo
y asi te señalo que te den quinientos Reales de la
renta de los Prados de Chossas miraflores
y Guadalix, y con el poder que remiti a Don
Ignazio para la assistenzia de el Patronato
de San francisco tambien le encargo la de la
renta que como nombrara has gozado y que
[fol. 2v]
procure em parte lo atrassado se te de y te asista su administrador al podatario o persona que
tu remitieres Con dicha renta pues los merca-
deres de essa villa tomaran el encargo Y en
ellos te puedes Valer ya que Don Ygnazio sus
Sus ocupaziones no te pueden servir y he sentido
el Mal logro del Chocolate y fue fortuna
rezibieras el Socorro de los zinquenta pesos en
medio del Ynfortunio del que los llevava y a
Dios querida hermana de Mis ojos que mientras viva me tienes mas que Padre para Servirte
pues de Corazon te amo y estimo y en todo
me resigno en la Voluntad divina que te guarde felizes años Villa de Santa fee y henero 8
de 1704 años.

^2Besa tu Mano tu Hermano

que te quiere y estima de
Corazon Y en Nuestro señor se Resi-
gna el Bolberte a Veer

el Marques de la Naba
de Brazinas ˆ

Mi querida hermana y sseñora Doña Antonia de Vargas

———

55. *Diego de Vargas to José de Vargas, Santa Fe, 9 January 1704,* AMNB, LS.

[fol. 1r]
[cross top center]
Hyjo querido mio Recivo La de Vuestra merced
de la Nava del Rey Con el gusto de saver
de su buena Salud y La de mi querida
hija Doña Juana y nietos que a todos
hecho Mi Vendizion estimo y amo
tiernamente Y aunque escribo a mi hermana Doña Antonia de Vargas algo mas
largo al pressente en esta solo le dize a Vuestra merced Mi afecto por esse poder
Como ya que Nuestro señor fue Servido de
llevarse a mi hijo Don Juan Manuel de Vargas que embida no podia Separar
nada de mis mayorazgos atendiendo
a su empleo y assenzos y que se hallase assistido Con su renta y en mi intenzion estava Yndependente de ella
la de Emparte de recompenza de Dote
por Junto a Vuestra merced en una porzion remitirle pero Ya que la fortuna me
deshizo los medios y nuestro señor a mi
querido hijo Se llevo para Si quiero
que Vuestra merced reconozca mi Cariño en
esse poder que le remito para que

[fol. 1v]

administre ese mayorazgo de tordelaguna que
poseo goze sus frutos y rentas Como en
el dicho Poder Se refiere y en esta le encargo mucho a la Conzervazion de sus heredades
en el Cultivo de ellas y reparo de la casa
grande del Cosso del dicho Mayorazgo pagando puntualmente las cargas y penzio-
nes que tubiere de Sus memorias y asi
mesmo a mi querida hermana Doña Antonia
de Vargas quinientos Reales al año que le
Señalo en la renta que se incluye en el
poder que a Vuestra merced remito de los prados y
zercas de Miraflores de la Sierra Chozas
Y Guadalix, y dicho poder Se lo remito
a Vuestra merced Como en el Se refiere lo uno en
recompenza de parte de Dote y lo otro por
el tiempo de mi Voluntad que nuestro señor fuere Servido darme de Vida y Me dilatare
en estos Reynos y asi no tengo mas con que
a Vuestra merced Mi afecto le Corresponda pues Vien
de repente le llega a su mano este Socorro
asegurandose el tiempo sera el que acredite lo que le estimo y quiero a mi querida hija Doña Juana en cuya Compa-
ñia y de la de mis nietos guarde a Vuestra merced
muchos años Villa de santa fee y henero 9 de 1704 años.

^2Besa la Mano de Vuestra merced su Padre
que le estima y su bien Desea

el Marques de la Naba
de Brazinas ^

Mi querido hijo Don Joseph de
Vargas.

56. *Diego de Vargas, Power of attorney to José de Vargas, Santa Fe, 11 January 1704, AMNB, DS.*

[fol. 1r]
Primer duplicado.
Numero 25
Numero 101
[cross top center]
En la Villa de santa fee cavezera Capital deste Reyno y
Provinzias de la nueba Mexico en onze dias del mes de henero
de mill setezientos y quatro años Yo el Maestre de Campo
     Lorenzo
Madrid Alcalde de Primer Voto desta dicha Villa haviendo
entrado en las cassas Reales y Palazio donde Vive el señor Don
Diego de Vargas zapata Lujan Ponze de Leon Marques de la
Nava de Brazinas governador y Cappitán general deste dicho
     Reyno y sus
Provinzias nuebamente restituido y prorrogado por Su
Magestad Su Conquistador Pazificador Poblador y Castellano de
sus fuerzas y pressidios que doy fee Conozco a su
Señoría, y estando en su sala con assistenzia de los testigos de mi assistenzia Como Juez Receptor por no haver
escribano publico ni Real en esta Villa y dicho Reyno ni en mas de doszientas y sesenta leguas dixo dicho
señor Marques governador y Cappitán general que le era pressizo
     remitir
poder a España a uno de Sus Yernos y poniendolo en
execuzion lo otorga ante mi dicho Maestre de Campo cumplido quan bastante de derecho se requiere nessezario
a Don Joseph de Vargas Vezino de la Villa de tordelaguna y
rezidente en el Lugar de la Nava de el Rey en los Reynos
de Castilla y Cassado segun orden de la santa Madre Yglesia
con Doña Juana de Vargas Pimentel su hija segunda y
a dicho su Yerno hijo Don Joseph, otorga su dicho Poder en recompenza de parte de dote que tiene y possee
dicho señor Marques de la Nava de Brazinas en la dicha Villa de tordelaguna que fundaron Juan de Zalinas el
biejo, y Juan de Zalinas el Mozo, y Doña Catarina Velez
de Guebara Su Muger, que se Compone de mas de ziento

y quinze alanzadas de Viñas, y muchas tierras de sembradura, assi en dicha Villa Como en los lugares de torremo-
[fol. 1v]
cha, talamanca, Baldepielagos, el Vellon, el Espartal, y el Molar, que seran por todas mas de setezientas
fanegas de tierra de Sembradura, y assimesmo y assimesmo
en dicha Villa pobedas, y algunos olibos en las dichas
Viña Como assimesmo la cassa grande del dicho Mayorazgo que tiene en el Cosso Con su huerta Con Sus
tapias y en ella Un olibar grande que dexo de mas
de quatrozientos pies de olibo, y assimesmo los patronatos de las dos Capillas de San Juan, y Santiago que
estan al lado de la Epistola, y Evangelio de la Capilla
mayor del Combento de San Francisco assimesmo la renta
de las quatro zercas, y Prados en los lugares de Miraflores de la Sierra, y assimesmo la renta de dos mill Reales de Vellon que le paga en cada un año el Excelentísimo señor
Duque del Ynfantado, y Pastrana por la Dehessa de las
Gariñas que alinda Con el Vozque, que dicho señor Duque
tiene en su Villa de Bustrago, y assimesmo de la media
dehessa de Viñaderos, que deve pagar su renta desta los
Herederos que fueren de Martin de Ahedo Vezino
de dicha Villa de Bustrago, o la perssona a quien en
la auzienzia de dicho señor Marques, y en Virtud de Su
poder la hubieren arendado pues la otra media Dehessa de Viñaderos, al tiempo que passo a las Yndias
en el año de Seiszientos y setenta y dos la posseia
dicho Martin de Ahedo, y Juntamente la otra media
que perteneze a dicho señor Marques Cuya renta devera en Caso
de que no conste por Cartas de pago de Sus podatarios
haverla pagado sus herederos, y la persona que hubiere
gozado las Yerbas, y passos de dicha media dehessa de Viñade-
[fol. 2r]
ros, y assimesmo la Venta de Rebollo y enzina que
se bende para Carbon, y empie segun husso, y estilo
en el Corte para que buelba de nuebo a criarse dichos
Arboles Cuyos frutos de dichas Heredades assi el de las
viñas Como el de los olibares pan de renta por dichas
tierras de Sembradura de pan llevar, trigo, Zenteno, y zebada, renta de dichas zercas, y Prados en los dichos lu-

gares de Miraflores de la Sierra, Chozas y Guadalix
se lo zede y da y otorga dicho señor Marques este dicho
poder al dicho su Yerno hijo Don Joseph de Vargas
por el tiempo que nuestro señor fuere Servido de darle
de Vida en el que se dilatare en este Reino y por el
que fuere Su Voluntad la qual dicha renta de dicho
Mayorazgo y dicha Cassa grande del se le da por este dicho poder en recompenza de parte de Dote al
dicho Don Joseph de Vargas su Yerno hijo Como esposso Marido y ConJunta perssona de la dicha Doña
Juana de Vargas Pimentel su hija segunda con el
gravamen de haver de pagar la penzion, y Carga que
tubiere y memoria de los fundadores del dicho Mayorazgo, y en Segundo le Señala a su hermana Doña Antonia de Vargas de dicho señor Marques religiosa profesa
de Nuestra señora de la Consepzion de nuestro Padre san francisco
de dicha Villa de tordelaguna quinientos Reales en cada
un año en la renta de los dichos Prados, y zercas
de Miraflores de la Sierra Chozas, y Guadalix, y
assimesmo de los dos mill Reales de la Renta de
[fol. 2v]
la dehessa de las Gariñas dicho Don Joseph de Vargas
a de gastar al año a lo menos un mill Reales de
dicha Renta en el trasejo, y reparo que pidieren las
dichas cassas, y mas si fuere nessezario para Su Conzerbazion siendo como son el lustre y memoria de
los fundadores de dicho mayorazgo, y assimesmo
el gran cuidado en la Lavor de dichas Viñas y Sus
olivares procurando plantar y amogronar de nuebo
de suerte que esten pobladas de zepas y no yermas
Su tierra, y las de Sembradura procure la de Sus
apeos Con autoridad de la Justizia ordinaria de
los terminos, y Jurisdizion a donde Se hallaren y
pressizo fuere y para Su Seguridad tambien se
amojonen Con assistenzia de dicha Justizia y escribano, y personas mas anzianas, y de notizia ynteligenzia y Conzienzia pagando el costo de los derechos y el que fuere pressizo hazer a costa de la
renta de dicho Mayorazgo pidiendo se zite a los
linderos Dueños de las dichas tierras, y Heredades

y tambien assistan los renteros labradores para Su
Conozimiento, y memoria pertenezer y zer de dicho Mayorazgo el qual devajo de dichas Calidades expresadas
le otorgo el dicho poder para que goze la dicha renta
y para ello por el, revoco el poder que Yncluye
este dicho mayorazgo en el general que otorgue y di en
la Ciudad de Mexico en treinta y un dias del mes
de Diziembre del año de setezientos y dos ante Juan
de Valdes escribano Real y Publico de dicha Ciudad a los
[fol. 3r]
Señores Marques de Vargas Cavallero del orden de
Calatrava del Consejo de Su Magestad en el de
hazienda y al Conde de la Puebla de los Valles
Cavallero de dicho Orden, y a mi Primo Don Sancho
Chacon Bullon Caballero del Orden de Santiago
gentil hombre de la boca de Su Magestad a los quales
dichos señores otorgue, di, y remiti el poder general
dicho que Comprehende^ia^ los Mayorazgos que poseo de
los Vargas de Madrid, y el de los Caramancheles, y
el de las Camarmas del Caño Esteruela y de ensima
que estan a dos leguas antes de la Villa de Alcala de
HeNares el Juro de ocaña Patronatos de las Parrochi-
as de san Pedro, y el de San francisco de dicha Villa de
Madrid que fundaron mis tias Doña Aldonsa, y Doña
Antonia Lujan Su Capilla de los Vargas al lado
del Evangelio en la mayor de dicha Yglesia de
san francisco y las demas Clausulas, y puntos que se refieren ya que me remito en el dicho poder inclu-
iendo en el el de el dicho mayorazgo de tordelaguna
que al presente excluyo revoco y anulo en Virtud
de este dicho poder por la razon dicha, y ruego y
Suplico a dichos señores assi lo executen y Cumplan
revocando el que hubiere^n^ dado en las personas que
hubieren señalado y sostituido para la administrazion de este dicho mayorazgo de tordelaguna
y si las dichas Viñas y olibares las hubieren dado
a renta Solamente la tenga por el tiempo de tres
[fol. 3v]
años el que las hubiere arendado pagando
la dicha renta al dicho mi hijo Don Joseph de
Vargas Como a persona que zedo en el todo

la de el dicho Mayorazgo su administrazion y
goze en recompenza de parte de Dote como
marido, y ConJunta persona de la dicha mi hija
Doña Juana de Vargas Pimentel por el tiempo como
dicho es de mi Voluntad y de la que nuestro señor fuere
Servido de darme de Vida, y me dilatare en
estos Reynos, y para ello Segun y Como puedo
en la forma de derecho quan bastante se requiere nessezario, otorgo y doy el dicho poder ante
dicho Maestre de Campo lorenzo Madrid en la forma que se refiere y Con el gravamen que se expresa assi lo otorgo, y firmo ante mi dicho Alcalde ordinario lorenzo Madrid Como Juez Rezeptor y Con los testigos de mi assistenzia que
fueron el Cappitán Juan Paez Hurtado theniente del
señor governador y Cappitán general y el Cappitán Don
    Pheliz Marti-
nes, que lo es del Pressidio de esta Villa de Santa
fee y los testigos instrumentales lo fueron el
Ayudante del señor governador Y Cappitán general Don Antonio
    Maldo-
nado Zapata y el Capitán Don Alphonsso Rael de
Aguilar Secretario de governacion y guerra y Don Joseph
Manuel Gilthomey Soldado deste Pressidio que doy
fee Conozco y lo firmaron en esta dicha Villa de
santa fee en dicho dia onze del Presente mes de
[fol. 4r]
henero y año de mill setezientos y quatro años y
va en papel blanco ordinario porque el sellado
no Corre en estas partes assi lo Sertifico y doy
fee Como Juez Rezeptor Con dichos testigos de
assistenzia y lo firme fecho Ut Supra.

^2el Marques de la Naba
de Brazinas^

^3Testigo de Asistencia
Phelix Martinez^

^4Testigo de asistencia
Juan Paez Hurtado^

Ante mi Como Jues Resetor de que doi fee
Lorenzo de Madrid

------

57. *Diego de Vargas to Juana de Vargas Pimentel, Santa Fe, 9 January 1704*, ARGD, LS.

[fol. 1r]
[cross top center]
HyJa querida mia de mis ojos Recivo la tuya
su fecha de mayo del año passado en que me das
notizia de buestra resoluzion en Volver a essa
Villa de Tordelaguna con mi hijo Don Joseph
y mis queridos nietos, y haviendo sido nuestro señor
servido de la muerte de mi querido hijo tu
hermano Don Juan Manuel de Vargas Pimentel en henero
del año passado de Setezientos y tres remiti poder
para la administrazion de la Hazienda de Granada a mi Primo Don fernando de Teruel conde
de Villamena para que lo sostituyese en la
persona mas de su Satisfazion con todos los
reparos y prevenziones pues lo primero le digo
que de no serlo al propozito Don Diego de Oblera
por hallarse con su familia en Madrid lo uno
y el otro reparo que yo he hecho ha ssido el de
su carta significandome los cortos medios
que para tanta familia, y obligaziones tiene
tu Cuñado Don Ygnazio entrando en rezelo
que maltendra de prompto Con que pagar
qualquiera libranza que remitiere expuesto
Yo a quedar mal por razon de que el dicho
Don Diego assista a su amo y mi hijo dicho
Don Ygnazio Con lo que le mandare le de y a mi
me de por descargo que no podia faltar ni
hazer menos este reparo he considerado para
[fol. 1v]
en esta ocazion dar orden que no se le de ni
Sostituya en el dicho poder.

Remiti tambien en dicho mes de henero del año
passado de Setezientos y tres poder general para la
administrazion de los Mayorazgos de Madrid y
de essa Villa de tordelaguna, y demas rentas
que me pertenezen al Marques de Vargas al
Conde de la Puebla de los Valles, a mi primo
Don Sancho Bullon Chacon, y haviendo reconozido buelbo a dezir buestra resoluzion
me ha parezido tambien Considerando a que
somos Mortales remitir el poder a tu esposso
y mi hijo Don Joseph de Vargas en recompensa de la parte de dote que mi Cariño te
ofreze señalandote la renta del mayorazgo
de essa Villa para que el dicho tu marido y
mi hijo Don Joseph en Virtud del poder
la administre y goze el tiempo que nuestro señor
fuere servido darme de Vida y me dilatare en estas partes juntamente Con la renta de los
dos mill Reales de la dehessa de las Gariñas con
obligazion de pagar todas las Cargas y memorias de los fundadores y de emplear Un
mill Reales cada año por lo menos en el de dicha renta de las gariñas en el aderezo y reparo de las
cassas del Cosso grandes de dicho mayorazgo haziendo la justa Confianza de dicho tu esposso
y mi hijo Don Joseph en la conservazion y
assistenzia a la labor de las Viñas y olibares y en los pedazos que pidiere plantas de
[fol. 2r]
nuebo y poner Mogrones lo haga de suerte
que frutifiquen y se logre las cosechas
Con todo augmento pues sera en util suyo y assi
no me dilato mas pues Ya tambien te escribi la notizia de mi entrada y possezion
de este govierno y te la doy segun la carta que
escribo a tu tia y mi hermana Doña Antonia de Vargas de señalarla quinientos Reales
Cada año en la Renta de los Prados de
Miraflores de la Sierra chozas y Guadalix
Como lo expezifico en dicho poder que

remito a mi hijo *Don* Joseph y de esta
Suerte la d*i*cha mi hermana ocurrira
a Vosotros desde su zelda ya que sus
achaques la tienen tan mala, y tambi-
en tendras gusto de que mediante la renta de esse Mayorazgo que te señalo sea
la que te asegure en essa Villa Dios te de
la Vida que deseo y a mis queridos nietos
a quien hecho mi Bendizion *f*echa en esta
Villa de *s*a*n*ta fee y hen*e*ro 9 de 1704 años

ˆ2tu P*a*dre que te quiere y
estima de Corazon y tu
Bien Desea

el Marques de la Naba
de Brazinas ˆ

Mi querida hija D*o*ña Juana de Vargas
Pimentel

———

58. *Diego de Vargas to Isabel María de Vargas Pimentel, Santa Fe, 12 January 1704, ARGD, LS.*

[fol. 1r]
[cross top center]
HyJa querida mia de mis ojos rezivo
La tuya que trujo el aviso que llego a
quinze de Jullio del año passado Con las notizias del Ynfeliz susesso de la flota
que despues de n*u*est*r*o se*ñ*or haverla librado del
enemigo y dado tiempo para asegurar los
imbios y haz*i*e*n*da de los que en Confianza las
entregan en medio del afan con que adquie-
ren qualquier p*e*so en este R*e*ino fineza en la
demostrazion de Su generoso Corazon y
amor Con q*u*e Cada uno Corresponde a Sus

obligaziones bastantemente puede Dolerme
la perdida despues de lo prinzipal de mi
querido hijo tambien de Sus Vienes
que le havia dado y dinero que havra
corrido el mismo riezgo y pague el
Ynterez de Un Viente porziento sin lo
demas Con que le alaxe de plata labra-
da y otras alajas y curiozidades de china y un Caxon Con nuebe *arrobas* de chocolate neto de todo regalo para el hazerlo a las personas de Su Cariño y con ta-
legas de polvillo de Guajaca ropa blanca
y galas, el Y su criado todo lo qual me
[fol. 1v]
Costo Una porzion bien Considerable y Un
mill Doblones que le di el dia que Salio
de Mexico y todo el avio Costeado *hasta*
la Veracruz y mis criados que le acompa-
ñasen Con mulas Cav*allos* y el tren de las de
carga Con sus harrieros y el regalo para el Camino y para la Mar que ni el
hijo de Un grande de españa podia el Yr
Con Mas Sobra y luzim*iento* tambien le di libranzas que Conoziendo Su Natural entregue el dinero a la persona que se los havia de pagar en Cadiz que Correria el
mesmo riezgo a D*on* fausto de Bustamante le entregue tres Caxones de Chocolate Con sus Costos de fletes Yndultos Carga y descarga en los puertos y los derechos
R*eales* para las aduanas hasta la entrega en
essa Corte a manos de tu Esposso y mi hijo
el s*eñor* D*on* Ygnazio sin tener que pagar nada
Considera Vien q*uan*to me empeñaria en el despacho de mi querido hijo Difunto y
que por omission de las personas en quien re-
cayeron la tenenzia de d*ichos* Vienes se *h*aya
perdido tambien Doy grazias a N*uestr*o s*eñor* por
todo que asi lo permite y quedo bueno
grazias a N*uestr*o s*eñor* en este govi*er*no dando a mi

Corazon el dessahogo que requiere en tanto
Ynfortunio y Contratiempo y assi no me
dilato mas en esta por quanto te tengo
[fol. 2r]
notiziada mi entrada en este Govierno y poze-
zion que se me dio Cuyo testimonio remiti a dicho tu esposso y mi hijo el
mes Passado de Diziembre y assi me remito en
todo a ella y a las antezedentes y Solo
te añado la notizia de la resoluzion
que *he* tomado y escribo a mis apoderados
en el poder que remito en recompenza
de parte de Dote a Don Joseph de Vargas mi
hijo Como marido de mi hija Doña
Juana de Vargas tu hermana del mayorazgo de tordelaguna Yncluyendo
la renta de los dos mill *Reales* de la dehessa
de las garinas y la de los prados de miraflores Chozas, y Guadalix le señalo en
ellos a mi hermana Doña Anttonia de Vargas
quinientos *Reales* y dicho poder se lo doy por
el tiempo de mi Voluntad y del que
nuestro señor fuere Servido de darme de Vida y me dilatare en estos Reinos pues
no era razon me diera por desentendido desta tan pressiza obligazion y somos Mortales y no eternos y haviendo
nuestro señor dispuesto llevarse para si a mi querido hijo corre en mi esta razon quan-
do el no haver tomado esta resoluzion lo ocaziono el tener librada la
hazienda Para la de su desempeño y assistenzia del dicho mi hijo Cuyos enpeños
[fol. 2v]
que Contrajo para pasar a las Yndias se
Cumpliran en este año de Setezientos y quatro y se
havran Cumplido para executar la dispossizion
y resoluzion mia que embirtud de poder general
Con dicha notizia de dicha Muerte Remito
y assi mi hijo Don Ygnazio Se hallara sin

esse embarazo pues assi me lo escribio y por lo
que mira a mis dependenzias en el Consejo
y pretenziones le dejo la Voluntad libre
prometiendome de ella assistira Sienpre a Sus
grandes obligaziones y deSiando en to-
do Sus augmentos y que Nuestro señor te guarde en
Su Compañía Y de mis queridos nietos que
hecho mi Vendizion muy felizes años Santa fee y henero 12 de 1704 años

^2tu Padre que te quiere y estima de Corazon y Veerte desea

el Marques de la Naba
de Brazinas ^

Mi querida hija Doña Ysabel Maria de Vargas.

---

59. *Diego de Vargas to Ignacio López de Zárate, Santa Fe, 13 January 1704,* ARGD, LS.

[fol. 1r]
[cross top center]
Hyjo y señor mio Recivo La de Vuestra Señoría en el aviso
que llego a Mexico su notizia el dia 15 de
Jullio del año passado y veo goza salud y mi
querida hija Doña Ysabel y nietos que a todos
hecho mi Vendizion y tierna y amorosamente les
doy en mi deseo muchos abrasos resignandome
todo en la Voluntad divina pues bien ha menester mi aflixido corazon toda su asistenzia divina Considerando deshecha mi fortuna consumida en un pleito de seis años y prision todo lo que pudiera Ser de alibio acre-
ze de mi cassa y gusto de gozar de mi tierra
de mis queridos hijos y nietos y no al contrario Con empeños que me obligan a tante-

ar el tiempo que me pueden servir de molestia
y tambien el que a este govierno se le quito la
terzia parte dando su Magestad Como dio
el pressidio del Passo Separandolo deste y la
de Su Jurisdizion y fronteras razones que
tengo escritas a Vuestra Señoría para todo su empeño en
la recompensa que pido a su Magestad y assi en
todo me remito a las que tengo por Duplicado
y repetido escripto a Vuestra Señoría el año passado en las
ocaziones que se ofrezieron de Navios de franzia
y avissos al Excelentísimo señor Virrey y tambien lo hize
[fol. 1v]
al señor Marqués de rivas con el poder para mis pretenziones, y propossizion para fazilitar mas
vien y assi lo repito en esta en todo se este y
Vuestra Señoría tambien pues tambien le escribi se asegurase la Merced del havito que Su Magestad el Rey nuestro
señor que Santa gloria haya hizo a mi querido
hijo Difunto y assi se puede asegurar tambien segun lo que tengo escripto de que recaya
en mi o en la persona que fuere de mi Voluntad.

Tambien Vuestra Señoría me da a entender Con palabras
Confussas que pueda tener algun estorbo tan
superior que me haga apetezer la mansion en este Reino Lo qual a Dios grazias he sido tan libre
en mi Voluntad que aunque en tan dilatado tiempo de mi assistencia En las Yndias no la he prendado
de suerte que no sea muy dueño acsoluto de mi
y solo el contratiempo susodicho del Pleito yn-
justamente movido puede haver fustrado mi
deseo pues a haver passado a esse Reino no hay duda que en el estado presente procurara acabar
mis dias con la quietud que del Santo Matrimonio Se Sigue y Mas quando ni Una Vara de
zinta Pidiera Con la persona que elixiera y
en esta Supozission pudiera enlazarme Con
lo que quisiera a mi Ygual Correspondiente
y la edad no se atendiera esto digo a Vuestra Señoría por
satisfazerle a su Vago pensamiento

En quanto a las diligenzias que hizo de Ynquirir
los Vienes de dicho mi hijo Difunto las re-
[fol. 2r]
conozco por las Cartas que *Vuestra Señoría* me remite y
los sufraxios por su Alma y missas los
hize en Mexico Con la notizia que se me dio
desde la Havana; Tengo librado el dinero
que en libranza le di y assi mesmo el que Se
le hallo y remitido poder a los Suxetos en
cuyo poder quedaron Sus Vienes y assi
hasta tener de ellos notizia no puedo asegu-
rarme Siendo personas de toda Confianza
y Credito la perdida en el todo y por Ultimo
sea lo que nuestro señor fuere servido y la relazion tocante a este punto se la escribo a mi
querida hija Doña Ysabel que reconozera *Vuestra Señoría*
Tambien en quanto a la dispossizion de essos mayorasgos haviendo faltado mi querido hijo atendiendo a ser de mi pressiza obligazion en recompensa de parte de Dote remito el poder a
mi hijo Don Joseph de Vargas para que goze
en administrazion el Mayorazgo de tordelaguna Yncluyendo en el la renta de los
dos mill *Reales* de la Dehessa de las gariñas y la
media dehessa del Viñaderos, y la renta de los Prados y zercas de Miraflores de la Sierra
chozas, y Guadalix Con la obligazion de
pagar quinientos *Reales* cada año que la Señalo en esta Renta a mi hermana Doña Antonia de Vargas y mas la de haver de gastar
Un mill *Reales* en cada Un año, y mas se lo pidiere en trastejo y aderezo de las Cassas
grandes del cozo las cargas y memorias que
[fol. 2v]
tubiere el dicho mayorazgo y dejaron sus fundadores, y assi atendiendo a que Somos mortales quiero emparte dejar mi Conzienzia como
pide Satisfaziendo a tan Justificada atenzion
y obligazion mia en dicha recompensa de dote ya
que el Motivo de no haverlo hecho antes han sido los dos de hazerlo por mi mano en esse Rey-

no quando se me detubo de Salir deste govierno y se
me mobio el pleito y el segundo el vivir el
dicho mi hijo difunto a quien en el todo le
havia dado dicho poder general y con la notizia
de Su Muerte y la de mis empeños y gastos tan
cressidos ocasionados de Su Venida y de Su
despacho y tornaviage se me han caussado pagando tan cressidos ynteresses que en mi discurso
hallo por forssosa la assistenzia y empleo en el
Servizio de Su Magestad en el que fuere la divina
Servido se me de en recompenssa y assi Solo a Vuestra Señoría
en este punto le digo este a todas las cartas que
en dicho año passado le tengo escriptas Con el
memorial y planta para dicha pretenzion que
esta dejo al señor Marqués de rivas Como primo
de Vuestra Señoría haziendo de Su persona la justa Confianza y que estimara la recomendazion assi
mesmo de Don Miguel de Ubilla Cavallero
del orden de Santiago y Contador Jubilado
del tribunal de quentas su primo y mi grande
amigo y assi no dudo Vuestra Señoría havra ocurri-
do a Conferir la dicha mi pretenzion Con
dicho señor Marqués y que su Señoria assimesmo
[fol. 3r]
lo habra hecho pues de ella resultara en mi
la resoluzion sobre todo procurando en este tiempo de su dilazion la forma por mi
determinada y dispossizion para la administrazion de essos Mayorazgos y Su desempeño
por el que consta tienen y dejo en el año
de Noventa Y nuebe tenian por el testimonio
que dicho mi hijo difunto me trajo para
mi Satisfazion y que creyese no era pa-
zion la que tenia a Vuestra Señoría sino para que yo
con su vista reconoziera y aplicara los medios
que havia ocasionado la de no haver pagado
Vuestra Señoría los Sensos de la Cassa en que ha vivido
y assimesmo los demas de la de la Plaza y
Con la autoridad de Su plaza y persona no
haverle Compelido para ello esto Veo por
el testimonio del Concurso puesto quando

el que govierna Mis dispossiziones y no informe que
mi querido hijo Difunto me diesse Contra
Vuestra Señoría Sino Solo el de la Merced que le tenia pedido no la aguardase hasta que el fuesse que
no le constava Como Vuestra Señoría me dezia el haverla adquirido la omizion que tubo en el despacho de las Reales Zedulas que mi hermano el Marqués de la florida fue el que las
ajenzio y remitio a cadiz para que me las
truxese y por la fecha de ellas reconosco lo
Veridico de su informe segun el testimonio de
el empeño con que se hallava essa hazienda de
los atrasados corridos de sus Sensos y demas
pensiones, y assi Vuestra Señoría no tiene que tener queja ni
[fol. 3v]
fundar sentimiento quando ha sido el Ynteresado
no solo en essa hazienda Sino en lo que le he remitido y el que con razon pudiera estar quejoso
y sentido soy yo pues solo Vuestra Señoría en su Satisfazion no me la da que me pueda persua-
dir quando en todo me falta y ha faltado
de lo que en sus cartas del año de Noventa Y nueve
y noventa Y ocho me escribio y tengo en mi
poder y no dudo dejaran de llegar a sus manos Mis cartas y con ellas los Ynstrumentos
de la eleczion y titulo que hize ante el Excelentísimo
señor Virrey que fue Conde de Montezuma de
Marqués de Nava de Brazinas y por Duplicado le
tengo a Vuestra Señoría remitido el testimonio y pedido
el ajuste del entero de la Media aNata Y
demas derechos que se deven pagar a Su Magestad
pidiendo en la forma que se acostumbra la
de su Real Zedula pues mi hijo que goze de
Dios tambien me dio razon de haver de parte
del consejo yntentado el cobro de dicha Media
anata queriendo en los alquileres de essa cassa y demas posseziones hechar embargo.

Tambien tengo remitido a Vuestra Señoría por Duplicado el testimonio de haverseme declarado por bu-
en Juez en la rezidenzia.

Assimesmo el testimonio por Duplicado
del tribunal de quentas de no dever nada a Su
Magestad antes si haver resultado a mi fabor
el alcanze que se me mando pagar.

Tambien tengo remitido a *Vuestra Señoría* el testimonio
por duplicado de la Sentenzia a mi fabor
[fol. 4r]
pronunziada en Vista y revista de los autos
que contra mi fulmino *Don* Pedro Cubero mi
antessezor y haverseme mandado despachar
en Virtud de la *Real* zedula de *merce*d a este govierno.

Tambien despache a *Vuestra Señoría* por Duplicado que
es el que me da en la suya notizia el testimonio de haver contra*dic*ho al Juez de la media
*a*nata no dever pagar la que por via de deposito Se me mando enterar en la *Real* Caxa de
Mexico hasta que Con vista del el consejo
de hazi*en*da determinase Su presidente y s*señor*es y
Vuestra Señoría podia haverme remitido Su resoluzion
pues mediante ella Se reconosiere ser Justa
mi representazion la qual pido a *Vuestra Señoría* me la
remita o la Conzedan o la nieguen pues Yo
me fundo en la *Real* Zedula de Su Magestad
y en los exemplares de los que no la *h*an pagado aun
no assistiendoles las caussas de tanta atenzion y Justificazion que en mi assisten
y que en *dic*ho s*eñor* Virrey Conde de Montezuma Por su decreto assi se lo propone a *dic*ho
señor Juez de la media *a*nata.

Y por Ultimo remiti a *Vuestra Señoría* el mes de Diziembre Pasado de Setezi*ent*os y tres el testimonio por Duplicado de haver tomado possezion deste govi*er*no
y Cappit*a*nia gener*al* deste govierno ~~del~~ mes de Noviembre en esta *Vi*lla de S*a*nta fee que me dio su Yllu*str*e Cavildo Justizia y Reximi*ent*o y en el se refiere Con la aclamazion y aplausso que fui rezivido y lo

gustosso que se hallava dicho Reino
[fol. 4v]
Tambien remiti a Vuestra Señoría la notizia de haver
escripto dicho Yllustre Cavildo a su Alteza en Su
Real Audienzia de Mexico haziendo relazion
del prozeder Contra mi del dicho Don Pedro Rodriguez Cubero mi antessezor y ellos ser
unos pobres hombres y temorosos del Natural violento de dicho governador y lo mas el poner-
les por delante eran Contra la Real hazienda
y devian en todo firmar Contra mi cuyos
escritos les dava para que lo hysiesen y assi
mesmo el Procurador que en Su nombre havia
estado en Mexico le dava al mes zinquenta pesos
y fomentava y Costeaba Contra mi el dicho
pleito en el todo por cuya dispossizion y por
la de Su Secretario Domingo de la Varrera y de
Mexico por la de Don Juan de Saldua apoderado
de dicho Don Pedro que tambien lo tenia y coste-
ava por su quenta y la del avogado y Procurador de
la Real Audienzia y sus Secretarios y en
todo era el dueño acsoluto que hazia y
deshazia y que ygnoravan todo quando contra
mi dicho governador Don Pedro les havia hecho firmar deponian y demandavan Cuya Satisfazion Con dicha Su relazion me davan
para descargo de Sus Conzienzias y que pedian a su Alteza Como lo hazian y Suplicavan revocavan el poder dado y firmas
en blanco al dicho Procurador Joseph Garzia Jurado
que dicho Don Pedro Cubero les havia hecho le diesen y firmasen y la firma en blanco para
[fol. 5r]
que en casso nessesario de dar qualquier escripto
Contra mi le hiziesen segun paresiese al dicho
apoderado Don Juan de Saldua y procurador y abogado y demas personas que por quenta de dicho Don Pedro entendian en el dicho Pleito que por interes
suyo de mantenerse en este govierno y embarazarme el de su entrada de dicha merced como lo ha-

via logrado en seis años y mas Con dicho pleito
por cuya razon Suplicavan y pedian a su alteza
a Su Magestad el Rey nuestro señor que Dios guarde assi se lo Yn-
formasen en su nombre Revocando assimes-
mo y anulando el poder dado y remitido
y firmas en blanco al apoderado de dicho Don
Pedro Cubero y a su primo al Contador de Real
Consejo de Yndias Don Alonsso de Buendia
la direczion y assistenzia en el todo pidiendo
a Su Magestad en Sus Secretarias de Camara y
la de Yndias Se haga notorio para que no
usen del dicho poder dando por nulo qualquier escripto y pedimento que en su nombre
que en virtud de el Se hubiere dado y presentado antes y despues desta y de su relazion

Y de la mesma Suerte escribieron a su Excelencia al
Excelentísimo señor Virrey Duque de Alburquerque en su Real
acuerdo y dichos sseñores de dicha Real audienzia para que en ambos tribunales conste.

Tambien a el Rey nuestro señor en su Supremo y
Real Consejo de Junta de guerra de Camara de
Yndias que remiti a Vuestra Señoría para que por su mano
Corriese el ocurrir a la Secretaria y asegurar
Se viesse y de lo que resultase y se mandase por
[fol. 5v]
Su Magestad Se hiziese por Vuestra Señoría la de la assistenzia
y se asegurase la remission a Mexico como des-
pacho de Su Magestad para que llegase a este Reyno Viniendo Su direczion en el Caxon de la
Real audienzia Con orden se remitiesse testimonio de Su rezivo del escribano de Cavildo
deste Reino

No dudo Vuestra Señoría Con vista de dicho despacho
pedira a Su Magestad la Justa satisfazion y recompensa que se me deve dar quando ha sido
tan considerable el agravio y daño Con la
perdida de mi Caudal la puede dar y Don Pedro

salio deste Reino y passa a esse Con Yntenzion
de presentarse y en el Consejo Yndultando-
se y relevandose de dar la rezidenzia y que
queden los querellosos y agraviados demandantes sin la Satisfazion que les corresponde
y Yo soy el que mas que todos Juntos tengo
que pedir en tanta perdida y assi Vuestra Señoría por
todas maneras este en la Ynteligenzia
[fol. 6r]
para que el dicho Don Pedro el Yndulto
no le logre pues en daño de partes no se
que sea Justizia y por ahora no escribo mas
a Vuestra Señoría que lo pressizo y remitiendome a las
antesedentes deseando nuestro señor guarde a Vuestra Señoría
muchos
y felizes años en Compañía de mi querida
hija Doña Ysabel y Nietos que tanto
estimo y hecho mi bendizion Santa
fee y henero 13 de 1704 años

^2Besa la Mano de Vuestra señoría su Padre
y Mas Seguro Servidor que lo
estima y Ama de Corazon

el Marques de la Naba
de Brazinas^

Señor Don Ygnazio lopez de Zarate mi hijo

---

60. *Diego de Vargas to Diego de Olvera, Santa Fe,* 13 *January* 1704, *ARGD, LS.*

[fol. 1r]
[cross top center]
Recivo La de Vuestra merced y del afecto que tenia a mi
hijo que goze de Dios Vien reconozco quan Sensible le seria la de su temprana muerte cuya

notizia me ha motibado el remitir el poder general
para essos Mayorazgo exonerando deste cuidado a mi hijo el señor Don Ygnazio y para el
de tordelaguna en recompenza de Dote se lo
remito por el tiempo de mi Voluntad a Don Joseph
de Vargas mi hijo como marido y conJunta
persona de mi hija Doña Juana de Vargas tan-
vien remiti poder para el Mayorazgo de granada a mi Primo el Conde de Villamena para que lo Sostituyese en la persona que fuese
mas de Su Satisfazion y a Vuestra merced le pidiesse la
quenta del tiempo que lo ha administrado y del
Consumo de la Cantidad que mi hijo le dejo
y La Segunda que le remitio desde Mexico
Y haviendo discurrido que Vuestra merced assiste a mi
hijo Don Ygnazio en Su Servizio Con Su familia en Su Cassa no es bien le Separe
Yo de ella ni de esta Combenienzia y seguridad en cuya atenzion remito en la ocazion
presente Carta al dicho mi primo Conde Vi-
[fol. 1v]
llamena Sostituya el poder en la persona que
le paresiere de mas abono y esta la Considero Solo en la que le assiste para la
cobranza de sus rentas y Mayorazgos
y le Suplico Cada año le de la quenta Y en si
dicho mi Primo recaude Y retenga la dicha
renta y Cantidad que Dios nuestro señor fuere
Servido de dar de dicho mayorazgo para que
pueda Yo Con este Seguro de liberar y Satisfazer a quien devo pues no era bien me
pusiese a librar empersona que lo pudiese
haver desparramado esta Satisfazion doy
a Vuestra merced porque no Juzgue de mi mas razon que la de atender con puntualidad
a la Satisfazion de mis devitos empersona
tal Como el dicho mi primo y no por mano
de otro y no me negare a tenerle a Vuestra merced
muy presente en mi memoria dejando en
todo mi Voluntad en la resignazion Di-

vina que es la que me mantiene Con la
esperanza de Volver a essa tierra y *guarde nuest*ro *señor*
a V*uestra* m*erced* mu*ch*os años *San*ta fee y henero 13 de
    1704 años

^2De V*uestra* m*erced* quien Mas
le estima y su bien Desea

el Marques de la Na-
ba de Brazinas ^

S*eñor* D*on* Diego de Oblera

———

61. *Juan Páez Hurtado to Ignacio López de Zárate,*
    Santa Fe, 20 April 1704, AMNB, ADS.

[fol. 1r]
[cross top center]
Muy s*eñor* mio Por ser pressizo y de mi Primera obligazion el dar notizia a V*uestra Señoría* como persona tan ymmediata Al s*eñor* Marqu*és* de la Nava
de Brazinas doy notizia a V*uestra Señoría* de su falle-
zim*ient*o que fue desta suerte Haviendose
aRojado al Puesto de Vernalillo (los Yndios
gentiles de la Nazion apacha que son los
que continuam*ent*e obstilizan este R*ei*no con muertes Y Rovos) y sacado de la cassa del cap*itá*n
D*on* fernando Duran y Chavez Vez*ino* de d*ic*ho
Pu*est*o Como zien Resses bacunas salio luego que las hecho menos d*ic*ho D*on* fernando Con algunos Vez*ino*s y siete soldados
que se hallavan en d*ic*ho parage y alcan-
sando al enemigo en una Sierra trava-
ron batalla con el y le quitaron como quarenta cavezas de d*ic*ho ganado y con esta
notizia que tubo por carta d*ic*ho s*eñor* Marques salio em persona sin Reparar en lo

rexido de los temporales deste Reino ni a su
mucha edad por que era tal su zelo y aplicazion en el Real Servizio que no omitia
diligenzia por pequeña que fuese y que
[fol. 1v]
condugese a la conservazion de lo que
con tanto travajo conquisto y Reconquisto en este
Reino a que personalmente no assistiesse y por
castigar la osadia de dicho enemigo salio
el dia Veinte y siete de Marzo deste presente año desta Villa de santa fee con
un trozo de gente de guerra Y algunos Yndios amigos y haviendo marchado con
dicho campo como quarenta leguas desta
Villa siguiendo el Rastro a el enemigo
le dio Un grave aczidente de Calenturas
caussado de haversele Resfriado el esto-
mago y viendolo tan fatigado el Reverendo
Padre Predicador fray Juan de Garaycoechea Capellan de
dicho campo le Hizo instanzia a que
se Volviesse por que lo veia muy fatigado y le Respondio a dicho Padre que donde mas bien perdida la Vida que en
servizio de Dios y El Rey nuestro señor mas
no obstante como era tan grave el
aczidente a fuerza de instanzias y su-
plicas hubo de Volverse en hombros de
Yndios al Pueblo de Vernalillo distante
desta Villa como diez y seis leguas donde lo estava Yo esperando con algunas
medizinas para su curazion que estas
no hizieron ningun efecto por no haver
suxeto en que obrase la Virtud de ellas
llego como digo el dia zinco del Presente mes de la fecha donde despues
de haver confessado Repetidas veses
y pedido el havito de la terzera orden
de penitenzia y professado en ella
[fol. 2r]
y hecho testamento el dia siete (el

qual vera V*uestra Señoría*) Un testimonio del que
Remito a D*on* Miguel de Ubilla albasea
de d*icho se*ñor Marqu*és* en un testam*ent*o que hizo
en Mexico en Primero de Junio de
mill setez*ient*os y tres y en este hultimo
corrobora y confirma todo lo hecho
en el Primero y el dia ocho del corriente mes como a las zinco del tarde
entrego el alma a su criador dejando a este aflixido R*ei*no Huerfano pues
era P*adr*e de todos sus moradores y a mi
con mas Razon pues en diez y siete a*ño*s
que *ha* que passe a este R*ei*no de la N*uev*a España de los de Castilla no conosi otro
y asi me *ha* faltado todo mi consuelo
y alibio aunque con haverme hallado
a su cavezera hasta que espiro me *ha* dejado con Mu*cho* Consuelo pues piadozam*ent*e
creo esta en el zielo por la gran despos-
ssizion y conformidad con la Voluntad de Dios pues solia Repetir muchas
veses Dominus Dedit Dominus abstulit
Premisas claras de su salvazion y assi por ser
de mi obligazion doy a V*uestra Señoría* este aviso para que
no se la Retarden los sufraxios que V*uestra Señoría*
como buen hijo Juntam*ent*e con mi ss*e*ñora Doña
Ysabel cuyos pies Besso Rendidam*ent*e deseando se halle V*uestra Señoría* a la *f*echa desta
con perfecta salud a cuyo servizio
ofrezco la que goso Rendido a sus Plantas deseando tener en este R*ei*no (donde me
dejo d*icho se*ñor Marques por su albasea
[fol. 2v]
y then*ient*e gener*al* del hasta que el Ex*celentí*simo se*ñor*
Duque de alburquerque embie persona que
lo govi*er*ne) muchas ordenes del obsequio de V*uestra Señoría*
que executara mi humildad siegam*ent*e
y en tanto pido a N*uest*ro se*ñor* me *guard*e a V*uestra Señoría*
felis-
sisimos a*ño*s Villa de santa fee Cavezera des-

te Reino de la Nueva Mexico y Abril 20 de
1704 años

Mui Señor mio
Besa La Mano de Vuestra Señoría su mas
afecto y reconozido Servidor

Juan Paez Hurtado

señor Doctor Don Ygnazio lopez de zarate muy señor mio.

———

62. *Ignacio López de Zárate to Diego de Vargas, Madrid, 26 June 1704,* AMNB, *c, inc.*

[fol. 1r]
[cross top center]
perssona, queden eternizados en esse
Reyno, quando por Uno, y por otro
deve Vuestra Señoría persuadirse, y asegurarse
han de ser siempre en esto muy aten-
didos, para que Vuestra Señoría tenga en el
todos los puestos, que le son tan Correspondientes, y hoy mas que nunca
haçe mas preçissa esta Consideraçion
haviendo faltado mi Hermano, y querido Don Juan Manuel de Vargas,
pues de esta Suerte se Consigue el
mayor Ynteres de Vuestra Señoría no solo en la
Conservazion del Lustre de sus mayorazgos, y Cassa de Vuestra Señoría sino tambien
su mayor aumento Vuestra Señoría Como se lo
Supplico disponga el darnos este Consuelo a todos sus hijos, y Nietos
en Cuyo nombre hago tambien

esta Supp*l*ica a V*u*estra Señoría pues basta
[fol. 1v]
el dilatado tiempo q*ue* V*u*estra Señoría se halla
en esse Reyno, y las Ultimas
tropelias, q*ue* ha padeçido para escar-
mentar de su residençia, y en todo
lo referido Solo, me muebe Mi
Cariño Obligazion y desseo de Veer
a V*u*estra Señoría Con todos los gustos y feliçidades q*ue* devo soliçitar a V*u*estra Señoría

En todas mis anteçedentes tengo partiçipado
Yndividualm*en*te todo lo que se ofreçe
en lo general de las dependiençias
de V*u*estra Señoría y me alegrare *h*ayan llegado todas mis cartas, y duplicados
a manos de V*u*estra Señoría deviendo añadir
q*ue* en la pretenssion de los Goviernos, se
Continuan las diligençias, y que
espero lograr la fortuna de Servir
a V*u*estra Señoría Como la tube remitiendo a
V*u*estra Señoría los despachos de la Confirmazion
[fol. 2r]
de la encomienda de 4U *Reale*s de a ocho p*o*r
lo q*ue* toca a la Segunda Vida, y Çierto
q*ue* no se puede Creer lo que questa *h*oy qualquiera pretenssion mayorm*en*te hallandose
el Rey (dios le gu*ar*de) en Campaña en la
Guerra de Portugal, y respecto de ser
todo aquel clima de la estremadura
tan ardiente, y el tiempo tan adelan-
tado, se discurre, q*ue* muy en breve
se retirara Su M*a*gestad a esta Cortte
*h*asta q*ue* el tiempo refrezque, y en
ella estamos todos muy Alborozados
Con esta notiçia pues nada nos Ymporta
mas q*ue* su Vida, y estando aqui su
M*a*gestad se podra Con mas façilidad disponer el que V*u*estra Señoría quede p*o*r mi parte
Obedeçido

Estos dias nos hallamos en esta de V*uestra* Señoría todos
Summ*amen*te afligidos y desconsolados
[fol. 2v]
Con la notiçia q*ue* Reçivimos la Semana
passada de *h*aver muerto el tio el
señor d*o*n Gregorio Pimentel, despues de
Una penossa, Y dilatada enfermedad
q*ue h*a sido gran lastima, y para noso-
tros de gran ternura, y desconsuelo
p*or* lo mucho q*ue* le estimavamos, y
queriamos i p*or* lo mucho, q*ue* le deviamos,
y solo tenemos el Consuelo de que
su muerte fue muy Correspondiente
a su Exemplar Vida, porque estara
gozando de dios, q*ue* es lo prinçipal

Y rremitiendome en todo a las q*ue* tengo escriptas anteçedentem*en*te a V*uestra* Señoría y sus
duplicados, p*or* no ofreçerse Cossa
particular, q*ue* añadir, devo deçir
a V*uestra* Señoría q*ue* los Subçessos de la g*ue*rra
Con Portugal Van muy favorables,
y q*ue* esperamos, q*ue* N*ue*stro señor se ha de
[fol. 3r]
Servir Continuarlos, y dar a nuestro
Rey (dios le g*uar*de) todas las feliçidades,
q*ue* mereçe y Combiene a esta Monar-
chia su divina Magesta*d* lo permita assi
y g*uar*de a V*uestra* Señoría mi señor y mi Padre
los muchos, y dilatados años, que
puede, desseo, y tanto he menester
Madrid, y Junio 26 de 1704.

señor d*o*n diego de Var*g*as zapata, Y Lujan, Ponce
de Leon, Marqués de la Nava de Varçinas, mi señor y mi P*adr*e

———

63. *Isabel María de Vargas Pimentel to Antonio de León, Bishop of Arequipa, Madrid, 14 April 1705, AMNB, L.*

[fol. 1r]

*I*lus*t*trisimo señor

Señor, Aunque no he solizitado ^nunca^
en las Ocassiones ~~ultimas~~ que se *h*an Ofrezido ponerme a la Ob*e*diencia de V*uestra* sSeñoría Puedo
asegurar ha sido Originado mi silen-
zio de la atenzion de no embarazar
a V*uestra* sSeñoría con mis cartas pero ~~no pudien-~~
~~do dejar~~ no pudiendo llebar ya en
Pasienzia el no saver ^de la Salud^ de V*uestra* sSeñoría Passo en
Cumplim*ie*nto de mi devida Obligazion a
a Manifestar a V*uestra* sSeñoría el desseo q*ue* me asiste de que V*uestra* sSeñoría la experimente tan
perfecta, y cumplida, como tanto he men*e*st*e*r
Y gozando la mia de esta combenienzia
(a Dios grazias) la repito como siempre
a la disposizion y serv*i*cio de V*uestra* sSeñoría como tan
reconoçida servidora de V*uestra* sSeñoría a los particu-
lares favores q*ue* me dispensso V*uestra* sSeñoría quando se hallava en torrelaguna y nunca
puede faltar en mi ~~esta tan~~ la grande
obligazion y aprezio a ellos;

Pongo en la Notizia de V*uestra* sSeñoría como n*u*est*r*o
[next word below the line] Señor
[fol. 1v]
Fue servido llebarse para si el año
pasado a mi tio Don Gregorio Pimentel
despues de una penosa y dilatada enfermedad, Y *h*aviendo prezedido la muerte de mi aguelo, mi s*e*ñora Doña Ysavel
de Olazaval, dejo a la considerazion
de V*uestra* sSeñoría de quanto dolor, y quebranto
*h*abra sido para mi una y otra Pena,
y solo en ambas tube el consuelo

de que mi tio el Marques de la Florida ^havia tomado mucho antes la resoluz*i*on de llebarse^
~~se llevo~~ quando passo a servir el empleo de Castellano de Milan a mis
Primos Sevastian y Gregorio que
si esto no se *h*ubiese logrado, se Vie-
ran estos Pobres muchachos en el todo perdidos, y desamparados y *h*oi se
hallan en carrera de hazer fortuna, pues ya Sebastian se halla Cappi*tán*
de Cavallos en aquel estado, y Gregorito, espero lo sea q*uan*to antes y ambos
*h*an logrado el hallarse en ~~estas~~ ^todas las^ cam-
pañas que *h*a havido en *d*icho estado

En estos Navios ultimos que havio,
[fol. 2r]
el Duque de Alburq*u*erque Virrey de
nueva españa rezivi la fatal notisia
de la muerte de mi Padre (que *santa* gloria
*h*aya) con q*ue* puede reconocer V*uestra s*Señoría la
particular asistenzia q*ue h*abre havido
menester, de N*uest*ro señor para Resignar-
me a su *ss*antísima Volunt*ad* en este tan
gran contratiempo conq*ue* en el todo
pareze *h*a querido su Mag*es*t*ad* que yo
Experime*n*te tan grandes Golpes a que
se añade tambien, el q*ue* haviendo
pasado mi herm*a*no Don Juan Man*uel*
~~p~~-a Mexico por Veer y conozer
a mi Padre y procurar si podia
reduzirle a que se bolbiese a españa
no pudiendo conseguirlo, resolbio
executarlo el con la ocassion de la
Ultima flota y en la trabesia de la
Veracruz a la Habana de Una Yn-
temperia de ayre ~~bolbio~~ murio
Cuasi repentiname*n*te confiesso a V*uestra s*Señoría
~~no tengo~~ que no se como tengo
[fol. 2v]
[written vertically in left margin] Ill*ustrí*simo señor Don

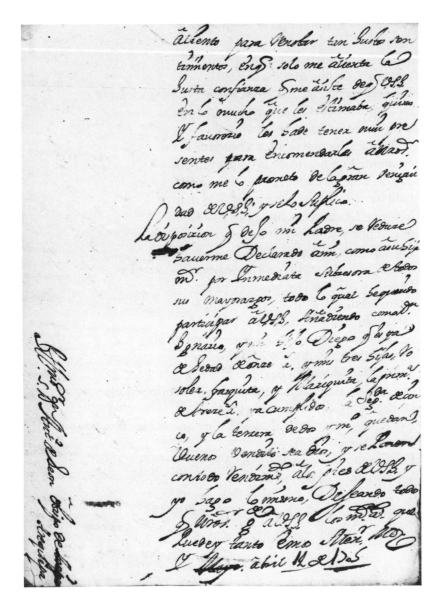

Folio 2v of Isabel María de Vargas Pimentel to Antonio de León, Bishop
of Arequipa, Madrid, 14 April 1705 (draft).
   Archivo del Marqués de la Nava de Barcinas, Madrid.

Antonio de Leon obispo de ~~Areqpa~~
Arequipa
aliento para renobar tan Justos sen-
timientos, en q*ue* solo me alienta la
Justa confianza q*ue* me asiste de q*ue* V*uestra* s*Señoría*
en lo mucho que les estimaba quisso
Y favorezio les ha de tener mui pre-
sentes para encomendarles a N*uest*ro señor
como me lo prometo de la gran Venigni-
dad de V*uestra* s*Señoría* y se lo Suplico
La disposizion q*ue* dejo mi Padre se reduze
haverme Declarado a mi como a su hija
m*a*yor por Ynmediata Subzesora de todos
sus mayorazgos, todo lo qual he querido
participar a V*uestra* s*Señoría* Añadiendo como Don
Ignazio y mi hijo Diego q*ue* es ya
de hedad de onze años y mis tres hijas Rosolea frazquita y Mariquita la prim*e*ra
de treze años ya cumplidos la Segu*n*da de cinco y la terzera de dos y m*edio* quedan
Vuenos Vendito sea Dios, y se Ponen
con todo Rendim*ien*to a los pies de V*uestra* s*Señoría* y
yo hago lo mismo Deseando todo
q*ue* N*uest*ro señor g*uar*de a V*uestra* s*Señoría* los muchos
    años que
Puede y tanto *h*emos Meneste*r* Madri*d* y
Y ~~Mayo~~ abril 14 de 1705

————

64. *Juan Manuel de Vargas Zapata Luján to Ignacio López de Zárate, Mexico City, 7 October 1706, ARGD, ALS.*

[fol. 1r]
[cross top center]
el *Señ*or Marques mui *Señ*or mio doi noticia a
V*uestra Señoría* Como quiso lo felis de mi Suerte acrisolar
mas mi fortuna con la dicha de rrezebir la con que

Vuestra Señoría se sirbe de honrrarme i faborezerme, en pliego
de el Señor Arzediano de esta Santa Yglezia cuyas honrras i fabores creo no llegaran a tener fin de lo fino de Vuestra Señoría como lo demuestran dichos rrenglones i asi
paso yo por esta a rretornar los pesames debidos al ta-
maño de la Sensible muerte de mi Padre y señor que en
gloria yaze; a Vuestra Señoría pues me puede crer que a tanta pena muda se haya la lengua para poder explicar el dolor conserniente a tanta falta; pero el
Autor divino como çiensia ynfinita lo dispuso, o, para premiar el anhelo con que procuro Serbir a entre
ambas magestades o para Castigo de mis culpas; pues
para mi ha sido el mayor que podia temer;

Pero señor Causa algun alivio a el torzedor de mi pena
el que si de antes desabrigado con dicha falta me
    comtemplaba
ahora me veo aun mas que antes amparado: por que si es
comun, afixarse mas con una palabra de un grande que
promete, que no con con lo valido de una escriptura
que da indisios de seguridad: me pareze que ba tanta
[fol. 1v]
Seguridad tengo en que Vuestra Señoría me ha de amparar,
pues veo asi lo pronuncia, i demas lo firma de su mano
y mas quando le incumbe la obligasion de su mesma
grandeza de Vuestra Señoría, i demas la lastima i fraternidad
que quiso el çielo contraxessemos dandome a mi
i a mis hermanos el mesmo Padre; que si no procxime
alminus rremote que a Vuestra Señoría pues es Esposo de mi
    queri-
da hermana y Señora Doña Ysabel, de quienes fue tan
grande la Confianza que hizo dicho mi Padre i Señor que me
dixo en varias ocaziones i en articulo de muerte
valete de mi hijo el Señor don Ygnacio i Doña Ysabel i tendras en ellos, tanto amparo como en mi, i asi fiado
en esto y sobre todo en la Soberania de la Grandeza de Vuestra Señoría postrado y rrendido a sus plantas, le
pido Se Compadesca de mi neçesidad, i de la de mis
dos, hermanos, pues nos, vemos Sin tener en esta tierra
ni un rreal de que poder pazar, por que aunque yo, i mi

hermano Yldefonso procuramos valernos de el *Señor*
Duque de Alburquerque, para que nos, acomodase, en algunos ofisios, para, mantenernos, con el punto de hijos de tal padre, i amparar a nuestra hermana la Donsella, que por Causa tan piadoza como
esta creo lo pudiera hazer, como no tuvimos, rreales
competentes a la rregalia usada no nos quiso amparar, aunque rrepresentamos los grandes meritos
de mi *Padre* i *Señor* no ignorados asi en estos rreinos, y los cortos mios de *h*aber Serbido a mi
[fol. 2r]
Rey i *Señor* con la plansa de Alferez Real: pasando tan graves Contratiempos como los que aquel
Reino causa, i sobre todo la gran fineza de mi *Padre*
de que viendose ya cargado de años i falto de Salud, Saliesse a la Campaña en que murio Sin Tener
mas forma de rremedio que el divino porque de
el humano caresia,

Y asi demas doi noticia a *Vuestra Señoría* como fue dios Servido
   de
llebarse a mi *Madre* el dia 11 de septiembre de este año de
la *f*echa quedando co*n*migo la familia de *d*icha mi *Madre* de
donde puede Considerar *Vuestra Señoría* qual me vere cargado de Cuidados, i destituido asi yo como mi hermano
de tener Con que pazar, i poder mantener i poner en
estado a mi hermana i asi aconsexado de Varios caballeros de esta çiudad, fiado en su palabra de *Vuestra Señoría*
i demas en su poder, Le Suplico me saque, un ofiçio
para estos reinos, o vien sea un ofiçio de Contador en
esta R*e*al Caxa, de esta Çiudad, o vien alguna alcaldia mayor, quales, O mestitlan de la Sierra, o S*a*n
Miguel el Grande; o, otra la en que *Vuestra Señoría* hallare lug*a*r
que pueda proverseme que mediando la autoridad
de la persona de *Vuestra Señoría* me prometo desde luego: la
   Conse-
quicion: Supliendome asimesmo, los gastos, de despachos, *Vuestra Señoría* en esa Corte a los quales, i su paga me
   obligo

porque luego que tenga yo por mano de Vuestra Señoría (Como me

lo prometo), alguna merzed, de las dichas no ha de faltar quien me de los rreales para pagar a Vuestra Señoría puesto en esa, Corte, quedando yo a ser firme Esclabo de
[fol. 2v]
Vuestra Señoría i quedando deudor a tanta fineza i benefiziencia
Y asi hagalo por mostrar Su grandeza; y por amparador
al desvalido, que ya diga que Sacandome dicha
merzed, de un ofisio, puede Vuestra Señoría librar para que
yo entere dichos Costos; otrosi de Conseguir i haserme
fabor Vuestra Señoría, benga por triplicado para mayor Seguridad
ˆi demas una carta de fabor para ʾel Señor Virrey que fuere en estos,
reinos, a la rrespuesta
de estaˆ

Y en tanto quedo pidiendo a Dios Nuestro Señor quiera mi dicha
Se mantenga Vuestra Señoría en la Salud, que mi afecto le desea;
i he menester para nuestro amparo, la que me asiste esta
promta a executar hordenes de Vuestra Señoría i de mi Señora Doña
Ysabel cuyas plantas beso, i a quienes a el par de
Vuestra Señoría se le ofreze cariñosa i rrendida mi hermana deseando sus Saludes i besando Sus manos, cesando
aqui de Canzar i molestar a Vuestra Señoría de esta Su Casa
y Mexico y Octubre 7 de 1706 años.

el Señor Marques, mui señor mio

Besa Las Plantas de Vuestra Señoría
Su Menor mas Seguro i afecto
Servidor i Esclabo,

Juan Manuel de Vargas
Zapata Luxan

Appendix: Genealogy

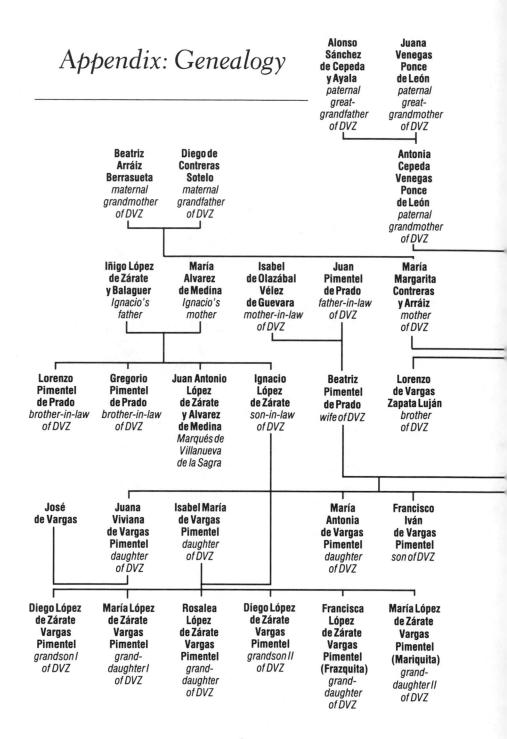

Alonso Sánchez de Cepeda y Ayala
paternal great-grandfather of DVZ

Juana Venegas Ponce de León
paternal great-grandmother of DVZ

Beatriz Arráiz Berrasueta
maternal grandmother of DVZ

Diego de Contreras Sotelo
maternal grandfather of DVZ

Antonia Cepeda Venegas Ponce de León
paternal grandmother of DVZ

Iñigo López de Zárate y Balaguer
Ignacio's father

María Alvarez de Medina
Ignacio's mother

Isabel de Olazábal Vélez de Guevara
mother-in-law of DVZ

Juan Pimentel de Prado
father-in-law of DVZ

María Margarita Contreras y Arráiz
mother of DVZ

Lorenzo Pimentel de Prado
brother-in-law of DVZ

Gregorio Pimentel de Prado
brother-in-law of DVZ

Juan Antonio López de Zárate y Alvarez de Medina
Marqués de Villanueva de la Sagra

Ignacio López de Zárate
son-in-law of DVZ

Beatriz Pimentel de Prado
wife of DVZ

Lorenzo de Vargas Zapata Luján
brother of DVZ

José de Vargas

Juana Viviana de Vargas Pimentel
daughter of DVZ

Isabel María de Vargas Pimentel
daughter of DVZ

María Antonia de Vargas Pimentel
daughter of DVZ

Francisco Iván de Vargas Pimentel
son of DVZ

Diego López de Zárate Vargas Pimentel
grandson I of DVZ

María López de Zárate Vargas Pimentel
grand-daughter I of DVZ

Rosalea López de Zárate Vargas Pimentel
grand-daughter of DVZ

Diego López de Zárate Vargas Pimentel
grandson II of DVZ

Francisca López de Zárate Vargas Pimentel (Frazquita)
grand-daughter of DVZ

María López de Zárate Vargas Pimentel (Mariquita)
grand-daughter II of DVZ

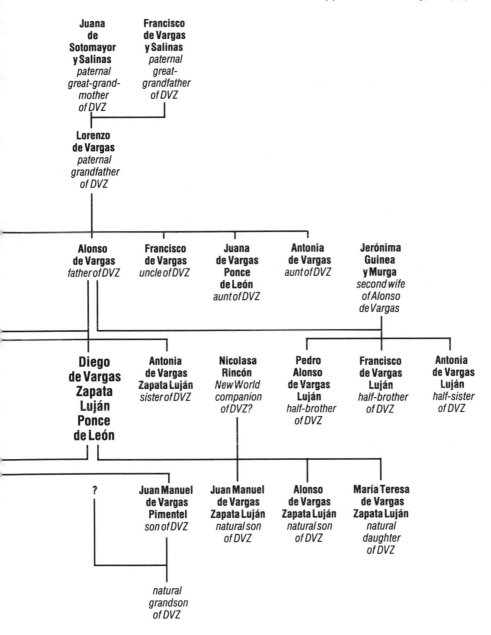

A concordance for the Spanish transcripts for *Remote Beyond Compare* is also available. The concordance includes a semipaleographic transcription of the complete text, an alphabetical keyword and text reference list, and a summary vocabulary and frequency list. The concordance should make the texts available to scholars interested in linguistic studies of Early Modern Spanish, particularly as used on the far northern frontier of New Spain.

Works Cited

ARCHIVAL MATERIALS

Archivo General de Indias, Seville, Spain
    Audiencia de Guadalajara 3; 73; 138:22; 139:4–6; 141:7, 20, 22–27; 142:16, 20
    Audiencia de México 276; 379; 1.102; 1.216
    Contaduría 776; 780
    Contratación 5.429; 5.450:47; 5.459:20, 97; 5.546
    Indiferente General 123; 162; 3.054
    Registro de Partes, Libro 44
Archivo General de la Nación, Mexico City, Mexico
    Civil 77:3; 1743:7
    Genealogía y Heráldica, LDS microfilm 035,750
    General de Partes 16:10
    Historia 37:1, 2, 3, 6
    Indios 25:232; 28:79
    Provincias Internas 30:8
    Reales Cédulas 34:181
    Universidades 148:221
    Vínculos 14; 125
Archivo General de Notarías del Distrito Federal, Mexico City, Mexico
    Notarías 7 (1700–1701); 11 (1680); 13 (1703); 379 (1682); 687 (1673); 692 (1702–1704)
Archivo Histórico Nacional, Madrid, Spain
    Consejos 4.424 (1627):126; 4.445:39; 8.975:127
    Ordenes Militares, Santiago 1.267, 1.268, 1.830, 6.471, 6.472; Casamientos 10.461; Consejo, Santiago 146
Archivo Histórico de Protocolos de Madrid, Madrid, Spain
    Protocolos 5.113; 6.587; 7.213–14; 7.514–16; 8.609; 9.012; 10.118; 10.120; 10.125; 10.126; 10.956; 11.431; 12.118; 13.146; 14.744
Archivo Histórico Provincial, Cadiz, Spain
    Protocolos de Cádiz 5.299

Archivo Histórico Provincial y Universitario, Valladolid, Spain
    Libros de incorporación y matriculación
Archivo del Marqués de la Nava de Barcinas, Madrid, Spain
Archivo de Rafael Gasset Dorado, Madrid, Spain
Archivo de Notarías, Torrelaguna, Spain
Biblioteca Nacional de México, Mexico City, Mexico
    Archivo Franciscano, New Mexico Documents 3:1; 4:4; 4:30; 6:3–4
The John Carter Brown Library, Providence, Rhode Island
    Planta de las pensiones y cargas anuales
Church of Jesus Christ of Latter-Day Saints, Genealogical Library, Salt
Lake City, Utah
    LDS microfilm 036,415
The Henry E. Huntington Library, San Marino, California
    Rare book 70361
New Mexico State Records Center and Archives, Santa Fe, New Mexico
    Alice Scoville Barry Collection
    Spanish Archives of New Mexico I:1027; II:59, 94a, 99, 100
New York Public Library, New York, New York
    Rich Collection, vol. 39
Parroquia de Nuestra Señora de la Encarnación, Huéscar, Spain
    Registro de bautismos
Parroquia de Nuestra Señora de la Soledad (la Paloma), Madrid, Spain
    San Pedro el Real, Difuntos, Libro 4
Parroquia de Santa María Magdalena, Torrelaguna, Spain
    Bautismos, Libros 4, 5; Difuntos, Libro 2; Matrimonios, Libro 3
The University of New Mexico, Zimmerman Library, Special Collections,
Albuquerque, New Mexico
    Thomas Benton Catron Collection, Box 1, Folder 1

OTHER WORKS

Adams, Eleanor B. *Bishop Tamarón's Visitation of New Mexico, 1760.* Pub-
    lications in History, 15. Albuquerque: Historical Society of New Mexi-
    co, 1954.
———. "Two Colonial New Mexico Libraries." NMHR 19 (Apr. 1944):
    135–67.
Adams, Eleanor B., and Fray Angelico Chavez, eds. and trans. *The Mis-
    sions of New Mexico, 1776: A Description by Fray Francisco Atanasio
    Domínguez, with Other Contemporary Documents.* Albuquerque: Univ.
    of New Mexico Press, 1956.
Alcocer y Martínez, Mariano, and Saturnino Rivera. *Biobibliografías de
    juristas notables.* Vol. 5 of *Historia de la Universidad de Valladolid.*
    Valladolid: Imprenta Castellana, 1924.

Alonso-Cadenas López, Ampelio, Julio de Atienza et al. *Elenco de grandezas y títulos nobiliarios, 1981*. Madrid: Ediciones de la revista Hidalguía, 1981.

Alvarez y Baena, Joseph Antonio. *Hijos de Madrid, ilustres en santidad, dignidades, armas, ciencias y artes: Diccionario histórico por el órden alfabético de sus nombres*. 4 vols. Madrid: Oficina de d. Benito Cano, 1789.

Arteaga y Falguera, Cristina. *La Casa del Infantado: Cabeza de los Mendoza*. 2 vols. Madrid: Duque del Infantado, 1944.

Atienza, Julio de. *Nobiliario español: Diccionario heráldico de apellidos españoles y de títulos nobiliarios*. 3d ed. Madrid: Aguilar, 1959.

Bakewell, P. J. *Silver Mining and Society in Colonial Mexico: Zacatecas, 1546–1700*. Cambridge: Cambridge Univ. Press, 1971.

Ballesteros Robles, Luis. *Diccionario biográfico matritense*. Madrid: Imprenta Municipal, 1912.

Bancroft, Hubert Howe. *History of Arizona and New Mexico, 1530–1888*. 1889. Reprint. Albuquerque: Horn and Wallace, 1962.

———. *History of Mexico: Vol. 3, 1600–1803*. Vol. 11 of *The Works of Hubert Howe Bancroft*. San Francisco: A. L. Bancroft and Co., 1883–88 (Vols. 9–14 of his works).

Bano, José de. *Instrucciones para el cultivo de la vid: Zonas vitícolas del país*. Mexico City: Dirección General de la Agricultura, 1919.

Belda, Joaquín. *Vinos de España*. Madrid: Compañía Ibero-Americana de Publicaciones, 1929.

Bleiberg, Germán. *Diccionario de historia de España*. 2d ed. Corrected and enlarged. Madrid: Ediciones de la *Revista de Occidente*, 1969.

Bloom, Lansing B. "The Vargas Encomienda." NMHR 14 (Oct. 1939): 366–417.

Bolton, Herbert Eugene. *Rim of Christendom: A Biography of Eusebio Francisco Kino, Pacific Coast Pioneer*. 1936. Reprint. Tucson: Univ. of Arizona Press, 1984.

Boylan, Leona Davis. *Spanish Colonial Silver*. Santa Fe: Museum of New Mexico Press, 1974.

Brading, D. A. *Miners and Merchants in Bourbon Mexico, 1763–1810*. Cambridge: Cambridge Univ. Press, 1971.

Bromley, J. S., ed. *The Rise of Great Britain and Russia, 1688–1715/25*. Vol. 6 of *The New Cambridge Modern History*. Cambridge: Cambridge Univ. Press, 1970.

Brown, Jonathan M. "Herrera the Younger: Baroque Artist and Personality." *Apollo* 84 (July 1966): 34–43.

Burrus, Ernest J. "A Tragic Interlude in the Reconquest of New Mexico." *Manuscripta* 29 (Nov. 1985): 154–65.

Canedo, Lino Gómez. *Evangelización y conquista: Experiencia franciscana en Hispanoamérica*. Mexico City: Editorial Porrúa, 1977.

Carrera Stampa, Manuel. "The Evolution of Weights and Measures in New Spain." *Hispanic American Historical Review* 29 (Feb. 1949): 2–24.

Chanes, Rafael, and Ximena Vicente. *Descubrir el Madrid antiguo*. Madrid: privately printed, 1976.

Chavez, Fray Angelico, O.F.M. *Archives of the Archdiocese of Santa Fe, 1678–1900*. Publications of the Academy of American Franciscan History. Bibliographical Series, 3. Washington, D.C.: Academy of American Franciscan History, 1957.

————. *The Origins of New Mexico Families in the Spanish Colonial Period in Two Parts: The Seventeenth (1598–1693) and the Eighteenth (1693–1821) Centuries*. 1954. Reprint. Santa Fe: William Gannon, 1975.

Corominas, Joan, and José A. Pascual, collab. *Diccionario crítico y etimológico castellano e hispánico*. 5 vols. Madrid: Editorial Gredos, 1980.

Davies, Reginald Trevor. *Spain in Decline, 1621–1700*. 5th ed. London: Macmillan, 1970.

Deleito y Piñuela, José. *Sólo Madrid es corte: La capital de dos mundos bajo Felipe IV*. 3d ed. Madrid: Espasa-Calpe, 1968.

Diccionario de autoridades. Biblioteca Románica Española. 3 vols. 1726–37. Facs. ed. Madrid: Editorial Gredos, 1979.

Diccionario de la lengua española. 18th ed. Madrid: Espasa-Calpe, 1956.

Diccionario Porrúa de historia, biografía y geografía de México. 4th ed. Corrected and enlarged, with a supplement. 2 vols. Mexico City: Editorial Porrúa, 1964, 1976.

Dictionary of American Biography. New York: Charles Scribner's Sons, 1928-.

Diputación Provincial de Madrid. *Guía de la provincia de Madrid: Torrelaguna*. Madrid: Diputación Provincial de Madrid, n.d.

Dirección General de Archivos y Bibliotecas. *Guía de los archivos de Madrid*. Madrid: Ministerio de Educación Nacional, 1952.

Documentary Relations of the Southwest, Biofile.

Domínguez Ortiz, Antonio. *El antiguo régimen: Los Reyes Católicos y los Austrias*. Serie Alfaguara, Historia de España Alfaguara, vol. 3. Madrid: Alianza Editorial, 1981.

————. *Las clases privilegiadas en la España del antiguo régimen*. Colección Fundamentos, 31. Madrid: Ediciones ISTMO, [1973].

————. *Política y hacienda de Felipe IV*. Madrid: Editorial de Derecho Financiero, 1960.

————. *La sociedad española en el siglo xvii*. 2 vols. Madrid: Consejo Superior de Investigaciones Científicas, 1963.

————. "Un virreynato en venta." *Mercurio Peruano* 453 (Jan.-Feb. 1965): 43–51.

Elliott, J.H. *The Count-Duke of Olivares: The Statesman in an Age of Decline*. New Haven: Yale Univ. Press, 1986.

————. *Imperial Spain, 1469–1716*. New York: St. Martin's Press, 1964.

————. *The Revolt of the Catalans: A Study in the Decline of Spain, 1598–1640*. Cambridge: Cambridge Univ. Press, 1963.

Ellis, Bruce. *Bishop Lamy's Santa Fe Cathedral: With Records of the Old Spanish Church (Parroquia) and Convent Formerly on the Site*. Albuquerque: Univ. of New Mexico Press, 1985.

————. "Santa Fe's Seventeenth Century Plaza, Parish Church, and Convent Reconsidered." In *Collected Papers in Honor of Marjorie Ferguson Lambert*. Edited by Albert H. Schroeder. Papers of the Archaeological Society of New Mexico, 3. Albuquerque: Archaeological Society of New Mexico, 1976.

Enciclopedia italiana di scienze, lettere ed arti. 40 vols. Rome: Istituto della Enciclopedia Italiana, Fondata da Giovanni Treccani, 1949.

Enciclopedia universal ilustrada europeo-americana. 70 vols. (23 supplements; Index 1934–80.) Barcelona: Hijos de J. Espasa, eds., 1907–30.

Escriche, Joaquín. *Diccionario razonado de legislación y jurisprudencia*. 4 vols. Edited by Juan B. Guim. Bogotá: Editorial Temis, 1977.

Escudero, José Antonio. *Los secretarios de estado y del despacho, 1474–1724*. 4 vols. Madrid: Instituto de Estudios Administrativos, 1969.

Espinosa, Fray Isidro Félix de. *Crónica de los Colegios de Propaganda Fide de la Nueva España*. New ed. with notes and introduction by Lino G. Canedo. Washington, D.C.: Academy of American Franciscan History, 1964.

Espinosa, José Manuel. *Crusaders of the Río Grande: The Story of Don Diego de Vargas and the Reconquest and Refounding of New Mexico*. 1942. Reprint. Salisbury, N.C.: Documentary Publications, 1977.

————. *First Expedition of Vargas into New Mexico, 1692*. Coronado Cuarto Centennial Publications, 1540–1940, vol. 10. Albuquerque: Univ. of New Mexico Press, 1940.

————. "The Legend of Sierra Azul with Special Emphasis on the Part It Played in the Reconquest of New Mexico." NMHR 9 (Apr. 1934): 113–58.

————. "Notes on the Lineage of don Diego de Vargas, Reconqueror of New Mexico." NMHR 10 (Apr. 1935): 112–20.

————. "Population of the El Paso District in 1692." *Mid-America* 23 (Jan. 1941): 61–84.

Fayard, Janine. "La Guerra de Sucesión, 1700–1714." In *La frustración de un imperio, 1476–1714*. Edited by Manuel Tuñón de Lara. Vol. 5 of *Historia de España*. Barcelona: Editorial Labor, 1982.

————. *Les membres du Conseil de Castille a l'époque moderne, 1621–1746*. Geneva: Droz, 1979.

Fernández, Fray Alonso. *Historia y anales de la ciudad y obispado de Plasencia*. Madrid: Juan González, 1707.

Fernández de Oviedo y Valdés, Gonzalo. "Noticias de Madrid y de las familias madrileñas de su tiempo." *Revista de la Biblioteca, Archivo y Museo* 16 (Jan.-July 1947): 287–88.

Fisher, Lillian Estelle. *Viceregal Administration in the Spanish-American Colonies.* University of California Publications in History, vol. 15. Berkeley: Univ. of California Press, 1926.

Forbes, Jack D. *Apache, Navaho, and Spaniard.* Norman: Univ. of Oklahoma Press, 1960.

García Carraffa, Alberto, and Arturo García Carraffa. *Diccionario heráldico y genealógico de apellidos españoles y americanos.* 88 vols. Madrid: Nueva Imprenta Radio, 1943.

García de Diego, Vicente. *Gramática histórica española.* Madrid: Editorial Gredos, 1951.

García Fuentes, Lutgardo. *El comercio español con América, 1650–1700.* Publicaciones de la Excelentísima Diputación Provincial de Sevilla. Sección Historia Serie 1A, 16. Publicación de la Escuela de Estudios Hispano-Americanos, 265. Seville: Escuela de Estudios Hispano-Americanos, Consejo Superior de Investigaciones Científicas, 1980.

García Rodrigo, Francisco Javier. *El cuerpo colegiado de la nobleza de Madrid.* 2d ed. Madrid: Imprenta de la Viuda e Hija Fuentenebro, 1884.

Gebhardt, Victor. *Historia general de España y de sus Indias, desde los tiempos más remotos hasta nuestros días.* 6 vols. in 7. Barcelona: Librería del Plus Ultra, 1863.

Gerhard, Peter. *A Guide to the Historical Geography of New Spain.* Cambridge: Cambridge Univ. Press, 1972.

———. *The North Frontier of New Spain.* Princeton: Princeton Univ. Press, 1982.

Gibson, Charles. *The Aztecs under Spanish Rule: A History of the Indians of the Valley of Mexico, 1519–1810.* Stanford: Stanford Univ. Press, 1964.

Gran enciclopedia Larousse en veinte volúmenes. 20 vols. Paris: Larousse, 1962.

Grimes, Ronald L. *Symbol and Conquest: Public Ritual and Drama in Santa Fe, New Mexico.* Ithaca: Cornell Univ. Press, 1976.

Gutiérrez Coronel, Diego. *Historia genealógica de la Casa de Mendoza.* Vol. 1. Biblioteca Conquense, 3. Cuenca: Instituto Jerónimo Zurita del Consejo Superior de Investigaciones Científicas, Ayuntamiento de la ciudad de Cuenca, 1946.

Hackett, Charles Wilson, ed. *Historical Documents relating to New Mexico, Nueva Vizcaya, and Approaches thereto, to 1773.* 3 vols. Washington, D.C.: Carnegie Institution of Washington, 1923–37.

———, and Charmion Clair Shelby, trans. *Revolt of the Pueblo Indians of New Mexico and Otermín's Attempted Reconquest, 1680–1682.* 2 vols.

Coronado Cuarto Centennial Publications, 1540–1940, vols. 8–9. Albuquerque: Univ. of New Mexico Press, 1942.

Hamilton, Earl J. *War and Prices in Spain, 1651–1800.* Cambridge, Mass.: Harvard Univ. Press, 1947.

Hanke, Lewis, ed., in collaboration with Celso Rodríguez. *Los virreyes españoles en América durante el gobierno de la Casa de Austria: México.* Biblioteca de Autores Españoles, desde la formación del lenguaje hasta nuestros días (continuación), vol. 277. Madrid: Ediciones Atlas, 1978.

———. *Los virreyes españoles en América durante el gobierno de la Casa de Austria: Perú.* Biblioteca de Autores Españoles, desde la formación del lenguaje hasta nuestros días (continuación), vol. 284. Madrid: Ediciones Atlas, 1979.

Haring, Clarence Henry. *The Spanish Empire in America.* 1947. Reprint. New York: Harcourt, Brace and World, Inc., Harbinger Books, 1963.

Hodge, Frederick Webb, George P. Hammond, and Agapito Rey, eds. and trans. *Fray Alonso de Benavides' Revised Memorial of 1634: With Numerous Supplementary Documents Elaborately Annotated.* Coronado Cuarto Centennial Publications, 1540–1940, vol. 4. Albuquerque: Univ. of New Mexico Press, 1945.

Hughes, Anne E. *The Beginnings of Spanish Settlement in the El Paso District.* 1914. Reprint. University of California Publications in History, vol. 1, no. 3. Berkeley: Univ. of California Press, 1935.

Jago, Charles. "The Influence of Debt on the Relations between Crown and Aristocracy in Seventeenth-Century Castile." *Economic History Review* 2d ser., 26 (1973): 218–36.

Jones, Oakah L., Jr. *Pueblo Warriors and Spanish Conquest.* Norman: Univ. of Oklahoma Press, 1966.

Kagan, Richard. *Students and Society in Early Modern Spain.* Baltimore: The Johns Hopkins Univ. Press, 1974.

Kamen, Henry. "The Destruction of the Spanish Silver Fleet at Vigo in 1702." *Bulletin of the Institute of Historical Research* (Univ. of London) 39 (1966): 165–73.

———. *Spain in the Later Seventeenth Century, 1665–1700.* London: Longman, 1980.

———. *The War of Succession in Spain, 1700–15.* Bloomington: Indiana Univ. Press, 1969.

Kessell, John L. "Diego de Vargas: Another Look." NMHR 60 (Jan. 1985): 11–28.

———. *Kiva, Cross, and Crown.* Washington, D.C.: National Park Service, U.S. Dept. of the Interior, 1979.

———. *The Missions of New Mexico since 1776.* Albuquerque: Univ. of New Mexico Press, 1980.

———. "Vargas or DeVargas: A Modest Justification of Both Forms." In

Collected Works in Honor of Charles H. Lange. Edited by Anne V. Poore. Santa Fe: Ancient City Press, 1988.

Klein, Julius. The Mesta: A Study in Spanish Economic History, 1273–1836. Cambridge, Mass.: Harvard Univ. Press, 1920.

Kubler, George. Building the Escorial. Princeton: Princeton Univ. Press, 1982.

Le Flem, Jean-Paul, Joseph Pérez et al. La frustración de un imperio, 1476–1714. Edited by Manuel Tuñón de Lara. Vol. 5 of Historia de España. Barcelona: Editorial Labor, 1982.

Leonard, Irving A. Baroque Times in Old Mexico: Seventeenth-Century Persons, Places, and Practices. Ann Arbor: Univ. of Michigan Press, 1959.

Lohmann Villena, Guillermo. Los americanos en las órdenes nobiliarias, 1529–1900. 2 vols. Madrid: Consejo Superior de Investigaciones Científicas, Instituto "Gonzalo Fernández de Oviedo," 1947.

———. El corregidor de indios en el Perú bajo los Austrias. Madrid: Ediciones Cultura Hispánica, 1957.

———. Las minas de Huancavelica en los siglos xvi y xvii. Publicación de la Escuela de Estudios Hispano-Americanos, 50. Seville: Escuela de Estudios Hispano-Americanos, 1949.

López de Zárate Vargas, Diego Joseph. Breve descripción genealógica de la ilustre, quanto antiquíssima Casa de los Vargas de Madrid. Madrid: privately printed, 1740.

Lucena Salmoral, Manuel. Nuevo Reino de Granada: Real audiencia y presidentes. Vol. 3, pt. 1 of Historia extensa de Colombia. Bogotá: Ediciones Lerner, 1965.

Lynch, John. Spain under the Habsburgs. 2 vols. 2d ed. New York: New York Univ. Press, 1984.

Maas, Otto, ed. Misiones de Nuevo Méjico: Documentos del Archivo General de Indias (Sevilla) publicados por primera vez y anotados. Madrid: Imprenta Hijos de T. Minuesa de los Ríos, 1929-.

Mackenzie, David. A Manual of Manuscript Transcription for the Dictionary of the Old Spanish Language. 4th ed., by Victoria A. Burrus. Madison: The Hispanic Seminary of Medieval Studies, Ltd., 1986.

MacLeod, Murdo J. Spanish Central America: A Socioeconomic History, 1520–1720. Berkeley: Univ. of California Press, 1973.

Madoz, Pascual. Diccionario geográfico-estadístico-histórico de España y sus posesiones de ultramar. 16 vols. Madrid: P. Madoz y L. Sagasti, 1845–50.

———. Madrid: Audiencia, provincia, intendencia, vicaría, partido y villa. 1848. Reprint. Madrid: José Ramón Aguado, 1981.

Magdaleno, Ricardo. Títulos y privilegios de Nápoles, siglos xvi-xvii: Catálogo 28 del Archivo de Simancas. 1 vol. Valladolid: Archivo General de Simancas and Consiglio Nazionale delle Ricerche, 1980.

Martin, Norman F., ed. *Instrucción reservada que el Obispo-Virrey Juan de Ortega Montañés dio a su sucesor en el mando el Conde de Moctezuma.* Mexico City: Editorial Jus, 1965.

Martínez, Santiago. *La diócesis de Arequipa y sus obispos.* Arequipa: TIP Cuadros, 1933.

Martínez Cosío, Leopoldo. *Los caballeros de las órdenes militares en México: Catálogo biográfico y genealógico.* Mexico City: Editorial Santiago, 1946.

Maura y Gamazo, Gabriel. *Carlos II y su corte.* 2 vols. Madrid: Librería de F. Beltrán, 1911–15.

———. *Vida y reinado de Carlos II.* 2d ed. 2 vols. Madrid: Espasa-Calpe, 1954.

Maza, Francisco de la. *San Miguel de Allende: Su historia, sus monumentos.* Mexico City: Instituto de Investigaciones Estéticas, Universidad Nacional Autónoma de México, 1939.

Mesonero Romanos, Ramón de. *El antiguo Madrid, paseos histórico-anecdóticos por las calles y casas de esta villa.* New ed. 2 vols. 1861. Reprint. Madrid: Oficinas de la Ilustración Española y Americana, 1881.

Micheli y Márquez, José. *Tesoro militar de cavallería. Antiguo y moderno modo de armar cavalleros, y professar, segun las ceremonias de qualquier orden militar:. . . .* Madrid: Diego Díaz de la Carrera, 1642.

Molina Campuzano, Miguel. *Planos de Madrid de los siglos xvii y xviii.* Madrid: Instituto de Estudios de Administración Local, Seminario de Urbanismo, 1960.

Momplet Míguez, Antonio, and María Victoria Chico Picaza. *El arte religioso en Torrelaguna.* Serie Monográfica. Madrid: Academia de San Dámaso, Archidiócesis de Madrid-Alcalá, 1979.

Moore, John Preston. *The Cabildo in Peru under the Habsburgs: A Study in the Origins and Power of the Town Council in the Viceroyalty of Peru, 1530–1700.* Durham, N.C.: Duke Univ. Press, 1954.

Moorhead, Max L. "The Presidio Supply Problem of New Mexico in the Eighteenth Century." NMHR 36 (July 1961): 107–22.

Muro Orejón, Antonio, ed. *Cédulas de Carlos II, 1679–1700.* Vol. 1 of *Cedulario americano del siglo xviii: Colección de disposiciones legales indianas desde 1680 a 1800, contenidas en los Cedularios del Archivo General de Indias.* Publicaciones de la Escuela de Estudios Hispano-Americanos, 99. Seville: Escuela de Estudios Hispano-Americanos, Consejo Superior de Investigaciones Científicas, 1956.

Naylor, Thomas H., and Charles W. Polzer, S.J., comps. and eds. *The Presidio and Militia on the Northern Frontier of New Spain: A Documentary History, 1500–1700.* Vol. 1. Tucson: The Univ. of Arizona Press, 1986.

Núñez de Castro, Alonso. *Historia eclesiástica y seglar de la muy noble y muy leal ciudad de Guadalaxara*. Madrid: Pablo de Val, 1653.

Ortiz, Alfonso, ed. *Southwest*. Vol. 9 of *Handbook of North American Indians*. Washington, D.C.: Smithsonian Institution, 1979.

———. *Southwest*. Vol. 10 of *Handbook of North American Indians*. Washington, D.C.: Smithsonian Institution, 1983.

Parry, J.H. *The Sale of Public Office in the Spanish Indies under the Habsburgs*. Ibero-Americana, 37. Berkeley: Univ. of California Press, 1953.

Pérez Balsera, José. *Laudemus viros gloriosos et parentes nostros in generatione sua*. Madrid: Tipografía Católica, 1931.

Phelan, John Leddy. *The Kingdom of Quito in the Seventeenth Century: Bureaucratic Politics in the Spanish Empire*. Madison: Univ. of Wisconsin Press, 1967.

Pierce, Donna, ed. *Vivan las Fiestas*. Santa Fe: Museum of New Mexico Press, 1985.

Porras Muñoz, Guillermo. *La frontera con los indios de Nueva Vizcaya en el siglo xvii*. Mexico City: Fomento Cultural Banamex, 1980.

Quintana, Jerónimo de. *Historia de la antigüedad, nobleza y grandeza de la villa de Madrid*. Edited by E. Varela Hervías. 1629. Reprint. Madrid: Artes Gráficas Municipales, 1954.

Real Díaz, José J. "El consejo de cámara de Indias: Génesis de su fundación." *Anuario de Estudios Americanos* 1st ser. 19 (1962): 725–58.

Recopilación de leyes de los reynos de las Indias. 4 vols. 1681. Reprint. Foreword by Ramón Menéndez y Pidal, and a preliminary study by Juan Manzano Manzano. Madrid: Ediciones Cultura Hispánica, 1973.

Ringrose, David R. *Madrid and the Spanish Economy, 1560–1850*. Berkeley: Univ. of California Press, 1983.

Rivera Cambas, Manuel. *Los gobernantes de México: Galería de biografías y retratos de los vireyes, emperadores, presidentes y otros gobernantes que ha tenido México, desde Hernando Cortés hasta el C. Benito Juarez*. 2 vols. Mexico City: Imprenta de J. M. Aguilar Ortiz, 1872–73.

Robles, Antonio de. *Diario de sucesos notables, 1665–1703*. Edited by Antonio Castro Leal. Colección de Escritores Mexicanos, 30–32. 3 vols. Mexico City: Editorial Porrúa, 1946.

Romero, Carlos A. "La virreina gobernadora." *Revista Histórica* (Lima) 1 (Mar. 1906): 39–59.

Romero Flores, Jesús. *Iconografía colonial*. Mexico City: Museo Nacional, 1940.

Rubio Mañé, J. Ignacio. *Introducción al estudio de los virreyes de Nueva España, 1535–1746*. 4 vols. Publicaciones, 32. Mexico City: Universidad Nacional Autónoma de México, Instituto de Historia, Ediciones Selectas, 1955.

Sarfatti, Magali. *Spanish Bureaucratic-Paternalism in America*. Berkeley: Institute of International Studies, Univ. of California, 1966.

Schäfer, Ernesto. *El Consejo Real y Supremo de las Indias: Su historia, organización y labor administrativa hasta la terminación de la Casa de Austria*. Vol. 1: *Historia y organización del Consejo y de la Casa de Contratación de las Indias*. Seville: Centro de Estudio de Historia de América, Universidad de Sevilla, 1935. Vol. 2: *La labor del Consejo de Indias en la administración colonial*. Seville: Escuela de Estudios Hispano-Americanos, 1947.

Scholes, France. "Civil Government and Society in New Mexico in the Seventeenth Century." NMHR 10 (Apr. 1935): 71–111.

———. "Problems in the Early Ecclesiastical History of New Mexico." NMHR 7 (Jan. 1932): 32–74.

Scholes, France V. and Lansing B. Bloom. "Friar Personnel and Mission Chronology, 1598–1629." NMHR 19 (Oct. 1944): 319–36.

Sheldon, Addison E. "The Massacre of the Villasur Expedition at the Forks of the Platte River, August 12, 1720." *Nebraska History* 7 (July-Sept. 1924): 68–81.

Sigüenza y Góngora, Carlos de. *Mercurio volante con la noticia de la recuperación de las provincias del Nuevo México conseguida por d. Diego de Vargas, Zapata, y Luján Ponze de León, governador y capitán general de aquel reyno*. Mexico City: Imprenta de Antuerpia de los Herederos de la Viuda de Bernardo Calderón, 1693.

———. *The Mercurio Volante of don Carlos de Sigüenza y Góngora: An Account of the First Expedition of don Diego de Vargas into New Mexico in 1692*. Quivira Society Publications, 3. Translated with an introduction by Irving A. Leonard. Los Angeles: The Quivira Society, 1932.

———. *Relaciones históricas*. Selection, prolog, and notes by Manuel Romero de Terreros. Mexico City: Universidad Nacional Autónoma de México, 1940.

Simmons, Marc. *Albuquerque: A Narrative History*. Albuquerque: Univ. of New Mexico Press, 1982.

Simón Díaz, José. *Historia del Colegio Imperial de Madrid*. 2 vols. Madrid: Consejo Superior de Investigaciones Científicas, Instituto de Estudios Madrileños, 1952–59.

Snow, David H. "A Note on Encomienda Economics in Seventeenth Century New Mexico." In *Hispanic Arts and Ethnohistory in the Southwest: New Papers Inspired by the Work of E. Boyd*. Edited by Marta Weigle. Santa Fe: Ancient City Press, 1983.

———. "Santiago to Guache: Notes for a Tale of Two (or more) Bernalillos." In *Collected Papers in Honor of Marjorie Ferguson Lambert*. Edited by Albert H. Schroeder. Papers of the Archaeological Society of New Mexico, 3. Albuquerque: Archaeological Society of New Mexico, 1976.

Soldevila Zubiburo, Fernando [Soldevila, Ferran]. *História de Catalunya*. 2d ed. Barcelona: Alpha, 1963.

Solórzano Pereira, Juan de. *Política indiana*. Preliminary study by Miguel Angel Ochoa Brun. Biblioteca de Autores Españoles, desde la formación del lenguaje hasta nuestros días (continuación), vols. 252–56. Madrid: Ediciones Atlas, 1972.

Stanislawski, Dan. *Landscapes of Bacchus: The Vine in Portugal*. Austin: Univ. of Texas Press, 1970.

Stevens, Capt. John. *A New Spanish and English Dictionary: Collected from the Best Spanish Authors, Both Ancient and Modern*. 2 vols. London: George Sawbridge, 1706.

Stokstad, Marilyn Jane. *Santiago de Compostela: In the Age of the Great Pilgrimages*. Centers of Civilization, 35. Norman: Univ. of Oklahoma Press, 1978.

Strout, Clevy Lloyd, ed. and trans. "Santa Fe Rediviva: The Muster Roll of the Juan Páez Hurtado Expedition of 1695." Thomas Gilcrease Institute, Tulsa, Okla., [c1978].

Texeira, Pedro. *Topographía de la villa de Madrid descrita por don Pedro Texeira, año 1656*. New ed. Madrid: Ayuntamiento de Madrid, 1980.

Thomas, Alfred Barnaby, ed. and trans. *After Coronado: Spanish Exploration Northeast of New Mexico, 1696–1727*. Norman: Univ. of Oklahoma Press, 1935.

Tormo y Monzó, Elías. *Aranjuez*. Madrid: Gráficas Marinas, [1930?].

Twitchell, Ralph Emerson, trans. "The Justification of Don Diego de Vargas, 1704." *Old Santa Fe* 2 (July 1915): 57–65.

———, comp. *The Spanish Archives of New Mexico: Compiled and Chronologically Arranged with Historical, Genealogical, Geographical, and Other Annotations, by Authority of the State of New Mexico, by Ralph Emerson Twitchell*. 2 vols. Cedar Rapids: The Torch Press, 1914.

Vázquez de Prada, Valentín. *Los siglos xvi y xvii*. Confederación Española de Cajas de Ahorros. Fondo para la Investigación Económica y Social, 52. Vol. 3 of *Historia económica y social de España*. Madrid: Confederación Española de Cajas de Ahorros, 1978.

Vilar, Pierre. "The Age of Don Quixote." In *Essays in European Economic History, 1500–1800*. Edited by Peter Earle. Oxford: Clarendon Press, 1974.

Villagrá, Gaspar Pérez de. *History of New Mexico*. Translated by Gilberto Espinosa. Introduction and notes by F.W. Hodge. Quivira Society Publications, 4. Los Angeles: The Quivira Society, 1933.

Villars, Pierre, Marquis de. *Memoires de la cour d'Espagne de 1679 à 1681*. Edited and annotated by A. Morel-Fatio. Introduction by the Marquis de Vogüé. Paris: E. Plon, Nourrit et Cie., 1893.

Walz, Vina. "History of the El Paso Area, 1680–1692." Ph.D. diss., Univ. of New Mexico, 1951.

Warner, Ted J. "Don Félix Martínez and the Santa Fe Presidio, 1693–1730." NMHR 45 (Oct. 1970): 269–310.

Weddle, Robert S. *Wilderness Manhunt: The Spanish Search for La Salle.* Austin: Univ. of Texas Press, 1973.

West, Robert C. *The Mining Community in Northern New Spain: The Parral Mining District.* Ibero-Americana, 30. Berkeley: Univ. of California Press, 1949.

Whitaker, Arthur Preston. *The Huancavelica Mercury Mine: A Contribution to the History of the Bourbon Renaissance in the Spanish Empire.* Cambridge, Mass.: Harvard Univ. Press, 1941.

Wilson, Christopher M. "The Santa Fe, New Mexico Plaza: An Architectural and Cultural History, 1610–1921." M.A. thesis, Univ. of New Mexico, 1981.

Wright, L.P. "The Military Orders in Sixteenth and Seventeenth Century Spanish Society: The Institutional Embodiment of a Historical Tradition." *Past and Present* 43 (May 1969): 34–70.

Ximénez, Fray Francisco, comp. *Historia de la provincia de San Vicente de Chiapa y Guatemala de la Orden de Predicadores.* Prolog by J. Antonio Villacorta C. Biblioteca "Goathemala" de la Sociedad de Geografía e Historia, vol. 1, no. 1. Guatemala City: Tipografía Nacional de Guatemala, 1929.

Ya-hya ibn Mu-hammad. *Libro de agricultura.* Edited by Claudio Boutelou. Translated by José Banqueri. 2 vols. in 1. Seville: Administración de la Biblioteca Científica-Literaria, 1878.

Zavala, Silvio A. *La encomienda indiana.* 2d ed. Mexico City: Editorial Porrúa, 1973.

Index

NOTE ON THE INDEX

Entries and subentries are alphabetical with the following exceptions. Spanish geographical names incorporating the articles "el," "la," or "del" are alphabetized by the name rather than the article, though the articles appear in the index. Surnames with "de la" and "del" are alphabetized by "de la" and "del." General references precede those modified by subentries.

References to note numbers follow the number of the page on which the note begins and are preceded by a "n." Definitions of terms are indexed by the page reference followed by a "d." Numbers in italics are references to maps, and numbers in bold type are references to illustrations. Italicized index entries refer to glossary items.

Entries for many people provide additional information, reflecting their relationship to Diego de Vargas (DVZ) or their professions. Places in Spain are identified by their modern provinces in parenthesis, those in New Spain, the focus of the book, by their colonial designation. Other Latin American and European place names are given with their modern locations.

Letters written by or to individuals are referenced at the end of an entry.

The Contents, Illustrations and Maps, Note on Spanish Monies, Chronology, and the Spanish text have not been indexed.